ABSTRACT

OF

NORTH CAROLINA WILLS

COMPILED FROM

ORIGINAL AND RECORDED WILLS IN THE
OFFICE OF THE SECRETARY OF STATE

BY

J. BRYAN GRIMES

SECRETARY OF STATE

Baltimore
GENEALOGICAL PUBLISHING COMPANY
1967

Originally Published
Raleigh, 1910

929.3
N 81a
62681
Sept. 1968

Reprinted
Genealogical Publishing Company
Baltimore, 1967

INTRODUCTION.

The increasing interest of the public in the old wills filed in the office of the Secretary of State has caused the Trustees of the Public Libraries to authorize the Secretary of State to prepare the within publication. An abstract of every will found in the office of the Secretary of State is published herein. These abstracts show the name of the testator, place of residence, names of wife, children, legatees, witnesses, probate officer, etc.; also, names of plantations mentioned and remarkable items or noteworthy passages in wills.

The first record I have been able to find providing for the keeping of wills in the office of the Secretary of State is the following order:

Order'd that a Commission be Deliver'd to ye Honble Majr Samuel Swann Esqr Secretary of State for this province Impowering him to keep an office for ye proving of Wills Granting administrats & probetts and all other Matters for ye Ordering & Securing of Dead Mens Estates according to ye foll Rules.

1. The Honble Secretary of State for ye time being shall atend ye Secretaries Office att ye Genrll Court House ye first thursday in every mo who shall have full power to prove Wills grant probetts & administrations & take care of Dead Mens Estates.

2. No will shall be proved or administration ordered either in ye Genrll Court or in ye precinct Court of Chowan Pequimans or Pascotant after ye first day of August next but only before ye sd Officer appoynted as afs'd and ye Clarks of each Respective precinct aforesd are hereby required to Return all papers and wrightings Relateing to wills & administrations and all other Concerns relating to Dead Mens Estates which shall Ly in their Respective offices into ye Secretaryes office within two mo.

3. Iff no person with in 2 months after ye Date of any person Dying Intestate appeare to sue for administration it shall be in ye power of ye sd officer to assigne an administrator.

4. Iff an Executor shall neglect to make proof of the will wthin 6 mo ye time Limitted by Law it shall be in ye power of ye sd Officer to Grant administration to the nearest of kinn if any sue for ye same if not to such pesons as he shall think fitt.

5. And ye sd Officer shall not grant administran or probatt of Will till Certificate be produced of ye Register ye Death of ye pson decd in ye Respective Registers as ye Law Directs.

6. And every prson suing for Admintrat Shall give in Sufficient Security before ye sd Officer & before whom all Evidence shall be brought to prove wills.

7. And every prson who shall obtain admintrati or Probett shall within one year after such adminstrat. or probatt obtaind bring in a true Inventory with acct of ye Estate in their hands until they shall obtaine further time which ye sd Officer hath power & liberty to grant.

The original of this paper was found by the late J. R. B. Hathaway in the courthouse at Edenton.[1] This order is without date, but was issued about 1700, as Samuel Swann was Secretary of State in that year and the first of his records are dated at that time.

The next legislation I find in reference to wills is an act of the General Assembly of 1715, chapter 48, the caption and first three sections of which are as follows:

AN ACT CONCERNING PROVEING WILLS AND GRANTING LETTERS OF ADMINISTRATION AND TO PREVENT FRAUDES IN THE MANAGEMENT OF INTESTATES ESTATES.

I. Be It Enacted by his Excellency the Pallatine & and the rest of the True & Absolute Lords Proprietors of the Province of Carolina by & with the advice & consent of the rest of the Members of the General Assembly now met at Little River for the No. East part of the province & by the Authority of the same.

II. It is Hereby Enacted & declared that all Wills & Administrations heretofore proved & granted by the Council, General Court, Precinct Court or by powers or Commission heretofore granted by any Governor, Deputy Governor, President & Council to any particular person or persons shall be deemed adjudged & taken to be good & effectual to all Intents & Purposes whatsoever as if proved before Or granted by any Ordinary or other Ecclesiastical Judge or person.

III. And Be It Further Enacted by the Authority afors'd that it shall & may be lawfull for the Governor or Commander in Chief for the time being the General Court or Precinct Court to have Wills proved before them and Grant Orders for Administration. Provided the same be not repugnant to the Rules & Methods prescribed in this Act And Provided that the Granting Letters Testamentary or Letters of Administration allways Excepted which shall be allways from & after the Ratification of this Act signed by the Governor or Commander in Chief for the time being and sealed with the Colony seale & only Issuing out of the Secretary's Office & Counter signed by the Secretary or Deputy. * * * * * * * *

This act validates probates up to that time, confirms letters of administration previously granted and provides for the better regulation of these matters.

---

[1]Published in *The North Carolina Historical and Genealogical Register*, Vol. III, p. 57.

In 1723 a law was enacted more rigidly enforcing the making and filing of inventories. Both the acts of 1715 and of 1723 were brought forward and confirmed in 1749.

During Governor Dobbs' administration, in 1760, acts were passed[2] "to establish Inferior Courts of Pleas and Quarter Sessions in the several counties in this Province," and[3] "for establishing Superior Courts of Pleas and Grand Sessions and regulating the proceedings therein." These acts provided for the filing and recording of wills in the clerk's office, which is still the law.

In an act of the General Assembly of 1754, ch. 6, sec. 8,[4] it was recited that "many original wills, patents and deeds have been lost for want of convenient offices to keep the same." The various migrations of our capital since that date have undoubtedly added to these losses.

Many of the wills here are in bad order, decayed, foxed and faded, and some of them are illegible. Where there is doubt as to correct recording of a will it is so stated or queried. The earliest will found is that of Mary Fortsen, which was made in 1663, but there are not many before 1690. There are a few wills filed here since 1760 which have been included in the abstract list. Occasionally it is found that a testator who was known to be an educated person signed his will by making his mark, so it is not always an evidence of illiteracy when the will is signed by a mark, nor is the signature to the will generally a satisfactory signature of the testator, as often he was sick, weak or infirm in body at the time of signing the will. The original spelling has been preserved in making abstracts of wills and the same name is often found spelled in several different ways. It will be observed that the terms "father-in-law" or "mother-in-law" often mean stepfather or stepmother; sometimes they

---

[2]Col. Rec., Vol. XXV, p. 405.
[3]Col. Rec., Vol. XXV, p. 433.
[4]Col. Rec., Vol. XXV, p. 306.

are referred to as "father" or "mother." The term "cousin" will be frequently found to mean nephew or niece.

It is interesting to note that in wills prior to 1752, two years are generally named for dates in the months of January, February and March; for instance, January 20, 1718-9; but this was not always the case, and occasionally only one year is given. As examples, see wills of

CATHERINE BUSBEY, made January 22, 1738-9. Proved February Court, 1738.

THOMAS BARCLIFT, made November 14, 1750. Proved at January Court, 1750.

NICHOLAS BLACKMAN, made August 26, 1730. Probated March 11, 1730.

On the continent and in Scotland the Gregorian Calendar was in use, but it was not adopted in England until 1751, when Parliament passed "An Act for Regulating the Commencement of the Year, and for Correcting the Calendar now in use." This act provided that the year begin on the first day of January, 1752, and not on the twenty-fifth of March, as was then the usage. The same act provided that eleven days be omitted in September, 1752,[5] "and that the natural Day next immediately following the said second Day of September, shall be called, reckoned and accounted to be the fourteenth Day of September, omitting for that Time only the eleven intermediate nominal Days of the common Calendar, and that the several natural Days which shall follow and succeed next after the said fourteenth Day of September shall be respectively called, reckoned and numbered forwards in numerical Order from the said fourteenth Day of September, according to the Order and Succession of Days now used in the Present Calendar." If this is kept in mind, it will reconcile many apparently contradictory dates.

The abstracts were prepared by Messrs. WM. H. SAWYER

[5]Statutes at Large, Vol. VII, 1747-1756; 24 Geo. II., C. 23, A. D. 1751, and as amended by 25 Geo. II., C. 30 A. D. 1752.

and JOSEPH E. SAWYER, the proof read by Messrs. W. P.
BATCHELOR and JOSEPH E. SAWYER, and the index made by
Mr. W. P. BATCHELOR. To these gentlemen I desire to
make acknowledgment for their faithful service.

It is expected that this work will be interesting and helpful
in genealogical research and especially valuable as illustra-
tive of the domestic history of our people. It will also be
found useful in tracing titles to properties.

J. BRYAN GRIMES.

ABSTRACT OF WILLS.

ABERCROMBIE, HANNAH. **Pasquotank County.**

August 12, 1754. January Court, 1755. *Daughter:* CATHRINE CHAMBERLIN. *Grandchildren:* LUCY and JEREMIAH CHAMBERLIN, DANIEL EVERTON, WILLIAM, HANNAH and JAMES EVERTON, COURTNEY and ABY CHAMBERLIN. *Executrix:* CATHERINE CHAMBERLIN. *Witnesses:* THOMAS TAYLOR, WILLIAM COALE. *Clerk of the Court:* THOMAS TAYLOR. Executrix qualified before ROBERT MURDEN.

ABINGTON, JOSEPH. **Currituck County.**

January 2, 1734–1735. July Court, 1735. *Son:* WILLIAM (land on the Banks). *Daughter:* MARY ABINGTON. *Executor:* HENRY WOODAS. *Witnesses:* MATHIAS and MARY TOLER, FRANCIS HODGES, OTHO HOLLAND. *Clerk of the Court:* JAMES CRAVEN.

ABINGTON, THOMAS. **Pasquotank Precinct.**

November 13, 1707. December 28, 1707. *Legatees:* MARY TULLY, GEORGE ELLIS, CHARLES GRIFFIN, ELIZABETH HECKLEFIELD. *Executors:* TOBIAS KNIGHT, JOHN and THOMAS PALIN. *Witnesses:* JOHN HECKLEFIELD, FRANCIS GILBERT, MARY COOKOO. Proven before W. GLOVER.

ADAMS, ABRAHAM.

(No date). *Sons:* ABRAM ADAMS (land lying on Pamlico River), RICHARD ADAMS (land on Pamlico River), WILLIAM ADAMS and WILLOBY ADAMS. *Daughter:* OBIA. *Wife:* BATHIA, who is appointed executrix. Part of this will is missing and no dates are given.

ADAMS, ABRAHAM.

October 3, 1733. *Witnesses:* PHILIP and MARY SHUTE, JOHN COLLISON. Only last page of will is found.

ADAMS, ABRAHAM. **Bath County.**

December 18, 1734. Probate not dated. *Sons:* JAMES and JOSEPH (lands on Kengens Mill Creek and Old Town Swamp). Negroes bequeathed to sons. *Daughters:* SARAH ADAMS, ELIZABETH ADAMS. *Wife and Executrix:* ANNE. *Guardian and Trustee:* JOHN HODGSON. *Witnesses:* JOHN COLLISON, JAMES ADAMS, PETER CAILAG (or Cailaugh). Proven before GAB. JOHNSON.

ADAMS, CHARLES.   Craven County.

March 21, 1757. April 20, 1757. *Wife:* MARGARET. *Executor:* JOHN STARKEY. *Witnesses:* JER. VAIL, NATHL. RICHARDSON, VINYD. BOND. Proven before ARTHUR DOBBS.

ADAMS, JOHN.   Bath County.

February 17, 1733-1734. No probate. *Sons:* ABRAHAM, JAMES, EMANUEL, JOHN, THOMAS. *Daughters:* MARTHA, RACHEL and MARY ADAMS. *Executors:* ABRAHAM and JAMES ADAMS (sons). *Witnesses:* OLIVER BLACKBURN, ROBERT SHARPLES, JOHN ALDERSHIRE.

ADAMS, JOHN.   Craven County.

September 19, 1750. *Friends:* JOSEPH BALCH and JOHN GOWEL, FRANCIS MERRINGER and WM. HERRITAGE. *Wife:* MARY ADAMS, to whom is devised a sloop called "Adventure." *Executors:* JOSEPH BALCH and MARY ADAMS. *Witnesses:* GEARSHAM SPEAR, RD. LOVETT. Will proven by J. VAIL. *Clerk of Court:* PHIL SMITH.

ADAMS, MARGARET.   Craven County.

July 8, 1765. September 1, 1773. *Executor and sole legatee:* BERNARD PARKINGTON. *Witnesses:* MARY HAWKS, AMBCOX BAYLEY, PERRIGAN COX. Proven before Jo. MARTIN.

ADAMS (spelled ADDOMES), MATTHEW.   Chowan Precinct.

August 9, 1703. November 25, 1708. *Wife and Executrix:* SARAH. *Son:* MATTHEW. *Daughter:* ELIZABETH. *Witnesses:* THOMAS BLOUNT, THOMAS BLOUNT, JR., JAMES BONNER. Proven before THOMAS CARY. Seal of the Colony affixed on probate.

ADAMS, PETER.   Chowan County.

December 13, 1745. March 31, 1746. *Sister:* MARY MOUNCE of Crediton in Devonshire. *Son:* JOHN. Wife not named. *Executors:* WILLIAM HOSKINS, HENRY BONNER, and JOHN LEWIS. *Witnesses:* JOHN HULL, WILLIAM LUTEN and WILLIAM LEWIS. Proven before E. HALL, C. J.

ADAMS, ROGER.   Bladen County.

August 2, 1739. August 6, 1739. *Wife and Executrix:* FRANCES. *Other legatees:* LUCY and JOHN GREEN, GABRIEL JOHNSTON, SAMUEL WOODWARD, JAMES INNES, JAMES MURRAY. *Witnesses:* THOMAS HART, ROBERT KNOWLS, JAMES MENZIES. Proven before GABRIEL JOHNSTON.

ADDISON, RICHARD.   Chowan County.

August 12, 1720. January Court, 1724. *Wife and Executrix:* SARAH. *Witnesses:* SAMUEL SPRUILL, ROBERT FEWOX, CHARLES CRADOCK. *Clerk of the Court:* ROBERT FOSTER.

AHIER, JOHN.   Onslow County.

January 11, 1744-1745. October Court, 1746. *Son:* WILLIAM. *Daughter:* ELIZABETH AHIER. *Wife and Executrix:* ELIZABETH. *Witnesses:* STEPHEN HOWARD, STEPHEN HOWARD, JR. *Clerk of the Court:* WILL HEDGES.

ALBERTSON, ALBERT, SR.   Perquimans Precinct.

February 10, 1701. April 14, 1702. *Sons:* PETER, NATHANIEL, ALBERT and EASAW. Wife not named. *Executors:* PETER and NATHANIEL ALBERTSON (sons). *Witnesses:* JOHN FALCONER, NATHANIEL NICKOLSON, JOSEPH SUTON. *Clerk of the Court:* JOHN STEPNEY.

ALBERTSON, ISAAC.   Pasquotank County.

February 12, 1759. March Court, 1759. *Wife and Executrix:* JEMIMA· *Daughter:* RUTH ALBERTSON. *Witnesses:* THOMAS CRAGHILL, ISAAC SITTEN (or Litten), SARAH MARTIN. *Clerk of the Court:* THOS. TAYLOR.

ALBERTSON, JOSHUA.   Perquimans County.

August 5, 1753. October Court, 1753. *Son:* FRANCIS (plantation). *Daughters:* ELIZABETH, MARY and PENELOPY ALBERTSON. *Wife and Executrix:* MARY. *Executors:* AARON and WILLIAM ALBERTSON (brothers). *Witnesses:* PHINEUS NIXON, NATHANIEL ALBERTSON, JOHN ANDERSON. *Clerk of the Court:* EDMUND HATCH.

ALBERTSON, MARY.   Perquimans County.

Will not dated. Probated January 10, 1720-1721. *Son:* ALBERT. *Grandchildren:* MARY, JOHN and ELISABETH ALBERTSON. *Executor:* ALBERT ALBERTSON (son). *Witnesses:* THOMAS STAFFORD, ALBERT ALBERTSON, JR. *Clerk of the Court:* RICHARD LEARY.

ALBERTSON, NATHANIEL.   Perquimans County.

December 4, 1751. January Court, 1752. *Sons:* JOSHUA (land on Long Branch and Creek Swamp), WILLIAM ("my manner plantation"), AARON. *Grandsons:* BENJAMIN and CHALKLEY ALBERTSON. *Daughters:* HANNAH ALBERTSON, ELIZABETH NEWBY, LYDDA TRUEBLOOD. Negroes bequeathed to sons. Three sons appointed executors. *Witnesses:* JOSHUA PERISHO, JAMES HENBE, MARY MORRIS. *Clerk of the Court:* EDMUND HATCH.

ALDERSON, SIMON.   Beaufort County.

Will not dated. Probated at December Court, 1740. *Sons:* LEVIN and JOHN. *Daughters:* ELIZABETH and SARAH ALDERSON. *Other legatee:* JOHN ODEON. No executor appointed. *Witnesses:* ROBERT HOWARD, WILLIAM MARTIN. *Clerk of the Court:* ROGER JONES.

ALDRIDGE, JOHN. County not given.

December 28, 1705. April 2, 1706. *Wife and Executrix:* DOROTY. *Witnesses:* SAMUL SLOCUMB, RICHARD SMITH, JOHN WILSON. *Clerk of the Court:* LEVI TRUEWHITT.

ALEXANDER, ANTHONY. Tyrrell County.

July 29, 1741. November 3, 1741. *Sons:* ANTHONY, JOSEPH, LAMUEL, BENJAMIN, ISAAC, JOHN (plantation known by name of Mockason), JOSIAS (plantation known as Tuttellfields), GIDDEON, JOSHUA. *Daughters:* ANNE, RACHEL, PRISCILLA, SARAH, JANE, NAOMI, CASIAH, SETH. *Son-in-law and Executor:* THOMAS BATEMAN. *Witnesses:* BENJAMIN GIDGOOD, THOMAS BEST, CHRISTIAN ALEXANDER. Proven before J. MONTGOMERY.

ALFORD, JABEZ. Chowan Precinct.

July 9, 1705. July Court, 1706. *Legatees:* GEORGE TAYLER, ESAYAH HENLY, LUKE HAMAN, JAMES DAMEVALL, MARY DAMEVALL, THOMAS DANIELL, SARAH JONES. *Executor:* THOMAS POLLOCK. *Witnesses:* THOMAS JONES, HENRY BROOKS, JAMES FITZGERALD. *Clerk of the Court:* N. CHEVIN.

ALFORD, JOHN. Albemarle County.

April 16, 1691. May 4, 1691. *Daughters:* TABITHA and SARAH. *Executor:* CHARLES JONES (father-in-law). *Witnesses:* JOHN HUNT, WILLIAM PINDOR, HANNAH WOOD. *Clerk of the Court:* RICHARD PLATER.

ALLDAY, THOMAS. Bertie County.

March 16, 1754. May Court, 1754. *Sons-in-law:* WILLIAM and BENJAMIN COWARD (land on Cotahney). *Other legatees:* THOMAS HIGHMAN, ISAAC, (a molato boy), WILLIAM HIGHMAN, DIANA SANDERLIN. *Executors:* HENRY HUNTER and JOHN SMITH. *Witnesses:* JOHN BROGDEN, THOMAS HYMAN, MOSES HUNTER, PETER BROGDEN. *Clerk of the Court:* SAMUEL ORMES.

ALFORD, JOSEPH. Albemarle County.

December 8, 1689. No probate. *Wife and Executrix:* ANN. *Witnesses:* CHARLES JONES, JOHN BARBER, LUDFORD IVY.

ALLEN, ANDREW. Dobbs County.

October 29, 1762. November 18, 1762. *Wife:* PRISCILLA. *Devisees:* THOMAS WALTON, HANNAH WALTON, GRACE MEERS, GILBERT KER, JOHN VANSSELT, JOSEPH PARKER. *Executors:* JACOB VANSSELT, PRISCILLA ALLEN, JOSEPH KERR. *Witnesses:* ANTHONY VANSSELT, FREDERICK GIBBLE, ANNA GIBBLE. Name of Clerk of Court is torn off.

ALLEN, ELEAZAR.   New Hanover County.

January 1, 1742. *Wife and Executrix:* SARAH. *Nephews and Niece:*
WILLIAM, DANIEL and CATHERINE WILLARD, children "of JOSIAH WILLARD,
of Boston, by my sister, CATHERINE WILLARD." *Executors:* JAMES HAS-
SELL and NATHANIEL RICE. *Witnesses:* SUSANN HASELL, JAS. HASELL,
Clerk of the Court: ISAAC FARIES. Impression of rope and anchor on
seal.

ALLEN, HUGH.   Chowan County.

July 5, 1752. No probate. *Sons:* JOSIA, JOHN and GEORGE. *Daughters:*
EALCE, MARY and SARAH. *Wife and Executrix:* ELIZABETH. *Witnesses:*
RICHARD BOND, RICHARD STALLINGS, JAMES BOND.

ALLEN, JAMES.   Edgecombe County.

December 4, 1733. February Court, 1733. *Legatees:* JAMES KELLEY,
JOHN NAIRNE (executor). *Witnesses:* WILLIAM BELL, ANNE and JOHN
STONE. *Clerk of the Court:* ROBERT FORSTER. Impression of head on
seal.

ALLEN, JOHN.   Bertie County.

January 8, 1735-1736. August Court, 1736. *Sons:* WILLIAM and
RICHARD. *Daughters:* CATHRINE and MARGARET ALLIN. *Wife and Exec-
utrix:* ELIZABETH. *Witnesses:* THOMAS MANDEN, ISAAC RICKS and
HENRY TUDOR. *Clerk of the Court:* JNO. WYNNS.

ALLEN, SARAH, wid. of ELEAZAR ALLEN.   New Hanover Co.

January 28, 1761. April 1, 1761. "My body I commit to the earth, to
be buried as near the remains of my late husband as not to hurt the founda-
tions of his tomb, which was bestowed on him by my beloved niece, MRS.
SARAH FRANKLAND.

"It is my will that all my just debts and funeral charges be paid * * *
hoping that THOMAS FRANKLAND, my said niece's husband (whose mortgage on the said ELEAZAR ALLEN'S estate may perhaps go near to swallow
the whole), will not avail himself of that mortgage so as to cut off the just
demands of my other creditors.

"To my beloved niece, MRS SARAH FRANKLAND, my wedding ring (plain
gold) as a particular mark of my affection and a memento of my conjugal
happiness, not doubting hers is equal, and may it be as lasting. Item: To
my beloved niece, MRS. MARY JANE DRY, I give and bequeath my gold
watch (not of modern taste, but an excellent piece of mechanism), the gold
chain and all the trinkets belonging thereto * * *. Item: To my beloved nieces, the daughters of my sister MOORE, MRS. SARAH SMITH of
Charlestown, MRS. MARY HARLSTON of the same place, and MRS. ANN
SWANN of Cape Fear, I give a mourning ring to each of them * * *. Item:

To my beloved grandniece, MISS MARY FRANKLAND, I give and bequeath my silver-chased teakettle and cream pot and lamp, also my walnut tree fineered tea chest containing three pieces of plate chased as the teakettle, in the form of urns for tea and sugar * * *. Item: I give to my grandniece, MISS HARIAT FRANKLAND, my largest silver waiter * * *. Item: To my grandniece, MISS REBECCA DRY, * * * a dozen teaspoons and strainer in a black shagreen case, designated to accompany an eight-sided silver coffee pot, put into her possession when I went to England in the year 1756, together with a shagreen writing stand, quite new, to encourage her in that part of her education in which she seems to be making great progress * * * To my beloved niece, MRS. MARY JANE DRY, one silver saucepan. I give to my grandniece, SUSANNAH HASELL, a mahogany dressing-table and a little gilt smelling bottle. I give to my grandniece, MARY HASELL, a little mahogany tea chest. I give all the books of modern taste to my grandnieces, REBECCA DRY and SUSANNAH HASELL. I give to my generous and constant friend, WILLIAM DRY, a mourning ring. I give to my friend, MRS. DEROSSETT, SR., my silver etice in a black shagreen case. As to all my other letters to and from my several correspondents abroad and in America, etc., etc.

"It is my will that one acre of ground around the tomb of my said husband be reserved sacred for the use of our cemetery when the rest of the plantation of "Lilliput" shall be sold † † †.

Executors: JAMES MURRAY, WILLIAM DRY, HENRY HYRNES, FREDERICK JONES of the OAK & WILLIAM BAMPFIELD of South Carolina. *Witnesses*: GEORGE MOORE, ELIZABETH CATHERINE DEROSSET, JAMES COLSON. Proven before ARTHUR DOBBS. Coat of arms on seal at top of first page of will.

ALLIGOOD, RICHARD.   Beaufort County.

January 22, 1751. September 19, 1752. *Sons:* HILLERY, WILLIAM. *Daughter:* MATHEW BAUER. Sons appointed executors. *Witnesses:* GEORGE JENKINS, JOHN ALLEGOOD and MARTHA JENKINS. *Clerk of the Court:* WILL ORMOND.

ALSTON, JOHN.   Chowan County.

February 20, 1755. December 2, 1758. *Sons:* JOSEPH JOHN ALSTON (land on White Oak River), SOLOMON ALSTON (one negro), WILLIAM and PHILLIP ALSTON, JAMES ALSTON. *Daughters:* MARY SEWARD, ELIZABETH WILLIAMS, SARAH KEARNY, CHARITY DAWSON. *Grandchildren:* JOHN, ELIZABETH, PATTY and WILLIAM ALSTON. *Executor:* JAMES ALSTON (son). *Witnesses:* SCASBROOK WILSON, THOMAS BYARD, JOSEPH PARKER. Proven before ARTHUR DOBBS.

AMBLER, WILLIAM.   Perquimans County.

April 27, 1745. July Court, 1745. *Friends:* JOHN STEVENSON, WILLIAM STEVENSON (land on Perquimans River), ZACHARIAH NIXON, ELIZA-

BETH PHELPS, HENRY PHELPS, JONATHAN PHELPS, JOHN BARCLIFT of Wearneck, ELIZABETH WILLIAMS, BENJAMIN BAPTIST, JOHN READ, ELIZABETH REED, JOSEPH SUTTON. *Executor:* JOHN STEVENSON. *Witnesses:* SAM SCOLLAY, WILLIAM HAROLD, FRANCIS LAYDEN. *Clerk of the Court:* EDMUND HATCH.

AMBROS, DAVID. Chowan County.

July 14, 1745. August 1, 1745. *Sons:* DAVID, WILLIAM, JESSE and ISRAEL. *Daughters:* MARY, SUSANNAH and MORNING AMBROS. *Wife and Executrix:* SUSANNAH. *Witnesses:* JACOB PRIVETT, DAVID BUSH, JAMES CRAVEN. Proven before ENOCH HALL, C. J. Coat of arms on seal.

ANDERSON, CAROLUS. Northampton County.

February 10, 1752. February Court, 1753. *Daughters:* RACHEL WARREN and MARY ANDERSON (land and negroes), SARAH ANDERSON (land on Kubys Creek). Wife and Executrix not named. *Witnesses:* NICHOLAS and WILLIAM BOONE. *Clerk of the Court:* I. EDWARDS.

ANDERSON, ELIZABETH. Bertie Precinct.

November 5, 1732. August Court, 1733. *Sons:* JAMES, CARROLUS. *Daughter:* ELIZABETH PITMAN. *Granddaughters:* ELIZABETH and SARAH ANDERSON (executrix) *Witnesses:* ELIAS FORTT, EALCER FORTT, HENRY CROMPTON. *Clerk of the Court:* ROBERT FORSTER.

ANDERSON, ELISABETH. Perquimans County.

May 25, 1757. January Court, 1760. *Sons:* JOHN and SAMUEL, *Daughter:* ABIGAIL CHARLES. *Granddaughters:* ELIZABETH and SARAH HENBE. *Grandsons:* WILLIAM ARNOLD and JOSHUA ALBERTSON. *Executors:* WILLIAM ARNOLD, JOHN ANDERSON and WILLIAM ALBERTSON. *Witnesses:* JOHN BOSWELL, JOSEPH BOSWELL, SARAH ANDERSON. *Clerk of the Court:* MILES HARVEY.

ANDERSON, GEORGE. Granville County.

July 6, 1757. March 7, 1758. *Wife and Executrix:* MARY. *Daughter:* EAVE ANDERSON. *Brother:* WILLIAM ANDERSON. *Nephew:* GEORGE ANDERSON (son of William). *Other legatees:* ELIZABETH and JOHN UNDERWOOD. *Executor:* OSBORNE JEFFREYS. *Witnesses:* JAMES BRAEZAR, WILLIAM ANDERSON, THOMAS SMITH. *Clerk of the Court:* DANIEL WELDON.

ANDERSON, JAMES. Perquimans County.

February 6, 1741-1742. December 14, 1742. *Sons:* JAMES and JOHN. *Executor:* RICHARD SKINNER. *Witnesses:* THOMAS JESSOP and THOMAS BATEMAN. Proven before W. SMITH.

ANDERSON, JOHN.   Perquimans County.

January 27, 1744-1745. March 5, 1745. *Executors:* CHRISTOPHER
SUTTON and ABRAHAM MULLEN. *Other legatee:* JANE MULLEN. *Witnesses:*
GEORGE WOOD, ELENDER MULLEN. Proven before GAB JOHNSTON.

ANDERSON, JOSEPH.   Chowan County.

1750. January Court, 1750. *Daughter:* MARY ANDERSON. *Guardians
of daughter:* THOMAS BARKER, DR. SAMUEL SABINE PLOMER and WILLIAM
MEARNS. *Brother:* JAMES ANDERSON, near Lundy. *Sister:* MARGARET
ANDERSON, in Bonnetown, near Leish. *Daughters-in-law:* LUCY and
AGNES MARTIN. *Executors:* THOMAS BARKER and JOSEPH BLOUNT.
Wife: ANN. *Witnesses:* JOHN HALSEY, WILLIAM LUTEN and JAMES
CRAVEN. Codicil bearing date December 24, 1750, makes further pro-
vision for daughter and confirms appointment of THOMAS BARKER as
executor. *Witnesses to Codicil:* PETER PAYNE and JOHN McKILDO.
Clerk of the Court: WILL MEARNS.

ANDERSON, JOSEPH.   Perquimans County.

September 23, 1751. October Court, 1751. *Daughter:* ELIZABETH
(land on Moses Creek, and two negroes). *Executor:* ZACHARIAH NIXON.
Witnesses: JAMES and SILVANUS HENBE, SAMUEL ANDERSON. *Clerk of the
Court:* EDMUND HATCH.

ANDREWS, JOHN.   Rowan County.

October 3, 1756. No probate. *Sons:* JAMES and JOHN. *Daughter:*
JANET. *Wife:* AGNES. *Executors:* THOMAS DOUGLAS and JAMES AN-
DREWS. *Witnesses:* JOHN MARTIN, WILLIAM NIBLACK, ELISABETH LAW-
RENCE. Codicil dated October 3, 1756, makes provision for minor children.
Witnesses: ELISABETH LAWRENCE, WILLIAM NIBLACK, JOHN MARTEN.

ANDREWS, THOMAS.   Bertie Precinct.

January 12, 1736-1737. March 31, 1737. *Legatees:* ROBERT BELL,
THOMAS ANDREWS (executor). *Witnesses:* THOMAS DAVY, ANN and PENE-
LOPE BELL. Proven before W. SMITH, C. J.

ANDREWS, WARREN.   Tyrrell County.

May 4, 1772. February 28, 1774. *Sons:* LEVI, EDMUND and ETHEL-
DRED ANDREWS. *Daughters:* MILLEE BLUNT, MARTHA PEARSE, ELISA-
BETH ANDREWS. *Wife:* SARAH. Three sons appointed executors. *Wit-
nesses:* WILLIAM ELLIS, ROBEN SHERROD. Proven before JO MARTIN.

ANELYN, PETER.

March 14, 1710. No probate. *Sons:* HENRY, PETER and JOHN.
Daughter: ANN. *Executor:* THOMAS POLLOCKE. *Witnesses:* LAURANCE
SARSON, ROBERT WEST, JOHN JONES, THOMAS ASHLY

ANSELL, JOHN.　　　　　　　　　　Currituck County.

September 12, 1738. April Court, 1740. *Son and Executor:* JOHN. *Daughter:* SARAH ROBERTS. *Grandson:* JAMES ROBERTS. *Witnesses:* HENRY WHITE, HILARY WHITE, LEADY WHITE. *Clerk of the Court:* WILLIAM SHERGOLD.

ANSELL, JOHN, "of Netsiland."　　　Currituck County.

April 6, 1753. March Court, 1755. *Sons:* JOHN, WILLIAM, JAMES, CALEB. *Daughters:* MARY and LETESSHA. Wife not named. *Executor:* JOHN ANSELL (son). *Witnesses:* CALEB WHITE, JOSHUA WHITE, PAUL ELISON. *Clerk of the Court:* WILLIAM SHERGOLD.

ANSLEY, SOLOMON.　　　　　　　　Tyrrell County.

August 27, 1750. March Court, 1750. *Daughters:* MARY, SARAH, ELIZA-BETH, ANN, RACHEL and EASTER ANSLEY. *Sons:* JOHN and JOSEPH. *Wife and Executrix:* SARAH. *Witnesses:* SAMUEL SPRUILL, MATTHEW CARSWELL, SAMUEL SPRUILL, JR. *Clerk of the Court:* EVAN JONES.

ARDERNE, JOHN.

October 22, 1707. May 17, 1712. *Kinsman:* WILLIAM DUCKENFIELD (tract of land known by name of Salmon Creek, "all negro, indian, molato slaves, all horses, mares, cobbs, cattle, hoggs, young and old, and everything else in America, England, or any other part of the world.") *Executor:* WIL-LIAM DUCKENFIELD, Esq. *Witnesses:* HENRY LYSLE, THO. ARNOLD, GEO. BLAINYE, CHARLES BARBOUR, JOHN TALOR.

ARENTON, CHRISTOPHER.　　　　　Chowan County.

April 22, 1753. July Court, 1753. *Son:* WILLIAM. *Daughter:* ABE-GELL HUBARD. *Wife and Executrix:* SARAH. *Witnesses:* THOMAS PEIRCE, MARY CREECY, JOHN FENNELL. *Clerk of the Court:* WILL HALSEY.

ARENTON, WILLIAM.　　　　　　　Craven County.

January 23, 1761. *Daughters:* REBECKAH, MARY and LEAH. *Wife:* MARY. *Executor:* HENRY SHIPPARD. *Witnesses:* EDMUND HATCH, MAR-TIN SHIPPARD. No probate.

ARMSTRONG, JEAMS.

June 22, 1684. November 2, 1685. *Executor and sole legatee:* RICHARD CRAGE (1). *Witnesses:* HENRY WHITE and WILLIAM JACKSON. No pro-bate officer.

ARLOW, JAMES.

December 27, 1757. February Court, 1758. *Nephew:* JOHN ARLOW. *Wife and Executrix:* BRIDGET (house and lot in Wilmington). *Executor:*

BENJAMIN MORISON. *Witnesses:* BEN WHEATLEY, ARTHUR MABSON, JOHN JONES. *Clerk of the Court:* JA. MORAN.

ARMOUR, JOHN.   Pasquotank County.

March 21, 1728. March Court, 1729. *Son:* JOHN. *Daughters:* MARY, ANN. *Other legatees:* JOHN DAVIS and WILLIAM DAVIS (brothers of former wife). Wife and Executrix not named. *Executor:* DAVID BARLY (father-in-law). *Witnesses:* (Signatures of witnesses, probate and portion of will missing.)

ARMOR, WILLIAM.   Pasquotank Precinct.

December 13, 1719. January 25, 1719. *Legatees:* THOMAS and THEOPHILUS ARMOR (sons), ROBERT and JOHN ARMOR and ANN MEADS, WILLIAM BROTHERS. *Executor:* JOHN ARMOR. *Witnesses:* WILLIAM JAMES, THOMAS CRANK. Proven before JNO. PALIN.

ARMSTRONG, JOHN.   Currituck County.

March 28, 1753. March Court, 1755. *Wife and Executrix:* ASIAH. *Witnesses:* THOS. WILLIAMS, JOSHUA BRENT, LUCY PUTT. *Clerk of the Court:* WILLIAM SHERGOLD.

ARNOLD, EDWARD.   Chowan County.

February 23, 1748. April Court, 1752. *Son and Executor:* EDWARD. *Daughter:* HANNAH STALLINGS. *Wife:* PLEASANT (plantation and negroes). *Witnesses:* JOHN SUMNER, RICHARD BROTHERS, APSILLA WEBB. *Clerk of the Court:* JAMES CRAVEN. Impression of lion rampant on seal.

ARNOLD, JOHN.   Perquimans Precinct.

March 21, 1723. July 14, 1724. *Sons:* JOHN, LAWRENCE, WILLIAM and JOSEPH. *Daughter:* ELIZABETH ARNOLD. *Wife and Executrix:* MARY. *Witnesses:* WILLIAM HAN, JAMES JONES, ABRAHAM REIGS, JOHN REIGS. *Clerk of the Court:* RICHD LEARY.

ARNOLD, JOHN.   Perquimans County.

April 11, 1735. July 21, 1735. *Son:* JOHN. *Wife and Executrix:* ELIZABETH (land at Deep Creek). *Executor:* SAMUEL PARSONS. *Witnesses:* JAMES GIBSON, WILLIAM ARNELL. *Clerk of the Court:* JAMES CRAVEN. Crest on seal.

ARNOLD, JOSEPH.   Perquimans County.

November 30, 1751. April Court, 1752. *Daughter:* MARY. *Executors:* WILLIAM and LAWRENCE ARNOLD (brothers). *Witnesses:* JAMES GIBSON and WILLIAM BATEMAN. *Clerk of the Court:* EDMUND HATCH.

ARNOLD, LAWRENCE.   Albemarle County.

   December 14, 1691. February 2, 1691. *Son and Executor:* JOHN. *Other legatee:* LAWRENCE GODFREY. *Witnesses:* ELIZABETH JENKINS, ISAAC ROWDEN. *Clerk of the Court:* RICHARD PLATER.

ARRINGTON, WILLIAM.   Northampton County.

   January 11, 1750. February Court, 1752. *Sons:* BRIGGS and WILLIAM (plantation to each). *Other legatees:* JAMES ROSS, NATHANIEL WILLIAMS. *Executors:* JOHN DAWSON and NATHAN WILLIAMS. *Witnesses:* HENRY DAWSON, JOHN PITMAN, JOHN BROCK. *Clerk of the Court:* I. EDWARDS.

ARTHUR, JOHN.   Chowan County.

   May 29, 1735. October Court, 1735. *Legatees:* WILLIAM FALAW, JACOB PRIVIT, JOHN HANAH. *Executors:* THOMAS LUTEN and CONSTANT LUTEN. *Witnesses:* WILLIAM GOOLDSBERRY, HUMPHREY WEBB, EDWARD HOWCOTT. *Clerk of the Court:* JAMES CRAVEN.

ARTHUR, JOHN.   Craven County.

   January 7, 1751. March 2, 1751. *Sons:* JOHN, JAMES, MATTHEW and WILLIAM. *Daughters:* ANN and MARY. *Wife and Executrix:* BRIDGET. *Witnesses:* CHARLES EVITT, ROBERT MOORE, AMMEY MOORE. Proven before GABRIEL JOHNSTON.

ASHE, JOHN BAPTISTA.   Bath County.

   November 2, 1731. November 15, 1734. *Sons:* JOHN and SAMUEL. *Daughter:* MARY. *Brothers:* JOHN and SAMUEL SWANN. *Other legatees:* JOHN RUSSELL, DANIEL HENDRICK of South Carolina. The following lands devised: "lands up the northwest branch of Cape Fear River, called Ashwood, situated between the lands of JOHN PORTER of Virginia, merchant, and the plantation whereon DANIEL DONAHO now lives." "My other lands on the north side of the river directly opposite to those aforementioned"; * * * land on Stumpy Sound called Turkey Point; 100 acres called Stumpy Island or New River Banks; 400 acres "above WILLIAM LEWIS's plantation on the Main Branche of Old Towne Creek"; 2,560 acres near Rockfish Creek on the northwest branch of Cape Fear River; 640 acres of land on the northeast branch of Cape Fear River." The following item may be of interest: "I will that my slaves be kept to work on my lands and that my estate be managed to the best advantage so as my sons may have as liberal an education as the profits thereof will afford; and in their education I pray my executors to observe this method: Let them be taught to read and write and be introduced into the practical part of Arithmetick, not too hastily hurrying them to Latin or Grammar; but after they are pretty well versed in these, let them be taught Latin and Greek. I propose this may be done in Virginia; after which let them learn French; perhaps some Frenchman at Santee will undertake this. When they are arrived to years of discretion let them study the Mathematicks. To my sons when they arrive at age I recommend the pursuit and study of some profession or business (I could wish the one to ye Law, the other to Merchandize), in which let them follow their own inclinations. I will that my daughter be taught to write and read and some feminine accomplishments which may render her agreeable; and that she be not kept ignorant of what appertains to a good housewife in the management of household affairs. Item: I give to each of my executors a gold ring as a token of the respect, etc. I will that a brick Vault may be built at Groveley and my Dear Wife's body taken up out of the Earth and brought and laid there; if it should be my fortune to die in Carolina so as my corpse may be conveyed thither, I desire that one large Coffin may be made and both our bodys laid together therein and lodged in the said Vault." *Executors:* EDWARD MOSELEY, ROGER MOORE, NATHANIEL RICE, SAMUEL and JOHN SWANN, WILLIAM DOWNING and EDWARD SMITH. *Witnesses:* MEHITTOBEL RUTTER, JOHN HAWKINS, CORNELIUS DARGAN, MICH RUTTER. Codicil dated October 16, 1734, appoints JOB HOWS and THOMAS JONES *Executors* and directs interest in sawmill owned by testator and MATT ROWAN to be sold. *Witnesses:* JAMES INNES, JOSEPH WALTERS, EDWARD SMITH. Proven before GAB JOHNSTON. *Executors* qualified before W. SMITH, C. J. Impression of dragon's head on seal.

ASHLEY, JOHN.   Anson County.

February 1, 1759. No probate. *Sons:* JOHN, FRANCIS and WILLIAM (land on Bare Creek), JURDEN. *Daughters:* MARY ANN FRANKS, ELINOR SUTTON, ROSE TOUCHSTONE, SARAH ASHLEY. *Wife and Executrix:* MARY. *Witnesses:* RICHARD YARBOROUGH, CHRISTOPHER TOUCHSTONE, FREDERICK ———.

ASKUE, JOHN.   Isle of Wight County.

Not dated. No probate. *Son:* WILLIAM. *Brother and Executor:* NICHOLAS ASKUE. *Witnesses:* JOHN BROWNE, WILL WILLIAMS, ELIZABETH BROWNE. Original missing. Abstract made from recorded copy, Book 1712-1722, page 31.

AVENT, THOMAS.   Northampton County.

April 15, 1751. February Court, 1752. *Brother and Executor:* WILLIAM AVENT. *Wife:* USLEA. Children not named. *Executor:* JOHN MOORE. *Witnesses:* RICHARD MOORE and JOHN DAVIS. *Clerk of the Court:* I. EDWARDS.

AVERITT, NATHANIEL.   Onslow County.

December 4, 1755. Probate not dated. *Sons:* JOHN, ARTHUR, BENJAMIN NATHANIEL, EPHALY AVERITT. *Son-in-law:* JONATHAN ENNETT. *Daughter:* NANCY AVERITT. *Executors:* STEPHEN LEE, JOHN MILTON and Captain JOHN ASHE. *Witnesses:* NATHANIEL KNOTT, ELIZABETH CAREY, JOHN HUNT. *Clerk of the Court:* WILL CRAY. Crest on seal.

AVERY, JOHN.   Hyde County.

October 27, 1740. Probate not dated. *Wife:* JANE. *Other legatees:* MARTHA SMITH, AGNES SLADE, THOMAS, WILLIAM and SAMUEL SMITH (sons of John), LYDIA (wife of Benjamin Russell), ELIZABETH and DORCAS SMITH, JOHN SMITH, DARCAS WORLDLY, JAMES AVERY, GILBERT MACKNARY, KEZIA HADLEY, ELIZABETH (daughter of Uriah Collins), FOSTER JERVIS, LYDIA CATHRIGHT, JAMES AVERY. *Executors:* JOHN SMITH and FOSTER JERVIS. *Witnesses:* URIAH COLLINS, WILLIAM SILVESTER, WILLIAM GIDDENS. *Clerk of the Court:* WILLIAM BARROW.

BADHAM, WILLIAM.   Chowan Precinct.

October 28, 1736. November 3, 1736. *Devisees and legatees:* ELLEN and MARY DUNSTON (daughters of Martha and John Dunston), BARNABY STELY DUNSTON (son of John), RICHARD WILLIAM DUNSTON (son of John), JOHN LAPORTE. The following lands devised: Plantation on Machecomock Creek; lots Nos. 1, 2 and 3 in town of Edenton; land on Rockahock Creek, in Chowan; plantation on Chinkapin Swamp, in Bertie; 640 acres in Bertie precinct; plantation near Edenton, "whereon I now live"; back plantation called "Heldersham"; 305 acres in Chowan. About ten negroes bequeathed. *Wife and Executrix:* MARTHA. *Executors:* THOMAS JONES and JOSEPH ANDERSON. *Witnesses:* THOMAS JONES, BENJAMIN HILL and THOMAS JACKSON. Proven before W. SMITH. Original of this will is missing. Abstract made from recorded copy, No. 136, in Land Grant Records, Book 4.

BAGGETT, NICHOLAS.   Bertie County.

January 9, 1753. April Court, 1755. *Sons:* BENJAMIN, NICHOLAS, ABRAHAM, JOSEPH, BARNABEY, THOMAS ("the plantation whereon I now live"), HARDY, JOHN. *Daughters:* MARY WEST, MARTHA BAGGETT, ELIZABETH WARD, SARAH BAGGETT. *Wife:* MARY. *Executors:* JOSEPH and THOMAS BAGGETT (sons). *Witnesses:* CHARLES HORNE, JOHN HOOKS. *Clerk of the Court:* BENJAMIN WYNNS.

BAGLEY, THOMAS.

July 19, 1727. *Sons:* THOMAS ("plantation whereon I now live"), WILLIAM (land on Great Branch). *Daughter:* HANNA BAGLEY. *Wife:* SU-

SANA. *Executors:* SUSANA BAGLEY (wife) and JOSEPH JESSOP. *Witnesses:* RICHARD WOOD, JOSIAS BAGNE, WILLIAM SHARBO. *Clerk of the Court:* CHARLES DENMAN.

BAILEY, DAVID.   Pasquotank County.

October 6, 1745. March 29, 1746. *Sons:* JOSEPH (one plantation, three negroes, one whipsaw, one steel trap, one corn mill), BENJAMIN (land bought of Ebenezer Hall, and one negro), ROBERT (land and plantation, "The Folly," two negroes, half of new schooner), SIMON (plantation called "Piney Point" lying at Core Sound, one negro). *Daughters:* ELIZABETH BRYANT, SARAH SNOWDON and TAMAR BAILEY. Stock mark of testator, swallow fork in right ear, the left ear off; also poplar leaf in "ye left ear and a crop and a slit in ye right." To daughter TAMAR is bequeathed one woolen wheel made at Core Sound. *Other legatees.* MIRIAM OVERMAN and DAVID WALLIS (children of second wife). *Wife:* THAMAR. *Executors:* JOSEPH BAILEY (son) and SIMON BRYANT (son-in-law). *Witnesses:* THOS. WEEKS, PATRICK BAILEY, JOHN BAILEY. Proven before ENOCH HALL, C. J.

BAILY, JOHN.   Hyde County.

July 23, 1749. March Court, 1758. *Daughter and Executrix:* MARGARET BAILY. *Friend:* THOMAS BARLOW (son of Elizabeth Kelly). *Witnesses:* THOS. LOACH, JOHN SMITH, WM. CARDING. *Clerk of the Court:* STEPHEN DENNING.

BAILEY, JOSEPH.   Pasquotank County.

June 17, 1749. August 4, 1749. *Daughter:* ANNE BAILEY ("plantation whereon I now live"). *Brothers:* SIMON and ROBERT BAILEY. *Sisters:* THAMAR BAILEY, SARAH SNOWDON. *Executors:* ROBERT BAILEY (brother), PATRICK POOL. *Witnesses:* PATRICK BAILEY, DAVID BAILEY, HENRY DE SON. Will proven before GAB. JOHNSTON at Eden House. Coat of arms on testator's seal.

BAIRD, RICHARD.

Sons-in-law: WILLIAM BOGE and ———BOGE. *Wife:* JEANE. *Cousin:* CATHERN CLARKE. *Other legatees:* JAMES LOADINAR, MARGREETT BOGE. *Executors:* JAMES and CHRISTOPHER———. *Witnesses:* PETER OREY, PATRICK———. On the back of this will appears another will of RICHARD BIARD, in which appear the names of JAMES LADMAN, CATRING CLARKE, HANNAH BARD, JANNE BIARD (wife), WILLIAM MOORE, JOHN LILEY (executor), WILLIAM BOGE, WILLIAM LARNESS, CHARLES MCDANIEL, RICHARD HICKNEY, HANNAH HILLE.

BAKER, HENRY.   Chowan County.

January 9, 1737. May 1, 1739. *Sons:* HENRY ("All the land whereon
I now live * * * these negroes vizt: Guy, Clouse, Bob, Caesar, Ned, Jacob,
Young Diner and Hagar * * * my watch, seal, desk, 6 Russia chares, ye
great glass, my sword, one deal table"); JOHN ("All my land at a place
called Little Town and my land joining on Banks Wynn & Askue, and the
land bought of WILLIAM GARRET in Bertie precinct * * * these negroes,
vizt, Arthur, Juno, Finney, Little Bobb and Dick * * *"); BLAKE ("land
bought of John and Thomas Wilkins in Chowan * * * land on Ahoskie
Marsh in Bertie and the stock thereto belonging * * * these negroes, vizt,
Cipio, Joe, Patt and Argalus"); DAVID ("130 acres of land at Meherring
Landing adjoining to the ferry"). *Daughters:* MARY and SARAH (two negroes to each), RUTH. *Son:* ZADOCK, (twenty shillings). *Wife:* RUTH (six
negroes). *Brothers* and *Executors:* WILLIAM, JAMES and LAWRENCE BAKER.
Witnesses: EDWARD VANN, JOHN BRADY, EDWARD WARREN. Proven
before W. SMITH, C. J.

Original of this will is missing. Abstract made from recorded copy No.
81 in Land Grants, Book 4.

BAKER, MOSES.   Chowan County.

January 26, 1723. January Court, 1724. *Sons:* BENETT, WILLIAM.
Wife and three daughters mentioned but not named. *Executors:* Wife
and RICHARD MINSHON. *Witnesses:* AARON BLANCHARD, WM. HILL,
WILLIAM WESSON. *Clerk of Court:* ROBERT FORSTER.

BALCH, JOSEPH.   Craven County.

December 18, 1750. February 13, 1752. *Friend:* JOHN MARKS. *Wife:*
SUSANNAH BALCH. *Her daughters:* PHOEBE and MARY. *Nephew:* JOSEPH
BALCH (son of Benjamin Balch). *Executor:* JOHN STARKEY. *Witnesses:*
ROBERT MOORE, JNO. SNEAD, CHRISTOPHER NEAL. *Deputy Clerk of
Court:* SOL. REW.

BALEY, JOHN.   Chowan County.

July Court, 1716. *Wife:* MAREY. *Friends:* HENREY CLARK, JEFERY
LYLES. *Executrix:* MARY BALEY (wife). *Witnesses:* HENREY CLARK,
JEFERY LYLES, WILL MITCHELL. *Clerk of the Court:* R. HICKS.

BALL, JOHN.   Carteret County.

November 10, 1749. December Court, 1749. *Sons:* NATHAN ("houses
and plantation whereon I now live"), STEPHEN (150 acres land on "west
side of Brice's plantation"), JAMES (150 acres land "adjoining plantation
whereon I now live"). *Daughters:* SARAH BALL, RACHEL BALL. *Wife:*
MAGDALENE BALL. *Executors:* MAGDALENE BALL (wife) and SAMUEL
NOBLE. *Witnesses:* DAVID TURNER, FRANCIS EGLETON, REBECCA TUR-
NER. *Clerk of the Court:* GEO. READ.

BALL, THOMAS.   Chowan Precinct.

March 28, 1722. April 17, 1722. *Son:* WILLIAM (200 acres land on Corsaks Swamp; 200 acres land; 400 acres of land). *Daughter:* ANN BALL. *Wife and Executrix:* ELIZEBETH. *Executor:* THOMAS YETTS. *Witnesses:* JOSEPH HUDSON, JOHN BUCKLER, THOS. OLDNEE. *Deputy Clerk of the Court:* W. BADHAM.

BALLARD, ABRAHAM.   Perquimans County.

November 9, 1753. April Court, 1754. *Sons:* JETHRO ("plantation whereon I now live"), KEADAH. *Daughters:* APSILLA BALLARD, BATHSHEBA BALLARD. *Wife:* ELIZABETH. *Executors:* ELIZABETH (wife) and JOHN SUMNER. *Witnesses:* SARAH NORFLEET, PHILLISIA NORFLEET, JOHN SUMNER. *Clerk of the Court:* WILLIAM SKINNER.

BALLARD, JOHN.   Chowan Precinct.

July 12, 1736. November 26, 1736. *Wife:* MARY. *Daughter:* ANN BALLARD. *Daughter-in-law:* SARAH. *Executors:* JOHN LEWISS, JOHN JONES, JR. *Witnesses:* BENJAMIN TALBOT, WILLIAM FALLOW. Proven before W. SMITH.

BALLARD, JOSEPH.   Chowan County.

July 21, 1729. October 14, 1729. *Sons:* JOHN, JOSEPH ("my plantation"), ELISHER, ELIAS. *Daughters:* MARTHA, SUSANNE, ESTHER. *Wife:* ANNE. *Executor:* JOSEPH BALLARD (son). *Witnesses:* JAMES MANY, JOHN HOOKS, JOHN PURVIS. Will proven before RICHARD EVERARD, at Edenton.

BALLENTINE, GEORGE.

January 14, 1723. *Wife, Executrix and sole legatee:* DINAH. *Witnesses:* AARON OLIVER, ALEXANDER BALLENTINE, ELINER WENTFORD.

BANGS, ABIAH, widow of JONATHAN.   Craven County.

June 3, 1755. *Cousin:* ELIZABETH HOBBS ("my lot in Newbern Town"). *Daughter:* BETTY BANGS. *Sisters:* ELIZABETH and MARY CARRUTHERS. *Brothers:* JOHN CARRUTHERS, WILLIAM CARRUTHERS. *Executors:* WILLIAM CARRUTHERS (brother), ROBERT JONES, "oturney at law." *Witnesses:* WILLIAM CREEKMORE, RUBIN HAMMONTREE, WILLIAM CARRUTHERS, SR. No probate.

BANGS, JONATHAN.   Craven County.

October 7, 1743. June 15, 1744. *Wife:* ABIAH. *Daughter:* BETTY BANGS. *Sister:* THANKFULL COVELL. *Executors:* JOHN CARRUTHERS (uncle), ABIAH BANGS (wife). *Witnesses:* FRANCIS BRINLEY, JNO. CARRUTHERS, JO. RD. HICKSON. *Clerk of the Court:* W. ROUTLEDGE. Coat of arms on seal.

BANKS, WILLIAM.   Craven County.

April 7, 1772. May 27, 1772. *Wife:* ANNE. *Daughters-in-law:* SU-
SANNAH and FILLDER MOORE. *Sons-in-law:* JOHN MOORE, WILLIAM
MOORE. *Brother:* JONATHAN BANKS. *Executors:* JONATHAN BANKS
(brother) and CHRISTOPHER NEALE. *Witnesses:* JAMES COOR, BENJA-
MIN FORDHAM, JOHN MOORE. Will proven before Jo. MARTIN.

BAPTIST, BENJAMIN.   Chowan County.

March 24, 1752. April Court, 1752. June 15, 1752. *Son:* EDMUND.
Wife: MARY CLARK BAPTIST. *Executors:* MARY C. BAPTIST (wife),
EDMUND BAPTIST (son) and EDMUND HATCH. *Witnesses:* J. PALMER (?),
EDMUND HATCH, SARAH ARNOLD. *Clerk of the Court:* JAMES CRAVEN.
Executrix qualified before————BLOUNT.

BARBER, JOHN.   Albemarle County.

June 10, 1692. April Court, 1693. *Servant:* ROBERT HARPER, 10
pounds, and servant to be set free at date of death. Remainder of estate
to ANN BOYCE, wife of William Boyce, debarring said William Boyce from
any claim or possession of any of said estate. *Witnesses:* THOMAS PALIN,
EM. NISCON, EDWARD MAYO. *Clerk of the Court:* EDWARD MAYO.

BARCLIFT, JOHN.   Perquimans County.

April 23, 1759. July Court, 1759. *Wife:* ELIZABETH BARCLIFT.
Sons: ASA BARCLIFT, DEMSON BARCLIFT, BENJAMIN BARCLIFT, JOHN
BARCLIFT, NOAH BARCLIFT. *Daughters:* MARY BARCLIFT, ELIZA SAN-
DERSON. *Executors:* SAMUEL SUTTON and THOMAS STEVENSON. *Wit-
nesses:* JAMES GIBSON, SAMUEL BARCLIFT, MATHIAS JOHNSON. *Clerk of
Court:* MILES HARVEY.

BARCLIFT, JOSHUA.   Perquimans County.

November 29, 1755. January Court, 1756. *Sons:* WILLIAM ("planta-
tion whereon I now live"), JAMES, BLAKE. *Daughters:* MIRIAM BARCLIFT,
ANN BARCLIFT. *Wife:* MARY. *Executors:* JOHN BARCLIFT (cousin),
JOSEPH ROBINSON, WILLIAM TRUMBALL (nephew). *Witnesses:* JAMES
GIBSON, TULLE WILLIAMS, GEORGE LEE. *Clerk of the Court:* MILES
HARVEY.

BARCLIFT, THOMAS.   Perquimans County.

November 14, 1750. January Court, 1750. *Sons:* WILLIAM, THOMAS
and JOSEPH. *Daughters:* SARAH BIDGOOD, ELIZABETH WRIGHT, MARY
JACKSON, ANNE GORDEN. *Wife and Executrix:* ELIZABETH. *Witnesses:*
JAMES GIBSON, JOHN BARCLIFT. *Clerk of the Court:* EDMUND HATCH.

2

BARCLIFT, WILLIAM.   Perquimans Precinct.
July 25, 1733. December 19, 1733. *Son:* WILLIAM. *Wife:* SARAH.
Executors: SARAH BARCLIFT (wife) and JOSHUA WHITE. *Witnesses:*
JOHN ARNELL, NEHEMIAH WHITE. *Clerk of the Court:* ISAAC PALMER.

BARCLIFT, WILLIAM.   Perquimans County.
March 22, 1747-1748. January Court, 1748. *Sons:* JOSHUA ("use
and occupation of my mannor plantation for two years"), SAMUEL, JOSEPH,
THOMAS, JOHN. *Daughter:* MARY GIBSON. *Grandson:* WILLIAM BAR-
CLIFT (son of Joshua). *Executors:* JOHN BARCLIFT (cousin), EDMUND
HATCH. *Witnesses:* JOHN NICKOLS, JOHN BARCLIFT, EDMUND HATCH.
Clerk of the Court: EDMUND HATCH. Courthouse at Phelps Point.

BARCOCK, WILLIAM.   Pasquotank Precinct.
March 5, 1730. July 10, 1731. *Sons:* THOMAS (100 acres land upper
end of my Island"), WILLIAM, DANIELL (100 acres adjoining Thomas),
PETER (100 acres adjoining Daniell), JOHN (100 acres "on bee tree neck"),
JOSEPH ("plantation I now live on," containing 140 acres), LUKE.
Daughters: JANE and ANN. *Wife and Executrix:* JANE. *Witnesses:* JAMES
FORBUS, REBECCA FORBUS, JOHN BELL. *Clerk of the Court:* WILLIAM
WYOTT.

BARECOCK, THOMAS.   Pasquotank County.
January 1, 1721. January 17, 1721-1722. *Sons:* WILLIAM and THOM-
AS BARECOCK. *Daughters:* ELIZABETH UPTON, SARAH SANDERLIN, PRIS-
CILLA GREGORY, MARGARET GREGORY, REBEKAH FORBUS and MARTHA
FORBUS. *Granddaughter:* MARGARET DAVIS. *Grandson:* CALEB GREG-
ORY. *Executors:* WILLIAM BARECOCK and MARGARET GREGORY. *Wit-
nesses:* BALEY FORBUS, JOHN BELL, GEORGE LUMLEY. *Clerk of the
Court:* EDWARD GALE.

BAREFIELD, RICHARD.   Bertie County.
November 22, 1728. February Court, 1728. *Sons:* RICHARD, ISHAM,
SOLOMON, JAMES, HENRY, WILLIAM, THOMAS. *Grandson:* RICHARD
BAREFIELD. *Wife:* MARY BAREFIELD. *Executors:* RICHARD BAREFIELD
(son) and WILLIAM MORE. *Witnesses:* WILLIAM JONES, THOMAS WHIPPLE,
ALEXANDER COTTON. Letters were issued August 8, 1729.

BAREFIELD, JOHN, on New River.   Onslow County.
November 24, 1742. *Son:* LUKE. *Daughters:* MARY EDWARDS, SARAH
JONES, ROSE, JUDITH. *Wife and Executrix:* ELIZABETH. *Witnesses:*
JAMES BARFIELD, RICHARD JOHNSTOUN, JOHN QUARLAY. No probate.

BARFIELD, RICHARD.   Duplin County.

May 1, 1754. *Sons:* HENRY ("plantation I now live on"), JESSE, SOLOMON. *Daughters:* MARY BARFIELD, BETH BARFIELD, AN GRADY, CATTREN TATER. *Granddaughter:* BETH TATER. *Executors:* SOLOMON and JESSE BARFIELD (sons). *Witnesses:* JAMES BARFIELD, JOHN MORRIS, SOLOMON BARFIELD. *Register:* JOHN DUCKSON (or Dickson).

BARLOW, ROBERT.   Hyde County.

November 24, 1751. March. 1752. *Legatees:* FOSTER JERVIS, DINAH SMITH, MARTHA SMITH, HANNAH MCNALLIN, WILLIAM SILVESTER. *Executor:* WILLIAM SILVESTER. *Witnesses:* BENJA. RUSSELL, JOEL BARTON. *Clerk of the Court:* FRAN. EGLETON. Courthouse at Woodstock town.

BARNETT, EDWARD.

November 13, 1687. *Wife:* SARAH. *Daughter:* ELENER CONET. *Witnesses:* THOMAS MONEY, THOMAS BUTLER. No probate.

BARNES, JOSEPH.   Northampton County.

April 7, 1751. August Court, 1751. *Sons:* JACOB, MYCAH, DEMSEY, JETHRO, JAMES. *Wife:* ELIZABETH. No executor named. *Witnesses:* JOSEPH CARISSUR, HENRY GAY, CHARLES SKINNER, JULION WHITLEY. *Clerk of the Court:* I. EDWARDS.

BARNES, JOSEPH.   Onslow County.

July 4, 1755. *Son:* HEZEKIAH (land and plantation). *Wife:* ANN. *Executors:* ANN BARNS (wife) and JONATHAN METTON. *Witnesses:* JOHN CHAPMAN, MARGRET MORTON. *Clerk of the Court:* WILL. CRAY.

BARNSFELD, ANNE.   Pasquotank County.

April 23, 1721. July 8, 1721. *Daughters:* ANN COWLES, ELIZABETH ROYAL. *Granddaughter:* ELIZABETH ROYAL. *Executor:* CORNILUS ROYAL. *Witnesses:* ROBERT PALMER and EVAN JONES. Will proven before JOHN PALIN, J. P.

BAROS, MOSES.

March 14, 1733. *Devisee:* MARY LESON. *Executor:* ROBERT PEYTON. *Witnesses:* WILLIAM LANE, TOBE LANE, ROBERT PEYTON, HENRY CRAFTON and EDWARD HADLEY, Justices of Bath Court. JOHN COLLISON, Clerk of Bath Court.

BARROW, EDMUND.   Northampton County.

March 22, 1758. July Court, 1758. *Sons:* BENJAMIN, JOHN, JAMES. *Daughters:* ELIZABETH BARROW, MARY BARROW. *Wife:* MARY. *Execu-*

tors: MARY BARROW (wife), Major NICHOLAS MASSENBURG. *Witnesses:* JOHN TURNER, JAMES CARY, JR. *Clerk of the Court:* I. EDWARDS.

BARROW, JAMES.   Chowan County.

June 17, 1718. *Sister:* JOHANAH. *Brother:* JOSEPH. *Wife:* SARAH. *Daughter:* SARAH BARROW. *Cousin:* SARAH BARROW. *Executrix:* SARAH BARROW (wife). *Witnesses:* FRANCIS SMITH, THOMAS PEIRCE, JOHN ANDERSO. Will proven in Perquimans County. *Clerk of the Court:* RICHARD LEARY.

BARROW, JOHN, SR.   Perquimans County.

March 1, 1718. August, 1718. *Sons:* JOHN and JOSEPH ("my manner plantation"), JAMES (300 acres land). *Friend:* JOHN MIDDLETON. *Executors:* JAMES and JOSEPH BARROW. *Witness:* FRANCIS SMITH. Will proven before CHARLES EDEN, Governor and Ordinary.

BARROW, JOHN.   Perquimans Precinct.

June 11, 1718. August 12, 1719. *Son:* JOHN ("all my lands"). *Daughters:* SARAH, REBECCA, ELISABETH, MARGARET. *Wife:* RACHELL. *Executors:* JOSEPH BARROW (brother) and RACHELL BARROW (wife). *Witnesses:* FRANCES SMITH, JAMES BARROW, JOHN WILLIAMS, JOHN LENDION. *Clerk of the Court:* RICHARD LEARY.

BARROW, JOHN.   Perquimans County.

February 17, 1742. March 5, 1742. *Sisters:* SARAH ASHLEY, MARGARET BARROW. *Cousins:* JOHN ASHLEY, JOSEPH ASHLEY. *Executors:* ZACHARIAH NIXON, FRANCIS ETOMS (_). *Witnesses:* JAMES SKINNER and JOSEPH BARROW, JR. (Quakers), WILLIAM JONES. Proven before W. SMITH.

BARROW, JOHN.   Hyde County.

August 23, 1748. September Court, 1748. *Brothers:* ZACHARIAH BARROW ("my house and plantation"), MOSES, THOMAS, GEORGE, FREDERICK. *Sisters:* ANN DOWNING, REBACA BARROW. *Executor:* JOHN BARROW (uncle). *Witnesses:* NATHANIEL EBORNE, JOHN HARVEY, THOMAS SIMONS. *Clerk of the Court:* THOMAS LOACK.

BARROW, JOSEPH.   Perquimans County.

March 17, 1754. January Court, 1755. *Sons:* JOHN ("lower part of my manner plantation"), WILLIAM (300 acres land). *Daughters:* ELIZABETH BUNDAY, ANN and ORPAH BARROW. *Grandson:* WILLIAM BARROW. *Wife:* SARRAH. *Witnesses:* THOMAS PEIRCE, JOHN SWAIN, JOSHUA LANG. *Executors:* JOSIAH BUNDAY, JOHN BARROW, WILLIAM BARROW (sons), ANN BARROW and ORPAH BARROW (daughters). *Clerk of the Court:* RICHARD CLAYTON.

BARROW, JOSEPH.   Beaufort County.

June 19, 1752. *Sons:* JEAMS (plantation bought of John Vernon), JOHN (plantation bought of Thomas Little), JOSEPH and daughter MARY ("place where Davis lives"). *Executors:* Brother JOHN BARROW and wife JEAN BARROW. *Witnesses:* JOHN BERGERON, ROBERT FLAKE, WILLIAM MITCHELL. *Clerk of the Court:* WILL ORMOND.

BARROW, JOSEPH, JR.   Perquimans County.

February 14, 1753. April Court, 1753. *Wife:* SARAH BARROW. *Son:* WILLIAM BARROW. *Executrix:* SARAH BARROW. *Witnesses:* JOSEPH WHITE, MARY SHERWOOD. *Clerk of the Court:* EDMUND HATCH.

BARROW, REBEKAH.   Perquimans Precinct.

January 13, 1721. October 23, 1722. *Sister, Executrix and sole devisee and legatee:* SARAH BARROW. *Witnesses:* WILLIAM DAVIS, JACOB BUTLER and CHRISTOPHER BUTLER. Will proven before C. GALE, Chief Justice.

BARROW, WILLIAM.   Hyde County.

January 8, 1715. October 23, 1716. *Sons:* WILLIAM, JOHN, RICHARD (manor plantation, 1400 acres), SAMUEL, JOSEPH, JAMES (1000 acres land on Broad Creek). *Daughters:* ANN and SARAH BARROW. *Wife:* ELIZA. *Executors:* ELIZA (wife) and WILLIAM (son). *Witnesses:* THOS. BONNER, THOS. MARTIN, JOHN COSTER. Will proven before C. GALE, Chief Justice.

BARROW, WILLIAM.   Hyde County.

April 25, 1746. *Sons:* JOHN, THOMAS ("my manner plantation"), GEORGE, MOSES, ZACHARIAH and HEDRICK (to the two latter sons "land lying on Jacks Creek"). *Daughters:* REBEKAH BARROW and ANNE DOWNING (wife of WILLIAM DOWNING). *Executors:* JOHN BARROW (brother), JAMES COLES (son-in-law), JOHN SMITH. *Witnesses:* NATHANIEL EBORNE, HENRY EBORNE, REBEKAH EBORNE, MARTHA EBORNE, JOHN BARROW. *Clerk of the Court:* THOMAS LOACK.

BARROW, WILLIAM.   Edgecombe County.

October 20, 1758. December Court, 1758. *Son:* WILLIAM BARROW (plantation lying on Kehukey Swamp). *Daughter:* ANNA FORT. *Granddaughter:* ELIZABETH FORT. *Executor:* WILLIAM BARROW. *Witnesses:* JAMES BARNES, DREW SMITH, WILLIAM BARNES. *Clerk of the Court:* JOS. MONTFORT.

BARRY, WILLIAM.   Bath County.

December 14, 1721. *Brothers:* DAVID BARRY, MARION BARRY. *Executor:* THOMAS MORRIS. *Witnesses:* RICHARD HARVEY, ANN GREEN. *Clerk of the Court:* RT. FORSTER.

BARTLETT, WILLIAM.   Albemarle County.

March 14, 1694-1695. July Court, 1698. *Eldest son:* WILLIAM (plantation adjoining William Arnold). *Son:* THOMAS (land from branch adjoining home plantation to Thomas Godfrey's line). *Executors:* ELIZA-
BETH and WILLIAM BARTLETT. *Witnesses:* THOS: TWEDY, JOHN NORTH-
COAT, GILBERT GOODALL. *Clerk of the Court:* WILLIAM GLOVER.

BARTON, VALLENTIN.   Albemarle County.

March 6, 1685. March 24, 1686. *Wife:* HANNAH. *Brothers-in-law:*
WILLIAM FYAM, JOSEPH WILLIAMS. *Friends:* HANNA FORD, LEDY HAR-
RISON. *Executors:* HANNA BARTON (wife) and GEORGE FORDISE (brother-
in-law). *Witnesses:* ANN SYMONS, RICHARD FOUNTAIN, WILLIAM WILKJON.
Will proven before WILLIAM WILKJON.

BARTRAM, ELIZABETH, relict of WM. BARTRAM.   Bladen Co.

December 27, 1771. August Court, 1772. *Daughters:* SARAH BROWN
(husband, Thomas Brown), MARY ROBESON (husband, Thomas Robeson).
Executors: THOMAS BROWN (son-in-law) and SARAH BROWN (his wife).
Witnesses: JNO. JONES, HENRIETTA JONES, MARY SYON (LYON). *Clerk
of the Court:* MATURIN COLVELL. Will also proven before the Governor
and Council, February 2, 1773, as attested by J. BIGGLESTON. Executor qualified before JO. MARTIN, at New Bern, February 3, 1773. Sealed
with signet ring.

BASS, EDWARD.   Northampton County.

July 25, 1748. August Court, 1750. *Sons:* BENJAMIN (plantation on
Quarter Swamp), JOSEPH (50 acres of land and orchard), SAMPSON (50
acres land on Quarter Swamp), EDWARD (50 acres of land), JAMES (50
acres land), REUBEN ("my mannor plantation"). *Grandson:* ELIJAH
BASS. *Daughters:* KATHERINE ANDERSON, DINAH BASS, KIZIAH BASS,
MARY BASS. *Wife:* LOVEWELL BASS. *Executor:* BENJAMIN BASS (son).
Witnesses: WILLIAM BASS, DINAH BASS, JOHN SUTTON. *Clerk of the
Court:* I. EDWARDS.

BASS, JOHN.   Bertie Precinct.

January 18, 1732. February Court, 1732. *Sons:* MOSES (all land on
north side of "Baire Swamp"), JOHN, EDWARD ("my maner plantation"),
WILLIAM ("my land at ye Beaver dam"), ARON ("plantation on south
side of Baire Swamp"). *Grandson:* ARON JOHNSTUN (100 acres of land).
Daughters: JEUDATH CANADY (100 acres of land), SARAH ANDERSON (100
acres of land), LOVEY BASS (100 acres land), MARY (100 acres land), PACE-

UNCE BASS ("plantation on south side of Baire Swamp"). *Wife:* MARY. *Executors:* JOHN and EDWARD BASS (sons). *Witnesses:* THOMAS BRYANT, JAMES GUIE, EDWARD BASS. *Clerk of Court:* RT. FORSTER.

BASTABLE, WILLIAM.   Perquimans Precinct.

March 9, 1727-1728. *Wife:* HANNAH. *Daughter:* HANNAH BASTABLE. *Other legatees:* MARY and ANN SCETTISON (daughters of JAMES SCETTISON), RACKES WHITE. *Executors:* SAMUEL PHELPS and ROBERT WILLSON. *Witnesses:* JONATHAN SHEARWOOD, JOHN HARRES, BENJAMIN SANDERS. *Clerk of the Court:* CHARLES DENMAN.

BATCHELOR, EDWARD.

September 21, 1706. *Wife:* (Mentioned, but not named). *Friend:* ROBERT FEWOX. *Executor:* JOHN FEWOX. *Witnesses:* SAMUEL BREUITT, JOHN GATE. No probate.

BATCHELOR, EDWARD.   Newbern, Craven County.

1777. *Sons:* JOHN BATCHELOR (tract of land on Susquehanna, in "Pensilvania"), EDWARD BATCHELOR. *Daughters:* FRANCIS BATCHELOR and ELIZABETH BATCHELOR. *Wife:* FRANCIS BATCHELOR. *Friend and partner in business:* THOMAS ASHETON. *Executors:* THOMAS ASHETON, of Philadelphia; DR. THOMAS HASTINE, Newbern; FRANCIS BATCHELOR (wife). This will was not signed, which fact is explained by affidavits of RICHARD COGDELL (taken by JOSEPH LEECH, J. P.), MICH'L. GORMAN (taken by JOSEPH LEECH), THOMAS FLYNN (taken by JOSEPH LEECH, J. P.). Executors qualify before RICHARD CASWELL, Governor.

BATE, HENRY LAWRENCE.   County not given.

May 12, 1740. July 9, 1740. *Son:* AUGUSTINE BATE (land bought of Jonathan Taylor). *Wife and Executrix:* MARTHA. *Sister:* ANN BATE (one gold ring). *Mother:* SARAH SANDERS. *Executors:* HUMPHREY BATE (brother), THOMAS WHITMELL (brother-in-law). *Witnesses:* WILL CATHCART, HENRY HUNTER, SARAH HUNTER. Proven before GAB. JOHNSTON. Coat of arms, a shield bearing a lion rampant on seal.

BATEMAN, JOHN.   Perquimans County.

February 4, 1747-1748. July Court, 1750. *Nephew:* THOMAS BATEMAN ("plantation whereon I now live," also plantation called "Broad Neck"). *Brother:* THOMAS BATEMAN (father of nephew THOMAS), MARY HAWKINS (daughter of nephew JOHN HAWKINS), ELIZABETH PHELPS (daughter of brother JONATHAN BATEMAN), MARY PHELPS (daughter of brother THOMAS), WILLIAM BATEMAN (son of brother THOMAS), SARAH BUTTERRE (daughter of brother JONATHAN). *Executors:* THOMAS BATEMAN (brother), WILLIAM BATEMAN (nephew). *Witnesses:* SAMUEL

SWANN, FRANCIS LAYDEN, CATHERINE DAVIS.   *Deputy Clerk of Court:*
BENJ. SCARBOROUGH, for EDMUND HATCH, Clerk.   Coat of arms on seal.

BATEMAN, JONATHAN.   Albemarle County.

January, 1694-1695. February 25, 1695. *Wife:* ELIZABETH. *Sister:*
MARGARET. *Sons:* JONATHAN, JOHN, THOMAS. *Daughter:* MARY. *Ex-
ecutor:* JONATHAN (son). *Witnesses:* THOMAS HASSALE, JOHN TWIGGER,
DIANA WHITE. *Clerk of the Court:* W. GLOVER.

BATEMAN, WILLIAM.   Currituck Precinct.

March 30, 1703. April 25, 1704. *Daughters:* MARY, ELIZA and ISA-
BELL (300 acres of land "back in the woods"). *Son:* JOSHER (or JOSEPH)
("dwelling plantation"), WILLIAM, SAMUELL. *Executrix:* Wife (not
named). *Witnesses:* ROBERT SMITH, DANNIELL MAKEFASHION and AN-
DREW MAKEFASHION. *Clerk of the Court:* EDWD. TAYLER.

BATTERS, THOMAS.

November 29, 1733. June 11, 1734. *Daughters:* MARY and DIANA
BATTERS ("my manor plantation"). *Wife and Executrix:* DARKERS.
Witnesses: ELIZABETH COUPPER, PHILO. WILLIAMS, SAMUELL COUPPER.
Will proven at Bath town. *Justices:* ROBT. PEYTON, BENJ'N PEYTON,
ROGER KENYON, EDWD. HADLEY. *Clerk of the Court:* JNO. COLLISON.

BATTLE, JOHN.   Bertie County.

April 22, 1740. May Court, 1740. *Sons:* WILLIAM, JESSE. *Daughters:*
PRISSILLA BATTLE, SARAH BATTLE. *Wife:* SARAH. *Executors:* SARAH
BATTLE (wife), WILLIAM BATTLE (brother). *Witnesses:* WILLIAM KNIGHT,
JAMES GRIFFEN, MARTHA KNIGHT. *Clerk of the Court:* JNO. WYNNS.

BAYER, DAVID.   Chowan County.

August 8, 1696. October, 1696. *Clerk of the Court:* THOS. CHEVIN.
Witnesses: THOS. LUTEN, CASTEN ROBISON. This will is illegible.

BAYES, EDWARD.   Albemarle County.

August 8, 1696. October Court, 1696. *Son:* JOHN BAYES. *Daughters:*
ELIZ., MARY and ANN BAYES. *Executrix:* MARY BAYES. *Witnesses:*
THOS. LUTON and COTTON ROBISON. *Clerk of the Court:* NATHL. CHEVIN.

BEASLEY, FRANCES.   Albemarle County.

April 17, 1719. May 20, 1719. *Son:* JEAMES (a tract of land on the
south side of Perquimans River), ROBERT (a tract of land on the north
side of Morattock River). *Wife:* MARY BEASLEY. *Executors:* JEAMS

BEASLEY (brother) and friend JOHN SMITHWICK. *Witnesses:* JOHN LESSHONS, WILLIAM MIZELL, JOHN BENTLEY. Proven before CHAS. EDEN, Governor and Ordinary.

BEASLEY, JAMES.   Bertie County.

January 2, 1758. January Court, 1758. WILLIAM BENTLEY (son of JOHN BENTLEY). *Godson:* LUKE SMETHWICK. *Executors:* JOHN SMETHWICK, JNO. WARD. *Witnesses:* JON. SMETHWICK, EDMUND SMETHWICK. *Clerk of the Court:* BENJ'N WYNNS.

BEASLEY, SAMUEL.   County not given.

November 13, 1735. *Brothers:* FRANCIS and THOMAS. *Other legatees:* JOHN BEASLEY, MARY BEASLEY (grandmother), THOMAS HUTSSOON, JAMES BEASLEY, JUNR. No executor. *Witnesses:* WILLIAM CROPLY, THOMAS BENTLEY, ELIZABETH WELLS. No probate.

BECTON, JOHN.   Craven County.

January 13, 1753. May Court, 1753. *Sons:* FREDERICK, GEORGE (340 acres land at "ye little creek"), EDMOND (land "known by ye name of Jacobbs Wells"), MICHAEL (lands "called the Snow Hills"). *Daughters:* MARY and SARAH. *Wife:* ANN. *Executors:* FREDRICK ESLER, FREDRICK BECTON (son). *Witnesses:* WALTER JONES, THOMAS BRANTON, CLEMENT DYSON. *Clerk of the Court:* SOL. REW.

BEELS, JACOB.   Pasquotank County.

May 15, 1746. July Court, 1746. * *Daughters:* TABITHA and MARY (manor plantation), BARBRAY, ELIZABETH. *Brother:* JOHN BEELS. *Executor:* JOHN BEELS (brother). *Witnesses:* CHARLES WRIGHT, WILLIAM ANDREWS, MARY WRIGHT. *Clerk of the Court:* THOS. TAYLOR.

BEELS, JAMES.   Pasquotank County.

November 3, 1721. April 17, 1722. *Wife and Executrix:* ANN. *Son:* JOHN BEEL (plantation). *Witnesses:* JOHN PERKENS, HENRY CREECH, GEORGE LUMLEY. *Clerk of the Court:* EDW'D GALE.

BEEZLEY, THOMAS.   No county given.

April 15, 1733. July 3, 1733. *Sons:* JOHN and THOMAS. *Wife:* ELIZA. *Friend:* THOMAS OWIN. *Executors:* ELIZABETH BEEZLEY (wife), JOHN BEEZLEY (son). ·*Witnesses:* JNO. FREDERICK, JOHN KING. *Clerk of the Court:* WM. CRAWFORD (or CRANFORD).

BEFRET, BENJAMIN, Mulberry Neck, New Hanover County.

October 25, 1749. August 24, 1753. August 30, 1753. *Son:* BENJAMIN (plantation and lands). *Executors:* HENNERY CASTER and THOMAS

KENNAN. *Witnesses:* WILLIAM SAVAGE, HOUGH MCCANNE, JOHN DICKSON, Register of Duplin County; JOSEPH WILLIAMS, Justice of the Peace; JA. MURRAY, Sec. *Remarks:* This will mentions wife and four children, but does not name the wife, and names only one of the children.

BELL, CORNELIUS.   Beaufort and Hyde Precincts.

August 26, 1729. December Court, 1729. *Sons:* CORNELIUS ("third part of my land"), GEORGE ("one third part of my land"). *Daughter:* MARY. *Grandson:* JAMES NEVEL. *Friend:* JOHN LATHY BELL. *Executor:* CORNELIUS BELL (son). *Witnesses:* EDWD. HADLEY, THOMAS TULLE. *Clerk of the Court:* JOHN MATTOCKE.

BELL, ELIZABETH.   Tyrrell County.

June 16, 1750. November 30, 1750. "Sister Margarett's daughter in London" (wedding ring and necklace). CAPT. WILLIAM MACKEY, deceased husband's nephew (all residue of estate). *Executors:* CULLEN POLLOCK and WM. MACKEY. *Witnesses:* THOS. LEE, JOHN GORMAN, BEDFORD FAGON Proven before GAB. JOHNSTON, at Eden House.

BELL, GEORGE.   Edgecombe County.

December 21, 1751. February Court, 1752. *Sons:* ARTHUR, GEORGE, WILLIAM. *Daughter:* ELIZABETH FLOYD. *Granddaughter:* MARY BELL. *Executors:* FRANCIS FLOYD and ARTHUR BELL. *Witnesses:* WILLIAM PARTIS, THOS. BELL, THOS. FLOYD. *Clerk of the Court:* BENJAMIN WYNNS.

BELL, GEORGE.   Edgecombe County.

February 18, 1755. May, 1755. *Sons:* JOHN ("plantation whereon I now live"), DAVID, GEORGE. *Wife:* SARAH BELL. *Executors:* SARAH BELL (wife) and JOHN BELL (son). *Witnesses:* ARTHUR BELL, GEORGE BELL, RAFE CHANNEL. *Clerk of Court:* JOS. MONTFORT.

BELL, JOHN.   Pasquotank County.

March 1, 1720. March 29, 1721. *Sons:* JAMES ("all my land att Alegator"), JOHN, WILLIAM, GEORGE, NATHANIEL (to these four "all my land on the north side of Pasquotank River"), HENRY, JOSEPH, BENJAMIN. *Daughter:* MARY BELL. *Wife and Executrix:* MARY. *Witnesses:* WILLIAM WILLSON, SAMUEL COCK, DARBEY SIVILENANT. Will proven before R. HICKS, Clerk, at Court held at Queen Anne's Creek, in Chowan Precinct.

BELL, JOSEPH.   Carteret County.

March 12, 1744. June Court, 1745. *Wife:* MARGRIT. *Son:* THOMAS ("my plantation"). *Friend:* JOHN NELSON. *Executors:* JOHN NELSON and THOMAS BELL. *Witnesses:* THOMAS HARRISS, RACHEL BOOTH, MARTHA BOOTH. *Clerk of the Court:* GEO. READ.

BELL, ROSS.   Carteret County.

January 24, 1726. *Sons:* GEORGE, ROSS, JOSEPH. *Daughter:* MARY
BELL. *Executor:* JOSEPH BELL. *Witnesses:* GEO. WHITAKER, JAMES
HINES, MARGRETT BELL. *Clerk of the Court:* JOHN GALLAND.

BELL, THOMAS.   Chowan County.

December 11, 1733. January Court, 1733. *Cousins:* WILLIAM BELL
(land in Perquimans called "Matthew's Point"), THOMAS BELL (land on
Kendricks Creek), ANNE and JANE BELL (daughters of brother JOHN BELL),
WILLIAM MACKAY. *Wife and Executrix:* ELIZABETH. "It is my will that
no sale be made of any slaves, but that my estate be kept intire except my
Sloop————". *Witnesses:* SAML DURRANCE, W. DOWNING, HANAH
GIRKIN. *Clerk of the Court:* MOSELEY VAIL.

BELL, THOMAS.   Chowan County.

August 28, 1751. October Court, 1751. *Cousins:* (the surviving children of ROBT. MCCLEE and JAMES OAR. *Friend:* CAPT. WILLIAM MACKEY.
Executors: ALEXANDER STEWART (brother-in-law), JAMES WADDAL. *Witnesses:* JAMES TROTTER, JEMIMA ALLEN, JAMES CAMPBELL. *Clerk of the
Court:* JAS. CRAVEN.

BELL, WILLIAM.   Currituck County.

August 27, 1721. August 31, 1721. *Son:* WILLIAM. Wife and children mentioned, but not named. *Witnesses:* THOMASIN ONEAL, MARY
ONEAL, DEBORAH PELL, SARAH WALKER. Proven before THOS. TAYLOR,
JOHN WOODHOUSE. This is a nuncupative will proven by witnesses after
testator's death.

BELL, WILLIAM.   Edgecombe County.

December 1, 1752. May and August Courts, 1754. *Sons:* ARTHUR
BELL (390 acres land in the River Island), JOSHUA BELL (plantation
where he now lives). *Daughters:* MARY PYRENT, ANNE BELL. *Executors:* ARTHUR and JOSHUA BELL. *Witnesses:* JAMES ATKISON, WILLIAM
CAIN, REBECAH CAIN. *Clerk of Court:* BEN'J. WYNNS.

BELLMAN, JOHN.   Perquimans County.

July 10, 1740. October, 1740. *Wife:* MARY. *Daughter:* SARAH BELL-
MAN. *Executors:* MARY BELLMAN (wife), ROBERT WILLSON, JAMES SIT-
TERSUN, ZACK ELSON. *Clerk of the Court:* JAMES CRAVEN.

BELMAN, JOHN.   Pasquotank Precinct.

November 5, 1706. January Court, 1706-1707. *Sons:* JOHN and ROB-
ERT. *Wife and Executrix:* SARAH. *Witnesses:* THO. BOYD, BENJ'N WEST.
Clerk of the Court: THO. ABINGTON.

BENBOW, GERSHON.   Bladen County.

January 12, 1750. *Sons:* POWEL, RICHARD and EVANS. *Daughter:*
SUSANNAH. *Executors:* POWELL BENBOW (son) and CHARLES BENBOW
(brother). *Witnesses:* ABRAM SANDERS, RICHARD MAY, JOHN JONES.
No probate.

BENBURY, WILLIAM.   Chowan County.

April, 1755. *Wife:* BRIGETT. *Sons:* WILLIAM, JOHN, JOSEPH, JAMES,
MILES, EDMOND. *Brother:* JOHN BENBURY. *Daughter:* SARAH. *Execu-
tors:* JOHN BENBURY, WM. BENBURY and wife of testator. *Witnesses:*
JOHN BEASLEY, SAMUEL BENBURY, J. BENBURY. *Clerk of the Court:* WILL
HALSEY.

BENDER, MARTIN.   Craven County.

October 19, 1750. December Court, 1750. *Sons:* DANIEL (plantation),
JOHN (150 acres land in Carteret County on the north side of White Oak
River). *Daughters:* SALOME and MARY BENDER (250 acres land on north
side of White Oak River). *Executors:* JOHN SIMMONS and JOHN GRANADE.
Witnesses: BENJAMIN SIMMONS and ELIZABETH MORREY. *Clerk of the
Court:* PHIL. SMITH.

BENNET, JOHN.   Currituck Precinct.

December 10, 1710. *Sons:* JOSEPH ("my plantation"), BENJAMIN (land
bought of JOSEPH NICKER). *Wife and Executrix:* MARY. *Brother:* JOSEPH
BENNET. Portion of lands devised to use of poor "old men and women
who have been honest, etc.," and portion left for education of poor children. *Witnesses:* GEORGE and ANN THOMPSON, EDWARD COB and ED-
WARD STAFFORD. Recorded in Book 1712-1722, page 49. Original missing.

BENNET, JOSEPH.   Currituck Precinct.

March 9, 1751–1752. April 9, 1723. *Sons:* JOSEPH ("plantation now
dwell on") WILLIAM, SAMUEL (84 acres land), JOHN. *Daughters:* MARY
SAYRS, ALICE BENNET. *Wife:* ANNE. *Executors:* ANNE BENNET (wife)
and JOSEPH BENNET (son). *Witnesses:* JOHN WILSON, EDWARD COX.
Clerk of the Court: JAMES WICKER.

BENNET, NEHEMIAH.   Currituck County.

March 11, 1753. April Court, 1753. *Sons:* JOHN ("plantation I now dwell
on"), JOSIAH ("lands on west side of the road"). *Daughter:* SUSAN BEN-
NET. *Wife and Executrix:* ELIZABETH. *Witnesses:* JAMES BURNHAM,
GEORGE DAVIS, SOLOMON BENNET. *Clerk of the Court:* WILLIAM SHER-
GOLD.

BENNET, SOLOMON.   Currituck County.

March 23, 1753. March Court, 1755. *Sons:* MOSES (plantation), BEN
JAMIN (150 acres of land on Mozark Creek). *Daughters:* REBECKER BEN
NET, MARY BENNET, BETSSE BENNET. *Wife and Executrix:* DARKES
BENNET. *Witnesses:* PHILIP NORTHERN, MARY ETHERIGS, TIMOTHY ETH
RIGS. *Clerk of the Court:* WILLIAM SHERGOLD.

BENTLEY, JOHN, OF MORATOCK RIVER.

December 15, 1728. July 15, 1741. *Sons:* WILLIAM ("plantation he
now lives on"), JOHN and JOSEPH ("my manner plantation to be equally
divided between them"), JEREMIAH ("plantation at Tuttsnia"), JAMES,
("plantation at fork of Rockner's"). *Daughters:* MARY BENTLEY, LIDIA.
Grandson: JOHN BENTLEY. *Granddaughter:* HANAH BENTLEY. *Wife:*
SARAH. *Executors:* SARAH BENTLEY (wife), WILLIAM BENTLEY (son).
Witnesses: WILL LATTIMER, MOSES GROOME, ELIZABETH LATTIMER. Will
proven before GAB. JOHNSTON, at Eden House.

BENTLEY, JOHN.   Perquimans Precinct.

October 15, 1695. November, 1695. *Brother:* RICHARD BENTLEY.
Cousin: ELIZABETH LEARY. *Wife:* ANN. JOHN and ROGER WILLIAMS
(sons of brother-in-law, JENKINS WILLIAMS). *Brother-in-law:* WILLIAM
BARROW. *Friend:* JONATHAN ASHFORD. *Executors:* ANN BENTLEY (wife)
and WILLIAM BARROW (brother-in-law). *Witnesses:* JOHN BARROW, ELIZ
ABETH GARDINER, GEORGE BARROW. *Clerk of Court:* W. GLOVER.

BENTLEY, JOHN.   Bertie County.

March 12, 1754. May Court, 1754. *Sons:* WILLIAM ("plantation
whereon I now live"), JOHN (lands known as "Island lands"). *Sister-in-
law:* ANN BENTLEY. *Executor:* RICHARD TOMLINSON. *Witnesses:* JOHN
HYMAN, JOHN WARD, REBEKAH WARD. *Clerk of the Court:* SAMUEL
ORMES.

BENTLEY, JOHN.   Albemarle County.

October 15, 1695. November Court, 1695. *Brother:* RICHARD BENT
LEY. *Cousin:* ELIZABETH LERRY. JOHN WILLIAMS and ROGER WILLIAMS,
WILLIAM BARROW. *Executor:* WILLIAM BARROW. *Witnesses:* JOHN BAR
ROW, ELIZABETH GARDNER, GEORGE BARROW. *Clerk of the Court:* W.
GLOVER.

BENTLEY, JOHN.   Tyrrell County.

March 25, 1754. June Court, 1754. *Wife:* SARAH. *Son:* ISAAC.
Brothers: WILLIAM BENTLEY and JAMES BENTLEY. *Executors:* WILLIAM
GARDNER, JAMES and ISAAC GARDNER. *Witnesses:* LUKE MIZELL, MARY
GARDNER, SARAH MIZELL. *Clerk of the Court:* EVAN JONES.

BENTLEY, RICHARD.   County not given.

April 6, 1697.   May 27, 1697. *Executrix and sole legatee:* DIANA WHITE. *Witnesses:* JAMES BASET (?), ALEXANDER LILLINGTON.   *Clerk of the General Court:* W. GLOVER.   Coat of arms on seal.

BENTON, JOHN.   Chowan County.

February 28, 1748–1749.   October Court, 1750. *Sons:* EPOPHRODITUS, ELIJAH, JETHRO ("manner plantation"), JOHN, MOSES. *Daughter:* JUDITH RABEY, MARY PARKER, CHARITY PARKER. *Grandsons:* WILLIAM PARKER (son of MARY), JAMES PARKER (son of CHARITY). *Executors:* JOHN and JETHRO BENTON (sons). *Witnesses:* HENRY MORGIN, JOHN WEAVER, WILLIAM PARKER. *Clerk of the Court:* JAMES CRAVEN.

BERGERON, JUDITH.   Beaufort County.

November 14, 1742. December Court, 1742. *Sons:* ELIAS, JOHN. *Daughters:* JUDETH WILKINS, JEAN BARROW, MARGRET GIDDINS. *Executor:* ELIAS BERGERON (son). *Witnesses:* MIKEL WARD, JACOB MERCER, THOMAS MERCER. *Clerk of the Court:* JOHN FORBES.

BERRY, CORNEALUS.   Currituck County.

April 17, 1751.   April 7, 1752. *Wife:* COMFORT. *Other legatees:* LITTLETON BERRY, CORNEALUS BERRY and JOHN BERRY (presumably sons). *Executrix:* COMFORT BERRY (wife). *Witnesses:* WILL WHITE, THOMAS MILLER. *Clerk of the Court:* WILLIAM SHERGOLD.

BEVANS, RICHARD.   Hyde County.

1744. *Wife:* MARY. All the land of the testator is bequeathed "to the Baptism ministers that Coms heare to the County of hide to preach the gospel." *Executor:* ROBERT SPRING. *Witnesses:* TIMOTHY ALLEN, PASHE BARTLETT, NAITHANE DAVIS. Will proven before ENOCH HALL, C. J.

BEVERLEY, JOHN, SR.   Bertie County.

December 22, 1737. February Court, 1737. *Sons:* JOHN and ROBERT (to whom is bequeathed "the manner plantation"). *Daughters:* SARAH COX, MARY PEEK. *Granddaughters:* RACHEL BEVERLEY, SARAH BEVERLEY. *Grandsons:* WILLIAM COX, WILLIAM and HENRY BEVERLEY. *Wife:* MARGARETT BEVERLY. *Executors:* JOHN JONES and JOSEPH JONES. *Witnesses:* JAMES DOUGLASS, ELIZA DOUGLASS and JOHN SUTTON. *Clerk of the Court:* JOHN WYNNS.

BEVINS, MARY.   Hyde County.

July 27, 1753. December Court, 1754. *Sons:* JOHN and ROBERT. *Daughters:* ELIZABETH, MARY, ANN. *Granddaughters:* MARY ARTRY, ANN

DICKS. *Friend:* JAMES CHAPMAN. *Executors:* ROBERT and JOHN BEVINS (sons). *Witnesses:* ABRAHAM COX, THOMAS MACKWILLIAMS, SARAH MATHERS. *Clerk of the Court:* STEPN. DENNING.

BEXLEY, WILLIAM.

March 13, 1745. *Daughter:* REBECKAH BEXLEY. *Witnesses:* WM. LANE, NICHS. ROUTLEDGE, PHILIP KESSLER, KATHN. COLESTON, CHARLES STEWART, PETER HENDRIKSON, ELIZTH. HENDRICKSON. Will proven before WM. LANE. This is a nuncupative will.

BIDDLE, JACOB.   Onslow County.

February 24, 1755-1756. April Court, 1758. *Sons:* JACOB ("a pease of land lying on the North side of the Branch that runs by plantation and binding on John Simson's Branch"), ISAAC. *Wife:* ANNE. *Grandsons:* WILLIAM BIDDLE (son of ISAAC), ISAAC BIDDLE (son of ISAAC). *Other legatees:* ABRAM SIMSON, ANTHONY and JACOB CHARLESCRAFT. *Executors:* ANNE BIDDLE (wife) and ISAAC BIDDLE (son). *Witnesses:* SAMUEL PEIRSON, WILLIAM GIBSON, JAMES ATKINS. *Clerk of the Court:* WILLIAM CRAY, Court House on New River. JNO. STARKEY and others, *Justices.*

BILLET, JOHN.   Pasquotank Precinct.

February 29, 1719–1720. April 19, 1720. *Son:* DANIEL (plantation adjoining BENJAMIN PRITCHARD). *Daughter:* SARAH. *Son-in-law:* JAMES BELL. *Wife and Executrix:* ALLICE. *Witnesses:* W. NORRIS, THOS. SAWYER, JONTH. JONES, JAMES BELL. Recorded in book 1712–1722, page 223. Original missing.

BIRNIE, WILLIAM.   New Hanover County.

September 28, 1752. December 14, 1752. *Wife:* ILLIN. *Executors:* ILLIN BIRNIE (wife) and MOSES JNO. DEROSSET. *Witnesses:* JOHN CAMPBELL, MARY MASON, JOHN MAULTSBY. *Clerk of the Court:* ISAAC FARIES.

BIROTE, PETER.   Edenton in Chowan County.

January 15, 1742. April 21, 1743. *Son:* BENJAMIN BIROTE ("all my estate"). *Executor:* PETER PAYNE. *Witnesses:* BENJAMIN TALBOT, HUMPHRY ROBINSON, WM. ARKILL. *Codicil:* January 22, 1742. MARY GASTON "one bed." *Witness:* BENJA. TALBOT. *Clerk of the Court:* RICHARD MCCLURE.

BISHOP, GEORGE.   Onslow County.

December 20, 1743. September Court, 1743. *Brothers:* STOAKLEY (325 acres land in Onslow Co.), JAMES SIDBURY ("one Indian man"), WOODMAN STOAKLEY SIDBURY. *Sister:* BETTIE DUDLEY. *Cousins:* BISHOP DUDLEY,

ESTER DUDLEY, COMFORT SIDBURY, MOSES SIDBURY. *Mother:* ELIZABETH BISHOP. *Father and Executor:* GEORGE BISHOP. *Other legatees:* JANE MORGAN, MORGAN MORGAN, JR. *Witnesses:* RICE RICE, MORGAN MORGAN, JAMES SMALLWOOD. Will proven in New Hanover Court. JAMES SMALLWOOD, *Deputy Clerk.*

BLACK, ISAAC.   New Hanover County.

June 22, 1754. August Court, 1754. *Brother:* JOHN BLACK. *Sisters:* ELIZABETH WOODS, JANE BLACK. *Executor:* JOSHUA TOOMER. *Witnesses:* WILLM. GREGORY, JAS. CAMPBELL, MARK GIBBINS. *Clerk of the Court:* ISAAC FARIES.

BLACK, MICHAEL.   Craven County.

January 16, 1760. May 3, 1760. *Friend: Executor and sole legatee:* JOSEPH WILLIS. *Witnesses:* JACOB MILLER, GEORGE FISHER, JAMES WILLIS. Will proven before ARTHUR DOBBS, at Newbern.

BLACKALL, ABRAHAM.   Edenton, Chowan County.

February 1, 1739–1740. February 23, 1749. January Court, 1749. *Wife:* SARAH. *Daughters:* PENELOPE and SHARLOT. *Executrix:* SARAH BLACKALL (wife). *Witnesses:* RD. FORSTER, JAMES PATTER, JAMES TROTTER. Executrix qualified before JOS. ANDERSON, Justice of the Peace. Will proven before WILL MEARNS, *Clerk of the Court.*

BLACKALL, SARAH.   Edenton, Chowan County.

January 29, 1754. April Court, 1754. *Daughters:* SARAH ROWDEN, PENELOPE, CHARLOT. *Deceased husband:* DR. BLACKALL. *Executor:* DR. SAMUEL LABAN PLOMMER. *Witnesses:* FRANCIS OLIVER, ABIGAIL SLAUGHTER. *Clerk of the Court:* WILL HALSEY. Coat of arms on seal.

BLACKLEDGE, RICHARD, SENR.   Craven County.

February 20, 1776. October 15, 1777. *Wife:* ANN. *Sons:* RICHARD ("manor plantation and ½ of 275 acres land on Pecoson Point"), WILLIAM, BENJAMIN ("200 acres Moseleys Creek," this to three sons above named), THOMAS ("land bought of Wm. Farmer and wife and 100 a. on Bever Dam"). *Sons-in-law:* SPYERS SINGLETON, CAP. JOHN JONES. *Daughters:* ELLENER (wife of CAPT. JOHN JONES), ANN BLACKLEDGE. *Friends:* MRS. MARY NEALE and MRS. BETSEY BAKER (ten pounds for mourning ring and gold buttons). *Father:* BENJAMIN BLACKLEDGE, SR. *Executors:* JACOB BLOUNT, CHRISTOPHER NEALE, RICHARD BLACKLEDGE, JR. (son) and SPYERS SINGLETON (son-in-law). *Witnesses:* J. BLOUNT, HENRY CANNON, READING BLOUNT. Will proven before RD. CASWELL.

BLACKMAN, JOHN. Bertie County.

November 19, 1736. November Court, 1736. *Wife:* SARAH. *Sons:* JOHN, BENNET, ARTHUR, JOSEPH, STEAVEN. *Daughter:* ELIZABETH. *Executors:* BENNET BLACKMAN (son) and THEOPHILUS WILLIAMS. *Witnesses:* WILLIAM TAYLOR, ARTHUR MAIKDSUNACE, PHEBE JERNIGAN. *Clerk of the Court:* JNO. WYNNS.

BLACKMAN, NICHOLAS. Bertie Precinct.

August 26, 1730. March 11, 1730. *Wife:* ALLISON. *Sons-in-law:* GEORGE SMITH and WILLIAM SMITH. *Executrix:* ALLISON BLACKMAN (wife). *Witnesses:* EDWD. COLLINS, RICHARD MOORE, JAMES BAKER. Will proven before GEO. BURRINGTON, Governor.

BLAKE, DAVID. Currituck Precinct.

October 9, 1714. January 13, 1714–1715. *Sons:* THOMAS, DAVID. *Daughters:* SARAH, ELIZABETH, MATHEW. *Friends:* MATHIAS TOWLER, JOHN MASON. *Executors:* RALPH MATHAM, JNO. MASON. *Witnesses:* THOMAS EVANS, JOHN EVANS, RICH'D SMITH. *Clerk of the Court:* JO. WICKER.

BLANCHARD, BENJAMIN. Upper part of Nansimond County.

June 5, 1719. *Sons:* ROBERT ("land on Beverdam Swamp in Chowan Precinct in North Carolina"), ABSALOM, BENJAMIN ("land on Beverdam"). *Son-in-law:* WILLIAM WESTON (wife CATHERINE). *Wife:* CATHERINE. *Executors:* CATHERINE (wife) and ROBERT (son). *Witnesses:* WILL. HILL, JAMES GRISING, THOMAS ROUNTREE. No probate.

BLANCHARD, EPHRAIM. Chowan County.

July 22, 1745. April, 1749. *Son:* AARON ("plantation on west side of Beaverdam Swamp." "Land on Walroy Swamp;" "100 acres in Pasquotank known by the name of the Sound Neck;" "place in Pasquotank called Nobbs Crook"). *Son:* EPHRAIM ("100 acres in Chowan Co.;" "100 acres on Walroy Swamp;" "200 acres in Pasquotank County on Sound Neck;" "50 acres at the head of Nobbs Crook in Pasquotank"). *Son:* MICAJAH ("manor plantation on east side of Beaverdam Swamp–450 acres;" "50 acres at Nobbs Crook"). *Granddaughter:* MARY GRIFFIN. *Wife:* ISABEL BLANCHARD. *Executors:* ISABEL BLANCHARD (wife) and EPHRAIM BLANCHARD (son). *Witnesses:* THOS. ROUNTREE, SR., CHAS. ROUNTREE, THOMAS ROUNTREE. *Clerk of the Court:* WILL MEARNS.

BLANING, HUGH. Bladen County.

May 10, 1751. March Court, 1752. *Wife:* ELIZABETH. *Wife's children:* WILLIAM and ELIZABETH HALL. *Sister:* SARAH STAR. *Executors:* ELIZA-

3

BETH BLANING (wife), MATTHEW ROWAN. *Witnesses:* ROBERT DOWIE, THOS. HALL and ———. *Clerk of the Court:* THOS. ROBESON. Coat of arms on seal.

BLICHENDEN, THOMAS.   Perquimans County.

April 12, 1744. July Court, 1745. *Sons:* JOHN (plantation on Sound Side), WILLIAM ("plantation whereon I now live"), ABRAHAM. *Daughter:* SARAH. *Wife:* MARY. *Executors:* MARY BLICHENDEN (wife), ABRAHAM and WILLIAM BLICHENDEN (sons). *Witnesses:* MAC. SCARBOROUGH, NATH'L CARRUTHERS, ZACH. CHANCEY. *Clerk of Court:* EDMUND HATCH. Courthouse on Phelps Point. Coat of arms on seal.

BLIN, DANIEL.   Bath Town, Beaufort County.

September 23, 1742. March 13, 1753. *Wife, Executrix and sole devisee:* MORNING BLIN. *Witnesses:* MARY SMITH, JOHN RIEUSSETT, PATRICK BRAHAM. *Clerk of the Court:* WILL ORMOND.

BLISH, JOHN.   Pasquotank County.

November 17, 1718. *Devisees:* MARTHA FOSTER (daughter of THOMAS FOSTER), ELIZABETH FLEMEN, EDWARD JAMES, STEPHEN SALL, WILLIAM WILLSON (mairener). *Executor:* WILLIAM WILLSON. *Witnesses:* JOSEPH CAPE, MARY MILLER, JOHN BETT Senor. No probate.

BLOUNT, BENJAMIN.   Tyrrell County.

February 1, 1739. June Court, 1740. *Sons:* JAMES, JACOB, EDMUND, ISAAC and BENJAMIN (to the latter is given "my manner plantation"). *Daughters:* ESTHER, MARY, SARAH. *Wife:* ELIZABETH. *Executors:* BENJAMIN (son) and ELIZABETH (wife). *Witnesses:* ANN HALLIS, ZACHARIAH GURKIN. *Justice of the Peace:* JAMES TURNBULL. *Deputy Clerk of the Court:* THOS. LEARY.

BLOUNT, EDMUND.   Tyrrell County.

February 12, 1754. June Court, 1754. *Son:* EDMUND ("manner plantation") *Wife:* ELIZABETH. *Executors:* ELIZABETH BLOUNT (wife), BENJAMIN BLOUNT. *Witnesses:* BENJAMIN BLOUNT, JACOB BLOUNT. *Clerk of Court:* EVAN JONES. Other children are mentioned, but not named.

BLOUNT, ELIZABETH.   Chowan County.

February 8, 1732. March 12, 1732. *Sons:* JOHN, THOMAS, JAMES, JOSEPH, CHARLES (to the two latter is bequeathed land at Bare Swamp and Haughton land). *Daughters:* ANNE WARLEY, RACHELE. *Executors:* JOHN LOVICK, SAMLL. PAGETT and JONATHAN JACOCKS. *Witnesses:* R.

HICKS and MARY COLESON. Will proven before GEORGE BURRINGTON, at Edenton. A tract of land at Barrow's Hole is ordered sold and proceeds applied to payment of doctor.

BLOUNT, JOHN. Chowan County.

January 27, 1725–1726. May 18, 1726. *Sons:* JOHN, THOMAS (manor, fronting on Albemarle Sound, John to have eastern and Thomas western portion), JAMES and CHARLES (land on Welches Creek), JOSEPH (land at Mattehapungo, known by the name of Goshen). *Wife:* ELIZABETH (land at Bear Swamp and at Barrow Hole). *Daughters:* MARY JACOCKS, ELIZA PAGET, SARAH LOVICK, MARTHA WARSLEY and HESTER WORLEY. *Executrix:* ELIZABETH BLOUNT (wife), to be assisted by friends JOHN LOVICK and THOS. POLLOCK. *Witnesses:* SAMLL. WARNER, WM. BENBURY, MAGNES PLOWMAN. Will proven before RICHARD EVERARD, Governor, etc.

Codicil to will of JOHN BLOUNT. Dated January 27, 1725–1726. *Daughters:* ANN and RACHEL (a gold ring each). CHRISTOPHER GALE appointed assistant together with JNO. LOVICK and THOS. POLLOCK. Coat of arms on seal of both will and codicil. The testator mentions in the will having broken the entail.

BLOUNT, ——————. County not given.

Dates missing. *Wife:* ELIZABETH. *Sons:* JOHN and THOMAS ("Beech Island land and land on Welches' Creek up Moratock;" JOSEPH (land at Matchapungo known by name of "Goshan"); JAMES (land at Bear Swamp). *Daughters:* MARY JACOCS, ELIZABETH PAGET and MARTHA WEST. Remainder of will missing.

BLOUNT, JAMES. Albemarle County.

March 10, 1685. July, 1686. *Sons:* THOS. BLOUNT and JOHN BLOUNT. *Son:* JAS. BLOUNT. *Daughters:* ANN SLOCUM and ELIZ. HAWKINS. *Grandchildren:* JAMES and SARAH BLOUNT and ANN SLOCUM, and JOHN HAWKINS. *Wife:* ANN BLOUNT. *Executrix:* ANN BLOUNT. *Witnesses:* JNO. HALL, JANE MILLER and WM. DOBSON. Proven before SETH SOTHELL.

BLOUNT, JAMES. Chowan County.

February 12, 1716. March 27, 1717. *Wife:* ELIZABETH. *Daughters:* ANNE BLOUNT ("my plantation with 240 acres of land"), ELIZABETH YELVERTON, MARY. *Sons:* JOHN BLOUNT, JAMES BLOUNT and JOHN YELVERTON. *Grandsons:* JAMES YELVERTON and JOHN YELVERTON. *Granddaughter:* SARA PHILLIPS. *Executrixes:* ELIZABETH BLOUNT (wife) and ANNE BLOUNT (daughter). *Witnesses:* J. TURNER, ANNE DUGLES, JOHN YELVERTON. *Clerk of Court:* R. HICKS.

BLOUNT, JOHN.   Chowan County.

December 8, 1753. April Court, 1754. *Sons:* JAMES (plantation and three negroes), FREDERIC (four negroes), WILSON (three negroes). *Sister-in-law:* Mrs. MARY MOOR. *Daughters:* ELIZABETH, MARTHA, MARY. *Wife:* SARAH (three negroes). Chaise, boat, blacksmith tools and watch ordered sold. *Brothers:* CHARLES BLOUNT and JOSEPH BLOUNT (*executors*). *Witnesses:* J. HALSEY, JNO. SMITH, JOHN BEASLEY, RICHARD DUNBAR. *Clerk of the Court:* WILL HALSEY. The following item may be of interest: "My Will and desire is * * * * That no Stranger shall be admitted to live on any part of the back land to destroy the timber and that no Person shall on any Consideration whatsoever be admitted to live on any part of my land excepting an overseer."

BLOUNT, THOMAS.   Kendricks Creek, Albemarle County.

September 3, 1701. March 28, 1706. *Sons:* JOHN and JAMES. Following lands devised: "Midle plantation; land at the mouth of Kendricks Creek, whereon I now live; land called Cabbin Necke." *Daughters:* BILLAH (wife of KELLEM TYLER), SARAH PEIRCE, CHRISTIAN LUDFORD and ANN WILSON. *Wife:* MARY. *Executor:* JAMES BLOUNT (son). *Witnesses:* WM. WILLSON, JOHN BLOUNT, THOMAS GREEN. Proven before THOMAS CARY.

BLYE, WILLIAM.   Bertie County.

November 29, 1748. May Court, 1749. *Sons:* WILLIAM ("manner plantation"), THOMAS. *Daughters:* SARAH BLYE, ELIZABETH BLYE. *Wife:* ELIZABETH. *Executors:* WILLIAM BLYE (son), ELIZABETH BLYE (wife). *Witnesses:* JOHN THOMAS, NATHANIEL WILLIAMS, TIMOTHY WILLIAMS. *Clerk of the Court:* JOHN LOVICK.

BOBBIT, JOHN.   Bertie County.

May 7, 1736. November 6, 1736. *Son:* WILLIAM (100 acres land in the "Orraneechey Neck"). *Son:* THOMAS (100 acres land in the "Orraneechey Neck"). *Daughters:* FRANCIS, MARY and AMEY. *Executors:* WILLIAM BOBBIT, ROBERT GREEN, JOHN MASSY and JAMES BROGDEN. *Witnesses:* FRANCIS BETTES, RICHARD MASSY, FRANCIS MASSY, and C. EVANS. *Clerk of the Court:* JOHN WYNNS.

BOGE (or BOGUE), JOSIAH.   Perquimans County.

March 1, 1752. July Court, 1752. *Sons:* JESSE, JOSEPH, JOBE ("all my lands"). *Daughters:* MARY BOGE, MIRIAM BOGE, LIDY BOGE. *Wife:* DEBORAH. *Executors:* DEBORAH BOGE (wife), JOHN MOOR, TRUMAN MOOR. *Witnesses:* JOSHUA PARISHE, JOSHUA HASKET, THOMAS HOLLOWELL. *Clerk of the Court:* EDMUND HATCH.

BOGE, WILLIAM.   Perquimans Precinct.

December 20, 1720.   April 11, 1721.   *Sons:* WILLIAM and JOSIAH ("my manner plantation").   *Daughters:* ELIZABETH HILL, JEAN BOGE, MYRIAM BOGE, RACHEL BOGE.   *Wife:* ELLENDER.   *Grandson:* WILLIAM HILL. *Executors:* WILLIAM BOGE (son), JACOB HILL (son-in-law).   *Witnesses:* BENJAMIN MUNDY, JOHN MOOR.   *Clerk of the Court:* RICH'D LEARY.

BOGUE, WILLIAM.   Perquimans County.

June 29, 1744.   October Court, 1745.   ("On the North East side of Perquimans River").   *Wife and Executrix:* SARAH.   *Sons:* WILLIAM BOGUE (100 acres land on the East side Sutens Creek"), JAK BOGUE. *Witnesses:* JOHN MORE, THOMAS BAGLEY.   *Clerk of Court:* EDMUND HATCH.   Courthouse on Phelps Point.

BOND, JOHN.   Beaufort County.

July 8, 1749.   September Court, 1749.   *Sons:* WILLIAM (land on the West side of Middle Swamp), JOHN, JAMES (land on South side Pamplico River), ROBERT ("plantation I now live on"), RICHARD (land called Piners).   *Daughters:* MARY and ANNA, and SARAH.   *Wife:* (mentioned, but no name given).   *Executors:* WILLIAM, JOHN and JAMES BOND (sons). *Cousin:* MARTHA SPRING.   *Witnesses:* ABRAM PRITCHETT, JOHN TURNER, PHILLIP PRITCHETT, JOSHUA PRITCHETT.   *Clerk of Court:* JOSIAH PRATHER.

BOND, LEWIS.   Chowan County.

February 22, 1753.   April Court, 1753.   *Sons:* RICHARD ("my mannar plantation"), WILLIAM, JOHN,   *Daughters:* ELISABETH and SARAH BOND. *Wife:* REBECKER.   *Executor:* RICHARD BOND (brother-in-law).   *Witnesses:* JAMES BOND, DEMSEY CASTEN, ROBERT STEWART.   *Clerk of the Court:* JAS. CRAVEN.

BOND, RICHARD.   No county.

January 15, 1725.   *Sons:* RICHARD and HENRY (land on Maidenhare Creek), HANCE, WILLIAM, LEWIS ("maner plantation").   *Daughter:* MARY BOND.   *Executrix:* Wife (mentioned, but not named).   This is a copy of Bond's will and no signature, witness or probate appears.

BOND, ROBERT.   Craven Precinct.

January 6, 1737.   June, 1738.   *Son:* FRANCIS ("plantation whereon I now live").   *Daughters:* SARAH BOND (100 acres land at Broad Creek), ELISEBETH (50 acres of land), MARTHA BOND.   *Wife and Executrix:* SARAH.   *Witnesses:* F. DAWSON, JOHN GOOD.   *Clerk of the Court:* JAMES COOR.

BOND, SAMUEL.   Perquimans County.

October 12, 1721. March 26, 1723. *Sons:* SAMUELL (land on Per-
quimans River), LUKE (land on Perquimans River). *Daughters:* MARY,
SUSANA, ELIZEBETH BOND, JANE BOND. *Friends:* JOSEPH SMITH, TIMO-
THY CLEARE, JOS. JESSOP. *Executor:* SAMUELL BOND (son). *Witnesses:*
JAMES SMITH, SUSANA SMITH, JOSEPH JESSOP. Will proven before C.
GALE, Chief Justice.

BOND, VINYARD.   Beaufort County.

March 25, 1762. November 8, 1762. *Wife:* SARAH. *Son:* SWEETING.
Daughter: SARAH. (Plantations on Care Point, Trent River and Town
Creek to wife and children for support of children). *Sisters:* SUSANNAH
KERSHAW, SARAH, MARY and MARGARET. *Executors:* SARAH BOND (wife)
and JOHN CARRUTHERS (brother of wife). *Witnesses:* WILL'M PEYTON,
WILL'M TRIPPE, HENRY LOCKEY, THOMAS LEE. Will proven before
ARTHUR DOBBS at Newbern.

BOND, WILLIAM.   Beaufort County.

November 6, 1757. December Court, 1757. *Sons:* JOHN ("plantation
wheareon I doe live" and one-half of the "Old Box Neak," together with
one negro). WILLIAM (land "where Samuell Daves lives and land where
Jarves Smith did live, one par of Silver Shue buckles, one par of Nea
buckles and one Stock Buckall"). *Daughter:* REBECCA (one negro). *Other
legatees:* KNIGA (?) and MARY ERKMAN. *Executors:* JAMES and RICHARD
BOND and SAMUELL DAVES. *Witnesses:* FRS. GILBERT, FRANCES WARNER,
ANN MAYO. *Clerk of the Court:* WALLEY CHAUNCEY.

BONNER, HENRY.   Chowan County.

September 1, 1738. October 7, 1738. *Sons:* HENRY (plantation lying
in Greenhall), THOMAS (three plantations called "Brins," "Hales's" and
"Jones's"). *Grandson:* RICHARD LEWIS ("Bayes plantation"). *Daughters:* ELIZABETH, DEBORAH and MARY. *Granddaughters:* SARAH LEWIS
and DEBORAH LEWIS. *Executor:* HENRY BONNER (son). *Witnesses:* JOS.
ANDERSON, ABRA'M BLACKALL, JAMES POTTER. *Clerk of the Court:* W.
SMITH.

BONNER, JOHN.   Chowan County.

November 11, 1753. January Court, 1754. *Cousins:* WILLIAM, ELIZA-
BETH, MARY and EDWARD HOWCOTT (negroes). *Godson:* THOMAS ECLES-
TON (one negro). *Brother:* THOMAS BONNER (plantation). *Executors:*
JOHN BENBURY and HENRY BONNER. *Witnesses:* JEREH MICHENER,
JOHN SMITH, GEORGE LILES. *Clerk of the Court:* WILL HALSEY.

BONNER, MARY.   Chowan County.

January 30, 1749–1750. July Court, 1750. *Friend:* DEBROH THOMP-
SON. Two brothers and a sister mentioned, but not named. *Executor:*
JAMES TOMPSON. *Witnesses:* JOHN LEWIS, JOHN LEWIS, JUNIOR. *Clerk
of the Court:* WILL MEARNS.

BONNER, THOMAS.   County not given.

March 6, 1685. November 24, 1685. *Son:* THOMAS. *Wife and Executrix:* MARY. *Witnesses:* HENRY BONNER, SAMUEL WARREN, WILLIAM
BONNER. Proven before WM. WILKISON.

BONNER, THOMAS.   Bertie County.

November 11, 1755. April Court, 1756. *Sons:* THOMAS, HENRY,
MOSES. *Daughters:* ESTER MORE, ELISEBATH WHELER, ANNA BYRDE,
SARAH WHARTON, PACHENCE BYRDE. *Wife:* ELISEBATH BONNER. *Ex-
ecutrix:* ELISEBATH BONNER (wife). *Witnesses:* MOSES BONNER, EDMON
BYRDE, ARTHUR MOOR, ABRAHAM BLITCHENDEN. *Clerk of the Court:*
BENJN WYNNS. WM. WYNNS, P. J.

BOON, JOSEPH.   No county given.

February 19, 1728. *Sons:* JAMES, JOSEPH, THOMAS, RATLIF. *Sister:*
MARTHA BAYLEY. *Daughters:* MARY and ELIZABETH. *Executrix:* ——
BOON. *Wife:* Not named. *Witnesses:* THOMAS BOON, NATHANIEL COOPER.
No probate.

BOONE, JAMES.   Bertie Precinct.

June 8, 1733. March 31, 1735. *Sons-in-law:* JOHN EARLY (one negro
woman and fifty apple trees); JOHN WYNNS (my negro man called Charles
and 1000 foot of plank); CULLINEUR SESSUMS (one negro). *Daughters:*
MARY WYNNS, ELIZA EARLY. *Grandsons:* GEORGE AUGUSTUS WYNNS,
JAMES EARLY. *Other legatees:* WILLIAM BURKE, JOHN ASSKEW, MARTHA
DAVIS. *Wife and Executrix:* ELIZABETH. *Witnesses:* JOHN WILLSON,
THOMAS LEE, JAMES MARTIN. Proven before GAB. JOHNSTON.

BOON, NICHOLAS.   No date and no county given.

Sons: NICHOLAS (dwelling plantation), WILLIAM, JOSEPH. *Daughters:*
MARY, MARTHA and ANN. *Wife:* MARY. *Executors:* MARY BOONE (wife),
WILLIAM BOON (brother) and THOMAS BOON, JUNR. *Witnesses:* JOHN
STRICKLAND, JOHN FORD, NATHANIEL COOPER. No probate.

BOOTH, GEORGE.   Knott's Island, Currituck County.

February 12, 1729. July 7, 1730. *Sons:* JOHN and GEORGE (land
lying in "Viriana"). *Daughter:* HANNAH SIMMONS. *Wife:* MARY BOOTH.
Executrix: MARY BOOTH. *Clerk of the Court:* J. MARTYN.

BOOTH, JAMES.   Newton in Cape Fear.

February 12, 1737–1738. February 18, 1737–1738. *Devisees:* ROGER
ROLFE, JONATHAN OGDEN, SEN'R, and JONATHAN OGDEN. *Executors:*
JONATHAN OGDEN and ROGER ROLFE. *Witnesses:* RICHARD OGDEN, ANN
SHIRLEY, ANN ROLFE. (Seal with coat of arms.) Proven before GAB.
JOHNSTON, *Governor*, etc.

BOOTH, JOHN.   Carteret County.

December 14, 1751. March Court, 1752. Nuncupative will spoken to
JOHN SIMPSON and GEORGE BELL, who made oath to same before RICHARD
WARD   Estate left to *Wife*, RACHEL, and *Children* (not named). *Clerk of
the Court:* GEO. READ.

BOOZMAN, RALPH.   Perquimans County.

January 1, 1744–1745. January Court, 1750. *Sister:* MARY BULLOCK.
Executors: JOSEPH BULLOCK and THOMAS BULLOCK. *Niece:* SARAH BUL-
LOCK (daughter of MARY BULLOCK). *Witnesses:* JOSHUA HOBART, JAMES
LITTLETON, JR., HANNAH LITTLETON. *Clerk of the Court:* EDMUND HATCH.

BORDEN, WILLIAM.   Carteret County.

February 10, 1748–1749. August 1, 1749. *Son:* WILLIAM ("my man-
ner plantation" and also 800 acres of land on Harlor's Creek and Core
Creek). *Daughters:* ALICE STANTON, KATHERINE BORDEN, HANNAH BOR-
DEN, SARAH PRATT. *Nephew:* WILLIAM BORDEN. *Brothers:* THOMAS
BORDEN, BENJAMIN BORDEN. *Sister:* AMY CHASE. *Executors:* BENJA-
MIN BORDEN (brother). HENRY STANTON (son-in-law), SUSANNAH BOR-
DEN (wife). *Witnesses:* SAMUEL NEWBY, JOSEPH NEWBY, JOSEPH ROBIN-
SON. Will proven before GAB. JOHNSTON, *Governor*, at Edenhouse.

BOSWELL, GEORGE.   Perquimans County.

December 30, 1741. January 7, 1741. *Sons:* GEORGE ("my dwelling
plantation"), ISAC. *Daughter:* EZIBELL. *Sister-in-law:* HANNAH MOR-
GIN. *Executors:* THOMAS HALLOWELL, CHARLES OVERMAN, HANNAH MOR-
GIN. *Witnesses:* THOMAS NICHOLSON, JOHN BOSWELL, JOSIAH BUNDY.
Will proven before J. MONTGOMERY, C. J.

BOSWELL, WILLIAM.   Perquimans Precinct.

February 1, 1734–1735. February 17, 1734. *Sons:* THOMAS (land at
the head of Little River), JOHN (one-half of plantation "that I now dwell
on"), ICHABOD ("remainder part of said tract"). *Daughter:* MARY BOSWELL.
Executors: THOMAS OVERMAN and THOMAS NICHOLSON. *Witnesses:* JOHN
BOSWELL, GEORGE BOSWELL, WM. BUNDY. *Codicil:* Places children in
hands of executors to be brought up. Will and codicil proven before GAB.
JOHNSTON, *Governor*, at Edenton.

BOSWORTH, JOSEPH. Carteret Precinct.

June 18, 1734. June 3, 1735. *Sons:* JOSEPH, EPHRAIM and ROBERT. *Wife:* MARY. *Executors:* MARY BOSWORTH (wife), JOSEPH WEEKS, DR. SOLOMON BACON. *Witnesses:* JAMES BALL, EPHRAIM CHADWICK, WILLIAM WALDRON. *Clerk of the Court:* JAS. WINRIGHT. All estate of testator is ordered sold and proceeds deposited with some person at Boston for use and benefit of wife and children.

BOTNETT, JOHN. Albemarle County.

October 30, 1703. April 17, 1704. *Friend and Executor:* DAVID PRICHARD. *Witnesses:* WM WARREN, WM JOY, MARGARE JOY. Will proven before WM ROLFE.

BOUDE, JOHN. Bertie County.

May 18, 1738. August 25, 1738. *Wife:* KATHERINE. *Reputed son* (son of Catherine Deed), 603 acres land. *Brother:* THOMAS BOUDE, of Philadelphia. *Friends:* JAMES WILKINGS, THOMAS BOXLY. *Cousin:* JOHN BOUDE. *Executors:* KATHERINE BOUDE, GODFREY LEA, EDWARD BARNS, JOHN DAYTON. *Witnesses:* ROBERT MACRAE, JAMES WILKINS, MARY HARBERTT, SARAH LEE. Proven before W. SMITH, C. J.

BOULD, GEORGE. Craven County.

July 12, 1745. September Court, 1745. *Brother:* JOSEPH BOULD. *Friends:* FRANCIS STRINGER, JOHN SNEAD (ten acres of marsh "opposite to Newbern Town"), GEORGE POWELL, son of JOHN POWELL. *Wife:* MARY BOULD. *Executrix:* MARY BOULD. *Witnesses:* FEILDER POWELL, JAMES COAR, THOS. FOX, MARY COAR. *Clerk of the Court:* JNO. RICE.

BOUND, RICHARD. Perquimans Precinct.

November 22, 1720. July 11, 1721. *Sons:* EDWARD (200 acres of land), SAMUELL (200 acres of land). *Daughters:* ELIZABETH, HORNER, ABIGALL. *Wife:* ABIGALL. *Executors:* ABIGALL BOUND (wife) and JAMES MINGE. *Witnesses:* HANAH BURROES, ELIZABETH PHETTS. *Clerk of the Court:* RICH'D LEARY.

BOUREN, EDMUND. Currituck Precinct.

July 29, 1711. No probate. *Son:* JOSEPH (land on Youpim Ridge). *Daughters:* SARAH, JANE and SUSANNAH BOUREN. *Wife and Executrix:* SARAH. *Witnesses:* WILLIAM WILLIAMS, JO WICKER, THOMAS POYNER. Original missing. Recorded in Book 1712–22, page 42.

BOYCE, ISAAC. Perquimans County.

January 15, 1750. July Court, 1751. *Uncles:* NICHOLAS and ELIAS STALLINGS. *Sons:* JOB, JOSEPH and BENJAMIN. *Wife:* JUDE. *Executors:* JOS. NICHOLAS and ELIAS STALLINGS. *Witnesses:* ABRAHAM SANDERS, WHITE, ELIZABETH SANDERS. *Clerk of Court:* EDMUND HATCH.

BOYCE, JOHN.　　　　　　　　　　　　　　Perquimans County.

February 12, 1748.　July Court, 1749.　*Sons:* ISAAC, JOHN, MOSES. *Daughters:* JEAN, ELIZABETH, RACHEL.　*Grandson:* JOB BOYCE.　*Wife:* SUSANNAH BOYCE.　*Executors:* SUSANNAH BOYCE (wife) and ISAAC BOYCE (son).　*Witnesses:* NICHOLAS STALLINGS, WILLIAM EASON, HENRY STALLINGS.　*Clerk of the Court:* EDMUND HATCH.

BOYCE, WILLIAM.　　　　　　　　　　　　　　Albemarle County.

August 30, 1688.　April Court, 1693.　All estate, real and personal, to *wife*, ANN BOYCE.　*Executrix:* ANN BOYCE.　*Witnesses:* PAUL LATHAM, JOHN BARBER, JACOB FIELDS.　*Clerk of the Court:* EDWARD MAYO.

BOYCE, WILLIAM.　　　　　　　　　　　　　　Perquimans County.

June 11, 1703.　October 12, 1703.　*Mother:* MARY (of Yarmouth, England).　*Friends:* MR. JULIAN LAKERS, MR. ROBERT BRADLEY (Prince George Co., Maryland).　Gold rings to following parties: COLL. WM. WILKINSON, his wife, MRS. JULIANA LAKERS, JAMES STODDART (Prince George Co., Maryland), his wife, JNO. COBB, PETER GODFREY.　*Executrix:* JOANNA KESLER.　*Witnesses:* DAVID HARRIS, ELIZ. STUART, P. GODFREY.　*Clerk of the Court:* THOS. SNODEN.　　Coat of arms on seal.

BOYD, JOHN.　　　　　　　　　　　　　　　　Chowan County.

October 9, 1737.　July Court, 1738.　*Son:* WILLIAM.　*Daughters:* ANNE, MARION and LYDIAR BOYD.　*Wife:* LYDIA.　*Executors:* LYDIA BOYD (wife), PHILIP AYDLETT (of Virginia), ANDREW IRVING.　*Witnesses:* JOHN ROWSOM, JAS. WILLIAMS, EDWARD SILK.　*Clerk of the Court:* JAMES CRAVEN.

BOYD, JOHN.　　　　　　　　　　　　　　　Pasquotank County.

January 29, 1741.　July Court, 1742.　*Sons:* WILLIAM ("Westeard parte of my land"), THOMAS ("Eastard part of my land").　*Daughter:* WINEFRUIT BOYD.　*Wife and Executrix:* ANN BOYD.　*Witnesses:* JOHN McKEEL, WM. WALLIS, ANTHONY MARKHAM.　*Clerk of the Court:* THOS. TAYLOR.

BOYD, THOMAS.　　　　　　　　　　　　　　Bath County.

December 17, 1725.　April Court, 1726.　*Son:* JOHN.　*Wife:* KATHERINE (use of plantation on Broad Creek, "where I now dwell").　*Friends:* COL. EDWARD MOSELEY, ROBERT TURNER (five pounds for ring), CAPT. SIMON ALDERSON.　*Executors:* EDWARD MOSELEY, SIMON ALDERSON.　This is a holograph will and a caveat was entered thereto by one John Bond. Several affidavits, together with portions of briefs and argument of counsel are filed with the original.

BOYD, WINEFRED.　　　　　　　　　　　　　Pasquotank County.

June 15, 1720.　July 19, 1720.　*Sons:* JOHN and THOMAS BOYD (negroes). BENJAMIN and CHARLES WEST (executors).　*Witnesses:* LEWIS KNIGHT, RICHARD STAMP.　Recorded in Book 1712–22, page 242.　Original missing.

BOYINTONE, JOSEPH.   Chowan Precinct.

September 25, 1738. January, 1738. *Brother and Executor:* BENJA-
MIN BOYINTONE of Gloster, New England. *Friend:* JOHN RICHARDS of
Edenton. *Witnesses:* ABNER BLACKALL, THOS. MORTIMORE, JAMES MITCH-
ELL. *Clerk of the Court:* JAMES CRAVEN.

BOYKIN, THOMAS.   Northampton County.

April 13, 1748. February Court, 1750. *Wife:* MELDRED. *Son:* THOMAS
(land and plantation). ANN CRAFORD, MARTHA THORNTON, ELIZABETH
STRICKLAND and PATTIENCE STRICKLAND (one shilling each). *Executors:*
MELDRED BOYKIN (wife) and THOMAS BOYKIN (son). *Witnesses:* JNO.
SIMPSON, JOSEPH ROGERS, JOHN REYNOLDS. *Clerk of the Court:* I. ED-
WARDS.

BOYKIN, EDWARD.   Northampton County.

June 8, 1743. *Sons:* THOMAS (lands lying between Richard Walls and
Meadow Branch), SOLOMON (lands above Meadow Branch), HARDY (land
on Cypress Swamp), EDWARD, BENJAMIN. *Daughter:* RACHEL HERON.
Grandson: HENRY BOYKIN. *Wife:* JUDITH. *Executors:* JUDITH (wife) and
SOLOMON BOYKIN (son). *Witnesses:* CHAS. CAMPBELL, RICHARD WALL.
Clerk of the Court: I. EDWARDS.

BRACK, GEORGE.   Onslow County.

September 25, 1750. April 2, 1751. *Sons:* GEORGE (160 acres land on
"head of the Rich Neck"), ELIAZAR, RICHARD, WILLIAM (160 acres of land
"whereon I now live"). *Grandson:* JOHN LEWIS. *Daughter:* ELIZABETH
BRACK. *Son-in-law:* MATHEW LEWIS. *Wife:* GEAN. *Executors:* MA-
THEW LEWIS, GEORGE BRACK (son). *Witnesses:* LIONEL BOUTWELL,
MOURNING LEWIS, SUSANER MORRIS. *Clerk of the Court:* THO. BLACK.

BRADDY, JAMES.   Chowan County.

August 17, 1750. January Court, 1750. *Sons:* JOHN and JOSEPH,
JAMES ("plantation whereon I now live"). *Grandson:* JAMES CONNER.
Wife: GRACE. *Executors:* GRACE BRADDY (wife) and JAMES BRADDY (son).
Witnesses: ED. WARREN, MARY POWELL, HENRY GOODMAN. *Clerk of the
Court:* WILL MEARNS.

BRADEY, JOHN.   Craven County.

October 11, 1753. November Court, 1753. *Wife:* ABIGAIL. *Executor:* JEREMIAH RHEAM. *Witnesses:* DANIEL PERKINS, JEREMIAH RHEAM.
Clerk of the Court: SOL REW.

BRADFORD, NATHANIEL.   Edgecombe County.

October 2, 1756. February Court, 1757. *Sons:* JOHN ("plantation whereon I now live"), NATHANIEL ("remainder of my lands"). *Daughters:* MARY BRADFORD and PATIENCE BRADFORD. *Wife:* SARAH: *Executors:* JOHN BRADFORD and JOSEPH LANE. *Witnesses:* SAM'L HARVY, JAMIMA SIMMONS. *Clerk of the Court:* JOSEPH MONTFORT.

BRADLEY, RICHARD.   Currituck County.

April 13, 1756. June Court, 1756. *Sons:* HANER, WILLIAM, ABEL, JOHN, RICHARD. *Daughters:* ANN ETHERIDGE, ALIDEA CORBILL, MARY BRADLEY, ELIZABETH BRADLEY. *Wife:* DORITY BRADLEY. *Executors:* DORITY BRADLEY (wife) and WILLIAM BRADLEY (son). *Witnesses:* KEDAR MARCHANT, JOSIAH DOUGH, ELIZABETH DENBY. *Clerk of the Court:* WILLIAM SHERGOLD.

BRADY, JOSEPH.   Chowan County.

November 19, 1752. July Court, 1753. *Daughters:* ELIZABETH HARTLOCK, BARSHEBA JONES, MARY JONES. *Son:* JOHN BRADY. *Grandson:* JOHN DICKINS (*mother,* SUFFRAH DICKINS). *Granddaughters:* TAMER BRADY and EADY DICKINS. *Witnesses:* JACOB ROGERS, JOSEPH BRADY, TAMER BRADY. *Clerk of the Court:* WILL HALSEY.

BRANCH, FRANCIS.   County not given.

November 14, 1739. December 4, 1739. *Daughter:* SARAH DONNAVAN. *Wife:* ANNE. PHILLIP MAGNIER, PHILLIP MAGNIER, JR., SAMUEL MAGNIER. WILLIAM BRANCH (son of ISAAC BRANCH). *Executors:* JAMES DONNAVON, ANNE BRANCH (wife). *Friends:* WM. ARKILL, WM. LUTEN. *Witnesses:* CONST. LUTEN, WM. LUTEN, WM. LEWIS. Will proven before W. SMITH, C. J.

BRANCH, WILLIAM.   Chowan County.

November 24, 1720. January Court, 1721. *Wife:* MARGRET ("lott of land in Edenton on Queen Anne Creek"). *Sons:* WILLIAM (plantation near Edenton), ISSACHAR (plantation on the southwest side of Mattchacomak Creek), SOLOMON. *Daughter:* ELIZABETH. *Executors:* MARGRET BRANCH (wife), FRANCIS BRANCH (brother). *Witnesses:* JNO. NEW, ANNE BRANCH, THOMAS BRANCH. *Clerk of the Court:* (name torn from will).

BRAND, ISABELLA CAMERON, relict of ANDREW BRAND,
                                        Basterin Cannongate, Scotland.

This is an assignment to ALEX CUNNYNGHAM of Cannongate, Scotland, in case of the death of testatrix who is about to set forth for Carolina and names as legatees, *Nephew:* JOHN MURRAY (son of ROBERT MURRAY of Glencarnock) and ROBINA CAMERON, his wife, and as *Executor,* JOHN RUTH-

ERFORD (Merchant in Cape Fear).   This will (or assignment) is written on stamped paper. *Witnessed by* THOMAS AINSLEE and DUN MCDONALD, and proven at August Court, 1748, before JAS. MORAN, *Clerk of the Court,* by ALEXR DUNCAN by "Parity of Hands."

BRASKE, LAURENCE.   Pasquotank County.

June 1, 1687. July 2, 1687. *Devisees:* MARGARET BROWNE and ELIZABETH CRADUCK. *Executrix:* MARGARET BROWNE and ELIZABETH CRADUCK. *Witnesses:* JOHN BROWNE, WM. WOOD, JOHN WILLSON. Will proven before SETH SOTHELL.

BRASWELL, ROBERT.   Bertie Precinct.

September 14, 1734. November Court, 1736. *Sons:* ROBERT, JOHN, RICHARD ("plantation whereon I now live"), VALENTINE (100 acres land). *Daughters:* SARAH DOUGHTRY, JEAN BRASWELL, MARY BRASWELL. *Godson:* DIOMEE SUMNER (100 acres land). *Wife:* SARAH. *Executors:* JAMES BRYANT, JOSHAWAY DAUGHTREY. *Witnesses:* THOS. BRYANT, NICHOLAS BAGET, PACCENCE BRYANT. *Clerk of the Court:* JNO. WYNNS.

BRAY, HENRY.   Pasquotank County.

September 20, 1745. *Sons:* WILLIAM, CHRISTOPHER, JOHN, GEORGE, DANIEL (one shilling each), JEREMIAH ("my plantation containing 100 acres land"), JACOB. *Daughters:* MARY SHAWDAILY, SARAH SQUIERS, ELIZABETH FORBES (one shilling each). *Wife and Executrix:* DINAH. *Witnesses:* JAS. FORBES, JNO. CARTRIET, WILLIAM WRIGHT. Probate illegible.

BRAY, WILLIAM.   Pasquotank Precinct.

August 23, 1725. January 18, 1725. *Sons:* HENERE (the tract of land "that he now liveth on"), GEORGE (plantation "where I now live"). *Executors:* WILLIAM BURGES and GEORGE BRAY. *Witnesses:* STEPHEN BURGES, THOMAS BURGES, ELIZABETH BURGES. *Clerk of the Court:* THO. WEEKES. Executor qualified before Jo. PALIN.

BRENT, JAMES.   Currituck County.

February 7, 1753. April Court, 1753. *Sons:* RICHARD ("plantation whereon I now live"), JAMES ("plantation called "Tuckers Ridg"). *Daughter:* ANN BRENT. *Wife and Executrix:* KIZIAH. *Witnesses:* ABSALOM LEGETT, JOHN SIMMONS, HENRY SIMMONS, JR. *Clerk of the Court:* WILLIAM SHERGOLD.

BRENT, THOMAS.   Currituck County.

January 1, 1726. April 11, 1727. *Son:* JAMES (150 acres land known as "Wolfpoint Ridge"). *Wife:* ANN. *Executrix:* ANN BRENT (wife). *Witnesses:* THOS. WILLIAMS, HOLLAND HEATH, CHARLES BRENT. *Clerk of the Court:* J. MARTYN.

BREWER, JANE.   New Hanover County.

August 18, 1739. September 25, 1739. *Daughters:* CATHERINE and
HANNAH. *Son-in-law:* RICHARD HOTT. *Executors:* DANIEL DUNBIBIN
and RICHARD HOTT. *Witnesses:* RUFUS MARSDEN, ROGER ROLFE, JAMES
BROWN. Will proven before GABRIEL JOHNSON, *Governor, etc.,* at Newton.

BREWER, GEORGE.   Northampton County.

January 25, 1757. August Court, 1757. *Sons:* RAWLE, GEORGE,
MATTHEW, JOHN. *Wife and Executrix:* MARY. *Witnesses:* JOSEPH SCOULS,
ELIZABETH WHITINGTON, WILLIAM CHAPMAN. *Clerk of the Court:* I.
EDWARDS.

BRIANT, SAMUEL.   Chowan County.

June 6, 1717. July Court, 1717. *Executor and sole legatee:* JOHN FISHER.
Witnesses: FRANCIS JOHNSON, EDWARD PHELPS. *Clerk of the Court:* R.
HICKS.

BRICE, WILLIAM.   County not given.

November 16, 1718. May 1, 1719. *Sons:* FRANCIS and WILLIAM.
Daughter: ELIZA BRICE. *Wife and Executrix:* ANN. *Executor:* THOMAS
HARVEY. *Witnesses:* THOMAS HARVEY, ELIZ. HARVEY, MARTIN FRANK.
Clerk of the Court: CALEB METCALFE. Recorded in Book 1712–22, page
226. Original missing.

BRICKELL, JAMES.   Beaufort County.

April 22, 1746. June Court, 1746. *Son:* JAMES (land joining Mr.
Ormond's lands). *Daughters:* ANN BRICKELL (land joining Mr. Barrow's
lands). *Son of* ELIZABETH GRAY (one cow). *Executors:* WYRIATT OR-
MOND, *Atty.-at-Law;* ABRAHAM DUNCAN, *Gent.,* and JAMES BRICKELL (son).
Witnesses: MARY DUNCAN, MARY BRICKELL, WILLIAM GRAY. *Clerk of
the Court:* JOHN FORBES.

BRIDGEN, SAMUEL.   Ludlow Castle, New Hanover County.

November 30, 1757. February Court, 1758. *Trustees:* JOB HOWES,
SEN'R, and JOB HOWES, JR., to whom is conveyed in trust for *daughter,*
JANE BENNETT, a tract of land on Old Town Creek. In trust for *son,*
EDWARD BRIDGEN, of London, a plantation called "Bridgen's Hall,"
"Ludlow Castle" and "Bridgen's Pastime." *Daughter:* ELIZABETH
CATHARINA, wife of ARMOND DEROSSETT. *Wife:* SARAH. *Brother:*
REV. JOHN BRIDGEN (Professor of Gresham College, London). *Nephew:*
WILLIAM BRIDGEN (Alderman of London). *Witnesses:* JOHN MOTT,
HANNAH MOTT, ARTHUR HOWES. *Clerk of the Court:* JA. MORAN.

BRIDGERS, WILLIAM. Bertie Precinct.

March 11, 1728–1729. November Court, 1729. *Sons:* WILLIAM ("plantation whereon I now live"), JOSEF ("plantation on Fishing Creek"), JOHN (100 acres land). *Daughter:* SARAH BRIDGERS. *Brothers:* BENJAMIN BRIDGERS, WILLIAM BRYANT. *Father:* JOHN DEW. *Wife:* SARAH. *Executors:* WILLIAM BRYANT and JOHN DEW, SENOR. *Witnesses:* JOHN DAWSON, WILLIAM BRYANT, MARY HUISE, RICHARD HUISE. *Clerk of the Court:* RT. FORSTER.

BRIDGERS, WILLIAM. Bertie County.

November 2, 1729. May Court, 1730. *Sons:* JOSEPH, BENJAMIN ("my plantation"), Samuel. *Daughters:* MARY, ELIZABETH. *Executor:* SAMUEL BRIDGERS (son). *Witnesses:* JOHN WEVVRILL, JOHN BARDIN, EDWARD CHITTY. *Clerk of the Court:* RT. FORSTER.

BRIDGERS, WILLIAM. Johnston County.

September 30, 1751. December Court, 1751. JOEL MARTIN and LUCRECE, *legatees. Executor:* PHILIP JONES. *Witnesses:* JAS. BRYANT, JAMES ACOCK, JOS. GOODING. *Clerk of the Court:* CHAS. YOUNG.

BRIDGESS, SAMUEL. Northampton County.

December 13, 1748. February Court, 1756. *Daughters:* MARY BRIDGESS, PATIENCE BRIDGESS (to both are bequeathed 200-acre tracts of land on the Tarkill Branch). *Executor:* WILLIAM BOON. *Witnesses:* JOHN CORE, JESSE CARDIN, JOSEPH BRIDGESS. *Clerk of the Court:* I. EDWARDS.

BRIGGS, RICHARD. Chowan County.

March 2, 1754. July Court, 1754. *Sons:* JOHN, SOLOMON, JAMES, MOSES, RICHARD and CHRISTIAN. *Daughters:* TILPAH and RACHEL. *Wife:* ELIZABETH BRIGGS. *Executors:* JOHN DAVIS and JOB HARRISS. *Witnesses:* JOHN DAVIS, JOBE HARRISS, JESSE EASON. *Clerk of the Court:* WILL HALSEY.

BRIGHT, HENERY. Pasquotank County.

July 8, 1734. October Court, 1739. *Son:* ADAM. *Daughter:* LEVINAH UPTON. *Wife and Executrix:* ELIZABETH. *Witnesses:* WILLIAM OVERENTON, JOSEPH MAKEFARSON. *Clerk of the Court:* JAMES CRAVEN.

BRIGHT, HENRY. Currituck County.

May 23, 1749. July Court, 1749. *Sons:* CALEB, SILAS, JOHN, HENRY. *Daughters:* BRIDGES, MARY ANN, SUSY, CORTNEY. *Executor:* HENRY BRIGHT (son). *Witnesses:* JAMES BURNHAM, SAMUEL BRIGHT, ANN BRIGHT. *Clerk of the Court:* RICH'D McCLURE.

BRIGHT, JAMES.   Hyde County.

March 29, 1735. *Wife, Executrix and sole devisee:* ANN. *Witnesses:*
GILES WILLIAMS, HANAH ADAMS, RICH'D WM. SILVESTER. *Clerk of the
Court:* JNO. COLLISON.

BRIGHT, RICHARD.   Currituck County.

December 12, 1734. *Sons:* EPHRAM, WILLIAM. *Daughters:* CASIAH,
ELIZABETH. *Wife:* ELIZABETH (who is appointed executrix). *Witnesses:*
SAMLL. BALLANCE, JOHN WEST, MOSES LINTON. *Clerk of the Court:*
THOMAS LOWTHER.

BRIGHT, RICHARD.   Currituck County.

February 20, 1733. July 1, 1740. *Sons:* RICHARD, HANSON, SOLLOMON,
("ye maner plantation"), WILLIAM, JAMES, SAMLL. *Daughters:* ANN COX,
ELENER ETHERIDGE, EDEE BRIGHT. *Executor:* JOHN ETHERIDGE (son-in-
law). *Witnesses:* RICH. ETHERIDGE, HENRY FORSHAW, SAMLL. LEE.
Clerk of Court: WM. SHERGOLD.

BRIGHT, SIMON.   Dobbs County.

November 23, 1775. January 18, 1777. *Sons:* SIMON ("the plantation
wheron I now live," together with 200 acres of land on the Briery Branch),
GRAVES (lands known by name of Haskins land), JAMES (500-acre and
160-acre tracts of land). *Daughters:* MARY BRIGHT, NANCY BRIGHT,
SALLY BRIGHT, ELIZABETH BRIGHT. *Wife:* MARY. *Executors:* RICHARD
CASWELL and JOHN COOKE (friends) and JAMES BRIGHT (brother). *Wit-
nesses:* E. COOKE, RD. CASWELL and J. GLASGOW. Will proven before
RD. CASWELL, at New Bern.

BRIGHT, SOLOMON.   Currituck County.

February 4 (no year). June, 1755. *Sons:* HANCE and SOLOMON
(plantation). *Wife and Executrix:* MARY BRIGHT. *Witnesses:* THOS.
WILLIAMS, WILLIAM WILLIAMS. THOMAS DAVIS. *Clerk of the Court:*
WILLIAM SHERGOLD.

BRIGHT, WILLIAM.   Craven County.

January 12, 1754. November 6, 1754. *Son:* STOCWELL ("all my land
down the Riever * * * * one plantation on Orched Creek and one Do.
on Loer Broad Creek"). *Daughters:* SUSANAH BRIGHT, ELENAR BRIGHT,
MARY BRIGHT, SARAH BRIGHT, ANN NELSON. *Grandson:* HARMON GAS-
KINS. *Granddaughters:* MARY and SARAH BRIGHT. *Wife and Executrix:*
ANN. *Witnesses:* JAMES ARTHER, SARAH ARTHER, W. CARRUTHERS,
JUNR. *Clerk of the Court:* SOL. REW.

BRILL, WILLIAM.   County not given.

November 27, 1752.   April 2, 1753.   *Sons:* WILLIAM ("my Richland plantation"), RIGDON ("plantation I now dwell on"), ACTON, FRANCIS. *Executors:* FRANCIS BRIN, SAMELL HATCH and NATHAN SMITH.   *Witnesses:* MARY MOORE, BENETA SMITH, MATTHEW SAMIN (?), JOSEPH BATCHER. Will proven before MATT ROWAN.

BRITT, WILLIAM.   County not given.

June 25, 1711.   No probate.   *Daughter:* MARY.   *Wife:* ELIZABETH. *Executors:* SAMUEL EDMUNDS, ROBERT and THOMAS WEST.   *Witnesses:* JOHN JORDAN, MATT ADAMS, MARY ADAMS.   Will recorded in book 1712–22, page 34.   Original missing.

BROCHETT, BENJAMIN.   Craven County.

July 9, 1750.   August Court, 1758.   *Wife and Executrix:* SARAH.   *Witnesses:* MARY GARDNER, MARY PRINGELL, JOHN GRANADE.   *Clerk of the Court:* PETER CONWAY.

BRODERICK, THOMAS, late of the Island of Granada,
                              but now of Wilmington.

May 6, 1770.   May 16, 1770.   *Friends:* "MR. PARNERA, *Priest of the Roman Catholic Religion* in Philadelphia" (30 pounds "Pensilvania Currency"), MR. HARDIN, *of the same Profession*"), CHRISTIAN CAIN, Wilmington (40 gallons of rum).   *Nephew:* ANDREW BRODRICK (son of brother DAN'L BRODRICK, of Philadelphia).   *Executor:* CORNELIUS HARNETT.   *Witnesses:* JAMES McCAN, THO. LOYD, ARCHY WARD.   Will proven before WM. TRYON, at Wilmington.   *Executor* qualified before FRED'K GREGG.

BROMLEY, GEORGE.   Bertie Precinct.

March 21, 1726.   September 20, 1728.   *Friend and sole legatee and devisee:* THOMAS BETTERLEY.   *Witnesses:* GO. ALLEN, WILL'M WILLIAMS, JNO. MATHEWS, W. BIGGS.   Will proven before RICH'D EVERARD.

BROOKS, JOHN.   Currituck County.

July 9, 1707.   April 27, 1708.   *Son:* JOHN ("plantation whereon I now live").   *Daughters:* ELIZABETH BROOKS, FRANCES BROOKS, MARY BROOKS. *Son-in-law:* WILLIAM SCOTT.   *Wife:* MARY.   *Executrix:* MARY BROOKS (wife).   *Witnesses:* WM. SWANN, JAMES BETTS.   *Clerk of the Court:* EDWARD TAYLOR.

BROTHERS, JOHN.   Pasquotank Precinct.

November 28, 1733. April 8, 1735. *Sons:* JOSEPH (200 acres of land known as Kirks plantation), WILLIAM (150 acres of land), JOHN (100 acres of land on North side of Gum Pole Swamp), SAMUELL (129 acres of land), THOMAS, RICHARD, SAMUEL. *Daughter:* ELIZABETH BROTHERS. *Wife:* MARY. *Executors:* MARY BROTHERS (wife), JOSEPH BROTHERS (son), WILLIAM BROTHERS (brother). *Witnesses:* THOMAS WOODLEY, MARY WOODLEY, JAMES CRAVEN. *Clerk of Court:* JOS. SMITH. Court-house in Broomfield.

BROTHERS, WILLIAM.   Pasquotank Precinct.

January 3, 1711. *Sons:* WILLIAM (126 acres of land), THOMAS (126 acres of land), RICHARD (126 acres of land), JOHN (126 acres of land), BENJAMIN. *Daughters:* ELINOR CARP, ELIZABETH, MARY, HANAH, SARAH, REBEKAH, DOROTY. *Wife and Executrix:* SARAH BROTHERS. *Witnesses:* HOWELL BROWNE. No probate.

BROWN, FRANCIS.   Bertie County.

November 7, 1748. May Court, 1750. *Sons:* FRANCIS (plantation purchased from Dan'l Brown), WILLIAM (150 acres of land), JOHN (land in Cypress Swamp), BENJAMIN. *Daughters:* ANNE, MARY, SARAH, JANE and ELIZABETH. *Executor:* JOHN WYNNS. *Witnesses:* ISAAC HILL, DAN'L VANPELT, GEORGE RIVET. *Clerk of the Court:* SAM'L ORMES.

BROWN, JAMES.   Currituck County.

April 5, 1721. *Wife and Executrix:* MARY. *Son:* WILLIAM (plantation). *Witnesses:* JAMES ADAMS, JOSEPH SANDERSON, ELIZABETH SANDERSON, *Clerk of the Court:* ———.

BROWN, JAMES.   Bath Town, Beaufort County.

November 13, 1746. *Daughters:* MARY BROWN and ANN BROWN. *Wife:* DOROTHY. *Executors:* MITCHELL COURTANCH (?), ABRAHAM DUN-CAN. *Witnesses:* DAN'L BLIZ, RICHARD BASSETT, JAMES RIGNEY. No probate.

BROWN, JAMES.   Edgecombe County.

March 26, 1773. March 25, 1774. *Son:* JAMES ("my plantation"). *Daughters:* MOLLY BROWN, RACHEL BROWN, CATHARINE BROWN, SALLY BROWN, ANNY BROWN. *Executor:* BENJAMIN AMASON. *Witnesses:* JAMES AMASON, JESSE AMASON, WILLIAM AMASON. Will proven before JO. MARTIN.

BROWN, JOHN.   Pasquotank Precinct.

February 15, 1698–1699.   October 17, 1699.   *Sons:* DANIEL and PEETER ("my plantation"). *Daughters:* MARGARET and JEAN. *Executrix:* WIFE (not named). *Witnesses:* DANIEL AKEHURST, WILLIAM REED. *Clerk of the Court:* THO. ABINGTON.

BROWN, JOHN.   Edgecombe County.

March 13, 1758.   June Court, 1759. *Sons:* NATHAN ("land, still and cyder hogsheads"), HARDY. *Daughters:* PATIENCE POPE, ELISABETH EDWARDS, PRISCILLA BROWN, HANRENITTIA BROWN, SARAH BROWN, OLIVE BROWN. *Grandson:* BURAL SHELTON. *Wife:* PATIENCE. *Executors:* NATHAN BROWN, SAMUEL EDWARDS and SOLOMON. *Witnesses:* JOHN POPE, GEORGE CRUDUP, NICHOLAS DIXON. Will proven in Halifax Court. JOS. MONTFORT, *Clerk.*

BROWN, JONAS.   Northampton County.

January 26, 1741. August Court, 1743. *Brother:* WM. BROWN. *Nephew:* JONAS BROWN (son of William). *Wife and Executrix:* EDITH BROWN. *Witnesses:* WM. BODDIE, MARY BODDIE. *Clerk of Court:* I. EDWARDS.

BROWN, PHILIP.   Bertie County.

December 10, 1725. *Wife:* TEMSIN. *Friend:* JOHN MCHARLIN. *Executors:* TEMSIN BROWN (wife) and JOHN MCHARLIN. *Witnesses:* WILL ADAMS, JOHN WHITE, BENJAMIN SANDERS. No probate.

BROWN, RICHARD.   Bertie County.

April 8, 1734. May Court, 1736. *Sons:* DANIEL, RICHARD, WILLIAM, JAMES, STEPHEN. *Daughters:* ELIZABETH, AGNIS, MARGARETT. *Wife:* MARGARETT. *Executrix:* MARGARETT BROWN (wife). *Witnesses:* NICHS TAINLESS, EDWARD TIDMAN, AGNIS BROWN. *Clerk of the Court:* JNO. WYNNS.

BROWN, THOMAS.   Chowan County.

April 1, 1718. October 21, 1718. *Sons:* THOMAS, JOHN, HOWELL, JAMES. *Daughter:* SARAH MACDONEL. *Wife:* CHRISTIAN. *Witnesses:* JUDETH PERRY and THOMAS PERRY. *Clerk of the Court:* R. HICKS.

BROWN, THOMAS.   New Hanover County.

July 16, 1748. May 10, 1749. *Wife:* FORTUNE (400 acres land on the Sound). *Daughters:* ISABELLA (plantation "up the North West"), ELIZABETH ("plantation I purchased of WILLIAM SALTER"). *Executors:* JOHN BROWN (brother), RICHARD QUINCE. *Witnesses:* GEO. MERRICK, HENRY WRIGHT, ANN WRIGHT. Will proven before E. MOSELEY, *Associate Justice,* at Wilmington.

BROWN, WILLIAM.   Chowan Precinct.

December 15, 1718.   July 21, 1719.   *Sons:* JOHN ("ye manner planta-
tion"), THOMAS (150 acres of land), JACOB (150 acres of land).   *Daughters:*
ANN, MARTHA, MARY, SARAH (each 150 acres of land).   *Executors:* THOMAS
MONDERS.   *Witnesses:* THOMAS MONDERS, THOMAS SMITH, MARTHA
BROWN.   *Clerk of the Court:* R. HICKS.   *Wife* of testator mentioned, but
not named.

BROWN, WILLIAM.   Beaufort County.

September 9, 1751. December 10, 1751.   *Wife:* ELIZABETH. *Son:*
JOHN BROWN. *Daughters:* MARY BROWN and SARAH BROWN. *Executrix:*
ELIZABETH BROWN (wife).   *Witnesses:* JOHN LINTON, JOHN CHESTER,
SAMUEL COAKSON.   *Clerk of the Court:* WILLIAM ORMOND.

BROWNE, JOHN.   Chowan County.

November 28, 1718.   October 21, 1718.   *Wife:* ANNE. *Stepson:* JACOB
PRITCHARD.   *Witnesses:* JAMES ROBERTSON, ELIZA SWANN, EDW'D MOSE-
LEY.   *Clerk of the Court:* R. HICKS.   *Remarks:* The date of probate of
this will is prior to date of signing.

BROWNE, WALTER.   Bertie County.

October 17, 1735. February Court, 1735.   *Son:* JOSIAH BROWNE
("dwelling plantation").   *Cousin:* JESSE DRAKE.   *Wife:* MARY BROWNE
("plantation on the South side of Cattawaske marsh").   *Executrix:* MARY
BROWNE.   *Witnesses:* JESSE BROWNE, JOHN BATTLE, JOHN BROWNE.
Clerk of the Court: JOHN WYNN.   *Remarks:* The date of probate is evidently
incorrect, as the will is dated eight months later.   Probably this date was
1736, as the will was recorded March 2, 1736.

BROWNING, JOHN.   Albemarle County.

April 29, 1723. September 4, 1733.   *Wife:* MARGETT. *Son:* JOHN
(plantation 250 acres).   *Daughters:* ELIZABETH BROWNING, DARKESS.
Executors: WIFE, son JOHN BROWNING, MR. COLLIN POLLOCK.   *Witnesses:*
THOS. HOBBS, JOHN COOTHEN.   Will proven before W. LITTLE, C. J.

BRYAN, ANNE.   Craven County.

October 25, 1767. March 9, 1773.   *Sons:* WILLIAM, JOHN and JESSE.
Daughters: MARY COOK and ELIZABETH DAWSON.   *Grandsons:* JOSEPH
STOCKLEY and JOHN DAWSON.   *Executors:* WILLIAM, JOHN and JESSE
BRYAN (sons).   *Witnesses:* JAMES CARRAWAY, ANN CARRAWAY, ELIES
JUSTES, GIDEON CARRAWAY.   Proven before JO. MARTIN.

BRYAN, EDWARD.   Craven County.

January 28, 1745. May 9, 1746. *Sons:* JOHN BRYAN (220 acres land
bought of Martin and Edward Frank, called "New Germany"), WILLIAM
BRYAN (300 acres land, called "New Germany"), EDWARD BRYAN (lot in
Newbern). *Daughter:* PENELIPY BRYAN (lot in Newbern). *Wife:* ANN
BRYAN ("one plantation, called paradice"). *Executors:* ANN BRYAN (wife),
HARDY BRYAN (brother), LEWIS BRYAN (brother). *Witnesses:* WM. WHIT-
FORD, JANE HAND, RICHARD HART. Will proven before E. HALL, Chief
Justice of North Carolina.

BRYAN, HARDY.   Craven County.

February 28, 1760. May 6, 1760. *Sons:* THOMAS, WILLIAM, HARDY
(one-half of manor, including houses), NATHAN, LEWIS (lots in Newbern),
ISAAC. *Daughter:* MARY (front lot in Newbern). *Wife:* SARAH. *Executors:* THOMAS and WILLIAM BRYAN (sons). *Witnesses:* JAMES REED, SHAD-
RACH ALLEN, MATTHEW ARTER. Will proven before ARTHUR DOBBS.

BRYAN, SIMON.   Bertie County.

November 26, 1751. May Court, 1753. *Son:* DAVID. *Wife:* ANN.
Brother: EDWARD BRYAN. *Executors:* ANN BRYAN (wife), EDWARD BRYAN
(brother) and DAVID BRYAN (son). *Witnesses:* MARTHA BRYAN, ISABEL
DEAL, JAS. LOCKHART, LILLINGTON LOCKHART. *Clerk of the Court:* BENJ.
WYNNS. The will mentions three children, but names only one.

BRYAN, THOMAS.   County not given.

December 1, 1760. *Wife:* RACHEL BRYAN. *Daughters:* SARAH and ANN
BRYAN. *Executors:* RACHEL BRYAN, WM. BRYAN (brother of testator)
and JOHN LAVENDER. *Witnesses:* SARAH BRYAN, HARDY BRYAN, WM.
WHITE. No probate appears.

BRYAN, WILLIAM.   Craven County.

December 12, 1746. June Court, 1747. *Wife:* ANNE. *Sons:* WILLIAM,
LEWIS, JOHN, JESS. *Daughters:* ELIZABETH and ANNE. *Executors:* ANNE
BRYAN (wife), JOSEPH BRYAN (brother) and WILLIAM BRYAN (son). *Wit-
nesses:* LAZARUS PEARSE, JAMES CARRAWAY, WILLIAM CARRAWAY, JR.
Clerk of the Court: WILL HEDGES.

BRYANT, JAMES.   Bertie Precinct.

March 11, 1731. *Son:* WILLIAM BRYANT. JOHN DEW, RICHARD BRAS-
WELL, JAMES BRYANT, THOMAS BRYANT and MATTHEW TELAR are named
as *children.* *Executors:* JOHN DEW and JAMES BRYANT. *Witnesses:* ARON
DRAKE and JOHN DANIEL. No probate.

BRYANT, JOHN.   Edgecombe County.

September 14, 1734. May Court, 1735. *Wife:* ELIZABETH. *Sons:*
WILLIAM BRYANT (tract of land known by the name of Ballards), ARTHUR
BRYANT and DAVID HOPPER. *Friend:* JAMES TURNER. *Executors:* WM.
BRYANT and DAVID HOPPER (sons). *Witnesses:* ROBT. REDFORD, ARCH-
BALD THOMPSON and ANN FRAZIER. *Clerk of the Court:* ——(?).

BRYANT, WILLIAM.   Edgecombe County.

September 21, 1749. February Court, 1749. *Sons:* JOSEPH, WILLIAM.
Daughter: PATIENCE ("my house, land and plantation"), SARAH MYHAND.
Grandson: JAMES MCDANIEL. *Friends:* THOMAS HUYANDINE. *Execu-
tors:* ABRAM DEW and EDWARD BROWN. *Witnesses:* THOS. POPE, WM.
ANDREWS, JAMES MYHAND. *Clerk of the Court:* BENJ'N WYNNS.

BUCKLY, ELENDER.   Pasquotank County.

February 26, 1704. April 17, 1705. *Sons:* HENRY, JORGE. *Daugh-
ter:* ELIZABETH BUCKLY. *Executor:* SON (not named). *Witnesses:* WM.
SIMSON, MARY SIMSON, JOANA PRITCHARD. *Clerk of the Court:* THOS.
ABINGTON.

BUCK, JOHN.   County not given.

June 27, 1710. *Sons-in-law:* LEM'LL. BARBER and JACOB BARBER (all
lands after wife's decease). JOSHUA BARBER (son to CHARLEY BARBER),
BENJAMIN TULLE. *Executrix:* ANNE BUCK. *Witnesses:* RICHD. THEARSSE,
ELIZA BEAY and JNO. WICKER. *Clerk of the Court:* ROBERT BUCKNER.

BUGNION, RALPH.   New Hanover County.

December; 1751. February 25, 1754. *Wife and Executrix:* ELIZABETH.
Sister: MARGARET BUGNION. *Witnesses:* CALEB GRAINGER, JOHN DAVIS,
JUNR. *Clerk of the Court:* ISAAC FARIES.

BUMPAS, JOB.   Onslow County.

September 5, 1746. October, 1746. *Sons:* DAVID (200 acres of land on
the North East of New River adjoining the Desert), CORNELIUS (300 acres
of land on the North side of the North East of New River with a grist mill
on the same), JOHN (320 acres of land on the South side of the North East
of New River). *Daughter:* ABIGGAIL LEWIS. *Executors:* DAVID and COR-
NELIUS BUMPAS (sons). *Witnesses:* ELMAR ANDERSON, TABAS BUMPAS,
ANN HALL. *Clerk of the Court:* WILL HEDGES.

BUN, JOHN.   Bertie County.

January 27, 1727. *Sons:* JOHN (300 acres land on South side Orreroy
Swamp), DAVID ("plantation lying in Verjenea"), BENJAMIN ("plantation

where I now live"). *Daughter:* ANN. *Wife and Executrix:* ELEANER BUN. *Witnesses:* WM. RICH, RICHARD HAREN, WILLIAM BUN. (Two wills, one original and one copy.) No probate.

BUNDY, ANNE.   Pasquotank County.

November 16, 1743. December, 1744. *Sons:* GIDEON (wife MIRIAM), ABRAHAM. *Granddaughter:* LYDIA BUNDY. *Executors:* GIDEON and ABRAHAM BUNDY (sons). *Witnesses:* JACOB OVERMAN, ABRAHAM HENDRICK, THOS. WILKES. *Clerk of the Court:* THOS. TAYLOR.

BUNDY, BENJAMIN.   Pasquotank County.

October 5, 1728. October 26, 1728. *Wife:* HANNAH BUNDY (plantation of 1,200 acres). *Brother:* SAMUEL BUNDY. *Executors:* HANNAH BUNDY and SAMUEL BUNDY. *Witnesses:* ZACHARIAH FEILD, THOMAS WOODLEY, JOHN PHITT. Will proven before C. GALE, C. J.

BUNDY, CALEB.   Pasquotank Precinct.

Brothers: WILLIAM and JOHN BUNDY. *Executor:* WILLIAM BUNDY (brother). *Witness:* RUTH RECTON. *Clerk pro tem. of the Court:* J. PALIN.

BUNDY, CALEB.   Pasquotank Precinct.

April 27, 1721. *Sons:* JOHN ("land I bought of THOMAS STANTON"), BENJAMIN ("tract of land whereon I now dwell"), SAMUEL ("all my land up Little River"). *Daughter:* MARY BUNDY ("tract of land I bought of my brother SAMUEL BUNDY"). *Granddaughter:* LIDAY BUNDY (daughter of son WILLIAM BUNDY). *Executors:* JOHN and BENJAMIN BUNDY (sons). *Witnesses:* THOMAS WOODLEY, RUTH RETTON, JOHN SYMONS. *Clerk of the Court*: EDW'D GALE.

BUNDY, DAVID.   Perquimans County.

January 22, 1749. April Court, 1750. *Brothers:* JEREMIAH, MOSES and CALEB BUNDY. *Uncle:* JOSIAH BUNDY. *Executor:* JOSIAH BUNDY. *Witnesses:* RICHARD SKINNER and GRAHAM SANDERS. *Clerk of the Court:* EDMUND HATCH.

BUNDY, SAMUEL.   Pasquotank County.

January 6, 1737. July Court, 1740. *Friend:* THOMAS NICHOLSON. *Sons:* WILLIAM, ABRAHAM, GIDEON, JOSIAH. *Daughter:* JANE PIKE, wife of BENJAMIN PIKE. *Wife:* ANNE. *Cousin:* SAMUEL BUNDY. *Executors:* ANNE BUNDY (wife) and THOMAS NICHOLSON. *Witnesses:* JOHN NIXON, PHINEAS NIXON, JOSEPH ROBINSON. *Clerk of the Court:* JAMES CRAVEN.

BUNDY, WILLIAM.   Perquimans County.

December 12, 1749. January Court, 1749. *Daughter:* SARAH BARROW ("plantation whereon I now live"). *Wife:* MARY BUNDY. *Executor:*

JOSEPH BARROW (son-in-law). *Witnesses:* THOMAS OVERMAN, CHARLES OVERMAN, PETER MUNDEN. *Clerk of the Court:* EDMUND HATCH. Codicil to this will.

BURGESS, STEPHEN.   County not given.

December 19, 1729. January 13, 1729–1730. *Sons:* STEPHEN (plantation called "Beach Reag"), THOMAS (100 acres of land "commonly called Bridg Nack"), ("all the rest of my children one shilling starling money apeas"). *Wife and Executrix:* ELIZABETH. *Witnesses:* GEORGE BRAY, HENRY BRAY, WILLIAM BRAY. *Clerk of the Court:* W. MINSON.

BURGESS, STEPHEN.   Pasquotank County.

January 21, 1734–1735. April 13, 1736. *Sons:* THOMAS ("plantation I now live on"), STEPHEN (plantation called Beach Ridge), DAVID (plantation called Bridg Nack). *Wife:* ELIZABETH. *Executors:* ELIZABETH BURGES (wife) and WILLIAM BURGES (brother). *Witnesses:* PETER BROWN, MATTHEW HARENDEEN, SARAH BROWN. *Clerk of the Court:* JAS. SMITH.

BURKETT, JOHN.   Perquimans County.

February 4, 1728–1729. March 7, 1728. *Sons:* JOHN, JOSEPH. *Executor:* JOSEPH BURKETT (son). *Witnesses:* CHARLES DENMAN, JOSIAH GILBERT, JANE ALMES. Will proven before RICH'D EVERARD.

BURLEIGH, ROBERT.   Wilmington, New Hanover County.

September 12, 1757. *Wife:* SARAH. *Sons:* ROBERT and JAMES. *Executors:* DANIEL DUNBIBIN, CORNELIUS HARNETT. *Witnesses:* SAM'LL GREEN, THOS. JAMES, THOMAS NEWTON. *Clerk of the Court:* JAMES MORAN. Will orders that houses and lots in Wilmington be sold.

BURNASS, JOHN.   Onslow County.

March 11, 1741–1742. January Court, 1744. Children mentioned, but not named. *Executor:* JOHN STARKEY. *Witnesses to Will:* JOHN MCGRAH, JACOB BIDDLE, ISAAC EVANS. *Witnesses to Codicil:* STEPHEN LEE, RICH'D ——and JACOB BIDDLE. *His Majesty's Justices:* JOHN STARKEY, ABM. MITCHELL, JOHN HOWARD. *Clerk of the Court:* ANDR. MURRAY.

BURNBY, JOHN.   Pasquotank Precinct.

April 8, 1705. August 19, 1707. *Son:* JOHN. *Grandson:* JOHN MASON. *Granddaughters:* MARGUERITT BURNBY, ELIZABETH BURNBY, ELIZABETH COBB, SARAH MASON, MARY MASON. *Wife and Executrix:* ELIZABETH. *Witnesses:* SAMUEL PIKE, GORG ELLES, JOHN CORP. *Clerk of the Court:* THO. ABINGTON.

BURNBY, THOMAS.   Pasquotank County.

May 12, 1687.   October 6, 1687.   *Wife:* HANNAH.   *Brothers:* EDWARD and WILLIAM STANLY, JOHN and WILLIAM BURNBY.   *Father:* JOHN BURNBY.   *Executrix:* HANNAH BURNBY.   *Witnesses:* QUITH CRADDOCK, ELIZABETH MABRY, DORITHY SHILO, JOHN BULL.   Proven before SETH SOTHELL.

BURNET, GEORGE.   Bertie County.

September 11, 1752.   August Court, 1753.   *Wife:* SUSANNA (*Executrix and sole devisee*).   *Witnesses:* JOSEPH MINTON, WILLIAM CARTER.   *Clerk of the Court:* SAM'L ORMES.

BURNHAM, ELIZABETH.   Currituck County.

April Court, 1755.   *Witnesses:* GEORGE BURGES, WILLIS MILLER, PHILIP NORTHERN.   *Clerk of the Court:* RICH'D McCLURE.   This will is illegible, except the names above given.

BURNHAM, ESEBEL.   Currituck County.

January 1, 1749--1750.   *Sons:* SOLOMON BENNET, JOHN BENNET, NEHEMIAH BENNET.   *Daughter:* SUSIAS ABIAR.   *Granddaughter:* ISABEL ARMSTRONG.   The probate and signatures of testatrix and witnesses are missing.

BURT, MARY, Widow of WM. BURT.   Bertie County.

September 10, 1724.   February Court, 1724; January 2, 1724.   *Sons:* JAMES and EGO GLYON.   *Daughter:* MARY GLYON.   *Witnesses:* JOSEPH HUTSON, JAMES KEETER, JOYCE HOKINS.   Proven before E. MOSELBY.   *Clerk of the Court:* R. W. MILLERTON.

BURTENSHALL, RICHARD.   Tyrrell County.

September 15, 1740.   September Court, 1743.   *Wife:* MARGARET BURTENSHALL.   *Daughters:* SUSANNA COFFT, DOREAS WATTS, ELIZABETH WEST, PRISCILLA SMITH.   *Grandson:* RICHARD BURTENSHALL.   *Executrix:* MARGARET BURTENSHALL.   *Witnesses:* MARY ROGERS, MARY TURNER, JOSHUA TURNER.   *Clerk of the Court:* J. J. BARRETT.

BUSBEY, CATHERINE.   Bertie Precinct.

January 22, 1738--1739.   February Court, 1738.   THEOPHILUS WILLIAMS ("my plantation liing on the North side of Roneoake River").   HESTER WILLIAMS (daughter of THEOPHILUS), JESSE PAGE (1 cow and calf).   *Executor:* THEOPHILUS WILLIAMS.   *Witnesses:* NEEDHAM BRYAN, H. BATE, SUSAN BRYAN.   *Clerk of the Court:* JNO. WYNNS.

BUSH, WILLIAM, SR.   Chowan Precinct.

April 5, 1716.   October Court, 1716.   *Sons:* WILLIAM ("that plantation whereon he now lives"), JOHN ("plantation whereon I now live").   *Daughters:* MARY EARLY, MARTHA WILLIAMS, ROSE WINNS, ELINORE MACLENDAN (one shilling each), ELIZABETH BUSH.   *Wife and Executrix:* MARTHA BUSH.   *Witnesses:* WILLIAM CRANFORD, JOHN SMITH.   *Clerk of the Court:* R. HICKS.

BUTLER, JACOB.   Chowan County.

May 24, 1745.   *Wife:* MARY.   *Son:* CHRISTOPHER BUTLER (dwelling and plantation).   *Daughter:* SARAH BUTLER.   *Grandson:* JACOB SIMONS.   *Executors:* CHRISTOPHER BUTLER (son) and MARY BUTLER (wife).   *Witness:* CHRIS'R BUTLER.   *Clerk of the Court:* JOS. CRAVEN.   This will is proven by affidavits of JOSEPH MING and DAVID BUTLER.

BUTLER, DAVID.   Chowan County.

August 13, 1742.   October Court, 1749.   *Wife and Executrix:* MARY (all land and estate of testator in trust for children).   *Witnesses:* NATHANIEL MING, MARTHA MING.   *Clerk of the Court:* WILL MEARNS.

BULTER, JOHN.   Tyrrell County.

December 24, 1772.   October 14, 1773.   *Wife:* ELIZABETH.   *Sons:* WILLIAM, JOHN, JAMES (plantation on Turkey Swamp).   *Daughters:* PHEREBY McHENRY (wife of GEORGE AUGUSTUS McHENRY, "manner plantation"), ELIZABETH JOHNSON, SARAH GARNER, MARTHA CHERRY, MARY LEGGITT.   *Granddaughters:* SARAH ANN McHENRY, SUSANNA McHENRY, WINEFORD McHENRY, ELIZABETH CHERRY (daughter of ARTHUR GARNER and SARAH)   *Grandsons:* JAMES CHERRY (son of MARTHA), JAMES GARNER (son of ARTHUR and SARAH GARNER), SIMON BUTLER (son of JOHN), JOHN BUTLER (son of JAMES).   *Executors:* ELIZABETH BUTLER (wife), JOHN and JAMES BUTLER (sons).   *Witnesses:* EDMUND ANDREWS, JOHN WHITEHURST, SOLO. WILSON.   Will proven before JO. MARTIN.

Codicil to Will of JOHN BUTLER: Dated November 5, 1773.   *Grandson:* ANDREW BUTLER.   *Granddaughter:* ELIZABETH CHERRY.   *Daughter:* PHEREBY McHENRY.   *Witnesses:* JACOB HARRIS, SOLO. WILSON.

BUXTON, SAMUEL.   Northampton County.

February 11, 1743–1744.   February Court, 1743.   *Sons:* SAMUEL, WILLIAM, GEORGE, JACOB.   *Daughters:* ANN BUXTON, PETRONELIA BUXTON (to each of the above-named children is bequeathed five pounds Virginia currency).   *Son:* LEWIS ("my plantation and land").   *Wife and Executrix:* ANN.   *Witnesses:* ELIZABETH EDWARDS, ISAAC EDWARDS, J. EDWARDS.   *Clerk of the Court:* I. EDWARDS.

BYRD, JOHN. Chowan County.

September 13, 1716. October Court, 1716. *Son:* JOHN ("tract of land, 640 acres lying at New Market). *Son:* EDWARD (365 acres land), WILLIAM (365 acres land). *Son:* RICHARD ("plantation I now live upon"). *Wife:* REBECCA. *Daughter:* ANNE. *Executors:* REBECCA BYRD and JOHN HARDY. *Witnesses:* JNO. CRAMBIE, SUSANNAH WILLIAMS, MARY DAMRELL. *Clerk of the Court:* R. HICKS.

BYRD, THOMAS. Bertie County.

December 14, 1742. February Court, 1742. *Sons:* THOMAS (water mill), EDMAN (still). *Daughters:* HONER BAKER, ELIZABETH JONES, MARGERRIT HOLLOMAN, SARAH BIRD, ANN BIRD. *Wife:* ELIZABETH (*Executrix*). *Witnesses:* CHRISFOR HALLOMON, THOMAS BAKER, ANTHO. WEBB. *Clerk of the Court:* HENRY DESON. Court held at the house of John Collins.

BYROM, THOS. Pasquotank County.

March 13, 1709–1710. *Friend:* BENJAMIN WEST. *Executors:* JOHN PALIN, BENJAMIN WEST. *Witnesses:* ARTHUR HATCH, BARTHOLEMEW HEWITT. Coat of arms seal. No probate.

CAIN, HARDY. Edgecombe County.

December 21, 1754. May Court, 1755. *Daughters:* ISABELL CAIN ("plantation whereon I now live"), PLURITY. *Wife and Executrix:* RACHEL. *Brother and Executor:* JAMES CAIN. *Witnesses:* WALLIS JONES, JAMES CORRELL. *Clerk of the Court:* JOS. MONTFORT.

CAIN, JOHN. Edgecombe County.

February 9, 1755. February Court, 1757. *Sons:* JONATHAN, ABIJAH (dwelling plantation). *Daughter:* ZIPPORAH. *Executor:* JONOTHAN CAIN (son). *Witnesses:* JAS. DEHORTY, JOHN TANNER, REBEKAH DEHORTY. *Clerk of the Court:* JOS. MONTFORT.

CAIN, WILLIAM. Bertie Precinct.

March 3, 1732. *Sons:* HARDY ("my plantation"), WILLIAM (290 acres of land), JAMES (upper part of dwelling plantation). *Daughters:* PATIENCE CAIN, UNIS CAIN, SARY CAIN, RACHELL CAIN. *Wife and Executrix:* ELIZABETH. *Witnesses:* RICHARD PACE, JUNR., WILLIAM CANE. No probate.

CALDWELL, ROBERT. Bladen County.

March 24, 1749. June 20, 1750. *Brother:* JOSHUA CALDWELL. Wife and two sons mentioned, but not named. *Friend:* WILLIAM NEALE. *Executors:* JOSHUA CALDWELL (brother), JOSEPH CLARK. *Witnesses:* GERSHAN BENBOW, JOHN LEARY, SAMUEL NEALE. *Clerk of the Court:* THOS. ROBESON.

CALLAWAY, CALEB.   County not given.

June 10, 1706.   June 13, 1706.   *Son and Executor:* JOSUA (plantation on Yawpim).   *Daughter:* RACHEL, wife of JOHN WIATT.   *Granddaughter:* ELIZABETH WIATT, daughter of JOHN WIATT (one negro).   *Wife:* ELIZABETH.   *Witnesses:* THOMAS LONG, JOHN BARROW, ANTHONY WHERRY. *Clerk of the Court:* THOS. SNODEN.

CALLAWAY, JOSHUA.   Perquimans County.

February 23, 1741.   July Court, 1742.   *Sons:* THOMAS ("plantation whereon he now lives"), JOHN, CALEB.   *Daughter:* ELIZABETH HARMAN. *Granddaughter:* ELIZABETH CALLAWAY (daughter of CALEB).   *Wife and Executrix:* ELIZABETH.   *Executor:* JOHN CALLAWAY (son).   *Witnesses:* WILLIAM WYATT, THOMAS LONG, JOHN STEPNEY.

CALLIO, JOSEPH.   County not given.

April 29, 1719.   July 22, 1719.   *Wife and daughter:* JANE and ELIZABETH CALLIO (*Executors*).   *Witnesses:* THOMAS HARRYS, ADAM MOORE, LOUIS THOMAS.   Recorded in Book 1712–1722, page 217.   Original missing.

CAMBRELL, ALEXANDER.   Chowan Precinct.

February 4, 1726.   February 21, 1726.   *Wife and Executrix:* ANNE. *Daughter:* SARAH CAMBRELL.   *Executor:* WILLIAM COTRELL.   *Witnesses:* ROBERT JEFFRYS, PAUL BUNCH, THOMAS MUNS.   Will proven before RICH'D EVERARD.

CAMBRIDGE, FRANCIS.   Upper Parish of Nansemond County.

February 2, 1710.   *Wife and Executrix:* ELIZABETH.   *Witnesses:* ANDREW ROSS, JAMES HAWARD, JNO. SUMNER.   Recorded in Book 1712–1722, page 36.   Original missing.

CAMBRILL, ANNE.   Chowan Precinct.

February 16, 1726.   February 21, 1726.   *Sole devisee and legatee:* DAUGHTER (not named).   *Witnesses:* ROBERT JEFFREYS, THOMAS SMITH.   Will proven before RICH'D EVERARD.

CAMERLEN, DANIEL.   Northampton County.

January 7, 1747.   May Court, 1752.   *Son:* PHILIP ALEXANDER CAMERLEN.   *Daughters:* RACHEL CAMERLEN, ANN WHITLEY, BRIDGET GODWIN, ELEZIN TEWE, MARY BEST, ELISABETH WHITLEY.   *Grandson:* JOSEPH GODWIN.   *Granddaughter:* BELASON.   *Wife and Executrix:* ANN.   *Witnesses:* WILLIAM WHITLEY, JOSHUA WILLIAMS.   *Clerk of the Court:* I. EDWARDS.

CAMPBELL, HUGH.   County not given.

January 28, 1737. February 20, 1737. *Executors:* ROGER MOORE, ELEAZAR ALLEN. *Wife and Executrix:* MAGDALEN CAMPBELL. *Witnesses:* CORNELIUS HARNETT, RICHARD SHAW. Will proven before GAB. JOHNSTON. No devisees or legatees in this will.

CAMPBELL, JAMES.   New Hanover County.

July 30, 1759. October 10, 1759. Wilmington. *Brothers:* WILLIAM CAMPBELL (½ of land on North West Brown Marsh, one lot in Wilmington on Market Street, also 3 other lots in Wilmington), ROBERT CAMPBELL (other half of lands on Brown Marsh, three lots in Wilmington), SAMUEL (tract of land on Hammond Creek in Bladen Co.), lots in Wilmington. *Executors:* MOTHER (not named) and WILLIAM CAMPBELL (brother). *Witnesses:* MARMADUKE JONES, CALEB GRAINGER, MOSES JNO. DEROSSET. Will proven before ARTHUR DOBBS at Brunswick.

CAMPBELL, JOHN.   New Hanover County.

February 4, 1770. May 16, 1770. *Wife and Executrix:* MARY. *Daughters:* MARY CAMPBELL, RACHEL CAMPBELL, ANN CAMPBELL. *Executor:* HENRY TOOMER. *Witnesses:* THOS. HENDERSON, ROBERT WEIR, DAVID ROSS. Will proven before WM. TRYON at Wilmington. Executrix qualified before CORNELIUS HARNETT, *Justice of the Peace.*

CAMPBELL, WILLIAM.   Beaufort County.

October 8, 1743. March Court, 1743. *Wife and Executrix:* ANN. *Son:* WILLIAM ("all my lands"). *Son-in-law:* JOHN LEWINTON. *Brother-in-law:* JOHN BARROW. *Witnesses:* MARY HOWARD, JOHN EVERTON, ROBERT HOWARD. *Clerk of the Court:* M. GOOLD. (?)

CANADY, RICHARD.   Tyrrell County.

April 20, 1744. October 23, 1749. *Son:* JOHN ("plantation whereon I now live"). *Daughter:* KEZIA. *Wife:* KATHERINE. *Executors:* JOHN CANADAY (son) and STEVENS LEE. *Witnesses:* RICHARD DRAPER, EVAN JONES. *Clerk of the Court:* JOSIAH HART. Executors qualified before STEVENS LEE.

CANADY, SAMUEL.   County not given.

January 2, 1727–1728. *Sons:* WILLIAM, SAMUEL ("my manor plantation"). *Daughter:* ELIZABETH. *Executors:* WILL BENETT and JOHN BARFIELD. *Witnesses:* JOHN PUFFIELDS, MARGRET WASTANDS, JOHN SMITH. No probate.

CANLEPI, MICHAEL.   Craven County.

October 31, 1743. December 22, 1743. *Godson and Executor:* JOHN
FONVILLE. *Witnesses:* JOSEPH HANNIS, JOSEPH HANNIS, SR., JNO.
MARTIN. *Clerk of the Court:* N. ROUTLEDGE.

CANNINGS, JOSEPH.   Albemarle County.

October 12, 1728. September 22, 1729. *Wife and Executrix:* REBEKA.
Friends: JOSHUA TURNER and MARY TURNER (gold ring to each). *Wit-
nesses:* JONATHAN BATEMAN, THOMAS BATEMAN, ELIZABETH BATEMAN.
Will proven before RICH'D EVERARD.

CANNON, EDWARD.   Beaufort and Hyde Precinct.

June 10, 1729. *Sons:* EDWARD, DENNIS, WILLIAM, HENRY, DAVID,
JOHN ("my plantation"). *Daughters:* MARGARET, SARAH WOODARD, JANE,
MARY, OLIF, RUTH. *Wife and Executrix:* SARAH. *Witnesses:* JOHN
KNOWIS, JOHN LAWHON, RICHARD ABEL. *Clerk of the Court:* JNO. MAT-
LOCK.

CAPPS, DENNIS.   Currituck County.

April Court, 1749. *Sons:* EDWARD ("land he now lives on"), MOSES
("eastern part of my land"), WILLIAM ("western part of my land"),
HENRY (one shilling), DENNIS (one shilling), PHILLIP ("all ye rest of my
estate"). *Grandson:* ENOCH CAPPS. *Daughters:* SARAH BARRY, MILL-
BOROUGH BRYAN, MARY STRIPES, ELIZABETH CAPPS. *Exccutors:* WIFE
(not named), MOSES CAPPS (son). *Witnesses:* ROBERT SIMMONS, WILLIS
SIMMONS, ELIAS CORNISH, DOYLEY LATTER. *Clerk of the Court:* RICHARD
McCLURE.

CAR, PATRICK.   Bertie County.

November 7, 1742. February Court, 1742. *Sons:* JONATHAN ("plantation whereon I now live"), THOMAS. *Daughter:* MARGARET CAR. *Wife
and Executrix:* TAMAR. *Executor:* RICHARD WILLIAMS. *Witnesses:* MI-
CAJAH HINTON, ELIZABETH BENTON, ROSANNAH WOOD. *Clerk of the
Court:* HENRY DESON.

CARLETON, ARTHUR.   Chowan Precinct.

January 9, 1718–1719. April 22, 1719. *Wife:* (mentioned, but not
named). *Witnesses:* JAMES WARD, WM. HOUGHTON, WM. GROSSVENOR.
Clerk of the Court: R. HICKS.

CARMAN, WILLIAM.   County not given.

August 12, 1725. November 1, 1727. *Wife and Executrix:* ELIZABETH.
Granddaughters: ANN CARMAN and SARAH SIMMONS. *Witnesses:* TIMOTHY
WINSLOE, WILLIAM TATE, GILBERT ———. Will proven before RICH'D
EVERARD.

CARR, WILLIAM.   Duplin County.

December 5, 1753. October Court, 1754. *Son:* ARCHBALD (plantation and houses). *Daughter:* JANE CARR. *Wife and Executrix:* HANNAH. *Witnesses:* JOHN DICKSON, WILLIAM McREE, SUSANNAH McALEXANDER. *Clerk of the Court:* JOHN DICKSON.

CARRAWAY, JAMES.   Craven County.

March 9, 1773. *Sons:* ENOCH (100 acres of land on Bay River), FRANCIS (150 acres of land on Bay River), JOSEPH, GIDEON. *Daughters:* NANCY, FANNY. *Wife:* ANN. *Executors:* JOSEPH and GIDEON CARRAWAY (sons). *Witnesses:* THOS. NELSON, THOMAS CARRAWAY, JESSE BRYAN. Will proven before JO. MARTIN.

CARRUTHERS, JOHN.   Perquimans County.

February 2, 1751–1752. April Court, 1752. *Wife and Executrix:* ELIZABETH ("plantation whereon I now dwell lying on Yopim"). *Brothers:* JAMES and JACOB (tract of land on Deadman's Swamp), NATHANIEL and ROBERT (land up Roanoke). *Executor:* JOHN WILKINS. *Witnesses:* J. HALSEY, DEBROH WILKINS, JAMES BRINKLEY. *Clerk of the Court:* EDMUND HATCH.

CARRUTHERS, JOHN.   Craven County.

September 20, 1751. February Court, 1752. *Daughters:* SARAH RICE (gold buttons), ROCKSOLANAH WITHERINTON (1 lot in Newbern joining Pollock Street and Eding Street, known as No. 98), FRANCES HODGES (cattle and one slave). *Sons:* JOHN ("riding sadal & bridle, one pr. large money seals and silver shu-buckels and Knee Buckels"), JOSEPH (6 large silver tea spoons, silver tea tongs and strainer and four large silver spoons), WILLIAM. *Sons-in-law:* FRANCES HODGES and JOHN WITHERINTON. *Wife:* CONTENT. All lands and lots in Newbern (including the two where "the long house stands"), together with slaves, ordered to be sold and proceeds divided among three sons. *Executors:* JOHN and JOSEPH (sons). *Witnesses:* SARAH BETSWORTH, ABIAH BANGS, SOL. REW. *Clerk of the Court:* PHIL. SMITH.

CARRUTHERS, NATHANIEL.   Perquimans County.

June 22, 1745. January Court, 1750. *Sons:* JAMES, JACOB and JOHN. *Executors:* JAMES and JOHN CARRUTHERS (sons). *Witnesses:* JOHN STEPNEY, JOHN RONSHAM, JACOB CARRUTHERS. *Clerk of the Court:* EDMUND HATCH. *Justice of the Peace:* PETER PAYNE.

CARRUTHERS, ROBERT.   Newbern, Craven County.

March 14, 1758. March 27, 1758. *Wife and Executrix:* UNICE. *Daughter:* LYDIA RALIER. (To these two is devised "all my lotts in New Bern and all my land in this Province.") *Witnesses:* MICH SMITH, THOS. HASLEN, RD. COGDELL. Will proven before ARTHUR DOBBS at New Bern.

CARTER, ANN. Onslow County.

July 21, 1770. July 25, 1770. *Legatees and Devisees:* MARY CLEAREY (of Philadelphia), ABRAHAM DAWS, WILLIAM JAMESON, STEPHEN LEE. *Executors:* WILLIAM JAMESON and STEPHEN LEE. *Witnesses:* EDWARD MOREY, LYDIA GILLESPYE, JOSEPH LITTLEBRIDGE. *Clerk of the Court:* WM. CRAY. Will proven before Gov. WM. TRYON.

CARTER, HENRY. Bath, Beaufort and Hyde.

February 3, 1735–1736. March 9, 1735. *Sons:* JOHN ("plantation I now live on"), HENRY, SOLOMON, WALTER. *Wife and Executrix:* MARGRET. *Executor:* JOHN CARTER (son). *Witnesses:* EDW'D HADLEY, GILBERT MCNEARY, GILD SILVERTHORN. *Justices:* ROBT. TURNER, SIMON ALDERSON, SETH PILKINTON. *Clerk of the Court:* JOHN COLLISON.

CARTWRIGHT, GRACE. Pasquotank Precinct.

December 30, 1728. June 3, 1729. *Daughter:* ELIZABETH TRUEBLOOD. *Son:* JOSEPH. *Other legatees:* JOSIAH TRUEBLOOD, JOSHUA TRUEBLOOD, JOHN TRUEBLOOD, ELIZABETH TRUEBLOOD, MIRIAM TRUEBLOOD, ELIZABETH MURDEN, JEREMIAH MURDEN, MARY MURDEN, JOHN MURDEN, JOB CARTWRIGHT, SENR, BENJAMIN CARTWRIGHT (son of Joseph), ELIZABETH CARTWRIGHT (daughter of Joseph), THOMAS CARTWRIGHT (son of THOMAS). *Executor:* JOSEPH CARTWRIGHT (son). *Witnesses:* BENJAMIN MILLER, WILLIAM LEWIS, MARTHA LEWIS. Will proven before RICHARD EVERARD.

CARTWRIGHT, JOHN. Pasquotank Precinct.

April 23, 1714. *Brothers:* JOB CARTWRIGHT, THOS. CARTWRIGHT, JOS. CARTWRIGHT. *Sisters:* ELIZA CARTWRIGHT, CATHERINE CARTWRIGHT. *Friend:* JOHN MURDEN (son of JERROM MURDEN). *Executors:* THOMAS and JOB CARTWRIGHT (brothers). *Witnesses:* GRAN CARTWRIGHT, WILL NORRIS. No probate.

CARTWRIGHT, ROBERT. Pasquotank County.

April 15, 1746. July Court, 1746. *Sons:* HEZEKIAH ("plantation whereon I now live"), JOSIAH, EZEKIEL. *Daughter:* MARTHA CARTWRIGHT. *Grandson:* CLAUDIUS CARTWRIGHT. *Wife and Executrix:* MARTHA. *Executor:* HEZEKIAH CARTWRIGHT (son). *Witnesses:* JAMES PIKE, EDWARD TADLOCK, JOS. MARTIN. *Clerk of the Court:* THOS. TAYLOR.

CARTWRIGHT, THOMAS. Pasquotank Precinct.

March 4, 1706. April 15, 1707. *Sons:* THOMAS, ROBERT, JOB, JOHN, WILLIAM. *Daughters:* CATREN, MARY, ELISABETH. *Wife and Executrix:*

GRACE CARTWRIGHT. *Executor:* JOHN CARTWRIGHT (son). *Witnesses:* THOMAS TWIDDY, GEORGE HARRIS and WILLIAM WARREN. *Clerk of the Court:* THO. ABINGTON.

CARTWRIGHT, WILLIAM.   Chowan or Pasquotank County.

February 2, 1731. February 16, 1730. *Brothers:* ROBERT and THOMAS. *Other legatees:* OWEN REES, HANNAH STAFFARD, JOSEPH STOCKLEY, MARY REES (sister), ELIZABETH CLARK. *Executors:* JEREMIAH MURDEN and STEPHEN DELEMARE. *Witnesses:* ELISABETH CLARK, JONATHAN HIBBS, MARY MURDEN. Proven before RICHARD EVERARD.

CARTRIGHT, WILLIAM.   Pasquotank County.

January 15, 1733. April Court, 1734. *Sons:* THOMAS, ROBERT, JOSEPH ("plantation whereon I now dwell"), CALEB and DAVID (land called the Sandy Run), JOHN. *Daughters:* HANNAH CARTRIGHT ("land above the pigpens"), TAMER CARTRIGHT (tract of land called the Little For). *Other legatees:* OEN RESE, ELIZABETH CARTRIGHT, daughter of son JOHN, deceased (forty acres of land on the South side of the Creek swamp known by the name of Maverts). *Wife and Executrix:* SARAH. *Witnesses:* EDWARD WHORTEN, JOHN RICHARDSON, JAMES GREAVES. *Clerk of the Court:* JOSEPH ANDERSON.

CARVER, JAMES.   Bladen Precinct.

May 7, 1738. June 7, 1739. *Sons and Executors:* JAMES (land on North side of the North West River), Samuel. *Daughters:* MARY BENBOW, ANN CARVER. *Wife and Executrix:* ELIZABETH. *Witnesses:* RICHARD HELLIER, ANN HELLIER. Will proven before GAB. JOHNSTON.

CARVER, JAMES.   Bladen County.

February 27, 1753. June Court, 1753. *Son:* JOB (house and land "where I now live"). *Daughter:* ELIZABETH CARVER. *Brother:* SAMUEL CARVER. *Executors:* SAMUEL CARVER (brother) and ELIZABETH CARVER (wife). *Witnesses:* RICHARD MALLINGTON, PATRICK MCCONKEY, GEORGE WILLISS. *Clerk of the Court:* THOS. ROBESON. The testator devises two acres of land "where the meeting house now stands," "to our society of People called Quakers."

CARVER, SAMUEL.   Bladen County.

April 23, 1758. July Court, 1758. *Wife and Executrix:* ARCADIA. *Sons:* SAMUEL ("plantation whereon I now live"), JAMES (lot in Wilmington). *Daughters:* SARAH and MARY CARVER. *Brother:* WILLIAM MAULTSBY. *Witnesses:* SAML. MILHOUS, CHARLES BENBOW, RICHARD MARLINGTON. *Clerk of the Court:* C. BURGWIN.

5

CASTELLAW, WILLIAM.   Bertie County.

June 18, 1749. August Court, 1749. *Mother and Executrix:* SARAH
CASTELLAW. *Brothers:* JOHN, JAMES and THOMAS CASTELLAW. *Sisters:*
BATHIAH, SARAH and KATHERINE CASTELLAW. *Executor:* THOS. WHIT-
MELL. *Witnesses:* SARAH SANDERSON, HARDY MOORE. *Clerk of the
Court:* JOHN LOVICK.

CASWELL, RICHARD.   Dobbs County.

July 2, 1789. January Court, 1790. Revokes will made at death of
son, WILLIAM CASWELL. One-half acre of ground reserved as burying
ground at place called "The Hill," where mother and father are buried;
one-half acre near "Red House," where wife and son WILLIAM are buried.
Disclaims any interest in land of MARTIN CASWELL. SAMUEL CASWELL
and NATHANIEL BIRD mentioned. Land near MRS. SHINES' dwelling to
ELEANOR CASWELL, wife of SAMUEL CASWELL, dec'd, until her son SHINE
CASWELL becomes of age. *Grandsons:* RICHARD WILLIAM CASWELL and
RICHARD FRANCIS MACKILEWEAN. Land bought of RICH'D CASWELL,
JR'S., estate to be sold to JONATHAN MORRIS, if he desires it. *Daughter-
in-law:* MRS. RICHARD CASWELL, 1½ lots in Kinston. *Granddaughter:*
MARY CASWELL, mentioned. *Daughter:* ANNA FONVILLE, land called
"Walnut Hill." *Sons:* WINSTON, DALLAM and JOHN. *Daughter:* SUSAN-
NAH. *Executors:* WINSTON, DALLAM and JOHN. *Friend:* JAMES GLASGOW,
to advise them. *Friends:* SPYERS SINGLETON, ROBERT WHITE, JOHN
HERRITAGE, JESSE COBB, FRANCIS CHILD, SIMON BRIGHT, JOSHUA CROOM,
BENJAMIN CASWELL, JOHN COART, to divide all other property into five
equal shares, after inventory, one share for wife, SARAH CASWELL, and
one share each for WINSTON, DALLAM, JOHN and SUSANNAH CASWELL.
⌐ A codicil includes further disposition of property to sons WINSTON,
DALLAM and JOHN, and daughters ANNA and SUSANNAH. *Witnesses:*
SIMON BRIGHT, JAMES BRIGHT. *Clerk of Court:* N. CASWELL.

Attested as a true copy of will on file in office of Clerk of the Court of
Lenoir County, July 20, 1799.   S. BRIGHT, *Clerk.*

CASWELL, MATTHEW.   Tyrrell County.

March 24, 1754. June Court, 1754. *Sons:* MATTHEW (plantation
"formerly belonging to Edward Phelps"), SAMUEL ("my Log house
plantation"), ELISHA ("my manner plantation"). *Daughters:* JOANNA
(land called the Red Banks), ELIZABETH CASWELL (plantation known by
the name of Briffit's Island and also land on Scuppernong River), TABITHA
CASWELL (land known by the name of the Loghouse land adjoining
brother Samuel). *Other legatee:* CASWELL HASSELL. *Wife and Executrix:*
ELIZABETH. *Executors:* SAMUEL SPRUILL (father-in-law) and MATTHEW
CASWELL (son). *Witnesses:* JOSHUA TURNER, ROBERT ELTON, EDWD.
PHELPS. *Clerk of the Court:* EVAN JONES.

CAVENA, CHARLES.   Edgecombe County.

April 8, 1756. February Court, 1757. *Sons:* DAVID (one shilling),
NEEDHAM (50 acres of land on Beech run), AQUILLA (60 acres land on
west side of Beech Run), NICOLAS (one shilling), ARTHER (60 acres of
land "joining to Needham land on the River"), CHARLES and HENRY
("the remainder of my land"). *Daughter:* MARY CAVENA (300 acres land
"on the south side of Northuntee Mach"). *Witnesses:* JOHN FOUNTAINE,
JOHN MURPHREE, ABIGAL PITTMAN. *Clerk of the Court:* JAS. MONTFORT.

CAWDREY, THOMAS.   Craven County.

August 1, 1748. December, 1748. *Executor and sole devisee and
legatee:* JOHN BROWN. *Witnesses:* PETER GLAIR, PATTERSON GILLETT and
JOHN HARPER. *Clerk of the Court:* ———SMITH.

CHADWICK, SAMUEL.   Carteret County.

October 4, 1749. December 5, 1749. *Sons:* THOMAS, JOSIAH, GAYER
("my manner plantation"). *Daughters:* TAMAR CHADWICK, SARAH CHAD-
WICK, MARY CHADWICK. *Wife:* MARY. *Executors:* SAMUEL WHITHURST,
THOMAS CHADWICK, ISAIAH CHADWICK. *Witnesses:* JOSEPH BRAY, RE-
BECKAH CHADWICK, RACHEL YOUNG. *Clerk of the Court:* GEO. READ.

CHALKHILL, JOHN.   New Hanover County.

November 14, 1757. February Court, 1758. *Wife:* DORCAS. *Daughters:* MARY (my ring), LYDIA. *Wife's daughter:* RACHEL HOWISON. *Executors:* GEORGE MOORE and WM. DRY. *Witnesses:* RD. HARDY, DAVID
BROWN, MARGARET McCORKHILL. *Clerk of the Court:* JA. MORAN.

CHAMBERLAIN, JOHN.   Pasquotank County.

January 10, 1743-1744. April Court, 1753. *Sons:* JOHN ("plantation
whereon I now live"), WILLIAM (land on Brights Branch), JEREMIAH ("plan-
tation joining upon his grandfather's, Jeremiah Everton"). *Daughters:*
MARY BRIGHT (wife of ISACK BRIGHT), ANN CHAMBERLIN, BETTIE CHAM-
BERLIN, LUCY, AMY and MARTHA CHAMBERLIN. *Executors:* JOHN CHAM-
BERLIN (son) and ISACK BRIGHT. *Witnesses:* SAM'L ETHERIDGE, GABR.
BURNHAM, ROBERT CHAMBERLIN, BENJAMIN BURNHAM. *Clerk of the
Court:* THOMAS TAYLOR.

CHAMBERS, EDMOND.   County not given.

December 3, 1693. January 2, 1693. *Friend:* FRANCIS HENRY. *Witnesses:* HENRY PALIN, ANN MADREN. *Clerk of the Court:* EDWARD MAYO.

CHAMPION, EDWARD.   Chowan Precinct.

January 6, 1717-1718. April Court, 1718. *Sons:* JOSEPH (land on the
West side of Miery Branch), THOMAS (land on the East side of Miery

Branch), EDWARD. *Daughters:* ELIZABETH CHAMPION, MARY CHAMPION *Wife and Executrix:* MARY. *Witnesses:* WILLIAM SADLER, HENRY LISLER. *Clerk of the Court:* R. HICKS.

CHAMPEN, JOHN.   Chowan County.

October 10, 1749. April Court, 1751. *Grandsons:* CHAMPEN SPIVEY, son of NATHANIELL and MARTHA SPIVEY (250 acres land on South side of Stoping Creek), JAMES BLY, son of WILLIAM and ELIZABETH BLY (250 acres land "whereon I now dwell"), PETER COPELAND, son of WILLIAM and SARAH COPELAND (250 acres of land). *Daughter:* MARGRET WARD (250 acres of land). *Wife:* SARRAH. *Executors:* SARAH CHAMPEN (wife), NA-THANIEL SPIVEY (son-in-law). *Witnesses:* JOHN ARLIN, MARY ARLIN, ROBT. ELLIOTT. *Clerk of the Court:* JAS. CRAVEN.

CHAMPION, ORLANDO.   Chowan County.

December 13, 1744. January 9, 1744. *Daughter and Executrix:* ELIZA-BETH NEAL ("plantation I now live on"). *Other legatees and devisees:* MARY, wife of WILLIAM RICHARDS; ANN, the wife of JOSEPH ANDERSON; EDWARD CHAMPION (brother), WILLIAM RICHARDS. *Executors:* JOSEPH ANDERSON and JOSEPH BLOUNT. *Witnesses:* NATHANIEL MATTHEWS, JOHN VERLIN, JAMES FENNISON. *Justice:* J. HALSEY. Will proven before GAB. JOHNSTON, *Governor.*

CHANCEY, EDMUND.   Pasquotank County.

March 15, 1753. July Court, 1754. *Grandsons:* EDMUND CHANCEY, son of STEPHEN ("eastermost part of my plantation"), EDMUND CHANCEY, son of JACOB ("middlemost part of my plantation"), EDMUND CHANCEY, son of ZACHARIAH ("my Sand Hills land"). *Sons:* DANIEL (a riding horse, saddle and bridle, dozen spoons, pair of brass scales, large Bible and three young horses); ZACHARIAH (one shilling "sterling money to cutt him off from my rail and personal Estate because of the Wickedness that he committed in my House in the time of my Absence"). *Daughter-in-law:* RACHEL CHAN-CEY (16 barrels of corn, 450 lbs dried meat, 3 gallons fatt, "my wheat patch, all my black pepper and all my flax and wool and one half of my sweeten-ing"). *Granddaughters:* MARY and HANNAH CHANCEY. To JAMES FUR-BUSH is bequeathed book "No Cross, No Crown." Children of *Daughter* RUTH: JOHN BAKER, MARY DEGRAFINRED, BLAKE BAKER, SARAH, RUTH and ZADOCK BAKER. *Executor:* JOHN BAKER. *Witnesses:* ROBT. HALL, WM. SWANN. *Clerk of the Court:* THOS. TAYLOR.

CHANCEY, WILLIAM.   Pasquotank County.

April 18, 1736. May 13, 1736. *Father:* WILLIAM CHANCEY. *Brother:* JEREMIAH CHANCEY. *Sisters:* ANN BOID, ELESABETH SUTTON, MARY CHAN-CEY, DEBORAH CHANCEY. *Cousins:* JOSEPH SUTTON, DEBORAH SUTTON,

JOHN SYMONS. *Executors:* JEREMIAH CHANCEY, JOHN BOIDE (brothers). *Witnesses:* JOE SYMONS, MARY LOWRY. Will proven before W. SMITH, C. J.

CHANCEY, WILLIAM. Pasquotank County.

July 17, 1746. August 4, 1749. *Daughters:* ANN WHEEDBEY, MARY COMMANDER, DEBORAH BALEY. *Grandsons:* WILLIAM CHANCEY ("plantation whereon I do now live"), WILLIAM BOYD, WILLIAM CHANCEY COMMANDER, JOSEPH SATTEN, THOMAS BOYD. *Granddaughters:* DEBORAH SATTEN, ELIZABETH BOYD, WINEFRED BOYD, ANN BALEY, MARY BALEY. *Executors:* JOSEPH BALEY and JOSEPH COMMANDER (sons-in-law). *Witnesses:* WILLIAM BROTHERS, DARCUS BROTHERS, ROBERT LOWRY. Will proven before *Gov.* GAB. JOHNSTON at Eden House.

CHAPMAN, CHAS. Northampton County.

May 19, 1753. November Court, 1753. *Sons:* CHARLES (100 acres land), HENRY (100 acres), WILLIAM ("my plantation"), DANIEL HAWKINS (100 acres on East side of cedy branch). *Wife and Executrix:* FRANCIS. *Witnesses:* DANIEL HAWKINS, CHARLES CHAPMAN, HENRY CHAPMAN. *Clerk of Court:* I. EDWARDS.

CHAPMAN, JOHN. Carteret County.

November 2, 1770. December 10, 1770. *Sister and Executrix:* SARAH CHAPMAN ("all my lands"). *Brother and Executor:* SAMUEL CHAPMAN. *Witnesses:* MICAJAH FRAZIER, JOB CALLOWAY. Will proven before *Gov.* WM. TRYON.

CHAPMAN, MARY. Pasquotank County.

September 2, 1728. December 9, 1729. *Daughters:* ELIZABETH LANDWELL, SARAH DAVIS (wife of ROBERT DAVIS). *Granddaughter:* MARY DAVIS. *Executor:* ROBERT DAVIS. *Witnesses:* ABRAHAM WHITE, JER. SYMONS. Will proven before RICHD. EVERARD.

CHAPPEL, RICHARD. Chowan County.

March 5, 1734–1735. October Court, 1735. *Sons:* MOSES, MICHAIAH, RICHARD. *Daughters:* JUDAH and SARAH CHAPPEL. *Wife and Executrix:* ELIZA. *Executor:* MOSES BAKER. *Witnesses:* MICHAEL BRINKLEY, WM. TREVETHAN. *Clerk of the Court:* JAMES CRAVEN.

CHARLES, DANIELL.

April 17, 1687. *Brothers:* JOHN CHARLES, SAMUELL CHARLES. *Sister:* JEANE CHARLES. *Executors:* FRANCIS TOMAS, CHRISTOPHER————. *Witnesses:* DAVID BLAKE, DAVID SHERROD, PETER GREY. No probate.

CHARLES, JOHN.   County not given.

Sisters: JANE and ELIZABETH CHARLES.   Brother: SAMUEL CHARLES.
Friends: MARY TONIE and WILLIAM BOGE.   No probate.   Endorsement:
"David Sharpe owes me fourteen shillings, John Steyne twenty shillings,
Edward Mayo owes me 3 L D."

CHARLES, HANNAH.   Perquimans County.

October 1, 1750. July Court, 1752. Son: EDWARD MOUDLIN. Daugh-
ters: ELISABETH WHITE, SARAH PERRY, ANN COX. Grandsons: JOHN
MOUDLIN and JOHN COX. Granddaughters: MARY MOUDLIN (daughter of
JOHN MOUDLIN). Son-in-law: ROBERT COX. Executors: JOHN MOUDLIN
(grandson), ROBERT COX (son-in-law). Witnesses: JACOB MARGIN, HAN-
NAH MOUDLIN, DAVENPORT GOODING. Clerk of the Court: EDMUND HATCH.

CHARLES, JEANE.   Perquimans Precinct.

July 11, 1688. Aunt: MARIE STEPNEY. Other legatees: JOHN STEPNEY,
brother and sister (not named), father (not named). Executors: CRISTIFER
NISBRALE, FRANCES TOMES. Witnesses: THOMAS STEELL, JOHN STEELL,
JOHN HARLEE. No probate. Coat of arms on seal.

CHARLES, SAMUEL.   Perquimans County.

March 12, 1727–1728. Sons: SAMUEL ("plantation whereon I now live),
JOHN (tract of land on gum swamp and Bull Branch), JOSUAY (tract of
land on gum Swamp). Daughters: LIDEY CHARLES, SARAH CHARLES, HAN-
NAUGH. Granddaughter: ELIZABETH OAVERMAN. Executors: SAMUELL
and JOHN CHARLES (sons). Witnesses: JOHN KEATTEN, NATHANIEL AL-
BURT, EDWARD MOUDLIN. Clerk of the Court: CHARLES DENMAN.

CHARLES, WILLIAM.   County not given.

April 7, 1687. Brother: JOHN CHARLES (120 acres of land). Daughter:
JANN CHARLES ("plantation I now live on"). Wife: ELIZABETH. Friend:
JAMES HOGG. Executors: FRANCIS TOMES (father), JONATHAN PHILIPS.
Witnesses: JAMES HOGG, DANIELL PINBROW. No probate.

CHARLTON, JOHN.   Chowan Precinct.

May 13, 1735. April 15, 1736. Sons: JOB ("plantation whereon I now
live"), JOHN (land called "Stacyes"), WILLIAM (fifty pounds). Wife and
Executrix: SARAH. Executor: WILLIAM HASKINS. Witnesses: SARAH
WARDNAR, RICHARD FITCHJARREL. Clerk of the Court: JAMES CRAVEN.

CHEASTEN, RICHARD.   Perquimans County.

October 22, 1715. November 22, 1715. Wife: ANNE. Son: RICHARD
("all my real estate"). Grandson: DANIELL LAYTON. Executors: JOSEPH
JESSOP, RICHARD CHEASTEN (son). Witnesses: ANTHONY HASKIT, TABI-
THA HASKIT, ANNE HASKIT. Secretary to the Governor: J. KNIGHT.

CHEEK, RICHARD.   Beaufort County.

September 29, 1743.   April 30, 1745.   *Sons:* RANDOLPH ("plantation I
now live on"), WILLIAM (150 acres land), JAMES (140 acres of land), JOHN
(150 acres land), ROBERT (150 acres of land).   *Daughters:* ELIZBETH
BURNEY, JANE CHEEK, ANN CHEEK.   *Wife:* JANE.   *Executors:* WM. CHEEK,
RICHARD CHEEK, JR., and JOHN BURNEY.   *Witnesses:* WM. HIX, JOHN
THIGPEN, ROBT. CHEEK.   Will proven before E. MOSELEY, *Chief Justice.*
Clerk of the Court: JOHN FORBES.

CHERRY, SAMUEL.   Beaufort County.

July 14, 1754.   September Court, 1754.   *Sons:* JOHN ("manner planta-
tion"), WILLIAM (400 acres land on the Beaverdam), CADO (400 acres of
land on Briery Swamp), CHARLES (land on Meadow Branch), SAMUEL, SOL-.
OMON, SAMUEL, GEORGE, WILLIS.   *Daughters:* ELIZABETH, ABIGAIL, PA-
TIENCE, MARY and COURTNEY CHERRY, REBECKAH HODGES.   *Executors:*
JOHN CHERRY (son) amd WM. WILLIS.   *Witnesses:* WM. WILLIS, GRIFFIN
FLOYD, PETER FLOYD.   *Clerk of the Court:* WALLEY CHAUNCY.

CHESTER, JOHN.   Bertie Precinct.

January 22, 1728.   February Court, 1728.   *Daughters:* ELIZABETH
CHESTER (land lying on Apple tree, Meratuck, and a place called frog Hall),
MARY CHESHER ("all my tract of land I now live on"), SARAH CHESHER
(land "betwixt the land of John Bowds and the land I now live on").
Son-in-law: JAMES FALK (land on Buck Horn).   *Wife and Executrix:* ELIZ-
ABETH.   *Executors:* ARTHUR WILLIAMS, JOHN DEW.   *Witnesses:* JOSEPH
DARDEN, WILLIAM SMITH.   *Clerk of the Court:* RT. FORSTER.

CHESSON, ANNE.   Perquimans County.

January 3, 1727.   January 17, 1727.   *Sons:* JOHN, JAMES and JOSHUA.
Sister: ESBELL GARRET.   *Executors:* DANIEL and WILLIAM GARRETT
(brothers).   *Witnesses:* JOSEPH OATES, JEAN AMES.   Will proven before
RICH'D EVERARD.

CHESSON, JAMES.   Perquimans County.

May 19, 1729.   *Sons:* JOHN ("all my right of land lying in the crik fork
in jowan), JAMES (land "where I now dwell").   *Wife and Executrix:* ANN.
Executor: WILLIAM EGERTON.   *Witnesses:* JEREMIAH PRATT, WILLIAM
EGARTON, JOB. PRATT.   Will proven before RICH'D EVERARD, *Governor.*

CHESTER, JOHN.   County not given.

December 18, 1733.   *Son:* JOHN.   *Daughters:* LEATH ADAMS, RACHELL
HOCKINGS, MARY CHESTER, SARY CHESTER, ELIZABETH CHESTER.   *Son-
in-law:* BENJAMIN HOCKINGS.   *Executors:* SIMON ALDERSON, WILLIAM
ADAMS.   *Witnesses:* ANNE JACKSON, PHILO. WILLIAMS.   *Clerk of the
Court:* JNO. COLLISON.

CHESTER, SAMUEL.   Wilmington, New Hanover County.

October 10, 1758. November Court, 1758. *Wife and Executrix:*
MARTHA. *Children:* mentioned, but not named. *Witnesses:* WILLIAM
VAUGHAN, WM. WILKINSON, ROBERT FREEMAN. *Clerk of the Court:* JA.
MORAN.

CHEVIN, NATHANIEL.   Pasquotank Precinct.

March 3, 1719–1720. *Son of wife:* NATHANIEL CALEY. *Other legatees:*
DANIEL RICHARDSON, JOHN FARRY, EDW'D BAPER, LEVI MARCUM, CHARLES
MARCUM, ROBERT KEELS. *Executors:* DANIEL RICHARDSON and JOHN
FARRY. Proven before JOHN PALIN and RICHARD SANDERSON. Recorded
in Book 1712–1722, page 219. Original missing.

CHEW, HENRY, SR.   Carteret County.

May, 1753. March 9, 1758. *Sons:* HENRY, JOSEPH ("plantation where-
on I now dwell" and 640 acres of land on Newport River). *Daughters:*
SARAH DEAL, JANE PARKER, ELISABETH HUNT. *Friend:* CALEB MARY-
LAND. *Executors:* JOSEPH CHEW (son) and ELISABETH HUNT (daughter).
Witnesses: ANN READ, MARY LUDFORD and GEORGE READ. WM. ROBERT-
SON, *Clerk of the Court.*

CHURCH, JOSEPH.   Currituck Precinct.

February 28, 1722–1723. April 9, 1723. *Son:* RICHARD. *Daughters:*
LEDY WHITE, ANN CHURCH, *Wife and Executrix:* JULIAN. *Executor:*
RICHARD CHURCH (son). *Witnesses:* HESTER JARVES, SENR., AZRIAM PAR-
KER, THOMAS PARKER. *Clerk of the Court:* JOS. WICKER.

CLAPHAM, JOSEPH.   Bertie Precinct.

March 25, 1733. May 8, 1733. *Sons:* SAMUELL ("my farm and stock
in the parish Dewsbery in Yorkshire in old England"), JOSIAS (plantation
lying on Long Marsh at the head of Tuckahoo creek in Queen Anne Co.,
Maryland, also plantation in Bertie precinct on the Runaray Marshes).
Executor: JOSIAS CLAPHAM (son). *Witnesses:* JUDETH WALKER, HENRY
WALKER, JOHN NAIRNS. *Clerk of the Court:* RT. FORSTER.

CLARE, HANNAH.   Perquimans Precinct.

August 26, 1726. *Daughters:* HESTER WINSLOW, HANNAH BUNDY
(husband BENJAMIN). *Granddaughter:* MARY JONES. *Grandson:* WIL-
LIAM JONES. *Son-in-law and Executor:* BENJAMIN BUNDY. *Witnesses:*
JOHN BUNDY, ELIZA BUNDY, JOHN SIMONS. *Clerk of the Court:* THOS.
WEEKES.

CLARK, GEORGE.   Bertie Precinct.

February 25, 1723–1724. July 31, 1724. *Friends:* THOMAS TAYLOR, JOHN SWAN, JONATHAN TAYLOR. *Wife:* ELISABETH. *Executor:* JONATHAN TAYLOR. *Witnesses:* JNO. SMITHWICK, GEORGE SMITH, PATRICK SMITH. Will proven before C. GALE, *Chief Justice. Clerk of the Court:* JOHN CARNICK.

CLARK, JAMES, SENR.   Bladen County.

April 26, 1757. On Cow Branch upon Drowning Creek. This is more a deed of assignment than a will and assigns all right, title and interest of JAMES CLARK of "the plantation I now live upon" to JOHN STACK. *Witnesses:* WILLIAM BARTRAM, JOHN MITCHELL.

CLARKE, JOHN.   County not given.

May 30, 1689. *Wife and Executrix:* MARY. *Guardians of children:* DANIEL AKHURST, JOHN WEST and EDWARD SMITH. *Friend:* WILLIAM CURRY. *Witnesses:* HENRY PALIN, SENR., JOHN HAWKINS, JOHN CABEY. Will proven before SETH SOTHELL.

CLARK, JOHN.   Perquimans County.

September 3, 1716. November 14, 1717. *Sons:* JOHN and THOMAS (estate divided between them). *Wife:* ANN. *Other legatees:* SIMON and THOMAS TROMBELL, SARAH TROMBELL, ELIZABETH TROMBELL. No Executor named. *Witnesses:* RICHARD SANDERSON, JOHN GRAY, SIMON TRUMBELL. Will proven before CHARLES EDEN.

CLARK, ROBERT.   Edgecombe County.

December 12, 1752. August Court, 1753. *Sons:* WILLIAM, MOSES, AARON, ROBERT, LEVI. *Daughters:* ANN TATUM, JEAN CLYBUN, MARY DUGLIS, RACHEL ETHEREDG, AGNESS ETHEREDG, HANNAH UNDERWOOD. *Wife:* JEAN. *Executor:* THOMAS TATUM. *Witnesses:* WM. WIGGONS, MARY WIGGONS. *Clerk of the Court:* BENJ'N WYNNS.

CLARKE, THOMAS.   Bertie Precinct.

April 25, 1728. *Sons:* THOMAS, LEWIS, WILLIAM, JOHN, MATTHEW. *Daughters:* ELIZABETH, MARY, GRACE and BRIDGET. *Executors:* WIFE (not named) and THOMAS CLARKE (son). *Witnesses:* NEHEMIAH JOYNER, ELLIS BRADEY, EDWARD HOOD. No probate.

CLAYTON, ELIZABETH.   Perquimans County.

January 13, 1737–1738. February 2, 1737. *Daughter:* MARY CLAYTON. *Executors:* JOHN STEVENSON, JOHN BARCLIFT. *Witnesses:* CHRISTIAN REED, BENJAMIN BAPTISTE, MARY DURANT. Will proven before W. SMITH, C. J.

CLAYTON, HENRY.   Chowan Precinct.

January 20, 1725.   July 26, 1725.   *Wife:* ELIZABETH.   *Daughter:* SARAH CLAYTON.   *Trustees for daughter:* CHRISTOPHER GALE, JOHN LOVICK and WILLIAM LITTLE (to whom is conveyed tract of land on Perquimans River called the "Vinyard," in trust for daughter SARAH).   *Brother:* RICHARD CLAYTON (of London).   *Executors:* CHRISTOPHER GALE (father-in-law), JOHN LOVICK and WILLIAM LITTLE.   *Witnesses:* WILLIAM WILLIAMS, BARTHALM SCOTT, JOHN———.   Will proven before RICH'D EVERARD, *Governor.*   Coat of arms on seal.

CLEARE, TIMOTHY.   Perquimans County.

November 10, 1724.   November 17, 1724.   *Daughters:* MARY MAYO, ELIZABETH WINSLOWE, JANE JESSOP, SARAH WHITE, HANNAH CLEARE, HEPZIBAH BERRY.   *Sons-in-law:* THOS. WINSLOW (his sons, TIMOTHY and JESSE), THOMAS JESSOP.   *Grandson:* JOHN ROBINSON.   *Wife:* HANNAH.   *Executors:* THOS. WINSLOW and THOS. JESSOP (sons-in-law).   *Witnesses:* THOMAS BAGLEY, SMITH COLLA, J. JESSOP.   *Clerk of the Court:* E. MOSELEY.

CLEMENT, JOHN.   Bertie Precinct.

January 2, 1734.   January 29, 1734.   *Friends:* JOHN BELL (*Executor*), ARCHIBALD BELL, GEORGE BELL, ROBERT BELL, PENELOPE BELL.   *Witnesses:* ROBT. SHARMAN, MIKEL KING, LUCY SHARMAN.   Will proven before GAB. JOHNSTON, *Governor,* at Edenton.

CLEMENTS, GEORGE.   Bertie County.

February 22, 1729.   May Court, 1730.   *Sons:* BENJAMIN and GEORGE.   *Daughter:* ELIZABETH CLEMENTS.   *Wife and Executrix:* SUSANNA.   *Witnesses:* THOMAS BUSBY, GEORGE FRENCH, WILLIAM SMITH.   *Clerk of the Court:* RT. FORSTER.

CLIFFORD, THOMAS.

October 9, 1735.   "Late of Charlestown in South Carolina, but at present residing in New Hanover Precinct in North Carolina."   *Wife and Executrix:* MARY.   *Witnesses:* M. MOORE, ELIZA SWANN, E. MOSELEY.   Proven before GAB. JOHNSTON.

CLOASE, GEORGE.   New Hanover County.

August 8, 1750.   April 28, 1760.   *Father-in-law:* NEWORK INGRIM.   *Mother:* JEAN INGRIM.   *Executor:* ALEXANDER DUNCAN.   *Witnesses:* A. McKEITHEN, JAS. CAMPBELL, JR.   Will proven before ARTHUR DOBBS.

COEN, BENJAMIN.   Pasquotank Precinct.

November 29, 1734. January 4, 1734. *Son-in-law:* JAMES MACK-
BRIDE. *Daughter:* BELEY COEN. *Wife:* BRIDGET. *Executors:* CHARLES
SAWYER, BENNETT MORGAN. *Witnesses:* CALEB KOEN and BENNETT
MORGAN. *Clerk of the Court:* JOS. SMITH.

COFFINE, MARY.   Perquimans County.

June 17, 1707. July 8, 1707. *Deceased husband:* JOHN THURSTON.
Daughter: HANNAH THURSTON. *Granddaughter:* SARAH ROSE. *Executor:*
EDMOND MODLIN. *Witnesses:* GILBERT SMITH, DERBY BRAYEN. *Clerk of
the Court:* THOS. SNODEN.

COGWELL, HENRY.   Perquimans Precinct.

February 26, 1716. October 3, 1719. *Daughters:* BETTIE COGWELL
("land whereon I now live"), SARAH COGWELL (75 acres of land in Chowan
precinct). *Wife and Executrix:* MARY. *Executor:* PETER JAMES. *Witnesses:* JOHN JONSON, WM. EGERTON, JAMES WILSON. *Clerk of the Court:*
RICH'D LEARY.

COKER, CALEB.   Edgecombe County.

June 11, 1748. November Court, 1748. *Wife:* MARY. *Sons:* RICHARD,
JAMES and THOMAS. *Daughters:* MARY NARRON, ANN BRUN, FRANCIS
WALL, ELIZABETH SPEIR, SARAH COKER, AGNES COKER. *Executors:* MARY
COKER (wife) and JAMES SPEIR. *Witnesses:* MARGRET COKER and JAMES
COKER. *Clerk of the Court:* BENJ'N WYNNS.

COKER, RICHARD.   Beaufort County.

March 26, 1756. June Court, 1756. *Wife and Executrix:* MARGREAT.
Executor: WM. SPEIR. *Witnesses:* JOHN SPEIR, WM. SPEIR, ELIZABETH
SPEIR. *Clerk of the Court:* WALLEY CHAUNCEY.

COLEMAN, WILLIAM.   Edgecombe County.

December 29, 1749. February Court, 1752. *Son:* SAMUEL ("plantation whereon I now live"). *Daughters:* SARAH, SUSANNAH. *Wife and Executrix:* JANE. *Executor:* ROBERT COLEMAN (brother). *Witnesses:* MOSES
COLEMAN, CORNELIUS JORDAN, ELIN JORDAN. *Clerk of the Court:* BENJ'N
WYNNS.

COLEMAN, ROBERT.   Bath County.

July 9, 1721. September 25, 1721. March 29, 1722. *Wife and Executrix:* MARY. *Daughters:* ELIZABETH ISLER, MARY WHITE. *Granddaughter:* MARY ISLER. *Grandson:* DAVID DUPUISE. *Wife's son:* DENNIS ODIER.

Son-in-law and Executor: CHRISTOPHER RUNNILLS. *Witnesses:* RICHARD CARY, JOHN BUTLER, PETER GREEN. *Clerk of the Court of Isle of Wight Co., Virginia:* W. BRIDGERS. C. GALE, C. J.

COLEMAN, WILLIAM.   Anson County.

May 1, 1750. June Court, 1750. *Sons:* WILLIAM, THOMAS, JOHN, JAMES and SAMUEL (To the 1st three is given "the plantation whereon I now live" and to the other two is given "plantation lying upon mountain creek"). *Wife and Executrix:* ELISABETH. *Executor:* JOSEPH WHITE. *Witnesses:* JOHN HAMER, MARY COLEMAN, ANTHONY HUTCHINGS. *His Majesty's Justices:* JAMES McCWEAN, JOSEPH WHITE, CHARLES ROBINSON, EDM'D CARTLIDGE, SAM DAVIS, ALEX'R OSBORN. *Clerk of the Court:* THOMAS JONES.

COLES, JAMES.   Perquimans Precinct.

February 20, 1711. *Daughter:* ELIZABETH COLES (tract of land in Nansemond County, Va., "whereon my father James Coles lived"; tracts of land at Somertowne and Buckland). *Wife and Executrix:* MARY. *Witnesses:* RICH FRENCH, ELIZ. FRENCH, SARAH EVENS. *Clerk of the Court:* HENRY CLAYTON. Coat of arms on seal.

COLESON, WILLIAM.   Bertie Precinct.

February 9, 1736. *Brothers:* ABRAHAM and JOSEPH COLESON. *Sister:* SARAH LUNDY. *Executors:* THOMAS WHITMELL and EDWARD COLLINS. *Witnesses:* EDW'D COLLINS, JAMES WARD, THOMAS FALCONER. Will proven before W. SMITH, C. J.

COLLEY, MAGDALEN.   Albemarle County.

December 10, 1699. Ratifies and confirms will of MATTHEW COLLEY, except one feather bed and appurtenances which she wills to *daughter* REBECCA. *Witnesses:* HENRY WHITE, JACOB OVERMAN.

COLLEY, MATTHEW.   Albemarle County.

April 16, 1699. *Children:* ELIZABETH, JOHN and REBECCA, one plantation each. JOHN NUBY. No Executor. No probate. *Witnesses:* FENN. WHITE, JAMES DAVIS.

COLLEY, ROBERT.   Craven County.

April 15, 1744. June 26, 1744. *Son:* JAMES. *Wife:* KATHERINE. *Executor:* DR. FRANCIS STRINGER. *Witnesses:* WM. BUIE, ED. WARNSLEY, ANDREW BASS. *Clerk of the Court:* N. ROUTLEDGE.

COLLIER, CORNELIUS. Beaufort County.

September 6, 1741. December 8, 1741. *Friends:* ABRAHAM GRAY, REBECKAH GRAY, CORNELIUS GRAY, ELIZABETH GRAY. *Executor:* RICHARD NEWMAN. *Witnesses:* WM. BARROW, JONAS SQUIRES. *Clerk of the Court:* JOHN FORBES.

COLLINS, CHARLES. Newberne, Craven County.

March 3, 1738. March 7, 1738. *Wife, Executrix and sole legatee and devisee:* ANN. *Witnesses:* JOHN REED, MARG'TT REED, JNO. WILLIAMS. Will proven before GAB. JOHNSTON.

COLLINS, JAMES. Perquimans County.

April 15, 1730. May 19, 1730. *Sons:* WILLIAM, THOMAS. *Daughter:* ALIE COLLINS. *Wife and Executrix:* LUIEE. *Executor:* WILLIAM COLLINS (son). *Friend:* JOSEPH JESSOP. *Witnesses:* THOS. LILLEY, SARAH LILLEY. Will proven before RICH'D EVERARD, *Governor.*

COLLINS, JOHN. Craven County.

February 20, 1748–1749. March Court, 1750. *Sons:* SAMUEL, JOSEPH. *Granddaughters:* ELISEBETH JONES, MARY JONES, VINI JONES. *Wife and Executrix:* MARY. *Executor:* SAMUEL COLLINS (son). *Witnesses:* WILLIAM SMITH, GEORGE BARBER, JACOB TAYLER. *Clerk of the Court:* PHIL SMITH.

COLLINS, JOHN. Bertie County.

December 27, 1749. March 18, 1752. *Sons:* WILLIAM (land on Casshi River purchased of Jonathan Standley), JOHN and DAVID (bible to each), JOSEPH (plantation on Guy hall swamp purchased of Hardy Keele), MIKELL (survey on Redbud), DEMSEY (plantation on Gie hall Swamp "where Henry Ballentine formerly lived"), JESSE ("my plantation"), ABSOLUM (247 acres of land on the Deep Branch). *Grandsons:* JOHN KEEN and JOHN COLLINS. *Wife and Executrix:* MARY. *Witnesses:* MOSES HILL, JETHRO ROUNTREE. Proven before GAB. JOHNSTON.

COLLINS, LUIEE.

April 18, 1730. May 19, 1730. *Son-in-law:* WILLIAM COLLINS. *Son:* THOMAS. *Daughter-in-law:* ALLIE COLLINS. *Executor:* JOSEPH JESSOP. *Witnesses:* SUSANAH SMITH, MARTIN ASPILL, ELIZABETH FERRILL. Will proven before RICHARD EVERARD.

COLLINS, RICHARD. Bath County.

September 23, 1707. October, 1707. *Legatees and devisees:* EDMON PARSE, ANN NOLSON, JOHN BUNTING. *Executor:* ROGER MOUNTERY. *Witnesses:* EDWARD PITT, JOSEPH HALEBROOK, JAMES PEIRCE. *Clerk of the Court:* LEVI EMEWHITT.

COLLINS, URIAH.   Hyde County.

January 3, 1751–1752. March Court, 1752. *Son:* HENRY ("house and plantation"). *Daughters:* ELIZABETH COLLINS and HANNAH COLLINS. *Executor and Guardian of Children:* TIMOTHY GRADLESS. *Witnesses:* JOEL BARTRE, RICHARD WOOD. *Clerk of the Court:* FRANCIS EGLETON. Courthouse in Woodstock town.

COLLINGS, WILLIAM.   Pasquotank Precinct.

April 8, 1706. July 19, 1709. *Wife and Executrix:* ELISIBETH. *Cousin:* THOMAS WODLEY. *Witnesses:* (CAPT.) JOHN HUNT, SAMUELL DAVIS, ELISIBETH DAVIS. *Clerk of the Court:* JOHN BISHOP.

COLLIS, THOMAS.   Pasquotank Precinct.

September 3, 1719. *Legatees:* GEORGE LUMLEY, SAMUEL BARNET (*executor*). *Witnesses:* GRIFFITH JONES, EDWARD COOPER, EDWARD FAIRCLOTH. Recorded in Book 1712–22, page 217. Original missing.

COLLSON, JOHN.   Bertie Precinct.

May 3, 1730. February Court, 1736. *Sons:* JOHN, THOMAS, JACOB, SANDOWS and JOSEPH (land on Rognes Swamp to be equally divided between them). *Daughters:* MARY and MARTHA COLLSON. *Wife:* SUSANNAH. *Executors:* SUSANNAH COLLSON (wife), JOHN COLLSON (son), THOS. BLOUNT, THOS. WHITMELL. *Witnesses:* AGNESS LEAGETT, JOHN LEAGETT, CHARLES HA'VENTON. *Clerk of the Court:* JOHN WYNNS.

COLSTON, MARY (Widow of Jacob).

July 20, 1732. *Son:* WILLIAM COLSTON. *Daughter:* SARAH LUNDY. *Executors:* JOHN GRAY, THOMAS WHITTMEAL. *Witnesses:* JOHN LEGGET, THOS. KEARNY. No probate.

COLTEN, JAMES.   Bertie County.

January 14, 1758. April Court, 1758. *Sons:* JAMES ("plantation where I now live"), HENRY, SOLOMON, THEOPHILUS. *Daughter:* CHRISTIAN COLTEN. *Wife and Executrix:* SARAH. *Executors:* ARTHUR and JOHN COLTEN (brothers). *Witnesses:* SAMUELL COLTEN, THOMAS ROCHE, MARY ROCHE. *Clerk of the Court:* BENJ. WYNNS.

COMBS, WINNIFITT.   Tyrrell County.

October 31, 1749. March Court, 1750. *Sons:* ROBERT and SAMUELL. *Daughters:* MARY COMBS, ELISEBETH BRADY, ANN WREN. *Grandson:* JAMES COMBS. *Executor:* ROBT. COMBS (son). *Witnesses:* DAVID DUNCAN, JOHN WARD, JOHN COMBS. *Clerk of the Court:* EVAN JONES.

COMMANDER, JOSEPH MATTHEW.

April 23, 1698. *Sons:* THOMAS and JOSEPH. *Executors:* JAMES TUKE, JOHN TUKE. *Witnesses:* DANIEL AKEHURST, THOMAS BLOUNT, JEREMIAH SYMONS, WILLIAM NICHOLSON. *Clerk of the Court:* W. GLOVER.

COMMANDER, THOMAS.   Pasquotank County.

August 25, 1739. October Court, 1739. *Sons:* JOHN ("the west side of my land"), SAMUEL ("land east of the flat branch"), BENJAMIN ("great iron pott"). THOMAS and JOSEPH. *Daughters:* MARY and SARAH. *Executors:* THOMAS and JOSEPH COMMANDER (sons). *Witnesses:* SIMON BRYAN, T. SWEENY, THOMAS SYMONS. *Clerk of the Court:* JAMES CRAVEN. Executors qualified before W. SMITH, C. J.

COMMANDER, THOMAS.   Pasquotank County.

February 16, 1741–1742. April Court, 1742. *Son:* JOSEPH ("all my land"). *Wife and Executrix:* ELISABETH. *Brother and Executor:* JOSEPH COMMANDER. *Sisters:* SARAH COMMANDER and MARY COMMANDER. *Witnesses:* ROBERT LOWRY, ANN OVERMAN, SIMON BRYAN. *Clerk of the Court:* THOMAS TAYLOR.

COMMINFORT, HENDRICK.   Currituck Precinct.

July 7, 1712. *Sons:* WILLIAM, ANDREW (*executor*). *Daughter:* MARGARET. *Witnesses:* RICHARD BALLANCE, JANE VANDERMULER, EVAN MILLER and THOMAS VANDERMULER. Recorded in Book 1712–22, page 44. Original missing.

COMINFORT, RICHARD.   County not given.

December 7, 1704–1705. *Legatees:* THOMAS VINCE, RICHARD CANNADY, THOMAS VANDERMULEN, JANE VANDERMULEN, MARY VINCE (sister), MARGARET and SARAH VINCE. *Mother and Executrix:* HENDRICK COMINFORT. *Witnesses:* WILL SWANN, JOHN BROWN, THOMAS PLATT. *Clerk of the Court:* JOSEPH WICKER. Recorded in Book 1712–22, page 244. Original missing.

CONGLETON, WILLIAM.   Beaufort County.

July 21, 1755. December Court, 1755. *Sons:* JAMES, WILLIAM ("my plantation on the Briery Branch"), JOHN ("plantation that George Hill now lives on"), HENRY and DAVID ("plantation whereon I now live"). ABRAHAM (my still). *Daughter:* ELIZABETH CONGLETON. *Wife:* SARAH. *Executors:* JAMES and WILLIAM CONGLETON (sons) and SARAH CONGLETON (wife). *Witnesses:* JAS. BONNER, THOS. BONNER, JUNR., WILLM. PHELPS. *Clerk of the Court:* WALLEY CHAUNCEY.

CONNER, ANDREW.   Bath Town.
January 14, 1754. March Court, 1754. *Friends:* ROGER and HENRY
ORMOND, sons of WYRIOTT ORMOND (972 acres of land on North side of
Pamplico River). *Daughter:* SARAH CONNER. *Executor:* WYRIOTT OR-
MOND. *Witnesses:* WILLM. MORE, WILL ORMOND, JAS. ELLISON, THOMAS
WILLIAMS. *Clerk of Craven County Court:* JNO. SNEAD.

CONNER, DEMSEY.   Pasquotank County.
December 5, 1753. January Court, 1754. *Daughter:* ANNLATITIA
CONNER. *Wife and Executrix:* MARY. *Witnesses:* MATTHIAS JORDAN,
JOSEPH JORDAN, ELIZABETH JORDAN. *Clerk of the Court:* THOS. TAYLOR.

CONNER, JOHN.   Pasquotank County.
October 5, 1753. October Court, 1753. *Sons:* JOHN, CADOR. *Daughters:* MARY CONNER and RUTH CONNER. *Wife and Executrix:* ELISEBETH.
Executor: JOS. SCOTT. *Witnesses:* JOS. JORDAN, PENELOPE JORDAN. *Clerk
of the Court:* THOS. TAYLOR.

CONNERLY, JOHN.   Johnston County.
October 17, 1751. March Court, 1751. *Sons:* WILLIAM and CULLEN
(300 acres of land in Duplin Co.). *Wife:* KESIAH. *Daughter:* PATIENCE.
Brothers: RICHARD JONES, STEPHEN HERRING. *Executor:* ANTHONY HER-
RING. *Witnesses:* ELIZABETH JONES, GRIFFIN JONES. *Clerk of the Court:*
CHAS. YOUNG.

CONWAY, MARY.   New Bern, Craven County.
August 17, 1774. August 26, 1774. *Son:* WILLIAM CONWAY ("lands
and lotts in the town of New Bern, together with all negroe slaves, two
pair of gold Buttons and the residue of My Gold Rings * * * * And I
do earnestly intreat my Executors to pay strict regard to the education
of my said son in such manner as shall be necessary to qualify him for
such Business or profession as his Genius shall most incline to"). *Other
legatees:* MARY GORDON, SUSANNAH (wife of EDMUND WRENFORD) and
ELIZABETH ELMSLEY (silk and linen wearing apparel). *Executors:* JOHN
HAWKS and EDMUND WRENFORD. *Witnesses:* JOHN BONNER, JOSEPH
DOWSE and HENRY VIPON. Proven before JO. MARTIN.

COOK, JOHN.   Bertie County.
November 24, 1744. January 30, 1745. *Sons:* SAMUEL (plantation on
Black Walnut Swamp), ISAAC (100 acres land), DAVID (100 acres of land
on Salmon Creek). *Daughters:* SARAH, ELIZABETH and ANNA COOK.
Wife and Executrix: ANNA. *Executor:* ISAAC COOK (son). *Witnesses:*
THOS. RYAN, WM. BALL, ISAAC RATLIFF. Will proven before GAB.
JOHNSTON at Eden House.

COOK, SAMUEL.   Bertie County.

October 2, 1756.   January Court, 1757.   *Sons:* JOHN ("my plantation, containing 162 acres), JESSE (100 acres of land at the head of Black Walnut), BENJAMIN, WILLIAM.   *Daughters:* FRANCES, MARY and ELIZABETH COOK.   *Wife and Executrix:* MARY.   *Executors:* EDWARD BRYAN, JOHN COOK (son), ROBERT WEST.   *Witnesses:* JOHN BURN, JOHN PERRY, ROBERT WEST.   *Clerk of the Court:* BENJ. WYNNS.

COOK, JOHN.   County not given.

August 19, 1696.   *Son:* THOMAS.   *Wife and Executrix:* ELIZABETH.   *Witnesses:* HENDERSON WALKER, ANN WALKER, ARGELL SIMONS.   *Clerk of the Court:* W. GLOVER.

COOK, THOMAS.   Chowan County.

November 20, 1734.   January 20, 1734.   *Legatees:* GRIZELL BULL ("houses and lots in Edenton and negroes), JOHN COOK (uncle).   *Executors:* JOHN PAYLEN and EDMUND GALE.   *Witnesses:* CHARLES WESTBEERE, SAMUEL SNOWDEN, PETER YOUNG.   Proven before GABRIEL JOHNSTON. Recorded in Book 1722–35, page 344.   Original missing.

COOK, WILLIAM.   Northampton County.

April 3, 1758.   October Court, 1758.   *Sons:* WILLIAM, JAMES, ELIMELEACH, JOHN, LAZARUS, DANIEL, HENERY, EPHRAIM, MERCURIUS (to each is bequeathed one shilling).   *Daughters:* ELIZABETH COOK, MARY COOK (one shilling each).   *Wife and Executrix:* NEOMY (balance of estate). *Witnesses:* EMELIUS DERING, RICHARD WORRELL, THOMAS PAIRE.   *Clerk of the Court:* I. EDWARDS.

COOPER, JOSEPH.   Pasquotank County.

April 3, 1753.   April Court, 1754.   *Sons:* JOSEPH, JAMES.   *Daughters:* SARAH and MARY COOPER.   *Wife and Executrix:* SARAH ANN COOPER. *Witnesses:* JARVIS JONES, ANTONY FOREHAND, BRIDGITT JONES.   *Clerk of the Court:* THOS. TAYLOR.

COPELAND, JAMES.   Chowan County.

March 13, 1752.   *Son:* JAMES (tract of land on Chowan River).   *Daughter:* MARY COPELAND.   *Wife and Executrix:* DIANA.   *Witnesses:* JAMES FALLAW, ISAC WILLIAMS, JOHN THACH.   No probate.

COPELAND, WILLIAM.

October 23, 1720.   *Sons:* WILLIAM ("plantation whereon I now live"), JOHN, JAMES and CHARLES ("land betwixt Sandy Run and Bear Swamp"). *Daughters:* CHRISTIAN and SARAH COPELAND.   *Wife and Executrix:*

6

CHRISTIAN. *Witnesses:* JOHN EARDAN, GEORGE TURNEDGE, ELIZABETH TURNEDGE. Will proven before CHRISTOPHER GALE. *Clerk of the Court:* JOHN CARNICK.

COPELAND, WILLIAM.   Chowan Precinct.

January 26, 1753. April Court, 1753. *Sons:* WILLIAM ("plantation whereon I now live"), JESSE. *Daughters:* ANNE COPELAND, JUDATH COPELAND. *Wife and Executrix:* SARAH. *Witnesses:* EVERARD GARRETT, THOMAS SMALL, CHARLES COPELAND. *Clerk of the Court:* JAS. CRAVEN.

CORBETT, THOMAS.   Albemarle County.

January 10, 1692. April 3, 1693. *Legatees and Devisees:* SARAH LILY (daughter of JOHN LILY), REBEKAH, ANN, JONATHAN and RICHARD VINS (children of RICHARD VINS, SR.) *Executor:* RICHARD VINS, SR. *Witnesses:* BENJAMIN GIDON, JOHANNAH GIDON, ANTHONY DAWSON. *Clerk of the Court:* JOHN STEPNEY.

CORBIN, JEAN (widow of FRANCIS CORBIN), Chowan County.

February 10, 1775. April 3, 1775. *Legatees:* JOHN RUTHERFORD, JR., WILLIAM GORDON RUTHERFORD and FRANCIS RUTHERFORD, "children of my good friend JOHN RUTHERFORD of New Hanover County" (1,260 acres of land on the East Branch of Long Creek; plantation on the North east side of the North West branch of Cape Fear adjoining Henry Simmons; plantation in Bladen County adjoining Macknights on the West side of the Northwest branch of Cape Fear River, together with all negroes, household furniture and personal estate of testatrix). *Executors:* LEWIS HENRY DeROSSET, JOHN RUTHERFORD and THOMAS HOLLOWAY. *Witnesses:* SAM ASHE, DANIEL and DAVID MORGAN. Proven before JO. MARTIN. Executor qualified before RICHARD CASWELL.

CORE, THOMAS.   Northampton County.

October 26, 1751. May Court, 1752. *Sons:* THOMAS, ARTHUR. *Daughters:* MARGET COOPER, MARY HOLLAND, ELIZABETH CORE, GRACE CORE. *Wife and Executrix:* MARGITT. *Executor:* ARTHUR CORE (son). *Witnesses:* JAMES BOYTE, JOHN RIGHT, WM. MURFREE. *Clerk of the Court:* I. EDWARDS.

COREY, JOHN.   Pasquotank County.

February 18, 1757. March 25, 1757. *Sons:* JOHN, THOMAS and JOSEPH. *Wife and Executrix:* LUCA. *Executor:* THOMAS COREY (son). *Witnesses:* ANN COAK, JOHN McKEEL. *Clerk of the Court:* THOS. TAYLOR.

CORP, JOHN.

December 20, 1718. February 10, 1718-1719. *Son and Executor:* WILLIAM. *Daughter:* ELNER CORP. *Wife and Executrix:* ELINOR. *Brother:*

RICHARD CORP. *Brother-in-law:* RICHARD BROTHERS. *Witnesses:* J. PALIN, CHAS. BULL, SARAH BULL. Will proven before JOHN ROBISON, *Justice of the Peace.*

CORP, JOHN.   Pasquotank County.

March 10, 1753. April Court, 1753. *Brother and Executor:* WILLIAM KNIGHTS. *Wife and Executrix:* ELIZABETH. *Witnesses:* THOMAS MC-KEELS, EDWARD KNIGHTS. *Clerk of the Court:* THOS. TAYLOR.

CORPREW, THOMAS.   Chowan County.

August 18, 1748. January Court, 1748. *Sons:* JOHN (400 acres land in Perquimans and 200 in Chowan Co.), GEORGE DURANT CORPREW ("planta-tion whereon I now live; plantation of 700 acres in Princess Ann County, Va."). *Wife:* SARAH. *Daughter-in-law:* MARY BUNCOMB. Poor of the PARISH of ST. PAUL in CHOWAN Co. (one negro man). *Executors:* SARAH CORPREW (wife), JOSHUA CORPREW (brother), BENJAMIN PAYTON, MILES GALE, WILLIAM HASKINS. *Witnesses:* CLEMENT HALL, JOHN REMBOUGH, JOHN ROSS. *Clerk of the Court:* WILL MEARNS. Executors qualified before JOS. ANDERSON, J. P.

CORREE, JAMES.   Bertie County.

October 22, 1750. May Court, 1754. *Sons:* JAMES ("manner planta-tion"), DAVID, JOHN and JACOB. *Daughters:* MARGRET CORREE, JANIT CORREE. *Wife and Executrix:* MARY. *Executors:* THOMAS WHITMILL, ARTHUR WILLIAMS. *Witnesses:* ABRAHAM JORDAN, HESTER BROADWELL, ARTHUR WILLIAMS. *Clerk of the Court:* SAML. ORMES.

COSTE, EPHRAIM.   County not given.

November 14, 1719. *God-daughter:* ELIZABETH MARKHAM. *Executor:* ANTHONY MARKHAM. *Witnesses:* LEVI MARKHAM LENERTON. No pro-bate.

COTTEN, JOHN.   Northampton County.

Date of death, February 2, 1741. *Sons:* JOHN ("plantation whereon I dwell"), BENJAMIN ("plantation whereon Philip Edens lives"). *Daugh-ters:* MARY BRUCLE (or Breecle) (land at Blue water), ANNE COTTEN, SARAH COTTEN (one negro). *Wife and Executrix:* ANNE. *Executor:* WILLIAM COTTEN (brother). *Witnesses:* RICHD. BARFIELD, THOMAS COWMAN, JOHN DAWSON. *Clerk of the Court:* I. EDWARDS. This is a nuncupative will proven before ISAAC HUNTER by the witnesses above named.

COTTEN, SAMUELL.   Northampton County.

January 16, 1774. May 18, 1774. *Sons:* SAMUELL ("my manor planta-tion"), JOHN. *Wife and Executrix:* LIDIA. *Wife's children:* ELISABETH COTTEN EWELL, SALLY COTTEN EWELL, RODERICK COTTON EWELL. *Other*

legatees: THOMAS THOMAS, EURIDICE GARDINAR (bound boy), JOHN FRANK-
LIN. *Executor:* ROBERT HILLIARD. *Witnesses:* C. E. TAYLOR, JNO.
BARNES, SARAH JOSSEY. Will proven before Jo. MARTIN at Halifax.

COTTEN, SARAH.   Northampton County.

December 7, 1753. February Court, 1754. *Sons:* WILLIAM BRIDGERS,
JOSEPH BRIDGERS, JOHN BRIDGERS, CHARLES COTTEN, WILLIAM COTTEN,
ROBERT COTTEN. *Daughters:* SARAH COTTEN, PATIENCE COTTEN, PRIS-
CILLA WILLS, MARY COTTEN, MARTHA SCOTT. *Executor:* WILLIAM BRIDG-
ERS (son). *Witnesses:* JOHN DAWSON, RICHD. WILLS, JOHN SCOTT. *Clerk
of the Court:* I. EDWARDS.

Codicil: Dated December 13, 1753. Mentions *sons:* JOSEPH BRIDGERS,
CHARLES, WILLIAM. *Witnesses:* JOHN DAWSON, JOHN SCOTT.

COTTON, JOHN.   Bertie County.

May Court, 1728. *Sons:* JOHN, WILLIAM, SAMUEL, THOMAS, ARTHUR,
JAMES, JOSEPH, ALEXANDER. *Wife:* MARTHA COTTON. *Sons-in-law:*
JOHN THOMAS, CAPT. JOHN SPEARS. *Daughters:* SUSANNAH and PRISCILLA
COTTON, MARTHA BENTON, widow of FRANCIS BENTON. *Executors:*
THOMAS BRYAN and WILLIAM BENNET. *Witnesses:* THOMAS BRYANT,
THOS. STRANGE, MARY PARKER. *Clerk of the Court:* RT. FORSTER. The
following lands devised: 320 acres on Ahoskey Marsh; 150 acres in the Ose-
row Meadow; land bought of Charles Stevenson; land called the Green
Pond Neck; lower survey on Fishing Creek; 400 acres of land in upper survey on Fishing Creek. Several negro slaves bequeathed, together with a
great quantity of personal property in the shape of wearing apparel, household furniture, etc.

COTTON, JOHN.   Pasquotank County.

March 1, 1791. July 4, 1792. *Son:* HUMFRE. *Executors:* THOMAS
SYONS, JARAMIAH SYMONS, JOSEPH COMMANDER. *Witnesses:* CALEB
BUNDY, JANE BUNDY. *Clerk of the Court:* PAUL LATHAM.

COULSON, WILLIAM.   County not given.

November 18, 1712. *Wife:* ELIZABETH. *Executors:* DAVID HENDER-
SON and JOHN BOYD. *Witness:* WM. DOWNING. Original missing. Recorded in Book 1712–1722, page 53.

COURTNEY, ROBERT.   Onslow County.

January 17, 1750. April 2, 1751. *Sons:* JOHN (1 shilling), ROBERT
(land on the Half Moon Creek on the East side of the Northwest branch of
New River called Wallins), JONATHAN (plantation whereon "I now live"),
ROWLAN (100 acres land on lower end of plantation). *Son-in-law:* RICH-
ARD CURTIS. *Friend:* BENJAMIN EASON. *Wife:* HANNAH. *Daughter:*

PHEBE CURTIS. *Executors:* ROBERT and JONATHAN COURTNEY (sons). *Witnesses:* MATTHEW LEWIS, JOS. STURGES, BENJAMIN EASON. *Clerk of Court:* THOS. BLACK.

COWARD, JOHN. Bertie Precinct.

March 8, 1737. August Court, 1737. *Sons:* WILLIAM and JOHN (plantation whereon I now live), BEVARD. *Wife:* ELISABETH. *Executor:* JOSEPH WIMBERLEY. *Witnesses:* EDWARD VANN, HENRY VANN, JOHNATHAN TALER. *Clerk of the Court:* JNO. WYNNS.

COWEN, GARRETT. Albemarle County.

July 6, 1720. April Court, 1721. *Son:* DANIEL. *Wife:* not named. *Witnesses:*——— and ELIZABETH KOWEN. *Clerk of the Court (pro tem.):* J. PALIN.

COWELL, BENJAMIN. Currituck County.

October 5, 1752. March Court, 1756. *Sons:* BENJAMIN, SOLOMON, WILLIAM, BUTLAR, EDMOND, JOHN, THOMAS. *Daughters:* REBECCA COWELL, ELIZABETH COWELL, DORCAS. *Wife and Executrix:* ELIZABETH. *Executor:* SOLOMON COWELL (son). *Witnesses:* JOS. CAMPBELL, JOHN WOODHOUSE, JORDAN ROGERS. *Clerk of the Court:* WILLIAM SHERGOLD.

COX, EDWARD. Currituck County.

September 26, 1748. July Court, 1751. *Sons:* THOMAS ("plantation whereon I now live"), ABSALOM (plantation of 75 acres), ELIJA ("remainder of my land"). *Daughter:* JEMIMA PARKER. *Executors:* THOMAS, ABSALOM, ELIJAH COX (sons). *Witnesses:* WM. SHERGOLD, NATHL. WILSON, MALACHI WILSON. *Clerk of the Court:* RICH'D McCLURE.

COX, CHARLES. Duplin County.

November 24, 1752. April 10, 1759. *Daughter:* ANNE COX (500 acres of land in the province of "pencelvany" (Pennsylvania) in the County of Newcastle). *Wife and Executrix:* FRANCESINA ("plantation whereon I now live"). *Executor:* JOSEPH WILLSON. *Witnesses:* AMBROSE DUDLEY, AARON HODESEN. *Clerk of the Court:* JOHN DICKSON.

COX, JOHN. Onslow County.

April 18, 1743. *Wife:* CHRISTIAN ("one-half my plantation"). *Daughter:* MARTHA COX (other half plantation). *Executor:* JOHN STARKEY. *Witnesses:* JAMES HOYLE, DANIEL SHORLY, MARY PELWOOD. *Clerk of the Court:* WM. CRANFORD.

COXE, ROBERT. Little River Precinct.

February 21, 1725. November 25, 1730. *Son:* ROBERT. *Daughters:* SARAH COXE, ANNE WEEKS. *Wife and Executrix:* ELIZABETH. *Witnesses:* MARY COLLINGS, JOHN BOSWEL. Will proven before RICHD. EVERARD.

COX, THOMAS.   Currituck County.

April 30, 1743.   July 5, 1743.   *Sons:* EDWARD (land called the "Wolfpit Ridge"), SOLOMON ("maner plantation"), MARMEDUKE (41 acres of land)· *Daughters:* MARY COX, DINAH COX, ANN COX.   *Wife and Executrix:* ANN. *Witnesses:* JOHN SHURLEY, LUCY PLATTS.   *Clerk of the Court:* JOHN LANG.

CRADDOCK, RICHARD.   Pasquotank County.

January 9, 1685.   *Wife, Executrix and sole legatee and devisee:* ELIZA-BETH.   *Witnesses:* ANTHONY HATCH, STEVEN STELL, JOHN BOWND, MAR-GRET BOWND.   No probate.

CRAIG, RICHARD.

February 9, 1695–1696.   April Court, 1696.   *Friends:* PATRICK BEALLY (*Executor*), JOHN and DAVID BEALLY (sons of PATRICK).   *Witnesses:* SAM-UELL DAVIS, JOHN DAVIS.   *Clerk of the Court:* EDWARD MAYO.

CRANFORD, WILLIAM.   Onslow County.

October 4, 1743.   April Court, 1745.   *Sons:* JAMES ("plantation where-on he now lives"), JOHN ("plantation whereon I now live").   *Son-in-law and Executor:* PHILLIP FINSINGER.   *Wife and Executrix:* KATHERINE. *Witnesses:* THOS. ROBERTS, RICHD. MELTEN, ROBERT MELTEN.   *Clerk of the Court:* ANDR. MURRAY.

CRAVEN, JAMES.

September 28, 1755.   October 11, 1755, "late of Droughton near Skip-ton in Craven in the County of York in Great Britain, now of Edenton in North Carolina."   "I give to my *wife* PENELOPE CRAVEN (formerly HODG-SON) all the Black cattle, sheep and hogs at the "Brick House" and the "Ould plantation called Pagetts Plantation" and in the Range commonly called the Great Marsh," together with ten negroes and all "the Craven Silver Plate" and furniture; fifty books and horse and side saddle.   *Other legatees:* "DOCKTER ABRAHAM BOULTON (brother), THOMAS CRAVEN HODG-SON ("my large gold seal"), WILLIAM BADHAM (six silver spoons), DOCTOR JOHN CRAVEN, MARY LEEMING (sister), PETER LEEMING.   *Executors:* FRANCIS CORBIN, WYRIOT ORMOND, WILLIAM HERITAGE of North Carolina and JOHN WATSON of Suffolk, Virginia.   *Witnesses:* SARAH BLOUNT, JO-SEPH HARRON, JOHN WILLIAMS, JOHN PINDOR.   Proven before ARTHUR DOBBS.

CRAWFORD, WILLIAM.   Chowan County.

May 12, 1732.   January 13, 1735.   *Daughters:* ELIZABETH, wife of ALEX-ANDER OLIVER; HONNER, wife of EDWARD DILLDAY.   *Granddaughter:* MARY OLIVER.   *Wife and Executrix:* MARY.   *Grandsons:* WM. CRAWFORD (*appointed Executor*), THOMAS JENKINS.   *Witnesses:* JOSEPH VAUN, ANNE VAUN, RICHARD TAYLOR.   Will proven before W. SMITH, C. J.

CREECH, HENRY.   Albemarle County.

August 16, 1709. No probate. *Son-in-law:* JOHN DAILIE (land at ye beetree neck). *Sons:* THOMAS and WILLIAM (land "called ye bald ridge"), RICHARD, HENRY. *Wife and Executrix:* JOYCE. *Witnesses:* ELENOR JAMES, TAMER CREECH, JOHN BELT. Original missing. Recorded in Book 1712–1722, page 28.

CRESSY, LEVI.   Perquimans County.

October 21, 1734. October 28, 1734. *Sons:* JOHN, JOSEPH. *Daughter:* ELIZABETH CRESSY. *Executors:* JOHN CRESSY (son) and ZACHARIAH CHANEY. *Witnesses:* NANN JONES, JOHN MOORE, ZACHARIAH CHANEY. Will proven before GEO. BURRINGTON.

CRICKET, JOHN.   Bertie County.

October, 1753. April Court, 1755. *Sons:* JOHN (300 acres of land on the Middle Swamp), THOMAS ("plantation whereon I now live" and land on South side of the Branch), CHARLES (land on the North side of the Branch). *Wife and Executrix:* MARY. *Executor:* JOHN CRICKET (son). *Witnesses:* ROT. LENOX, ALEXR. FORD, EDWARD RASON. *Clerk of the Court:* BENJAMIN WYNNS.

CRISP, NICHOLAS.   Chowan Precinct.

March 22, 1727. May 23, 1727. *Grandsons:* RICHARD CRISP (lands and plantations in Chowan precinct; plantation known by the name of Windlys; lot and warehouse in Edenton; land in Perquimans precinct known by the name of Fendals; the Island called Batts Grove), GEORGE DURANT. *Granddaughters:* MARY DURANT (plantation and lands in Perquimans precinct lying on Albemarle Sound between Norcombs and Col Harneys), SARAH DURANT ("all my lands lying on Moratoke River in Bertie Precinct at and near Shauwaukee and Hennunteh containing 1120 acres); ANN DURANT, ELIZABETH DURANT. *Daughter-in-law:* ELIZABETH CRISP (widow of son, JOHN CRISP). *Daughter:* HAGAR DURANT. *Executors:* EDWARD MOSELEY and JEREMIAH VAIL. *Witnesses:* WILLM. WILLIAMS, HUMPHRY ROBINSON, JAMES BUSH. Will proven before C. GALE, C. J.

CROCKER, PETER.   Edgecombe County.

October 24, 1752. August Court, 1753. *Wife:* SARAH. *Children:* mentioned, but not named. *Witnesses:* JAMES WILLIAMSON, THOMAS BARRAN, JOSEPH BRIDGERS. *Executors:* FRANCIS WILLIAMSON and SARAH CROCKER (wife). *Clerk of the Court:* BENJN. WYNNS.

CROFTON, HENRY.   Beaufort County.

October 6, 1756. March Court, 1757. *Sons:* THOMAS ("plantation whereon I now live"), THEOPHILUS, WILLIAM and AMBROS (plantation

lying in Crofton's Cut).   *Daughters:* ELIZABETH CROFTON, MARY and MAR-
THA.   *Executors:* JOHN BOYD (brother), EDWARD SALTER and JOHN SLADE.
Witnesses: SAM'LL DUNBAR, ROBT. PHILIPS, ELIZABETH CROFTON.   *Clerk
of the Court:* WALLEY CHAUNCEY.

CROKER, ANTONY.   Granville County.

July 28, 1754.   September 3, 1754.   *Sons:* THOMAS ("plantation where-
on I now live" on Sandy Creek), ARTER ("plantation he now lives on"),
JACOB.   *Executors:* ARTER and JACOB CROKER (sons).   *Witnesses:* JAMES
WHITE, EDWARD THOMAS, JOHN BRANTLY.   *Clerk of the Court:* DAN'L
WELDON.

CROMEN, MARTIN.   Bertie Precinct.

May 1, 1733.   August Court, 1733.   *Brother:* THOMAS CROMEN (of Bo-
lart in the County of Limerick, Kingdom of Ireland, "all my lands within
this province").   *Legatees:* WM. KENEDY, JR., FRANCIS KENEDY, JOHN
GRAY, JR., ELIZABETH FROST (daughter-in-law), THOMAS COPLAND (son-
in-law), JONATHAN RIDING, MICHAL ELLIS, WILLIAM KENEDY.   *Executors:* WM. KENEDY, JAMES CONER, JOHN GRAY.   *Witnesses:* MICHAEL
ELLIS, GRACE KENEDY.   *Clerk of the Court:* RT. FORSTER.

CRONEY, DINNIS.   Pasquotank Precinct.

March 24, 1735.   April 8, 1735.   *Son:* WILLIAM.   *Daughters:* ELENDER
CRONEY, MARY CRONEY, SARAH WALLARD.   *Wife:* ANNE.   *Executor:* WM.
CRONEY (son).   *Witnesses:* JOHN SCARBOROUGH, JEAN BILLITT.   *Clerk of
the Court:* JOSA. SMITH.

CROSLAND, ELIZABETH.   Albemarle County.

October 18, 1693.   April Court, 1694.   *Father:* RICHARD STIBETT
(STIVER).   *Witnesses:* CHRISTOPHER BUTLER, WILLIAM SPRICK, ANHO-
RETTA BUTLER.   No probate.

CROSLEN, JOHN.   Albemarle County.

May 6, 1693.   Chowan Court, April, 1694.   *God-daughter:* CONSTANT
STIVER.   ANN STIVER, HANER STIVER, RICH STIVER, JOHANER STIVER.
Executor: RICH STIVER.   *Witnesses:* JONES BREFOT, ARTHUR CARLETON,
COTTON COLLES.   *Clerk of the Court:* NATHANIEL CHEVIN.

CROPLEY, JOHN.   Albemarle County.

January 25, 1685.   March 29, 1686.   *Son:* VINS ("land where I now
live").   *Wife:* ANN.   *Wife's father:* JOHN VINS.   No executor named.
Witnesses: WILLIAM WILKJON, GEORGE FORDYSE, EDWARD HARRISON.
Will proven before WM. WILKJON.

CROPLEY, VINES.   Chowan Precinct.

April 10, 1719. July 31, 1719. *Son:* WILLIAM ("all my estate"). *Executor:* JAMES BEASLEY. *Witnesses:* JAMES BEASLEY, JACOB PRIVET, MARY BEASLEY. *Clerk of the Court:* R. HICKS. Coat of arms on seal.

CROSSOT, JOSEPH.   Carteret Precinct.

October 28, 1728. December 3, 1728. *Legatees:* DAVID SHEPHERD, JOSEPH FULFORD. This is a nuncupative will proven by the oaths of THOMAS DUDLEY,and ELIZABETH, his wife, before JOHN GALLAND, *Clerk of the Court.*

CRUISE, LAWRENCE.   Albemarle County.

January 13, 1690. *Daughter:* MARY CRUISE. *Friends:* ROBERT JENKISSON and wife, ELIZABETH. *Executor:* THOMAS CLARCK (of "yawe pime River"). *Witnesses:* WILLIAM PRIVIT, DAVID PERKINS. No probate.

CRUMP, JOSEPH.   Northampton County.

May 5, 1758. October Court, 1759. *Wife:* CASSANDRA. *Sons:* JOSIAS, RICHARD (in Virginia), CHARLES, JOSEPH. *Daughters:* PATTY CRUMP, KATY CRUMP. *Executrix:* CASSANDRA CRUMP (wife) and CHAS. CRUMP (son). *Witnesses:* WM. HALL, CLEMT. LANIER. *Clerk of the Court:* I. EDWARDS.

CRUMPTON, HENERY.   Bertie Precinct.

January 11, 1735. February Court, 1735. *Sons:* HENERY, WILLIAM. *Daughters:* SUSANNAH, ELIZABETH, JANE and ANNE (to each of the above named is given five shillings). *Friend and Executor:* SAMUELL PEACOCK ("all my land" on pattecasi Creek on the beaverdam). *Witnesses:* ABRAHAM BURTON, ARTHUR SELLERS, ARTHUR WILLIAMS. *Clerk of the Court:* JNO. WYNNS.

CUNNINGHAM, MORRIS.   Albemarle County.

July 19, 1696. *Executor and sole devisee and legatee:* MATHEW KELLEY. *Witnesses:* THOMAS SYMONS, ARNOLD WHITE. *Clerk of the Court:* EDWARD MAYO.

CURRIR, JOHN.

May 1, 1681. February 5, 1683. *Daughter:* SARAH. *Witnesses:* THOMAS LUTON, MARTHA CULLEN. Will proven before SETH SOTHELL.

DALRYMPLE, JOHN.   New Hanover County.

(Second son to Sir John Dalrymple of Cowsland, Baronet of the Kingdom of Scotland.) February 25, 1742–1743. January 26, 1767. *Wife and Executrix:* MARTHA. *Friend:* ROGER MOORE. *Brothers:* WM. WALTERS,

JOSEPH WALTERS, JOHN WALTERS, SAMUEL WALTERS. *Sisters:* SARAH LILLINGTON, ELIZABETH HAWES. *Executors:* ROGER MOORE, WM. and JOSEPH WALTERS. *Witnesses:* JNO. SWANN, GEO. LOCKHART, GEORGE MOORE. Assistant Judge of New Hanover County, THOS. LLOYD.

DAMERELL, JAMES.   Chowan Precinct.

June 22, 1692. October 3, 1704. *Daughters:* RACHELL DAMERELL. *Wife:* LUCY. *Witnesses:* DANIELL HALLSEY, WILLM. JONES. *Clerk of the Court:* NA. CHEVIN.

DANIEL, ELISABETH.   Tyrrell County.

March 1, 1752. June 9, 1752. *Sons:* ROBERT, THOMAS, JOHN ("my manner plantation"), WILLIAM, AARON, JOSIAH. *Daughters:* SARAH WILLSON, ELISABETH DANIEL, MARY WARD, RUTH DANIEL, PRICILAH DANIEL. *Executors:* THOMAS and JOHN DANIEL (sons). *Witnesses:* WM. WILLIS, JOHN BROWN, SENIOR, MARY WILLIS. *Clerk of the Court of Beaufort County:* WILL ORMOND.

DANIEL, JOHN.   Northampton County.

November 13, 1754. February Court, 1755. *Sons:* EZEKIEL ("my plantation"), EPHRAIM, JOSEPH, JOHN, ABRAHAM, ISAAC. *Daughters:* SARAH DANIEL, ELIZABETH DANIEL. *Wife and Executrix:* SARAH. *Executor:* JOHN DANIEL (son). *Witnesses:* SAMUEL PARKER, JOSEPH DANIEL. *Clerk of the Court:* I. EDWARDS.

DANIELL, OWEN.   Chowan Precinct.

March 7, 1700. *Executor:* THOMAS JONES (to take care of two of the testator's children until they arrive at age). *Son:* THOMAS (in care of THOMAS POLLOCK). *Daughter:* MARY (in care of JAMES HIRES (?)). *Witnesses:* CORNELIUS BENNINGTON, JOHN JONES. *Clerk of the Court:* N. CHEVIN.

DANIEL, THOMAS.   Tyrrell County.

July 11, 1749. September Court, 1749. *Sons:* ROBERT LANIER DANIEL, THOMAS, JOHN, WILLIAM, ARON, JOSIAH. *Daughters:* SARAH WILLSON, ELISABETH DANIEL, MARY DANIEL, RUTH DANIEL, PRISILIA DANIEL. (To all of the above named is bequeathed one shilling.) *Wife and Executrix:* ELISABETH ("all my estate"). *Witnesses:* WM. WILLISS, JOHN WILLSON, JOHN BROWN. *Clerk of the Court:* EVAN JONES.

DANIELL, WILLIAM.   Bath Town, Beaufort County.

December 31, 1740. March Court, 1740. *Wife and Executrix:* FRANCES. *Wife's Grandson:* WILLIAM DANIELL PENKET. *Witnesses:* JAS. CALEPS, THOMAS OWEN, WM. FOREMAN, ROGER JONES. *Clerk of the Court:* ROGER JONES.

DANN, JOHN, SENR.   Albemarle County.

January 7, 1696–1697. May Court, 1697. *Sons:* JOHN, LUIA. *Daughter:* ELIZABETH DANN. *Wife and Executrix:* JEANE. *Witnesses:* ARCHIBALD BURNETT, HUGH———, JONATHAN BURDET. *Clerk of the Court:* W. GLOVER.

DANSBE, DANIEL.   Edgecombe County.

January 21, 1749–1750. August Court, 1750. *Son:* ISOME ("my plantation"). *Daughters:* MARY, ELIZABETH and CLEAREMON DANSBE. *Wife and Executrix:* ELIZABETH. *Executor:* DAVID ROZIER. *Witnesses:* ROBERT TAYLOR, DAVID COLLINS, REUBEN ROZIER. *Clerk of the Court:* BENJ'N WYNNS.

DARDEN, JOSEPH.   Bertie Precinct.

February 18, 1732–1733. August Court, 1733. *Sons:* WEST (119 acres of land), JOSEPH (110 acres of land), HENAREY (320 acres of land on the horse pasture swamp). *Daughters:* AMERICA DARDEN, REBEC DARDEN. *Wife and Executrix:* ALSE. *Executor:* ARTHUR WILLIAMS. *Witnesses:* ELIZABETH JONES, MARY POWERS, JOHN EGERTON. *Clerk of the Court:* RT. FORSTER.

DARLING, RICHARD.   Chowan Precinct.

April 8, 1702. *Son:* THOMAS. *Wife and Executrix:* ELIZABETH. *Witnesses:* COLLUMB. FLYN, DANIEL DEENS, JAMES LONG. No probate.

DARNALL, ANN.   Currituck Precinct.

June 17, 1720. July 20, 1720–1721. *Son:* WILLIAM DARNALL. *Executor:* RICHARD DAUGE. *Witnesses:* PETER DAUGE, SUSANNAH DAUGE. *Clerk of the Court:* JOS. WICKER.

DAUGHTREY, THOMAS.   Northampton County.

November 15, 1757. November Court, 1757. *Sons:* SAMUEL ("plantation whereon I now live"), JOHN, THOMAS, JESSE. *Daughters:* MARY ROOKS, ELIZABETH WILLIAMS, SARAH RICE, MARTHA RUTLAND, PATIENCE MONSON, PLEASANTS DAUGHTREY. *Wife:* MARY. *Grandson:* JOHN DAUGHTREY. *Executors:* BRYAN DAUGHTREY (cousin), ROBERT PEELLE. *Witnesses:* SAMUELL PIRKINS, JOSHUA DAUGHTREY, ALEXANDRIA DAUGHTREY. *Clerk of the Court:* I. EDWARDS.

DAVENPORT, JACOB.   Tyrrell County.

July 29, 1746. *Wife:* RACHEL. *Daughter:* ANN. *Brothers:* JAMES and JOHN DAVENPORT (*Executors*), WILLIAM DAVENPORT. *Witnesses:* EDWARD PHELPS, JOHN BROWN, JOHN DAVENPORT, SENIOR.

DAVEY, WALTER.   Beaufort County.

June 22, 1743.   October 24, 1743, "late of the City of Dublin, now resident in Beaufort County." *Sons:* SAMUELL, JOSEPH. *Daughters:* JANE, MARGARETT and RACHELL. *Executor:* ABRAHAM DUNCAN. *Witnesses:* EDWARD HOWCOTT, JAMES BROWN, SAML. BUNDY. Will proven before J. MONTGOMERY, C. J.

DAVID, PHILIP.   Wilmington, New Hanover County.

August 5, 1747. December Court, 1747. *Son and Executor:* DAVID (land lying on North East River). *Daughter:* MARY McKEITHEN. *Executor:* JAMES SMALLWOOD. *Witnesses:* WM. HARRISON, CHARLOTTE SMALLWOOD, JOSEPH JONES. *Clerk of the Court:* JAMES SMALLWOOD.

DAVIES, FRANCIS.   County not given.

February 10, 1749. April 30, 1753. Cape Faire. *Wife and sole legatee and devisee:* JUDITH. *Witnesses:* BENJ'N MORISON, ROBERT HALTON. Will proven before MATT. ROWAN.

DAVIS, ARTHUR.   County not given.

February 2, 1733–1734. April 1, 1735. *Sons:* ARTHUR (land on "ye rainbow banks"), LEWIS (200 acres of land on Banbow Creek). *Son-in-law:* WILLIAM FORK (100 acres of land adjoining Lewis' plantation). *Wife:* ELIZABETH. *Executors:* ARTHUR and LEWIS DAVIS (sons). *Witnesses:* SAMUEL WHEATLEY, STEPHEN ANDREWS. Will proven before *Governor* GAB. JOHNSTON at Edenton.

DAVIS, DAVID.   Bladen County.

December 9, 1740. September Court, 1741. *Sister:* RACHEL DAVIS (plantation purchased of GABRIEL WAYNE). *Executor:* WILLIAM BARTRAM. *Witnesses:* JONATHAN EVANS, THOS. WALKER, THOMAS JONES. *Clerk of the Court:* JOHN CLAYTON. *Chief Justice:* J. MONTGOMERY.

DAVIS, HUGH.   County not given.

December 7, 1729. *Legatees and devisees:* JOHN HARMAN (plantation on the Sound Side), ROBERT HARMAN, MARY HARMAN, ANN LONGLAD. *Executrix:* JULIANA LAKER. *Witnesses:* THOMAS CALLOWAY, WILLIAM———. *Clerk of the Court:* EDWARD MOSELEY.

DAVIS, ISAAC.   Currituck County.

March 21, 1742. July 13, 1743. *Son:* CORNELIUS ("all my land and plantation"). *Wife and Executrix:* RACHEL. *Executor:* CORNELIUS JONES (father-in-law). *Witnesses:* DANIELL PHILLIPS, FRANCES HODGES, FRANCIS STAFFORD. *Clerk of the Court:* JOHN LURRY.

DAVIS, JAMES. County not given.

April 22, 1715. *Sons:* WILLIAM, JAMES, JOHN, ROBERT, HENRY. *Wife and Executrix:* ELIZABETH. *Executors:* ROBERT WHITE, JOHN WHITE and JOHN SYMONS. *Witnesses:* HENRY WHITE, ARNOLD WHITE, JR., DAMARIS WHITE, ARNOLD WHITE, SENR. No probate.

DAVIS, JOHN. County not given.

April 26, 1688. May 12, 1688. *Daughter:* ELIZABETH. *Friend and Executor:* WILLIAM WILKISON. *Witnesses:* MATHEW LYAL, WILLIAM ELFISK, JANE MILLER. Will proven before SETH SOTHELL.

DAVIS, JOHN. Hyde County.

December 17, 1751. March Court, 1752. *Sons:* SAMUEL (plantation on the river side), JOHN. *Daughters:* TEMPERANCE DAVIS, JEMIMA BALLARD. *Wife:* SARAH DAVIS. *Executors:* NATHANIEL DAVIS and THOS. SMITH. *Witnesses:* THOS. SMITH, JER. SLADE, RICHARD WOOD. *Clerk of the Court:* FRAN. EGLETON.

DAVIS, JOHN. Pasquotank County.

March 28, 1753. April Court, 1753. *Sons:* JOSEPH ("my plantation"), WILLIAM, JOHN, SAMUEL. *Daughter:* SARAH GORDEN. *Executors:* JOSEPH DAVIS (son), WILLIAM GORDEN (son-in-law). *Witnesses:* WILLIAM SYMONS, THOMAS LOWRY, MARY TART. *Clerk of the Court:* THOS. TAYLOR.

DAVIS, JOHN. Pasquotank County.

January 10, 1754. April Court, 1754. *Brothers:* SAMUEL and WILLIAM DAVIS. *Cousins:* JOHN DAVIS, JR., MARY DAVIS. *Friends:* JAMES TURNER, WILLIAM GORDEN, JOHN GORDEN. *Executor:* JOSEPH DAVIS (brother). *Witnesses:* JOHN TURNER, JOSEPH LOWRY, THEOPHILUS LEONARD. *Clerk of the Court:* THOS. TAYLOR.

DAVIS, PETER. Bertie Precinct.

April 29, 1719. May Court, 1723. *Daughter:* SARY DAVIS. *Brother:* DAVIS. *Cousins:* ARTHUR and HENERY CRAWFORD. *Executrix:* WIFE (mentioned, but not named). *Witnesses:* ARTHUR CRAFFORD (Crawford), WILLIAM CROFORD (Crawford). *Clerk of the Conrt:* RT. FORSTER.

DAVIS, RICHARD. Pasquotank County.

June 9, 1737. June 14, 1737. *Sons:* JOSHUA ("plantation whereon I now live"). *Daughters:* ALEE and ABIGILL (DAVIS). *Guardians:* ELIZABETH HALL and JAMES COPLAND. *Executor:* ZACH NIXON. *Witnesses:* RICHARD CHEASTEN, RALPH FLETCHER, SAMUELL MOORE. Will proven before W. SMITH, *Chief Justice.*

DAVIS, ROBERT.   Pasquotank County.

December 30, 1749. January Court, 1750. *Sons:* JAMES ("maner plantation"), THOMAS ("my other plantation which lies next to JAMES LOWRY"). *Daughters:* ELIZABETH, RUTH. *Wife:* SARAH. *Executors:* JAMES and THOMAS (sons). *Witnesses:* JOSHUA WHITE, JAMES NEWBY. *Clerk of the Court:* THOS. TAYLOR.

DAVIS, SAMUELL.   Albemarle County.

January 11, 1687–1688. *Wife:* ELIZABETH. *Witnesses:* ROBERT WALLIS, JOHN BILLITT. No probate. Device on seal is three arrows and tomahawk.

DAVIS, SOLOMON.   Pasquotank County.

January 12, 1737. January Court, 1739. *Daughters:* DOROTHY DAVIS, MARGARET FORSTER, ELIZABETH DAVIS. *Son-in-law:* CALEB COEN. *Grandson:* DANIEL KOEN. *Friend:* JOHN SAWYER. *Wife and Executrix:* SARAH. *Witnesses:* B. MORGAN, JOHN GRAY. *Clerk of the Court:* JAMES CRAVEN.

DAVIS, THOMAS.   Bath County.

February 15, 1711–1712. January 4, 1714. *Son:* PHILLIP ("my manner plantation on Oyster Creek, West side of Pamlico River), THOMAS (land on Matchepungo River). *Daughters:* SARAH, RACHELL, CHARITY and MARY DAVIS. *Wife and Executrix:* THOMESON. *Witnesses:* none given. No signature. Will proven by GYLES SHUTE and THOMASIN DAVIS. *Clerk of the Court:* JOHN DRINKWATER.

DAVIS, THOMAS.   Perquimans County.

December 14, 1745. April Court, 1746. *Son and Executor:* MOSES ("plantation whereon I now live"). *Daughters:* ELIZABETH DAVIS, SARAH BOND. *Wife and Executrix:* ELIZABETH. *Witnesses:* WILLIAM EASON, THOMAS EASON, ISAAC SPEIGHT. *Clerk of the Court:* EDMUND HATCH.

DAVIS, THOMAS.   Granville County.

August 20, 1754. March 7, 1758. *Sons:* JOHN, THOMAS, RUBIN and RICHARD. *Daughter:* MARY DAVIS. *Wife and Executrix:* ELISABETH. *Executors:* DANIEL UNDERWOOD, RICHARD PINNIL. *Witnesses:* JOHN GIBBS, THOS. COOK, THOMAS ZACEE. *Clerk of the Court:* DANIEL WELDON.

DAVIS, THOMAS.   Bladen County.

October 2, 1761. May Court, 1769. *Daughter-in-law:* KATHERINE GREADY. *Daughter:* MARY GREADY (500 acres of land adjoining "Secretary Rice's backland"). *Brother:* WILLIAM DAVIS. *Executors:* WILLIAM DAVIS and JOHN LUCAS. *Witnesses:* JNO. TURNER, RALPH MILLER,

THOS. NEWTON. Codicil to will appoints ANN DAVIS (wife) and THOMAS OWEN *Executors* in place of WILLIAM DAVIS and JOHN LUCAS. *Witnesses to codicil:* THOS. HALL, JOHN ROOT, RALPH MILLER. *Clerk of the Court:* ARTHUR HOWE.

DAVIS, WILLIAM.   Carteret County.

June Court, 1756. *Sons:* NATHAN, JOSEPH, WICKER, CALLIP, BENIE-MEN, WILLIAM, SOLOMON. *Daughter:* ABIGARL. *Wife and Executrix:* MARY. *Executors:* NATHAN and JOSEPH (sons). *Witnesses:* GEORGE BELL, RILIND BELL and JAMES SHAFORD (Shackleford). *Clerk of the Court:* JOHN SMITH.

DAVISON, JOHN.   Bertie County.

August 6, 1752. October Court, 1756. *Son and Executor:* JOHN ("plantation whereon I now live"). *Grandson:* JOHN DAVISON (land on Chinkopin Creek). *Granddaughter:* MARY DAVISON. *Wife and Executrix:* MARY. *Witnesses:* JOHN FREEMAN, ABRAM HARRILL, JACOB LASITER, THOMAS HARRILL. *Clerk of the Court:* BENJN. WYNNS.

DAVISON, JOHN.   Edenton, Chowan County.

November 1, 1773. December 9, 1773. *Wife:* ELESHEA CHRISTIANA DAVISON. *Brother and Executor:* ROBERT DAVISON. *Friends and Executors:* JOHN SMITH, ANDREW LITTLE. *Witnesses:* JOHN ROM COUGH, CHAS. BONDFIELD, GEO. GRAY. Will proven before Jo. MARTIN.

DAWE, WILLIAM.   Beaufort County.

January 20, 1745. March Court, 1745. *Son:* WILLIAM (100 acres of land on Durham's Creek), JOHN ("the plantation whereon I now live"). NICHOLAS and WILLIAM. *Daughters:* DIANA DAWE, SARAH DIXON, LYDIA COE. *Wife and Executrix:* DINAH. *Witnesses:* EDWARD CAMPEN, JOHN CORREE. *Clerk of the Court:* JOHN FORBES.

DAWS, WILLIAM.   Chowan Precinct.

July 21, 1719. October Court, 1719. *Sons:* WILLIAM and ELYJAH (268 acres of land). *Executors:* WILLIAM BAKER and JOHN BROWN. *Witnesses:* JOHN BROWN, JOHN MANEAR, ELIZABETH BAKER. *Clerk of the Court:* R. HICKS.

DAWSON, JOHN.   Edgecombe County.

November 22, 1748. May Court, 1749. *Sons:* JOHN, DEMEY, SOLLO-MON. *Daughters:* MARTHA, PATIENCE. *Wife and Executrix:* MARY. *Witnesses:* BENJ. CHAMPION, FRANCES BYTHELL HAYNES. *Clerk of the Court:* BENJN. WYNNS.

DEANE, GEORGE, SENR.   Albemarle County.

April 10, 1700. GEO. DEANE (150 acres of land). *Daughter:* CHRISTIAN.
HUMPHREY LEGG and JOHN BATCHELOR (150 acres each). *Executrix:*
ELIZABETH DEANE. *Witnesses:* JOHN PROCTOR, MARY SECHEWRAA,
HUMPHREY LEGG. (No probate.)

DEIPTT, JOHN.   Bath County.

January 17, 1723-1724. June 17, 1724. *Sons:* PETTER DEIPTT (plantation in Machapongo containing two hundred acres), JOHN (200 acres
of land). *Wife and Executrix:* PENON. *Daughter and Executrix:* ANN
DEIPTT. *Witnesses:* PETER HAND, JOHN FONVIELLE. *Clerk of the Court:*
JOHN CORNICK. *Clerk of the Court at Newbern:* C. METCALFE.

DELAMAR, FRANCIS.   Beaufort County.

May 15, 1739. March, 1741. *Son:* THOMAS ("plantation on the South
side of Broad Creek"). *Wife and Executrix:* SUSANNAH. *Son:* FRANCIS
("plantation whereon I now live"). *Witnesses:* ROBERT WENHAM,
BENJA. RICE, MARY RICE. *Clerk of the Court:* JOHN FORBES.

DELAMARE, STEPHEN.   Pasquotank Precinct.

October 2, 1732. October Court, 1732. *Nephew:* JOSEPH STOCKLEY
("plantation whereon I now live"), ISAAC STOCKLEY. *Cousin:* EDWARD
MAYO. *Sister and Executrix:* ANN STOCKLEY. *Brother:* FRANCIS DELA-
MARE. *Witnesses:* HARRAL BLY, SAMUEL REDING, JO. PALIN. *Clerk of
the Court:* H. MINSON.

DELOHOIDE, WILLIAM.   New Hanover County.

October 3, 1738. This is a nuncupative will proven by MRS. ELIZABETH
ROWAN, and provides for the lading of his sloop (WILLIAM O'BRYAN,
Master), and of his brig by CAPT. ROWAN and cargo delivered to THOMAS
FARREN and JOHN ———. Proven before ROBT. HALTON, J. P.

DENEHAM, ELIZABETH.   Bath County.

July 9, 1716. *Legatees:* ANN CLEWES, ELIZABETH LEIGH, JOSEPH
TREWETT, ELEZABETH DENEHAM, JOHN LEIGH, JOHN DENEHAM. *Wit-
nesses:* ELIZABETH LEE and JAMES LEE, JUNR. *Clerk of the Court:* JNO.
DRINKWATER.

DENSON, JAMES.   Onslow County.

May 3, 1756. *Legatees:* JAMES HOWARD, JOHN HOWARD, LUKE BARE-
FIELD, SARAH ASHBURN. *Wife and Executrix:* ELIZABETH. *Witnesses:*
WM. ROYAL, MOSES ANDERSON, JOSEPH STURGES. *Clerk of the Court:*
WILLM. CRAY.

Dept, Penelope.

March 25, 1732. August 27, 1735. *Sons:* Peter, John (*Executor*). *Daughters:* Ann, Jane and Elizabeth. *Witnesses:* Mary Lane, Elizabeth Norwood, Edward Broughton. Will proven before W. Smith, C. J. Executor qualified before C. Powell and N. Routledge.

Derby, William.

March 10, 1687. March 13, 1688. *Daughter:* Judith ("plantation whereon I now live"). *Witnesses:* John Privett, Robert Lindsay, John Dawley. Will proven before Seth Sothell.

Derham, Elizabeth.   Bath County.

July 17, 1716. *Legatees:* Anne Clows, Katherine Derham, Elizabeth Leigh, Joseph Truwitt, Elizabeth Derham, Joseph Derham, John Leigh, James Leigh. *Brother:* John Derham. *Father-in-law and Executor:* James Leigh. *Witnesses:* names not given. *Clerk of the Court:* John Drinkwater. Original missing. Recorded in Book 1712–22, page 125.

DeRosset, Moses John.   New Hanover County.

November 30, 1767. March 1, 1768. ("Practitioner in physic and surgery"). *Wife and Executrix:* Mary. *Daughter:* Magdalene Mary DeRosset. *Son:* Armond John DeRosset. *Executors :* Lewis Henry DeRosset (brother), John DuBois, James Moore and Marmaduke Jones. *Witnesses:* Ann Moore, A. Maclaine, E. Justuce (?). Will proven before Gov. Wm. Tryon at Wilmington.

Dexter, Hope.   New River, in Onslow County.

March 10, 1745. April 1, 1746. *Brother:* Phillip Dexter (all the land that lies between the main road and Mitiams Creek). *Friend:* James Thomson (land "between my land and the land above named"). *Nephew:* Hope Dexter (one watch). *Witnesses:* Daniel Mcfeters, John Holmes, Charles Stout, Joshua, James. *Clerk of the Court:* Geo. Clopton.

Devis, John.   Newberne, in Craven County.

March 11, 1754. March 25, 1754. *Legatees and Devisees:* John Freeman, Ann Nelson, John Starkey (*Executor*), Mary Wigmore, Richard Lyon. *Witnesses:* Euphemia White, Richard Lyon, Charles Farquharson. Will proven before Matt. Rowan.

Dew, John.   Bertie County.

September 5, 1740. November Court, 1744. *Sons:* John ("all my horses and mairs that run on the South side of the Meharin River"), Joseph

7

(land lying on the East side of the "Rode from Cornell hills ferry and also
land on Buckhorse swamp"), SPENSER ("plantation whereon I now live"),
WILLIAM, MORVEN. *Daughter:* PATIENCE. *Wife and Executrix:* SUSAN-
NAH. *Executor:* JOSEPH DEW (son). *Witnesses:* EDWARD MOSELEY, ALES
MOSELEY, CONSTANT DEW. *Clerk of the Court:* RT. FORSTER. (Northamp-
ton County.)

DIAS, HENRY.   Beaufort Precinct (Bath County).

December 8, 1737. March Court, 1737. *Sons:* RICHARD (plantation on
Blounts Creek), JOHN (land called Forke neck), THOMAS (land on WALLASES
Creek), HENRY ("plantation whereon I now live"). *Daughter:* ANN DIAS.
Wife and Executrix: REBECCA. *Executor:* JOHN PURSELL. *Witnesses:*
RICHARD EVANS, JAMES PERDUE, MARY PERKINS. *Clerk of the Court:*
ROGER JONES.

DICKENSON, JOHN.   Northampton County.

February 4, 1742. August Court, 1749. *Sons:* DANIEL, JOHN, DAVID,
ISAAC. *Daughters:* SARAH DANIEL, ELIZABETH FUTREL, REBECKAH NEW-
SOM, CHARITY DICKENSON, MARY DICKENSON. *Wife:* REBECCA. *Execu-
tors:* DANIEL and JOHN DICKENSON (sons). *Witnesses:* JOSEPH JORDAN,
ROBERT PEELLE, ISAAC PARKER. *Clerk of the Court:* I. EDWARDS.

DICKINSON, MARY.   Northampton County.

October 6, 1753. November Court, 1753. *Brothers:* DAVID, ISAAC
(*Executors*), DANIEL and JOHN DICKINSON. *Sisters:* CHARITY PEELLE,
SARAH DANIEL, ELIZABETH FUTRELL. *Kinsman:* WILLIAM ROWSUM.
Witnesses: JOHN BROWN, SUSANAH PARKER, SUSANAH HORTON. *Clerk of
the Court:* I. EDWARDS.

DICKINSON, REBECKAH.   Northampton County.

July 1, 1750. February Court, 1753. *Sons:* JOHN and ISAAC DICKIN-
SON (*Executors*), DAVID. *Daughters:* SARAH DANIEL, ELIZABETH FUTU-
RELL, REBECCAH NEWSOM, CHARITY DICKINSON, MARY DICKINSON. *Wit-
nesses:* ISAAC PARKER, JOHN HORTON. *Clerk of the Court:* I. EDWARDS.

DICKS, JOHN.   Chowan Precinct.

February 10, 1705. October 2, 1706. *Son-in-law:* RICHT LEWIS.
Wife and Executrix: PHELIS. *Witnesses:* THOS. LUTEN, JON JONES, JON
WHEATLY. *Clerk of the Court:* N. CHEVIN.

DICKSON, JOHN.   Dobbs County.

April 16, 1769. *Father:* JAMES DICKSON. *Mother:* JENNET. *Uncle:*
ROBERT GRACEY. *Friends:* JAMES CUMMIN, JAMES GIBSON (*Executor*),
JAMES LINDSAY (*Executor*). *Witnesses:* ANTHONY HERRING, CHRISTOPHER
BLANSHARD, CHARLES HINES. No probate.

DISCORAH, THOMAS.   Perquimans County.

January 11, 1726–1727. February 2, 1726–1727. *Legatees:* SAMUEL PHELPS, SARAH SHEARWOOD, MARY SHEARWOOD, JAMES SITERSON (*Executor*). *Witnesses:* RALPH BOOSMAN, R. WILSON. Will proven before RICH'D EVERARD.

DIXON, JOHN.   Beaufort County.

March 23, 1772. December 11, 1773. *Son and Executor:* CHOOSEWELL ("my land"). *Daughter:* BIATHA. *Witnesses:* NICHOLAS DAW, LEVIN STANFORD, THOMAS DIXON. Will proven before JO. MARTIN.

DIXON, ROBERT.   Bertie Precinct.

April 4, 1727. August Court, 1727. *Sons:* TOBIAS, JAMES, ROBERT. *Daughter:* FRANCES. *Wife and Executrix:* CHRISTIANA. *Executor:* JOHN LOWE. *Witnesses:* ABRAHAM BURTON, BEREBE MELTON, WILLIAM LOWE. *Clerk of the Court:* RT. FORSTER.   Coat of arms on seal.

DOBBS, ARTHUR.   Brunswick, in New Hanover County.

"Governor and Captain General of the Province of North Carolina." August 31, 1763. April 24, 1765. *Sons:* CONWAY RICHARD DOBBS, EDWARD BRICE DOBBS. *Wife:* JUSTINA. *Brother:* REVEREND DOCTOR RICHARD DOBBS. *Witnesses:* JAMES HASELL, LEWIS DEROSSET, JOHN SAMPSON. Proven before WM. TRYON. The following items are of interest: "instead of immoderate funeral expenses I desire that one hundred pounds Sterling money may be paid and distributed proportionately among the housekeepers of the Parrishes of Ballynure and Kilroot in the County of Antrim and Kingdom of Ireland, and one other hundred pounds of like money among the poor freemen House-keepers who reside within the county of the town of Carrick-fergus to be paid————out of my Demesnes at Castle Dobbs or out of the arrears of rents I reserved out of a Moiety of lands in that Kingdom during my life." All slaves, plate, etc., is bequeathed to wife, together with "the money and interest due to me by the General Assembly for the lands called Tower hill in Johnston County, purchased from me by the publick." "Whereas, I have a right to the Moiety of two hundred thousand acres of land granted to me by the Crown in Sixteen patents of twelve thousand five hundred acres each in Mecklinburgh (late Anson) County as one of the associates of HUEY and CRYMBLE ————etc." To each of children is bequeathed fifty pounds and to brother twenty pounds. "Item. Whereas I am entitled to a Moiety of Twelve Thousand acres of land by a purchase from MR. PATRICK SMITH of Waterford, merchant, for which a patent was granted to him as an associate of HUEY and CRYMBLE, subdivided from the great tract No. 4, the heirs and assigns of MR. JAMES BENNING of Lisburn, Ireland, being entitled to the other moiety." "I give and bequeath to my son CONWAY RICHARD DOBBS

— — — — — all my plate goods, Household furniture, arrears, Rents and other chattels whatsoever which are now belonging to me at my decease, which are now or hereafter may be at Castle Dobbs in the County of Antrim and Kingdom of Ireland." Sons and wife appointed executors and executrix. Impression of head on seal.

DOBSON, WILLIAM.   Chowan Precinct.

August 23, 1690. October 13, 1690. *Wife and Executrix:* KATEREN. *Witnesses:* JOHN LEWIS, THOMAS MUNS, JOHN WINGATE. *Clerk of the Court:* JOHN WINGATE.

DOLEER, GYLES.   Albemarle County.

February 26, 1687–1688. January 6, 1689. *Legatees and Devisees:* JOHN VALLENTINE ROE, DAVID PRITCHETT, ROWLAND BUCKLY, MARY GARNETT ("my plantation"). *Executor:* RALPH GARNETT. *Witnesses:* PAUL LATHUM, FRANCIS HENRY, ROWLAND BUSSLY. Will proven before THO. ROLFE, ROBERT WALLIS, PAUL LATHUM———, THOMAS SYMONS.

DONOHO, JOHN.   New Hanover County.

June 6, 1743. June 24, 1743. *Friend, Executor and sole legatee and devisee:* WILLIAM WHITE of Wilmington. *Witnesses:* JAMES SMALLWOOD, GEO. OWEN, ANN HIGGINES. *Clerk of the Court:* JAMES SMALLWOOD.

DOOLES, THOMAS.   Edgecombe County.

November 28, 1756. May Court, 1757. *Sons:* JOSEPH ("plantation whereon I now live"), JOHN. *Daughters:* SARAH, CATTEREN, BITHA. *Wife:* PATIENCE. *Executors:* JOSEPH DOOLES (son), ROBERT PURRER. *Witnesses:* JAMES MYHAN, MOSES HORNE, ROBERT PURYEAR, JOSEPH DOOLES. *Clerk of the Court:* JOS. MONTFORT.

DOUGE, TULL.   Currituck County.

May 18, 1746. July 1, 1746. *Brother and Executor:* JAMES DOUGE. *Brother:* JOHN DOUGE. *Sisters:* SARAH SOREY, SUSANNAH CLASCO (or GLASCO), MARY DOUGE. *Other legatees:* PETER SOREY, CALEB GLASCO. *Witnesses:* JOSA CAMPBELL, HENRY SIMMONS, JOAB DOUGE. *Clerk of the Court:* RICHARD MCCLURE.

DOUGHTY, JOHN.   Wilmington, New Hanover County.

June 9, 1742. August 31, 1749. *Wife:* MARIAN. *Witnesses:* THOMAS CHINAGAM, JOSA GRAINGER. *Clerk of the Court:* ISAAC FARIES.

DOUGLASS, DAVID.   Northampton County.

March 29, 1753. November Court, 1753. *Sons:* WILLIAM ("land whereon he now lives"), JOHN ("manner land and plantation"). *Daughters:* MOLLEY CARRILL, ELIZABETH HARWELL, SUSANAH DOUGLASS. *Grand-*

daughter: Elizabeth Carril.   *Wife and Executrix:* Elizabeth.   *Executor:* William Douglass (son).   *Witnesses:* Chrismass Ray, John Douglass.   *Clerk of the Court:* I. Edwards.

Douglas, James.   Bertie County.

October 6, 1750.   July 11, 1752.   *Sons:* Kesia (plantation), James.
Daughter: Ann.   *Granddaughter:* Elizabeth Douglas.   *Wife and Executrix:* Elizabeth.   *Witnesses:* John Brown, Elizabeth Robertson,
Joseph Madlin.   *Secretary to the Governor:* Saml. Ormes.   Lands on
Hoskie Swamp devised to children.

Doway, Robert.   Bladen County.

January 30, 1756.   January Court, 1758.   *Sons:* James and Robert.
Daughter: Elizabeth.   *Wife:* Catherine.   *No executors.*   *Witnesses:*
John Stack, Henry Lewis, James White.   *Clerk of the Court:* J. Burgwin.

Downer, William.   Brunswick, New Hanover County.

December 10, 1745.   March Court, 1745.   *Executors:* Capt. Hugh
Blaning and Capt. Richard Quince.   The will directs the executors to sell so much of the estate as may be necessary to pay the
debts of the testator and to pay to themselves 80 pounds each in addition
to their legal fees of seven and one-half per cent, and to ship the remainder
to William Wynn and wife Ruth at Aldgate in the City of London, and
Benjamin and Mary Sandwell in Wapping, London.   *Witnesses:* Hugh
Mackay, Ralph Sugnion, Thomas Campbell.   *Clerk of the Court:* James
Smallwood.

Downing, William.   Tyrrell County.

April 1, 1739.   April 6, 1739.   *Sons:* William ("my plantation, except
sawmill, which is bequeathed to Cullen Pollock and Stephen Lee, proceeds to be applied to debt due Samuel Herring of London, woolen draper).   *Brothers-in-law:* Ebenezer Slade (450 acres of land on Moratock
River), Henry Slade.   *Son-in-law:* Thomas Lee.   *Executors:* Cullen
Pollock, John Montgomery, Stephen Lee, Peter Payne.   *Witnesses:*
Wm. Maxwell, Sam Scollay, David Coltrane.   Codicil bearing same
date as will provides for working slaves in mill.   Will proven before W.
Smith, C. J.

Downing, William.   Tyrrell County.

February 24, 1748.   March 7, 1748.   *Son:* Henry ("plantation whereon
I now dwell").   *Wife:* Ann.   *Daughters:* Mary, Elizabeth.   *Friend:*
John Hughes.   *Executors:* Stevens Lee, John Barrow.   *Witnesses:*
Jacob Blount, James Jones, Mary Jones.   *Clerk of the Court:* Evan
Jones.

DRAKE, JOHN.   Bertie Precinct.

January 5, 1728. May Court, 1729. *Son:* JAMES ("my manner plantation"). *Wife:* SARAH. *Executor:* JAMES BRYANT (father-in-law). *Witnesses:* JOHN SUTTON, JOHN DICKINSON, RICHARD SUMNER. *Clerk of the
Court:* RT. FORSTER.

DREDING, JOHN.   Craven County.

December 22, 1757. February Court, 1758. *Executor:* JOSEPH PRIN-
GLE ("plantation whereon I now live"). *Wife and Executrix:* CHARITY.
Witnesses: SAMUEL SLADE, JOHN SLADE, SAMUEL SLADE, JUNR. *Clerk of
the Court:* PETER CONWAY.

DRINKWATER, JOHN.   Bath County.

August 7, 1717. May 30, 1718. *Devisees:* PHILLIP SHUTE, son of
GYLES and CHARITY SHUTE (plantation containing 820 acres, lying be-
tween Mallard Creek and Goose Creek; 320 acres on South Dividing
Creek; house and lot in Bath Town; money and plate on hand), GYLES
SHUTE (wearing apparel), CHARITY SHUTE (all lands in event of death of
PHILLIP. *Executors:* GYLES and CHARITY SHUTE. *Witnesses:* PATRICK
CAVAN, ELIZABETH ELLEBAR. Will proven before CHAS. EDEN, at Bath
Town.

DUBOIS, JOHN.   Wilmington, New Hanover County.

September 13, 1767. March 1, 1768. *Sons:* PETER, WALTER, JOHN
(house in Dock Street, also plantation on Smith Creek containing 300
acres; also a large diamond ring), ISAAC (two houses in Dock Street),
JAMES (two lots in front street and houses thereon). *Daughters:* ANNE
JEAN DUBOIS, MAGDALENE MARGARET DUBOIS (two brick houses on Dock
Street and two diamond rings), MARGARET DUBOIS (lot on the north side
of Market Street.) *Wife and Executrix:* JEAN. *Friends:* CALEB and
CORNELIUS GRAINGER (sons of COLONEL CALEB GRAINGER). *Executors
and Guardians of children:* JEAN DUBOIS (wife), PETER, WALTER and
JOHN DUBOIS (sons), LEWIS HENRY and MOSES JOHN DEROSSET. *Wit-
nesses:* J. EUSTACE, EDWARD CHIVERS, ARCHIBALD MACLAINE. *Secretary:*
BENJ'N HERON. Will proven before WM. TRYON at Wilmington.

DUCKENFIELD, NATHANIEL.   Utkinton, in the County of
                                          Chester, England.

July 4, 1746. January Court, 1756. *Wife and Executrix:* MARGRET
(lands in County of Chester during widowhood, leasehold estate in Lud-
gate Street, London). *Friend and Executor:* JOSEPH COLLET, merchant of
London (lands in North Carolina to be sold and proceeds applied according
to directions). *Brother and Executor:* JOHN CHORLEY. *Nephew:* JOHN
CHORLEY (son of sister, JANE CHORLEY). *Nephew and Executor:* SAMUEL

DUCKENFIELD (son of JOHN DUCKENFIELD of Bristol). *Witnesses:* WILLIAM PRIOR, JOSEPH COLLET, DOROTHY POTTS. Will proven before ROBERT CHAPMAN, Doctor of Laws, Surrogate to JOHN BETTESWORTH, certified by THOMAS, Archbishop of Canterbury, over the seal of the town of London. *Deputy Registers:* WM. LEGARD, PETER ST. ELY, HEN. STEPHENS. JOSEPH COLLET refused the trust imposed by this will in a writing witnessed by SAMUEL DUKINFIELD and BENJAMIN ROSEWELL. Letters of administration granted to MARGARET DUCKINFIELD by Bertie County Court, January, 1756. *Clerk of the Court:* BENJ. WYNNS. This will is illegible, but is recorded in Bk. Wills, 1755–58, at page 144.

DUCKENFIELD, WILLIAM.   Chowan Precinct (formerly of Cheshire, in Great Britain).

May 17, 1720. February 27, 1721. *Brother:* JOHN DUCKENFIELD. *Cousins:* CHARLES BARBER, NATHANIEL DUCKENFIELD (son "of my brother, SIR ROBERT DUCKENFIELD, BARONET"), MARY, ANN, SUSANNA, JANE, SARAH, KATHERINE and JUDITH DUCKENFIELD (sisters of NATHANIEL). *Executor:* NATHANIEL DUCKENFIELD. *Witnesses:* THOMAS ASHLY, JOHN POWELL, BENJA. SOAMES, JOHN CHERYHOLME, JOHN DUCKENFIELD, E. MOSELEY. Will proven before CHAS. EDEN, *Governor.* Coat of arms on seal.

DUDLEY, CHRISTOPHER.   Onslow County.

March 19, 1744–1745. February 26, 1746. *Sons:* EDWARD, WILLIAM, THOMAS and CHRISTOPHER DUDLEY (land on "the River"). *Grandsons:* GEORGE (son of EDWARD) and CHRISTOPHER (son of THOMAS) DUDLEY. *Daughter:* ANN HOUSTON (one negro). Other negroes bequeathed to wife and sons. *Wife and Executrix:* MARY. *Executor:* JOHN STARKEY. *Witnesses:* JANE SIMPSON, JOHN SIMPSON, MARY TROTT. Proven before GAB. JOHNSTON.

DUDLEY, EDWARD.   County not given.

January 22, 1744–1745. April 3, 1745. *Son:* GEORGE. *Daughters:* HANNAH, ANNE, MARY. *Executors:* JOHN STARKEY and JOHN DUDLEY. *Witnesses:* JOHN HENAGAN ("nicknamed SWENNY"), WILLIAM SIMPSON, HANNAH PITTS. Will proven before GAB. JOHNSTON. *Chief Justice:* E. MOSELEY.

DUDLEY, JOHN.   Onslow County.

September 12, 1748. April 2, 1751. *Sons:* JOHN and DAVID ("my cow pen land to be equally divided between them"), WILLIAM ("my manor plantation"). *Daughter:* SARAH. *Wife:* ELIZABETH. *Executors:* JOHN STARKEY and THOMAS DUDLEY. *Witnesses:* JOHN WELLS, NATHNELL BURNAP, RICHARD STEVENS. *Clerk of the Court:* THOS. BLACK. Courthouse at Johnston, on New River.

DUDLEY, THOMAS.   Carteret County.

May 13, 1753. June Court, 1753. *Sons:* CHRISTOPHER (250 acres of land on East side of White Oak River), ELIJAH, JACOB, STEPHEN, ABRAHAM and THOMAS (to the last two is bequeathed "plantation where I now live"). *Daughters:* ELISABETH DUDLEY, SARAH GILLITT. *Granddaughters:* ELIZABETH and SARAH GILLITT. *Son-in-law:* JOHN GILLITT. *Wife:* ELIZABETH. *Executors:* JOHN STARKEY and MOSES HOUSTON. *Witnesses:* CHARLES COGDELL, EZEKILL HUNTER, WILLIAM HOUSTON. *Clerk of the Court:* GEO. READ.

DUDLEY, THOMAS.   Currituck County.

December 15, 1755. March, 1757. *Sons and Executors:* WILLIAM, THOMAS ("one-half of the plantation whereon I now live"). *Grandson:* MALAKIE DUDLEY ("one-half of the plantation whereon I now live"). *Daughter:* MARY WILLIAMS. *Wife:* MARY. *Witnesses:* CHARLES WILLIAMS, THOMAS WILLIAMS, SOLOMON ASHLEE, OEN SLATTER. *Clerk of the Court:* WILL MEARNS.

DUGGAN, THOMAS.   Tyrrell County.

May 9, 1754. June Court, 1754. *Sons:* THOMAS, JESSE. *Apprentice:* JOHN SEALS. *Wife and Executrix:* MARY. *Executor:* CAPT. JOHN HARDISON. *Witnesses:* JNO. BENNET, HIGASON KING, WILLIAM KING. *Clerk of the Court:* EVAN JONES.

DUNBAR, DUN.   Beaufort County.

May 18, 1747. December Court, 1747. *Son:* SAMUELL (300 acres of land on the West side of Goos Creek). *Daughters:* ELISABETH DUNBAR (300 acres of land on Rush Marsh and Goose Creek), SARAH DUNBAR (tract of land and also "plantation I now live on"), MARY DUNBAR ("small neck of land" on "the River and South Dividing Creek") HANNAH DUNBAR (tract of land on the South side of a creek formerly called Hendersons), ESTER (stock of hogs and cattle). *Wife and Executrix:* SARAH BARR. *Executors:* JOSIAH JONES, JOHN TRIPPE, JUNR. *Witnesses:* JOSHUA PRITCHET, EDMOND CAMPEN, ROBERT CAMPEN. *Clerk of the Court:* JOHN FORBES.

DUNCAN, ABRAHAM.   Beaufort County.

February 3, 1749. June Court, 1751. *Wife and Executrix:* MARY (land on Kenyon's Savannah; house and storehouse in Bath Town; lot No. 65 in Bath Town). *Nephews:* GEORGE and ABRAHAM DUNCAN, sons of JOHN DUNCAN of Londonderry, New England (my plantation on the South Side of Pamplico River, land on Southside of Tar River, land on Swifts Creek). *Brothers:* JAMES, WILLIAM, JOHN and ROBERT. *Sister:* HESTER

CASON. *Witnesses:* THOMAS PEARSON, JOHN SIMPSON, JUNR., JAMES ADAMS, W. ORMOND, *Clerk of the Court:* WILLIAM ORMOND. Coat of arms on seal.

DUNCAN, ALEXANDER.   Wilmington, New Hanover County.

May 11, 1767. May 18, 1768. *Brother:* ROBERT DUNCAN. *Other legatees:* ALEXANDER PURVES of Edinburgh, JOHN CLARK GOLDSMITH, THOMAS SMITH, JOHN RUTHERFORD (1000 pounds sterling), JAMES MOORE (eight young negroes), THOMAS CUNNINGHAM, JR., FRANCES RUTHERFORD, daughter of JOHN RUTHERFORD (8 young negroes), JOHN WALKER, CORNELIUS HARNETT, MARY, wife of CALEB GRAINGER, MAURICE MOORE and WIFE, CAPT. JOHN FORSTER and WIFE, ALEXANDER CHAPMEN (20 pounds to each), ARTHUR BENNET, ROBERT SCHAW, JOHN ANCRUM (two last named appointed executors). Proven by THOMAS COBHAM and WILLIAM LORD before WM. TRYON.

DUPEE, ELIAS.   Craven County.

August 14, 1750. February Court, 1754. *Father and Executor:* DANIEL DUPEE ("my share of all prize money to me belonging while on board his Majesty's Ship 'Bedford,' CAPT. JAMES CORNWELL, Commander"). *Witnesses:* JOHN MILL, FRAN. FONTAINE, JNO. FOSTER. *Clerk of the Court:* SOL. REW.

DURANT, ANN, widow of GEORGE.   Albemarle River.

January 23, 1694. June 22, 1695. *Son and Executor:* THOMAS DURANT. This is a nuncupative will proven by JOHN NORTHCOATE, JOHN CLAPPAR, ELENOR MOLINES, before WILLIAM DUCKENFIELD. *Clerk of the Court:* W. GLOVER. *Executor* qualified in Palatine Court—JOHN ARCHDALE, *Governor,* DANIEL AKEHURST, FRANCIS ———, BENJAMIN LATEN. Seal of the Palatine on probate.

DURANT, GEORGE.   Albemarle County.

October 9, 1688. April 26, 1693–1694. *Sons:* JOHN ("½ of my plantation"), THOMAS ("ye other half"). *Nephews:* GEORGE DURANT, HENRY DURANT (son of brother JOHN). *Daughters:* SARAH, MATYTYA, PERTYENIA, and ANN DURANT. *Wife and Executrix:* ANN. *Witnesses:* JOHN PHILPOTT, FRANCES HOSSTEN, JOHN CULLY. *Clerk of the Court:* EDWARD MAYO.

DURANT, GEORGE.   Albemarle County.

May 25, 1730. September 29, 1730. *Son:* GEORGE. *Daughters:* ANNE DURANT, MARY DURANT, SARAH DURANT, ELIZABETH DURANT. *Friend:* ANNE LONGLARTHER. *Executors:* ZEBULON CLAYTON, RICHARD WHIDBEE (brothers). *Witnesses:* THOMAS SNOWDEN, ELIZABETH GIBSON, JOHN STEVENS. Will proven before RICHARD EVERARD.

DURANT, THOMAS.   Perquimans Precinct.
May 8, 1728. April 15, 1734. *Sons:* ABRAHAM JETNETT and AARON
MOSES DURANT. *Friend:* JOSHUA DICKS. *Witnesses:* ZEB CLAYTON,
JOHN MITCHELL, PELEG ROGERS. *Justice of the Peace:* SAMUEL SWANN.
Clerk of the Court: CHARLES DENMAN.

DURRANCE, SAMUEL.   Tyrrell County.
November 21, 1756. December Court, 1756. *Sons:* WELLCOM, WIL-
LIAM, FRANCIS ("all my land to be equally divided between them").
"Ungratefull wife, Late": ELIZABETH DURANT. *Executors:* WILLIAM
SWINSON, FRANCIS WARD. *Witnesses:* ALEXANDER MACCLELEAN, MARY
COMBS, FR. WARD. *Clerk of the Court:* FR. WARD.

DWIGHT, MATHEW.   Chowan County.
February 27, 1737–1738. *Executrix, Wife and sole legatee and devisee:*
ELIZABETH. *Witnesses:* CHARLTON MIZELL, SUSANNAH MIZELL. Probate
illegible.

EADEY, HENRY.   Pasquotank County.
April 11, 1750. July Court, 1750. *Brother:* JOHN EADEY (land in Curri-
tuck County). *Daughter-in-law:* MARY WALSON. *Wife and Executrix:*
ELIZABETH. *Witnesses:* SARAH WILLSON, PETER WREN, SAMUEL LOW-
MAN. *Clerk of the Court:* THOS. TAYLOR.

EAGAN, JAMES.   "Cape Fare, in Bladen Precinct."
October 30, 1737. March Court, 1738. *Executor:* WILLIAM CARY.
Wife and daughter: mentioned, but not named. *Witnesses:* THOMAS LOCK,
WILLIAM BARTRAM, ARTHUR DANIEL. *Clerk of the Court:* RICHARD HET-
EIER.

EAGLE, RICHARD.   Brunswick County.
March 23, 1769. March 31, 1769. *Son:* JOSEPH ("House, plantation,
saw and grist mills"). *Daughter:* SUSANNAH EAGLE. *Wife:* MARGARET
HENRIETTA EAGLE (formerly BUGNION). *Cousins:* JEAN and ELIZABETH
DAVIS. *Sister:* ELIZABETH DAVIS. *Other legatees:* JEANET MCFARLING,
JOHN EAGLESON. *Executors:* JOHN GIBBS, ROBERT SHAW, JOHN ANCRUM
and THOMAS OWEN. *Witnesses:* JOHN WALKER, JOHN FERGUS, MARY
WALKER. Will proven before WM. TRYON. Codicil to this will, of even
date. Confirms title to MR. WM. DRY in and to a tract of land "bought of
my father, RICH'D EAGLES."

EARLY, ELIONOR.   Albemarle County.
September 2, 1732. *Grandsons:* THOS. SUTTON, JAMES CURLEE. *Granddaughters:* SARAH SUTTON, MARY DALE (my plantation called by the name
of "Blew Water"). *Executrix:* MARY DALE. *Witnesses:* ROBT. EVANS,
NICHOLAS FAIRLESS, NATHANIEL KEELE. No probate.

EARLY, JOHN. Bertie County.

August 6, 1740. October 20, 1740. *Son:* JOHN (plantation on horse swamp). *Daughters:* MARGARET MACHENRY, MARTHA THOMSON, MARY BLAKE, SARAH REEF, ELISABETH WILLSON, BETHSHABA MORRIS, REBEKAH MORRIS. *Wife:* ANN. *Executors:* JOHN EARLY (son), WILLIAM WILLSON (son-in-law). *Witnesses:* JOHN WILLIAMS, EDWARD WILLIAMS, WILLIAM WILLSON. Will proven before GAB. JOHNSTON at Eden House.

EASON, WILLIAM. Perquimans County.

January 20, 1718–1719. July 14, 1719. *Sons:* WILLIAM (land on South side of Cypress Swamp), THOMAS, GEORGE ("plantation whereon I now live"). *Daughters:* MARY, SUSANNA, RACHEL and JANE EASON. *Wife and Executrix:* MARY. *Witnesses:* THOMAS DAVIS, ELISEBETH DAVIS, THO. SPEIGHT. *Clerk of the Court:* RICHD. LEARY.

EASON, WILLIAM. Bertie Precinct.

January 27, 1734. May Court, 1736. *Sons:* WILLIAM and GEORGE. *Wife:* ANNE. *Executors:* THOMAS and GEORGE EASON (brothers). *Witnesses:* HENRY BAKER, JUNR., SAMUELL SMITH, JOHN HENNARD. *Clerk of the Court:* JNO. WYNNS.

EASTER, ABRAHAM. Hyde County.

November 18, 1751. December Court, 1751. *Son:* JAMES ("choice of two plantations my father left me"). *Daughter:* MARY EASTER (fifty-three acres of land on Swan Quarter"). *Wife:* ELIZABETH. *Brothers and Executors:* JOHN and THOMAS EASTER. *Witnesses:* WILLIAM CARON, SABBASTIN SILVERTHORN, URIAH COLLINS. *Clerk of the Court:* THOS. LOACK.

EASTER, JOHN. Hyde Precinct.

October 27, 1732. March Court, 1733. *Sons:* ABRAHAM ("my plantation"), THOMAS. *Daughters:* SARAH and DINAH. *Wife and Executrix:* Mentioned, but not named. *Witnesses:* EDWD. HADLEY, THOMAS GOODING, THOMAS RICHARDS. *Clerk of Beaufort Court:* JNO. COLLISON.

EASTER, JOHN. Hyde County.

January 17, 1751–1752. March Court, 1752. *Sister:* LIDA EASTER. *Friend:* ELIZABETH LOACK. *Brothers and Executors:* THOMAS and WILLIAM EASTER. *Witnesses:* JOHN HOUREN, JOHN WINLY, SARAH WINDLY. *Clerk of the Court:* FRANS. EGLETON.

EASTER, MOVY. Hyde County.

November 4, 1751. December Court, 1751. *Sons:* ABRAHAM, JOHN, WILLIAM and THOMAS. *Daughters:* LYDIA EASTER, MARY EASTER, ANN and SARAH EASTER. *Executors:* JOHN and THOMAS EASTER (sons). *Witnesses:* JOHN MASON, JACOB TULE, ANN JASPER. *Clerk of the Court:* THOS. LOACK.

EATON, JAMES.   Chowan Precinct.

December 11, 1729. January 6, 1729. *Wife:* MARY. *Executor:* WILLIAM WILLIAMS of Edenton. *Witnesses:* JOHN MATTHEWS, WM. BAELEY, DAVID DAVIS. Will proven before RICHARD EVERARD.

EATON, WILLIAM.   Granville County.

February 19, 1759. March 20, 1759. Saint Johns Parish in the County of Granville. *Sons:* WILLIAM (lands in Dinwiddie and Brunswick counties in Virginia, except land received of William Scoggan), THOMAS, CHARLES RUST. *Daughters:* JANE, wife of COLO. NATHANIEL EDWARDS; ANNE HAYNES, relict of ANDREW HAYNES; MARY, wife of ROBERT JONES; SARAH, wife of CHARLES JOHNSON; ELIZABETH, wife of DANIEL WELDON; MARTHA EATON. *Grandson:* EATON HAYNES. *Wife and Executrix:* MARY. The following lands devised: plantation in Granville "whereon I now live"; land in Granville called Bowsers; land where LEWIS BALLARD and CORMELIAL EARLS live; land in Northampton called Cumboes; lots in the town of Halifax; land "where Granville Court house is built"; land on Tabbs Creek; lot in the town of Petersburg; land in Granville called Gould's; land on Little Fishing Creek called Youngs; land on Andersons Swamp; two tracts on Smiths Creek called Hughes and Rayborn's; lot in Halifax adjoining the Market place and Main street. A large number of negroes bequeathed, some being on plantations at Tabbs Creek and others on Mush Island. *Witnesses:* WM. PERSON, JAS. PAINE, RICHD. COLEMAN. *Clerk of the Court:* DANIEL WELDON.

EBURN (or EBORNE), ELIZABETH.   Hyde County.

May 23, 1745. June Court, 1751. *Sons:* LITTLETON, HENRY, NATHANIEL. *Daughters:* ELIZABETH MACKNICOL, REBECCA JONES, ANN JONES. *Granddaughter:* MARY STEPHENS. *Executor:* HENRY and LITTLETON EBURN (sons). *Witnesses:* EDWARD DAVIS, ELISABETH BELL, WM. HARRIS. *Clerk of the Court:* THOS. LOACK.

EBORN, HENRY.   Hyde County.

October 20, 1732. March Court, 1732. Matchepungo in Hyde County. *Sons:* HENRY ("my plantation"), LITTLETON (land on Broad Creek and plantation Pantego; one negro). *Daughters:* MARY EBORN, RHODA LAYSON, ELIZABETH EBORN, ANNE JONES and REBECKER DEEDAN. *Other legatees:* NATHANIEL EBORN, son of HENRY and ELIZABETH EBORN (land between George Mixon and William Cambal on Matchepungo Creek); SALATHYEL LAYSON, son of EVENS RHODA LAYSON. *Wife and Executrix:*

ELIZABETH. *Executors:* WILLIAM BARROW, NATHANIEL EBORN and THOMAS SMITH. *Witnesses:* GEORGE MIXON, ELIZABETH WILLIAMSON, CHARLES JOHNSON. *Clerk of the Court:* JNO. COLLISON.

EBORN, LITTLETON.   Hyde County.

April 13, 1758. June Court, 1758. *Brothers:* AARON EBORN ("my dwelling plantation"), JAMES EBORN, WILLIAM EBORN. *Executors:* WILLIAM BOYD (brother-in-law), WILLIAM EBORN. *Witnesses:* WM. HARRIS, MARTHA EBORN, WILLIAM MACNORAL. *Clerk of the Court:* STEPHN DENNING.

EBORN, NATHANIEL.   Hyde County.

October 1, 1753. March Court, 1754. *Sons:* JAMES ("My plantation and one negro"), LITTLETON (plantation on Matchapungo Creek); WILLIAM (land on Matchapungo Creek adjoining HENRY EBORN, "holden by a bond in the hands of THOMAS, GEORGE and ZACERIA BARRAH," and 1 negro), AARON (land on Matchapungo adjoining THOMAS BARRAH, and one negro). *Daughter:* ELIZABETH EBORN (one negro). *Wife:* REBECCA. *Executors:* JAMES and LITTLETON EBORN (sons). *Witnesses:* ISRAEL WINDLY, ELIZABETH WINDLY, JOHN HOUREN. *Deputy Clerk:* STEPHEN DENNING.

EBORNE, REBEKAH.   Hyde County.

October 30, 1754. June Court, 1758. *Sons:* LITTLETON (*Executor*), WILLIAM and AARON. *Daughter:* ELIZABETH EBORNE. *Witnesses:* GEORGE BARROW, ZACHARIAH BARROW. *Clerk of the Court:* STEPN. DENNING.

EDEN, CHARLES.   County not given.

Governor of North Carolina, December 26, 1721. April 2, 1722. *Niece:* MARGARET PEUGH, daughter of ROBERT PEUGH. *Other legatees:* JOHN HOLLOWAY, DANIEL RICHARDSON, JAMES HENDERSON (land on Derhams Creek), JOHN LOVICK (executor). *Witnesses:* MARY BADHAM, H. CLAYTON, W. BADHAM. *Clerk of the Court:* W. BADHAM. Original missing. Recorded in Book 1712–1722, page 299.

EDMONDS (spelled EDDMONDS), RICHARD. Northampton Co.

September 26, 1750. November Court, 1750. *Sons:* THOMAS and DAVID. *Daughters:* MAREY, REBEKAH, ELIZABETH and SUSANNAH EDMONDS. *Wife:* ELIZABETH. *Executor:* BERABE MELTON. *Witnesses:* SAMUEL HACKNEY, SAMUEL JORDAN, JENINGS HACKNEY. *Clerk of the Court:* I. EDWARDS.

EDMONDS, SAMUEL.   Chowan County.

November 3, 1720. April Court, 1721. *Son:* HENRY ("my plantation") *Daughters:* SARAH EDMONDS, ANN SMITH, ELISABETH MEDLETON. *Wife:*

MARY. *Executor:* JOHN EDWARDS, SENR. *Witnesses:* JOHN WILLIAMS, GEO. EUBANK, THEOPHILUS WILLIAMS, EDWARD MORE. *Clerk of the Court:* THOS. HENMAN.

EDMONDSON, JOSEPH.   Craven County.

August 4, 1743. *Sons:* JOHN (*Executor*), THOMAS. *Daughter:* PRISE-LOW EDMONDSON. *Wife and Executrix:* PRISELOW. *Witnesses:* RICHD. BATH, ELIAS MARTIN, JOSEPH GAD. No probate.

EDNYE (EDNEY), ROBERT.   Pasquotank County.

April 4, 1752. December Court, 1758. *Sons:* SAMUEL, NUTON REN-SHER EDNYE. *Daughters:* ANN EDNYE (land on "the long ridge"), AHI-NOAM EDNYE (land on "ash branch"), ELIZABETH CARTWRIGHT (land on "broad neck branch"). *Wife and Executrix:* ANN. *Witnesses:* SAMUEL SMITH, JOSEPH SPENCE, THOS. LOADS (RHODES). *Clerk of the Court:* THOS. TAYLOR.

EDWARDS, CATHERINE.   Bladen County.

May 2, 1755. October Court, 1755. *Son:* ROBERT ("ye plantation I formerly lived on"). *Daughter:* ANN SUTTON. *Grandsons:* JOHN, SAMUEL and ISAAC HOLLINGSWORTH. *Executors:* ROBERT EDWARDS (son) and VALENTINE HOLLINGSWORTH. *Witnesses:* JAMES PROTHRO, JEREMIAH PROTHRO, ANN D. LAURENCY. *Clerk of the Court:* EDWARD NUGENT.

EDWARDS, EDWARD.   Northampton County.

February 27, 1758. July Court, 1758. *Wife and Executrix:* ANNE. *Witnesses:* JAMES LEAY, WILLIAM WINBORNE. *Clerk of the Court:* J. ED-WARDS.

EDWARDS, HENRY.   Edgecombe County.

January 14, 1758. June Court, 1758. *Sons:* NATHAN, BRITAIN and JESSE ("my plantation"), SAMUEL and HENRY (*executors*). *Witnesses:* ARTHUR BOWIN, JOHN NORWOOD. *Clerk of the Court:* JOS. MONTFORT.

EDWARDS, ISAAC.   Northampton County.

December 18, 1758. January Court, 1759. *Sons:* JOSIAH ("plantation whereon I now live, including all the lands lying between Roanoque River and Uraha Swamp"), JOHN (land on North side Uraha Swamp), THOMAS ("100 acres of land, including Davise's plantation"), WILLIAM. *Daughter:* ELIZABETH FERGUSON. *Son-in-law:* SAMUEL PHILIPS. *Grandchildren:* ELIZABETH PHILIPS, JOHN EDWARDS. *Daughter-in-law:* ANN EDWARDS. *Wife and Executrix:* ELIZABETH. *Witnesses:* JOHN SAWKILL, ROBERT DUKES, JOHN EDWARDS. *Clerk of the Court:* J. EDWARDS.

EDWARDS, JOHN.   New Hanover County.

June 19, 1743. May 15, 1744. *Sons:* JOHN, THOMAS. *Daughter:* CHARITY EDWARDS. *Wife and Executrix:* MARY. *Executor:* HENRY BARON. *Witnesses:* THOMAS HOBBY, WILLM. STEPHENS, HENRY BARON. Will proven before E. MOSELEY, *Chief Justice.*

EDY, JOHN.   County not given.

November 7, 1726. December 2, 1726. *Daughter:* DIANA EDY. *Brother:* HENRY EDY. This is a nuncupative will proven before THOS. TAYLOR by THOMAS SPENCER, HENRY EDEN and ESTHER DUDLY.

EGERTON (spelled EGGERTON), JAMES.   Perquimans County.

September 11, 1749. January Court, 1750. *Sons:* JAMES (plantation in Chowan County), WILLIAM (plantation on Mill Swamp). *Daughters:* ANN and MARY EGERTON. *Wife and Executrix:* SARAH. *Executors:* JOHN HALCEY, JOHN WILKINS. *Witnesses:* THOMAS CALLOWAY, WILLIAM HALL, RICHARD CLEMENS. *Clerk of the Court:* EDMUND HATCH.

ELDRIDGE, WILLIAM.   Northampton County.

May Court, 1751. *"Supposed son":* MATTHEW MOOR. *Wife:* MARY. *Other legatees:* MELA MOOR, CHARITY MOOR, PATTY PEACOCK (daughter of ELIZABETH PEACOCK). *Brother:* SAMUEL. *Sisters:* MARTHA, THOMAS NIXON, MARTHA MOOR. *Executors:* WILLIAM KECHEN, JAS. WASHINGTON, BENJN. DeBERRY. *Witnesses:* JNO. DEBERRY, WILLIAM RICHARDSON. RABACKAH DAWSON. *Clerk of the Court:* I. EDWARDS.

ELKS, JOHN.   County not given.

January 23, 1707–1708. *Sons:* JOHN ("my dwelling plantation"), THOMAS, AMANUEL (land called "rich neck"), MARMADUKE. *Wife and Executrix:* MARY. *Witnesses:* EDWARD OLD, JUNIOR, GEORGE WARRENTON, SENIOR, GEORGE WARRENTON, JUNIOR, REBEKAH OLD. *Clerk of the Court:* JOS. WAKER (or WALKER).

ELKS, RICHARD.   Albemarle County.

September 21, 1687. October 6, 1687. *Executor and sole legatee and devisee:* WILLIAM DARBY ("plantation upon Yawpin River"). *Witnesses:* THOMAS POLLOCK, HANNA HAILE, JOHN WOLFENDEN, JOHN LEWIN. Will proven before SETH SOTHELL, *Governor.*

ELLEGOOD, MATTHIAS.   Pasquotank County.

September 10, 1773. March 7, 1774. *Friends and Executors:* COLO. JOHN SAWYER, JONATHAN HEARRING. *Wife and Executrix:* MARGREAT. *Witnesses:* SAMUEL SPENCE, THOS. ETHERIDGE, THOMAS GRANDY. Will proven before JO. MARTIN.

ELIOTT, CHARLES.   Enfield.

October 15, 1753. May Term, 1757. *Executor and sole legatee:* HON.
JOHN RUTHERFORD. *Witnesses:* THOS. LOWE, JOHN LAWSON. *Clerk of
the Court:* I. EDWARDS.

ELLIOTT, GEORGE.   Pasquotank Precinct.

February 7, 1727–1728. April Court, 1728. *Daughter:* MARY WALLIS.
Other legatees: JOHN CLARKE, ANN ASKINS, ANN GRAY. *Executor:* RICH-
ARD GRAY. *Witnesses:* THOMAS BEDFORD, WILLIAM WALLIS, JAMES COL-
LINS. *Clerk of the Court:* WM. MINSON.

ELIOT, MICHEL.   Orange County.

October 25, 1756. December Court, 1756. *Executor and sole legatee
and devisee:* WILLIAM PHILLIPS. *Witnesses:* WILLIAM OFFILL, JAMES HOP-
KINS, WILLIAM HOPKINS. *Clerk of the Court:* JAMES WATSON.

ELLIOTT, MOSES.   Perquimans County.

February 22, 1756. January Court, 1756. *Sons:* JOSEPH, MOSES, BEN-
JAMIN. *Daughter:* MARGRET ELLIOT. *Wife and Executrix:* JUDAH. *Wit-
nesses:* ABRAHAM HASKIT, SAMUEL BAGLEY. *Clerk of the Court:* MILES
HARVY.

ELLIOT, THOMAS.   Perquimans County.

April 2, 1720. December 16, 1729. *Sons:* CALEB ("plantation on which
I now dwell"), JOSHUA (200 acres of land), ISAAC ("remaining part of ye
tract"), WILLIAM (1 shilling), THOMAS, ABRAHAM, SOLOMON, MOSES,
JOSEPH and BENJAMIN. *Daughters:* MARY BROWN, URSELY. *Wife and
Executrix:* MARGARET. *Witnesses:* SARAH WARNER, WILLIAM———, R.
WILSON. Will proven before RICH'D EVERARD.

ELLIS, GEORGE.   Pasquotank Precinct.

January 30, 1720. July Court, 1720. *Brother and Executor:* THOMAS
PALIN. *Daughter:* ANN ELLIS. *Wife and Executrix:* HANNAH. *Witnesses:* SARAH BULL, KATH. TOWER, JANE DANN. *Clerk of the Court pro
tem.:* J. PALIN.

ELLIS, MARY.   County not given.

Executor and Guardian of son: THOMAS CLARKE. *Witnesses:* ELIZABETH
WILLIS, ELLIS WILSON, JOHN WILSON. No probate.

ELLIS, ROBERT.   Northampton County.

January 28, 1740. February Court, 1743. *Son:* JNO. ELLIS (one shilling). *Grandsons:* ROBERT and JOHN ELLIS (160 acres of land to each).

Neighbor and Executor: PHIL SMITH ("plantation whereon I now dwell").
Witnesses: PHIL SMITH, MOSES BECK, ELIZABETH SMITH.   *Clerk of the
Court:* I. EDWARDS.

ELLISON, WILLIAM.   New Hanover County.
   June 23, 1737.   July 2, 1737.   *Brother and sole devisee and legatee:* AN-
DREW ELLISON.   *Executor:* JAMES MURRAY.   *Witnesses:* JA. PATERSON,
THOMAS CLARKE, JA. MURRAY.   Will proven before ROBT. HALTON and
GAB. JOHNSTON.

ELTON, ZACHARIAH.   Perquimans County.
   October 5, 1752.   October Court, 1752.   *Devisees and Legatees:* JONA-
THAN PHELPS, SEN., JOSEPH WHITE, MARY BARKER, WILLIAM LAMB.
Executors: JONATHAN PHELPS, JOSEPH WHITE.   *Witnesses:* WILLIAM
TOWNSEN, THOMAS MARTIN.   *Clerk of the Court:* EDMUND HATCH.

ENGEL, PETER.   Craven Precinct.
   September 20, 1722.   December Court, 1722.   *Godson:* WILLIAM MORE.
Other legatees: ANN CARTUS, SUSAN MOORE, SURITY MOORE, MARY LOTS,
ADAM MOORE, GEORGE MALS.   *Witnesses:* MATTHEW REASON, PETER
HAND.   *Clerk of the Court:* C. METCALFE.

ENGLISH, JOSEPH.   Beaufort County.
   November 20, 1744.   December Court, 1744.   *Friends:* MARY PALLEE,
DOCR. PETTER COLAXE.   *Executor:* PETTER SOLE.   *Witnesses:* JOHN
BROCK, JOHN FULKER, NATHAN ARCHBELL.   *Clerk of the Court:* FR. GOOLD,
JNO. TURNER.

ENNET, EDMUND.   New River.
   February 24, 1734.   April 11, 1735.   *Sons:* JOHN (land on Kisable
Creek), EDMOND and JOSEPH ("my dwelling plantation").   *Daughter:*
ELLINOR ENNET.   *Executors:* NATHANIEL EVERET and JOHN WARREN.
Witnesses: MARTHA HOLT, WILLIAM MARCHMENT, JONATHAN PIKE, MARY
PATTER.   Will proven before GOVERNOR GAB. JOHNSTON at New River.

ESPY, JAMES.   Brunswick, in New Hanover County.
   October 3, 1739.   October 9, 1739.   *Son:* USHER.   *Daughter:* SARAH
ESPY.   *Wife:* MARGARET.   *Executors:* JOHN MONTGOMERY and WILLIAM
DRY.   *Witnesses:* RICHARD HELLIER, WM. GRAY, JAMES LYON.   Will
proven before GAB. JOHNSTON at Newton.

ETHERIDGE, HENRY.   Currituck County.
   March 14, 1742–1743.   July Court, 1743.   *Sons:* SAMUEL, WILLIAM,
RICHARD, JOHN, HENRY.   *Daughters:* ANN ETHERIDGE, TEDY ETHERIDGE,

8

MARY ETHERIDGE. *Wife and Executrix:* SUSEY. *Witnesses:* JOHN BALLANCE, WILLIAM MAKEFASHION, MOSES LINTON. *Clerk of the Court:* JOHN LURRY.

ETHERIDGE, JOHN. Currituck County.

April 3, 1744. July Court, 1744. *Sons:* AMOS (land known as the "Bull yard"), WILLIS (411 acres of land), CALLIB (land known as "Northerns"), JAMES ("plantation where Henry Blount now liveth"), JOHN ("plantation whereon I now live"), JOSIAS ("plantation where Samuel Jones now liveth"). *Daughters:* SARAH BIGGS, DOROTHY ETHERIDGE. *Wife and Executrix:* ELINER. *Witnesses:* THOS. WILLIAMS, SOLOMON ETHERIDGE, JOHN PIRKENS, ABSALOM LEGETT. *Clerk of the Court:* RICHD. MCCLURE.

ETHERIDGE, LUKE. Currituck County.

February 25, 1732. *Daughters:* SARAH ETHERIDGE ("land I now live on"), ELIZABETH ETHERIDGE ("land in ye great swamp"), ANN ETHERIDGE. *Wife and Executrix:* CHRISTON. *Witnesses:* ELISABETH DANIEL, OTHO HOLLAND. *Clerk of the Court:* THOS. LOWTHER.

ETHERIDGE, MARMADUKE. Currituck County.

February 3, 1734. *Devisees and legatees:* CALEB, MARMADUKE and MARY BELL (children of Sarah Bell). *Executrix:* SARAH BELL. *Witnesses:* JOHN HOUREN, JOSEPH BOURN, PETER DOUGE. *Clerk of the Court:* THOS. LOWTHER.

ETHERIDGE, RICHARD. "Currituck Banks and Bay of Kitty Hawk."

February 12, 1739–1740. April Court, 1750. *Sons:* ADAM ("plantation whereon I now live, commonly known by the name of the Whale House"), SAMPSON. *Daughters:* DIANAH DOWE, HELLENA DOWDY, ELIZABETH DOWDY. *Grandson:* ROBERT TUCKER. *Granddaughters:* PRISSELLA ETHERIDGE, DEBORAH FEILDS. *Wife:* SARAH. *Executors:* ADAM, SAMPSON ETHERIDGE (sons). *Witnesses:* THOMAS MAYO, CHARITY SIVELLS, LENINE MAYO. *Clerk of the Court:* RICH'D MCCLURE.

ETHERIDGE, SOLOMON. Currituck County.

November 7, 1749. January Court, 1749. *Sons:* ABNER ("plantation I now live on"), SOLOMON, ABSALOM. *Daughters:* SARAH ETHERIDGE, LETTISHA ETHERIDGE, BARBY ETHERIDGE, REDAH ETHERIDGE. *Witnesses:* WILLIAM ETHERIDGE, CALEB ETHERIDGE. *Clerk of the Court:* RICHD. MCCLURE.

EUBANK, GEORGE. Bertie Precinct Society Parish.

March 2, 1732–1733. March 12, 1732. *Brother:* JAMES EUBANK. *Sisters:* ELIZABETH and ISABELL EUBANK. To brothers and sisters is devised all estate in Great Britain. *Other legatees:* Thomas, Elizabeth and Martha Whitmell, William Gray. *Executors:* James Castellaw, Thomas Whitmell and John Gray. *Witnesses:* James Bulock, John Barton. Proven before George Burrington.

Evans, Barwell. Beaufort County.

April 1, 1756. June Court, 1756. *Daughters:* Sarah Evans ("plantation whereon I now live and forty acres of land on the creek I live on"), Susannah Evans ("plantation whereon William Brantly lives and three hundred acres of land on the mill creek"). *Nephews:* Jacob and Barwell Evans. *Friend:* William Stokes. *Wife and Executrix:* Susannah. *Executors:* Jacob, Benjamin and Charles Evans (brothers). *Witnesses:* George Sugg, Peter Hull and Richard Hurley. *Clerk of the Court:* Walley Chauncey.

Evans, Charles. Tarr River, in Edgecombe County.

June 1, 1759. June Court, 1759. *Sons:* Jacob (land in Beaufort County), Benjamin, Charles (land on Tar river and town Creek). *Grandchildren:* Charles Evans (son of Benjamin), John Evans (son of Charles and Elizabeth), Ann Evans (daughter of Charles and Elizabeth). *Witnesses:* John Tison, Charles Evans, Jr. *Clerk of the Court:* Jos. Montfort.

Evans, Hunt. Pasquotank Precinct.

December 15, 1729. January 13, 1729. *Brothers:* Bartholomew Evans, Thomas Armore. *Father-in-law and Executor:* Louis Markham. *Witnesses:* Robert Keel, Ann Crank, Isaac Finney. *Clerk of the Court:* H. Minson.

Evans, John. Chowan County.

August 24, 1739. January 15, 1739. *Sons:* John ("plantation whereon I now live"), Thomas, Benjamin. *Daughters:* Jane Evans, Mary Evans, Rachel Evans. *Wife and Executrix:* Jane. *Witnesses:* John Evans, Charles Jordan. Will proven before W. Smith, *Chief Justice.*

Evans, Mary. Perquimans County.

April 8, 1720. March 7, 1723. *Son:* William. *Executors:* Francis Penrine, Darby Bryan. *Witnesses:* John Dick, Harris Willoughby, Francis Laydain. Will proven before Geo. Burrington, *Governor.*

Evans (spelled "Eivens"), Richard. Albemarle County.

September 7, 1692. October 2, 1693. *Sons:* Jonathan, Richard. *Daughters:* Rabakah Eivens, Ann Eivens. *Executors:* Elizabeth Eivens (wife), Alexander Lillington. *Witnesses:* David Shearwood, Jane Arnold, Benjamin Cidden. *Clerk of the Court:* John Stepney.

EVANS, RICHARD.   Beaufort County.

December 26, 1752. June Court, 1753. *Sons:* RICHARD and GEORGE
(lands in Onslow on the mouth of New River). *Daughter:* MARY EVANS.
About thirteen negroes bequeathed. *Executor:* MICHAEL CAUTANCHE.
Witnesses: EDMUND PEARCE, JOSHUA PEARCE, READING BLOUNT. *Clerk
of the Court:* WALLEY CHAUNCEY.

EVANS, ROBERT.   Perquimans County.

March 20, 1754. January Court, 1758. *Sons:* JOHN, ROBERT (*Executor*). *Daughters:* SARAH GRIFFIN, ELISABETH EVANS, MARY EVANS.
Grandchildren: DEMSEY, ARON, ROBERT and HULDAH BLANSHARD. *Witnesses:* WILLIAM KELLY, NATHAN CULLENS, DAVENPORT GOODING. *Clerk
of the Court:* MILES HARVEY.

EVANS, THOMAS.   Chowan Precinct.

February 29, 1731–1732. November 2, 1732. *Son and Executor:*
THOMAS ("my maner plantation"). *Daughters:* ALLIS WILLIAMSON,
SARAH BROWNEY, ELIZEBETH WALKER. *Wife and Executrix:* ELLENER.
Witnesses: THO. HOBBS, CORNELIUS COLLEHAN. Will proven before WM.
LITTLE, *Chief Justice.*

EVANS, THOMAS.   Tyrrell County.

March 14, 1744–1745. June Court, 1745. *Mother:* ELENER EVANS.
Daughters: ELIZABETH, MARY, CATHERINE, ALCE and SARAH EVANS.
Wife and Executrix: MARY. *Executors:* SAMUEL DURRANCE, MATHIAS
ADAMS. *Witnesses:* JOHN NICHALLS, JOHN GARRETT, JOHN WALKER.
Clerk of the Court: JAS. CONNER.

EVATT, WILLIAM.   Northampton County.

April 10, 1758. July Court, 1758. *Daughter:* MARY EVATT. *Wife
and Executrix:* SARAH. *Executor:* DANIEL DUNKIN. *Witnesses:* GERARD
YOUNG, THOMAS WILBORN. *Clerk of the Court:* I. EDWARDS.

EVERETT, JOHN.   Tyrrell County.

March 16, 1754. June Court, 1754. *Brother:* JOSHUA (145 acres of
land known as "the Stamping place"), THOMAS (*Executor*). *Father and
Executor:* NATHANIEL EVERETT. *Cousins:* JOHN and ELISABETH EVERETT.
Witnesses: SAMUEL DURRANCE, DANIEL YARRETT, NATHANIEL EVERITT.
Clerk of the Court: EVAN JONES.

EVERITT, NATHANIEL.   Tyrrell County.

November 2, 1749. December 5, 1749. *Legatees and devisees:* NATHAN-
IELL EVERITT of New River, NATHANIEL EVERITT of Mereland, NATHANIEL
EVERITT of the parish of St. Andrews ("my plantation"), MARY EVERITT,

ELISABETH RAY, SARY FUGGIN. *Executor:* NATHANIEL EVERITT of St. Andrews. *Witnesses:* THOMAS EVERITT, JAMES RHOUDES, ANN BEESLEY. *Clerk of the Court:* EVAN JONES.   Courthouse on Kindrecks Creek.

EVERTON, JEREMIAH.   Pasquotank County.
   January 3, 1736. October Court, 1740. *Sons:* SOLOMON (1 shilling), JAMES ("my dwelling plantation"). *Daughters:* SARAH FOREHAND, RACHEL EVERTON, KATHERINE CHAMBERLAIN. *Wife and Executrix:* HANNAH. *Witnesses:* JOHN SCARF, JAMES SCARF, THOMAS CROMWELL. *Clerk of the Court:* JAMES CRAVEN.

EYRES, RICHARD.   County not given.
   October 2, 1685. November 11, 1685. *Executor and sole legatee:* CHARLES PROWS. *Witnesses:* RICHARD ROOKE, MARY ROOKE.   *Clerk of the Court:* HENDERSON WALKER.

FAGAN, ENOCH.   Tyrrell County.
   January 16, 1777. April 29, 1777. *Daughter:* MARY FAGAN. *Wife and Executrix:* RUINA. *Executor:* BENJAMIN BLOUNT. *Witnesses:* SAMUEL BLACK, ISHAM WEBB, FR. WARD. Will proven before RD. CASWELL, *Governor.*

FALCONER, JOHN.   Chowan County.
   July 28, 1739. August 5, 1741. *Sons:* THOMAS, GEORGE. *Daughters:* ANN FALCONER, MARY FRAZIER, HESTER GRAVENOR. *Wife and Executrix:* SARAH. *Witnesses:* JOHN RONSHAM, EDWD. AURENDELL, PATINES EVERAY. Will proven before J. MONTGOMERY, C. J.

FALCONER, THOMAS.   Chowan County.
   February 1, 1756. April Court, 1756. *Nephew:* JAMES BEASLEY. *Wife:* SARAH (plantation and all personal property). *Other legatees:* SARAH FREEMAN, daughter of THOMAS FREEMAN; RICHARD LEARY of Tyrrell County; JOHN, son of JAMES BEASLEY; JAMES, son of JOHN BEASLEY and THOMAS son of JAMES BEASLEY; MARY PAIN, daughter of JAMES BEASLEY. *Executors:* JOHN HALSEY and CORNELIUS LEARY. *Witnesses:* ROBERT BEASLEY, JAMES FRANCIS, EDWARD ROBINS, ELIZABETH ROWSUM, THOMAS PEIRCE, JOHN CREECY. *Clerk of the Court:* THOMAS JONES.

FALK, RICHARD.   Chowan Precinct.
   March 15, ———. No probate. *Sons:* JONATHAN, WILLIAM, JOHN and RICHARD (lands on Maheron River). *Wife and Executrix:* ELIZABETH. *Witnesses:* RICHARD FALK, WILLIAM MAULE, THOMAS BUSBE. Original missing. Recorded in Book 1712-1722, page 27.

FARLEE, JAMES.   Chowan Precinct.

May 1, 1727. May 15, 1727. *Wife:* mentioned, but not named. Testator's lands left to JAMES BENTLEY, son of SARAH BENTLEY. *Guardians:* HENRY BONNER, SAMUELL PAGETT. *Executor:* EDWARD MOSELEY. *Witnesses:* ROBERT JEFFREYS, WM. HALLSEY, JOHN HALLSEY. Will proven before RICHARD EVERARD, *Governor.*

FARLEE, JAMES.   Chowan County.

January 12, 1750. January Court, 1750. *Sons:* SAMUEL ("all my land"), JAMES. *Daughters:* MARY PARKER, SARAH FARLEE, CHRISTIANA FARLEE. *Wife:* RACHEL. *Executor:* JOHN CAMPBELL. *Witnesses:* WILLIAM BOYD, AMOS PARKER, JOHN BACKCUS. *Clerk of the Court:* WILL. MEARNS. Executor qualified before JAMES CRAVEN.

FARR, RICHARD.   Onslow County.

November 8, 1757. July Court, 1758. *Sons:* RICHARD, TITUS GREEN FARR, WILLIAM, JAMES. *Executors:* HANNAH FARR (*wife*), STEPHEN LEE, JOHN MILTON. *Witnesses:* THOS. HILL, ROBERT MILTON, DNL. AUSTIN. *Clerk of the Court:* WILLIAM CRAY.

FARROW, FRANCIS.   Currituck County.

October 7, 1721. February 9, 1722–1723. *Wife and Executrix:* BARBARY. *Children:* mentioned, but not named. *Friend:* WILLIAM ROLLISON. *Witnesses:* DANIEL GUTHRIE, JOHN MACQUIN, RICHARD JOHNSON. Will proven before WM. REED, "presedent of North Carolina."

FEARE, OBADIAH.   Pasquotank Precinct.

June 5, 1719, "of Alligater in the presinck of Pascotank." *Legatees and Devisees:* WILLIAM LUDFORD (*Executor*), SARAH LUDFORD, ANNE LUDFORD, CHRISTIAN LUDFORD, MARY LUDFORD, MARTHA LUDFORD, TOMSON LUDFORD, THOMAS LUDFORD, ANN FEARE (wife). *Witnesses:* EDWD. LININGTON, JOSEPH WINSHAPP, ANDREW OLIVER. No probate.

FEILDS, JAMES.   Perquimans County.

February 15, 1750–1751. April Court, 1751. *Sons and Executors:* RUBIN, MOSES. *Daughters:* ANN FEILDS, ZEBIAH FEILDS. *Son-in-law:* JAMES PRICE (*Executor*). *Witnesses:* NICHOLAS STALLINGS, ELIAS STALLINGS, MOSES ROUNTREE. *Clerk of the Court:* EDMUND HATCH.

FEILD, RICHARD.   Onslow County.

June 24, 1742. January Court, 1744. *Wife and Executrix:* ANN. *Sons:* JOHN and SAMUEL (550 acres of land up White Oak river), RICHARD

and SMITH (my plantation), JAMES (300 acres land). *Executor:* JOHN
STARKEY. *Witnesses:* ABRA. MITCHELL, ABRAHAM MITCHELL, JAMES AT-
KINS. *Clerk of the Court:* ANDREW MURRAY.

FELTHEN, JAMES. Bertie County.

March 16, 1726. July, 1726. *Wife and Executrix:* ANN. *Witnesses:*
FRED. RASOR, CHRISTOPHER VANLUVAN, MARTHA HOOPER. Will proven
before RICHD. EVERARD.

FELTS, HUMPHREY. Perquimans County.

1726. July, 1726. *Son:* JOHN. *Daughter:* ELISABETH. *Executor:*
WILLIAM LONG. *Witnesses:* EDWD. STANDIN, JOSHUA LONG, SAMUEL
WIATT. *Clerk of the Court:* RICH'D LEARY. Court held at the house of
ROBERT MOORE.

FENDALL, JOHN. Chowan County.

December 17, 1695. April Court, 1696. *Wife:* ELIZABETH. *Brother:*
ROBERT FENDALL. *Father-in-law and Executor:* ALEXANDER LILLINGTON.
Witnesses: JOHN DIX, ANN WALKER, HENDERSON WALKER. *Clerk of the
Court:* NA. CHEVIN.

FENDALL, ROBERT. Perquimans County.

November 30, 1711. January, 1711–1712. *Daughter:* ELIZABETH LIL-
LINGTON. *Other devisees and legatees:* ISAAC WILLSON (land on Kendricks
Creek known as Hawkinses Neck), RICHARD LOWRY. *Executor:* THOMAS
LONG. *Witnesses:* JOHN WIAT, JOHN LONG, THOMAS WYATT. Will proven
in Council: N. CHEVIN, *Clerk.*

FEPS, WILLIAM. Beaufort County.

January 11, 1753. June, 1754. *Sons:* WILLIAM ("my maner planta-
tion"), NATHANIEL, JOSIAH. *Daughters:* LU. RAINER, MOLLE, SARAH
Wife and Executrix: MARY. *Witnesses:* ROBERT SPRING, CHARLES HOW-
ARD, WILLIAM MORRIS. *Clerk of the Court:* WALLEY CHAUNCY.

FERGUSON, ADAM. Craven Precinct.

October 13, 1715. February 15, 1715. *Son:* MARK ("my plantation").
Daughters: SARAH FERGUSON, JANE FERGUSON. *Wife:* ELIZABETH FER-
GUSON. *Executor:* DANIELL MCFARLAN. *Witnesses:* ROBT. RAMSEY,
PETER CROPELY, FRANCIS HUTSON. *Clerk of the Court:* DANIELL MCFAR-
LAN.

FERGUSON, MARK. Craven County.

April 16, 1751. September Court, 1751. *Sons:* ADAM (350 acres of
land on the East side of Slocumb's Creek), SLOCUMB (800 acres of land on

Mill Creek). *Cousin:* BENJAMIN CUMMINGS (land on East side of Adams Creek). *Wife and Executrix:* ELIZABETH. *Witnesses:* ADAM WALLIS, ROBERT WALLIS, JOHN CUMMINGS. *Clerk of the Court:* PHIL. SMITH.

FERIEL, RICHARD.   Pasquotank County.

January 31, 1738–1739. July Court, 1740. *Sons:* ERASMUS and JOHN (*Executor*). *Witnesses:* JOHN HOUREN, THOMAS and WILLIS JAMES. *Clerk of the Court:* JAMES CRAVEN.

FERRIL, WILLIAM.   Currituck County.

November 7, 1742. January Court, 1742–1743. *Sons:* JOSEPH, CALEB, SAMUEL. *Daughters:* TAMER, MARY and ANN FERRIL. *Sister:* ESBEL BURKET. *Wife and Executrix:* SARAH. *Witnesses:* GEORGE FEREBEE, JOSEPH FEREBEE, WILLIAM FEREBEE. *Clerk of the Court:* JOHN LURRY.

FEWOX, JAMES.   County not given.

March 2, 1710. January 9, 1711–1712. *Son:* ROBERT. *Wife:* ANN. *Other legatees and devisees:* JNO. LAWSON, MARY LAWSON, SAMUEL HARDY, son of WM. HARDY. *Executrix:* MARY LAWSON, widow of NATHANIEL LAWSON. *Witness:* GEO. GLADSTAIN. Codicil, dated May 5, 1711, provides for use of gristmill. *Witnesses:* GEO. GLADSTAIN, JOSEPH FANINGS, JOHN SNELL. Will proven in Council: ROBERT BUCKNER, *Clerk*.

FIGURES, BARTHOLOMEW.   Northampton County.

March 16, 1758. July Court, 1758. *Sons:* JOHN (700 acres of land), RICHARD (275 acres of land), BARTHOLOMEW ("my plantation"), JOSEPH ("land whereon he now lives"), WILLIAM (700 acres of land). *Daughters:* REBEKAH DERRING, ELIZABETH LEWIS. *Witnesses:* JOSEPH DEW, CHARLES DEW, WILLIAM SHERARD, JOHN DEW. Codicil to this will of even date makes more bequests to JOHN and BARTHOLOMEW. *Executors:* JOHN and BARTHOLOMEW FIGURES. *Clerk of the Court:* I. EDWARDS.

FILLIAW, JOHN.   Craven County.

August 31, 1747. March 15, 1748. *Sons:* JOHN, JOSEPH, JAMES. *Daughters:* ANN FILLIAW, PRISILLAR FILLIAW, MARY FILLIAW. *Wife and Executrix:* JANE. *Witnesses:* ALEXANDER BLACKSHIRE, N. WOLF, WM. GRAY. *Clerk of the Court:* JOHN RICE.

FILLINGHAM, JOHN.   Pitt County.

November 11, 1771. December 22, 1773. *Sons:* JOHN, ROBERT, SAMUEL, JARVIS, BENJAMIN. *Daughters:* MATHEW WHITE, MARY HAYS. *Wife:* MARGARET. *Executors:* JOHN and ROBERT (sons). *Witnesses:* JOSIAH LITTLE, ALEXR. STEWART. Will proven before JO. MARTIN.

FISH, WILLIAM.   Bertie County.

August 10, 1750. May Court, 1751. *Sons:* JOHN, WILLIAM ("plantation whereon I now live"). *Daughters:* ANN FERRILL, MARY FISH ("100
acres of land in Johnston County on Marsh Branch"). *Grandsons:* JOHN
and WM. FISH. *Wife:* MARY. *Executor:* SAMUELL WILLIAMS. *Witnesses:*
SARAH LEE, SAMUEL WILLIAMS, MARY CALVART. *Clerk of the Court:* BENJ.
WYNNS.

FISHER, JAMES.   County not given.

August 13, 1702. No probate. "This being my last desire from all
wills that all my whole estate both real and personal I give to my *wife and
to my children* and my deare friend MR. WILLIAM WILKESON. I would
have you if you please to assist them, that they may not be wronged."
Witnesses: WILLIAM LONG, PETER JONES.

FISHER, RANDOLPH.   Craven County.

March 31, 1747. June Court, 1751. *Sons:* THOMAS and GEORGE (*Executor*). *Witnesses:* GEORGE GRAHMS, THOS. MATCHETT, RICHD. BATH.
No signature to probate.

FITZGARRALD, JOHN.   Johnston County.

August 14, 1749. September Court, 1751. *Sons:* JOHN and THOMAS.
Son-in-law: ARTHUR PEIRCE (*Executor*). *Wife:* ANN. *Executor:* RICHARD
PEIRCE. *Witnesses:* ROBT. BUTLER, ANTHONY FULGHAM, ANNE PEIRCE.
Deputy Clerk of the Court: JAMES OATES.

FITZPATRICK, BRYAN.   Allegator Creek, in Chowan County.

March 26, 1709. *Sons:* CORNELIUS, VINNEY, DINIS ("my dwelling
plantation called Hunts"). *Son:* CONRELIUS, appointed *Executor*. Negroes
bequeathed to sons. *Witnesses:* SAMUEL BROOKE, DAVID ELDER, JOHN
MACKER. Original missing. Recorded in Book 1712–22, page 64.

FITZPATRICK, CORNELIUS.   Allegator, in Albemarle County.

August 21, 1716. *Wife and Executrix:* ELIZABETH. *Sons:* JOHN, COR-
NELIUS and BRYANT. *Daughters:* ELENDER, MARY, SARAH, ELIZABETH.
Other legatees: GEO. WHIDBEE, JOHN WOODLAND, ELIZABETH WHIDBEE,
RICHARD WHIDBEE, JOHN MARKE. *Witnesses:* JOHN WOODLAND, GEORGE
WHIDBEE, RICHARD WHIDBEE. Will proven before THOS. POLLOCK,
May 4, 1722.

FLANAKIN, RICHARD.   South Dividing Creek, in Bath Co.

September 5, 1739. June Court, 1741. *Sons:* JAMES ("the mannour
plantation"), THOMAS, RICHARD, WILLIAM. *Daughter:* LEAH FLANAKIN.

Wife: KATHERINE.   *Executors:* ABRM. PRITCHETT (brother), JAMES FLAN-
AKIN (son).   *Witnesses:* PORTER FINCH, DOROTHY FINCH, SAMUEL GOODIN.
Clerk of Beaufort Court: ROG. JONES.

FLEMING, GEORGE.   Pasquotank Precinct.
   May 27, 1694. July 16, 1694. *Daughter:* ELIZABETH FLEMING.
Friends: THOMAS ELLIOTT, JAMES ROBINSON. *Executor:* SIMON RICE.
Witnesses: WILLIAM BRAY, ISAAC GILFORD, ELIZEBETH JONES, JOHN
PHILPOTT.   *Clerk of the Court:* EDWARD MAYO.

FLEMING, ROSANNA.   Perquimans County.
   May 20, 1758. October Court, 1758. *Son:* JAMES (*Executor*). *Daugh-
ters:* SARAH SCRIMSHER, MARTHA FLEMING, ELIZABETH FLEMING, MARY
FLEMING. *Witnesses:* ZACHARIAH WEBB, SENR., JAMES GIBSON, ZACHARIAH
WEBB, JUNR.   *Clerk of the Court:* M. HARVEY.

FLETCHER, CURTIS.   County not given.
   March 28, 1671. April 15, 1671. *Legatees:* WILLIAM BRAY, THOMAS
TULLEY, BENJAMIN TULLEY. *Witnesses:* WILLIAM BAYS, DAVID PRISHET.
Proven before RICHARD FOSTER and PATRICK WHITE.

FLETCHER, FRANCIS.   Pasquotank County.
   January Court, 1743. *Wife and Executrix:* MARGARET. *Witnesses:*
BENJAMIN BAPTISTE, JONATHAN LANGATHEN, WILLIAM DELENY. *Clerk
of the Court:* THOS. TAYLOR.

FLETCHER, RALPH.   Perquimans County.
   February 20, 1726–1727. January 21, 1728. *Sons:* RALPH ("my
manner house & plantation"), GEORGE ("my lower house and plantation"),
JAMES, JOSUA. *Daughters:* JANE and ELIZABETH FLETCHER. *Executors:*
RICHARD SKINNER and RICHARD CHEASTEN. *Witnesses:* ELIZABETH
FRENCH, SARAH SKINNER, THOMAS RATTLIFF. *Clerk of the Court:* THOMAS
CREW.

FLETCHER, RALPH.   Perquimans County.
   April 5, 1752. July Court, 1752. *Sons:* RALPH ("the manner planta-
tion"), JOSHUA. *Daughters:* JANE, MIRIAM and RUTH FLETCHER, MARY
RATTLIFF. *Wife:* MARY. *Executors:* JOSEPH RATLIFF (son-in-law). *Wit-
nesses:* FRANCIS TOMS, FRANCIS NEWBY, WILLIAM LASEY. *Clerk of the
Court:* EDMUND HATCH.

FLETCHER, THOMAS.   Chowan County.
   May 10, 1727. April Court, 1734. *Wife:* DOROTHA. *Son:* THOMAS.
Witnesses: ROBERT LACITER, GEORGE LACITER. *Clerk of the Court:*
MOSELY VAIL.

FLOOD, JAMES.   "Cape Fare."

1731. June 10, 1736. *Wife and Executrix:* ELIZABETH. *Witnesses:*
TUNIS VAN GOLDER, ELIZABETH HARNETT, MARY PARKER. *Clerk of the
Court:* HUGH CAMPBELL.

FLOOD, JAMES.   Chowan County.

November 15, 1750. November 30, 1750. *Wife and Executrix:* ELIZA-
BETH. *Children:* WILLIAM and ANN BRASWELL. *Executors:* JAMES
CRAVEN and THOMAS BARKER. *Witnesses:* EDMUND HATCH, JOHN MC-
KILDO, RICHARD MCCLURE. Will proven before *Gov.* GAB. JOHNSTON.

FLOVELL, WILLIAM.   Newton, county not given.

December 18, 1737. March 1, 1737. Two hundred pounds South
Carolina currency to be paid towards the erection of an English Church.
Niece: ELIZABETH CALLETON, wife of GEORGE CALLETON of South Carolina.
Uncle: WILLIAM HALE ("late of Nassau in New Providence"). *Executors:*
WILLIAM ROPER, ELIZABETH CALLETON, RUFUS MARSDEN, JOHN DAVIS
and JOSEPH WRAGG. *Witnesses:* ROGER ROLFE, ARMAND DEROSSET,
M. D., MICH. HIGGINES. Will proven before GAB. JOHNSTON. Coat of
arms on seal.

FLOYD, JOHN.   Northampton County.

August 3, 1756. November Court, 1756. *Sons:* MORRISE (80 acres of
land in King William County, Va.), THOMAS ("plantation whereon I now
live"), STEPHEN, JESSEE, JOHN and WILLIAM. *Daughter:* ELIZABETH
COOKER. *Executors:* THOMAS and WILLIAM (sons). *Witnesses:* CHAS.
CAMPBELL, JAMES STANTON. *Clerk of the Court:* I. EDWARDS.

FLYN, COLLUMB.   Bath County.

August 22, 1721. September 9, 1737. *Son and Executor:* COLLUMB
("all my real estate"). *Daughters:* MARY SMITH, MARGARET PRITCHARD.
Witnesses: MARTIN FRANCK, ANDREW BALLEAU, THOS. BOYD. Will proven
before GAB. JOHNSTON at Newton.

FOGG, MOSES.   Craven County.

December 3, 1751. March 20, 1751. *Legatees and devisees:* GRACE
FOGG (daughter of JOHNWATS FOGG, 300 acres of land on Nuse River),
MATHIAS BENSTON. *Executor:* JOHN LANE. *Witnesses:* JOHN DUNCAN,
NICHOLAS ROUTLEDGE and NATHAN ALEXANDER. *Clerk of the Court:*
JNO. SNEAD.

FONVIELLE, JOHN.   Craven County.

January 24, 1773. January 27, 1773. *Sons:* JOHN ("240 acres of land
where he now lives; 120 acres of land between ISAAC FONVIELLE and

ARTHOR BLACKMAN; lot No. 6 in Newbern"), WILLIAM BRICE FONVIELLE (640 acres of land where he now dwells; Lot No. 5 in Newbern), FRANCIS (510 acres of land where he now lives; lot No. 7 in Newbern), FREDERICK ("land where he now lives and lot in Newbern"), STEPHEN ("500 acres of land where he now lives on New River; my lower tract on Stone Bay"), JEREMIAH ("770 acres of land in the mouth of Stone Creek; upper part of the lower tract on Stone Bay; half lot in Newbern"). *Daughters:* MARY HATCH (two half lots in Newbern and two hundred acres of land on the North side of Nuce River), ELIZABETH HATCH (lot in Newbern by the West gate; 360 acres of land in New Hanover County), EASTER FONVIELLE (one lot in Newbern). *Granddaughter:* ELIZABETH FONVIELLE. *Wife:* MARY. *Executors:* JOHN, WILLIAM BRICE and FRANCIS FONVIELLE (sons). *Witnesses:* JOHN TURNER, WILLIAM BALLARD, ISAAC ESLECK. Will proven before JO. MARTIN.

FORASTER, JAMES.   Orange County.

September 5, 1755. December Court, 1755. *Sons:* WILLIAM, JAMES (to both is given land on Eno River), BENJAMIN and THOMAS ("my plantation"). *Son-in-law:* JOHN MANNING (200 acres of land on Eno River). *Wife and Executrix:* ANN. *Witnesses:* PATT MCCULLOCH, HUGH WOOD. *Clerk of the Court:* JAS. WATSON.

FORBES, JOHN.   Pasquotank County.

November 24, 1747. July Court, 1750. *Son:* JAMES. *Wife and Executrix:* MARTHA. *Witnesses:* PETER BROWN, SARAH BROWN. *Clerk of the Court:* THOS. TAYLOR.

FOREHAND, CORNELIUS.   Pasquotank County.

February 24, 1727. July 26, 1728. *Sons:* JOHN, CORNELIUS, JAMES, RICHARD, THOMAS. *Daughters:* ELIZEBETH and MARY FOREHAND. *Wife and Executrix:* ELIZABETH. *Witnesses:* ISAAC JONES, WILLIAM PHILLIPS and JOHN KIGHT. *Clerk of the Court:* R. EVERARDE. Executrix qualified before JOHN SOLLEY.

FOREMAN, JOHN.   Hyde County.

September 25, 1744. December Court, 1744. *Sons:* CALEB, JOHN FYDINGS FOREMAN, ALEXANDER, WILLIAM, JOSHUA, JOSEPH, LAZARUS (plantation on North side of Pongo Creek). *Daughters:* CHARITY LUCAS, DOROTHY KIPPS. *Wife and Executrix:* MARGARET. *Witnesses:* THOS. LOACK, ELIS LOACK, JOSHUA FOREMAN. *Clerk of the Court:* THOS. LOACK.

FOREMAN, JOHN TIDINGS.   Hyde County.

April 1, 1758. September Court, 1758. *Wife and Executrix:* MARGARETT. *Brother and Executor:* SANDERS FOREMAN. *Nephew and Executor:* JOHN FOREMAN (son of SANDERS). *Witnesses:* WM. DUNBARR, SAMUEL DUNBARR. *Clerk of the Court:* STEPHEN DENNING.

FORT, GEORGE. Chowan Precinct.

May 15, 1719. October 2, 1719. *Sons:* ELIAS, GEORGE, BENJAMIN, JOHN, SAMUELL. *Daughters:* PHELIS FIBATH, ELIZEBETH FORT, CATHERINE FORT, ALICE FORT. *Wife:* ELISABETH FORT. *Executor:* ELIAS FORT. *Witnesses:* WILLIAM BOON, NICCOLIS BOON. *Clerk of the Court:* R. HICKS.

FORT, JOHN. Craven County.

August 6, 1745. March Court, 1745–1746. *Sons:* ARTHUR, JOHN (plantation and mill at Conohoe) DUNLY (550 acres of land on lower side of falling Creek), MOSES (400 acres land on Cohary Swamp). *Daughters:* JERUSHAH FORT. *Wife and Executrix:* MARY. *Executors:* ARTHUR and JOHN FORT. *Witnesses:* JOHN PIPKIN, JOHN FORT, JUNIER. *Clerk of the Court:* JOHN RICE.

FORT, JOHN. Johnston County.

May 16, 1748. June Court, 1748. *Brothers:* MOSES and ARTHUR and DRULY. *Sister:* JERUSHA. *Executors:* WILLIAM HOLMES (father-in-law). DRULY FORT (brother). *Witnesses:* ROBERT BUTLER, JOHN PIPKIN, JETHRO PIPKIN. *Deputy Clerk of the Court:* RICHARD CASWELL.

FORT, RICHARD. Craven County.

March 6, 1745. December Court, 1746. *Brothers:* THOMAS, ELIAS and WILLIAM FORT. *Sisters:* SARAH WALL, MARY BYNUM, HANNAH PHILLIPS. *Nephew:* AUTHOR FORT. *Executors:* THOMAS and ELIAS FORT. *Witnesses:* JOHN PHILLIPS, ROBERT HOOD, AMBRUS PITTMAN, BENJAMIN BLACKBURN. *Deputy Clerk of Johnston County Court:* WM. CASWELL.

FORTSEN, MARY. County not given.

January 28, 1663. November 15, 1665. *Son:* THEOPHILUS. *Witnesses:* JU. LAWRENCE, WM. EMLY, ELIZABETH ROSY, ELLINER WARDELL. *Clerk of the Court:* THOMAS HARRIS.

FOSCUE, JOHN. Hyde County.

November 18, 1751. March Court, 1752. *Sons:* MOSES ("my mannor plantation"); JOHN, WILLIAM. *Daughters:* MARY and LYDIA FOSCUE. *Executors:* WILLIAM SLADE and ABIGAIL FOSCUE (wife). *Witnesses:* SIMON FOSCUE, MARY HAMILTON, URIAH COLLINS. *Clerk of the Court:* FRAN. EGLETON.

FOSCUE, SIMON. Hyde County.

November 11, 1751. December Court, 1751. *Sons:* RICHARD, BELL (my mannour plantation), SIMON, WILLIAM, LUKE, JOHN. *Daughters:*

MARY SILVERTHORN, SARA SANDERSON, BARBARIE BAILEY. *Executors:*
LUKE, JOHN and BELL (sons). *Witnesses:* URIAH COLLINS, ABRAHAM
EASTER, COMFORT RUE. *Clerk of the Court:* R. LOACK.

FOSTER, HANNAH.   Perquimans County.

June 27, 1727. July Court, 1728. *Grandson:* SAMUEL RIT. *Grand-
daughter:* COMFORT RIT. *Daughter-in-law:* JEMINAH RIT. *Executors:*
THOMAS AWEEDY, GEORGE GORDIN. *Witnesses:* THOS. and JEMINAH WRIT.
Clerk of the Court: R. EVERARD.

FOSTER, JAMES.   County not given.

October 23, 1726. March 29, 1727. *Friend:* SAMUEL WITE (son of "old
SAMUEL WITE"). *Wife:* HANNAH. *No Executor. Witnesses:* ELIJAH
STANTON, ELEZBETH STANTON. Will proven before *Governor* RICHARD
EVERARD.

FOSTER, JOHN.   Craven County.

October 9, 1754. November Court, 1754. *Son:* THOMAS. *Daughter:*
LYDIE FOSTER. *Wife:* ELIZABETH. *Executors:* JEREMIAH VAILE, ZECHA-
RIAH SAWTELL (uncle). *Witnesses:* WM. WRIGHT, CHARLES COGDELL, jun.,
WILL. MONAT. Codicil of even date makes bequests to *son*, PARKER,
wife, ELIZABETH, and *uncle*, ZACHARIAH SAWTELL. Same witnesses.
Clerk of the Court: SOL. REW. Coat of arms on seal.

FOSTER, ROBERT.   Bertie County.

February 12, 1739–1740. May Court, 1740. *Grandchildren:* JOHN
BROWN, ANN BROWN, JEMIMA COTTEN and SUSANNA COTTEN (land on
Meherin Creek), MARY BROWN. *Son-in-law:* ALEXANDER COTTEN. *Daugh-
ter:* ANN COTTEN. *Wife's grandson:* WILLIAM NIGHT. *Executrix:* WIFE
(not named). *Witnesses:* WM. WHITFIELD, CHRISTIAN DENTON, MAR-
GREAT LACEY. *Clerk of the Court:* JNO. WYNNS.

FOSTER, WILLIAM.   County not given.

October 9, 1687. *Son:* FRANCIS. *Daughter:* ELIZABETH FOSTER.
Wife: DIANA. *Witnesses:* JONATHAN HOLEMAN, WILLIAM HUGHES, SAM-
UEL PRICKLOVELL. No Executors. No probate.

FOURRE, JOHN.   Pasquotank County.

March 13, 1730. April Court, 1732. *Sons:* ISAAC ("ye mannor plantation"), NATHANIELL (plantation on Lettel River). *Daughters:* ELIZABETH
FOURRE, MAHER FOURRE. *Sister:* MARY CORRY. *Wife and Executrix:*
mentioned, but not named. *Witnesses:* JNO. MILLS, JO. CORRY, THOMAS
CORRY. *Clerk of the Court:* W. MINSON.

FOURREE, PETER.   Albemarle County.

August 6, 1697. November 3, 1697. *Son:* JOHN. *Daughters:* NICOLE, MARGUERITT, MARY. *Wife and Executrix:* CATHERINE. *Witnesses:* ANTHONY MARCKHUM, FRANCIS DELAMARE. *Clerk of the Council:* W. GLOVER.

FOX, JAMES.   Tyrrell County.

August, 1754. June Court, 1755. *Son and Executor:* THOMAS. *Daughters:* ANN FOX (*Executrix*), SUSANNA ALEXANDER, MARY WISE. *Witnesses:* JOSHUA ALEXANDER, ABRAHAM JENNET, BENJAMIN CHAPMAN. *Clerk of the Court:* FR. WARD.

FRANCK, JOHN MARTIN.   Craven County.

November 3, 1744. *Sons:* JOHN and EDWARD. *Wife:* SEVIL. *Daughters:* SUSANNAH, SEVIL, BARBARA and CATHERINE FRANCK, MARY WORSLEY, ELIZABETH HARROLD. *Executor:* FREDERICK ISLER. *Witnesses:* CHRISTIAN ISLER, MELCHER REMM, FREDERICK ISLER. The following lands devised: plantation called "Chinpin"; 500 acres on Trent River adjoining Chinpin; 640 acres commonly called "James Marchels plantation." About 20 negroes bequeathed. To each of children is bequeathed cattle and riding horses, and to each of sons is bequeathed a watch. No probate.

FRASER, DUNCAN.   Craven County.

September 8, 1773. September 23, 1773. *Legatees:* PEGGY and JOHN ("two mulatto children, the offspring of Phillis, a free negro woman now in my possession"). *Executor:* JOHN MCKAY of Newbern. *Witnesses:* THOS. SITGREAVES, JOHN SITGREAVES. Will proven before JO. MARTIN.

FRAZIER, DAVID.   County not given.

September 20, 1729. October Court, 1729. *Executor and sole legatee:* ROBERT BELL. *Witnesses:* JOHN CLEMET, GEORGE BELL. Will proven before RICHD. EVERARD.

FRAZIER, SAMUEL.   Craven County.

May 3, 1772. May 20, 1772. *Wife:* MARY. *Daughter:* MARY. *Sisters:* JANE FRUME and ELIZABETH HEADLY. *Father:* SAMUEL. *Mother:* ELIZABETH. *Executors:* JOHN HAWKS and JAMES COOR. *Will proven before:* JO. MARTIN. *Witnesses:* CORNELIUS GROENENDEYK, JNO. TURNER, JUN., JOSEPH RAWLINGS.

FREEMAN, JOHN.   Chowan Precinct.

February 19, 1729–1730. *Sons:* JOHN, JAMES, MATHEW. *Wife:* MARY. *Executors:* WILLIAM FREEMAN (brother), JOHN FREEMAN (son) and MICHEALL WARD. *Witnesses:* EDWARD WOOD, GEORGE WHITE, THOMAS ROWNTREE. No probate.

FREEMAN, JOHN.   Beaufort County.

December 19, 1752. March 13, 1753. *Son:* JOHN. *Wife:* MARY (lots
in Bath Nos. 16, 17 and 18). *Executors:* WIFE and SON, who are author-
ized and directed to sell 1300 acres of land on Tarr River and 1900 acres on
Core Creek for the payment of debts. *Witnesses:* JAMES CALEF, JAMES
PILKINGTON, WY. ORMOND. *Clerk of the Court:* WILL. ORMOND.

FREEMAN, WILLIAM.   Chowan County.

February 7, 1736. August 13, 1737. *Sons:* JOHN ("plantation whereon
he now lives"); WILLIAM, THOMAS, RICHARD, ARON, SAMUEL (plantations
to each). *Wife and Executrix:* MARY. *Witnesses:* WALTER DROUGHAN,
JOHN FREEMAN, JUNER, THOMAS ROWNTREE. Will proven before W.
SMITH, C. J.

FRENCH, RICHARD.   Perquimans County.

December 17, 1712. April 13, 1716. *Wife and Executrix:* ELIZABETH.
Witnesses: THOMAS BLICHENDEN, RICHARD SKINNER, JUNR., SARAH EVENS.
Clerk of the Court: RICH'D LEARY.

FRESHWATER, JOHN.   Pasquotank County.

April 9, 1753. July Court, 1753. *Sons:* WILLIAM ARMSTED FRESH-
WATER, JOHN FRESHWATER. *Daughters:* FRANCES ARMSTEAD FRESHWATER
and PHADDUS FRESHWATER. *Wife and Executrix:* ELIZABETH. *Witnesses:*
JOSEPH PENDLETON, ABRAHAM HOSEA, ANN PENDLETON. *Clerk of the
Court:* THOS. TAYLOR.

FROST, WILLIAM.   Albemarle County.

May 30, 1717. April Court, 1718. "Kisey River in Albemarle County."
Sons: JAMES, WILLIAM. *Daughters:* ELENOR FROST, MARY JOHNSON.
Wife: JOAN. No Executor named. *Witnesses:* WILL LATTIMER, JOHN
STANCELL. *Clerk of Chowan Court:* R. HICKS.

FRY, THOMAS.   Bath County.

March 18, 1724–1725. January Court, 1726. "Late of London in
Great Britain, now of Bath County in N. C." *Mother:* ELIZABETH FRY of
Milton in Southton. *Wife and Executrix:* ELIZABETH. *Witnesses:* PAT-
RICK MAULE, THOMAS HARDING, SARAH SWANN, JNO. BAPTA. ASHE. *Clerk
of the Court:* THOMAS JONES.

FRYLY, WILLIAM.   Tyrrell Precinct.

August 28, 1737. March 7, 1737. *Daughter and Executrix:* MARY JONES.
Grandsons: EVEN and FRYLY JONES. *Wife and Executrix:* GRACE. *Wit-
nesses:* STEVENS LEE, ROBERT MCBRIE, THOMAS LEE. *Clerk of the Court:*
ANDERSON LEGGET. Executor qualified before JAMES CRAVEN, *Clerk of
Court.*

FULLERTON, ROBERT.   Chowan County.

December 30, 1749. January Court, 1750. *Daughters:* MARY TOMSON, SUSANNA. *Wife:* MARY. *Executors:* JOHN THOMPSON and MATTHIAS FULLERTON. *Witnesses:* JOHN LEWIS, DAVID BUSH, LEWIS JONES. *Clerk of Court:* WILL. MEARNS.

FURBISH, THOMAS.   Pasquotank County.

April 26, 1732. July Court, 1732. *Sons:* WILLIAM, THOMAS, ISAAC. *Wife:* ABIGAIL. *Executor:* THOMAS BURGES. *Witnesses:* ALICE FURBISH, MARY JONES, JUDA HANBURY. *Clerk of the Court:* H. MINSON.

FUSSEL, THOMAS.   Parish of Cartee.

June 4, 1735. *Son:* AARON (*Executor*). *Daughters:* ELIZABETH WEAVER (husband GILBERT), MARY RAINWATER (wife of JOHN), MARTHA ARNAL (wife of JOHN), SARAH, ANN. *Witnesses:* WILLIAM WEAVER, RICHARD HEAD, JOHN COOK. No probate.

GAD, JAMES.   Pasquotank County.

March 1, 1699. July 15, 1701. *Wife and Executrix:* SARAH. *Sister:* ELIZABETH RIGGENS. *Brother-in-law:* WM. TRANES. *Sister-in-law:* MARJORY LOMBROSER. *Witnesses:* SAMUEL AKEHURST, STEPHEN SCOTT, KATHERN TONER. *Clerk of the Court:* THO. ABINGTON.

GAINER, MARY.   Edgecombe County.

October, 1751. November Court, 1751. *Legatees:* HESTER GAINER, MARTHA GAINER (sister), LIDDAY LASATER (sister), WILLIAM GAINER (brother). *Executor:* WILLIAM GAINER. *Witnesses:* ARTHUR BELL, MARTHA GAINER, ESTER BELL. *Clerk of the Court:* BENJAMIN WYNNS.

GAINER, SAMUEL.   Tyrrell County.

October 1, 1751. June Court, 1752. *Sons:* JAMES, SAMUEL, WILLIAM, THOMAS, ARTHER, ' JOSEPH, BENJAMIN. *Daughters:* MARY WHITTEY, ELIZABETH GRIFFEN, SARY GAINER. *Executors:* WIFE (not named), SAMUEL (son). *Witnesses:* WILLIAM GAINER, THOMAS GAINER, JOSEPH GAINER. *Clerk of the Court:* EVAN JONES.

GAINER, WILLIAM.   Edgecombe County.

March 11, 1746. November Court, 1750. *Wife and Executrix:* HESTER. *Sons:* WILLIAM and JOSEPH. *Daughters:* MARTHA, MARY, LYDDA, ELIZA. *Executors:* WILLIAM and JOSEPH (sons). *Witnesses:* JOHN COLLINS, WILLIAM BELL, MATTHEW LOWRY. *Clerk of the Court:* BENJAMIN WYNNS.

GALE, CHRISTOPHER.   County not given.

February 17, 1734. March 12, 1734. "Born at York in the kingdom of Great Britain, but now Collector of his Majestys Customs at the port

9

of Roanoak." *Executors:* SARAH CATHERINE GALE (wife), EDMOND GALE
(brother) and MILES GALE (son). *Daughter:* PENELOPE LITTLE. *Granddaughter:* SARAH CLAYTON. *Nephews:* EDMOND GALE, ROGER GALE.
Friends: DAVID O'SHEAL, of Nancimond in Va. and WILLIAM BADHAM.
Witnesses: E. MOSELEY, LOUIS ALLAIRE, MARGARET ALLAIRE. Will
proven before GAB. JOHNSTON at Edenton. Coat of arms on seal.

GALE, EDMOND.   Chowan County.

December 6, 1738. January 27, 1738. *Sons:* ROGER and EDMOND.
Wife and Executrix: MARY. *Witnesses:* THOS. BLOUNT, HENRY BONNER,
JOS. ANDERSON. Will proven before W. SMITH, C. J.

GALLEY, JOHN.   Pasquotank County.

October 6, 1729. October 15, 1729. *Sole legatee:* PATRICK LAUGHLIN.
Witnesses: THOS. GREORGY, RICHARD GREORGRY, JOHN BELL. *Clerk of
the Court:* WM. MINSON.

GALLUAY, THOMAS.   Chowan County.

July 27, 1753. October Court, 1753. *Executors and sole devisees:*
JACOB ODOM, MARY GALLUAY (mother). *Witnesses:* WILLIAM FRYER,
THOMAS FRYER, JEAMES FRYER. *Clerk of the Court:* WILL. HALSEY.

GAMBELL, ADAM.   County not given.

November 14, 1694. November, 1694. "Glaskow in the Kingdom of
Scotland." *Legatees:* JOHN GAMBELL, JOHN LOVE (both of London),
ADAM HILL (of Glascow), JOHN ARGY (of Arranthrew), ROBERT, THOMAS
and JOHN WEST (sons-in-law of THOMAS POLLOCK), CAPT. JOHN HUNT,
JAMES GAMBELL (brother, of Glascow). *Executors:* COL. THOS. POLLOCK,
CAPT. JOHN HUNT. *Witnesses:* HENE MCGREGORE, ELIZABETH HUNT,
MICH. LYNCEY (or LYNCH). Will proven before W. GLOVER.

GAMMIDGE, FRANCIS.   Currituck County.

October 19, 1719. January 6, 1738. *Cousin, Executor and sole legatee:*
HUMPHREY VINCE. *Witnesses:* MOSES PRISCOD, ISABELL PRISCOD, AND.
PEACOCK. *Clerk of the Court:* JOSN. SMITH.

GARDNER, JOHN.   Tyrrell County.

April 13, 1749. June 6, 1749. *Son:* JAMES SMEATHWICK GARDNER.
Daughters: DUNSILA and ANN GARDNER, JEMIMAH WALLBUTON, ELISA-
BETH MOY, ASHE MOY, REBECCAH WARD. *Wife:* ELISABETH. *Executors:*
JOHN WALLBUTTON, JOHN WARD. *Witnesses:* WILLIAM GARDNER, WIL-
LIAM GARDNER, JUN., EDWARD GRIFFEN. *Clerk of the Court:* EVAN JONES.

GARDNER, MARTIN. Bertie County.

October 6, 1755. January Court, 1760. *Sons:* JOHN, WILLIAM, JAMES, MARTAIN. *Daughters:* ANN, ANNAH and JANE. *Wife and Executrix:* ANNAH. *Executor:* NEEDHAM BRYAN. *Witnesses:* BENJAMIN CARTER, JOSEPH HOLLAND. *Clerk of the Court:* BENJAMIN WYNNS.

GARDNER, WILLIAM. Tyrrell County.

February 11, 1754. June Court, 1754. *Sons:* WILLIAM, THOMAS, SAMUEL, ISAAC ("ye manner plantation"). *Friend:* MARY COOPER. *Executors:* WILLIAM and SAMUEL GARDNER. *Witnesses:* THOMAS and ISAAC GARDNER, CLOANAH SMITHWICK. *Clerk of the Court:* EVAN JONES.

GARFORT, GREGORY. Albemarle County.

October 1, 1703. July Court, 1704. "To my mate WILLIAM PARGITER all my whole estate reall & personall * * * *." *Executor:* WM. PARGITER. *Witnesses:* FRANCIS TOMES, JR., MARGARETT TOMES, THO. HOUGHTON. *Clerk of the Court:* THO. SNODEN.

GARNER, JOHN. Northampton County.

March 23, 1746. February Court, 1755. *Son and Executor:* JOHN. *Grandsons:* JOHN GARNER and THOMAS MACKOONE. *Daughters:* MOURNING HARE, HANNER. *Wife and Executrix:* MARY. *Witnesses:* BENET SMITH, JOHN MACKCONE, SAMUEL WARREN. *Clerk of the Court:* I. EDWARDS.

GARNER, RALFE. Albemarle County.

May 31, 1695. August Court, 1695. *Daughters:* MARY, ELIZABETH and ESTOR. *Executrix:* JOAN GARDNER. *Witnesses:* THOMAS BARKOCK, GARRETT KEEN. EDWARD MAYO, *Clerk of the Court.*

GARRET, JOHN. Currituck Precinct.

January 27, 1734–1735. July 1, 1735. *Wife and Executrix:* SARAH. *Sons:* JOHN and JONATHAN. *Witnesses:* JOHN HAWREN, SAMUEL STEVENS, SAMUEL JARVIS. *Clerk of the Court:* JAMES CRAVEN.

GARRETT, THOMAS. Chowan Precinct.

January 30, 1733. January 31, 1734. *Sons:* HUMPHREY (*Executor*), THOMAS. *Daughters:* CATREN WHITE, SARAH GARRETT, ANN LASITTOR, JANE GARRETT, MARY GARRETT, LETTES GARRETT, PRUDENCE GARRETT. *Executor:* HUMPHREY GARRETT (son). *Wife:* mentioned, but not named. *Witnesses:* ORLANDO CHAMPION, WILLIAM HASE. Will proven before GAB. JOHNSTON, Jan. 31, 1734, at Edenton.

GARRET, WILLIAM.   Albemarle County.

   March 23, 1734. March 27, 1735. *Wife and Executrix:* MARY. *Other legatees:* JAMES CHASON, THOMAS HARDISON, RICHARD HARDISON, JOSEPH HARDISON. *Witnesses:* JOHN HARDISON, JASPER HARDISON. Will proven before GAB. JOHNSTON at Edenton.

GASKILL, WILLIAM.   Pasquotank County.

   May 4, 1703. July 20, 1703. *Sons:* WILLIAM, THOMAS. *Daughters:* JEAN and FANE GASKILL, ELIZABETH DURANT. *Wife and Executrix:* JANE. *Witnesses:* THO. ABINGTON, RICHARD NETT, WM. HARLOW. *Clerk of the Court:* THO. ABINGTON.

GASKINS, CATRIN.   Pasquotank County.

   August 25, 1755. September Court, 1755. *Son and Executor:* THOMAS. *Daughter:* ANN CARTRIGHT. *Witnesses:* SAMUEL DAVIS, JOSEPH PINDLETON. *Clerk of the Court:* THOS. TAYLOR.

GASKINS, FISHER.   Craven County.

   November 15, 1757. August Court, 1758. *Son:* JOSEPH. *Daughter:* ANN GASKINS. *Wife and Executrix:* ANN. *Executor:* THOMAS GASKINS (brother). *Witnesses:* ANN BRIGHT, SARAH ARTHER. *Clerk of the Court:* PETER CONWAY.

GASKINS, WILLIAM.   Pasquotank County.

   November 4, 1711. *Sons:* WILLIAM (plantation at mouth of Great Flatty Creek), BENJAMIN (plantation in "letel flate creek"). *Executrix:* WIFE (not named). *Witnesses:* EVAN JONES, JOSEPH PEGS. No probate.

GATHIN, EDWARD.   Craven Precinct.

   January 3, 1725–1726. March 5, 1725–1726. *Sons:* JOHN. *Wife:* ELIZABETH. *Executors:* JOHN and ELIZABETH (son and wife). *Witnesses:* ROBERT PITTS, MARY PITTS, CALEB METCALFE. *Clerk of the Court:* C. METCALFE.

GEORGE, DAVID.   Pasquotank County.

   February 29, 1747–1748. July Court, 1748. *Sons:* JAMES, DAVID ("plantation whereon I now live"). *Daughter:* MARGARET GEORGE. *Wife and Executrix:* ELIZABETH. *Trustees:* JOHN BARCLIFT (brother) and JOHN EVERIGIN. *Witnesses:* WILL GREGORY, STEPHEN SCOTT, SAMUEL SCOTT. *Clerk of the Court:* THOS. TAYLOR.

GEORGE, HENRY.   County not given.

   December 3, 1711. *Legatees:* SUSANNAH and ELIZABETH MITCHELL, WILLIAM MITCHELL, JOHN BROWNING, SARAH and JANE BROWNING. *Ex-*

ecutor: JOHN BROWNING. *Witnesses:* JOHN BROWNING, FECEY TICEHORE, JOHN JORDAN. Original missing. Recorded in Book 1712–1722, page 34.

GERFORT, GREGORY.   Perquimans County.

 October 1, 1703. July 11, 1704. *Friend, Executor and Sole Legatee:* WILLIAM PERGIFER. *Witnesses:* FRANCIS TOMES, MARGARET TOMES, THO. HAGHTON (or RAGHTON). *Clerk of the Court:* THOS. SNODEN.

GEWIN, CHRISTOPHER.   Edgecombe County.

 April 2, 1748. February Court, 1749. *Son and Executor:* CHRISTOPHER. *Daughter and Executrix:* MARY HARRELL. *Grandsons:* LOT, ABELL and CHRISTOPHER HARRELL. *Witnesses:* JAMES BRASWELL, BENJAMIN BRASWELL, ABRAHAM DEW. *Clerk of the Court:* BENJN. WYNNS.

GIBLE, DEDERICK.   Pasquotank County.

 June 25, 1720. July 19, 1720. *Sons:* DEDERIK and FREDERICK. *Daughter:* MARY GIBLE. *Wife and Executrix:* MARY. *Witnesses:* JOHANN BARNHART SCHONNEWOLF, ANN———. *Clerk of the Court:* W. NORRIS.

GIBBLE, DEDERICK.   Carteret County.

 August 25, 1754. September Court, 1754. *Sons:* DEDERICK, FREDERICK. *Daughter:* SUSANNAH GIBBLE. *Wife and Administratrix:* HANNAH. *Witnesses:* JOHN KILBE, DANIEL REESE, PRUDENCE LEWIS. *Clerk of the Court:* GEO. READ.

GIBSON, THOMAS.   Cumberland County.

 February Court, 1762. This is a nuncupative will proven by JOHN CAMPBELL, NEILL MCNEILL and CATHERINE MCNEILL. *Wife:* MARY. *Brother:* WALTER GIBSON. *Executors:* MARY and WALTER GIBSON and ROBERT SMITH. *Justices:* HUTON MCNEILL, ALEZR MCALISTER, FERGD CAMPBELL. *Clerk of the Court:* RICH'D GROVE.

GIDDINGS, THOMAS.   Johnston County.

 July 13, 1747. September 5, 1747. *Sons:* JACOB, WILLIAM, ISAAC, BENJAMIN, ABRAHAM. *Granddaughter:* ELIZABETH. *Executor:* JACOB GIDDINGS. *Witnesses:* GEORGE DYCKES, THOS. GRISARD, TH. LAMBERTHSON. Will proven before E. HALL, C. J.

GIDDINGS, WILLIAM.   Hyde County.

 November 10, 1757. March Court, 1758. *Sons:* THOMAS, JACOB, JOHN. *Daughters:* AGNIS, LIDEA and DARKIS GIDDINGS. *Wife and Executrix:* FRANCES. *Executor:* JOHN SLADE. *Witnesses:* TIMOTHY GREEN, BENJAMIN SLADE, KEATREN LEATH. *Clerk of the Court:* STEPHN DENNING.

GILBERD, THOMAS.   Chowan Precinct.

October 14, 1719. October 20, 1720. *Sons:* THOMAS ("plantation whereon I now live"), WILLIAM, JOHN. *Executor:* JOHN BRYAN. *Witnesses:* JOHN BRYAN, PHILIP BROWN, TOMSIN BROWNE. *Clerk of the Court:* THOMAS HENMAN.

GILBERT, FRANCIS.   Bath County.

December 30, 1725. July Court, 1726. *Sons:* FRANCIS and HENRY GILBERT. *Wife and Executrix:* ELIZABETH. *Witnesses:* WM. SPARRY, SAMUEL PEEK, WILLIAM MOOR. *Clerk of the Court:* THO. JONES (Clerk of Beaufort and Hyde prect. court).

GILBIRT, JOSIAH.   Perquimans County.

March 14, 1758. April Court, 1760. *Wife and Executrix:* SARAH. *Sons:* JOSEPH (*Executor*); JEREMIAH, THOMAS, JOEL. *Daughter:* JEMIMA COX. *Witnesses:* JOSEPH WHITE, MARY STEWART, DINAH GILBIRT. *Clerk of the Court:* MILES HARVEY.

GILFORD, JOHN.   Pasquotank County.

January 15, 1741. July Court, 1743. *Brother and Executor:* JOSEPH GILFORD (100 acres of land on the Northeast side of Pasquotank River known as "Cabbing Ridge"). *Witnesses:* BENNETT MORGAN, PETER SAWYER. *Clerk of the Court:* THOS. TAYLOR.

GILLETT, JOHN.   Craven County.

May 17, 1749. October 18, 1749. *Sons:* JOHN, PATTERSON, ANDERSON, MOSES. *Executors:* JOHN HARPER, PRISCILLA HALL. *Witnesses:* JOHN SIMMONS, EMMANUEL SIMMONS, MARY DUDLEY. Will proven before GAB. JOHNSTON.

GILLETT, JOHN.   Carteret County.

September 29, 1753. *Daughters:* BETTY and SARAH GILLET. *Brothers:* PATERSON and ANDERSON and MOSES GILLETT. *Executors:* MOSES GILLETT and MOSES HOUSTON. *Witnesses:* EML JONES, JOHN PEGGOTT, EZEKIL HUNTER. No probate.

GILLYAM, THOMAS.   County not given.

October 10, 1702. *Wife and Executrix:* SARAH. *Witnesses:* WM. WILKJON, JOHN TYLER, MARGRETT HOLBROOK. No probate.

GLADSTAINE, GEORGE.   Scuppernong, county not given.

November 6, 1712. *Legatees:* EDWARD PHELPS and MARY LAWSON. *Witnesses:* ROBERT HICKSON, JOHN HASTEL, SAMLL BRIFFET. Original missing. Recorded in Book 1712–1722, page 44.

GLAISTER, MARY.   Pasquotank County.

June 9, 1740. October Court, 1740. *Cousins:* HENRY PALIN (son of
Thomas), THOMAS PALIN (son of THOMAS), ANN READING and MARY
GLAISTER PALIN (daughters of THOMAS PALIN), MARY CLARK PALIN
(daughter of JOHN PALIN), JOHN PALIN (son of JOHN), SARAH PALIN, SU-
SANNAH PRITCHARD. *Other legatees:* ELISABETH SCOTT (daughter of STE-
PHEN SCOTT), MARY JONES, MARY MORRIS, SAMIVEL NEWBY, SARAH MAR-
TIN (wife of NATHANIEL). Other bequests made to negro slaves. *Execu-
trix:* SARAH and MARY CLARK PALIN. *Witnesses:* DAVID GEORGE, JOHN
HENLEY, JOSHUA SCOTT. *Clerk of the Court:* JAMES CRAVEN.

GLASCO, ROBERT.   Chowan Precinct.

March 26, 1690. October 6, 1690. *Wife and Executrix:* JAN. *Witnesses:* RICHARD SKEBELL, JOHN CROSSLLAN, RICHARD WOLLARD. *Clerk
of the Court:* JOHN WINGATE.

GLASGOW, WILLIAM.   Currituck County.

September 30, 1746. April 7, 1747. *Son:* CALEB GLASGOW. *Daugh-
ters:* SARAH, ABIAH, ELIZABETH, LOWDENNER. *Wife and Executrix:* SU-
SANNAH. *Witnesses:* WILLIAM SHERGOLD, PETER DAUGE, WILLIAM BRAY.
Clerk of the Court: RICHD. MCCLURE.

GLAUSTER, JOSEPH.   Pasquotank County.

January 27, 1718–1719. February 11, 1718–1719. *Wife and Execu-
trix:* MARY. *Daughters:* RUTH and SARAH GLASTER (or GLAUSTER).
Friend: NATHANIEL MARTIN. *Cousin:* THOMAS PALIN. *Witnesses:* JNO.
PALIN, CHAS. BULL, SARAH BULL. Will proven before JOHN ROBISON,
Justice of the Peace.

GLIN, RICHARD.   Chowan Precinct.

October 5, 1728. November 4, 1728. *Cousins (nephews):* WILLIAM
POWELL, son of sister ELIZABETH GLYN; JOHN THORNTON. *Executor:* JOHN
AVERETT. *Witnesses:* JOHN POWELL, JAMES STONE, JOHN ROBERTSON.
Will proven before RICHD. EVERARD.

GLISHAN, JOHN.   Runeroy Marshes, Bertie Precinct.

September 20, 1734. *Wife and Executrix:* JEAN. *Witnesses:* THEOPH-
ILUS WILLIAMS, LAZARUS BENTON, THOMAS JONES. No probate.

GLOVER (spelled "GLOVEYER"), WILLIAM. Northampton Co.

July 30, 1754. August Court, 1754. *Sons:* JOHN, WILLIAM, GEORGE,
JOSEPH, BENJAMIN. *Daughters:* LIDDY HARRIS, SARAH PARRISH. *Grand-*

daughter: MORNING HARRIS. *Wife:* MARY. *Executors:* JOHN and WILLIAM GLOVER (sons). *Witnesses:* JOHN DAY, SILVESTER EASTIS, SAMMUEL HARRIS. *Clerk of the Court:* I. EDWARDS.

GODBY, CARY. Onslow County.

September 17, 1758. February 28, 1759. *Son:* WILLIAM. *Daughters:* SARAH, ELIZABETH, RACHEL and MARY. *Wife:* ANN. *Executor:* JOHN STARKEY. *Witnesses:* HENRY GODBE, W. MOLSEED, JAMES FOYLE. Will proven before *Governor* ARTHUR DOBBS. *Secretary to the Governor:* RICHD. SPAIGHT.

GODFREY, FRANCIS. Albemarle County.

October 20, 1675. November 5, 1675. *Sons:* WILLIAM, JOHN. *Wife and Executrix:* JOANE. *Witnesses:* PAUL LATHUM, WM. WESTERMAN, JOHN CULPEPER. *Reg. Pub.:* THOMAS HARRIS. *Clerk of the Court:* RALPH COATES.

GODFREY, MATTEW. Craven County.

December 8, 1744. *Sons:* MATHEW, JAMES. *Daughters:* SARAH GODFREY, ANN GODFREY, FILLAMER GODFREY. *Executors:* JOSIAH MASTRES, ELISABETH SIMENS. *Witnesses:* THOS. MASTRES, DAVID RAMSEY, THOS. ABETT. No probate.

GODFREY, THOMAS. Perquimans County.

November 26, 1748. April Court, 1749. *Sons:* WILLIAM, THOMAS, FRANCIS ("my plantation"), JOSEPH. *Daughters:* SARAH GODFREY, ELLINOR GODFREY. *Wife and Executrix:* ELLINOR. *Witnesses:* JAMES GIBSON, BENJAMIN BIDGOOD, AMEY STAFFORD. *Clerk of the Court:* EDMUND HATCH.

GODLY, JOHN. Bertie County.

January 22, 1731–1732. May Court, 1732. *Sons:* NATHAN ("plantation on Tarr River known by ye name of Tubbago's folly"), JOHN (300 acres of land on South side of Swifts Creek), THOMAS ("plantation on Lookinglass Swamp whereon I now live"). *Daughters:* MARY and AMY GODLY. *Wife and Executrix:* KATHERINE. *Executor:* JOHN EDWARDS "of Roneoke." *Witnesses:* ANN WILLIAMS, SAMUELL HENLEY, WILLIAM PORGEN. *Clerk of the Court:* RT. FORSTER.

GODWIN, NATHAN. Beaufort County.

February 27, 1751–1752. June 9, 1752. *Executors:* JOSEPH BARROW, GEORGE SUGG, MARY GODWIN (wife). *Daughter:* MARY GODWIN. *Witnesses:* RICHD LATTEN, MARY WILLIAMS, ELISEBETH CHURCH. *Clerk of the Court:* WILL. ORMOND.

GODWIN, WILLIAM.   Bertie County.

May 4, 1752. May Court, 1753. *Sons:* BARNSBY, WILLIS, KEARNEY, JOSIAS. *Wife:* MARTHA. *Daughters:* JULIAN, SILVIA GODWIN, COURTNEY GODWIN, MARTHA GODWIN. *Executor:* JOHN BRICKELL. *Witnesses:* JOHN BROWN, RICHARD ROBERTS, GILSTRAP WILLIAMS. *Clerk of the Court:* BENJN. WYNNS.

GOFFE, ARTHUR.   Craven County.

November 29, 1725. June Court, 1737. *Friend, Executor and sole legatee:* JAMES WINRIGHT. *Witnesses:* TH. BELL, TH. WILSON, PATR. OGILBY. *Clerk of the Court:* JAMES COOR.

GOMM, JOHN.   Tyrrell County.

March 25, 1754. June Court, 1754. *Godson:* GODFREY GRAY, son of HENRY GRAY (tract of land known as Stults Hall). *Wife and Executrix:* MARY. *Witnesses:* JOHN PAGETT, SAMUEL NORMAN, JOSEPH NORMAN. *Clerk of the Court:* EVAN JONES.

GONSOLVO, LAURENCE.   County not given.

December 25, 1687. *Wife and child:* mentioned, but not named. *Witnesses:* WILLIAM PRIVIT, WILLIAM STEWART, RICHARD WILLIAMS. No probate.

GONSOLVO, LAWRENCE.   Albemarle County.

July 2, 1698. July Court, 1698. All worldly goods bequeathed to *father-in-law and mother.* *Witnesses:* THOS. NORSEM, ALICE CHEW, MARY NORCOMB, SARAH BLANK. *Clerk of the Court:* JOHN STEPNEY.

GONSOLVO, THOMAS.   County not given.

1698. Bequeathed all estate to *Mother and Father-in-law,* who are not named. *Witnesses:* THOMAS NORCAM, ALISE OHONE, MARY NORCAM, SARA BLANCK. *Clerk:* JOHN STEPNEY.

GOODALL, GILBERT.   Albemarle County.

September 3, 1712. *Legatees:* ELIZABETH HOSEA, THOMAS ARNOLD, JR., JOHN WINBERY, WILLIAM COLLSON, GEORGE TAYLOR, SARAH WHIDBE, CHARLES BARCLIF, GEORGE DURANT, JOHN STIVERS, RICHARD WHIDBE (*executor*). *Witnesses:* WILLIAM STEVENS, MARGARETT SLATER, MARY DURANT. Original missing. Recorded in Book 1712–1722, page 47.

GOREHAM, JOHN.   Chowan Precinct.

September 30, 1717. October Court, 1717. *Wife and Executrix:* ELINOR ("plantation on Queen Anne Creek I now dwell on"). *Nephew:* JOHN

GOREHAM (land on Darby Creek "called in Indian Renocooset," and also lands on Kesiah River). *Witnesses:* R. HICKS, JOSEPH YOUNG, JOHN CASS.

GORDEN, GEORGE.   Perquimans County.

August 14, 1748.   January Court, 1748.   *Sons and Executors:* NATHANIEL and WILLIAM ("land I now live on").   *Daughter:* HANNER.   *Granddaughter:* TAMER.   *Witnesses:* ELIJAH STANTON, WM. TOMBLIN, JEREMIAH HENDRECK.   *Clerk of the Court:* EDMUND HATCH.

GORDON, JOHN.   Perquimans County.

April 25, 1754.   April Court, 1758.   *Sons:* JOHN ("plantation whereon I now live"), GEORGE.   *Grandchildren:* MARY and JACOB GORDON, MARMADUKE NORFLEET.   *Executors:* JOHN and GEORGE GORDON (sons).   *Witnesses:* JESSE EASON, MOSES EASON, JOSHUA SMALL.   *Clerk of the Court:* MILES HARVEY.

GORDEN, NATHANIEL.   Perquimans County.

July 14, 1755.   January Court, 1756.   *Sons:* NATHANELL ("plantation and house whereon I now live"), GEORGE.   *Daughters:* ELIZABETH and TAMER.   *Wife and Executrix:* ANN.   *Witnesses:* ELIJAH STANTON, THOMAS, BARTLET, SAMUILL DAVIS.   *Clerk of the Court:* MILES HARVEY.

GORDON, PATRICK.   County not given.

(Attorney-at-law.)   November 5, 1773.   November 12, 1773.   *Wife and Executrix:* MARY.   *Witnesses:* JOHN BURNSIDE, ARCHD NELSON.   Will proven before JO. MARTIN.

GORMACK, PATRICK.   Pasquotank County.

April 9, 1708.   July 21, 1708.   *Wife and Executrix:* ELIZABETH.   *Other legatees:* JOHN and ALEXANDER CRUIKSHANK, sons of PATRICK CRUIKSHANK and JOANE GORMACK; CAPT. JOHN ROBISON.   *Witnesses:* RICHARD MADREN, GEORGE HARRIS, SR., ANN MADREN, GEORGE HARRIS, JR.   *Clerk of the Court:* J. PALIN.

GOSBE, JOHN.   County not given.

August 17, 1693.   October 2, 1693.   *Son:* JOHN.   *Executors:* SAMUELL and JOSEPH NICHOLSON (cousins).   *Wife:* mentioned, but not named.   *Witnesses:* RICHARD DORMON, FRANCES TOMES, JOSEPH SUTTEN.   *Clerk:* JOHN STEPNEY.

GOUGH, THOMAS.   County not given.

December 18, 1694.   April 8, 1695.   *Sons:* ROBERT GOUGH.   *Daughter:* SARAH GOUGH.   *Wife and Executrix:* SARAH.   *Witnesses:* ANTHONY DAWSON, JOHN WILLIAMS, JULIAN TAYLOR.   *Clerk of the Court:* JOHN STEPNEY.   *Clerk (probably of the Council):* W. GLOVER.

GOURLEY, JOHN.   Onslow County.

January 2, 1746. January 7, 1747. *Mother:* ELIZABETH GOURLEY. *Brother:* GEORGE GOURLEY. *Sisters:* GRISLE, MARY. *Executor:* SAMUEL JOHNSTON. *Witnesses:* JAMES GLAUSTER, GEORGE COHERNAN, JOHN DAVIS. Proven before GAB. JOHNSTON at Eden House. Testator left in hands of his executor "forty pounds currency or four pounds sterling to be laid out in Bibles and New Testaments to be distributed among poor children on New River."

GRAINGER, CALEB.   New Hanover County.

1763. October 31, 1765. *Sons:* CALEB (houses and lands on Smiths Creek and No. Et. River, north side of the Main or King's Road); CORNELIUS HARNETT GRAINGER (houses and lands on Smiths Creek on South side of the Main Road); WILLIAM (land on the Sound). *Daughter:* MARY GRAINGER. *Wife and Executrix:* MARY. *Executors:* MAURICE MOORE, CORNELIUS HARNETT, ALEXANDER DUNCAN. *Witnesses:* SAMUELL GREEN, ANTHONY WARD, JOSEPH STOCKLEY. Testator was a Mason and desired to be buried with Masonic honors. Codicil to will dated October 5, 1765, provides for child *in ventre sa mere*, and also for erection of sawmill. *Witnesses to codicil:* MARY GRAINGER, MARGARITT DOUGLASS, EDMOND FOGER. Will proven before the Lieutenant Governor, as evidenced by letter from FOUNTAIN ELWIN.

GRAINGER, JOSHUA.   New Hanover County.

Sons: CALEB and JOSHUA. *Wife and Executrix:* ELIZABETH. *Daughter:* ANN, ——— DeROSSET, JNO. SITE (?), ——— BRADDISH. No probate. Will almost illegible.

GRANBARY, SAMUEL.   Craven County.

January 15, 1760. *Sons:* JOHN ("plantation whereon I live"), WILLIAM. *Wife and Executrix:* FRANCES. *Executor:* WILLIAM SPEIGHT. *Witnesses:* DAVID LEWIS, WM. WEST, JOELL KING. No probate.

GRANGE, JOHN.   New Hanover County.

January 20, 1739–1740. June 4, 1740. *Sons:* JOHN and JAMES ("estate whereon I now live consisting of 1000 acres of land up the No. West River"), HUGH (640 acres in New Hanover County commomly called "Old Town"). *Executors:* JAMES GRANGE (brother), JOHN and JEHN DAVIS (brothers-in-law). *Witnesses:* WM. FORBES, CHA. CODGAN, PAUL GUERAR, ELIZ. GARRAD. Will proven before GAB. JOHNSTON.

GRANT, ALEXANDER.   Onslow County.

June 9, 1738. January 2, 1738. *Sons:* SOLOMON, ALEXANDER, JOHN. *Daughter:* MARY. *Neighbor and Executor:* JOHN STARKEY. *Wife:* mentioned, but not named. *Executors:* JOHN and ALEXANDER (sons). *Witnesses:* SAMLL. NOBLE, JOSEPH SMITH, RACLL. (RACHEL) NOBLE. *Clerk of the Court:* WM. CRANFORD.

GRANT, WILLIAM.   Dobbs County.

September 23, 1773. November 11, 1773. *Sole legatee and devisee:* JANE BRODIE. *Executors:* JANE BRODIE, THOMAS SCOTT. *Witnesses:* WILLIAM HOOKS, JOHN TILTEN. Will proven before JO. MARTIN.

GRAVES, RICHARD.   Craven Precinct.

April 11, 1730. September Court, 1730. *Sons:* THOMAS GRAVES. *Daughter:* MARY GRAVES. *Cousins (nephews):* RICHARD and FRANCIS GRAVES (sons of brother, THOMAS GRAVES). *Son-in-law:* FERNIFOLD GREEN. *Wife and Executrix:* HANNAH. *Witnesses:* JAMES GREEN, ——— JONES, JNO. RICHARDS. *Clerk of the Court:* C. METCALFE.

GRAVES, RICHARD.   Craven County.

May 3, 1774. June 4, 1774. *Nephews:* GRAVES BRIGHT ("my land & mills known as Jumping Run"), RICHARD FONVIELLE (son of WILLIAM BRICE FONVIELLE). *Wife:* ANN. *Mother:* SARAH FONVIELLE. *Executors:* SIMON BRIGHT, CHRISTOPHER NEALE. *Witnesses:* CHRIS'R DAWSON, THOMAS DRINY, SARAH BENSON. Will proven before JO. MARTIN. R. G. monogram on seal.

GRAY, ALEN (ALLEN).   Onslow County.

January 17, 1755. July Court, 1755. *Sons:* WILLIAM, JOHN, HUGH, THOMAS and JAMES. *Daughters:* JENOT, MARY, ELINOR and SARAH. *Wife and Executrix:* MARY. *Executor:* HUGH GIDDINGS. *Witnesses:* THOS. JENKIN, CASSON MOORE, SAMUEL ALEXANDER. *Clerk of the Court:* WILLM. CRAY.

GRAY, ANN.   Pasquotank Precinct.

March 4, 1731. April Court, 1732. *Sons:* WILLIAM and VALLENTINE WALLIS. *Daughters:* JANE, MARY and SARAH WALLIS, ANN KENNEKUM. *Executor:* WILLIAM WALLIS. *Witnesses:* JOHN MCKEEL, JOHN BOYD, RICHARD GRAY. *Clerk of the Court:* H. MINSON.

GRAY, GRIFEN.   County not given.

October 24, 1684. February 4, 1684. *Son and Executor:* GRIFEN. *Wife:* HANNAH. *Witnesses:* SAMUELL DAVIS, THOMAS FRINCH. Will proven before SETH SOTHELL.

GRAY, JAMES.   Onslow County.

October 21, 1757. January Court, 1758. *Son:* JAMES ("my manner plantation"). *Daughter:* ELIZABETH. *Wife and Executrix:* HANNAR.

Executors: THOMAS JENKINS and HENRY RHODES.   *Witnesses:* MARY GRAY, MARGET JENKINS, MARTHA KEEN.   *Clerk of the Court:* WM. CRAY.   Seal of testator bears impression IG.

GRAY, JOHN (SURVEYOR).   Bertie County.
September 20, 1745. November 16, 1750. *Sons:* JOHN ("my lands in Northampton and Edgecombe"), WILLIAM ("my plantation"). *Daughters:* JANET McKINZIE, BARBARA, ANN, LUCRETIA, AMELIA, LOUISA. *Wife:* ANN. *Executors:* EDWARD BRYAN (brother), THOMAS WHITMELL (nephew). *Witnesses:* JAS. WATSON, DUGALD McKITHAN.   No probate.

GRAY, RICHARD.   Pasquotank County.
October 6, 1729. October 15, 1729. *Wife and Executrix:* ANN. *Son:* RICHARD (land on the Sound Side and Flatty Creek). *Daughter:* ANN. *Overseer of son's estate:* LEWY MARCKHAM. *Witnesses:* CHARLES WEST, ALEXR. CRUICKSHANK, ANN CRUICKSHANK. *Clerk of the Court:* H. MINSON.

GREEN, JACOB.   Chowan County.
January 9, 1751. April Court, 1752. *Cousins (nephews):* RICHARD and WILLIAM GREEN (sons of brother, THOMAS GREEN). *Executors:* THOMAS GREEN (brother), THOS. HARRELL. *Witnesses:* JAMES WIAT, ANN EVANS, THOS. HARRELL. *Clerk of the Court:* JAS. CRAVEN.

GREEN, JOHN.   Bladen County.
April 28, 1749. June Court, 1749. *Sons:* JAMES, ROBERT, JOHN. *Daughter:* SARAH. *Wife:* mentioned, but not named. *Executors:* JAMES GRANGE and JAMES CARR. *Witnesses:* JOHN ELISS, JOHN STUBBS, JAMES JONES, DAVID MONLEY. *Clerk of the Court:* THOS. ROBESON.

GREEN, RICHARD.   Chowan County.
September 13, 1742. October Court, 1742. *Sons:* JOHN, THOMAS, LEONARD, JACOB, WILLIAM. *Daughters:* ELSE, CATHERINE and MARY GREEN. *Wife and Executrix:* ELEE (or ELSE). *Witnesses:* WILLIAM WHITFIELD, JOHN SPARKMAN, HENRY GOODMAN. *Clerk of the Court:* RICH'D McCLURE.

GREEN, SUSANNAH.   "Bath County, in Craven Precinct."
June 29, 1732. September 17, 1735. *Son:* JOHN BIGGS. *Granddaughter:* MARY BIGGS. *Executors:* JOHN BIGGS and ROBERT BOND. *Witnesses:* WILLIAM BRIGHT, ROBERT BOND. *Clerk of the Court:* CALEB METCALFE.

GREGORY, JUDATH.   Pasquotank County.
October 21, 1753. January Court, 1754. *Sons:* ISAAC, DEMSEY. *Daughters:* MARY, LOUCY. *Friend:* MARY LOYED. *Brother and Executor:* JOSEPH MORGAN. *Witnesses:* WM. BURGES, JOSEPH EVERIGIN, SAMUEL SCOTT. *Clerk of the Court:* THOS. TAYLOR.

GREGORY, MARGARET.　　　　　　　　　Pasquotank County.

February 3, 1746–1747. July Court, 1753. *Sons:* RICHARD, JAMES,
JOHN, CALEB. *Daughters:* MARY UMPHERIS, MARGARET BARBER, SARAH
GRANDY. *Granddaughter:* SARAH UMPHERIS. *Executor:* JAMES GREGORY
(son). *Witnesses:* JAMES FORBES, ELIZABETH FORBES, REBECCA HARD-
ING. *Clerk of the Court:* THOS. TAYLOR.

GREGORY, RICHARD.　　　　　　　　　　Currituck County.

October 7, 1758. December Court, 1758. *Sons:* GRIFFITH, CORNELIUS,
ROBERT ("Easter end of my plantation"), WILLIAM ("dwelling planta-
tion"), JOSEPH ("remainder of my land"). *Daughters:* JUDAH SAWYER,
EASTER SAWYER and BRIDGET SAWYER; RUTH GLASGOE, ANNE GREGORY,
CHARITY GREGORY. *"Dividers":* JAMES GREGORY (brother), ISAAC and
WILLIAM BRIGHT (brothers-in-law). *Executors:* JAMES GREGORY (brother),
ROBERT GREGORY (son). *Witnesses:* RICHD. STANLEY, THOMAS HUTCH-
INGS, AMEA HUTCHINGS. *Clerk of the Court:* WM. MEARNS.

GREGORY, SAMUEL.　　　　　　　　　　Chowan County.

February 5, 1744. August 4, 1747. *Sons:* SAMUELL and LUKE (107
acres of land in Perquimans County), THOMAS ("Hous & lot in Edenton
that I now dwell in"). *Daughter:* ELIZEBETH GREGORY. *Wife and
Executrix:* ELIZEBETH. *Witnesses:* DAVID BUTLER, JOSEPH MING. Will
proven before ENOCH HALL.

GREGORY, THOMAS.　　　　　　　　　　Pasquotank County.

April 10, 1736. June 23, 1740. *Sons:* NATHAN ("my manner planta-
tion"), SAMPSON, JACOB, JOB, RICHARD, WILLIAM. *Daughters:* ELISABETH
GODFREE, PRISILLA GRAY. *Grandson:* FREDERICK GREGORY. *Executors:*
JACOB and JOB (sons). *Witnesses:* JOHN BELL, JOHN ROBERTS, JOHN
BEARCOCK. Will proven before W. SMITH, C. J.

GREGORY, WILLIAM.　　　　　　　　　　Pasquotank County.

June 4, 1748. July Court, 1753. *Son:* JOHN (600 acres of land
on Cashie River, and 500 acres called "Goram's neck"). *Daughters:*
MARY and BARBRA GREGORY. *Wife:* SARAH. *Executors:* JOSEPH ANDER-
SON, DR. WILLIAM CALHEART, JOHN GRAY, SR., THOMAS WHITEMELL, JOHN
EVREGAN. *Witnesses:* ANN ANDERSON, ELISE SCOLLAY, THOMAS POL-
LOCK, Will proven in Chowan County before MATT. ROWAN. *Clerk of
Pasquotank County:* THOS. TAYLOR.

GREGORY, WILLIAM.　　　　　　　　　　Pasquotank County.

November 24, 1751. April Court, 1752. *Sons:* MARK (100 acres of
land on North River Swamp), DEMPSEY, ISAAC. *Daughters:* AFFIAH,

MARY, LOVEY. *Granddaughter:* ANN GREGORY. *Wife and Executrix:* JUDITH. *Witnesses:* JOHN RIDING, JOSEPH JONES, THOMAS RIDING. *Clerk of the Court:* THOS. TAYLOR.

GRICE, FRANCIS.   Johnston County.

April 28, 1750. December Court, 1750. *Sons:* THOMAS, ROBERT, JAMES, WILLIAM, JACOB, JOHN. *Daughters:* MARY LITTMAN, FAITH GRICE, ELIZABETH GRICE. *Wife and Executrix:* ELIZABETH. *Executor:* ROBERT (son). *Witnesses:* WILLIAM HALL, SAMUELL LITTMAN, JNO. SUTTON. *Clerk of the Court:* JAMES OATES.

GRIFFIN, EDWARD.   Tyrrell County.

April 27, 1753. March Court, 1754. *Sons:* EDWARD and WILLIAM (land in Bertie County on Crofoot Branch adjoining Mikell Hill's land). *Daughters:* MARY and SARAH GRIFFIN, ANN GRIFFIN, ELIZABETH COOPER. *Wife:* GRACE. *Executors:* JOHN GRIFFIN (brother), EDWARD COOPER. *Witnesses:* WILLIAM GARDNER, JOHN GRIFFIN, EDWARD COOPER. *Clerk of the Court:* EVAN JONES.

GRIFFEN, EPENETUS.   Tyrrell County.

July 30, 1755. December Court, 1756. *Sons:* ANDREW, EPENETUS, MATTHEW, JOHN (*Executor*). *Daughters:* SARAH COCKBERN, ELISABETH GRIFFEN, ANN GRIFFEN. *Wife and Executrix:* ANN. *Witnesses:* NATHL. COOPER, JOSEPH HILSON WORRIN. *Clerk of the Court:* FR. WARD.

GRIFFIN, JAMES.   On Kathrine Creek, Chowan County.

June 13, 1748. April Court, 1749. *Sons:* JAMES, JOSEPH and WILLIAM. *Wife and Executrix:* SARAH. *Witnesses:* WILLIAM HILL, WILLIAM COLTHRED, SUSANNAH OVERMAN. *Clerk of the Court:* WILL. MEARNS.

GRIFEN, MARTIN.   Chowan County.

June 3, 1718. July Court, 1718. *Sons:* EDWARD ("my plantation on the North side Cissai River), JOHN and WILLIAM (plantation on South side of Rokquis Creek), MARTIN (plantation on Rokquis Creek). *Daughters:* SARAH GRIFEN, ELIZABETH GRIFEN. *Wife and Executrix:* ELIZABETH. *Other legatees:* MARY STANSILL (daughter of MARY), WILLIAM STANSILL (son of JOHN and CATHERINE), JOHN RODGERS (son of THOMAS and FRANCES). *Witnesses:* THOMAS RODGERS, RICHARD PICKEREN, JOHN SMETHWICK. *Clerk of the Court:* R. HICKS.

GRIFEN, RICHARD.   Chowan County.

April 8, 1701. February 7, 1702–1703. *Executrix:* WIFE (not named). *Witnesses:* THOMAS JONES, WILLM. JONES, MARY SKITTLESHARP. *Son-in-law:* JOSEPH SKITTLESHARP. *Clerk of the Court:* N. CHEVIN.

GRIFFIN (spelled "GRIFFON"), WILLIAM.   Carteret Precinct.

June 20, 1681.   March 29.   *Wife and Executrix:* LIDDIA.   *Son:* WILLIAM.   *Witnesses:* WM. BATEMAN, ROGER MARTIN.   Will proven before THOMAS MILLER.

GRIFFIN, WILLIAM.   Bertie Precinct.

December 10, 1735.   February Court, 1735.   *Wife and Executrix:* MARY.   *Witnesses:* THO. WHITMILL, ALEX. THOMPSON, EDWARD MOORE.   *Clerk of the Court:* JNO. WYNNS.

GRIFFETH, JOHN.   Bertie County.

July 1, 1727.   February Court, 1727.   *Sons:* ARTHER (land on Meherrin Cypress Swamp), EDMOND (550 acres of land), JOHN (*Executor*).   *Wife and Executrix:* JEMIMA.   *Daughter:* MARY.   *Other legatees:* JOHN CLARKE, DANIEL RIGING.   *Overseer:* WILLIAM BOLDIN.   *Clerk of the Court:* RT. FORSTER.

GRIGGS, SAMUEL.   Kings County, New York.

September 3, 1749.   *Wife and Executrix:* ELIZABETH.   *Witnesses:* W. BETTS, JANE BROWN, MARY COGAN.   *Clerk of Craven County Court:* PHIL SMITH.   Will proven June 19, 1750.

GRILLS, RICHARD.

February 1, 1719–1720.   April 4, 1720.   *Wife and Executrix:* SARAH.   *Witnesses:* JNO. NEW, HANNAH DOWERS, PATRICK OGILBY.   Original missing.   Recorded in Book 1712–1722, page 221.

GRIMES, ABSOLOM.   Pasquotank County.

January 7, 1757.   March Court, 1757.   *Wife, Executrix and sole legatee:* LIDEA.   *Witnesses:* JOHN COX, J. BURGES.   *Clerk of the Court:* THOS. TAYLOR.

GRIST, RICHARD.   Beaufort County.

June 6, 1752.   March 13, 1753.   *Sons:* JOHN, WILLIAM, RICHARD ("my manner plantation").   *Daughters:* FRANCES NOUELL, MARY GRIST, ELIZABETH WALL.   *Wife and Executrix:* FRANCES.   *Witnesses:* WILLIAM WILLIS, WILLIAM LANIER, ELISABETH HILL.   *Clerk of the Court:* WILL ORMOND.

GROSVENOR, WILLIAM.   Perquimans Precinct.

November 5, 1702.   *Daughters:* SUSANNAH, ELIZEBETH and ESTER GROSVENOR.   *Wife and Executrix:* SARAH.   *Witnesses:* JONATHAN TAYLOR, J. WMSON. (WILLIAMSON).   No probate.

GUILLIAMS, GEORGE.   Chowan County.

September 22, 1746. April Court, 1747. *Sons:* ISAAC ("my manner plantation"), SAMUELL, GEORGE. *Executor:* SAMUELL GUILLIAMS (son). *Witnesses:* WILLIAM HUGHES, JUNR., GEORGE GUILLIAMS, SAMUEL GUILLIAMS. *Clerk of the Court:* HENRY DELON.

GUMBS, MATTHEW.   Chowan County.

February 9, 1754. April Court, 1754. *Sons:* ELISHA and ABRAHAM ("my manner plantation"). *Daughters:* SARAH, RACHEL, LEAH and RUTH GUMBS, MARY PATCHET. *Executors:* ELISHA and ABRAHAM GUMBS (sons). *Witnesses:* CHARLES ROBERTS, MARTHA JONES, MARY PREVIT. *Clerk of the Court:* WILL. HALSEY.

GUNTER, JOHN.   Beaufort and Hyde Counties.

March 28, 1722. July Court, 1725. *Executor and sole legatee:* JOHN ODEN. *Witnesses:* THOS. OLDNER, THOMAS WARSLEY, CHAS. ODEN. *Clerk of the Court:* JNO. SWANN.

GUTAN, JOSEPH.

January 30, 1770. *Wife's son:* JOHN SATCHWELL. *Wife's grandson:* JACOB DARDON. *Wife and Executrix:* REBECCA. *Witnesses:* ROBERT DIXSON, WALTER DIXSON, WY. ORMOND, ROGER ORMOND. No probate.

GUTHRIE, JOHN.   Pasquotank County.

October 12, 1748. April Court, 1750. *Uncles and Executors:* CHARLES KEEL and JOHN MCKEEL. *Cousin:* MARY MCKEEL. *Father-in-law:* HENRY PENDLETON. *Witnesses:* HENRY PENDLETON, MARY PENDLETON. *Clerk of the Court:* THOS. TAYLOR.

GUY, WILLIAM.   Perquimans County.

March 17, 1754. April Court, 1754. *Cousins:* JOHN and JAMES GUY (sons of JAMES GUY), BRIGGIT GUY. *Wife and Executrix:* MARY. *Executors:* THOMAS and CHRISTOPHER NICHOLSON. *Witnesses:* THOMAS CRAGHILL, SARAH BARROW, MARY KELLEY. *Clerk of the Court:* RICHD. CLAYTON.

HACKLEFIELD, JOHN.   Chowan County.

August 13, 1739. October 29, 1741. *Legatees:* THOMAS, WILLIAM and SARAH HOSKINS. *Executors:* WILLIAM HOSKINS and JOHN BENBURY. *Clerk of the Court:* J. MONTGOMERY.

HADLEY, EDWARD.   Hyde County.

January 22, 1740. June Court, 1743. *Wife and Executrix:* KEZIAH. *Witnesses:* GILBERT MCNARY, NATHANIEL TULE, JONATHAN BELL. *Clerk of the Court:* WM. BARROW.

10

HAIG, MARY, widow of WILLIAM.   Pasquotank County.

February 9, 1718. January 20, 1718–1719. *Son:* WILLIAM. *Other children:* mentioned, but not named. *Other legatees:* MARY WHITE, JOSEPH GLAISTER, MARY GLAISTER. *Executors:* GABRIEL NEWBY and JOSEPH GLAISTER. *Witnesses:* JNO. FOURRE, THOMAS PENDLETON, JOHN CARP. *Clerk of the Court:* W. NORRIS.

HAIG, WILLIAM.   Newbegin Creek, in Pasquotank County.

November 4, 1718. January 9, 1718–1719. *Wife and Executrix:* MARY. *Son:* WILLIAM ("my plantation"). *Daughters:* MARY, SARAH and ANN HAIG. *Witnesses:* JOHN MAN, JOHN CARP, RICHARD BROSSIERS. *Clerk of the Court:* W. NORRIS.

HAIG, WILLIAM.   Pasquotank County.

February 20, 1734–1735. July Court, 1735. *Son:* WILLIAM. *Wife:* SARAH. *Executors:* SARAH HAIG, WILLIAM HAIG, JOHN EVERIGIN. *Witnesses:* WILLIAM KELLY, JR., JOSEPH JORDAN, MARY JORDAN. *Clerk of the Court:* JOS. SMITH.

HAKONY, JOHN.   Albemarle County.

February 25, 1672. October 1, 1673. *Son:* JOHN. *Wife and other children:* mentioned, but not named. *Witnesses:* ABELL ROBETSON (?), FRANCIS MALLARD. Proven before JOHN JENKINS. *Clerk of the Court:* THOMAS HARRIS.

HALL, AN.   Perquimans County.

October 9, 1741. January Court, 1741. *Son and Executor:* SAMUEL. *Daughters:* SARAH WARRIN, MARY JENNET. *Granddaughter:* AN JENNET. *Witnesses:* THOS. CALLAWAY, JOSHUA HOBARD, SARAH CURLING. *Clerk of the Court:* EDMOND HATCH.

HALL, HEZEKIAH.   Carteret County.

January 9, 1733–1734. March Court, 1733–1734. *Daughter:* SARAH HALL. *Wife and Executrix:* ANN. *Executor:* DAVID SHIPURD. *Witnesses:* JOHN JERRETT, JNO. NELSON, J. HARRIS. *Clerk of the Court:* JAS. WINRIGHT.

HALL, JOHN.   Bertie Precinct.

August 9, 1736. February Court, 1736. *Wife:* MARY. *Executor:* JONATHAN STANDLEY. *Witnesses:* THOMAS WATSON, MARGRETT STANDLY, ELIZABETH KELLY. *Clerk of the Court:* JOHN WYNNS.

HALL, JOSEPH.   Onslow County.

December 16, 1747. July 5, 1748. *Daughters:* MARY BURNS, JANE
PARROTT. *Wife:* JANE. *Son:* EDWARD ("my plantation"). *Executors:*
JOHN STARKEY, EDWARD HALL (son). *Witnesses:* CHARLES SHARP, MARY
EVES, RALPH EVES. *Clerk of the Court:* THOS. BLACK.

HALL, NATHANIEL.   Pasquotank County.

January 31, 1734. February 17, 1734. *Sons:* JOSEPH ("my planta-
tion"), BENJAMIN ("plantation up the river" and also land at Banks called
Chickconacomock). *Wife and Executrix:* ELINOR. *Executor:* THOMAS
WEEKES. *Witnesses:* DAVID BALEY, ROBERT LOWRY, JR., PATRICK BALEY.
Proven before GAB. JOHNSTON at Edenton.

HALL, WILLIAM.   Bladen County.

February 6, 1764. April 21, 1765. *Wife and Executrix:* ELIZABETH.
Witnesses: A. GREEN, JAMES HENDERSON, MARY GREEN. Proven before
WM. TRYON at Wilmington.

HALSEY, DANIEL.   Albemarle County.

March 13, 1719. *Wife and Executrix:* MARY. *Witness:* THOMAS EVANS.
Original missing. Recorded in Book 1712–1722, page 222.

HALTON, ROBERT.   New Hanover County.

March 22, 1748. April Court, 1749. *Wife:* MARY (in England). *Sis-
ters:* SUSANNAH WILKINS, MARY, ELIZABETH. *Other legatees:* ELIZABETH
WILKINS (niece), MARY WILKINS (niece), GABRIEL JOHNSTON, DR. WM.
CATHCART, GEORGE GOULD, THOMAS BARKER, BENJAMIN HILL, JOHN
ASHTON (1000 acres of land on So. side Nuse River on Greens past.), SARAH
GRAVES, ROBERT HALTON, JR., son of SARAH GRAVES ("my seat called
Halton's Lodge"; two tracts in New Hanover Co. known as "Laban" and
"Brown Marsh," Laban lying on Mill Creek and Brown Marsh "on the
North East River of Cape Fear"). *Executors:* GABRIEL JOHNSTON, WM.
CATHCART, THOS. BARKER. *Witnesses:* SAML. ORMES, WM. CHURTON,
DAN. WELDON. *Clerk of the Court of Chowan County:* WILL MEARNS.

HAMAN, THOMAS.   Pasquotank County.

March 9, 1720–1721. March 30, 1721. *Son:* JOSEPH. *Wife and Exec-
utrix:* SARAH. *Daughters:* SARAH and JANE HAMAN. *Witnesses:* WM.
WILLSON, WM. BELL, JOS. BROWN. *Clerk of Chowan Precinct Court:*
R. HICKS.

HAMBLETON, JOSEPH.

April 1, 1737. April 11, 1737 ("late of Pensilvania but now of the Province of Carolina"). *Wife and Executrix:* RACHELL (plantation in Buck's

Co., Pa.). *Friends:* DAVID LOYD, CHARLES O'NEIL, EVEN EVENS. *Executors:* DAVID LOYD and THOMAS RUSS. *Witnesses:* WILLIAM SALTAR, MARY RUSS, CHARLES O'NEILL. Proven before GAB. JOHNSTON.

HAMBLETON, JANE.   Tyrrell Precinct.
    March 20, 173—. April 22, 1734. *Son and daughter:* JOHN GARRETT and MARY his wife (who are also appointed executors). *Witnesses:* SAMEL DURRANCE, MARY SKILES. Will proven before NATHANIEL RICE, *President.*

HAMBLIN, THOMAS.   Pasquotank County.
    December 31, 1757. March Court, 1758. *Son:* JOHN. *Daughters:* ELIZABETH and MARTHA HAMBLIN. *Wife:* MARTHA. *Executor:* CHARLES MARKHAM. *Witnesses:* LYMAN SPENCE, THOMAS MARKHAM, DAVID SINCLAR. *Clerk of the Court:* THO. TAYLOR.

HAMILTON, JOHN.
    Will torn and illegible.

HAMILTON, JOHN.   Nansemond County.
    February 25, 1706–1707. April 25, 1711. *Sons:* JAMES, WILLIAM and STEWART (land at Salem), JOHN and ANDREW. *Daughter:* MARY HAMILTON. *Daughter-in-law:* MARY HOBGOOD. *Wife and Executrix:* CATHERINE. *Witnesses:* RICHD. WYNNE, HENRY PULLEN, DANIEL ELLETT. *Deputy Clerk:* W. RAGSDALE. *Clerk of Court:* MICHL. ARCHIR. This is a copy of will.

HAMILTON, JOHN.   Bladen County.
    October 22, 1764. February Court, 1765. *Son:* JAMES. *Wife and Executrix:* ESTHER. *Other legatee:* ESABEL HAMILTON (probably daughter). *Executor:* WM. CREE. *Witnesses:* JOHN KENNEY, LEVI MOORE. *Justices:* GEORGE BROWN, JOHN SMITH, JOHN TURNER, GEORGE GIBBS, JOSEPH CLARK. *Clerk of Court:* MALUNN COLVELL.

HANBY, JOHN.   Perquimans County.
    May 5, 1752. July Court, 1752. *Son:* SALVANIAS ("the manner and plantation whereon I now live"). *Grandsons:* JOHN and DEMSIE HANBY. *Daughters:* MARY HANBY, HANNAH BISHOP, ELIZABETH GRIFFIN. *Friend:* ZACHARIAH NIXON. *Executors:* SELVANUS HANBY (son) and FRANCIS NEWBY. *Wife:* HANNAH. *Witnesses:* NATHAN NEWBY, SAMUEL ANDERSON, FRANCIS TOMES. *Clerk of the Court:* EDMUND HATCH.

HAND, PETER.   Craven Precinct.

February 1, 1730–1731. March 16, 1730–1731. *Wife and Executrix:*
ANN. *Daughters:* ELIZABETH, MARY and JEAN HAND. *Other legatee:*
RICHARD HART. *Executor:* JOHN DEPT. *Witnesses:* THOS. FOX, JAMES
GREEN, JOHN DEEP. *Clerk of the Court:* CALEB METCALFE.

HANCOCK, HECTOR.   Carteret County.

October 27, 1751. December Court, 1751. *Sons:* NATHANIEL, BENJA-
MIN, HENRY, JOSEPH, JOHN and WILLIAM. *Daughter:* MARY HANCOCK.
Wife: ANN. *Executors:* NATHANIEL and BENJAMIN HANCOCK (sons).
Witnesses: ANANIAS CAVENAGH, BENJAMIN HANCOCK, NATHANIEL HAN-
COCK. *Clerk of Court:* GEO. READ.

HANDCOCK, ELISEBETH.   Craven County.

January 20, 1743–1744. June 20, 1744. *Sons and Executors:* SIMON
and WM. BRIGHT. *Daughter:* LEDLAY HANDCOCK. *Witnesses:* WALTER
JONES, FRANCIS HODGES, HOWEL JONES. *Clerk of Court:* N. ROUTLEDGE.

HANDCOCK, WILLIAM.   Craven Precinct.

October 9, 1722. March 16, 1730–1731. *Son:* WILLIAM. *Grandsons:*
JOHN HANDCOCK ("my plantation"), WILLIAM HANDCOCK. *Granddaugh-
ters:* ELIZABETH and MARY HANDCOCK. *Wife and Executrix:* ELENOR.
Executors: WILLIAM HANDCOCK (son), RICHARD GRAVES, JOHN SLOCUMB
(cousin). *Witnesses:* JAMES KEITH, MOSES THOMAS, THOMAS KNIGHT.
Clerk of the Court: CALEB METCALFE.

HANDWORKER, DANIEL.   Perquimans County.

March 7, 1729–1730. April 4, 1730. *Wife, Executrix and sole legatee:*
KATHERINE. *Witnesses:* CHARLES DENMAN, SARAH DENMAN. Will
proven before RICHARD EVERARD.

HANNIS, JOSEPH.   Craven County.

June 30, 1745. September 7, 1745. "Christ Church Parish & County
of Craven." *Son and Executor:* JOSEPH. *Wife and Executrix:* CATHERINE.
Witnesses: FRANCIS STRINGER, WM. THOMPSON, JOSEPH CARRUTHERS,
GEORGE WIGGINS. *Clerk of the Court:* JNO. RICE.

HARBERT, EDWARD.   Craven County.

January 20, 1754. May Court, 1754. *Sons:* EDWARD ("200 acres of
land on the south side of Contentny"), JOHN. *Four other children:* mentioned, but not named. *Executor:* EDWARD HARBERT (son). *Witnesses:*
JAMES COMBS, HENRY GIBBINS, WILLIAM RIGGSBY. *Clerk of the Court:*
SOL. REW.

HARDESTY, THOMAS.   Carteret County.

July 16, 1758. September Court, 1758. *Sons:* THOMAS (land at Michael's Bridge), ROBERT HARDESTY, JOSEPH HARDESTY, SAMUEL HARDESTY. *Daughters:* MARY, LUCY and ANNA HARDESTY. *Wife and Executrix:* DOROTHA. *Witnesses:* LEWIS WELCH, HENRY CHEW, ROBERT WELCH. *Clerk of Court:* WILLIAM ROBERTSON.

HARDIN, WILLIAM.   Currituck County.

July 30, 1746. October 5, 1748. *Granddaughters:* JANE and ELIZABETH DUDLEY ("my land on Knott's Island whereon I live"). *Daughter:* ELISABETH DUDLEY. *Executors:* JANE HARDEN (wife) and HENRY WHITE. *Witnesses:* WILLIAM WHITE, THOMAS DUDLEY, JR., THOMAS WILLIAMSON. *Clerk of Court:* RICH'D McCLURE.

HARDING, JOSIAH.   Northampton County.

July 1, 1752. November Court, 1756. *Sons:* JOSIAH, THOMAS, JAMES. *Wife and Executrix:* ANN. *Witnesses:* J. EDWARDS, WM. WINBORNE. *Clerk of the Court:* I. EDWARDS.

HARDING, MARY.   Perquimans County.

October 22, 1743. November 8, 1744. *Legatees:* SARAH SKINNER, RICHARD SKINNER, SR., ZACHARIAH and SARAH SKINNER (children of JAMES). *Executor:* RICHARD SKINNER, SR. *Witnesses:* RICHARD SKINNER, JR., SAM'LL MOORE, SARAH CREECEY. Will proven before E. MOSELEY, *Chief Justice.*

HARDING, RICHARD.   Perquimans County.

December 6, 1741. January Court, 1741. *Wife and Executrix:* MARY. *Executor:* THOMAS PEIRCE. *Other legatees:* THOMAS GILBORD and JAMES SKINER. *Witnesses:* JOSEPH ASHLEY, PETER JONES, THOMAS PEIRCE, JR. *Clerk of the Court:* EDMUND HATCH.

HARDISON, JASPER.   Albemarle County.

May 8, 1733. November 5, 1733. *Sons:* JOHN ("land on South side of Deep run"), JASPAR (200 acres of land on Cheat Neck), CHARLES ("piece of land called Cheat Neck Island"), JOSUAH and THOMAS (land on Cheat Neck branch), RICHARD and JOSEPH ("rest of plantation known by the name of Roses Plantation"). *Other legatees:* MARY CARKEET, JUDAH SUTTON. *Executors:* MARY HARDISON (wife), JOHN HARDISON (son). *Witnesses:* JOSEPH HUDSON, SAMUEL DURRANCE. Will proven before GEO. BURRINGTON.

HARDY, JOHN.   Chowan County.

January 19, 1719. March 16, 1719. *Brothers:* WILLIAM, THOMAS and JACOB HARDY. *Daughters:* ELIZABETH and MARY. *Wife and Executrix:*

REBECCAH. *Other legatees:* KATHERINE STANCELL, RICHARD PICKERING, JOHN BUTLER. *Executors:* WILLIAM HARDY, THOMAS POLLOCK and ROBERT WEST. *Witnesses:* JOHN HOLBROOK, LAURENCE SARTON, JOHN LUERTON. Proven before C. EDEN.

HARDY, RICHARD.   Wilmington, New Hanover County.

May 20, 1758. August 6, 1758. *Executors:* DANIEL DUNBIBIN, FRANCIS BEITELLE (uncle). *Wife:* SARAH. *Witnesses:* JAMES GREGORY, AO. ROUTLEDGE, ZACK WEEKS. No signature of probate officer.

HARE, EDWARD.   Chowan County.

August 27, 1756. October Court, 1757. *Sons:* EDWARD (lands in Chowan), JOHN (lands in Bertie), THOMAS, BRYAN. *Daughters:* CHRISTIAN WEST, MARY BURGES, ANN SCOT. *Wife:* MARY. *Executors:* JOHN and EDWARD HARE (sons). *Witnesses:* WILLIAM SKINNER, JOSEPH ROOKS, JOSEPH SPEIGHT. *Clerk of the Court:* THOMAS JONES.

HARE, EDWARD.   Hertford County.

May 16, 1772. April 22, 1777. *Legatees:* THOMAS HARE (brother), MARY HARE (niece), WYNNE WEST (daughter of PETER WEST), MARY BURGES (sister), ANN SCOT (sister), LUKE LEWIS (son of JOHN LEWIS), LUCRETIA HARE (daughter of BRYAN HARE), EDWARD BRYAN HARE (son of BRYAN HARE), JOHN PIPKEN (son of ISAAC PIPKIN), BRAY WARREN (son of JOSEPH WARREN), EFF LEWIS (son of JOHN LEWIS), JOHN MILLER, EDWARD WARREN, JOHN HARE (brother), MILLS LEWIS (son of JOHN LEWIS), WILLIAM WARREN (son of EDWARD WARREN), PHILLIP LEWIS (son of JOHN LEWIS), JOHN GATTELLEN, ISAAC PIPKEN, JESSE BARNES, FRANCIS SPEIGHT, HENRY SPEIGHT, JOHN GOODMAN, BENJ. WYNNS, JUNR., SOLOMON KING, WILLIAM WEST. *Executor:* THOMAS HARE. *Witnesses:* SOLOMON KING, JOHN LEWIS, ISAAC PIPKIN, EDWARD WARREN. Will proven before *Gov.* RD. CASWELL at New Bern.

HARISON, JOHN.   Albemarle County.

February 18, 1693. April Court, Chowan, 1694. *Son:* WILLIAM HARISON. *Son:* JOHN HARISON. *Daughter:* ELIZABETH HARISON. *Son:* THOMAS HARISON. *Executrix:* MARY HARISON. *Witnesses:* GEO. HARDIE and JOHN WATKINS. *Clerk of the Court:* HENDERSON WALKER.

HARKEL, GEORGE.   Craven County.

May 2, 1746. March 17, 1746. *Sons:* GEORGE ("plantation whereon I now dwell"), JOSEPH. *Daughters:* MIRIAM, MARGARET and MARY HARKEL. *Wife and Executrix:* ELISABETH. *Executor:* JAMES CONAWAY. *Witnesses:* NICHOLAS HARPER, AMOS CUTHRIS, ISAAC BRAWLER. *Clerk of Court:* JNO. RICE.

HARKER, ELIZABETH.   Carteret County.

April 12, 1777. June 9, 1777. *Sons:* EBENEZER, JAMES, ZACHARIAH.
Daughter: SARAH FRESHWATER. *Other legatee:* JOHN BROOKS. *Executors:*
JAMES and ZACHARIAH HARKER (sons). *Witnesses:* JOSEPH YEOMAN,
SARAH HARKER, ELIAS REES. Will proven before RD. CASWELL.

HARMAN, CALEB.   Perquimans County.

October 2, 1773. March 9, 1774. *Sons:* ROBERT and JAMES ("my
plantation to be equally divided between them"), CALEB and JOSHUA.
Daughter: ORPAH HARMAN. *Wife and Executrix:* ELIZABETH. *Executor:*
THOMAS HARMAN (brother). *Witnesses:* J. CARRUTHERS, ZEBULON CAL-
LOWAY, MARY HARMAN. Proven before Jo. MARTIN.

HARMAN, ROBERT.   Perquimans County.

January 7, 1758. July Court, 1758. *Sons:* CALEB ("my plantation"),
JOHN (land in Beaver Cove), STEPHEN, THOMAS. *Daughter:* MARY HAR-
MAN. *Trustees and Guardians:* FRANCIS JONES, DANIEL SAINT and JOHN
WHITE, son of JOSEPH. *Wife and Executrix:* ELIZABETH. *Executors:*
CALEB HARMAN, JOHN WHITE. *Witnesses:* THOMAS LONG, ELISABETH
LONG, JOSEPH WHITE. *Clerk of the Court:* MILES HARVEY.

HARRELL, ABRAHAM.   Bertie County.

May 5, 1755. July Court, 1755. *Sons:* ABBE (or ABLE), JOHN ("my
manner plantation"), LOTT, ZACHARIAH, CHRISTOPHER. *Daughters:* ABBA-
GILL, GRACE, SUSANNAH. *Executors:* ABLE and JOHN HARRELL. *Witnesses:* GEORGE HOUSE, EDWARD TOOLE, ISRAEL HARDY HARRELL. *Clerk
of the Court:* BENJAMIN WYNNS.

HARRELL, EDWARD.   Bertie County.

August 17, 1752. May Court, 1754. *Sons:* HENRY, JOSHEWA, THOMAS.
Grandson: JESSE HARRELL. *Daughters:* MARY and REBECCA ANDREWS.
Wife: ANN. *Executors:* HENRY HARRELL (son) and HENRY ANDREWS
(son-in-law). *Witnesses:* JOHN HARRELL, ROBERT HOUSE, GEORGE HOUSE.
Clerk of the Court: SAML. ORMES.

HARRELL, JOHN.   Bertie County.

November 8, 1755. January Court, 1756. *Sons:* GEORGE (land between
THOS. WILLIAMS and JNO. RHODES), JESSE, ELISHA and BENJAMIN. To
these four sons is bequeathed several tracts bounded and described in the
will. *Daughter:* MARY. *Wife:* MARY. *Executors:* GEO. HARRELL (son),
JESSE and ISRAEL HARDY HARRELL (brothers), RICHARD WILLIAMS,
THOMAS WILLIAMS, WM. ANDREWS, JOHN RHODES. *Witnesses:* THOMAS
WILLIAMS, WM. ANDREWS, JOHN SKINNER. *Clerk of Court:* BENJAMIN
WYNNS.

HARRELL, JOHN.   Bertie County.

November 1, 1756. April Court, 1759. *Sons:* JESSE and DAVID (plantation to each, and three negroes), JOSIAH (land bought of THOMAS BARKER), EZEKIEL (160 acres of land). Negroes bequeathed to each of sons. *Grandsons:* ESIAS HARRELL (plantation "whereon JONATHAN SPIVEY now lives who married the widow of Esias Harrell deceased"). *Granddaughter:* SARAH HARRELL (one negro). Copper still bequeathed to four sons. *Executors:* JESSE, DAVID and JOSIAH. *Witnesses:* WM. WILLIAMS, EDWARD TOOLE, JONATHAN TOOLE. *Clerk of the Court:* BENJAMIN WYNNS. Codicil makes bequests to THOMAS WILLIAMS, husband of daughter, SARAH. Same witnesses to codicil.

HARRELL, JOSIAH.   Bertie County.

March 30, 1773. November 12, 1773. *Sons:* SOLOMON (land in Renneroy Marshes), JOSIAH ("my plantation"), WILLIAM. *Wife:* ANN. *Executors:* EDWARD TOOL, NOAH HINTON. *Witnesses:* JAMES CHURCHWELL, JONATHAN TOOL, MARY TOOL. Will proven before Jo. MARTIN.

HARRINGTON, HUMPHREY.   Perquimans Precinct.

November 2, 1713. *Daughter:* ANN. *Daughter-in-law:* ANN MAJOR. *Wife and Executrix:* ELIZABETH. *Witnesses:* RICHARD MORRIS and FRANCIS THOMAS. Original missing. Recorded in Book 1712-1722, page 18

HARRIS, JAMES.   Edgecombe County.

January 10, 1749-1750. February Court, 1749. *Sons:* JAMES ("my plantation"), ELI. *Wife and Executrix:* CHEARY. *Executor:* MATHEW JOYNER. *Witnesses:* WM. SKINNER, JOHN BLOUNT, JOHN CRUMPTON. *Clerk of the Court:* BENJAMIN WYNNS.

HARRIS, JOHN.   Craven County.

January 22, 1749. March Court, 1749. *Legatees:* BRICE and JOHN FONVIELLE, WM. BARRAN, JR. (land on Batchelor's Creek). *Executors:* JOHN FONVIELLE, THOMAS GRAVES. *Witnesses:* JOHN MCGIBBINS, AMBROSE FIELD, DOROTHY ROLTON. *Clerk of the Court:* PHIL SMITH.

HARRIS, THOMAS.   Currituck County.

November 7, 1749. January Court, 1749. *Wife:* ELENDER. *Son and Executor:* THOMAS. *Witnesses:* STEPHEN WILLIAMS, JOHN LURRY, LEVI STEWART. *Clerk of the Court:* RICH'D MCCLURE.

HARRISON, DANIEL.   Chowan County.

January 14, 1726-1727. *Son:* JOSEPH (100 acres of land). *Wife and Executrix:* ELIZABETH. *Friend:* HILL SAVAGE. *Executor:* EDWARD PADGGETT. *Witnesses:* WILLIAM WILLIAMS, JNO. FALCONAR, MARTHA HAMMOND. No probate.

HARRISON, JOHN.

November 19, 1710. *Brother and Executor:* THOMAS HARRISON. *Witnesses:* ANN MITCHELL and WILLIAM MITCHELL. Original missing. Recorded in Book 1712–1722, page 32.

HARRISON, ROBERT.

March 9, 1713–1714. *Sons:* ROBERT (land bought of GARRETT PURSELL), JOSEPH. *Daughters:* SARAH and ELIZABETH HARRISON. *Wife and Executrix:* SARAH. *Executor:* ROBERT HARRISON. Executors to sell land upon River adjoining CORNELIUS JONES. *Witnesses:* DAN'L GUTHRIE, ELIZABETH JONES, WILL VAUGHAN. No probate. Anchor on seal.

HARRISON, VINES.   Chowan County.

February 25, 1738. March 24, 1738. *Brothers:* WILLIAM and JOSHUAY HARRISON. *Executors:* EDMOND HARRISON. *Sister:* SARAH FELTE. *Witnesses:* THOMAS PEIRCE, THOMAS EVERENDEN, EDWARD LISTER. Proven before W. SMITH, C. J.

HART, MARY.   Northampton County.

July 12, 1750. November Court, 1751. *Sons:* BENJAMIN, JOSEE, JOHN, DAVID. *Daughters:* SARAH HART, LUSEE HART. *Executors:* JOHN LAMAN and GREEN HILL. *Witnesses:* JAMES WRIGHT, JOHN GOODEN, JESSE HART, GEORGE BRACE. *Clerk of the Court:* I. EDWARDS.

HART, JOHN.   Bertie Precinct.

November 13, 1741. May Court, 1746. *Sons:* BENJAMIN (plantation "at Pattycasey"), JESSE (plantation on South side of Tarr River), JOHN (land on Town Creek), DAVID ("plantation whereon I now live"). *Daughters:* SARAH and LUCE. *Other legatee:* THOMAS FOXHALL. *Executors:* ETHELDRED RUFFIN and ROBERT RUFFIN. *Witnesses:* JOHN LAMON, HOWILL BROWNE, JOHN DAVISON. *Clerk of Northampton Court:* RT. FORSTER.

HART, THOMAS.   Northampton County.

March 6, 1748. August Court, 1751. *Son and Executor :* HENRY (plantation in "The Meadowes"). *Grandchildren:* JOHN SANDERS, SARAH SANDERS, EURIDICE, THOMAS, MARY and ROSE SANDERS. *Wife:* MARY. *Witnesses:* JNO. SIMPSON, HOWILL BROWNE. *Clerk of the Court:* I. EDWARDS.

HARTLEY, FRANCIS.   Albemarle County.

February 4, 1691–1692. May 2, 1692. *Wife and Executrix:* SUSANNAH. *Other legatees:* ELIZABETH GLASCOINE, ELIZABETH GRAY, JABUS ALFORD, WILLIAM MORRIS, GEORGE MASCHAMP. *Executor:* THOMAS HARVEY.

Witnesses: G. MASCHAMP, RICHARD SLATER, FRANCIS PARROTT, ANN DURANT, THOMAS DURANT. *Clerk of the Court:* HENDERSON WALKER.

HARVEY, DOROTY.   Pasquotank County.

November 14, 1682.   January 20, 1682.   *Brother and Executor:* THOMAS TOOKE of Isle of Wight County in Virginia.   *Children of Brother:* JAMES, THOMAS, DOROTEY, JOHN, ABRAHAM, JOANE and WILLIAM TOOKE.   *Cousin:* THOS. HARVEY.   *Niece:* MARY CREW.   *Other legatees:* DORCAS, wife of THOMAS JARVIS, MARGARET, wife of CAPT. WM. CRAFORD; ABIAH, wife of CHRISTOPHER MERCHANT.   *Witnesses:* WILLIAM MICHALLE, JOHN HAWKINS, CHRISTOPHER MERCHANT, JOHN COLPEPER.   Proven before SETH SOTHELL.   This is a copy of will and not the original.

HARVEY, JOHN.   Hyde County.

February 26, 1759.   June Court, 1759.   *Sons:* JOSHUA, RICHARD, JOHN MARK HARVEY, ARTHUR.   *Daughters:* MARY MARTIN, REBECCA HARVEY. *Wife:* FRANCIS.   *Grandson:* JOHN HARVEY (house and lot in Woodstock). *Brother:* RICHARD HARVEY.   *Executors:* RICHARD and JOHN MARK HARVEY (sons).   *Witnesses:* STEPHEN DENNING, WILLIAM WEBSTER, JOHN WRIGHT.   *Clerk of the Court:* STEPN. DENNING.

HARVEY, RICHARD.

February 22. 1732–1733.   *Sons:* JOHN, RICHARD, PETER, SAMUEL, JAMES, JOSIAS.   *Daughter:* BRIDGET HARVEY.   *Wife and Executrix:* MARY.   *Witnesses:* SAMLL HARVEY, JOHN MILLS, ANDREW CONNER.   *Clerk of the Court:* JNO. COLLISON.

HARVEY, THOMAS.   Albemarle County.

March 31, 1696.   November 2, 1699.   *Wife and Executrix:* SARAH. *Son:* THOMAS (plantation called "ye Quarter").   *Daughter:* MARY HARVEY (land called Faulks Point and land on Perquimans River).   *Nephew:* THOMAS HARVEY.   *Brother:* ROBERT HARVEY.   *Witnesses:* HENRY NORMAN, ROBERT FENDALL, JOHN PEIRT, W. GLOVER.   Codicil to will dated March 23, 1698–1699.   Appoints COL. WM. WILKINSON executor of estate of JOHN HARVEY, dec'd, of which estate the testator was executor at the time of his death.   *Witnesses to Codicil:* RICHARD FRENCH, RUTH LUKER.   Codicil proven before HENDERSON WALKER.

HARVEY, THOMAS.   Perquimans County.

April 10, 1729.   November 10, 1729.   *Sons:* THOMAS ("Plantation whereon I now live"), JOHN (plantation called the Quarter), BENJAMIN (plantation called Foulks (or Foleks) Point), MILES (land on Chowan River in Rockahock Neck bought of SAMUEL WOODARD).   *Brother:* MILES GALE of Boston.   *Brother-in-law:* COL. ROBERT WEST.   *Nieces:* MARTHA, SAREY and MARY WEST (daughters of ROBT.).   *Sisters:* ELIZABETH CLAY-

TEN and PENELOPE LITTLE, wife of WILLIAM LITTLE. *Other legatees:* JAMES SITTERSON, WILLIAM TETTERTON; JOHN son of JOHN COLE of Nansemond, Virginia; JOSHUA WHERRY son of ANTHONY WHERRY; ELIZABETH WHERRY daughter of ANTHONY; EDWARD MOSELEY and THOMAS POLLOCK. *Wife and Executrix:* ELIZABETH. *Executors:* MILES GALE, WILLIAM LITTLE, EDWARD MOSELEY and THOS. POLLOCK, JOHN LOVICK. *Witnesses:* THOMAS NORCOMB, RICHARD SUTTON, JOHN WIAT, CHARLES DENMAN, JOHN MITCHELL. Proven before RICHARD EVERARD.

HARVEY, THOMAS.   Perquimans County.

November 21, 1748. January Court, 1748. *Brothers and Executors:* JOHN, BENJAMIN and MILES HARVEY. *Nephews:* THOMAS and JOHN HARVEY. *Sister-in-law:* HANNAH SALTER. *Cousin:* SARAH ALDERSON. *Aunt:* HANNAH SITTERSON. *Witnesses:* JOHN NICKOLS, STEPHIN MARTIN, JOSEPH ARNOLD. *Clerk of the Court:* EDMUND HATCH.

HARWOOD, EDWARD.   Onslow County.

October 21, 1735. October Court, 1737. *Executor:* JOHN STARKEY. *Witnesses:* EDMD. HUGGER, JOHN MIXON, ELIZA JONES, JOHN STARKEY. *Clerk of the Court:* WM. CRANFORD. The testator provides for the sale of all his effects, proceeds to go to his wife and child, who are not named.

HASKINS, HANNIBAL.

February 11, 1698–1699. *Friend and Executor:* JOHN PORTER. *Witnesses:* HUMPHREY LEGGETT, ARCHIBALD HOLMES, WILLIAM BARROW. No probate.

HASSELL, JOHN.   Tyrrell County.

March 25, 1754. June Court, 1754. *Sons:* JOHN (plantation on West side of Scuppernong river known by the name of Plains), JOSEPH (lands on East side of Scuppernong river), ISAAC (plantation on East side of Scuppernong River), BENJAMIN ("my manner plantation"). *Daughters:* MARY WYNNE, SARAH FOX, ESTHER HASSELL. *Wife and Executrix:* RACHELL. Negroes bequeathed to sons. *Witnesses:* THOS. WYNNE, JEREMIAH WYNNE, PETER WYNNE. *Clerk of the Court:* EVAN JONES.

HATCH, ANTHONY.   Perquimans Precinct.

August 1, 1726. November 18, 1726. *Sons:* EDMUND and LAMB (lands lying in Neuse in the County of Bath), ANTHONY ("my plantation"). Lands in Alligator held in common with GEORGE DURANT (brother-in-law) ordered sold. *Wife and Executrix:* ELISABETH. *Daughter:* ELISABETH HATCH. *Executors:* RICHD. WHIDBY and GEORGE DURANT (brothers-in-law). *Witnesses:* J. SWEENY, THOMAS PENRICE, JOHN STEVENS, PARTHENIA STEVENS. Proven before RICHARD EVERARD.

HATCH, ANTHONY.   Perquimans County.

September 30, 1744.   October Court, 1744.   *Sons:* ANTONY ("my manor plantation"), JOHN (plantation joining SOLOMON SNOWDEN).   *Wife and Executrix:* ELIZABETH.   *Executors:* COL. MCARORA SCARBOROUGH, EDMUND HATCH ("Brother GERMAN").   *Witnesses:* TULLE WILLIAMS, GEORGE DUVANT, SAM SCOLLAY.   *Clerk of the Court:* EDMUND HATCH.

HATCH, LEMUEL.   Craven County.

April 2, 1774.   February 3, 1777.   *Sons:* LEMUEL (two-thirds of dwelling plantation lying between Sted's and Reasonover's Runs and also land on Trent River), JOHN and EDMUND, DURANT, JOY, ANTHONY (to each is given land which is described in will).   *Daughters:* ELIZABETH and MARY HATCH.   *Wife:* MARY.   *Executors:* LEMUEL and JOHN HATCH (sons).   *Witnesses:* EDMD. HATCH, JAMES WATSON, CHAS. MARKLAND.   *Executor with sons:* FRANCIS FONVILLE.   Witnesses to codicil appointing *Executor:* STOKES NORMENT, ELIZABETH NORMENT, ELIZABETH ANDRESS, EDMD. HATCH, JAMES WATSON.   Will proven before RD. CASWELL.

HATTON, JOHN.   Pasquotank County.

March 15, 1697-1698.   August 16, 1698.   *Executor:* BARTHOLEMEW HEWIT.   *Friends:* JOHN CIRBY (or COBY), ELIZABETH FOX.   *Witnesses:* DANIEL AKEHURST, HENRY PALIN, JUNR., HUMPHRY BOLTON.   *Clerk of the Court:* EDWARD MAYO.

HAUGHTON, CHARLES.   Chowan County.

October 4, 1754.   *Sons:* JEREMIAH ("my plantation"), JOHN, CHARLES.   *Daughter:* ELIZABETH.   *Executors:* JEREMIAH and CHARLES (sons).   *Witnesses:* WILLIAM HASKINS, WILLIAM WILKINS, JOHN TALER.   No probate.

HAUGHTON, GEORGE.   Chowan Precinct.

December 16, 1718.   *Daughter:* ELIZABETH.   *Wife* and *Executrix:* JUDITH.   *Executor:* THOMAS HAUGHTON (brother).   *Witnesses:* JOSHUA PORTER and CHARLES HAUGHTON.   Original missing.   Recorded in Will Book 1712-1722, page 171.

HAUGHTON, JAMES.   Perquimans County.

March 8, 1758.   April Court, 1758.   *Nephews:* JOSHUA HAUGHTON (son of sister, EASTER GARRETT), HENRY and EDWARD HALL (sons of sister, RACHEL HALL).   *Niece:* MARY HALL.   *Executors:* EDWARD HALL, JOHN HALSEY, ANDREW KNOX.   *Witnesses:* JAMES EGGERTON, THOS. MING, SARAH ARRANTON.   *Clerk of the Court:* MILES HARVEY.

HAUGHTON, RICHARD.   Chowan County.

October 19, 1748. November 25, 1748. *Son:* RICHARD. *Wife and Executrix:* MARY. *Executors:* THOMAS WHITE and JOB CHARLTON. *Witnesses:* THOS. WHITE, CHRIS. BUTLER, LEEY HAMPTON. Will proven before J. HALL, J. P.

HAUGHTON, WILLIAM.   Chowan County.

November 17, 1749. January Court, 1752. *Sons:* JOSHUA, JAMES, JOB, DAVID (*Executor*). *Daughters:* RACHEL and EASTER HAUGHTON. *Granddaughters:* MARY and SARAH PENRICE, SARAH and MARY HAUGHTON. *Grandsons:* WILLIAM and JONATHAN HAUGHTON. *Wife:* MARY. *Witnesses:* J. BENBURY, RICHARD BRINN, THOMAS BURKIT. *Clerk of the Court:* JAS. CRAVEN.

HAUSINGTON, BENEDICTUS.   Bath County.

November 16, 1729. December 16, 1730. *Daughters:* CATTERN, ELISEBETH, DINAH, MARY, SARAH. *Wife and Executrix:* DINAH. *Witnesses:* ROBERT BOND, ANNE NORWOOD.

HAWKINS, JOHN.   Albemarle County.

March 1, 1687-1688. May 13, 1688. *Daughter:* MARY HAWKINS. *Executor:* WILLIAM WEST. *Witnesses:* WILL BENBOW, FRANCIS WELLS, WILL HANCKOCK. Proven before SETH SOTHELL.

HAWKINS, JOHN.   Chowan County.

February 8, 1716-1717. August 16, 1719. *Sons:* JOSHUA, JAMES. *Daughter:* ANNE. *Other devisees and legatees:* THOMAS HARTSHORN (plantation on Cushake Creek), ELIZABETH HARTSHORN (son and daughter of JOYCE HARTSHORN, who is appointed *Executor*). *Witnesses:* THOS. ROGERS, FRANCIS ROGERS, JOHN HARDY. Will proven before CHAS. EDEN.

HAWKINS, JOHN.   Perquimans County.

October 14, 1744. January Court, 1744. *Daughter-in-law:* MARY TRUMBULL. *Daughter:* MARY HAWKINS. *Wife and Executrix:* MARY. *Executors:* ROBERT HODGES and JAMES PEIRCE. *Witnesses:* FOSTER TOMS, JOHN BARCLIFT. *Clerk of the Court:* EDMUND HATCH.

HAWKINS, SARAH.   Pasquotank County.

October 19, 1719. November 2, 1722. *Legatees:* THOS. MERRIDAY, heirs of ELIZABETH STUBBLE, wife of JOHN STUBBLE of Wickham, England; MARY STUBBLE, GEORGE GRIFFING, JOHN CARTWRIGHT, JOHN KING, SUSANNAH TALKSEY, JOHN EVERIGIN, WM. EVERIGIN, JR., EMANUEL LOW, JOHN SYMONS, WM. EVERIGIN, SR. (last-named two appointed *Executors*). *Witnesses:* GARRETT PURSEY, ROBERT HARRISON, SARAH HARRISON. Proven before WM. REED.

HAWKINS, THOMAS.   Tyrrell County.

October 8, 1730. July 21, 1732. *Son:* THOMAS. *Daughters:* MARY,
ELIZABETH and SARAH. *Wife's daughter:* ELIZABETH. *Wife and Executrix:* ELIZABETH. *Witnesses:* RICHD. LEARY, JOHN BROWN, JOHN LONG.
Will proven before GEO. BURRINGTON.

HAWLEY, MIKELL.   Northampton County.

March 1, 1752. August Court, 1752. *Sons:* JOSEPH, WILLIAM, CHRISTOPHER, BENJAMIN. *Grandson:* WILLIAM MITCHELL. *Daughters:* ANN,
ELIZABETH and MARY. *Executor:* BENJAMIN HAWLEY (son). *Witnesses:*
ROBERT HARREN, JOHN JOHNSON, ROBERT SHARP. *Clerk of the Court:* I.
EDWARDS.

HAYMAN, HENRY.   Albemarle County.

August 29, 1709. *Sons:* HENRY and THOMAS ("land bought of EDWARD
MAIO"), CHARLES and JAMES (two Islands on North River next to Indian
Island). *Daughters:* MARY and ELINOR HAYMAN. *Wife and Executrix:*
MARTHA. *Witnesses:* JAMES FORBUS, ALICE FORBUS, METHUSALEM
VAUGHAN. No probate.

HAYMAN, HENRY.   Pasquotank County.

May 23, 1727. July 18, 1727. *Son:* WILLIAM. *Daughter:* ANN HAYMAN. *Wife and Executrix:* MARY. *Witnesses:* MAC. SCARBOROUGH, SARAH
FARECLOF, SARAH JONES. *Clerk of the Court:* THOS. WEEKES.

HAYWOOD, JOHN.   Edgecombe County.

July 23, 1756. December Court, 1758. *Sons:* WILLIAM, JOHN, EGBERT
and HARWOOD. *Daughters:* DEBORAH and MARY HAYWOOD (213 acres of
land devised to daughters). All six children appointed *Executors.* *Witnesses:* EDWARD CROWELL, WM. CAMPBELL, THOMAS MERRIT. *Clerk of the
Court:* JOS. MONTFORT.

HAYWOOD, JOHN.   Edgecombe County.

February 18, 1758. June Court, 1758. *Brothers:* EGBERT, WILLIAM and
SHERWOOD HAYWOOD. *Sisters:* DEBORAH and MARY HAYWOOD. *Father:*
not named. *Executor:* EGBERT HAYWOOD. *Witnesses:* ROBERT WARREN,
JOSEPH POPE, SAMUEL PITMAN. *Clerk of the Court:* JOS. MONTFORT.

HEARESON, JOHN.   Chowan Precinct.

February 18, 1693-1694. April Court, 1694. *Sons:* WILLIAM, THOMAS,
JOHN. *Daughter:* ELISABETH. *Executrix:* WIFE (not named). *Witnesses:*
GEORGE FORDYES, JOHN WATKENES, WILLIAM HEARESON. *Clerk of the
Court:* HENDERSON WALKER.

HEATH (spelled also "HATH"), NEHEMIAH.   Currituck Co.

January 2, 1749-1750. April Court, 1750. *Wife and Executrix:* ELIZA-
BETH. *Other legatee:* ROBERT HATH (or HEATH). *Witnesses:* WILLIS ETH-
ERIDGE, WILLIAM BLUNT, LAZERUS FLOWREY. *Clerk of the Court:* RICH'D
MCCLURE.

HECKLEFIELD, JOHN.   Chowan County.

May 30, 1721. August 8, 1721. *Son:* JOHN. *Other legatees:* Gov.
CHARLES EDEN (mourning ring with a deaths head and christal), EDMUND
GALE (1 diamond ring), GEORGE DURANT. *Sister-in-law:* MARY COX.
Executors: EDMUND GALE and GEORGE DURANT. *Witnesses:* WILLIAM
BARCLIFT, DARBEY BRYAN, ENOCH CAWEN. Will proven before CHAS.
EDEN.   There is filed with this will a memorandum or will made by testator
in 1718.

HEDGES, THOMAS.   New Hanover County.

March 23, 1745. November 27, 1746. *Son:* WILLIAM. *Daughter:* ANN
HEDGES. *Executors:* WILLIAM HEDGES (son), JAMES SMALLWOOD. *Wit-
nesses:* PHILLIP DAVID, DAVID DAVES, THOS. JAMES.   Will proven before
GAB. JOHNSTON.

HENBY, JOSEPH.   Perquimans County.

April 8, 1752. July Court, 1752. *Daughter:* CLARKEY HENBY. *Father:*
JOHN HENBY. *Sisters:* MARY HENBY, ELISABETH GRIFFIN. *Brothers:*
JAMES and SILVANUS HENBY. *Executors:* FRANCIS TOMES, JOSEPH RAT-
LIFF. *Witnesses:* JO. SUTTON, SAMUEL ANDERSON, JOHN HENBY. *Clerk
of the Court:* EDMUND HATCH.

HENDERSON, DAVID.   Bertie County.

February 13, 1735-1736. March 9, 1735. *Nephew:* GEORGE HENDER-
SON. *Sister:* JENNETT. *Executors:* COLO. ROBT. WEST, CULLEN POLLOCK,
GEORGE HENDERSON and CAPN. JOHN CALDEN. *Witnesses:* THOS. DAVIS,
SIMON DART, JAMES KEETER and ELIZABETH DART.   Proven before W.
SMITH, C. J.

HENDERSON, GEORGE.   Bertie Precinct.

October 15, 1736. November 27, 1736. *Legatees and devisees:* THOMAS
MOOR, JOHN RAY, RACHEL NELSON, MARY GREGORY, ANDREW MOOR, HUGH
SCOTT (land on Cashai River); ANDREW SCOTT, GEORGE SCOTT (sons of
ANDREW SCOTT, merchant in Glasgow). *Executors:* HUGH SCOTT (mer-
chant in Boston), ANDREW MOORE. *Witnesses:* JOHN RAY, GEORGE
STRACHAN, SAMUEL COOK.   Will proven before W. SMITH, C. J.

HENDERSON, HENMAN.

February 19, 1728.   February 21, 1728.   Boston in Massachusetts Bay. *Wife, Executrix and sole devisee:* MARY.   *Witnesses:* EB. YOUNGMAN, BEN SOPER, GEORGE WILLIAMS.   Proven before R. EVERARD.

HENDRICK, FRANCIS.   Pasquotank County.

May 5, 1714.   *Son and Executor:* THOMAS.   *Wife and Executrix:* MARY. *Witnesses:* W. NORRIS, LEVI CRESSEY, W. ROLFE.

HENDRICK, FRANCIS.   Craven County.

September 11, 1734.   December 17, 1734.   *Wife:* ELISHE.   *Sons-in-law:* JOHN HILL (*Executor*), MOSES ARNECH.   *Witnesses:* JOHN JEAMES, THOS. FISHER, GEORGE FISHER.   *Clerk of the Court:* CALEB METCALFE.

HENDRICK, JEREMIAH.   Perquimans County.

June 1, 1756.   January Court, 1756.   *Son:* GEORGE.   *Wife and Executrix:* SARAH.   *Executor:* ROBERT COCKS (father-in-law).   *Witnesses:* THO. WEEKES, THOS. CRAGHILL, THOS. WEEKES, JR.   *Clerk of the Court:* MILES HARVEY.

HENDRICKS, SOLOMON.   Perquimans County.

April 18, 1744.   October Court, 1744.   *Daughters:* MARY ("plantation whereon I now dwell"), SARAH and FRANCES HENDRICKS.   *Executors:* JEREMIAH HENDRICKS (brother), MARY HENDRICKS (wife) and SARAH HENDRICKS (daughter).   *Witnesses:* MICHAEL MURPHY, THOMAS OVERMAN, JAMES OVERMAN.   *Clerk of the Court:* EDMUND HATCH.

HENLEY, JOHN.   Pasquotank County.

March 21, 1726–1727.   July Court, 1728.   *Sons:* JOHN ("my plantation"), JESSE.   *Daughters:* MARY, MIRIAM and ELIZABETH.   *Wife and Executrix:* ISABELL.   *Executor:* JOHN HENLEY (son).   *Witnesses:* DANIEL GUTHRIE and ISAAIAH CULBERTSON.   *Clerk of the Court:* R. EVERARD.

HENLY, JOHN.   Onslow County.

January 14, 1747.   April Court, 1747.   *Sons:* JOHN, WILLIAM, EDWARD (to each is devised land), BENJAMIN.   *Daughter:* ELIZABETH HENLY. *Wife and Executrix:* ELIZABETH.   *Executor:* GEORGE CUPER (COOPER). *Witnesses:* RICHD. WHITHURST, HENRY BROWN, ANN EUERE.

HENLEY, JOHN.   Pasquotank County.

June 3, 1753.   April Court, 1754.   *Sons:* JOHN and JOSEPH ("my plantation to be divided between them").   *Wife and Executrix:* MARY.

11

Executors: JOHN HENLEY (son) and JOSEPH JORDAN (brother-in-law). *Witnesses:* LEML. COOK, ELIZABETH BROTHERS. *Clerk of the Court:* THOMAS TAYLOR.

HENLEY, PETER, "Chief Justice of the Province of North Carolina."

November 23, 1757.   July Court, 1758. *Son:* JOHN. *Executor:* JOHN CAMPBELL. This will provides for the payment of a debt of £400 due one AGNES TUCKER of Coryton, near Honiton, in the County of Devon, for advancement made by her in order to provide for the marriage of herself and testator, which marriage, "to the great disappointment of us both," says the testator, "was postponed to be compleated at a future day." Other creditors mentioned are: MR. SIMON BUNKER, of Axminster, in the County of Devon, attorney-at-law; MR. BENJAMIN MAYBERRY, Taylor of Craven Buildings, near Drury Lane, London. *Witnesses:* SARAH McCULLOCH, JOSEPH MONTFORT, RICHD. BROWNRIGG. *Clerk of the Court of Chowan County:* THOS. JONES. Endorsement on the will reads: "The last will and testament of PETER HENLEY, ESQR., who departed this life on Tuesday, the 25th day of April, 1738, about nine o'clock in the morning, and was interred in the Church in Edenton on the Evening the 27th of same month at six o'clock in the evening in a decent manner and much lamented by his acquaintance."

HERN, JAMES.   Beaufort County.

February 22, 1751–1752.   June 9, 1752. *Sons:* JAMES, WILLIAM, JOHN ("my plantation"), MASON. *Daughters:* MARY, ELLINDER, ELIZEBETH, SARAH and RACHEL HERN. *Wife and Executrix:* MASON. *Executor:* GEORGE SUGG. *Witnesses:* MARY MAYO, NATHAN GODWIN, MARY TYSON. *Clerk of the Court:* WILL ORMOND.

HERRENDEN, HEZEKIAH.

November 5, 1746.   May Court, 1754, "of Duxborough in the County of Plymouth in New England." *Wife and Executrix:* HANNAH. *Witnesses:* SILVANUS CURTIS, SAMUEL WESTON, SAMUEL WESTON, JUNR. *Clerk of Bertie Court:* SAML. ORMES.

HERRING, SAMUELL.   Johnston County.

October 22, 1750.   December Court, 1750. *Sons:* ANTONY, STEPHEN, MICHAEL ("plantation whereon I now live"). *Daughter:* BARTHENA HERRING. *Son-in-law:* JNO. CONNERLEY. *Executor:* ANTONY HERRING (son). *Wife:* not named. *Witnesses:* ANTONY HERRING and JOSEPH HERRING. *Clerk of the Court:* RICHD. CASWELL.

HERRITAGE, WILLIAM. Craven County.

March 8, 1769. *Sons:* HENEAGE ("plantation whereon I dwell, called Springfield"), JOHN ("plantation called Harrow"), WILLIAM MARTIN HERRITAGE. *Son-in-law:* RICHARD CASWELL. *Daughters:* ELIZABETH HERRITAGE, ANNA LOVICK (wife of GEO. LOVICK), SARAH (wife of RICHARD CASWELL), SUSANNAH. *Executors:* RICHARD CASWELL and JOHN and HENEAGE HERRITAGE. *Witnesses:* DANIEL BARRY, —— and ——. Several tracts of land, besides the ones above mentioned, are conveyed to sons and son-in-law, for description of which said lands see will. Codicil dated April 10, 1769, devises other lands to son HENEAGE, etc. *Witnesses to Codicil:* DAVID GORDON, MARGRET WIGGINS, ELIZABETH BLOUNT, RD. CASWELL. No probate.

HEWITT, BARTHOLOMEW. Pasquotank County.

July 16, 1719. *Legatees:* ROBERT LOWRY, SAMUEL DAVIS, THOMAS CARTRIGHT, SAMUEL NORRIS. *Executor:* WILLIAM NORRIS. *Witnesses:* WILLIAM JONES, JOHN MACKY. Original missing. Recorded in Book 1712–1722, page 243.

HIBBS, JONATHAN. Pasquotank County.

April 5, 1745. July 15, 1745. *Sons:* JOHN (420 acres of land), JONATHAN. *Executors:* DAVID BOLES and CALEB SAWYER. *Witnesses:* JOHN NORRIS, EDWARD SCOTT, WM. COALE. *Clerk of the Court:* THOS. TAYLOR.

HICKS, AFRICA. Pasquotank Precinct.

November 7, 1711. No probate date. *Two sons:* PATRICK MACKGREGORY and GREGORY MACKGREGORY. *Husband:* ROBT. HICKS. *Sister:* ANN PALIN (widow). *Executors:* PATRICK MACKGREGORY and GREGORY MACKGREGORY, to be in care of MR. JOHN PALIN and NATH. CHEVIN until they are 21 years of age. *Witnesses:* GEORGE ELLIS, ELIZA HARLOW. *Clerk of Court:* ROBERT BUCKNER.

HICKS, DAVID. Chowan County.

September 9, 1732. December 23, 1732. *Son-in-law:* THOMAS ASHLY, JR. *Daughter:* LUCRETIA. *Wife and Executrix:* ELIZABETH. *Other children:* mentioned, but not named. All land to be divided among children. *Witnesses:* MART. FRED RASOR, THOMAS ASHLY, LAMB HARDY. Will proven before GEORGE BURRINGTON.

HICKS, JOHN. Carteret County.

May 15, 1749. September Court, 1749. *Wife and Executrix:* HANNAH. *Brothers:* DAVID HICKS, THOMAS HICKS. *Executor:* DAVID HICKS. *Witnesses:* GEORGE MCKEAN, EVE LEWIS, MARTHA LEWIS. *Clerk of Court:* GEO. READ.

HICKS, THOMAS.

October 26, 1722. August 24, 1724. *Sisters:* HANNAH and ABIGAIL HICKS. *Executor:* JOSEPH SUTTON, JUNR. *Witnesses:* BENJAMIN JACKSON, NATHANIEL SUTTON, SENR., NATHANIEL SUTTON, JUNR. Will proven before C. GALE, C. J. This document is in the form of a power of attorney to JOSEPH SUTTON, JUNR., constituting him trustee for sisters above named, who reside in "ould England."

HIGGINS, MICHALL.   Craven County.

April 28, 1753. May Court, 1753. *Sons:* MICHAEL and WILLIAM. *Daughters:* MARY, SARAH, ANN and HANNAH HIGGINS. *Wife and Executrix:* ANN. *Executors:* MICHAEL HIGGINS, JEREMIAH VAIL. *Witnesses:* WM. WICKLIFFE, JOHN MURPHY, THOMAS EVENES. *Clerk of the Court:* SOL. REW.

HILL, BENJAMIN.   Bertie County.

June 20, 1752. August Court, 1753. *Son and Executor:* HENRY ("all my lands"). *Daughters:* MARY CAMPBELL, SARAH MCCULLOCH (400 acres of land on Roanoak River), PRISCILLA HILL. *Other legatee:* MARGARET COCKRAN. *Executor:* THOMAS JONES of Petty Shore. *Witnesses:* JESSE BROWNE, ROBERT HARDY, JOHN PITT. Codicil dated June 6, 1753, gives land in Cashia Neck to *grandson,* BENJAMIN MCCULLOCH. Same witnesses to codicil. *Clerk of the Court:* SAMUEL ORMES.

HILL, GEORGE.   Bath County.

April 17, 1722. March 30, 1723. *Sons:* JOHN, GEORGE, HARMAN, *Wife and Executrix:* MARY. *Daughter:* RACHEL. *Executors:* JOHN and GEORGE HILL. *Witnesses:* THOMAS GOODIN, JOHN LEATH, JOHN PROCTER. *Clerk:* JOHN CORNICK.

HILL, HARMAN.   Beaufort County.

December 4, 1752. March Court, 1755. *Sons:* HARMAN (land on Callums Creek), JAMES and WILLIAM. *Daughters:* ELIZ. HANCOCK, SARAH RICE, ANN SLADE (land on Pamplico River), MARY SMITH, RACHEL HILL. *Executors:* SARAH HILL (wife), JOSEPH SLADE, JOHN BARROW. *Witnesses:* EDMUND PEARCE, JOSHUA PEARCE, GRIFFETH HOWELL. *Clerk of Court:* WALLEY CHAUNCEY.

HILL, ISAAC.   Chowan Precinct.

March 3, 1710. *Sons:* MICHAEL, JOHN and ISACK, NATHANIEL. *Daughter:* MARTHA. *Executor:* ROBERT WEST. *Witnesses:* WILLIAM MAULE, EDWARD BRYAN, JOHN HALE. Original missing. Recorded in Book 1712–1722, page 34.

HILL, MOSES.   Chowan County.
    Will is illegible.

HILL, JOHN.   Bath County.
    March 27, 1731.   September Court, 1731.   *Sons:* JOSHUA, JOHN.
Friend: THOMAS TISON.   *Executors:* WIFE (not named) and EDMUND
PEARS.   *Witnesses:* THOMAS TISON, HARMAN HILL, WILLIAM NICHOLS.
Clerk of the Court: FRE. GOOLDE.

HILL, JOHN.   Northampton County.
    June 15, 1747.   August Court, 1747.   *Sons:* NATHANIEL ("plantation
he now lives on"), DANIEL ("plantation I now live on"), LEWIS ("remainer
part of my land"), PETER.   *Executors:* DANIEL and NATHANIEL HILL
(sons).   *Witnesses:* WILLIAM ADDISON, WILLIAM FLOARYDAY, HOSEA TAP-
LEY.   *Clerk of the Court:* RT. FORSTER.

HILL, RICHARD.   Craven County.
    February 17, 1728–1729.   March 18, 1729.   *Granddaughter:* ELISABETH
HILL.   *Executor:* FRANCIS HILL (brother).   *Daughter:* ANN JONES.   *Son-
in-law:* EVAN JONES.   *Witnesses:* JAMES TAYLOR, THOMAS JONES, JOHN
LEWEIS, JOHN CUMING.   *Clerk of the Court:* CALEB METCALFE.

HILL, ROBERT.   Tyrrell County.
    January 16, 1735–1736.   February 4, 1735–1736.   *Son:* ROBERT ("my
plantation").   *Wife:* ANN.   *Daughter:* SARAH HILL.   *Executors:* CULLEN
POLLOCK and ROBERT WEST.   *Witnesses:* SAMUELL DURRANCE, NATH'L
CARRUTHERS, PAUL THORP.   Proven before W. SMITH, C. J.

HILL, WILLIAM.   Northampton County.
    September 3, 1748.   November Court, 1748.   *Son:* WILLIAM ("my
plantation").   *Daughters:* ANN HILL, CELIA PHILLIPS.   *Wife and Executrix:* ANN.   *Witnesses:* JNO. SIMPSON, JACOB LITTLE, FRANCIS DELOATCH.
Clerk of the Court: I. EDWARDS.

HILL, WILLIAM.   Chowan County.
    March 10, 1750–1751.   April Court, 1751.   *Grandsons:* AARON and
ROBERT HILL.   *Sons:* WILLIAM and AARON (*Executor*).   *Son-in-law and
Executor:* THOMAS NICHOLSON.   *Daughters:* RACHEL HILL, SARAH BARROW,
wife of JOSEPH BARROW.   *Witnesses:* JAMES GRIFFIN, JETHRO RABEY,
ANN PETERS.   *Clerk of the Court:* JAS. CRAVEN.

HILLIARD, JOHN.   Northampton County.
    November 6, 1748.   November Court, 1748.   *Sons:* ROBERT ("my plan-
tation"), JOHN.   *Daughter:* SARAH HILLIARD.   *Wife and Executrix:* MARY.
Witnesses: JOHN MOREAN, WILLIAM LIVINGSTONE, JOHN MOLTAN.   *Clerk
of the Court:* I. EDWARDS.

HILLIARD, ROBERT.   Edgecombe County.

April 13, 1743. May Court, 1751. *Devisees and legatees:* JACOB HIL-
LIARD, ROBERT HILLIARD, JEREMIAH HILLIARD ("plantation on the falls of
Teare River"); SAMSONE HILLIARD, MARY HILLIARD (all children of JERE-
MIAH HILLIARD); WILLIAM HILLIARD, JEAMES HILLIARD (sons of WILLIAM
HILLIARD). *Wife:* CHARETY. *Executors:* WILLIAM HILLIARD and OS-
BORNE JEFFREYS. *Witnesses:* SAM'L HALLIMAN, WILLIAM SIRGENER, BENJ.
BOYKIN. *Clerk of Court:* BENJ'N WYNNS.

HILLIARD, WILLIAM.   Northampton County.

July 4, 1754. May Court, 1756. *Sons:* WILLIAM (land known by name
of "Hogpen Neck"), JAMES ("plantation whereon I dwell"), ISAAC (land in
Edgecombe County on Swift Creek), ELIAS (plantations in Northampton
and Edgecombe). *Daughter:* ANN HILLIARD. *Wife and Executrix:* ANN.
Executor: JAMES HILLIARD (son). *Witnesses:* HENRY HART, JOSEPH
BRIDGERS, NATHANIEL HOWEL, CHARLES COTTEN. *Clerk of the Court:* I.
EDWARDS.

HILORY, SAMEL.   Bath County.

March 20, 1712–1713. *Executor and sole legatee:* SAMUEL WOODARD.
Witnesses: ELLICKSANDER OLIVER, HENERREY TURNER. No probate.

HINTON, JOHN.   Chowan Precinct.

June 21, 1730. October Court, 1732. *Sons:* HARDY, JOHN, WILLIAM,
MALLACIE. *Executors:* MARY HINTON (wife), HARDIE HINTON (son), WIL-
LIAM HINTON (brother). *Witnesses:* JAMES HINTON, JOSEPH ASHLEY, THOS.
ROUNTREE. *Clerk of the Court:* RT. FORSTER.

HINTON, MICAJAH.   Bertie County.

October 5, 1756. January Court, 1757. *Son:* WILLIAM. *Daughter:*
ELIZEBETH HINTON. This is a nuncupative will proven before JOHN HAR-
RELL, J. P., by JOHN and JONAS HINTON and HEZEKIAH TOMSON. *Clerk
of the Court:* BENJAMIN WYNNS.

HOBBY, JACOB.   Edgecombe County.

January 22, 1758. September Court, 1758. *Son:* MATHEW (all "my
land"). *Daughters:* RHODA, SARAH and FRANCES HOBBY. *Wife and
Executrix:* JEMIME. *Executor:* JOHN BAKER. *Witnesses:* ANDREW IRWING,
BRACEWELL BRIDGES, JOSEPH KELLEY. *Clerk of the Court:* JOS. MONT-
FORT.

HOBS, JOHN.   Pasquotank County

October 29, 1728. October 14, 1729. *Wife and Executrix:* FRANCES.
Witnesses: JNO. GALLEY, JAMES SMITH, FRANCES SMITH, PATIENCE PRICK-

ETT. *Clerk of the Court:* H. MINSON. *Justices:* JON. PALIN, ROBT. MORGAN, JNO. ROLF, MCKRONA SCARBOROUGH, GABRELL BURNHAM, NATT HALL.

HOCKINGS (HAWKINS), JOHN.   Duplin County.

March 29, 1756. July Court, 1756. *Daughters and Executrices:* MARY, ANN and LATTESS HOCKINGS. *Witnesses:* BENJAMIN FUSSELL, JACOB FUSSELL, THOMAS DAVIS, RICHARD PENNEY, EDWARD SPEARMAN. *Clerk of Court:* JOHN DICKSON.

HOCUT, EDWARD.   Beaufort County.

January 19, 1749–1750. March Court, 1750. *Sons:* WILLIAM, NATHANIEL, EDWARD. *Wife and Executrix:* MARTHA. *Executor:* NATHAN ARCHEBALD. *Witnesses:* WALLEY CHAUNCEY, STEPHEN BUCKINGHAM, JOHN BOWIN. *Clerk of the Court:* JOHN ALDERSON.

HODGES, JAMES.   Chowan County.

September 23, 1722. October 10, 1722. *Cousin:* ELIZABETH HARRISON. *Wife and Executrix:* SARAH CATHERINE HODGES. *Witnesses:* C. GALE, ROGER HAZARD, SARAH HAZARD. Will proven before WM. REED, *President.* Coat of arms on seal.

HODGES, JAMES.   Pasquotank County.

February 2, 1758. March Court, 1758. *Sons:* JOSIAH (plantation and islands on the Northeast side of Pasquotank River bridge), WILLIS (one negro), JAMES (land and Marsh on West side of road going to "ye Great Bridge"), LAMB, PORTLOCK. *Daughters:* KESIAH CURLIN, MOLLY, FRANCES HODGES, MIRIAM HODGES. *Brother:* JOSEPH HODGES. Several negroes and a large quantity of personal property bequeathed to wife and children. Estate to pay for brick chimney to house. *Wife:* MARIAM. *Executor:* COLO. ROBERT MURDON. *Witnesses:* JOHN HARRIS, DANIEL KOEN, JOHN MURDEN. *Clerk of the Court:* THOMAS TAYLOR.

HODGES, RICHARD.   Beaufort County.

September 3, 1747. April 16, 1752. *Sons:* JOHN (400 acres of land on "Cochavinity Bay"), HENRY ("the manner plantation"). *Daughter:* SARAH HODGES. *Wife:* SARAH. *Executor:* JOHN HODGES (son). *Witnesses:* JAMES COUPPER, JAMES SINGLETON, THOMAS WILLIAMS. *Clerk of Anson County Court:* ANTHONY HUTCHINS.

HODGES, RICHARD.   Currituck County.

March 2, 1748. April Court, 1749. *Daughters:* SARAH BURNHAM, FRANCES BOWRIN, MARY, ELISEBETH and UPHAN HODGES. *Wife and Executrix:* FRANCES. *Witnesses:* CALEB WILSON, GEORGE POWERS, WILLIS ETHERIDGE. *Clerk of the Court:* RICHARD MCCLURE.

HODGSON, JOHN.   New Hanover County.

July 6, 1738.   December Court, 1738.   *Daughters:* MARY and MARGARET
HODGSON.   *Executor:* ROGER MOORE.   *Witnesses:* CORN'S HARNETT, CHAS.
HEPBURN, JOHN MARTINDALE.   *Clerk of the Court:* JNO. RICE.

HOGBIN, WILLIAM.   Albemarle County.

May 4, 1692.   July 4, 1692.   *Wife:* MARGETT.   *Daughters:* SARAH and
ELIZABETH HOGBIN.   *Executors:* THOMAS and JEREMIAH SIMONS.   *Witnesses:* PATRICK BAYLEY, JOHN RAPER.   *Clerk of the Court:* PAUL LATHUM.

HOG, RICHARD.   Bladen County.

June 18, 1768.   September 21, 1769.   *Sister:* ELIZABETH HOG of Tishe-
raw, in the parish of Inveresk in North Brittain.   *Executors:* ROBERT
JOHNSTON, ROBERT and JOHN HOGG.   *Witnesses:* WILLIAM BARTRAM,
THOMAS BAYLY, LILLAH JOHNSTON.   Proven before WM. TRYON.

HOGGES, ROBERT.   Bertie County.

March 30, 1740.   August Court, 1742.   *Sons:* JOHN and RICHARD and
ELIAS.   *Daughters:* ANN MOORE, OLIVE WIGONS and MATHEW WILLIAMS.
Wife: not named.   *Executors:* ELIAS and RICHARD HOGGES (sons) and
ISAAC WILLIAMS (son-in-law).   *Witnesses:* NEEDHAM BRYAN, ADAM RA-
BEY, WILLIAM BRYAN.   *Clerk of Court:* HENRY DELON.

HOLBROOK, FARMANESS.

March 8, 1683–1684.   This will is so torn and rotten as to be illegible.

HOLBROOK (or HOLEBROUGH), JOSEPH.   Bath County
                                    and "Pamlicoth Precinct."

October 18, 1711.   *Legatees:* ALEXANDER and ELIZABETH AVERA, SWAN
SWANSON.   *Brother and Executor:* JOHN HOLEBROUGH.   *Witnesses:* DANIEL
HALLSEY, JAMES LEIG.   Original missing.   Recorded in Book 1712–1722,
page 16.

HOLLADAY, THOMAS.   Chowan County.

August 30, 1744.   September 8, 1744.   *Legatees and devisees:* HARDY
HOLLADAY HUTSON, THOMAS HOLLADAY HUTSON, JOHN HOLLADAY HUT-
SON (land in Virginia to be sold and proceeds divided among above named),
WILLIAM HOLLADAY, HANNAH BEDARRIN, ELIZABETH BURTON (daughter).
Executrix: MARY HUTSON.   *Witnesses:* JOHN THACH, JOHN NICHOLLS, PRU-
DANCE GARRETT.   Will proven before GAB. JOHNSTON at Eden House.

HOLLADAY, WILLIAM.   Tyrrell County.

April 23, 1754.   June Court, 1754.   *Sons:* THOMAS, SAMMUELL (appointed
Executors).   *Wife:* ELIZABETH.   *Daughters:* mentioned, but not named.
Witnesses: WILLIAM JONES and JOHN BENNET.   *Clerk of the Court:* EVAN
JONES.

HOLLAND, DANIEL.   Craven County.
   March 16, 1771.   April 20, 1771.   *Wife and Executrix:* ANNIE.   *Witnesses:* JAMES REED, HANNAH REED, JOHN HOLLAND.   Will proven before WM. TRYON.

HOLLBROOK, JOHN.   Bertie County.
   April 29, 1740.   May Court, 1740.   *Son and Executor:* JOHN.   *Wife:* DOROTHY.   *Executors:* COLL. ROBERT WEST, THOMAS RYAN.   *Witnesses:* ROGER SNELL, THOS. ASHLY, JUNR., THOMAS ASHBURN.   *Clerk of the Court:* JNO. WYNNS.

HOLLERY, SAMUEL, and SAMUELL WOODARD.
   April 13, 1713.   This is a contract by the terms of which the survivor of the above-named parties shall take all estate of the other, at his decease, and is proven by HENRY TURNER and ALLIS GIVEN before WM. BRICE.

HOLLIS, JAMES.   Tyrrell County.
   May 20, 1735.   March Court, 1735.   *Son:* ARMIT.   *Wife and Executrix:* ANN.   *Executor:* THOS. HUBBS.   *Witnesses:* MARY FEWAX, WILLIAM TYSAR, MARY HUBBS.   *Clerk of Court:* JAMES CRAVEN.

HOLLOWAY, THOMAS.   Perquimans County.
   November 3, 1750.   January Court, 1750.   *Son and Executor:* JOHN (two plantations).   *Daughters:* ELIZABETH BARCLIFT, RACHEL TURNBULL, ANN SNODEN, MARY BATEMAN, SARAH COUPLAND, UPHERASHA HOLLOWAY.   *Witnesses:* JAMES GIBSON, THOS. BARCLIFT, ELIZABETH BARCLIFT.   *Clerk of the Court:* EDMUND HATCH.

HOLLOWELL, EDMUND.   Bertie County.
   June 17, 1729.   October 20, 1729.   *Brothers:* THOMAS HOLLOWELL (*Executor*), JOHN HOLLOWELL.   All land is bequeathed to JOHN BACON.   *Witnesses:* JOHN HOLLOWELL, RICHD. BACON, THOMAS HOLLOWELL, SENR.   *Clerk of the Court:* THOS. CREW.

HOLLOWELL, LUKE.   Perquimans County.
   March 22, 1734–1735.   April 21, 1736.   *Sons:* JOEL ("my dwelling plantation"), WILLIAM, JOHN.   *Wife and Executrix:* ELIZABETH.   Land in Virginia devised to son JOHN.   *Witnesses:* JAMES FEILD, THOMAS ROUNTREE, GILBERT SCOT.   Will proven before W. SMITH, C. J.

HOLLOWELL, RUBIN.   Perquimans County.
   January 23, 1753.   April Court, 1753.   *Brothers:* LEVY, JOHN and ABNER HOLLOWELL.   *Sister:* ANN BRINKLEY.   *Executors:* JOHN and LEVY HOLLOWELL.   *Witnesses:* NICHOLAS STALLINGS, THOMAS REDDICK, JOSIAH ROGERSON.   *Clerk of the Court:* EDMUND HATCH.

HOLLY, JOHN. Bertie Precinct.

December 23, 1728. February Court, 1728. *Wife and Executrix:* SARAH. *Son:* RICHARD. *Witness:* JOHN SWENNY (or SWENEY). *Clerk of the Court:* RT. FORSTER.

HOLMES, EBENEZER. Onslow County.

February 4, 1745–1746. April 1, 1746. *Sons:* JOHN, EBENEZER, SETH, BARNABAS (*Executor*). *Daughters:* REBECCA WRIGHT (wife of JOSEPH), HANNAH WILLIAMS, LYDEL HOLMES, ABIGIL HOLMES. *Wife:* HANNAH. *Witnesses:* ANDREW MURRAY, JAMES THOMSON, ANN HURLEY. *Clerk of the Court:* GEO. CLOPTON.

HOLMES, JOHN. Edgecombe County.

February 28, 1735–1736. May Court, 1736. *Sons:* JOHN, HARDY, EDWARD, GABRIEL. *Daughters:* ANN SANDERS, CHARITY BROWN, DOROTHY SPIER, ROSE. *Wife:* TAMAR. *Executor:* HARDY HOLMES. *Witnesses:* EDWD. BUXTON, WILLIAM DAVIES, ELIZABETH WELSH. *Deputy Clerk of Court:* THOS. KEARNY.

HOMES, EDWARD. Perquimans County.

April 14, 1702. *Sons:* THOMAS and JOHN. *Wife and Executrix:* ELIZABETH. *Witnesses:* names illegible. *Clerk of Court:* JOHN STEPNEY.

HOMES, EDWARD. Bertie County.

August 9, 1750. November Court, 1750. *Cousin and Executor:* WM. BIRD. *Wife and Executrix:* LIDDEA. *Witnesses:* HENRY BONNER, WM. MITCHELL and JOHN PADGE. *Clerk of the Court:* SAM'L ORMES.

HOOK, JOHN.

March 27, 1732. *Sons:* WILLIAM (*Executor*), ROBERT, THOMAS and JOHN. *Daughters:* ELISEBATH, MARY and SARAH. *Wife:* RUTH. *Witnesses:* JOHN MACKCONE, NATHAN BARNES. No probate.

HOOKER, GODPHREY. Bertie County.

April 2, 1729. *Son:* BENJAMIN ("the manner plantation"). *Daughter:* ELISABETH. *Wife and Executrix:* ELISABETH. *Executor:* ROBERT EVANS. *Witnesses:* ROBERT EVANS, JOHN MORRIS and ———. No probate.

HOOKER, WILLIAM. Chowan County.

June 8, 1716. October Court, 1717. *Sons:* WILLIAM ("plantation whereon I now live, on Barren Branch and Wickacorn Creek"), GODFREE two hundred and fifty acres of land adjoining COL. POLLOCK). *Daughters:* ANN EVANS, BRIDGETT MANN, MARGARETT LEWIS, JANE BROWN and ELIZABETH SISEMORE. *Son-in-law:* SAMUEL SISEMORE (land on the main road). *Grandson:* WILLIAM LEWIS. *Executor:* WILLIAM HOOKER (son). *Witnesses:* WILLIAM CRANFORD, FRANCIS BROWN. *Clerk of the Court:* R. HICKS.

HOOKER, WILLIAM.   Bertie County.

October 20, 1756. January Court, 1757. *Sons:* WILLIAM, JOHN, JAMES, STEPHEN, NATHAN. *Daughters:* ANN LASITER, SARAH HOOKER (*Executrix*). *Witnesses:* WM. WYNNS, JAMES WYNNES, BENJAMIN BAKER, BENJAMIN BAKER, JUNR. *Clerk of the Court:* BENJAMIN WYNNS.

HOOKS, WILLIAM.   Chowan County.

February 18, 1746–1747. April Court, 1751. *Son:* WILLIAM. *Grandsons:* WILLIAM, CHARLES, THOMAS and JOHN HOOKS. *Executor:* JOHN HOOKS. *Witnesses:* MARTHA SUMNER, ANN SUMNER, CHAS. KING. *Clerk of Court:* JAS. CRAVEN.

HOPKINS, JAMES.   Parish of Saint Matthews, Orange Co.

February 8, 1759. September Court, 1759. *Executors:* WILLIAM HOPKINS, WILLIAM PHILLIPS and JOHN HOPKINS. *Children:* mentioned, but not named. *Witnesses:* ALICKANDER FERGUSON, JOHN DOBBINS, DAVID SMITH. *Clerk of Court:* JAS. WATSON.

HOPKINS, JOHN.   Albemarle County.

October 14, 1721. November 8, 1721. *Sons:* mentioned, but not named. *Other legatees:* SARAH HOPKINS (granddaughter), CHARLES CRADOCK. No executor named. *Witnesses:* ANDREW OLOVER, CHARLES CRADOCK, ELESEBETH BATEMAN. *Clerk of the Court:* R. HICKS.

HOPKINS, JOHN.   Chowan County.

January Court, 1754. *Wife and Executrix:* MARY. *Executor:* JOHN HALSEY. *Witnesses:* THOMAS SUMNER, JNO. MCKILDO, WM. HORNSBY. *Clerk of the Court:* WILL HALSEY. No date of execution.

HORN, WILLIAM.

September 10, 1753. *Sons:* WILLIAM, HENRY, CHARLES, THOMAS, MOSES, MICHAELL (*Executor*). *Daughter:* MARGARET. *Witnesses:* WM. REYNOLDS, JOYCE REYNOLDS, ANN HILL. No probate.

HORTH, THOMAS.   Chowan Precinct.

October 29, 1735. January Court, 1735. *Grandchildren:* SARAH, MARY and THOMAS MING (land, cattle, hogs, horses, etc.). *Daughter:* MARTHA MING. No executor. *Witnesses:* LUKE GREGORY, WILLIAM POWEL. *Clerk of the Court:* JAMES CRAVEN. The original of this will missing. Abstract made from recorded copy in Grant Book No. 4, Will No. 28.

HOSEA, ABRAM.   Pasquotank County.
    May 31, 1771. December 22, 1773. *Wife:* MARY. *Daughter:* LOVEY,
wife of JOHN SMITH ("my manner plantation"). *Nephew:* ABRAM HOSEA
(land on Little Alligator, in Tyrrell County). *Brother:* ROBERT HOSEA.
Trustee: THOMAS NICHOLSON. *Executors:* JOHN POOL and JOHN SMITH.
Witnesses: MATTHEW PRITCHARD, LEMUEL STONE, PETER ROSHALL. Will
proven before JO. MARTIN.

HOSEA, JOSEPH.   Perquimans County.
    May 10, 1753. July Court, 1753. *Sons:* JOSEPH and WILLIAM HOSEA.
Wife and Executrix: MARY. *Executor:* JOHN HOSEA (brother). *Wit-
nesses:* JAMES GIBSON, WILLIAM TRUMBALL. *Clerk of the Court:* EDMUND
HATCH.

HOSEA, ROBERT.   Perquimans County.
    December 17, 1742. January Court, 1742. *Sons:* ABRAHAM, JOSEPH,
WILLIAM (*Executor*), THOMAS (*Executor*). *Wife:* ANN. *Witnesses:* JACOB
MULLEN and WM. TOMBLIN. *Clerk of the Court:* EDMUND HATCH.

HOSKINS, THOMAS.   Chowan County.
    October 24, 1733. April Court, 1734. *Son and Executor:* WILLIAM.
Daughters: SARAH CHASTLON, MATHEW MARY. *Son-in-law:* WM. LUTON.
Executor: JOHN BENBURY. *Witnesses:* JOHN MITCHENER, JAMES SMITH.
Clerk of the Court: MOSELEY VAIL.

HOSKINS, WILLIAM. "Matacomack Creek in Albemarle Co."
    January 20, 1692–1693. *Brother:* THOMAS HOSKINS. *Cousin:* DANIEL
COX, JR. *Executor:* DANIEL COX. *Witnesses:* THOMAS MORIS, NICHOLAS
DAW. No probate.

HOSMER, HANNAH.   Onslow County.
    March 26, 1773. May 18, 1773. *Sons:* JOHN and STANTON SPOONER.
Executor: STANTON SPOONER. *Other children:* mentioned, but not named.
Witnesses: REUBEN GRANT, EXPERIENCE GRANT. Will proven before JO.
MARTIN.

HOUGHTON, THOMAS.   Bladen County.
    January Court, 1743. *Daughter:* MARY HOUGHTON. *Executors:* ELIZA-
BETH (wife), JOSHUA and WILLIAM HOUGHTON (brothers). *Witnesses:*
DAVID BUTLER, MARY BUTLER. *Clerk of Court:* RICH'D MCCLURE.

HOUGHTON, WILLIAM.   Chowan County.
    February 28, 1744–1745. July Court, 1745. *Son:* JONATHAN. *Daugh-
ters:* MARY and SARAH HOUGHTON. *Wife and Executrix:* MARY. *Ex-

ecutors: WILLIAM HOUGHTON (father), DAVID and JAMES HOUGHTON (brothers). *Witnesses:* DAVID BUTLER, MARY HOUGHTON. *Clerk of the Court:* EDMUND HATCH.

HOUSE, GEORGE.   Bertie County.

September 28, 1770. January 3, 1771. *Son and Executor:* THOMAS. *Grandsons:* GEORGE, BALIS, JAMES and JOHN HOUSE. *Granddaughters:* SARAH HOUSE, EDITH HOUSE, ANN, MARY and ELIZABETH SMITH. *Daughters:* ANN AVERET, ELIZABETH MOORE. *Executor:* JAMES MOORE (son-in-law). *Witnesses:* BENJAMIN PARKER, LEWIS HAYLES, WILLIAM HOUSE. Proven before WM. TRYON. Lands on Flagg Run, Little Roquis and other waters devised to son and grandsons.

HOUSE, THOMAS.   Albemarle County.

July 4, 1733. *Sons:* GEORGE, BAYLIS (*Executor*). *Daughters:* ANN and EDITH HOUSE. *Witnesses:* ROBERT POWELL, MARMADUKE NORFLEET. No probate.

HOUSTON, MOSES.   Carteret County.

January, 1774. January 27, 1774. *Wife:* MARGRETT. *Daughter:* MERIAM WEST (plantation on Whittock River). *Grandson:* HOUSTON ROBERTS. *Granddaughters:* JAMIMA DUDLEY, BONETA WILLIAMS, FANNIE DUDLEY, SARAH MADDUX. *Other legatee:* CAPT. GEORGE MITCHEL. *Executors:* BAZELL SMITH, BRICE WILLIAMS and MICAJAH FRAZIAR. *Witnesses:* JAMES MEAD, WILLIAM RAMSEY, PASLEY JACOBS. Proven before JO. MARTIN.

HOUSTON, THOMAS.   Onslow County.

March 29, 1733. July 3, 1733. *Sons:* WILLIAM, MOSES, JAMES, THOMAS. *Daughter:* ELIZIBETH HOUSTON. *Wife and Executrix:* MARY. *Witnesses:* NICHOLAS HUNTOR, SAM'LL JONES, JR., REBECKAH HUNTER. *Clerk of the Court:* WM. CRANFORD.

HOUSTON, WILLIAM.   Carteret County.

May 6, 1760. January 2, 1761. *Son:* WILLIAM. *Wife and Executrix:* RACHEL. *Executors:* SAMUEL and JAMES NOBLE (brothers of wife). *Witnesses:* JOSEPH NOBLE, MARK NOBLE and BETTY NOBLE. Will proven before ARTHUR DOBBS.

HOVER, JOHN JACOB.   Craven County.

February 15, 1744. November 28, 1744. *Sons:* JACOB, JOHN (plantation on Beards Creek), HENRY, SAMUEL. *Daughters:* MARY SLABBACH, ELIZABETH SLABBACH, MARGARETH. *Wife and Executrix:* MARY MAGDA-

LENA. *Executor:* NICHOLAS PUREFOY. *Witnesses:* JOHN GRANADE, GEORGE GRAHAM, JAMES WILLCOCKS. Will proven before E. MOSELEY, *Chief Justice.*

HOWARD, CHARLES.   Craven County.

1754. *Son:* CHARLES. *Daughters:* SARAH BROOKS and COURTNEY IVES. *Son-in-law:* JACOB HANBOX (or HANCOX). To each of these is bequeathed 'one shilling apease as the Law directs." *Granddaughter:* SIBBE BROOKS ("land in the fork of Crounes creek, if not sold before I die, quietly to be possessed during her pleasure.") *Wife, Residuary Legatee, and Executrix:* MARY. *Witnesses:* FRAN. FONTAINE, WILLIAM ARTHER, ANN SPINKS. No probate.

HOWARD, JAMES.   Bertie Precinct.

October 6, 1729. *Sons:* SOLOMON ("my plantation"), JAMES, EDWARD, SAMUELL, JOHN. To these sons is conveyed lands in Virginia, and lands on Aharskey Swamp, Cooneriskratt Swamp, Horse Swamp, etc. *Daughter:* SARAH HOWARD. *Wife and Executrix:* SARAH. *Other legatees:* FRANCIS SPEIGHT of Chuckatuck parish in Nancemond County, Va., THOMAS DAVIS (land lying on Rattlesnake Branch). *Executor:* JAMES HOWARD (son). *Witnesses:* JOHN RAWLEY (?), MARY BARKETT, WM. CRAFFORD, GEO. OTWAY. Codicil dated October 9, 1729. *Witnesses to Codicil:* JAS. SPEIR, MARY BURKETT, ANN STONE, GEO. OTWAY. No probate.

HOWCOTT, JOHN.   Bertie Precinct.

July 28, 1732. September 12, 1733. *Sons:* EDWARD (land called by the name of Stancells); JOHN (dwelling plantation); RICHARD, NATHANIEL. *Daughters:* ELIZABETH BRANCH, MARY HOWCOTT. *Wife:* MARY. *Executors:* EDWARD HOWCOTT (brother) and EDWARD HOWCOTT (son). *Witnesses:* JOHN FRYARD, EDWARD HOWCOTT, ELIZABETH BRANCH. Will proven before GEO. BURRINGTON.

HOWELL, JOSEPH.   Edgecombe County.

January 10, 1749. May Court, 1750. *Sons:* JOSEPH, THOMAS (land on Herricks Creek). *Daughters:* MARY, MURPHREY and MARTHA. *Wife and Executrix:* MARGETT. *Executors:* JOSEPH HOWELL (son), COLL. J. DAWSON, SAMUEL RUFFIN, THOMAS HOWELL and JOSEPH HENDERSON. *Witnesses:* JOS. WILLIAMSON, JAS. BARRAN, THOS. BARRAN. *Clerk of Court:* BENJAMIN WYNNS.

HOWSON, WILLIAM.   Beaufort County.

November 13, 1713. April 5, 1715. Testator bequeathes all property to his mother, who is not named. *Witnesses:* HENRY SLADE, WILLIAM CORDING, JOHN STAFFORD. *Clerk of the Court:* JNO. DRINKWATER.

HUBBARD, RANE.

March 30, 1714. *Executors and legatees:* WILLIAM EVERIGIN, JOSEPH GLAISTER. *Witnesses:* WILLIAM SIMSON, MARY MURDEN, MARY MASON. No probate.

HUCKINS, DANIEL.   Bath County.

March 26, 1733. June Court, 1733. *Sons and Executors:* SOLOMON and VALLINTY. *Wife and Executrix:* ANN. *Witnesses:* JOHN JACOB HONOR, RICHARD SCOTT. *Clerk of the Court of Craven County:* CALEB METCALFE.

HUDDE, CHRISTOPHER.   Beaufort County.

July 27, 1714. January 5, 1714. *Daughters:* PRUSILY, ELIZABETH GREEN (*Executrix*). *Witnesses:* THO. HENDERSON, JOHN SNEAD. *Clerk of the Court:* JNO. DRINKWATER.

HUDSON, JOSEPH.

Letters issued May 30, 1745. *Sons:* JOSEPH (*Executor*), LEWIS. *Daughters:* SARAH NEKELLES, SUSANAH, ELESEBETH. *Wife and Executrix:* MARY. *Witnesses:* BENJAMIN CARTREET, JOHN DUGEN, JONATHAN BATEMAN. No probate or county given.

HUGGENS, ANN.   Onslow County.

February 30, 1745–1746. May 22, 1746. *Sons:* CHARLES and BENJAMIN (land in Maryland), MATTHEW and JACOB (*Executors*). *Grandson:* JACOB HURLEY (son of ANN HURLEY). *Granddaughter:* LUCREASEA HUGGENS (daughter of MATTHEW HUGGENS). *Witnesses:* R. CHEASTEN, JOHN NORMAN, CATRINE PAULL. Will proven before E. HALL, C. J.

HUGGINS, EDMOND.   Onslow County.

April 12, 1737. July 6, 1737. *Son:* PHILIP. *Other legatees:* ABRAHAM HUGGINS, MARY HUGGINS (daughter of NEHEMIAH), JOHN HUGGINS, THOMAS HILLIARD, THOMAS OWIN, EDWARD EDWARDS. *Executor:* JOHN STARKEY. *Witnesses:* ABRA. MITCHELL, THOS. OWIN. *Clerk of the Court:* WM. CRANFORD.

HUGGINS, JAMES.   Onslow County.

January 24, 1745–1746. May 22, 1746. *Sons:* CHARLES and BENJAMIN (lands in Maryland); JACOB and MATHEW (*Executors*). *Grandson:* JACOB (son of ANN HURLEY). *Granddaughter:* LUCRESEA (daughter of MATTHEW HUGGINS). *Witnesses:* R. CHEASTEN, JOHN NORMAN, CATRINE PAULL. Will proven before E. HALL, C. J.

HUGGINS, JOHN.   Onslow County.

July 15, 1745. February Court, ———. *Son:* JOHN ("plantation whereon I now dwell on Bear Creek"). *Brother:* NEHEMIAH HUGGINS.

Wife: MARY. *Executors:* JOHN and PETER STARKEY. *Witnesses:* SARAH STARKEY, DANIEL SHERLOW, JOSEPH WATTS. *Clerk of Court:* WILL HEDGES.

HULL, JOHN.   Edenton, Chowan County.

January 14, 1747. March 23, 1752. *Wife:* not named. *Sisters:* CATHERINE and MARY HULL (in Rhode Island). *Other legatee:* ANNAH MARTIN. *Executors:* MILES GALE and JAMES CRAVEN. *Witnesses:* HUMPHREY ROBINSON, SAMUEL ROBINSON, ALEXR. FORBES. Will proven before GAB. JOHNSTON and recorded by SAM'L ORMES, *Deputy Secretary.* The testator makes some interesting provisions as to his burial.

HUMES, JAMES.   Beaufort County.

February 6, 1745. March Court, 1745. *Wife:* ELISABETH. *Daughters:* ABIGAIL ("the plantation whereon I now live called by the name of Cappell Point"), ELISABETH HUCHLEROY, MARY (land on Thomases Creek on South Side of Bear River), RENNIS. *Executor:* JOSIAS JONES. *Witnesses:* WM. BETSWORTH, MARY CRICKMAN, URIAH LAMBERT. *Clerk of the Court:* JOHN FORBES.

HUMPHRIES, JOHN.   Pasquotank Precinct.

December 2, 1708. *Sons:* JOHN, WILLIAM, CHRISTOPHER and JOHN (two JOHNS named). *Daughters:* MARY GRAY, SARAH BRAY. *Son-in-law:* GRIFFITH GRAY. *Executor:* WILLIAM HUMPHRIES (son). *Witnesses:* JOHN ULAN, FR. MCBRIDE, SOL. HARAERY (?). No probate.

HUMPHRIES, RICHARD.   Albemarle County.

October 7, 1688. July 25, 1689. *Mother:* mentioned, but not named. *Other legatees:* WILLIAM NICKOLE, JOHN HUNT. *Executor:* THOMAS POLLOCK. *Witnesses:* ELIZEBETH BARCLIFF, JOHN ROPER, WILLIAM BARCLIFT. Will proven before SETH. SOTHELL.

HUMPHREY, JOSEPH.   Bladen County.

October 14, 1752. December Court, 1752. *Cousin:* SARAH ROBERTS. *Nephew:* JOSEPH HUMPHREY. *Friend:* EVAN ELLIS. To Carvers Creek Meeting is given three pounds. *Executors:* JONATHAN EVANS and ISAAC JONES. *Witnesses:* ALEXANDER MCCONKEY, THOMAS SPEIRS. *Clerk of the Court:* THOS. ROBESON.

HUNT, JOHN.   Little River (county not given).

April 7, 1710. August 26, 1710. *Grandsons:* JOHN HUNT EVANS, BARTHOLOMEW EVANS. *Granddaughter:* ELIZABETH EVANS. *Wife:* ELIZABETH. *Executor:* JAMES TOOKE (TOOLE). *Witnesses:* W. EVERIGIN, JOSEPH PARISE, THO. COMMANDER. Will proven before THOMAS CARY, *President.*

HUNT, THOMAS.   Pasquotank County.

May 7, 1688. October 2, 1696. *Brother and Executor:* ANDREW HUNT of Bucks County, England. *Other legatees:* JOHN and THOMAS HAWKINS (sons of JOHN HAWKINS). *Witnesses:* EDWARD SMITH, WILLIAM COLLINGS, JOHN CABAGE. *Clerk:* W. GLOVER.

HUNTER, ANN.   Chowan County.

May 24, 1749. October Court, 1751. *Sons and Executors:* WM. HUNTER and EDWARD ARNAL. *Daughters:* JUDITH BLAND, ANN WINBORN, HESTER KNIGHT, ALICE ARNAL. *Witnesses:* SARY OSBORN, WM. HUNTER, JOHN PARKER, JOSEPH PARKER. *Clerk of the Court:* JAMES CRAVEN.

HUNTER, ISAAC.   Chowan County.

April 17, 1752. April Court, 1753. *Sons:* ELISHA ("my plantation whereon I now live and plantation whereon he now lives, together with one negro), JESSE (land purchased of THOMAS MORRIS and one negro), ISAAC (land in Bertie, together with one negro), DANIEL (70 pounds "current money"). *Daughters:* HANNAH RIDDICK, ELIZABETH PERRY, ALCE HUNTER, RACHELL WALTON and SARAH HUNTER (one negro to each). *Grandchildren:* JESSE, PHILIP and MARY PERRIES and SARAH FIELD. *Other legatee:* ZILPHEA PARKER. Water-mill bequeathed to son JACOB. *Executor:* ELISHA HUNTER (son). *Witnesses:* MOSES SUMNER, SAMUEL SUMNER, JOHN SUMNER. *Clerk of the Court:* JAMES CRAVEN. Impression of dragon on seal.

HUNTER, JOHN.

June 13, 1753. October 25, 1756, "township of Little Brittan, County of Lancaster and province of Pencalvania." *Wife and Executrix:* AGNESS. *Daughters:* MARY and CATRIN. *Witnesses:* JOHN MCBURNEY, ADAM LECKY. *Deputy Register:* EDWARD SHIPPEN. This is a certified copy from the records of Lancaster County, Pa.

HUNTER, NICHOLAS.   Carteret County.

January 3, 1749–1750. March Court, 1749. *Sons:* STEPHEN ("all land on the West side of Gailes Branch"), EZEKELL, LEBBEUS, WILLIAM, JOAB. *Grandson:* GEORGE MILLCHELL. *Daughters:* E———, ZILLAH, REACHELL, KISIAH MILLCHELL, ELIZEBATH, SARAH, RUTH. *Wife and Executrix:* REBECCA. *Executor:* EZEKELL HUNTER (son). *Witnesses:* JOHN WILLCOCKS, MOSES HOUSTON, JOHN GILLETT. *Clerk of the Court:* GEO. READ.

HUNTER, ROBERT.   Bertie County.

June 3, 1753. August Court, 1753. *Sons:* HENRY, MOSES (*Executor*). *Daughters:* SARAH DOCTON, MARY GORDON, JUDITH PERRY, SUSANNAH

12

BENTON, ELIZABETH WILLIAMS. *Executor:* THOS. WHITMELL. *Witnesses:* JNO. HILL, JOHN SLATTER, OEN SLATTER, LITTLETON SLATTER, KEZIAH SLATTER, WILLIAM APPERSON. *Clerk of the Court:* SAM'L ORMES.

HUNTER, WILLIAM.   Chowan County.

January 4, 1732–1733. January 18, 1732. *Sons and Executors:* WILLIAM and EPHRAIM. *Daughters:* JUDITH, ALLISE and MARY HUNTER, ANN, EASTER. *Wife:* ANN. *Witnesses:* SPENCER COLE, ISAAC HUNTER, ROBERT HUNTER. *Clerk of the Court:* RT. FORSTER.

HUNTER, WILLIAM.   Chowan County.

March 21, 1749. April Court, 1750. *Sons:* JOHN, NICHOLAS, HARDY, WILLIAM, JOB, JAMES, TIMOTHY. *Wife and Executrix:* SARAH. *Executor:* JOHN HUNTER (son). *Witnesses:* ELISHA HUNTER, JOHN GOURDON, JOHN NORFLEET. *Clerk of the Court:* WILL MEARNS.

HURDLE, BENJAMIN.   Perquimans County.

February 14, 1734. July Court, 1735. *Legatees:* WILLIAM HURDLE, MORING HURDLE and ELIZABETH HURDLE (mother). No executor. *Witnesses:* NATHANIEL WILLIAMS, DANIEL RAGESON, JOSEPH RIDDICK. *Clerk of Court:* JAMES CRAVEN.

HUSBANDS, RICHARD.

August 16, 1732. September 15, 1732, "late of Barbadoes but now of ye Country of North Carolina in ye Cape Fear." *Sons:* RICHARD and JOHN ("now in Barbadoes"). *Executrix and Wife:* JANE. *Witnesses:* ELIZABETH HALL, ELIZABETH BRYAN, THOS. HALL. Will proven before GEO. BURRINGTON.

HUTSON, WILLIAM.   Craven County.

January 29, 1739–1740. March 3, 1739. *Wife:* FRANCES. *Executor:* JOSEPH MARR. *Witnesses:* JOSIAH HART, ELISHA JAQUES. Will proven before GAB. JOHNSTON.

HYRNE, HENRY.   New Hanover County.

September 9, 1772. October 26, 1773. *Nephews:* HENRY WALTERS (plantation called "New Hyrnham"; also 1,747 acres of land in New Hanover), JOSEPH and GEORGE WALTERS, MOSES, FRANCIS and HENERY BRITTON. *Niece:* MARY BRITTON. *Goddaughter:* ELIZABETH JONES (daughter of FREDERICK JONES). *Executor:* FREDERICK JONES (two volumes of Chambers' Dictionary). *Witnesses:* SAM'LL SWANN, JOHN BUFORD, BENJAMIN WILLIAMS, WILLIAM BUFORD. Codicil of even date disposes of wearing apparel. *Witnesses to Codicil:* JOHN BUFORD, WILLIAM BUFORD, BENJAMIN WILLIAMS. Proven before JO. MARTIN.

INGRAM, ABSALOM (or ABRAHAM). Onslow County.

October 20, 1744. November 24, 1744. *Sons:* DAVID (land known as "Weakes Iland"), ISAAC, ABRAHAM and JAMES (20 shillings each). *Executor:* DAVID INGRAM (son). *Witnesses:* JOHN WHITE, LAZARUS KENNY. *Justice of the Peace:* JOHN STARKEY. Will proven before GAB. JOHNSTON.

INNES, JAMES.

July 5, 1754. October 9, 1759. "Of Cape Fear in North Carolina. Col. of the Regement of sd Province raised for His Majesty's imediate Service and Commander in Chief of the Expedition to the Ohio against the French and there Indians who have most unjustly Invaided & Fortified themselves on His Majestys Lands." "Being now reddey to Enter upon action & of sound minde, Memory and understanding etc." "I direct a remittance may be made to Edinburgh Sufficient to pay for a Church Bell for the Parish Church of Cannesby in Caithness agreeable to my letter to MR. JAMES BROADEE Minister there." "I also give and bequeath att the death of my loving wife JEAN INNES my plantation called Point Pleasant & the opposite Mash land over the River for which there is a separate patent, two negro young women, one Negroe young man and there increase, all the Stock of Cattle and Hogs halfe the stock of horses belonging att the time to that plantation with all my Books and one hundred Pounds Sterling or the Equivalent there unto in the Currency of the Country For the Use of a Free School for the Benefite of the Youth of North Carolina." The colonel of the New Hanover Regiment, the Parson and Vestry of the Wilmington Church appointed trustees to carry out the foregoing provision. *Executrix:* JEAN INNES (wife). *Witnesses:* JOHN CARLYLE, W. COCKS, CALEB GRAINGER. Will made and executed at Winchester in Virginia. Proven before ARTHUR DOBBS.

IRBY, HENRY. Brunswick County.

January 30, 1733. February 12, 1733–1734. *Sons:* WILLIAM, HENRY ("plantation up North West and House and Lott in Cape Fair to hold in common with ELIZABETH, his sister, and FORTUNE HOLEDERLEY their mother"). *Daughters:* ANN and ELIZABETH IRBY. *Executrix:* FORTUNE HOLEDERLEY. *Witnesses:* JAMES ESPY, ROBT. EATON, WILLIAM POWER. Will proven before GEO. BURRINGTON.

IRVING, ROBERT. Currituck County.

February 16, 1735–1736. "According to the Computation of the Church of England, April 5, 1737." *Executor and sole legatee and devisee:* GEORGE POWERS. *Witnesses:* W. WHITE, CHARLES WALPOLE, HUMPHRY VINCE, RICHARD SPAN. *Clerk of the Court:* WM. SHERGOLD.

ISHAM, JAMES.   Duplin County.

November 2, 1752.   July Court, 1753.   *Sons:* JAMES, CHARLES.   *Daughter:* MARGARET.   *Wife and Executrix:* JANE.   *Executors:* EVAN ELLIS and EDWARD HARRISON, JUNIOR (brothers-in-law).   *Witnesses:* WM. HOUSTON, WM. MCKEE, JOHN DUNN.   *Clerk of the Court:* JOHN DICKSON.

ISLANDS (spelled also "ILANDS"), RICHARD.
Currituck Precinct.

March 7, 1733.   October Court, 1735.   *Sons:* ROBERT (150 acres of land in Princess Ann County), GEORGE (land in Currituck), RICHARD.   *Daughters:* SARAH ILANDS (100 acres of land in Princess Ann County), JANE WAYE, ELIZABETH ROULINGS.   *Wife and Executrix:* ELIZABETH.   *Witnesses:* FRANCIS MORSE, JOHN ROSE, MOSES FICHER.   *Clerk:* JAMES CRAVEN.

ISLER, CHRISTIAN.   Craven County.

October 4, 1747.   November 7, 1747.   *Sons:* JOHN ("one negro, and horse, saddle & bridle"), WILLIAM (plantation and two negroes).   *Daughters:* ELIZABETH and SUSANNAH ISLER.   *Wife:* ELIZABETH.   *Executors:* FREDERICK ISLER (brother), JOHN and WILLIAM ISLER (sons).   *Witnesses:* MELCHER REMM, JAMES MARSHEL, SARAH LICKBLAT.   Proven before E. HALL, C. J.

ISMAY, JOHN.   Edenton, Chowan County.

January 12, 1729.   August 5, 1732.   *Daughter:* NANCY (lots 11 and 12 in Edenton).   *Wife and Executrix:* SARAH.   *Trustees:* JOHN LOVICK and EDW'D MOSELEY.   *Witnesses:* SARAH ROWDEN, JNO. MATTHEWS, WILL'M WILLIAMS.   Will proven before GEO. BURRINGTON.

IVES, JOHN.   Craven County.

February 21, 1750.   August Court, 1752.   *Sons:* JOB ("½ of my land at the head of Broad Creek"), JONAS (" loer half of my land on Broad Creek").   *Daughters:* ESTHER (land on south side of Broad Creek called Giddinses Point).   *Executor:* JOB IVES (son).   *Witnesses:* JAMES WHITING, JACOB JONES, FRANCES NASH.   *Clerk of the Court:* PHIL. SMITH.

IVES, THOMAS.   Currituck County.

October 26, 1750.   April Court, 1751.   *Daughter:* ELISABETH IVES.   *Wife and Executrix:* MARY.   *Witnesses:* JOHN WOODHOUSE, JAMES PARKER, RODE ALLEN.   *Clerk of the Court:* RICH'D MCCLURE.

JACKSON, DANIEL.   Pasquotank County.

February 14, 1734–1735.   January 10, 1737.   *Sons:* DANIEL, SAMUEL, DAVID ("my plantation"), WILLIAM, JOAB ("long glade tract of land").

Daughters: RUTH, ANN and ELISABETH JACKSON. *Wife and Executrix:* ANN. *Executors:* ZACHARIAS and SAMUEL JACKSON (sons). *Witnesses:* WM. SIMSON, JR., JOHN SIMSON, JUNR. *Clerk of the Court:* JOS. SMITH. *Justice of the Peace:* JAMES CRAVEN.

JACKSON, DAVID.   Little River.

September 12, 1715. January 9, 1715–1716. *Son:* THOMAS. *Daughter:* ELIZABETH. *Wife and Executrix:* MARY. *Brothers:* WILLIAM and AARON DAVIS, SAMUELL JACKSON. *Cousin:* LUCY JACKSON. *Witnesses:* JOS. HORNY, SAMUELL DAVIS, DANIEL JACKSON. No signature of probate officer.

JACKSON, ISAAC.   Bath County.

September 7, 1716. April 2, 1718. *Son:* THOMAS ("my plantation"). *Daughters:* ELIZABETH CHESTER, RACHELL ADAMS, MARGRIT. *Friend:* JOHN JORDAN. *Wife and Executrix:* ELIZABETH. *Witnesses:* JOHN JORDAN, THO. MORRIS, ELIZABETH MORRIS. *Clerk of the Court:* JNO. DRINKWATER.

JACKSON, JOHN.   Bath County.

July 30, 1728. March Court, 1728. *Legatees:* JOHN CHESTER (*Executor*), EDWARD POYNER (*Executor*), NICHOLASS SMITH, ELIZABETH CHESTER, WILLIAM WHITFORD. *Witnesses:* NICHOLAS SMITH, WILLIAM WHITFORD, JEAN SMITH. *Clerk of the Court:* JOHN MATTOCKE.

JACKSON, ROBERT.   Chowan County.

January 21, 1757. October Court, 1757. *Wife and Executrix:* ANN. *Witnesses:* JASPER CHARLTON, ABIGAIL CHARLTON. *Clerk of the Court:* THO. JONES.

JACKSON, SAMUEL.   Pasquotank County.

December 3, 1748. January 19, 1748. *Sons:* JOHN ("upper part of plantation"), JOSHUA ("remainder of my land"). *Daughters:* ELISABETH BENTON, MIRIAM POOL, MARY CARTWRIGHT, MARY ANN LOVEL. *Wife:* ELISABETH. *Executors:* JOHN and JOSHUA JACKSON (sons). *Witnesses:* ABRAHAM RANKHORN, SAMUEL BENTON, JOSEPH ROBINSON. Will proven before GAB. JOHNSTON.

JACKSON, SAMUEL.   Pasquotank County.

March 20, 1750. April Court, 1750. *Sons:* ABSALOM ("plantashion whereon I now live"), MATHIAS (land described in will). *Daughters:* MARY and HANAH JACKSON. *Wife and Executrix:* MARY. *Executor:* DANIEL JACKSON (brother). *Witnesses:* JACOB MADREN, ANN JACKSON, ELIZABETH BENTON. *Clerk of the Court:* THOMAS TAYLOR.

JACKSON, THOMAS.   Bertie County.

March 15, 1746. May Court, 1753. *Sons:* THOMAS ("plantation known as Mount Garriot, together with my ferry"), WILLIAM (plantation bought of RICHARD MARTIN), JOHN (plantation in Northampton County), JAMES (plantation in Bertie County). *Wife's daughter:* ELIZABETH HAMMOND GRIFFIN. *Wife:* HESTER. *Executors:* JOHN BROWN, son of DR. JAS. BROWN, dec'd, BENJAMIN WYNNS and HESTER JACKSON. *Brother:* JEREMIAH JACKSON of Boston. Codicil dated April 9, 1749, changes division of land among sons, and appoints as *Executors:* BENJAMIN WYNNS, WILLIAM WYNNS and HESTER JACKSON. No witnesses or signature to codicil. *Witnesses to will:* WM. POWER, JAMES GRIFFIN, BETTY GRIFFIN, CATHERN CONNER. *Clerk of the Court:* BENJAMIN WYNNS.

JACKSON, WILLIAM.   Albemarle County.

March 3, 1694. *Sons:* ZACHARIAS and DANIELL. *Wife:* ELIZABETH. Will proven before W. GLOVER. Part of this will is torn away.

JACKSON, WILLIAM, SENR.   Albemarle County.

February 21, 1695–1696. March Court, 1697. *Sons:* WILL JACKSON, JR., ZACHARIAH, DAVID, SAMUEL, DANIEL (plantation on the eastermost branch of Herrin Creek). *Daughter:* RUTH DAVIS. *Wife:* ELIZABETH JACKSON. *Executors:* ZACHARIAH and DANIEL JACKSON. *Witnesses:* HUGH CAMPBELL, RICH'D PLATER, WM. SIMSON. *Clerk of the Court:* WILLIAM GLOVER.

JACKSON, WILLIAM, JR.   Perquimans County.

February 1, 1734. April 20, 1735. *Sons:* MOSES and AARON ("plantation whereon I now dwell"). *Daughters:* PARTHENIA and MARGARET JACKSON. *Wife and Executrix:* MARGARET. *Witnesses:* GEORGE GORDING, WM. JACKSON, SR., EDWARD JACKSON, THOMAS WEEKES. *Clerk of the Court:* JAMES CRAVEN.

JACKSON, ZACHARIAS.   Pasquotank County.

October 18, 1748. August 4, 1749. *Sons:* SIMON ("the plantation"), DEMCE (land bought of JOHN ALLBIRD), ACE (plantation bought of THOMAS HARRIS), LAMUEL. *Daughter:* DARKES JACKSON. *Wife:* ELIZABETH. *Executors:* WILLIAM and JOAB JACKSON (brothers). *Witnesses:* DAN'L JACKSON, SR., SAMUEL JACKSON, DAVID JACKSON. Will proven before GAB. JOHNSTON at Eden House.

JACOB, ISAAC.   Currituck County.

March 19, 1713–1714. July 14, 1714. *Daughters:* SUSANAH JACOB ("my manor plantation at New Corotuck"), JANE JACOB ("a tract of land in New Corotuck on ye head of Deep Creek"). *Overseers:* JOHN PROCKTER, BEN-

JAMIN SANDERSON. *Wife and Executrix:* SARAH. *Witnesses:* JOSEPH SANDERSON, DINAH, NELL, WILLIAM ASHLEY. *Clerk of the Court:* JOS. WICKER.

JACOCKS, THOMAS.   County not given.

May 2, 1692. August Court, 1692. *Executrix and sole legatee: Wife,* not named. *Witnesses:* PATRICK BEALLY (or BAYLEY), RICHARD ROOKE. *Clerk, Sect. Office:* W. GLOVER.

JAMES, EDWARD.   Pasquotank County.

February 8, 1720. April Court, 1721. *Sons:* EDWARD ("my manner plantation"), GILBERT. *Sons-in-law:* DOSER BETS, HEZEKIAH. *Cousins:* JOSEPH and MARY MURFEY. *Witnesses:* STEPHEN SAUL, MARY HUTCHENSON, JOHN MARTYN. *Clerk pro tem.:* JOHN PALIN.

JAMES, WILLIAM.   Pasquotank County.

May 31, 1733. May 9, 1733. *Sons:* THOMAS ("plantation whereon I now live"), WILLIAM ("plantation I bought of THOMAS PALMER"), SAMUEL. *Daughters:* REBECCA JAMES and FRANCIS MACKEELE. *Wife and Executrix:* JANE. *Executor:* THOMAS JAMES (son). *Witnesses:* SAMUEL BUNDAY, JEAN BUNDAY, J. SWEENY. Will proven before GEO. BURRINGTON.

JAMES, WILLIAM.   Pasquotank County.

September 18, 1757. September Court, 1757. *Son:* WILLIAM ("my plantation"). *Daughter:* MILLY. *Wife and Executrix:* ANN. *Executor:* JOSEPH POOL. *Witnesses:* MATTHEW DUAN, ELIZABETH JAMES. *Clerk of the Court:* THOS. TAYLOR.

JARMAN, THOMAS.   Onslow County.

April 5, 1759. January Court, 1760. *Sons:* THOMAS, JOHN, MOSES, LARRANCE, WILLIAM. *Daughter:* MARY JARMAN. *Grandchildren:* WILLIAM and MARY JARMAN (children of WILLIAM). *Wife:* not named. *Executors:* JOHN JARMAN and MIKEL KOONE. *Witnesses:* JOHN JARMAN, JACOB MANER. *Clerk of the Court:* WILL'M CRAY.

JARRATT, JOHN.   Carteret County.

April 13, 1745. June Court, 1745. *Sons:* JOHN, JACOB, ABRAHAM, ISAAC. *Daughters:* SARAH, SUSANNAH and ESTHER JARRATT, SARAH SHEPARD, ELISABETH DUDLEY, ANN GASKILL, MARGARET WORD. *Wife and Executrix:* CATHERINE. *Witnesses:* GEORGE BELL, THOMAS LEWIS. *Clerk of the Court:* GEORGE READ.

JARVIS, FOSTER.   Currituck County.

December 3, 1750. January Court, 1750. *Sons:* SAMUELL (100 acres of land adjoining JOHN WOODHOUSE), JONATHAN (200 acres adjoining tract above devised), MARTAIN (361 acres of land), WILLIAM (360 acres of land), FOSTER. *Daughters:* ELIZABETH and FRANCIS JARVIS. *Grandson:* SAMUEL JARVIS. *Executor:* MARTAIN JARVIS (son). *Witnesses:* SAMUEL SALYER, HILLARY WHITE, MICHAEL O'NEEL, HENRY KINZEY. *Clerk of the Court:* RICH'D McCLURE.

JASPER, RICHARD.   County not given.

October 30, 1722. *Son and Executor:* SAMUELL ("my plantation'). *Daughters:* ELIZABETH, ANN. *Wife and Executrix:* not named. *Witnesses:* CHARLES SMITH, CHARLES SMITH, JR., MARY SMITH.

JASPER, SAMUEL.   Hyde County.

March 29, 1752. March Court, 1753. *Sons:* SAMUEL ("all my land"), WILLIAM, JONATHAN and ISRAEL. *Daughters:* HANNAH LEATH (her children KEZIA and JOHN), ANN JASPER, MARY JASPER, LYDDELA JASPER. *Wife:* ANN. *Executors:* WILLIAM and JONATHAN JASPER (sons). *Witnesses:* ROGER MASON, JR., JOHN SLADE, JR., DORCAS LEATH. *Clerk of Court:* THOS. JORDAN.

JEFFREYS, CHRISTOPHER.   Perquimans County.

.January 23, 1735. April Court, 1736. *Legatees:* ELIZABETH and JOSEPH POTTLE, of Pasquotank. *Executor:* JOSEPH POTTLE. *Witnesses:* SAMUEL SWANN, JOHN WILLCOCKS, PATRICK QUIDLE. *Clerk of Court:* JAMES CRAVEN.

JEFFREYS, ELIZABETH.   Northampton County.

June 20, 1742. February Court, 1742. *Sons:* JOHN HILLIARD, OSBORNE JEFFREYS, ROBERT HILLIARD, WILLIAM HILLIARD. *Daughter:* ELIZABETH (wife of JOHN BODDIE). *Grandsons:* WILLIAM, JAMES, ISAAC and ELIAS HILLIARD (sons of WILLIAM), JEREMIAH, JACOB and JOHN HILLIARD. *Granddaughter:* SARAH HILLIARD. *Executors:* JOHN HILLIARD and OSBORNE JEFFREYS (sons). *Witnesses:* I. EDWARDS, DAVID DICSON, MARY DUKE. *Clerk of the Court:* I. EDWARDS.

JEFFREYS, ELIZABETH.   Northampton County.

January 28, 1742. February 1, 1742. May Court, 1743. This is a nuncupative will proven before JOHN DAWSON by OSBORN JEFFREYS and RACHEL BOLLEN, and bequeathes all property to daughter, ELIZABETH BODDIE. Property consists of land, stock and negroes. *Executor:* OSBORN JEFFREYS. *Clerk of the Court:* I. EDWARDS.

The original of this will missing; abstract made from recorded copy No. 142, in Grant Book 4.

JENKINS, CHARLES.   Hertford County.

September 26, 1772. November 25, 1773. *Sons:* WILLIAM, HENRY ("plantation he now dwells on"), CHARLES ("plantation I now dwell on").

Daughter: Elizabeth.   *Executors:* Henry Jenkins, Winbourne, William and Charles Jenkins (sons) and William Murfree. *Grandsons:* Charles and Shurard Jenkins (sons of William). *Witnesses:* Thomas Winborne, Sarah Winborn. Will proven before Jo. Martin.

Jennett, Abraham.   Perquimans County.

October Court, 1742. *Sons:* Isakiah, Abraham, Jeremiah. *Daughters:* Ann and Elisabeth Jennett. *Wife and Executrix:* Mary. *Executors:* John Moor, Samuel Hall, Ralph Doe. *Clerk of the Court:* Edmund Hatch.

Jennett, John.   Tyrrell County.

August 3, 1738. March Court, 1749. *Sons:* William ("all my land"), John and Jabez. *Daughters:* Elizabeth Alexander, Dorothy Poptewell, Jean. *Wife:* Dorothy. *Executor:* William Jennett (son). *Witnesses:* Henry Norman, Jos. Spruill, Sam'l Spruill. *Clerk of the Court:* Evan Jones.

Jennett, John.   Tyrrell County.

April 9, 1748. June Court, 1749. *Sons:* Abraham, John. *Daughters:* Ann and Elizabeth Jennett. *Grandson:* Abraham Jennett. *Wife and Executrix:* Ann. *Witnesses:* George Caron, Ann Jennett ("Jabez's Daughter"), Danll. Grandin. *Clerk of Court:* Evan Jones.

Jennings, John.   Pasquotank County.

April 15, 1751. July Court, 1751. *Son:* Isaac. *Other children:* mentioned, but not named. *Wife and Executrix:* Luse. *Witnesses:* Zachariah Keeton, Joseph Lambrosher, Nathan Overman. Clerk's signature missing.

Jennings, Mary.   Currituck County.

December 7, 1725. October 7, 1729. *Son:* John Relf. *Son-in-law and Executor:* John Norton. *Witnesses:* David Linsey, Henry Smith, John Martyn. *Clerk of the Court:* J. Martyn.

Jennings, Thomas.   New Hanover County.

December 23, 1744. *Son:* Thomas ("my plantation"). *Wife and Executrix:* Elliner. *Executor:* Michael Higgins. *Witnesses:* Jas. Mackilwean, Daniel Dupee, —— Sherlock. No probate.

Jennings, William.   County not given.

January 24, 1686–1687. April Court, 1687. *Son and Executor:* John. *Daughter:* Ann Lathum. *Son-in-law:* Ralph Garret. *Granddaughter:*

MARY GARRET.   *Godson:* WILLIAM BARKCAKE.   *Witnesses:* THOS. ROLFE, EDWARD CHAMBARS, WM. ROLFE.   Officer before whom probated not named.

JENNINGS, WILLIAM.   Currituck County.

July 11, 1713.   October Court, 1729.   *Wife, Executrix and sole legatee:* MARY.   *Witnesses:* JOHN BLISH, JOHN NORTON, MARGARET NORTON. *Clerk of the Court:* J. MARTYN.

JENOURE, JOSEPH, Surveyor General of North Carolina.

September 30, 1732.   January 13, 1732.   *Wife and Executrix:* ANN. *Son:* mentioned, but not named.   *Witnesses:* WM. LITTLE, R. FOSTER. Proven before GEO. BURRINGTON.

JERNAGAN, JOHN.   Bertie Precinct.

January 10, 1733.   February Court, 1733.   *Sons:* THOMAS and GEORGE ("200 acres of land"), DAVID, JAMES (100 acres of land).   *Executors:* TEMPERANCE JERNAGAN (wife), BENJAMIN HILL.   *Witnesses:* JOHN CARROL, BARZILLA HEWITT, BENJAMIN HILL.   *Clerk of Court:* RT. FORSTER.

JERNIGIN, HENRY.   Bertie Precinct.

May 9, 1736.   August Court, 1736.   *Sons:* HENRY (80 acres of land), JACOB ("my plantation"), JESSE (80 acres of land), DEMPSIE ("plantation I bought of THOMAS WATSON").   *Daughter:* ANN JONES.   *Wife:* PHEBE. *Executors:* HENRY and JACOB JERNIGIN.   To Henry is also given land in Va. in north side of Summersetts Creek.   *Witnesses:* THEOPHILUS WILLIAMS, JOHN JERNIGAN, BENNETT BLACKMAN.   *Clerk of the Court:* JOHN WYNNS.

JESSOP, JOSEPH.   Perquimans County.

March 12, 1735–1736.   August 29, 1735.   *Nephews:* THOMAS JESSOP ("plantation whereon I now live"), TIMOTHY and JONATHAN JESSOP. *Granddaughter:* MARY MAYO ("my plantation at the meeting house"). *Kinsman:* THOMAS PRITCHARD.   *Brother:* THOMAS JESSOP.   *Nieces:* MARY and ELIZABETH (daughters of THOMAS).   *Wife and Executrix:* MARGARET. *Executors:* THOMAS JESSOP (brother), WILLIAM WHITE.   *Witnesses:* THOMAS WINSLOWE, LEAH WINSLOWE, JOHN WILLSON.   Will proven before W. SMITH, C. J.

JEVINS, ELIZABETH.   Pasquotank County.

February 5, 1734–1735.   July 8, 1735.   *Son:* ISAM SWINNEY.   *Husband's nephew:* NATHANIEL CHEVIN.   *Executor:* STEPHEN SCOTT.   *Witnesses:* JOHN SCOTT, JOSEPH PINDLETON, J. JESSOP.   *Clerk of the Court:* JOS. SMITH.

JEVINS, JOHN.   Pasquotank County.

May 14, 1734. April Court, 1735. *Wife and Executrix:* ELIZABETH. *Friend:* EDWARD MAYO. *Witnesses:* EDWARD MAYO, MARY MAYO, ANN BRYAN. *Clerk of the Court:* JOS. SMITH.

JEWELL, JOHN.   Beaufort County.

December 10, 1744. March Court, 1744. *Daughter:* ANNE JEWELL ("plantation whereon I now live on the Eastern Branch of Old Town Creek"). *Wife and Executrix:* MARTHA. *Executor:* JAMES ADAMS. *Witnesses:* JAMES ADAMS, MARY ADAMS, JOHN FORBES. *Clerk of the Court "pro hac vice":* JNO. TURNER.

JEWEL, THOMAS.   Beaufort County.

December 24, 1735. March 9, 1735. *Sons:* JOHN, BENJAMIN, SAMUEL and JAMES ("all my land to be equally divided between them"). *Wife and Executrix:* FRANCES. *Executor:* JOHN JEWEL (son). *Witnesses:* DANIEL BLIN, ELIZ. BEAHAN, JNO. COLLISON. *Justices:* ROBT. TURNER, SIMON ALDERSON, SETH PILKINTON. *Clerk of the Court:* JOHN COLLISON.

JOHNSTON, GABRIEL, Governor of North Carolina.

Granville County.

May 16, 1751. April 4, 1753. *Wife:* FRANCES (plantation called Possum Quarter in Granville County; plantation called Conahoe in Tyrrell and plantation in Bertie County on Salmon Creek). *Daughter:* PENELOPE JOHNSTON. *Nephews:* SAMUEL and JOHN JOHNSTON, HENRY JOHNSTON ("now at school at Newhaven in the Collony of Connecticut"). *Sister:* ELIZABETH SMEAR, of the County of Fife in North Britain. *Executors:* JOHNSTON and WILLIAM CATHCART. *Witnesses:* ANDREW LEAKE, SAMUEL ORMES, THOMAS WHITMELL. Proven before MATT. ROWAN. The following real estate devised: lands lying in Bertie, Northampton and Granville; 1,000 acres on Cypress Creek on the south side of Trent River; 980 acres on Trent River; 400 acres on the head of Trent and New Rivers; 7,000 acres on Deep River in Bladen County; all the small islands in Roanoke River in the neighbourhood of Mount Gallard. The following are items of interest: "And in case my wife shall choose to remain in North Carolina and reside upon the lands of and live with my daughter * * * my will is that she, my said wife, shall have the use of all my said daughter's plantations and for her encouragement to cultivate and improve these plantations, especially in raising silk, etc. * * * And I earnestly request my dearest wife to be a kind, tender mother to my dear little girl and to bring her up in the Fear of God and under a deep sense of her being always in his presence and in Sobriety and moderation confining her desires to things plain, neat and elegant, and especially to take care to keep within the bounds of her income and by no means to

run in debt." "My books I leave to WILLIAM CATHCART after my wife
and brother have choose out of them any number not exceeding forty
each. To my sister ELIZABETH SMEAR my large gold watch * * * ."
Original missing. Recorded in Book 1755–1758, page 153.

JOHNSON, JAMES.   Albemarle County.

    August 21, 1694. October Court, 1694. *Children:* WM. JOHNSON,
JAMES JOHNSON and ELIZABETH JOHNSON. *Executor:* RICHARD ATKINSON.
Witnesses: PATRICK KENADY, ANDREW DAVIE. *Clerk of the Court:* JOHN
STEPNEY.

JOHNSON, JOHN.   County not given.

    September 10, 1693. *Son-in-law:* LAWRENCE GONSOLVO. *Wife and Exec-
utrix:* SARAH. *Overseers:* CALEB CALLOWAY, JAMES HOGG, THO. LEPPER,
THO. HAUGHTON, JOHN PORTER. No probate.

JOHNSON, JOHN.   Northampton County.

    January 27, 1745–1746. August Court, 1753. *Granddaughter:* MARY
JOHNSON BRIDGER. *Wife and Executrix:* MARY. *Witnesses:* JAMES JOHN-
SON, NICHOLAS BOON. *Clerk of the Court:* I. EDWARDS.

JOHNSON, JOHN.   Brunswick County.

    March 1, 1750. February Court, 1752. St. Andrews Parish in Bruns-
wick County. *Son and Executor:* WILLIAM ("my land and plantation").
Daughters: AMEY MITCHELL and ANN JELKS. *Granddaughters:* MARTHA
and ANNE (daughters of WILLIAM). *Witnesses:* JOHN CARRELL, WILLIAM
HOLLOWAY and WILLIAM MOSELEY. *Clerk of Edgecombe Court:* BENJ'N
WYNNS.

JOHNSON, JOHN.   Hyde County.

    September 1, 1756. March Court, 1757. *Son:* WILLIAM. *Daughter:*
CATHERINE. *Wife and Executrix:* SARAH. *Witnesses:* JOHN JENNETT,
THOMAS JONES, ABSALOM JONES. *Clerk of the Court:* STEPHEN DENNING.

JOHNSON, LEWIS.   Bath County.

    October 9, 1711. *Sons:* RICHARD and WILLIAM. *Executor:* FARNIFOLD
GREEN. *Witnesses:* CHRISTOPHER DAUSON, GEORGE GRAVE, ELIZABETH
HOG. Original missing. Recorded in Book 1712–1722, page 53.

JOHNSTON, SAMUEL.   Onslow County.

    November 13, 1756. January Court, 1736. *Sons:* SAMUEL and JOHN
(6,500 acres of land on Cape Fear River). *Daughters:* JOAN, PENELOPE,
ISOBELL, ANN, HANNAH (lands on Tuckahoe, together with negro slaves

belonging to testator). *Executor:* JOHN STARKEY. *Witnesses:* CARY GODBE, WILLIAM WILLIAMS, JOHN MILTON. *Clerk of the Court:* WILLIAM CRAY. Original missing. Recorded in Book 1753–1763, page 134.

JOHNSON, SUSANAH.   Chowan County.

August 13, 1717. July 29, 1718. *Son:* WILLIAM. *Grandson:* JACOB PARROT. *Daughter and Executrix:* FRANCES RASOR. *Granddaughters:* SUSANAH and ELIZABETH PARROT. *Godson:* EDWARD FREDERICK RASOR. *Friend:* JOHN HARDY. *Witnesses:* LAURENCE SARTON, E———z———, WILLIAM WALTERS, PATRICK CANADA. *Clerk of the Court:* R. HICKS.

JOHNSTON, THOMAS.   Onslow County.

August 13, 1751. April Court, 1752. *Sons:* THOMAS, BENJAMIN, JOHN ("plantation I now live on"). *Daughters:* SARAH POWELL, ANN WHIT-FIELD. *Granddaughters:* MARY, ANN and PRISCILLA KEEL. *Other legatee:* MARGARET HOENS. *Wife:* ANN. *Executor:* THOMAS JOHNSTON (son). *Witnesses:* ANTHONY LEWIS, JOHN BRABHAM, JOS. STURGES. *Clerk of Court:* THO. BLACK.

JOHNSON, WILLIAM.   Albemarle County.

January 10, 1689. October 7, 1689. *Sons:* BENJAMIN and THOMAS. *Guardians:* JOHN HAWKINS, THOMAS REFFER (?). *Wife and Executrix:* MARY. *Witnesses:* THOMAS PRISE (PRICE), THOMAS COPER (COOPER), THOMAS MILLER. *Clerk of the Court:* JOHN PHILPOTT. Will proven also before THOS. ROLFE.

JOHNSON, WILLIAM.   Carteret County.

November 5, 1726. March 5, 1727–1728. *Sons:* THOMAS, JOHN STE-PHEN and EZEKEL ("my land"). *Son-in-law:* THEO. NORWOOD. *Wife and Executrix:* SARAH. *Witnesses:* ENOCH WARD, RICH'D CANADY, JOHN SIMPSON. *Clerk of the Court:* JOHN GALLAND.

JONES, ARTHUR.   Bladen County.

October 21, 1750. December Court, 1750. *Sons:* LEWIS, SIPHRES. *Daughter:* ANN JONES. *Executors:* GERSHON BENBOW, GRIFFITH JONES. *Witnesses:* CYPRIAN SHIPHERD, SAMUEL PIKE. *Clerk of the Court:* THOS. ROBESON.

JONES, CHARLES.

April 25, 1693. July 15, 1695. *Legatees:* SARAH and TABYTHA ALFORD. *Executors:* THOMAS SYMONS, JOHN MEEDS. *Witnesses:* ELLINER MELINE. JACOB DENILLARD, JAMES DAMERELL. *Clerk Secretary's Office:* W. GLOVER.

JONES, CHARLES.   Bertie County.

February 5, 1739. February Court, 1748. *Sons:* CHARLES, JOHN, LANCE-
LOT. *Daughter:* SARAH OUGHTREE. *Wife's daughter:* MARY JONES (land
and plantation). *Wife and Executrix:* KATHIRAN. *Overseers:* CHRISTEFER
HOLLOMAN, WILLIAM RASBARNY. *Witnesses:* NATHANIEL NICKLESS,
JAMES OVERTON. *Clerk of the Court:* HENRY DELON.

JONES, CORNELIUS.   Albemarle County.

May 18, 1714. January 17, 1715. *Son:* CORNELIUS (land commonly
called James Robinsons). *Daughters:* ELIZABETH and ANN. *Wife and
Executrix:* ELIZABETH. *Witnesses:* WM. VAUGHAN, JOHN BLISH, FRANCES
HARRISON. Will proven before JOHN BLISH and JOHN BETS.

JONES, CORNELIUS.   Currituck County.

August 14, 1749. January Court, 1750. *Sons:* WILLIAM, CORNELIUS'
("my plantation"), TAYLOR. *Daughters:* RACHEL WHALE (?), ESTHER
WHITE, RHODA CASLE, SARAH MOLBRON, BRIDGET JONES. *Wife and
Executrix:* ELISABETH JONES. *Executor:* CORNELIUS JONES (son). *Wit-
nesses:* WILLIAM WHITE, JOHN ANSELL, WILLIAM DUDLEY. *Clerk of
Court:* RICH'D MCCLURE.

JONES, DANIELL.   Perquimans County.

October 10, 1713. February 21, 1714–1715. *Wife and Executrix:*
SARAH. *Executors:* ARTHUR JONES (brother), TIMOTHY CLARE. *Witnesses:* JAMES MINGE, MATHIAS GILES. Executors qualified before C. EDEN.

JONES, DAVID.   Hyde County.

January 9, 1753. March Court, 1753. *Sons:* MORIS, THOMAS, CHRISTO-
PHER and ABRAHAM (to these four is devised land in Currituck County),
RICHARD ("plantation I now live on"), CORNELIUS, SOLOMON (125 acres of
land on Strohorn's Neck). *Daughters:* ELISEBETH MASON, ANN. *Executors:* ELIZABETH JONES (wife), THOMAS and MORRIS JONES (sons). *Witnesses:* SAMUEL SELBY, WILLIAM SELBY, SARAH JONES. *Clerk of the Court:*
THOMAS JORDAN.

JONES, DAVID, SR.   Hyde County.

September 25, 1756. March Court, 1757. *Sons:* MORRIS ("my dwelling
place"), DAVID, ABSALUM. *Daughter:* ELEZEBETH JONES. *Executors:*
MORRIS and THOMAS JONES (brothers). *Wife:* ELEZEBETH. *Witnesses:*
BENJA. MASON, EDWARD SPENSER, ABRAHAM JONES. *Clerk of the Court:*
STEP'N DENNING.

JONES, EDWARD.   Pasquotank Precinct.

March 30, 1718.   July 15, 1720.   *Wife and Executrix:* ANN.   *Brother:* JAMES JONES.   *Daughters:* PRISCILLA JONES, ABIGALL JONES (land called the Ferny Ridge).   To wife is given land called Basteba.   *Brother-in-law:* WILLIAM ROOS.   *Witnesses:* WILLIAM PHILLIPS, SAMUEL RANSHER.   Original missing.   Recorded in Book 1712–1722, page 246.

JONES, EDWARD.   Bladen County.

October 8, 1751.   September Court, 1752.   *Son and Executor:* ISAAC. *Daughters:* HANNAH LOCK, JANE ENECKS.   *Grandsons:* ISAAC and WILLIAM ENECKS.   *Granddaughter:* ANN ENECKS.   *Wife:* SUSANNA.   To Carver's Creek meeting is given ten pounds.   *Witnesses:* JOHN SMITH, WM. SIBBLY, JOHN GRAY.   *Justices:* BENJAMIN FITZRANDOLPH, HENRY SIMMOND, JONATHAN EVENS.   *Clerk of the Court:* THOS. ROBESON.

JONES, EVAN.   Craven County.

June 10, 1750.   November Court, 1751.   *Sons:* EVAN (plantation on East side of Clubford's Creek), JAMES (plantation on the East side of Buck Creek), ROGER ("manner plantation on West side of Clubford Creek"), CHARLES (plantation on West side of Cohookey Creek).   *Wife:* ANN.   *Executors:* EVAN, JAMES and ROGER JONES (sons).   *Witnesses:* CATHARINE JONES, BRIGETT CANADY, WILLIAM FLOOD.   *Clerk of the Court:* PHIL. SMITH.

JONES, EVAN.   Craven County.

December 23, 1752.   March 19, 1753.   *Son:* LOVICK ("my plantation & lands on the East side of Clubfords Creek").   *Daughter:* SARAH JONES. *Executors:* THOMAS LOVICK and ROGER JONES.   *Witnesses:* JAS. JONES, JOHN TANEYHILL, CHARLES JONES.   Will proven before JAS. HASELL. *Clerk General Court:* JNO. SNEAD.

JONES, FRANCIS.   Edgecombe County.

January 14, 1750.   August Court, 1755.   *Sons:* NATHANIEL and TINGNALL (land on Crabtree Creek in Johnston County), JOHN (land on Crabtree Creek), MATTHEW (land on Swift Creek in Johnston County), FRANCIS (land on Jackit Swamp, Edgecombe County), ALBRIDGTON, RIDLEY.   *Son-in-law:* JOHN CULLERS (land on Crabtree Creek).   *Daughters:* JUDITH WILSON, MARY CULLERS, LUCY JONES, BETTE DAY JONES, LYDIA JONES, JEMIMA JONES.   *Executors:* MARY JONES (wife) and NATHANIEL JONES (son). *Witnesses:* THOS. WIGGINS, FRANCIS DRAKE.   *Clerk of the Court:* JOS. MONTFORT.

JONES, FREDERICK.   Chowan Precinct.

April 9, 1722. March 26, 1723. *Sons:* WILLIAM HARDING JONES (lands on the south side of Moratoke River), FREDERICK ("all my lands in Craven Precinct"), THOMAS (land at Maherrin and lands on north side of Moratoke River). To each of sons is bequeathed one diamond ring. Plate divided between sons. To brother THOMAS JONES of Virginia is devised lands in King William County, Virginia, called Horns Quarter. *Daughters:* JANE ("Indian girle, four negroes, diamond ring and diamond earrings, Gold watch with chain, seal, etc."), MARTHA (four young negroes, one diamond ring, diamond earrings, gold shoe-buckles, thimble, etc., and one dozen finest damask napkins, one dozen diaper napkins, Holland sheets, etc.), REBECKAH (one diamond ring, about three dozen damask and diaper napkins, table-cloths, sheets, etc.) *Executors:* THOMAS JONES, of Virginia (brother), WM. HARDING and FREDERICK JONES (sons). *Witnesses:* SARAH STEWART, ROGER HAZARD, JOHN ANSLEY, EDW'D MOSELEY. Codicil bequeathes gold rings to REBECAH JONES and silver-mounted pistols to EDWARD MOSELEY. Proven before C. GALE. Coat of arms on seal.

JONES, FREDERICK.   Craven County.

November 21, 1758. February Court, 1759. *Mother:* MARY MOORE. *Brother:* HARDING JONES. *Niece:* MARY JONES. *Executors:* HARDING JONES (brother) and JOSEPH LEECH. *Witnesses:* ELIZABETH SPAIGHT, MARY VAIL, JANE SWANN. *Clerk of the Court:* PETER CONWAY. Coat of arms on seal.

JONES, HENRY.   Northampton County.

November 14, 1733. November Court, 1757. *Sons:* HENRY (*Executor*), WILLIAM, JOHN (plantation on south side of Roanoke River), PHILIP, JAMES ("plantation whereon I now live"). *Daughter:* ELEZEBETH JONES. *Wife:* CATHERINE. Four oldest sons appointed trustees. *Witnesses:* NEEDHAM BRYAN, GEORGE SMITH, JOHN ELESS. *Clerk of the Court:* I. EDWARDS.

JONES, HENRY.   Northampton County.

November 26, 1751. February Court, 1752. Northwest parish in Northampton County. *Son:* HENRY RESTORE JONES ("my manor planta-tion"). *Daughters:* PRIOR, GRAY, MARY and KATY JONES. *Wife and Executrix:* SARAH. *Witnesses:* JOHN MANDAR, JOHN CORLEW, JUNR., JOEL MOSELEY. *Clerk of the Court:* I. EDWARDS.

JONES, HENRY.   Chowan County.

February 11, 1754. April Court, 1754. *Son:* WILLIAM. *Daughters:* MARY LOVEL, JANE CHAMPION, SARAH PARKER. *Wife and Executrix:* ELIZ-ABETH. *Executor:* BENJAMIN PARKER. *Witnesses:* HENRY BONNER, JOHN LUTEN, SAMUEL LUTEN. *Clerk of Court:* WILL HALSEY.

JONES, ISAAC.   Pasquotank Precinct.

January 7, 1734.   January 31, 1734.   *Sons:* JOHN ("my manner planta-
tion"), ISAAC ("my little plantation"), NEHEMIAH (land beginning at "ye
Fork Bridge, running, &c."), EVIN (100 acres of land).   *Daughters:* DORO-
THY and MARY JONES.   *Executors:* JOHN JONES (son) and JARNAS JONES
(brother).   *Witnesses:* ABEL ROSS, JOSHUA GAMBLING, JOHN WALLIS.
Will proven before GAB. JOHNSTON, at Edenton.

JONES, ISAM.   Edgecombe County.

April 24, 1753.   November Court, 1753.   *Wife:* MARY.   *Daughter:*
CREACY.   *Executor:* WALLIS JONES.   *Witnesses:* RICHARD BURD, MATTHEW
JONES.   *Clerk of the Court:* BENJ'N WYNNS.

JONES, JAMES.   Tyrrell County.

August 3, 1750.   No probate.   *Sons:* JAMES (150 acres of land),
TRALEY, EVAN, BENJAMIN (150 acres of land).   *Daughters:* MARY DRAPIR,
ANN and ELIZABETH JONES.   To JOHN RAY is given "the liberty of
dwelling on my land called the Folley."   *Wife and Executrix:* MARY.
Witnesses: JOHN RAY, WILLIAM HOWARD, ELIZABETH HOWARD.

JONES, JOHN.   Pasquotank County.

November 23, 1707.   January 20, 1707–1708.   *Son:* JOHN ("all my
land").   *Wife and Executrix:* ELIZABETH.   *Witnesses:* ROBERT WALLIS,
RICHARD MADREN, HENRY SAWYER.   *Clerk of Court:* JOHN PALIN.

JONES, JOHN.   Pasquotank County.

March 23, 1719–1720.   December 23, 1723.   *Father-in-law (meaning,
probably, stepfather):* JOHN ROLFE.   *Mother and Executrix:* ELIZABETH
ROLFE.   *Aunt:* MARY BARD.   *Witnesses:* JOHN SOLLEY, JNO. ROLFE.
Will proven before WILLIAM REED, *President.*

JONES, JOHN.   Pasquotank Precinct.

December 12, 1723.   *Legatees:* DORITY and ELE MACKDANIEL.   *Witnesses:* THOMAS HEARENDEEN, JOHN JENNINGS, BENJAMIN SAWYER.
Clerk of the Court: JOHN PARKER.

JONES, JOHN.   Chowan Precinct.

May 12, 1727.   May 15, 1727.   *Sons:* WILLIAM, JOHN, THOMAS, DAVID.
Daughter: ELISABETH.   *Granddaughter:* ELISABETH JONES (daughter of
DAVID).   *Friend:* HENRY BONER.   *Executor:* SAMUEL PADETH.   *Witnesses:*
THOS. JONES, DAVID JONES, WM. YATES.   Will proven before RICHARD
EVERARD.

JONES, JOHN.   Chowan County.

August 6, 1734. October 18, 1744. *Sons:* JOHN ("my plantation").
LEWES, SAMUEL. *Wife and Executrix:* FLORANCE. *Witnesses:* CONST.
LUTEN, JOHN LEWIS, JACOB PRIVETT. *Clerk of the Court:* EDMUND HATCH.

JONES, JOHN.   Chowan County.

February 2, 1735–1736. October Court, 1736. *Sons:* JAMES and DEM-
SEY ("all my land at the Loosing Swamp"). *Wife and Executrix:* ANN.
Executor: JAMES JONES (son). *Witnesses:* JOHN SUMNER, JAMES HUBARD.
Clerk of Court: JAMES CRAVEN.

JONES, JOHN.   Bertie County.

September 25, 1750. May Court, 1751. *Sons:* SOLOMON and JOSEPH
(plantation on Poplar Swamp), WILLIAM, JOHN and JAMES. *Daughter:*
MARY JONES. *Wife:* not named. *Executors:* JOHN BROWN, THOMAS
EASON. *Witnesses:* THOMAS EASON, JOHN ROBERSON, JOHN HARE, SOLO-
MON HOWARD. *Clerk of Court:* SAM'L ORMES.

JONES, JOHN.   Chowan County.

June 23, 1754. July Court, 1755. *Sons:* JAMES (plantation on Lousin
Swamp), JOHN ("plantation I bought of WM. ASHLEY"), JOSIAS ("my
manner plantation which I purchased of JOHN PERRY"). *Daughter:*
JUDITH JONES. *Wife and Executrix:* JUDITH. *Executor:* JAMES JONES
(son). *Clerk of the Court:* THOMAS JONES.

JONES, JOHN.   Edgecombe County.

October 24, 1757. June Court, 1758. *Sons:* WALLIS, ETHELDRED,
JOHN. *Sons-in-law:* THOMAS SPELL, CHARLES JERKINS, PETER MITCHELL.
Other legatees: ANN and BENJAMIN RICHARDSON, JOHN JONES. *Daughter:*
SARAH JERKINS. *Executor:* WALLIS JONES (son). *Witnesses:* HENRY
HORN, SIKON HORN, JOSIAH HORN. Codicil dated December 17, 1757,
mentions son FREDERICK JONES and makes bequests to other sons. Same
witnesses. *Clerk of the Court:* JOS. MONTFORT.

JONES, JOHN.   Duplin County.

March 15, 1759. January 12, 1759. *Sons:* WILLIAM ("plantation
whereon I now live"), THOMAS (100 acres of land), JOHN (*Executor*).
Daughters: PATTE, CATHERINE, ELIZABETH, MARY ANN and SARAH JONES.
Wife and Executrix: ANN. *Witnesses:* WILLIAM WHITFIELD, ANN JONES,
ANN WILLIAMS. *Clerk of Court:* JOHN DICKSON.

JONES, JOHN.   Northampton County.

June 24, 1759. October Court, 1759. *Daughter:* ELIZABETH. *Wife
and Executrix:* PRISCILLA. *Brother:* EDMOND JONES. *Friend:* SAMUEL

WELDON (lot No. 90 in town of Halifax). *Executor:* JOHN EDMUNDS. Land in Southampton County, Va., and lot No. 15 in Halifax given to executors to be sold for payment of debts. *Witnesses:* WILL CATHCART, WM. FANNING, JAMES DANCY. *Clerk of the Court:* I. EDWARDS.

JONES, JOHN, SR.   Bertie Precinct.

March 17, 1735. May Court, 1736. *Sons:* JAMES, FREDERICK ("my plantation"), JOHN, JOSEPH. *Grandson:* ABRAHAM JONES. *Daughters:* ANN COTTEN, MARY BONNER. *Wife:* MARTHA. *Trustees:* JOHN BROWN, JOHN BATTLE, WILLIAM MEARS. *Executor:* JOHN JONES (son). *Witnesses:* P. HANFORD, JAMES DOUGLASS, ELIZABETH OQUIN. *Clerk of the Court:* JOHN WYNNS.

JONES, JONATHAN.   Pasquotank County.

April Court, 1740. *Sons:* JONATHAN ("plantation at ye head of Sawyer's Creek"), CORNELIUS ("land below Sawyer's Creek"). *Daughters:* MARY, ELESEBETH, RUTH and DINAH JONES. *Wife:* SUSAN. *Executor:* JOSEPH HUMPHRIES. *Witnesses:* WILLIAM MACKDANIEL, CHRISTOPHER HUMPHRIES, DINAH HUMPHRIES. *Clerk of the Court:* JAMES CRAVEN.

JONES, JOSEPH.

September 10, 1756. *Sons:* JAMES and JOSEPH (land divided between them). *Daughters:* MARY, HANNAH, ELIZABETH and ANN. *Wife and Executrix:* MARTHA. *Executor:* WILLIAM VAUGHAN. *Witnesses:* JOHN WHITE, RICHARD NANSON. *Clerk of the Court:* ISAAC FARIES.

JONES, MARY.   Bertie County.

December 22, 1745. January 9, 1748. *Legatees:* ELISABETH SPRUELL (cousin), SARAH HAWKINS (daughter of THOMAS HAWKINS), THOMAS HACKMAN, THOS. SUTTON (nephew), ELIZABETH SUTTON (sister), JOHN SUTTON (nephew, to whom is bequeathed 100 acres of land "in Cishooke at the head of the Line"), GEORGE SUTTON (nephew). *Executors:* CHARLES JACOCKS, THOMAS and JOHN SUTTON. *Witnesses:* THOMAS HACKMAN, JOHN BURN. Will proven before GAB. JOHNSTON, at Eden House.

JONES, MORRIS.   Hyde County.

September 25, 1756. December Court, 1756. *Son:* HENRY ("my dwelling plantation"). *Daughters:* ELESEBETH, MARY, ANN, NEOMY and SARAH JONES. *Wife:* MARY. *Executors:* THOS. JONES (brother), HENRY GIBBS, JNR. *Witnesses:* BENJN. MASON, EDWARD SPENSER, SOLOMON JONES. *Clerk of Court:* STEPHEN DENNING.

JONES, PETER.   County not given.

April 2, 1731. *Sons:* PETER ("plantation whereon I now live"), ROBERT (374 acres of land on Mash Swamp). *Daughters:* SARAH and MARTHA JONES. *Wife and Executrix:* SARAH. *Witnesses:* WM. WILLIAMS, WILLIAM PAUL. No probate.

JONES, PETER.   Perquimans County.

February 17, 1753. April Court, 1753. *Sons:* THOMAS ("plantation whereon I now live"), ZEPHANIAH (land at head of land given to THOMAS), ZECHARIAH (land purchased of WM. WYATT), MALACHY (land on the Mile Branch). All of the sons to be given "Education to Reade & write a Ledgable hand and work Arithmitick through the single rule of three." *Daughter:* MARY JONES. *Grandson:* JOSEPH JONES. *Wife:* MARY. *Arbitrators to divide estate:* JOHN HARVEY, JOSEPH BARROW, JR., FRANCIS JONES, NATHAN and ROBERT NEWBY. *Executors:* JOSEPH WHITE, JOSEPH RATLIF, THOMAS JONES. *Witnesses:* EVAN SKINNER, WILLM. SKINNER, SARAH SKINNER. *Clerk of the Court:* EDMUND HATCH.

JONES, PETER, SENR.   Perquimans County.

May 15, 1751. April Court, 1752. *Sons:* JOHN ("plantation I now live on," plantation at the Mile Branch), WILLIAM (170 acres of land), PETER ("plantation whereon he now lives"). *Daughters:* MARY and HANNAH JONES, SARAH SUTTON, REBECCA DENMAN, MARGRET. *Grandson:* THOMAS SHERWOOD. *Executors:* JOHN JONES (son), MARY JONES (daughter), THOMAS NICHOLSON. *Witnesses:* MAC SCARBOROUGH, ELIZAB. SCARBROUGH, WILLIAM REED. *Clerk of the Court:* EDMUND HATCH.

JONES, ROGER.   Beaufort County.

July 25, 1741. September Court, 1741. *Sons:* ROGER, GEORGE. *Daughters:* JANE, MARGARET, MARY, HOLLAND and ELIZABETH (to the two last named is given plantation called Holland House, also a plantation on Massapungo Swamp. *Wife and Executrix:* REBECCA. *Witnesses:* JOHN BARROW, LITTLETON EBORN, ELIZABETH JONES. *Clerk of the Court:* JNO. TURNER.

JONES, SAMUELL.   Currituck County.

September 30, 1723. *Sons:* THOMAS (one shilling), SAMUEL and WILLIAM (land called Thurrefare Ridge), IZAYAH and ZACKARYATH ("my dwelling plantation"). *Executors:* WILLIAM WILLIAMS, THOMAS DAYES. *Witnesses:* MARGRET CROSSMAN, DANLL. PHILLIPS. *Clerk of the Court:* THOS. LOWTHER.

JONES, SARAH.   Bath County.

May, 1722. *Daughters:* MONING MITEM, CHARITY SHUTE, ELIZABETH CARNEY, MARY SMITH (*Executrix*). *Grandson:* JAMES SMITH. *Witnesses:* FRANCIS DELAMARE, JOHN MARTIN, THOMAS DAVIS. No probate.

JONES, THOMAS.   Bertie County.

1754. Petty Shore in Bertie County. *Legatees:* MARGRET WEBB (widow of SAMUEL WEBB), SAMUEL WEBB (son of MARGRET), HENRY HILL,

JOHN CAMPBELL (of Lazy Hill). *Executor :* JOHN CAMPBELL. No signature. No witnesses. Will proven before ARTHUR DOBBS by BENJAMIN WYNNS, ALEXANDER FORD and JOSEPH HERON, who made oath as to the handwriting of the testator.

JONES, WILLIAM HARDING.   Chowan County.

January 22, 1730. July 27, 1732. Eastern parish in Chowan County. *Wife:* ANN (4,000 acres of land on Roanoke River, together with "house and plantation whereon I now live with third part of the negroes * * * * except ye family pictures and Court of arms which I give to my well beloved brother FREDDICK JONES and likewise all ye books in ye said house which I give to my brothers FREDDICK and THOMAS JONES"). No executor appointed. *Witnesses:* GEORGE ALLEIGN, SAM'LL SNOWDEN, MATTHEW YOUNG. Proven before JNO. PALIN, C. J. Coat of arms on seal.

JONES, WILLIAM.   Chowan Precinct.

January 9, 1722. *Sons:* JOHN ("land whereon he now lives"), HENRY ("the plantation whereon I now live"), CHARLES (land on Deep run). *Grandson:* WILLIAM JONES. *Daughter:* JANE LISLES. *Granddaughter:* DOROTHY LISLES. *Grandsons:* WILLIAM LISLES (son of JANE), WILLIAM LEWSE (son of ELISABETH SPIER), WILLIAM JONES (son of HENRY JONES), WILLIAM WALSTON (son of DOROTHY WALSTON), WILLIAM JONES (son of JOHN JONES). *Other legatees:* HENRY LISLES, JR., and HENRY LISLES, SR. No executor appointed. *Witnesses:* FRANCES HOWCOTT, HANAH LUTEN, THOMAS LUTEN. No probate.

JONES, WILLIAM.   Chowan Precinct.

May 4, 1722. *Sons:* JOHN (land at "ye Rich Thick'tt in Virginia," after his decease to his sons, JOHN and JAMES), also one hundred acres of land on Deep Run Swamp to go to his sons, DAVID and WILLIAM, after his decease), HENRY ("the plantation whereon I now live," after his death to his son, WILLIAM), CHARLES (100 acres of land). *Daughters:* JEANE LYSLE, ELIZABETH SPIERS, DOROTHY WALSTON. *Other devisee:* WM. LYLES. *Executor:* THOMAS LUTEN. *Witnesses:* ROBERT FULLERTON, MARY FULLERTON, MARY DREACE. No probate.

JONES, WILLIAM.   Bertie Precinct.

March 15, 1736. May 20, 1736. *Son:* EPHRAME ("plantation whereon I now live"). *Wife:* ANN. *Executors:* FRANCIS HOPSON, HENRY JERNIGAN. *Witnesses:* BENNET BLACKMAN, HENRY BAKER, JR. Will proven before W. SMITH, C. J.

JONES, WILLIAM.   Beaufort County.

April 28, 1740. September 1, 1742. *Daughters:* ELISABETH, RUTH, ANN PRISKET, wife of JOHN PRISKET; HANER, wife of SOLOMON ROBSON; JANE, wife of ROBT. DUNBAR. *Grandchildren:* WM. QUINN and WM. ROBSON. *Executors:* MARGET JONES (wife), SOLOMON ROBSON. *Witnesses:* RICHARD CHEEK, WM. MITCHELL, JOHN BRYLY, JOHN HENINTON. Will proven before J. MONTGOMERY, C. J.

JONES, WILLIAM.   Edgecombe County.

November 27, 1749. August Court, 1750. *Sons:* DREURY, PETER ("plantation whereon I now live"), ISAM (grist mill). *Arbitrators to divide land:* THOMAS HILL, GEORGE NICHOLSON, JOHN CLARK, WALLIS JONES. *Executors:* SARAH JONES (wife) and WALLIS JONES. *Witnesses:* THOMAS THROWER, WILLIAM ATKISON, WINNIFRED ATKISON. *Clerk of the Court:* BENJAMIN WYNNS.

JONES, WILLIAM.   Perquimans County.

December 9, 1750. April Court, 1752. *Son:* WILLIAM. *Daughters:* ELISABETH BARBER, REBECKAH JONES. *Arbitrators to divide estate:* JOHN HARVEY, JOSEPH WHITE, JOSEPH RIBINSON, JOSEPH BARROW. *Executors:* PETER JONES (brother), MOSES BARBER (son-in-law), WILLIAM JONES (son). *Witnesses:* JOSEPH BARROW, JUNR., JOHN WILLIAMS, JOHN BARROW. *Clerk of the Court:* EDMUND HATCH.

JONES, WILLIAM.   Halifax County.

January 3, 1758. June Court, 1759. *Sons:* WILLIAM (land he now has possession of), HENRY (300 acres land), BRITTON (300 acres of land "adjoining my mill"), SIMON (500 acres of land with mill). *Daughters:* SARAH, WINNIFRED, AMEY, ELIZABETH, SILVA. *Wife and Executrix:* SARAH. *Executor:* WILLIAM JONES. *Witnesses:* AUGUSTINE BATE, NICHOLAS KILLINGSWORTH, SOLOMON HAWKINS, SARAH JONES. *Clerk of the Court:* JOS. MONTFORT.

JONES, WILLIAM.   Chowan County.

July 15, 1773. March 16, 1774. *Daughters:* CHARITY WALKER, RACHEL LUTEN, ESTER JOHNSTON, SARAH, AN and EDAH JONES. *Son:* JAMES ("my plantation"). *Executors:* THOMAS BONNER, JOHN LEWIS and JAMES JONES. *Witnesses:* JOHN MUSHROW, DANCY TROTMAN. Will proven before JO. MARTIN.

JORDAN, ARTHUR.   Northampton County.

November 13, 1751. May Court, 1752. *Sons:* GEORGE ("land where he now lives"), ARTHUR, JOHN and THOMAS ("land JOHN now lives on"), HENRY (150 acres of land), BENJAMIN ("plantation where I now live"). *Daughters:* ELIZABETH, FORTUNE. *Wife and Executrix:* SARAH. *Executor:* BENJAMIN JORDAN (son). *Witnesses:* CHARLES GREGORY, JAMES JORDAN, WILLIAM BARCROFT. *Clerk of the Court:* I. EDWARDS.

JORDAN, ARTHUR.   Northampton County.

September 14, 1754.   August Court, 1755.   *Sons:* SAMUEL and ARTHUR.
Daughters: REBECCA, MARY and SARAH.   *Wife and Executrix:* SARAH.
Witnesses: ARTHUR YOUNG, REUDEN ROGERS.   *Clerk of the Court:* I.
EDWARDS.

JORDAN, DEBORAH.   Bladen County.

September 4, 1769.   February 14, 1770.   *Brothers:* ITHAMAR and JOHN
SINGLETARY.   *Daughter:* MARGARET GIBSON.   *Niece:* DEBORAH SINGLE-
TARY (daughter of ITHAMAR).   *Executors:* JOHN SINGLETARY (brother) and
WALTER GIBSON (son-in-law).   *Witnesses:* JOHN RUSS, EPH'M MULFORD,
JOSEPH POWERS.   Will proven before WM. TRYON.

JORDAN, JOHN.   Hyde Precinct.

December 31, 1719.   *Son and Executor:* JOHN.   *Daughters:* MARGARET,
wife of JOHN FOREMAN; MARY JORDAN.   *Witnesses:* PETER McDULE,
THOMAS TYLER, ISAAC CHABANAS.   Original missing.   Recorded in Book
1712–1722, page 219.

JORDAN, JOSEPH.   Pasquotank County.

January Court, 1752.   *Witnesses:* SAMUEL HUGHE, DEMSEY CONNOR and
JOSEPH ROBINSON.   Will illegible.

JORDAN, SOLOMON.   Tyrrell County.

March 3, 1721–1722.   April 11, 1722.   *Sons:* ABRAHAM (200 acres of
land on north side of Cashia River and other tracts described in will).
Daughters: LUARRESIA, REBECCA.   *Wife:* not named.   *Executor:* MAJ.
ROBERT WEST.   *Witnesses:* REBECCA CORRY, RACHEL BUTTLOR, MARTIN
CREMEN.   Will proven before THOS. POLLOCK.

JORDAN, WILLIAM.   Tyrrell County.

July 4, 1732.   November 2, 1732.   *Sons:* JOHN ("my manner planta-
tion").   *Daughter:* ESTER.   *Wife and Executrix:* SARAH.   *Executor:*
NATHANIEL EVERETT.   *Witnesses:* THOS. HOBBS, WILLIAM GARRETT.
SAM'LL DURRANCE.   Will proven before WM. LITTLE, *Chief Justice.*

JOY, WILLIAM.   Pasquotank County.

December 17, 1725.   January 18, 1725.   *Wife and Executrix:* MARGERY.
Other devisees: SOLOMON and SARAH EVERTON.   *Witnesses:* JEREMIAH
EVERTON, FRANCES EVERTON.   *Clerk of the Court:* THO. WEEKES.   *Execu-
trix* qualified before GABRIEL BARNHAM.

KALBIN, JOHN.   Perquimans Precinct.

December 20, 1685.   *Executor and sole legatee:* ROBERT INBASON.   *Witnesses:* WILLIAM DANSE, ANDREW ROSS.   No probate.

KASEWELL, FRANCIS.   Pasquotank Precinct.

January 1, 1712–1713. Allegator in Albemarle County. No probate.
Daughters: MARTHA and MARY KASEWELL. *Wife and Executrix:* SARAH.
Witnesses: ANN WHITE, HANNAH MANSFIELD, EBENR. WAITE. Original
missing. Recorded in Book 1712–1722, page 42.

KEARSEY (spelled also CEARSEY), THOMAS.   Bertie County.

October 28, 1730. August Court, 1731. *Sons:* JOHN (land on Cashie
Swamp), THOMAS and WILLIAM (lands), JAMES and PETER. *Daughter:*
MARY POHAGON. *Wife and Executrix:* SUSANNA. *Grandson:* WILLIAM
KEARSEY. *Executor:* THOMAS KEARSEY (son). *Witnesses:* THOMAS KEAR-
SEY, JR., MARY POHEAGIN, JOSEPH DARDEN, ARTHUR WILLIAMS. *Clerk of
Court:* RT. FORSTER.

KEEFE, FREDERICK.   Bertie County.

November 10, 1723. February Court, 1723. *Wife and Executrix:* ELLI-
NOR. *Sons:* FREDERICK and JOHN. *Witnesses:* JAMES BATES, ELIZABETH
KEEFE, MARGRETT KEEFE. *Clerk of Court:* RT. FORSTER.

KEEL, JOHN.   Bath County.

November 18, 1736. *Legatees:* JOHN MAINNER, WILLIAM MAINNER
(sons of WM. and SARAH MAINNER). *Brother and Executor:* NATHANIEL
KEEL. *Witnesses:* JOB BROOKS, WILLIAM MAINNER. No probate.

KEEL, LEMUEL.   Pasquotank County.

February 11, 1747–1748. April Court, 1748. *Brother:* CHARLES KEEL.
Wife and Executrix: TAMER. *Witnesses:* HEN. PENDLETON, ROBERT
HOSEA. *Clerk of Court:* THOS. TAYLOR.

KEEL, TAMAR.   Pasquotank County.

December 14, 1748. January 19, 1748. *Legatees:* SUSANNAH, wife of
THOMAS MEADS; ELIZABETH, daughter of THOS. MEADS, and WILLIAM
DAVIS (*Executor*). *Witnesses:* JAS. GREGORY, WILLIAM WALLIS. Proven
before GAB. JOHNSTON.

KEELAND, JOHN.   Edgecombe County.

January 21, 1752. March 24, 1752. *Executor and sole legatee:* JAMES
CARTER. This is a nuncupative will proven by WILLIAM HORNSBY, WIL-
LIAM TAYLOR and CATTREN CARTER. *Clerk of Court:* BENJ'N WYNNS.
Proven before GAB. JOHNSTON.

KEETON, HENRY.   Pasquotank Precinct.

September 20, 1710. *Son:* JOSEPH (plantation at New Begun Creek).
Daughters: ELIZABETH and MERRIAM. *Overseers of will:* EDWARD MAYO,

BENJAMIN PRICHARD and JOSEPH GLAISTER. *Wife and Executrix:* ELISA-BETH. *Witnesses:* JOHN JENNINGS, W. NORRIS, JOHN SIMSON. No probate.

KEETON, ZACHARIAH, SR.   Pasquotank County.

April 28, 1743. January Court, 1743. *Sons:* ZACHARIAH and PATRICK. *Daughters:* MARY CORY, ELIZABETH WILLCOCKS. *Granddaughter:* ELINER WINBERG. *Wife:* SARAH. *Executors:* ZACHARIAH and PATRICK (sons). *Witnesses:* STEPHEN SCOTT, JOSEPH LOMBROSKER. *Clerk of Court:* THOS. TAYLOR.

KEILE, THOMAS.   Albemarle County.

September 19, 1682. March 6, 1682–1683. *Sons:* THOMAS, ROBERT. *Daughter:* SARAH. *Wife and Executrix:* MARY. *Guardian:* THO. ROLFE. *Witnesses:* THO. ROLFE, FRANCIS WARDE, WILLIAM BENTLEY. Proven before WILL. CRAFORD.

KELLEY, JOHN.   Pasquotank County.

October 22, 1758. December Court, 1758. *Son:* ASA. *Daughters:* MARY, ELIZABETH, MARTHA and NANNA KELLY. *Wife and Executrix:* ELISABETH. *Executor:* PATRICK KELLY (cousin). *Witnesses:* JOHN MAC-BRIDE, SAMUEL EDNY, SARAH MACBRIDE. *Clerk of the Court:* THOS. TAYLOR. Coat of arms on seal.

KELLEY, SARAH.   Pasquotank Precinct.

January 1, 1699. April 16, 1700. *Daughter:* SARAH KELLEY. *Executor:* JOHN MACKEELL. *Witnesses:* THO. BOYD, DANIEL MACKEEL, ELIZA-BETH ———. *Clerk of the Court:* THOS. ABINGTON.

KELLY, MATHEW.   Pasquotank County.

April 16, 1697. January 16, 1699. *Sons:* JAMES and JOHN. *Daughters:* ELIZABETH and REBECCA. *Executrix:* WIFE, not named. *Witnesses:* HENRY WHITE, JAMES DAVIS. MAGDALEN KELLY, probably wife of testator, adopts will as her own by writing dated December 10, 1699. *Witnesses:* HENRY WHITE, JACOB OVERMAN. *Clerk of the Court:* THO. ABINGTON.

KELLY, SMITH.   Perquimans Precinct.

February 2, 1734. April 15, 1734. *Son:* NICHOLAS. *Wife and Executrix:* MARY. No signature. No witnesses. *Clerk of the Court:* CHAS. DENMAN.

KEMP, GEORGE.   Pasquotank County.

January 20, 1723–1724. April Court, 1724. *Sons:* GEORGE and ALLEN (all my lands). *Daughter:* SARAH KEMP. *Wife and Executrix:* MARY. *Witnesses:* MAC. SCARBOROUGH, JOHN TOXEY, THO. HILLARD. *Clerk of the Court:* W. NORRIS.

KEMP, WILLIAM.   Anson County.

April 20, 1750. April Court, 1753. *Sons:* JOHN, WILLIAM, THOMAS, JOSEPH and STEVEN. *Daughter:* SARAH KEMP. To the sons is bequeathed land described in will. *Wife and Executrix:* ELIZABETH. *Executors:* JOHN and WILLIAM (sons). *Witnesses:* ANDREW MAREMAN, ANTHONY HUTCHINS. *Clerk of the Court:* JNO. DUNN.

KENEDY, WALTER.   Johnston County.

March 25, 1751. June Court, 1751. *Son:* JOHN. *Daughter:* MARY KENNEDY. *Wife and Executrix:* SARAH. *Witnesses:* JOHN KENNEDY, ROBT. FELLOW. *Deputy Clerk of the Court:* JAMES OATES.

KENT, JOHN.   Bath County.

September 28, 1719. *Wife and Executrix:* MARY. *Executor:* RICHARD HARVEY. *Witnesses:* ANTHONY MARKHAM, JOHN MCKEEL and JOHN HARVEY. Original missing. Recorded in Book 1712–1722, page 219.

KENYON, JOHN.   Perquimans County.

May 19, 1751   July Court, 1752. *Son:* JOAB ("my plantation"). *Wife and Executrix:* MARY. *Executors:* ABRAHAM HENDRIXON (brother-in-law) and JOHN WEAKES. *Witnesses:* JOHN MODLING, SAM'LL MOORE, HANNAH MODLING. *Clerk of the Court:* EDMUND HATCH.

KETON, JOHN, SR.   Perquimans County.

February 28, 1734–1735. October 1, 1735. *Sons:* JOHN, LEWIS, JOSEPH. *Daughters:* SARAH HUBBARD, ELIZABETH WIGGINS. *Wife and Executrix:* ELIZABETH. *Executor:* ZACHARIAH NICKSON. *Witnesses:* EDWARD MOORE, JOHN WILLCOCKS, ROBERT COCKS. *Clerk of the Court:* JAMES CRAVEN.

KIBBLE, ABRAHAM.   Onslow County.

December 6, 1750. April 2, 1757. *Son:* JAMES. *Daughter:* LUSE. *Stepsons:* THOMAS and DANIEL HIX. *Son-in-law and Executor:* JOSEPH WILLIAMS. *Wife and Executrix:* EDITH. *Witnesses:* THOS. JENKINS, JOSEPH LOYD, WILLIAM LOYD. Codicil provides for education of son "as far as the rule of three." *Witnesses:* THOS. JENKIN, JOSEPH LOYD, WILLIAM LOYD.

KILBEE, CHRISTOPHER.   Northampton County.

February 9, 1741–1742. May Court, 1752. *Sons:* EPAPHRODITUS, XPHER (to each is devised land). *Daughters:* SARAH, ELIZABETH, FRANCES. *Wife:* KATHERINE. *Executors:* MAJ. JOSEPH GRAY, THOMAS JARRELL. *Friends:* JOSHUA LEWIS and JOHN FORT. *Witnesses:* JOHN BRASSELL, THOMAS WESBROOK. *Clerk of the Court:* I. EDWARDS.

KILLINGSWORTH, FRANCIS.   Johnston County.

March 3, 1751. March Court, 1752. *Son:* NOLS. *Wife:* REBECKAH. *Executors:* ARTHUR FORT, SOLOMON HOMES. *Witnesses:* RACHEL STEPHENS, ELIZABETH PACE. *Deputy Clerk of the Court:* CHAS. YOUNG.

KILLINGSWORTH, RICHARD.   Edgecombe County.

December 3, 1733. *Wife and Executrix:* MARY. *Cousin:* RICHARD KILLINGSWORTH. *Witnesses:* BENJAMIN WOOD, FRANCIS WOOD, JNO. SPEIR. No probate.

KINCE, CHRISTIAN.   Brunswick County.

December 24, 1761. January 19, 1762. *Sons:* JOHN, EDWARD, WILLIAM. *Daughter:* ELIZABETH. *Executors:* JOHN and JOSEPH KINCE and EDWARD WILLIAMS. *Wife:* mentioned, but not named. *Witnesses:* JOHN FILLYAW, SAMUEL KINCE, JOHN HOWARD. Proven before ARTHUR DOBBS.

KINCHEN, WILLIAM.   Edgecombe County.

November 6, 1758. December Court, 1758. *Sons:* JOHN (land on the river adjoining Craghill), WILLIAM ("remainder of my land"). *Daughters:* MARTHA, ELIZABETH, MARY and TEMPERANCE. *Executors:* BLAKE BAKER, HENRY DAWSON (brothers), JOHN KINCHEN (son). *Witnesses:* HENRY CAMPBELL, PETER JONES, WILLIAM MOORE. *Clerk of Court:* JOS. MONTFORT.

KING, HENRY.   Chowan County.

February 24, 1714. April 16, 1716. *Sons:* MICHAEL, CHARLES and HENRY (lands in Chowan and in Virginia). *Daughters:* ELISABETH, CATREN and MARY KING. Signatures of witnesses torn off. *Clerk of the Court:* R. HICKS. *Names of witnesses appearing in probate:* CHRISTOPHER VANLUON, JOHN HAYES, JUDITH FOX.

KING, HENRY.   Bertie County.

July 1, 1750. May Court, 1751. *Daughters:* CATTREN, ANN and PRUDENCE KING. *Wife and Executrix:* ANN. *Executors:* ROBT. WEST, JOS. HARDY. *Witnesses:* AGNEE MARVELL KNOTT, HANNAH MALTIMER. *Clerk of the Court:* SAM'L ORMES.

KING, JOHN.   Onslow County.

January 5, 1743–1744. July 4, 1749. *Sons:* JOHN, CHARLES, WILLIAM, NICHOLAS, HENRY and JACOB, MICHAEL. *Wife:* PRISCILLA. *Executors:* LEWIS JENKINS and GEORGE BISHOP. *Witnesses:* ISABELLA JENKINS, ELIZABETH WINGATE, SARAH HIGMAN. *Clerk of the Court:* THOS. ——. Portion of this will missing.

KING, MICHAEL.   Bertie County.

May 20, 1741.   October 29, 1741.   *Sons:* MICHAEL, HENRY and JOHN.
Daughters: CATHERINE, ISBEL, PENELOPE and MARY KING.   *Wife and
Executrix:* ISBEL.   *Executors:* COLL. ROBERT WEST and his son ROBERT.
Witnesses: ROGER SNELL, JNO. HILL, J. HOLBROOK.   Proven before J.
MONTGOMERY, C. J.

KINGSTAN, JAMES.

July 12, 1748.   *Legatees and devisees:* JACOB BONI, JR., and WM.
THOMAS, JUNR.   *Executors:* JACOB BONI, SR., and WILLIAM THOMAS, SR.
Witnesses: WM. MCCANNE and NAT MCCANNE.   No probate.

KINSE, JOHN.   Perquimans County.

October 8, 1718.   April 14, 1719.   *Daughter:* ELIZABETH KINSEY.
Daughter-in-law: MARY NICKOLSON.   *Son-in-law:* SAMUEL NICKOLSON.
Wife and Executrix: PRESILLAH.   *Executor:* RICHARD RATLIFF.   *Witnesses:* EDWARD MAUDLIN, EZEKIEL MAUDLIN.   *Clerk of the Court:* RICHARD LEARY.

KINSEY, JOHN.   Craven County.

April 9, 1752.   May Court, 1752.   *Sons:* JOHN, JOSEPH, ABSALOM,
CHRISTIAN and SAMUEL.   *Daughter:* EASTER.   *Wife and Executrix:* MARY.
Executor: JOHN GRANADE.   *Witnesses:* JNO. SNEAD, HARDING JONES,
JOHN DUNN.   *Clerk of the Court:* PHIL SMITH.

KIRBY, THOMAS.   Chowan County.

May 7, 1718.   July 16, 1719.   *Sons:* THOMAS, CHARLES and EDWARD.
Daughters: MABEL and EASTER.   *Wife and Executrix:* EASTER.   *Witnesses:*
JOHN COLSON, RICHARD HORN, ROBERT SHARAR.   Proven before CHAS.
EDEN.

KISABLE, MICHAEL.   Craven County.

March 8, 1727–1728.   September 24, 1728.   *Daughter:* MARY FROWING.
Wife: mentioned, but not named.   *Daughter-in-law:* MARGET TEACHY.
Son-in-law: DANIEL TEACHY.   *Executors:* MATHEW RISNOVER and
FLETCHER MILLER.   *Witnesses:* ROBT. SMITH, ALEXANDER STEEL, JOHN
WAXFIELD.   *Clerk of the Court:* C. METCALFE

KITCHING, WILLIAM.   Perquimans Precinct.

May 4, 1736.   May 20, 1736.   *Devisees and legatees:* DANIEL ROGERSON
("plantation I now live on, called Mount Messeary"), JOSIAH ROGERSON,
CHRISTOPHER JACKSON, CHARLES DENMAN, CHRISTOPHER DENMAN, SARAH
DENMAN, THOMAS LILLY, JR., WILLIAM LILLEY, SARAH ROBERTS, GILBERT SCOT, JOHN LILLEY, CASIAH ROGERSON, MARGRET ROGERSON, ANN

MOORE, JEAN ASPELL.   *Executor:* DAN'LL ROGERSON.   *Witnesses:* WALTER ANDREW, WILLIAM ROBERTS, MARY ANDREW.   Proven before W. SMITH, C. J.

KNIGHT, LEWIS ALLEXANDER.   Pasquotank Precinct.

March 17, 1731. April Court, 1732. *Sons:* EMMANUEL and LEWIS (land "on ye River"). *Wife and Executrix:* ANN. *Witnesses:* JER. SWEENY, TIMOTHY MEADES, MARY SWEENY. *Clerk of the Court:* W. MINSON.

KNIGHT, TOBIAS.   Bath County.

June 11, 1719. July Court, 1719. *Wife and Executrix:* CATHERINE. All lands, etc., conveyed to wife and *daughter-in-law:* ELIZABETH GLOVER. *Witnesses:* JNO. HALTON, EDWD. CHAMBERLAYNE, PETER HAND. *Clerk of the Court:* JNO. HALTON.

KNIGHT, WILLIAM.   Bertie County.

December 3, 1751. February Court, 1752. *Sons:* JOHN, WILLIAM, NEMIAH. *Wife:* MARTHA. *Friends:* ISAAC CARTER, JOSEPH BENTHALL. *Executors:* ISAAC CARTER, JOHN KNIGHT (son). *Witnesses:* WILLIAM KNIGHT, SUSANNAH SKINER, JOSEPH BENTHALL. *Clerk of the Court:* SAMUEL ORMES.

KNOX, JOHN.   Chowan County.

February 11, 1729-1730. November 17, 1730. *Son:* THOMAS. *Wife and Executrix:* MARGRET. *Daughter:* MARY KNOX. *Guardian of daughter:* JOHN PORTER, SR. *Executor:* JOHN PORTER, JR. No witnesses. Proven before RICHARD EVERARD.

KORNEGEY, GEORGE.   Craven County.

November 2, 1773. November 29, 1773. *Sons:* DANIEL, ELIJAH (land in Dobbs County on Falling Creek), JOHN JACOB, GEORGE (250 acres of land in the fork of the Beaverdam in Duplin County), WILLIAM, DAVID, JOSEPH (500 acres of land on the northeast of Cape Fear), ABRAHAM. *Daughter:* MARY DEBRUHL. *Executors:* JOHN, JACOB and GEORGE KORNEGEY (sons). *Witnesses:* JOHN GRANADE, MORGAN SMITH SANDERS, RUBEN ANDREWS. Proven before JO. MARTIN.

LACYE, WILLIAM, SENIOR.   Albemarle County.

August 3, 1701. July Court, 1704. *Daughter:* BARBARY LACYE. *Granddaughter:* MARY LACYE. *Daughter-in-law:* MARY LACYE. *Son:* WILLIAM LACYE. BARBARY and MARY LACYE, daughters of WILLIAM LACYE, JR. *Executor:* WM. LACYE, JR. *Witnesses:* PETER GREY, SENIOR, PETER GRAY, JR., THOMAS HOLMES. *Clerk of the Court:* THO. SNODEN.

LACY, WILLIAM.   Perquimans County.

January 17, 1734–1735.   January 29, 1734.   *Sons:* WILLIAM and THOMAS ("land and plantation whereon I now live"), JOSEPH.   *Executors:* WIFE (not named) and RICHARD CHEASTEN.   *Witnesses:* JOHN POWELL, ARTHUR CRAXTON and ISAAC MACKEY.   Proven before GABRIEL JOHNSTON at Edenton.

LAFFITTE, TIMOTHY.   Edenton Precinct.

November 4, 1742.   March 24, 1742.   *Wife and Executrix:* SARAH. *Witnesses:* BENJN. TALBOT, JESSE BRENN, THOS. BLOUNT.   Proven before W. SMITH, C. J.

LAKARO (or LAKERS), BENJAMIN.   Perquimans Precinct.

April 7, 1701.   July 8, 1701.   *Wife and Executrix:* JULIANA (land on Parishes Creek).   *Daughter:* SARAH HARVEY (book, "Grantham's Church Principles").   *Friend:* GEORGE BLEIGHTON ("one book, being an Exposition upon the five books of Moses").   *Witnesses:* RICHARD FRENCH, ELIZABETH STEWARD, DEBORAH THURSTON.   *Clerk of the Court:* JOHN STEPNEY.

LAKER, JULIANA.   Perquimans County.

September 24, 1735.   January Court, 1738.   *Great-grandson:* BENJAMIN SCARBOROUGH, son of MACKEORA SCARBOROUGH (plantation called the Chenifen Ridge).   *Sister:* NEPTUANIA HUTSON.   *Daughter:* JOANNA PALMER.   *Other legatees:* HUTSON and JULIANA WORTHAM, MARTHA PALMER, SAMUELL PALMER.   *Executor:* MACKEORA SCARBOROUGH.   *Witnesses:* JOHN BANCKEY, PACIANA CREACY.   *Clerk of the Court:* JAMES CRAVEN.

LAMB, WILLIAM.   Perquimans County.

December 4, 1757.   April Court, 1758.   *Wife and Executrix:* MIRIAM. *Daughters:* ELIZABETH, MIRIAM and MARY.   *Brother and Executor:* WILLIAM NEWBY.   *Witnesses:* SAMUEL LITTESON (or SITTESON), DAVID POWELL, JACOB WILSON.   *Clerk of the Court:* MILES HARVEY.

LAMBERSON, HENRY.   Beaufort County.

February 17, 1743–1744.   June Court, 1744.   *Wife:* MARY.   *Son:* JOHN. *Executors:* JAMES HUMES, JESSE JONES and JOHN PHYSIOC and NATHANIEL DRAPER.   *Witnesses:* JOHN PHYSIOC, JAMES MACKELWAY, NATH'LL DRAPER.   *Clerk of the Court:* THE. GOOLD.

LANE, CHRISTIAN.   Edgecombe County.

October 5, 1747. May Court, 1748. *Daughters:* SARAH and MARY
LANE. *Son:* ABRAHAM. *Other legatees:* CHRISTIAN HILL. *Executor:*
ABRAHAM HILL. *Witnesses:* STEPHEN JACKSON, SARAH HILL. *Clerk of
the Court:* BENJ'N WYNNS.

LANE, EPHRAIM.   Craven County.

July 21, 1773. June 8, 1774. *Wife:* SARAH. *Other devisee and legatee:*
FREDERICK TODVINE. *Brothers:* SAMUEL and GEORGE LANE. *Executors:*
RICHARD CASWELL and FURNIFOLD GREEN. *Witnesses:* EDWARD HALLE,
WM. MIX, RICHARD TEER. Proven before Jo. MARTIN.

LANE, JOSEPH.   Edgecombe County.

December 6, 1757. November Court, 1758. *Brother:* WILLIAM LANE.
Sisters: FAITH BYNUM, DREWSILLER BRYANT. *Other legatee:* WINIFRED
POPE. *Executors:* JOHN BRADFORD and HENRY POPE. *Witnesses:* BEN-
JAMIN MERRYMAN, BARNABAS LANE, DAVID DICKSON. *Clerk of the Court:*
JOS. MONTFORT.

LANE, THOMAS.   Bertie County.

March 30, 1754. November Court, 1754. *Daughters:* ANN ROBESON,
ELIZABETH LANE, SARAH BERRY. *Son:* WILLIAM. *Executors:* JOHN
ROBINSON, ANN ROBINSON and ELIZABETH LANE. *Witnesses:* JOSEPH
BUTTERTON, WILLIAM PERSEY, SAM'LL O'STEEN. *Clerk of the Court:*
SAMUEL ORMES.

LANE, WALTER.   Newbern, in Craven County.

September 13, 1742. August Court, 1757. *Brothers:* WILLIAM, JOHN
and GEORGE LANE. *Sisters:* ELIZABETH MATTO, SARAH GODARD, ELENOR
HIXON, RACHEL. *Son:* GEORGE ("my lot in Newbern, No. 10"). *Grand-
sons:* WALTER LANE and WALTER HIXON. *Wife and Executrix:* MARY.
Executor: SAMUEL SWANN. *Witnesses:* JOHN LAPIERRE, JOHN BRYAN,
MARTIN FRANCK, DAN'LL GRANDIN. *Clerk of the Court:* PETER CONWAY.

LANIER, ROBERT.   Tyrrell County.

September 20, 1744. March Court, 1744. *Daughters:* JEAN, ELIZA-
BETH, SARAH, ANNANAZAH CRISTANAH, GRASE, SAMARIAH. *Sons:* WIL-
LIAM and JOHN (1 bible each). *Grandsons:* ROBERT DANIELL, JOHN
BRYAN. *Granddaughters:* SARAH and MARY GILBERT. *Wife and Execu-
trix:* SARAH. *Executors:* JOHN and WILLIAM LANIER (sons). *Witnesses:*
WILLIAM WILLIS, ROBERT LANIER DANIEL, JOHN LANIER. *Clerk of the
Court:* THOS. LEE.

LANKTON, THOMAS.

September 11, 1696. WM. STEVENS, JEBAZ. ALFORD, RACHEL and MARY DAMORELL, MR. FRANCIS PARROTT, "NEGRO BETTY" (one son about three years old), ANDREW JAMES. *Executor:* MR. WM. DUNKEN-FIELD. *Witnesses:* WM. JONES, JAMES DAMORELL. Proven by oath of JAMES DAMORELL before HONBLE. THOS. POLLOCK, *Lords' Deputy,* and by WM. JONES before CAPT. ANTHONY DAWSON, *Justice,* September 14, 1696.

LARKINS, JOHN.   New Hanover County.

May 15, 1737. September Court, 1738. *Sons:* WILLIAM and JOHN ("my plantation"), JAMES. *Wife and Executrix:* TABITHA. *Friend:* JAMES INNES. *Witnesses:* JOHN SMITHES, JAMES CARTER, JOHN INNES. *Clerk of the Court:* JNO. RICE.

LASEY, FRANCIS.   Perquimans County.

April 16, 1739. July Court, 1739. *Daughter:* JEMIMA LASEY ("planta-tion whereon I now dwell"). *Wife and Executrix:* MARY ANN LASEY. *Brother:* JOHN LASEY. *Executor:* WILLIAM BOGUE. *Witnesses:* FRANCIS JAMES, MOSES ELLIOTT. *Clerk of the Court:* JAMES CRAVEN.

LASHLY, PATRICK.   Granville County.

November 28, 1758. March Court, 1759. *Wife:* LIDDA. *Executor:* PHILIP PRYOR. *Witnesses:* MOSES SPAN, CHRISTIAN LANGSTON. *Clerk of the Court:* DANIEL WELDON.

LATHUM, PAUL.   Albemarle County.

October 7, 1692. July 31, 1693. *Son:* GEORGE ("my plantation"). *Daughter:* ELIZABETH LATHUM. *Wife and Executrix:* ELIZABETH. *Wit-nesses:* GEORGE FLEMMING, MARIA FLEMMING, JOHN PHILPOTT. *Clerk of the Court:* EDWARD MOOR.

LATTIMER, WILLIAM.   Bertie County.

August 21, 1750. February Court, 1750. *Wife and Executrix:* ELIZA-BETH. *Executor:* JAMES LEAGWIT. *Friend:* JAMES SMITH. *Witnesses:* RICHARD TOMLINSON, RICH'D BRADLEY, ROBERT ROGERS. *Clerk of the Court:* SAM'LL ORMES.

LATTIMORE, ELIZABETH.   Bertie County.

March 3, 1753. May Court, 1753. *Legatees:* MARY SMITH, JAMES SMITH, ABENEZAR TOMLINSON, RICHARD TOMLINSON ("all my lands and houses"). *Executor:* RICHARD TOMLINSON. *Witnesses:* LUKE MIZELL, JOHN OLIVER, ELIZABETH SMITH. *Clerk of the Court:* BENJ'N WYNNS.

LAWLER, PATRICK.   Chowan County.

November 29, 1728. January 22, 1728. *Sons:* DANBY ("my planta-
tion"), DAVID (appointed *Executor*). *Daughter:* ANN LAWTER. *Wife:*
PASHENT. *Witnesses:* THOS. ROUNTREE, JAMES HINTON, JOHN MARTAIN.
Proven before C. GALE and also before RICH'D EVERARD.

LAWRENCE, GEORGE.   Bertie County.

March 26, 1752. January Court, 1756. *Daughters:* ANN and SARAH
LAWRENCE. *Sons:* JOSHUA and GEORGE ("my lands"). *Wife and Executrix:* SARAH. *Executors:* THOMAS and JOHN LAWRENCE (brothers). *Witnesses:* GEORGE LAWRENCE, JOHN YEATS, ROBERT LAWRENCE, THOMAS
LAWRENCE. *Clerk of the Court:* BENJAMIN WYNNS.

LAWRENCE, WILLIAM.   Albemarle County.

July 5, 1694. August Court, 1694. *Daughters:* JANE and RACHELL
LAWRENCE. *Wife:* MARGARET LAWRENCE. *Cousin:* RACHEL SNELLING.
Cousin: WM. LAWRENCE. *Executors:* ISRAEL SNELLING and JOHN LAW-
RENCE. *Witnesses:* FRANCIS JONES, JR., CHRISTOPHER LACY, LAWRENCE
HUNT. *Clerk of the Court:* JOHN STEPNEY.

LAWSON, JOHN, Gent.   Bath County.

August 12, 1708. "To my dearly beloved HANNAH SMITH the house I
now live in * * * *." "Remainder of my estate real and personal to
my *daughter*, ISABELLA, of Bath County, * * * * *." Property to be
divided among daughter, ISABELLA, and any other child or children of her
mother, HANNAH SMITH, "by me." *Executrix:* HANNAH SMITH. *Witnesses:* RICHARD SMITH and JAMES LEIGH. Original missing. Recorded
in Will Book 1712–1722, page 39.

LAWSON, SAMUEL.   Craven County.

April 24, 1758. May 31, 1758. *Son:* DURRAM. *Daughter:* MARY PAL-
LIS LAWSON. *Wife and Executrix:* MARGARET. *Executors:* JOHN HILL and
WILLIAM MANSFIELD LIPSCOMB. *Witnesses:* JOHN HARDEE, WM. SPEIR
and BENJ'N PANE. Proven before ARTHUR DOBBS. To each of the children is devised a house and lot in Newbern.

LAWTER, DAVID.   Chowan County.

Will is not dated, nor is there any probate. *Wife and Executrix:* MARY
("my plantation" and also tract of land called the Cow Island). *Other
legatees and devisees:* WALTERS PHELPS (*Executor*), ELIZABETH HOMES,
EDWARD PILAND, DARBY LAWTER (brother), CHRISTIANA LOVEWELL, BEN-
JAMIN LOVEWELL. *Witnesses:* THOMAS PILAND, JOHN PHELPS and THOMAS
HOMES.

14

LAYDEN, FRANCIS.   Albemarle County.

February 23, 1727–1728. Probate not dated. *Wife and Executrix:*
ELIZABETH. *Sons:* WILLIAM ("the manor plantation"), FRANCIS (land
adjoining JOHN STEVENS), GEORGE and ISAAC. *Daughter:* MARY. *Cousin:*
WILLIAM MIDDLETON. *Witnesses:* JOHN STEVENS, WILLIAM MIDDLETON,
WILLIAM EVENS. *Clerk of the Court:* CHAS. DENMAN.

LAZY (or LACY), JOHN.   Perquimans Precinct.

December 1, 1682. No probate. *Wife:* ABIGAIL. *Daughter:* SARAH
LAZY (or LACY). *Witnesses:* JOHN STEPNEY, WILLIAM CHARLES, WILLIAM
LAURENCE. No executrix or executor appointed.

LEAR, JOHN.   Nansemond County.

November 21, 1695. December 12, 1695. *Daughters:* MARTHA BUR-
WELL, ELIZABETH LEAR. *Grandson:* JOHN LEAR. *Other legatees:* CHARLES
GOREMGE, JOHN GEORGE. *Executors:* LEWIS BURWELL, CAPT. THOMAS
GODWIN. *Witnesses:* WILLIAM COFFIELD, JOHN LOWE, ELIZABETH BRIDGER,
ANN COFFIELD. *Deputy Clerk of the Court:* ANDREW ROSS. This is a copy
of the original made by the deputy clerk of the Court.

LEARGE, JACOB.   Craven County.

1731. March Court, 1731–1732, "of the Switz Country being in Obar
Savenchal." *Sons:* JACOB and CHRISTIAN. *Daughter:* MARY LEARGE.
Executor: JACOB MILLER. *Witnesses:* PETER CORTNEY, GEORGE SLIDER,
VENDAL PHILER. *Clerk of the Court:* CALEB METCALFE.

LEARY, CORNELIUS.   Tyrrell County.

March 30, 1742. September Court, 1742. *Brothers:* JOHN and JAMES
LEARY. *Sisters:* SARAH, MARY and REBECCA LEARY. *Mother:* SARY
LEARY. *Executor:* JOHN LEARY (brother). *Witnesses:* RICH'D LEARY,
JAMES SUTTEN. *Clerk of the Court:* W. DOWNING.

LEARY, RICHARD.   Tyrrell County.

April 20, 1738. September 5, 1738. *Sons:* CORNELIUS and JAMES
("plantation whereon I now live to be equally divided between them"),
JOHN (three hundred acres of land commonly known as the Chincquapine
ridge), THOMAS, RICHARD. *Daughters:* SARAH, MARY and REBECKAH
LEARY. *Wife and Executrix:* SARAH. *Executor:* CORNELIUS LEARY. *Witnesses:* JOHN LONG, ELIZABETH LONG. *Deputy Clerk of the Court:* ANDER-
SON SAGG.

LEATH, JOHN, SR.   Hyde County.

April 9, 1750. June Court, 1751. *Sons:* THOMAS and SAMUEL (100
acres land), CHARLES and PETER (plantation bought of RICHARD LAMBIRT-

SON), JOHN. *Daughters:* SARAH, FRANCES, DORCAS, CASIA, MARY and CATHERINE LEATH, HANNAH HODGES SLADE, ELIZABETH SLADE. *Executors:* JOHN and CHARLES LEATH (sons), AARON TISON. *Witnesses:* AARON TISON, ROGER MASON, JUNR., WILLIAM RICHARD JASPER. *Clerk of the Court:* THOS. LOACK.

LEATH, JOHN.   Hyde County.

November 10, 1751. March Court, 1752. *Sons:* SAMSON ("my manner plantation"), JOHN. *Daughters:* LYDIA and KEZIAH LEATH. *Wife and Executrix:* HANNAH. *Executors:* AARON TISON and JONATHAN JASPER. *Witnesses:* GEORGE BELL, JONATHAN JASPER, ANN JASPER. *Clerk of the Court:* FRANCIS EGLETON.

LEATH, RICHARD.   Hyde County.

May 10, 1749. *Daughters:* AGNES and RACHEL LEATH. *Wife and Executrix:* MARY. *Witnesses:* HEZEKIAH SLADE, BENJAMIN JEWELL, MARY JEWELL. *Clerk of Court:* THOS. LOACK. Testator describes his stock mark as being "crop and under bit and a hole Left Eare, the right under bit and over bit."

LEE, GEORGE.   Pasquotank Precinct.

May 3, 1729. October 12, 1729. *Sons:* JOHN ("ye plantation whereon I now dwell"), EDWARD (land adjoining the plantation aforesaid), GEORGE and WILLIAM. *Daughters:* ELIZABETH, MARY and SARAH LEE. *Wife and Executrix:* ELIZABETH. *Witnesses:* THOS. WEEKES, ANNE WEEKES, ANNE BUNDY. *Clerk of the Court:* H. MINSON. *"Item:* I give and bequeath * * * * * all ye neat cattle that are to be found of ye following mark (viz.) a crop in ye right ear and two slits in ye left wch mark is recorded * * *."

LEE, JAMES.   Bertie Precinct.

January 17, 1731. November Court, 1732. *Sons:* JAMES ("the plantation whereon I now live"), ROBERT and WILLIAM ("a plantation at a place called Kinyard's"). *Wife and Executrix:* SARAH. *Witnesses:* JOHN MORE, RICHARD MORE, JR. *Clerk of the Court of Edgecombe Precinct:* RT. FORSTER.

LEE, MARY (wife of Capt. Thomas Lee),   Chowan County.

September 26, 1716. October 31, 1716. *Sons:* THOMAS BLOUNT (one-half of the "manner plantation with the manner house"), BENJAMIN and JACOB BLOUNT ("the Middle plantation"). *Daughter:* ZILPLIA BLOUNT ("the other halfe of the said manner plantation"). *Executor:* THOMAS BLOUNT (son). *Witnesses:* JERVIS COLEMAN, JOHN EDWARDS, GILBERT HOLLIDAY and WILLIAM SWINSON. *Clerk of the Court:* R. HICKS. Testatrix states that she is also "widdow of CAPTT. THOMAS BLOUNT of Chowan."

LEE, RICHARD.   Edgecombe County.

April 4, 1756. May Court, 1756. *Sons:* TIMOTHY (100 acres of land on "Contenteny Creek"), ARTHUR, RICHARD, SOLOMON (the plantation "which I now live on"). *Daughters:* ELISABETH LEE, RACHEL BRADLEY, SARRAH HORN, MARTHA LEE. *Witnesses:* ABSALOM HOLLIMAN, WILLIAM FOKES, JAMES PERMENTER. *Clerk of the Court:* JOS. MONTFORT. Stock mark of the testator is described as being "swallow fork in the right ear and a crop and half Crop in ye Left Ear."

LEE, STEVENS.   Tyrrell County.

February 2, 1746–1747. June Court, 1746–1747. *Son:* STEVENS (land on Kendricks Creek, ⅔ of grist mill; plantation on White Oak called Cedar Point). *Daughter:* FRANCES LEE ("plantation where I now live called Cabbin Neck"). *Wife:* ELIZABETH. *Executors:* ROBERT WEST, CULLEN POLLOCK, THOMAS LEE and ROBERT WEST, JR. *Witnesses:* WM. MACKEY, JOHN GOMM, JOHN HUGHES. *Clerk of Court:* EVAN JONES.

LEE, STEPHEN.   Onslow County.

January 25, 1772. December 8, 1773. *Son:* STEPHEN ("my plantation bought of WM. HOUSTON"). *Daughters:* MARY, SARAH and FERREBY LEE. *Wife:* FERREBEE. *Executors:* ROBERT ORME, EDWARD STARKEY, PETER STARKEY. *Witnesses:* STEPHEN GRANT, RICHARD OLDFIELD, SARAH WILLIAMS. Proven before JO. MARTIN. Provision is made for education of son at Boston or Philadelphia.

LEE, THOMAS.   Chowan Precinct.

March 14, 1716–1717. July 6, 1719. *Brother:* WILLIAM LEE ("my plantation called Cabbin Neck lying on the East side of Kendricks Creek"). *Children of brother William:* WILLIAM, ELIZABETH and EDWARD. *Friend:* ZILPHA BLOUNT. *Son:* STEPHENS ("all my lands and my mill"). *Wife:* MARY. *Executors:* FREDERICK JONES, EDWARD MOSELEY, WILLIAM DOWNING. *Witnesses:* C. GALE, JERVIS COLMAN, JOHN EDWARDS. Proven before CHARLES EDEN. To wife is given plantation at Conaby "on the east side of the Creek." "*Item:* It is my will that the ship or pink by me now intended to be built at Kendricks Creek shall be compleatly built, finished and launched, &c &c &c."

LEE, THOMAS.

July 23, 1722. July 28, 1722. *Brother:* WILLIAM LEE ("my third part of the Sloop Sea Flower"). *Daughters:* JANE and RACHEL LEE. *Executor:* COLL. MAURICE MOORE. *Witnesses:* GYLES SHUTE, ANTHONY GREEN, THOMAS PESKET (PRESCOTT). Proven before THOMAS POLLOCK, *President of the Council.*

LEE, THOMAS.   Tyrrell County.

   November 1, 1750.   April Court, 1753.   *Son:* THOMAS (lands between
Combee Creek and Morrattock River).   *Executors:* FRANCIS BRICE, WIL-
LIAM MACKEY, STEVENS LEE.   *Witnesses:* JOHN NICHOLLS, WILLIAM BAR-
RET, JAMES RHOADS.   *Clerk of the Court:* EVAN JONES.

LEE, THOMAS.   Bertie County.

   March 31, 1751.   February Court, 1752.   *Sons:* WILLIAM ("my planta-
tion"), STEVEN.   *Wife and Executrix:* MARY.   *Daughter:* PRISSILLA LEE.
Executor: BENJAMIN WYNNS.   *Witnesses:* JNO. HARRELL, THOS. HUDSON,
JACOB LEWESS, JNO. LEWESS.   *Clerk of the Court:* SAMUEL ORMES.

LEETH, JOHN.   Anson County.

   July 21, 1757.   *Legatees:* JOSEPH LEETH (son of GEORGE LEETH), MARY
WHITE (daughter of JOSEPH WHITE).   *Executor:* ANTHONY HUTCHINS.
Witnesses: JOHN THORMAIN, SAMUEL SMART, ANTHO. HUTCHINS, MARY
THURMAN.   No probate.

LEGITT, THOMAS.   Currituck County.

   April 10, 1749.   July Court, 1749.   *Wife and Executrix:* ELISABETH.
Daughter: ELISABETH LEGITT.   *Cousin:* JAMES LEGITT (son of ALEXANDER
LEGITT).   *Witnesses:* ROBERT SIMMONS, ELIASH CORNISH, MOSES CAPS.
Clerk of the Court: RICH'D MCCLURE.

LEIGH, ANN.   Beaufort Precinct.

   August 9, 1732.   March Court, 1732–1733.   *Sons:* SAMUEL DARDEN
(plantation and three negroes), JOSEPH DARDEN.   *Daughters:* ANN ADAMS,
JANE WATKINS.   *Grandsons:* JACOB DARDEN and JAMES ADAMS.   *Granddaughters:* SARAH ADAMS and MARY WATKINS.   *Executor:* SAMUEL DAR-
DEN.   *Witnesses:* ROBERT CAMPEN, JOHN MAYO, THOS. MALLDEN.   *Clerk
of the Court:* JNO. COLLISON.

LEIGH, JAMES.   Bath County.

   September 23, 1728.   October Court, 1728.   *Sons:* JAMES ("part of the
tract of land I now live on"), JOHN (land called the Accomack Entry),
Lyonall (land adjoining the Accomack Entry).   *Daughters:* SARAH LEIGH,
PATIENCE PURSER, ELIZABETH UNDERWOOD and MILLY DURHAM.   *Wife:*
ANN.   *Grandson:* PETER LEIGH.   *Executors:* JAMES and JOHN LEIGH
(sons).   *Trustee:* ROBERT RURNER.   *Witnesses:* ROBERT PEYTON, ROBERT
PEYTON, BENJA. PEYTON.   *Clerk of the Court:* JOHN MATTOCKE.

LEIRMONT, RICHARD.   Hyde County.

   February 24, 1752.   March Court, 1752.   *Daughters:* AMELIA WEBSTER
(plantation on Jordan's Creek commonly known by the name of LODOWICK

MARTIN's plantation), WILLIELMA LEIRMONT (one plantation on Jordan's Creek called Margaret Jordan's Fork), MARGARET LEIRMONT (land known as Hunt's Point). *Executors:* WILLIAM WEBSTER, THOMAS JORDAN and THOMAS SMITH. *Witnesses:* ROGER MASON, DINAH SMITH, THOMAS REW. *Clerk of the Court:* FRAN. EGLETON.

LENNON, JOHN.   Bladen County.
  October 13, 1757.   October Court, 1757.   Parish of St. Martin's. *Sons:* JOHN ("this land I now live on"), DENIS (land on Waccamaw Swamp), EPHRAIM. *Daughter:* PHILLIS ELLICE. *Wife and Executrix:* ANN. *Executor:* EVEN ELLICE (son-in-law). *Witnesses:* SAMU'L BAKER, WM. MCREE (or MCKEE), MARY MACKKEY. *Clerk of the Court:* JNO. BURGWIN.

LEPPER, THOMAS.   Bath County, in Craven Precinct.
  October 23, 1715.   July 22, 1719. *Legatees:* ANNE and KATHERINE NUSS. *Wife and Executrix:* ANNE. *Executors:* DANIEL MCFARLANE and RICHARD GRAVES. *Witnesses:* JOHN NELSON, ELIZABETH FERGUSON, MARY JONES and MARY RIDING. *Clerk of the Court:* C. METCALFE.

LEWERTON, EPHRAIM.   Chowan Precinct.
  October 10, 1713. *Cousins:* JOHN LEWERTON, son of JOHN LEWERTON (land on Salmon Creek); WILLIAM, son of WILLIAM JONES (land on Black Walnut Swamp); ELIZABETH LEWERTON, ANN and MARY JONES. *Sister:* MARY JONES. *Friend:* REBECCA HARDY. *Executor:* JOHN HARDY. *Witnesses:* WILLIAM JONES, JOHN HOLBROOK. Original missing. Recorded in Book 1712–1722, page 30.

LEWERTON, WILLIAM.   Chowan Precinct.
  January 3, 1698–1699.   April Court, 1699. *Sons:* WILLIAM and JOHN. *Daughters:* MARY and ELIZABETH. *Wife and Executrix:* ELIZABETH. *Witnesses:* NICHOLAS FILLBERT, JNO. DAVIS and NATH. CHEVIN. *Clerk of the Court:* NATH. CHEVIN.

LEWIS, DAVID.   Carteret County.
  October 6, 1773.   November 11, 1773. *Devisees and legatees:* JOHN SHEPARD ("plantation whereon I now dwell known by the name of Indian Town"), WILLIAM SHEPARD (plantation known as Glover's Hammock), DAVID SHEPARD, JOHN SIMMONS, DANIEL, JAMES and BENJAMIN SIMMONS, RICHARD SHEPARD. One hundred pounds is bequeathed toward building a church in Beaufort. *Wife and Executrix:* MARY. *Executors:* JOHN SHEPARD, SOLOMON SHEPARD and JOHN SIMMONS. *Witnesses:* WILLIAM BEVIN, JAMES FRAZIER, SARAH FRAZIER. Proven before JO. MARTIN.

LEWIS, EVAN.   Beaufort County.

June 26, 1713–1714.   January 3, 1714.   *Wife and Executrix:* ELIZABETH
LEWIS.   *Other legatee:* MARY MAYO.   *Witnesses:* SAM'LL MELTUM, SWAN
SWANSON.   *Clerk of the Court:* JNO. DRINKWATER.

LEWIS, WILLIAM.   Bath County.

December 11, 1731.   August 5, 1732.   *Daughters:* ELIZABETH SINCLARE,
MARY DUDLEY, MAGDALEN BIGFORD, EDY BENSON.   *Sons:* WILLIAM and
SOLOMON.   *Wife and Executrix:* MARY.   *Executor:* WILLIAM LEWIS (son).
Witnesses: ED. SMITH, JOHN HERBERT.   Proven before GEORGE BURRING-
TON.

LILE, GEORGE.   Chowan County.

October 29, 1752.   January Court, 1753.   *Sons:* GEORGE ("plantation
whereon I now live"), JOHN.   *Executors:* WILLIAM HOSKINS and HENRY
BONNER.   *Witnesses:* JOHN CARLTON, JEREMIAH HAUGHTON, JOHN HOS-
KINS.   *Clerk of the Court:* JAMES CRAVEN.   Six other children are mentioned, but not named.

LILLINGTON, ALEXANDER.   Perquimans Precinct.

September 9, 1697.   October 8, 1697.   *Sons:* JOHN ("plantation whereon
I now live and plantation that was formerly STEPHEN HANCOCKS and my
silver hilted sword"), GEORGE ("my plantation at Yawpim River and plan-
tation at Little River whereon FRANCIS PENRIE now lives").   *Daughters:*
ANN WALKER, ELIZABETH FENDALL, MARY LILLINGTON, SARAH LILLING-
TON.   *Sons-in-law:* HENDERSON WALKER and JOHN FENDALL.   *Wife:* ANN.
Executors: COL. WILLIAM WILKISON and HENDERSON WALKER.   *Witnesses:*
CALEB CALLAWAY, JOHN BARROW, ROBERT HARMAN.   *Clerk of the Court:*
W. GLOVER.   Coat of arms on seal.

LILLINGTON, ANN.   Chowan Precinct.

January 26, 1724.   April 1, 1725.   *Daughter:* ELIZABETH LILLINGTON.
Grandson and Executor: JOHN SIMONS.   *Witnesses:* JAMES BEASLEY, ANNA
STEWART, MARY STEWART.   Proven before GEORGE BURRINGTON.

LILLINGTON, ELIEZER.   Bath County.

April 28, 1729.   December Court, 1729.   *Wife:* ELIZABETH (also appointed *Executrix*).   *Witnesses:* JOHN BROCK, JOHN CLIFFORD, GILBERT
HALIDAY.   *Clerk of the Court:* JOHN MATTOCK.   The testator bequeathed
the following books: To NATHAN ARCHBALD, "one come and welcome to
Jesus Christ by John Bunyan, Mr. Baxters directions of Geting and attain-
ing peace of Conscience, Measons Hymne Book an old sermon book by
several divines called the farewell sermons."   To JOHN CLIFFORD: "Allens

call to the unconverted and Lees Triumphs of Mercy with a New England Psalm Book." To GILBERT HALIDAY: "Mathers remarkable Providences and an English Dictionary."

LILLINGTON, ÉLIZABETH.   Bath County.

July 8, 1734. *Sons:* RICHARD BARROW, JOSEPH BARROW, JAMES BARROW, WILLIAM, JOHN and SAMUEL BARROW (1 shilling each). *Daughters:* MARY BARROW and SARAH HARRIS. *Executors:* RICHARD and JOSEPH BARROW (sons). *Witnesses:* DELIVERANCE LATHAN, ELEANOR HOWARD, ROBERT HOWARD. *Clerk of Hyde County Court:* WM. BARROW. Five negro slaves are bequeathed.

LILLINGTON, JOHN.   Beaufort Precinct.

March 19, 1721–1722. July 2, 1723. *Son:* ALEXANDER (1,000 acres of land, two negro slaves, a family bible, etc.). *Daughters:* ELIZABETH, MARY, ANN. *Wife:* SARAH LILLINGTON. *Executors:* MAURICE MOORE, JOHN PORTER and JOHN BAPTISTE ASHE. *Witnesses:* PAT. MAULE, SAMUEL COOPER, JOHN TRANTER. *Clerk of the Court:* JOHN BAPTISTE ASHE. Five negroes, about sixty cattle bequeathed to children.

LILLY, JOHN.   Perquimans County.

January 26, 1753. April Court, 1753. *Wife and Executrix:* KAZEIAH ("plantation where I now dwell"). *Father-in-law:* DANIEL ROGERSON (163 acres of land in Chowan County called the "beverdams"). *Brother:* JOSHUA LILLY, "and my father-in-law, DANIEL ROGERSON" ("three hundred acres of land lying up the Ridges"). *Executor:* JOSIAH ROGERSON. *Witnesses:* NICHOLAS STALLINGS, JOSEPH LILLY, ISAAC LILLY. *Clerk of the Court:* EDMUND HATCH.

LILLEY, THOMAS.   Perquimans County.

October 12, 1735. January Court, 1735. *Sons:* JOHN ("plantation he now lives on"), THOMAS ("plantation whereon I now live"), WILLIAM (100 acres of land), TIMOTHY and JOSEPH (tract of land to be equally divided between them). *Daughters:* MARGARET REDDICK (wife of JOHN REDDICK), HANNA ROGERSON. *Wife and Executrix:* SARAH. *Executor:* THOMAS LILLEY (son). *Witnesses:* GEORGE SPIVE, DANIEL ROGERSON, GILBERT SCOTT. *Clerk of the Court:* JAMES CRAVEN.

LINDSAY, JAMES.   Dobbs County.

June 15, 1768. May 11, 1770. *Brothers:* PETER, WILLIAM and ROBERT LINDSAY. *Executors:* RICHARD CASWELL, JOHN DICKSON and ROBERT LINDSAY. *Witnesses:* FRAS. MACKILWEAN, RIGDON BRICE. *Clerk Superior Court:* AMBLOX BAGLEY.

LININGTON, EDWARD.   Craven County.

July 9, 1736. September Court, 1736. *Sons:* GEORGE and EDWARD
LININGTON. *Daughter:* MARY SHERLOCK. *Grandson:* FRANCIS SHERLOCK
("all my lands in Alligator"). *Executors:* DENNIS SHERLOCK and CAPT.
JOSEPH HANNIS. *Witnesses:* KATHERINE HANNIS, ANN DUPARTALL, GAS-
PAR VIALON. *Deputy Clerk of the Court:* WM. LANE. Provision in will
that "all the pitch and Tarr my negroes makes shall goe to pay my debts
&c."

LININGTON, GEORGE.   Craven County.

January 24, 1741–1742. June 16, 1742. *Daughters:* ANN HUTCHISON
LININGTON, ELIZABETH LININGTON, CHRISTIAN LININGTON. *Nephew:*
FRANCIS SHEARLOCK (640 acres of land on Neuse River). *Wife:* HANNAH.
Executors: WM. BRICE and RICHARD NIXSON. *Witnesses:* THOS. SMITH
and NATHAN SMITH. *Clerk of Court:* N. ROUTLEDGE.

LINSEY, DANIEL.   Currituck Precinct.

November 6, 1720. January 10, 1721. *Son:* DAVID (1 shilling). *Wife
and Executrix:* MARY. *Witnesses:* JOHN NORTON, WILLIAM JOHNSON, JOHN
MARTYN. *Clerk of the Court:* JO. WICKER.

LINSEY, DAVID.   Currituck County.

August 17, 1749. October Court, 1750. *Wife and Executrix:* ANN.
Mother: SARAH LINSEY. *Brother:* BENJAMIN LINSEY. To wife is be-
queathed "my house and plantation." *Witnesses:* HENRY WOODHOUSE,
SOLOMON SMITH, MENES SMITH. *Clerk of the Court:* RICH'D MCCLURE.

LINSEY, ROBERT.   Albemarle County.

May 16, 1689. July 25, 1689. *Executors:* JOHN WILSON and GEORGE
HARDIE. *Legatees and devisees:* ANN MATHEWS, COLLETON STURGON ("my
plantation at Yawpim"), MARY STURGON, (son and daughter of JOHN
STURGON). *Witnesses:* FRANCIS HARTLEY, THOMAS SLATER, MARGARET
SLATER. Proven before SETH SOTHELL.

LINTON, WILLIAM.   Bath County.

January 12, 1725–1726. June 20, 1727. *Wife and Executrix:* MARGA-
RET. *Sons and Daughters:* mentioned, but not named. *Witnesses:* ROB-
ERT WATSON, FRANCIS HILL. *Executor:* THOMAS MISTRES. *Clerk of the
Court:* CALEB METCALFE.

LITTLE, GEORGE.   Hertford County.

August 1, 1787. *Son:* WILLIAM. *Daughter:* PENELOPE. *Wife and
Executrix:* MARY LITTLE. *Witnesses:* GEORGE SWOPE, JOHN JENKINS,
ELIZABETH HURST, JAMES BROWN. No probate. All estate of the tes-
tator, both real and personal, is divided between son and daughter.

LITTLE, JOHN. Anson County.

December 8, 1755. No probate. *Sons:* THOMAS (of Rowan County), WILLIAM, JOHN, ARCHIBALD, JAMES and ALEXANDER. *Daughters:* MARGARET LITTLE and MARTHA REED, wife of JOHN REED. *Grandson:* THOMAS LITTLE. *Executors:* JOHN LITTLE (son) and JOHN CATHEY. *Witnesses:* CHARLES MOORE, HENRY JOHNSON and MARY RENICK. No probate.

LITTLE, WILLIAM.

June 25, 1734. September 5, 1734. *Sons:* GEORGE (lands in Meherrin Neck), WILLIAM (lands at Okaneechy). *Daughter:* PENELOPE LITTLE (mill at Hoskins). *Wife and Executrix:* PENELOPE. *Executors:* CRISTOPHER GALE, EDMUND GALE and EDWARD SALTER. *Brothers:* JOHN ARBUTHNOT (also *Executor*), ISAAC LITTLE. *Friend:* PENELOPE LOVICK (widow of JOHN LOVICK). *Witnesses:* JOHN BOND, JOHN CROWELL, JOHN PARKER. Proven before GEO. BURRINGTON. About ten negroes bequeathed.

LITTLE, WILLIAM. Beaufort County.

March 1, 1756. March Court, 1756. *Sons:* ABRAHAM (land on Cheek's Mill Creek), JACOB (100 acres of "the tract of Land whereon I now dwell"), WILLIAM, JAMES, ISAAC, JOHN, JOSEPH. *Daughter:* JANE MORING. *Wife:* MORNING. *Executors:* ISAAC and JACOB LITTLE (sons). *Witnesses:* AMOS ATKINSON, MARY JUDKINS, JANE ATKINSON. *Clerk of the Court:* WALLEY CHAUNCEY.

LOADMAN, JAMES. Albemarle County.

November 14, 1694. April Court, 1695. JANE BARFIELD, RICHARD BARFIELD, WILLIAM BUTLER, SARAH BEASLEY, TIMOTHY CLEAR, ELIZABETH PHELPS, JAMES KENIDAY. *Executor:* WILLIAM BOGUE. *Witnesses:* JOHANNA BEASLEY, JANE BYARD, PATRICK CENADY. *Clerk of the Court:* JOHN STEPNY.

LOCK, BENJAMIN. Bladen County.

April 25, 1756. January Court, 1757. *Son:* JOHN ("my land"). *Wife:* MIRIAM. *Executors:* NEIL BEARD (father) and JOHN LOCK (brother). *Witnesses:* THOMAS THEMS, DANIEL BEARD, ELIZABETH LOCK. *Clerk of the Court:* THOS. ROBESON.

LOCK, THOMAS. Bladen County.

August 29, 1739. December 19, 1739. *Wife and Executrix:* SUSANNAH. *Sons:* BENJAMIN, DAVID and LEONARD. JOSEPH (land on Northwest River). *Daughters:* ELIZABETH BARTRAM, MARY LOCK. *Witnesses:* THOMAS WIER, PETER WALLSON, WILLIS HUGHES. Proven before GAB. JOHNSTON at Brompton. Original missing. Recorded in Book 1738–1753, page 123.

LOCKEY, JOSEPH.   Beaufort County.

January 30, 1746. March Court, 1746. *Sons:* JOSEPH ("plantation whereon I now live"), HENRY (land on Barrows Creek), JAMES. *Daughters:* SARAH and FRAZER LOCKEY. *Wife and Executrix:* SARAH. *Executors:* LEVI ALDERSON, JOHN ODEN, JOHN SLADE. *"Item:* My will and desire is that my executors do finish the Brick House now A Building this Ensueing Summer, and that they putt Ten Large Sash Glass Windows therein." *Witnesses:* WM. DUNBARR, AARON SPRING, JOHN HILL. *Clerk of the Court:* JOHN FORBES.

LOCKHART, JAMES.   Bertie County.

December 7, 1753. May Court, 1754. *Wife and Executrix:* ELIZABETH. *Sons:* LILLINGTON ("plantation whereon I now live"), GEORGE ("my two plantations at Cashoak"), JAMES ("all the rest of my lands"). *Executors:* LILLINGTON LOCKHART, MICHAEL CONTANCH. *Witnesses:* EDWARD BRYAN, JOHN BURN, THOS. JACOCKS, ANDR. BURN. *Clerk of the Court:* SAML. ORMES.

LODMAN, JAMES.

November 14, 1694. April 8, 1695. *Legatees:* WM. BARFIELD, SARAH BASLY, TIMOTHY CLEAR, ELIZABETH PHELPS, JAMES KENEDY, WILLIAM BOOGE *(Executor)*. *Witnesses:* JOHANA PASLY, JEANE BYRD, PATRICK KENEDY. *Clerk of the Court:* JOHN STEPNEY.

LOFTIN, LEONARD.   Craven Precinct, Bath County.

April 11, 1720. June 21, 1721. *Sons:* CORNELIUS (220 acres of land where "he now lives"), LEONARD ("plantation I now live on"), BENONIEA. *Daughters:* PERCELLY, JANE and JOYCE. *Executors:* CORNELIUS and LEONARD LOFTIN (sons). *Witnesses:* WM. HANDCOCK, ANN METCALFE, CALEB METCALFE. *Clerk of the Court:* CALEB METCALFE.

LOGAN, ALEXANDER.

October 9, 1739. November 6, 1739. *Executors:* THOMAS BLOUNT of Cape Fear, THOMAS BLOUNT and JESSE BLOUNT of Chowan County. Executors are directed to sell the real and personal estate of the testator, and forward proceeds of sale to MESSRS. JOHNSTON & ROBINSON at Charlestown, to be by them forwarded to THOMAS KENNEDY of Bristol, to be applied by him as before directed. *Witnesses:* J. MONTGOMERY, JOHN DUNCAN, DENNIS SHERLOCK. Proven before W. SMITH, C. J.

LONG, DANIEL.   Perquimans County.

July 28, 1714. January 11, 1715–1716. *Wife:* ELIZABETH. *Friend and legatee:* ANN LONGLATHER, of King and Queen County in Virginia. *Executor:* JOSEPH JESSOP. *Witnesses:* RICHARD FRENCH, ROBERT MOORE. *Clerk of the Court:* RICH'D LEARY.

LONG, GILES.

February 12, 1691–1692. This is a nuncupative will, proven by the oaths of EDWARD SMITHWICKE and THOMAS ———, and gives all estate of the testator to his wife and child, who are not named. No probate.

LONG, JAMES.   Albemarle County.

November 24, 1678. October 7, 1680. Sons: JAMES, THOMAS and GILLES. Wife and Executrix: mentioned, but not named. Witnesses: JOHN WILSON, WILLIAM STANARD. No probate officer.

LONG, JAMES.   Chowan County.

November 15, 1711. July 29, 1712. Sons: JAMES, THOMAS ("the brick house plantation"), JOHN ("my plantation at Moratock"). Daughters: MARY and ELIZABETH. Wife and Executrix: ELIZABETH. Witnesses: JAMES HAWKINS, THOMAS HOOPPER, LEONARD LEFTIN. Court held at the house of CAPT. THOMAS LEES in Chowan County. Clerk of the Court: J. PALIN.

LONG, JAMES.   Chowan County.

September 1, 1731. April Court, 1734. Sons: JAMES, GILES, JOSHUA, JOHN, ANDREW (to each of these sons is devised land). Daughter: ELIZABETH LONG. Executor: GILES LONG (son). Witnesses: RICHARD LEARY, THOMAS LEARY, CORNELIUS LEARY. Clerk of the Court: MOSELEY VAIL.

LONG, JOSHUA.   Perquimans County.

May 20, 1741. July Court, 1741. Sons: THOMAS ("the manner plantation"), JOSHUA ("the land I purchased of JOHN BANKS, and one hundred acres of land on Yopim River"). Wife: ELIZABETH. Executors: THOMAS LONG (brother), WILLIAM HOSKINS and JOSEPH SUTTON. Witnesses: NATHANIEL CARRUTHERS, JOHN BANCKES, ROBERT HARMAN. Clerk of the Court: EDMUND HATCH. To two sons is bequeathed one "peryoger" (periagua).

LONG, JOSHUA.   Tyrrell County.

January 7, 1750. June Court, 1754. Daughters: PRISCILLA, KEZIAH and ESTER LONG. Nephew: STEPHEN LONG ("my plantation"). Wife and Executrix: JEMIMA. Executor: JOSHUA SWAIN. Witnesses: ANDREW LONG, PRISCILLA LONG, GILES LONG. Clerk of the Court: EVAN JONES.

LONG, SARAH.   Perquimans Precinct.

September 10, 1712. July 8, 1718. Legatees: THOMAS LONG (brother-in-law), MARY PERCE (sister), THOS. PERCE (brother-in-law), CORNELIUS LEARY (son of RICHARD LEARY), JOHN WIATT (cousin), JONATHAN and WILLIAM TAYLOR, JOSHUWAY LONG (plantation at creek's mouth), WIL-

LIAM LONG ("plantation whereon I now dwell"), JAMES CHESSON. *Executors:* THOS. PERCE and THOS. LONG. *Witnesses:* JAMES CHESSON, WILL'M TETHERTON, RICH'D LEARY. *Clerk of Court:* RICHARD LEARY.

LONG, THOMAS.   Perquimans Precinct.

September 21, 1721.   October 10, 1721. *Sons:* WILLIAM ("all my land up ye mill swamp"), JOSHUA ("ye land lying on MAJOR HARVES Quarter"), THOMAS ("my plantation whereon I now live, containing four hundred and seventy acres"). *Daughter:* SARAH LEARY. *Wife and Executrix:* REBECKAH. *Executor:* JOSHUA LONG (son). *Witnesses:* THOMAS PEIRCE, JOHN WIAT, JOSHUA CALLOWAY. *Clerk of the Court:* RICH'D LEARY. Court held at the house of MRS. ELIZABETH FRENCH.

LONG, THOMAS.   Perquimans County.

March 7, 1754. April Court, 1754. *Sons:* JOSHUA, THOMAS (plantation commonly known as DANIEL HALL'S plantation). *Wife and Executrix:* SARAH. *Executors:* JOSEPH CREECY, JOSHUA LONG (brother). *Witnesses:* THOMAS WILLIAMS, ROBERT TURNER, ANDR. KNOX. *Clerk of the Court:* WILL. SKINNER.

LONG, WILLIAM.   Perquimans Precinct.

June 2, 1701. July Court, 1712. *Nephews:* JAMES and WILLIAM LONG ("plantation whereon I now live"). *Brothers:* JOHN LONG and THOMAS LONG. *Wife and Executrix:* SARAH. *Witnesses:* THOMAS LONG, JOHN FOSTER, JOHN STEPNEY. *Clerk of the General Court:* J. PALIN.

LONG, WILLIAM.   Perquimans County.

July 4, 1758. April Court, 1759. *Sons:* SIMEON (part "of my manor plantation"), THOMAS ("part of my manor plantation"), REUBEN (land on Franks Creek), WILLIAM, JAMES (100 acres of land on the west side of Minses Creek). *Grandsons:* LEMUEL and ICHABOD LONG, JOSHUA WYATT. *Granddaughter:* MARY WYATT. *Wife and Executrix:* ANN. *Executors:* JAMES, THOMAS, REUBEN and SIMEON LONG (sons). *Witnesses:* THOMAS JONES, ZEPHANIAH JONES, WILL. SKINNER. *Clerk of the Court:* MILES HARVEY.

LONGLEATHER, DANIEL.   Perquimans Precinct.

July 28, 1714. *Legatees:* ANNE LONGLEATHER, of King and Queen County, Va., WILLIAM and JOSEPH STEWARD (sons of wife). *Wife and Executrix:* ELIZABETH. *Witnesses:* RICHARD FRENCH and ROBERT MOORE. Original missing. Recorded in Book 1712–1722, page 105.

LORD, WILLIAM.   Brunswick, in New Hanover County.

July 5, 1748. August Court, 1749. *Sons:* PETER, WILLIAM, THOMAS. *Daughters:* MARY, MARGARET, AMELIA. *Wife and Executrix:* MARGARET. *Witnesses:* RICH'D QUINCE, WILLIAM ROSS, GEO. NICHOLAS. *Clerk of Court:* ISAAC FARIES.

LOVE, AMOS.

August 15, 1770. October 30, 1773. *Sons:* AMOS, THOMAS, CHARLES. *Daughters:* WINNEFRED, MARY, MARGARET, ELISHE and ELIZABETH LOVE. *Wife and Executrix:* MARY. *Executor:* AMOS (son). *Witnesses:* JOSEPH CHATWIN, JOHN WILKINS, CHARLES HARDISON. Proven before JO. MARTIN.

LOVE, DANIEL.   Duplin County.

November 6, 1752. July Court, 1755. *Son:* JAMES. *Daughter:* SARAH LOVE. *Wife and Executrix:* CATHERINE. *Executors:* WILLIAM McKEE and JOHN SMITH. *Witnesses:* GEORGE PRICE, RICH'D COCKBURN, JAMES PARTON. *Clerk of the Court:* JOHN DICKSON.

LOVICK, JOHN.

August 27, 1727. November 10, 1733. *Nephew:* JOHN LOVICK, son of brother THOMAS LOVICK (plantation called the Horse Meadow or Pasture). *Wife and Executrix:* PENELOPE. *Friends:* RICHARD EVERARD, CHRISTOPHER GALE, EDMOND GALE, ROBERT FORSTER, WILLIAM LITTLE (to each is bequeathed a mourning ring). To WILLIAM LITTLE is bequeathed: "my best Hat, Wigg & Sword my Gold Buttons, all my Law Books & Lord Clarendons History." Testator was executor of the wills of JOHN PLOWMAN and CHARLES EDEN, and his will recites the following in regard to the will of EDEN: "forasmuch as the said CHARLES EDEN on his death bed did charge me if I met with any Trouble about his will from RODERICK LOYD or any of his family that I should not pay the legacy of five hundred pounds sterling in the sd CHAS. EDENS will given to Mrs. MARGARET PUGH, I do therefore forbid my said Executrix to pay the same I having met with great trouble, Vexation and Charge about the said Will from ye RODERICK LOYD and several of his Family and the sd Mrs. PUGH having once refused the said Legacy too and endeavoured to defeat and overthrow the said CHARLES EDENS Will." The depositions of CHRISTOPHER GALE, WILLIAM LITTLE and DR. ABRAHAM BLACKALL will be found filed with the copy of MR. LOVICK'S will from which this abstract is made.

LOVICK, THOMAS.   Carteret County.

April 4, 1759. June Court, 1759. *Wife and Executrix:* SARAH. *Son:* GEORGE PHENNEY LOVICK. *Sons-in-law:* JOHN BENNERS, JAMES PARKIN-

SON. *Grandson:* THOMAS LOVICK. *Granddaughter:* SARAH JONES. *Witnesses:* WILLIAM ROBERTSON, STEPHEN SMITH, ELIZABETH YARBROUGH. *Clerk of Court:* WILLIAM ROBERTSON.

LOW, EMANUEL.   Pasquotank Precinct.

March 2, 1726–1727. August 2, 1727. *Daughter:* ANN LETITIA LOW ("plantation whereon I now live; land called Town Point on the Mouth of the Northwest side of Newbegun Creek; one negro). *Grandson:* GEORGE LOW ("plantation where my cousin ROBINSON now lives and the plantation called New Abbey;" one negro boy and "my seal Scutcheon of arms"). *Wife and Executrix:* ANN. *Witnesses:* W. NORRIS, EDMD. GALE and CHAS. BULL. Codicil appoints daughter *Executrix* and bequeathes to one JOHANNA PEARCE ten pounds. *Witnesses to Codicil:* W. NORRIS, JOSEPH JORDAN, JOHN CONNER, JOSHUA SCOTT, JOHANA PEARCE. *Clerk of the Court:* THOS. WEEKES. *Executors* qualified before RICHARD EVERARD. Coat of arms on seal.

LOW, JOHN.   Pasquotank County.

May 11, 1755. March Court, 1759. *Sons:* THOMAS, JOHN LOW, BARNABE. *Daughter:* LIDIE LOW. *Wife and Executrix:* HANNAH. *Executor:* THOMAS LOWE (son). *Witnesses:* GEORGE LOW, EDWARD EDWARDS, JOHN COCKS. *Clerk of the Court:* THOS. TAYLOR.

LOWDEN, JOHN.   Pasquotank Precinct.

May 5, 1719. July 21, 1719. *Son:* ROBERT. *Daughters:* SARAH and ANN LOWDEN. *Witnesses:* SAMUEL COCK, JUN., HENRY HAYMAN. *Clerk of the Court:* W. NORRIS.

LOWE, ANNE.   Pasquotank County.

November 2, 1729. October Court, 1731. *Grandson:* GEORGE LOWE ("now in old England"). *Daughter and Executrix:* ANNA LATITIA LOWE. *Witnesses:* JNO. PALIN, STEPHEN SCOTT, JOHN SCOTT. *Clerk of the Court:* H. MINSON.

LOWE, WILLIAM.   Chowan County.

July 31, 1720. April 17, 1722. *Sons:* JOHN (land in Prince George County, Virginia), WILLIAM (land in Prince George County, Virginia). *Son-in-law:* ROBERT DIXON. *Daughter:* ELIZABETH PACE. *Wife:* ANN. *Executor:* ROBERT DIXON. *Witnesses:* THOMAS WHITMELL, THOMAS ARINGTON. *Clerk of Court:* N. BADHAM.

LOWELL, EDMUND.   Onslow County.

April 21, 1744. July Court, 1744. *Grandson:* EDMUND THORLA. *Daughter:* REBECCA THORLA. *Wife:* ABIGAILL. *Executor:* JOHN STARKEY. *Witnesses:* JOB HUNTER, WILLIAM WEBB, SARAH MIDDLETON. *Clerk of Court:* ANDREW MURRAY.

LOWRY, GEORGE.   Pasquotank County.

September 19, 1753. October Court, 1753. *Friends:* JOHN LOWRY
(*Executor*), WILLIAM, MARY and ELISABETH LOWRY. *Witnesses:* JOSEPH
LOWRY, WILLIAM LOWRY. *Clerk of the Court:* THOS. TAYLOR.

LOWRY, JOSEPH.   Pasquotank County.

March 23, 1754. April Court, 1754. *Sons:* BENJAMIN and NOAH
LOWRY ("all my lands"). *Daughters:* SARAH, LIDEA and HANNAH LOWRY.
Executors: SOLOMON POOL and JOSEPH DAVES. *Witnesses:* JOHN LOWRY,
THOMAS LOWRY, JAMES NEWBY. *Clerk of the Court:* THOS. TAYLOR.

LOWRY, ROBERT.   Pasquotank County.

October 19, 1750. July Court, 1752. *Sons:* WILLIAM, ROBERT and
JOHN LOWRY. *Daughters:* BETEY and MARY LOWRY ("my two Lots att
Nixson toune"). *Wife and Executrix:* ELIZEBETH. *Executor:* THOMAS
RELF. *Witnesses:* WILLIAM SYMONS, JOHN DAVIS, ANNE DAVIS. *Clerk of
the Court:* THO. TAYLOR.

LOWTHER, TRISTRIM.   Northampton County.

June 10, 1754. January Court, 1759. *Mother:* MARGERET. *Brothers:*
GEORGE, JOHN and WILLIAM LOWTHER. *Sisters:* NELLY and NANCY LOW-
THER. *Executor:* WILLIAM LOWTHER (brother). *Witnesses:* BARTHOLO-
MEW FIGURES, WILLIAM FIGURES, JOHN FIGURES. *Clerk of the Court:* I.
EDWARDS.

LOYDE (spelled also LIDE), JOHN.   Bertie County.

July 31, 1741. May Court, 1742. *Sons:* JOHN (200 acres of land in
James Citty County, Virginia), ROBERT ("my manner plantation"), THOMAS
(125 acres of land adjoining the "manner plantation"). *Daughter:* ELIZA-
BETH LOYDE. *Wife and Executrix:* SARAH. *Witnesses:* WILLIAM PACE,
BARRABEE MILTON, ANTONY TYE. *Clerk of Northampton Court:* I. ED-
WARDS.

LOYD, ROBERT.

December 10, 1726. October 8, 1728. Edenton. *Wife, Executrix and
sole legatee:* SARAH CATHERINE LOYD. *Witnesses:* WILL ROWDEN, SARAH
ROWDEN, JNO. SELLWOOD. Proven before RICHARD EVERARD.

LUARTON, JOHN.

August 28, 1722. July Court, 1723. Bath Town Creek. *Wife and Executrix:* ANNE. *Witnesses:* JOHN BUCK, THOS. COOKE, ELIEZR. LILLING-
TON. *Clerk of the Court:* JNO. BAPT. ASHE.

LUCAS, MARY.   Beaufort County.

March 24, 1761. April Court, 1761. *Daughters:* ANN ALDERSON (also appointed *Executrix*. *Grandsons:* JAMES ALDERSON, JOEL MARTIN, CHARLES ARDISON MARTIN. *Granddaughters:* FRANCES, SARAH, ANN, MARY and SUSANAH MARTIN. *Executor:* JAMES ELLISON. *Witnesses:* JOHN SMAW, SARAH HOWARD. *Clerk of Court:* JNO. SMITH.

LUDFORD, JOHN.   Tyrrell Precinct.

February 26, 1736. *Sisters:* SARAH and HANAH LUDFORD. *Brother:* THOMAS LUDFORD. *Other legatees:* ISACK FITZPATRICK. *Witnesses:* WILLIAM RAPHELL, WM. WILSON and SAMUEL HOPKINS. *Deputy Clerk of the Court:* ANDERSON SAGG.

LUDFORD, WILLIAM.

May 1, 1702. *Son:* WILLIAM. *Grandson:* WILLIAM LUDFORD. To both son and grandson is given a plantation. *Granddaughter:* SARAH LUDFORD. *Wife:* ANN. *Friend:* SAMUEL COOPER. *Executor:* WILLIAM LUDFORD (son). *Witnesses:* GODFREY SPRUILL, CANON SIMPSON and JOHN ANGELY. *Clerk of the Court:* N. CHEVIN.

LUDFORD, WILLIAM.   Of Allegator in the Precinct of Pasquotank.

October 2, 1732. April 2, 1733. *Sons:* WILLIAM, THOMAS and JOHN. *Daughters:* CHRISTIAN, ANN, MARTHA, MARY, TOMSON, RACHEL, SARAH, JOHANA. *Wife:* CHRISTIAN. *Executors:* EDWARD LININGTON, CAPT. SAMUEL SPRUILL, THOS. and JNO. LUDFORD (sons). *Witnesses:* G. LININGTON, BENJAMIN ALEXANDER, WILLIAM MAN. No signature of probate officer.

LUERTON, JOHN.   Bertie County.

August 23, 1740. February 23, 1742. *Nephew:* JOHN GREGORY. *Sister:* MARY JONES (*Executrix*). *Executors:* JAMES CASTELLAW, THOMAS OSBURN. *Witnesses:* JAMES LOCKHART, JOHN RAY, JOHN HILTON. Proven before GABRIEL JOHNSTON.

LUFMAN, WILLIAM.   Currituck Precinct.

April 1, 1728. July 10, 1728. *Sons:* WILLIAM and DANIEL. *Daughter:* MARY WHEATLEY. *Executors:* WILLIAM LUFMAN (son) and THOMAS DAVIS. *Witnesses:* ANDREW ETHERIDGE, WILLIAM TANT. *Clerk of the Court:* J. MARTYN.

LUFMAN, WILLIAM.   Currituck Precinct.

May 9, 1728. July 10, 1728. *Son:* WILLIAM ("all my lands"). *Executor:* THOMAS DAVIS. *Witnesses:* ANDREW ETHERIDGE, JR., DANIEL LUFMAN. *Clerk of the Court:* J. MARTYN.

15

LUFTY (or LUTTY), WILLIAM.

August 3, 1701.   July 11, 1704.   *Son:* WILLIAM.   *Granddaughter:* MARY LUFTY (or LUTTY).   *"Daughter in Lawe":* MARY LUFTY (or LUTTY).   *Executor:* WILLIAM LUFTY (son).   *Witnesses:* PETER GREY, SR., PETER GREY, JR., THOMAS HOMES.   *Clerk of the Court:* THOS. SNODEN.   This will is so torn and faded as to be almost illegible.

LUIS, RICHARD.   Chowan Precinct.

Not dated.   *Sons:* JOHN, BENJAMIN, WILLIAM.   *Daughter:* HUDSON. *Wife and Executrix:* ELIZABETH.   *Witnesses:* HENRY, WILLIAM and JANE LISLE.   Original missing.   Recorded in Book 1712–1722, page 177.

LUMBROSIER, JOHN.   Pasquotank County.

August 25, 1740.   April Court, 1744.   *Son and Executor:* JOSEPH. *Grandson:* JOHN DAWES.   *Granddaughter:* ELIZABETH BROSYER.   *Witnesses:* WILLIAM POWERS, JOSEPH COTTON, ROBT. KEELL.   *Clerk of the Court:* THOS. TAYLOR.

LURRY, WILLIAM.   Currituck County.

April 21, 1746.   July Court, 1746.   *Son:* THOMAS ("plantation whereon I now live").   *Wife:* MIRIAM.   *Executor:* WILLIAM MACKIE.   *Witnesses:* EDWARD COX, GEORGE GAINWELL, SUSANAH MACKIE.   *Clerk of the Court:* RICHARD McCLURE.

LUTON, ADAM.   Onslow County.

February 17, 1740.   April 2, 1746.   *Wife:* ELIZABETH.   *Daughter:* MARY LUTON.   *Executor:* THOMAS JENKINS.   *Witnesses:* THOMAS GANEY, CHARLES BRUTON, ZACHARIA BLACKMOOR.   *Clerk of the Court:* GEO. CLOPTON.

LYNCH, JOHN.   Granville County.

August 31, 1753.   March 7, 1758.   *Daughters:* ELIZABETH and NELLY ("plantation whereon I now live").   *Wife:* ELIZABETH.   *Executors:* JAMES JENKINS (son-in-law) and ROBERT BAKER.   *Witnesses:* THOMAS PARKER, JOHN BLAKENEY and WILLIAM FROHOCK.   *Clerk of the Court:* DANIEL WELDON.

LYON, JAMES.   Bladen County.

April 27, 1752.   June Court, 1752.   *Wife:* ZILLAH.   *Son:* GEORGE ("my watch").   *Daughters:* ANN (land on White Marsh), ELIZABETH LYON (land on White Marsh), MARY LYON.   *Executors:* ZILLAH LYON, MATT. ROWAN, JOHN LYON.   *Witnesses:* THOS. ROBESON, RICH'D MULLINGTON, ROBERT WILSON.   *Clerk of the Court:* THOS. ROBESON.

MABSON, ARTHUR.   Carteret County.

June 13, 1748. March Court, 1748. *Daughters:* ELIZABETH (wife of
NATHANIEL SMITH), SUSANNA. *Son:* ARTHUR. *Nephew:* WILLIAM COLE.
Grandson: WALTER SMITH. *Wife and Executrix:* MARY. *Executor:* JOHN
STARKEY. *Witness:* THOS. LOACK. *Clerk of the Court:* GEO. READ. Six
negroes are bequeathed and others mentioned.

MCADAM, JAMES.   Pasquotank County.

April 27, 1742. February 23, 1742. *Wife and Executrix:* SARAH.
Executor: JOSHUA WHITE. *Witness:* JAMES FENESON. Proven before
W. SMITH, C. J.

MCADAMS, SARAH.   Pasquotank County.

October 10, 1744. January Court, 1744. *Brothers and Executors:*
JOSHUA and NEHEMIAH WHITE. *Friend:* THOMAS NICHOLSON. *Son:*
JOSEPH MCADAM (all estate, both real and personal). *Witnesses:* CHARLES
TAILER, THOMAS NICHOLSON, JONATHAN LANGWORTHY. *Clerk of the
Court:* THO. TAYLOR.

MCALPIN, WILLIAM.   Craven County.

October 28, 1747. November 7, 1747. Formerly of Sterlingshire in
Scotland. *Wife:* HANNAH (in London). *Daughter:* HANNAH MCALPIN (in
London). *Mother:* JANE MACKEY (Earthtown in Sterlingshire, Scotland).
Executor: THOMAS RICHEY, of Jamaica. *Witnesses:* FRANCIS STRINGER,
HONNORA DUNCAN, CATHERINE LIDDLE. Proven before E. HALL, *Chief
Justice.*

MCCARTY, BAILEY.   Hyde County.

March 1, 1751. June Court, 1751. *Devisees and legatees:* LEAH ANDER-
SON, BENJAMIN CLEAVES, BAILY COLLINS. *Brother:* DENNIS MCCARTY
(land on Great Neck in Currituck). *Wife and Executrix:* ELINOR. *Executor:* THOMAS SMITH. *Witnesses:* THOS. SMITH, WILLIAM SMITH, JEREMIAH
SLADE. *Clerk of the Court:* THOS. LOACK.

MCCARTY, DENNIS.   Hyde County.

April 26, 1758. June Court, 1759. *Wife and Executrix:* MARY. *Other
devisee:* ABELL HUDSON (one hundred acres of land on Oyster Shell
Creek). *Witnesses:* LUKE FORTESCUE, RACHEL MASON, MARTHA BEETY.
Clerk of the Court: STEPHN. DENNING.

MCCLALLAND, ANDREW.   Bladen County.

March 21, 1752. *Grandchildren:* THOMAS, JANE, ANDREW and JAMES
MCCLALLAND. *Executor:* ANDREW MCCLALLAND (son-in-law). *Witnesses:*
GEORGE BROWN, BENJA. MOOR, BENJ. FITZRANDOLPH. *Clerk of the Court:*
THOS. ROBESON.

McCLAMMY, THOMAS.   New Hanover County.

May 2, 1772. September 27, 1773. *Sons:* PETER ("my plantation"),
LUKE (plantation called The Hammock), WONEY, MARK. *Daughters:*
ELLENDER NIXON, CATHERINE HYDLEBYRD. *Executors:* PETER, WONEY
and LUKE McCLAMMY. *Witnesses:* EDWARD PILCHER, ANNE SUTTAIN,
DAVID FALLE. Proven before JO. MARTIN.

McCLENDEN, DEBORAH.   Perquimans County.

February 8, 1728–1729. October 15, 1732. *Grandson:* JOSEPH SUTTON.
Son and Executor: RICHARD WHEEDBEE. *Witnesses:* CHARLES DENMAN,
JAMES ANDERSON, SENR., JAMES ANDERSON, JUNR. *Clerk of the Court:*
CHARLES DENMAN.

MacCLENDON, DENNIS.   Bertie County.

January 19, 1725–1726. *Sons:* DENNIS, JOHN (to each is devised a
plantation). *Daughters:* MARY and ELIZABETH MacCLENDON. *Wife:*
MARGARETT. *Executors:* JOHN EARLEY (father), FRANCIS and THOMAS
MacCLENDON (brothers). *Witnesses:* JAMES PAGE, NICHOLAS FAIRLESS.
No probate. "I desire my two negroes * * * in ye winter to make
pitch and tarr, and freight it away to New England for such goods as
shall best for my wife, etc."

McCORKEL, ROBERT.   Anson County.

No date given. *Sons:* ARCHIBALD and ROBERT (dwelling plantation
and plantation on "Catabee River"). *Wife and Executrix:* MARGARET.
Executors: JAMES McCORKEL and JAMES LINN. *Witnesses:* JOHN CROCK-
ETT, ROBT. McCLENACKEN. No probate.

McCOY, DANIELL.   Currituck County.

December 2, 1731. October Court, 1735. *Sons:* JOHN and WILLIAM
(plantation). *Daughter:* LIDEA McCOY. *Wife and Executrix:* CHRISTIAN.
Witnesses: MOSES LINTON, JAMES WILKINS, ELEZABATH WILKINS. *Clerk
of the Court:* JAMES CRAVEN.

MacCRARY, ROBERT.   Bertie County.

May 30, 1740. July 30, 1740. *Legatees and devisees:* ELIZABETH BAR-
FIELD, MARY BROWN, SARAH BROWN, PRISCILLA BROWN, ELIZABETH
BROWN. *Executor:* THOMAS BARFIELD. *Witnesses:* P. ROCHE, THOMAS
BARFIELD, MARY BARFIELD. Proven before W. SMITH, C. J.

McCULLOCH, HENRY.

October 25, 1755. November 15, 1755. "Secretary of the Province of North Carolina." *Wife:* MARY. *Daughters:* HENRIETTA MARY,
DOROTHY BERISFORD, ELIZABETH MARGARET and PENELOPE MARTHA.

Executor: JOHN CAMPBELL, of Bertie. *Witnesses:* WM. POWELL, GO. ARTHAUD, WM. ROBERTSON. Proven before ARTHUR DOBBS. Coat of arms on seal.

McDANIELL, DANIEL.   Bertie Precinct

April 16, 1733. May 2, 1734. *Sons:* NICHOLAS, DANIEL, JAMES (negroes to each). *Daughters:* ANN and SARAH McDANIEL. *Wife and Executrix:* SARAH. *Witnesses:* JOHN ANDERSON, ALEX. WIGHT, JOHN BRYAN. Original missing. Recorded in Book 1722–1735, page 295.

MacDANIEL, JAMES.   Craven County.

November 29, 1759. *Sons:* JAMES and JOHN (plantation to each), RISDON. *Daughter:* LEVINAH. *Wife and Executrix:* MARGERET. *Executor:* JOHN OLIVER. *Witnesses:* BASSETT SIMMONS, E. BRYAN, DAVID B———. No probate.

MacDANIELL, OWEN.   Bertie County.

February 7, 1742–1743. May Court, 1743. *Wife:* ELLENER. *Son-in-law and Executor:* JETHRO BUTLER ("my manner plantation and six negroes"). *Witnesses:* HENRY HORNE, JOHN CAMPBELL, RICHARD MEDLIN. *Clerk of the Court:* HENRY DeSON.

McDOWELL, JAMES.   Bertie County.

February 10, 1752. March 3, 1752. *Brother-in-law:* JOHN SMITH of Wigtown in Galloway in North Britain. *Sister:* CHRISTIAN McDOWELL. *Nephew and Executor:* JOHN SMITH. *Witnesses:* JAMES TROTTER, DANIEL GOLDSMITH, ANNE ORINDELL. Will proven before GAB. JOHNSTON at Edenhouse.

McDOWELL, JOHN.   Brunswick County.

March 27, 1735. April 19, 1735. "Master of the scooner called the Jolly Batchelor, now riding at anchor in Cape Fear River, But of Brunswick * * *." Ten pounds is bequeathed to the Presbyterian church at Dover, Delaware, and five pounds to the Episcopal Church at the same place. *Brother:* JAMES McDOWELL. *Sister:* ELEANOR NISBETT. *Friend:* LYDIA JONES. *Executors:* HUGH CAMPBELL and JAMES ESPY, of Brunswick. *Witnesses:* STEPHEN MOTT, A. DELABASTIE, ANDW. BLYTH, MAGDALEN CAMPBELL. Proven before GAB. JOHNSTON. Provision in will that "a small brick wall be put around my grave wt two marble stones sett up, one att the head and the other att the foot, as is commonly us'd in such cases att Philadelphia."

MACE, FRANCIS.   Pasquotank County.

February 7, 1748–1749. August 1, 1749. *Wife and Executrix:* ANN. *Sons:* JOHN and FRANCIS. *Daughters:* MARY SYMONS, ELIZABETH, SARAH,

HANNA. *Executor:* PETER SYMONS (son-in-law). *Witnesses:* SAMUEL NEWBY, JAMES NEWBY and WILLIAM NEWBY. Proven before GAB. JOHNSTON at Eden House.

MACE, WILLIAM.

May 10, 1757. *Son:* WILLIAM. *Brothers:* BENJAMIN MACE (30 pounds in Irish Money), JONAS MACE (40 pounds Proclamation Money). *Nephews:* WILLIAM MACE and WILLIAM MORRISON. *Wife and Executrix:* ANNE. *Witnesses:* ARTHUR WILLIAMS, BENJAMIN ELLIS, WILLIAM TEEL, WILLIAM PRESCOTT. The foregoing is made from a copy of the original will, and no probate appears. Provision is made for shipping a cargo of indigo.

McGEE, JOHN.   Guilford County.

November 22, 1773.   January 28, 1774.   *Sons:* SAMUEL, JOHN, ANDREW (plantation on the waters of the Alamance, known by the name of Graham's Place), WILLIAM ("plantation whereon I now live"). *Daughters:* JEAN (plantation on Shockley Creek), SUSANAH (plantation on Shockley Creek, known by the name of Jarrot Hays Place). *Wife and Executrix:* MARTHA. *Executor:* ROBERT LINDSAY (son-in-law). *Witnesses:* ANN LEWIS, JAMES MORGAN, THOMAS WELBORN, MARTHA McGEE. Codicil makes provision for burying-ground, and devises house and one acre of land to one GEORGE ALEXANDER, SENR., to be used as a meeting house. *Witnesses to codicil:* JAMES MORGAN, THOMAS WELBORN. Will and codicil proven before Jo. MARTIN.

McGREGOR, HUGH.   Pasquotank Precinct.

January 12, 1703–1704. February Court, 1704. *Sons:* PATRICK and GREGOR. *Brother-in-law:* JOHN McGREGOR. *Wife and Executrix:* AFRICA. *Witnesses:* WILLIAM BARNSFELD, THOS. PENDLETON, THO. ABINGTON. *Clerk of the Court:* THO. ABINGTON.

MacKANE, GEORGE.   Carteret County.

October 14, 1753. June 6, 1758. *Son:* JOHN. *Daughters:* SOPHIA, MARY and MARGERET. *Wife and Executrix:* MARY. *Witnesses:* ELIZABETH WALLACE, JOHN FINNY. *Clerk of the Court:* WM. ROBERTSON.

MacKARTY, TIMOTHY.   Chowan Precinct.

February 28, 1717–1718. July 15, 1718. *Godson:* WM. GULLIVER. *Wife:* MARY. *Executors:* MAJ. ROBERT WEST and HENRY SPELLER. *Witnesses:* ARTHUR DUGALL, WM. GADD, PATIENCE SPELLER. *Clerk of the Court:* R. HICKS.

MACKDANIELL, DANIEL.   Bertie Precinct.

April 16, 1733. *Sons:* DANIEL, ARCHBELL, ELEXANDER, JAMES. *Daughters:* MARY, ANN and SARAH MACKDANIELL. *Wife and Executrix:* SARAH. *Witnesses:* JNO. ANDERSON, ALEXR. WEIGHT, JOHN BRYAN. No probate.

MACKEELL, ANTHONY.   Bath County.

November 28, 1723.   January Court, 1723–1724.   Parish of St. Thomas.
Sons: ANTHONY (1 shilling), THOMAS (plantation), JOHN (plantation),
JOSEPH (plantation).   *Daughters:* ANN and SARAH MACKEELL.   *Wife and
Executrix:* RABACKEY.   *Witnesses:* WILLIAM PRICE, JOHN SOUTH, PHILIP
BAYNARD.   *Clerk of the Court:* JNO. BAPT. ASHE.

McKEEL, BENJAMIN.   Pasquotank County.

April 11, 1754.   July Court, 1754.   *Daughter:* SARAH McKEEL ("my
plantation").   *Wife and Executrix:* THAMAR.   *Executor:* JOHN McKEEL
(brother).   *Witnesses:* JOHN CLARK, JOHN LISTER.   *Clerk of the Court:*
THO. TAYLOR.

McKEEL, JOHN.   Pasquotank Precinct.

December 24, 1706.   April 15, 1707.   *Sons:* NATHANIEL and JOHN
("all my lands").   *Wife:* MARY.   *Brothers:* THOMAS and DANIEL McKEEL.
Executors: THOMAS McKEEL, JAMES TOOKES.   *Witnesses:* JOHN HUNTT,
THOMAS ABINGTON, WALTER TURNER.   *Clerk of the Court:* THO. ABINGTON.

McKEELL, JOHN.   Pasquotank County.

October 27, 1750.   January Court, 1750.   *Sons:* THOMAS and JOHN.
Daughter: SOPHIA.   *Wife:* MARGRETT.   *Executors:* THOMAS JAMES and
THOMAS McKEELL, JUNR.   *Witnesses:* THOS. McKEEL and EMANUEL
KNIGHT.   *Clerk of the Court:* THOS. TAYLOR.

McKEEL, REBECCA.   Bath County.

May 7, 1729.   December Court, 1729.   *Sons:* ANTHONY, THOMAS,
JOSEPH and JOHN.   *Executor:* JOHN BARROW.   *Witnesses:* RICH'D HAR-
VEY, LAM'LL HARVEY, PETER McDOULE (McDOWELL).   *Clerk of the Court:*
JOHN MATTOCKE.

McKEEL, THOMAS.   Pasquotank County.

December 13, 1729.   January 13, 1729.   *Sons:* BENJAMIN (plantation
called the Old Field), THOMAS and JOHN ("the manner plantation").
Daughters: ELIZABETH and MARY McKEEL.   *Executors:* BENJAMIN and
THOMAS McKEEL (sons).   *Witnesses:* JNO. McKEEL, LEVI MARKHAM,
JOHN POINTER.   *Clerk of the Court:* WM. MINSON.

McKEEL, THOMAS.   Pasquotank County.

May 3, 1753.   October Court, 1753.   *Daughter and sole devisee:* MARGA-
RET McKEEL.   *Executors:* ANTHONY and CHARLES MARKHAM.   *Witnesses:*
JONATHAN HOWELL, THOMAS COREY.   *Clerk of the Court:* THOS. TAYLOR.

McKEEL, THOMAS.   Pasquotank County.

March 31, 1754. July Court, 1754. *Daughters:* GRACE, WIHNEYFRUIT (WINNIFRED), MILLA and ELIZABETH McKEEL. *Wife:* MIRIAM. *Executors:* JOHN McKEEL (brother) and GRACE McKEEL. *Witnesses:* ANTONY MARKHAM, WINEYFRUIT (WINNIFRED) WOODLY. *Clerk of the Court:* THOS. TAYLOR.

McKEITHAN, DUGALD.   Bladen County.

January 1, 1750–1751. March Court, 1750. *Father:* DONALD McKEITHAN. *Brother:* JAMES McKEITHAN. *Wife:* MARY. *Cousins:* JOHN McKEITHAN, JAMES McKEITHAN. *Sisters:* NANCY McLAUCHLIN, SARAH McKEITHAN. *Son-in-law:* ROBERT HILLYARD. *Niece:* MARY McKEITHAN. No executor appointed. *Witnesses:* HECT. McNEILL, ALEXR. McALESTER, ANGUS SHAW. *Clerk of the Court:* THOS. ROBESON.

MACKELROY, JAMES.   Beaufort County.

April 23, 1773. October 20, 1773. *Sons:* DAVID ("my plantation"), ADAM (land on south prong of Trents Creek), JAMES (land in the fork of Trent Creek). *Daughters:* SARAH and ELIZABETH (land on Neales Creek), MARY CIRTIS (land on Raccoon Creek). *Grandsons:* JAMES and JOHN MACKELROY (land called Whites Old Field). *Wife and Executrix:* ELISABETH. *Executor:* FRANCIS DELAMAR. *Witnesses:* AMOS SQUIERS, THOMAS MACKELROY, ZEKILL HUDSON. Proven before Jo. MARTIN.

MACKFARRELL, JOHN.

November 27,———. December 1,———. This is a nuncupative will proven before JAMES HOYLE, J. P., by the oaths of WILLIAM HUNTER, BENJAMIN TURNER and JOSEPH BENIMAN, in which the testator desired all of his property sold and the proceeds invested for his son, JACOB MACKFARRELL, which son was to remain with his grandfather, JACOB LEWIS.

MACKGUE, LAWRENCE.   Bertie County.

April 26, 1740. May Court, 1740. All of estate, both real and personal, is left to grandchildren, children of daughter, ELICE BRYAN. *Executors:* ELICE BRYAN, JOHN BRYAN, EDWARD BRYAN. *Witnesses:* CHARLES, WILLIAM and JOHN RICKETS. *Clerk of the Court:* JNO. WYNNS.

MACKILWEAN, FRANCIS.   Dobbs County.

February 8, 1774. March 10, 1774. *Sons:* FRANCIS MACKILWEAN ("my New plantation" also plantation called Old Ford on Contentnea Creek), JOHN STRINGER (five negroes and three horses). *Daughters:* HANAH, ELIZABETH, GATSEY, MARY, ELINOR, NANCY, PENELOPY MACKILWEAN. *Wife and Executrix:* MARY. *Executors:* FURNIFOLD GREEN and RICHARD NIXON of Craven County. *Witnesses:* RD. CASWELL, JNO. SHINE, MARTIN

CASWELL, SIMON BRIGHT.   Proven before JO. MARTIN.   Will provides for division of negro slaves into nine parts, one part to each of children and one to wife.   *Codicil of even date makes bequest to brother:* JOHN MACKILWEAN. Same witnesses to codicil.

MACKINNE, BARNABEE, JR.   Edgecombe Precinct.

October 13, 1736.   November Court, 1736.   *Daughters:* PATIENCE and MARY MACKINNE.   *Other legatees:* BARNABY, son of JOSEPH LANE; BARNABY, son of WILLIAM MACKINNE; JOSEPH LANE, WILLIAM MACKINNE (brother), JOHN POPE, JAMES NOWELL, ROBERT and JOHN MACKINNE (brothers), NATHANIEL COOPER, JOHN LANE.   *Wife and Executrix:* MARY (five negroes).   Land devised to daughters.   Live stock and land devised to other legatees mentioned.   *Witnesses:* NATHANIEL COOPER, JOHN CROWELL, JNO. WATFORD.   *Clerk of the Court:* THOMAS KERNEY.   Original of this will missing.   Abstract made from recorded copy No. 58 in Grant Book, No. 4.

MACKINNE, JOHN.   Edgecombe County.

February 28, 1753.   May Court, 1753.   *Son:* BARNABY.   *Daughters:* MARY, MARTHA and PATIENCE MACKINNE, ANGELINA PARISH.   *Wife and Executrix:* MARY.   *Friend:* CANNON CUMBO.   *Executor:* MONTFORT ELBECK.   *Witnesses:* MONTFORT ELBECK, WILLIAM GADDY, MARY ELBECK. *Clerk of the Court:* BENJ'N WYNNS.   "I give and bequeath my loving wife * * * the use of my grist mill on Great Quonkee two years next ensuing for pay for the giveing each of my children before mentioned two years schooling."

MACKINNE, RICHARD.   Edgecombe County.

August 10, 1751.   August Court, 1755.   *Brother:* ROBERT MACKINNE. *Nephew:* BARNABY MCKINNIE.   *Wife and Executrix:* MARY.   *Executors:* WILLIAM KINCHEN and WILLIAM KINCHEN, JUNR.   *Witnesses:* W. KINCHEN, WM. BAKER, LEMUEL KINCHEN.   *Clerk of the Court:* JOS. MONTFORT.

MCKINNEY, MARY.   Edgecombe County.

October 13, 1754.   November Court, 1754.   "Imprimis.   I most humbly bequeath my Soul to God my Maker beseeching His most Gracious reception of it through the all sufficient merits and Meditations of my Most Compassionate Redeemer Jesus Christ, Who gave himself to be an atonement for my sins, and is able to save to the uttermost all that come unto God by him, Seeing he ever liveth to make intercession for them, and who, I trust will not reject me a returning penitent sinner, when I come to him for mercy; in this Hope & confidence I render up my soul with comfort humbly beseeching the most Blessed and Glorious Trinity, one God most holy, most merciful and gracious to prepare me for the time of my dissolution, and then to take me to himself unto that Place of Rest and incomparable Felicity which he has prepared for all that Love and fear his holy name Amen Blessed be God." (The foregoing is given as a specimen of the preambles to the wills of this period.) *Sons:* JOHN, BARNABY. *Daughters:* ANNJELEANY POPE, MARY, PATIENCE and MARTHA MCKINNE. *Executor:* BARNABY POPE. *Witnesses:* DAVID CRAWLEY, WM. GADDY, ROBERT BELCHER. *Clerk of the Court:* BENJ'N WYNNS.

McKINZIE, JOHN.   Nansemond County, Va.

March 2, 1754. April Court, 1754. *Sons:* JOHN (795 acres of land at Skeehawkee in Tyrrell County and 305 acres in the Island of Carolina in Bertie County), KENNETH (1000 acres of land at Skeehawkee), WILLIAM (300 acres of land on Ronoke River in Bartie County). *Daughters:* JANET and ANN. *Executors:* WM. GRAY (brother-in-law), CAPT. JOHN HILL of Bertie County and JAMES PUGH and PASCO TURNER of Nansemond County. *Witnesses:* JAMES PUGH, JAMES WRIGHT, CHRISTIAN GOOD. *Clerk of the Court:* SAMUEL RIDDICK. This is taken from a copy of the will of the above named McKINZIE certified to North Carolina by the Court of Nansemond County. Provision in will directs executors to provide for the removal of family to North Carolina.

MacLEARAN, ARCHIBALD.   Bladen County.

October 26, 1751. December Court, 1751. *Sons:* JOHN and ARCHIBALD (358 acres of land to be divided between them). *Wife and Executrix:* FLORANCE. *Executor:* DUNCAN MacLEARAN. *Witnesses:* DUSHEE SHAW, ARCHIBALD MacDONALD, DUNCAN MacFEE. *Clerk of the Court:* THOMAS ROBESON.

MACKLEMORE, ABRAHAM.   Bertie Precinct.

January 4, 1735. November Court, 1736. *Sons:* ATKIN, YOUNG ("manner plantation"), WILLIAM. *Wife and Executrix:* MARY. *Witnesses:* WILLIAM GILLIM, WILLIAM CLANTON, JOSEPH BRADY. *Clerk of the Court:* JNO. WYNNS.

MACKLEMORE, JAMES.

February 13, 1733. *Sons:* WILLIAM, JAMES, CHARLES, EPHRAIM (to each of the above named is given a plantation and cattle), JOHN. *Daughter:* MARGORY. *Wife and Executrix:* FORTAIN. *Witnesses:* JOHN DOYLE, ABRAHAM MACKLEMORE, THOMAS ROBERSON. No probate.

MACKLY, HENRY.   Pasquotank Precinct.

February 11, 1720. April Court, 1721. *Daughters:* MAREY MACKLEY (50 acres of land on the north side of Nuce River), ANNE MACKLEY (50 acres of land on the north side of Nuce River). *Son-in-law:* MARTIN MILLER (50 acres of land on the north side of Nuce River). *Wife and Executrix:* BAR-BERY. *Witnesses:* JANE RUSEL, ELIZABETH PALMER, EVAN JONES. *Clerk of the Court pro tem.:* JNO. PALIN.

MACMIEL, JOHN. Bertie Precinct.

February 26, 1729. February 22, 1730. *Devisees:* JOHN MYHAND (300 acres of land on Tar River), MARY MYHAND ("my plantation"), JOHN GRAY (*Executor*). *Witnesses:* JOHN HARRISS, ANN MIHAND, HENRY WALKER. Proven before RICH'D EVERARD.

MCNARY, GILBERT. Hyde County.

March 11, 1746–1747. June 2, 1747. *Son:* WILLIAM. *Daughters:* MARY and JANE. *Wife:* ELISABETH. *Executors:* JOHN SMITH, SR., and JOHN SMITH, JR. *Witnesses:* WM. SPEIR, THOMAS ALLEN, AARON TISON. *Clerk of the Court:* THOS. LOACK.

MACNAUGHTEN, RANALD. Bladen County.

October 5, 1752. December 19, 1752. *Sons:* NEILL and CHARLES. *Wife:* ISBELL. *Daughter:* MARY. *Executors:* DUNCAN and NEILL MAC-COULASKIE. *Witnesses:* ANGUISH SHAW, JOHN OPTAN, JOHN CAMPBELL. *Justices of Bladen County Court:* GRIFFITH JONES and BENJAMIN FITZRAN-DOLPH. *Clerk of the Court:* THOS. ROBESON.

MCREE, WILLIAM. Duplin County.

March 30, 1751. April 2, 1751. Goshen Settlement. *Sons:* JOHN, JAMES, WILLIAM, ROBERT, SAMUEL. *Daughters:* SARAH SMITH, ALICE WILLIAMS, SUSANNAH MCREE. *Executors:* JOHN SMITH and WILLIAM MCREE. *Witnesses:* WILLIAM KENNAN, SARAH MCALEXANDER, ELIZA-BETH CHAMBERS. *Clerk of the Court:* JOHN DICKSON.

MACKY, WILLIAM. Bertie County.

1730. *Son:* DANIEL. *Daughter:* MARGRET. All of estate, both real and personal, is devised and bequeathed to MARY JONES, daughter of HENRY JONES, of Greenhall, in Chowan County. No signature, witnesses or probate.

MADDOX, JOHN. Carteret County.

January 1, 1767. March 22, 1774. *Wife and sole legatee:* MIRIAM. *Executors:* MOSES HOUSTON, JAMES BARRY. *Witnesses:* WILLIAM HOUS-TON, DAVID WILLIAMS. Will proven before JO. MARTIN.

MADREN, RICHARD.

March 10, 1755. June Court, 1755. *Sons:* THOMAS ("my plantation"), REUBEN. *Daughters:* ELIZABETH, RUTH and ANN MADREN. *Wife and*

Executrix: SARAH. *Executors:* JACOB and JOSEPH MADREN (brothers). *Witnesses:* THOMAS PRITCHARD, JNO. SMITHSON. *Clerk of the Court:* THOS. TAYLOR.

MAKEE, DANIELL.   County not given.

July 15, 1694. July 15, 1695. *Sons:* DANIELL, JOHN. *Daughters:* CATHERINE, ELINOR. *Wife and Executrix:* ELINOR. *Witnesses:* G. MUSCHAMP, PIERRE LOURRE, ROBERT MELLYNE, WILLIAM BROWNE. *Clerk of the Court:* EDWARD MAYO.

MAN, JOHN.   Tyrrell County.

February 19, 1742–1743. March Court, 1744. *Sons:* JOHN, WILLIAM, THEOPHALOS ("land on ye South side of Mesus Creek known by ye name of Volls Island"), EDWARD ("ye southermost part of my plantation"), THOMAS ("land joining my son EDWARD'S"), JOSEPH ("ye other part of my maner plantation"). *Daughters:* DORRITY——— and ELIZABETH MAN. *Wife:* MARGIT. *Executors:* THEOPHALUS, JOSEPH and EDWARD MAN. *Witnesses:* BENJAMIN BIDGOOD, JAMES NAHALE. *Clerk of the Court:* THOS. LEE.

MAN, JOHN.   Northampton County.

April 19, 1757. November Court, 1757. *Sons:* FREDERICK, ABSOLOM, JESSE. *Daughter:* LIZEBETH. *Wife and Executrix:* LIZEBETH. *Witnesses:* JOSEPH SIKES, THOMAS TADLOCK. *Clerk of the Court:* I. EDWARDS.

MAN, THOMAS.   Bertie County.

September 30, 1735. November Court, 1735. *Sons:* JOHN ("my plantation and six hundred and forty acres of land"), THOMAS (plantation on Wickacone Creek). *Cousin:* WILLIAM CRAWMAN (land on Killam Swamp). *Daughter:* MARY. *Grandson:* GEORGE WILLIAMS. *Wife:* BRIDGETT. *Executors:* GEORGE WILLIAMS, SR., and THOMAS BUSBEY. *Witnesses:* CHARLES HORNE, GEORGE WILLIAMS, JUNR. *Clerk of the Court:* JOHN WYNNS.

MANDOVEL, JOHN.   Hyde County.

September 31, 1751. March Court, 1752. *Sons:* SAMUEL and JOHN (a plantation to each). *Daughters:* ELIZABETH, REBECKAH, DINEY. *Wife and Executrix:* ELIZABETH. *Executor:* LITTLE JARMAN. *Witnesses:* STEPHEN MANDOVEL, LITTLE JARMAN, JOSEPH GURGANUS. *Clerk of the Court:* FRAN. EGLETON.

MANDUE, THOMAS.   Bertie Precinct.

April 17, 1736. August Court, 1736. *Grandson:* MANDUE DOTHRY ("my plantation and orchards, and all my books except the ould Bible and the Whole Duty of Man"). *Granddaughter:* PERCILA DOTHERY.

Son: WILLIAM BUNN. *Daughter:* MARY. *Executor:* ARTHUR WILLIAMS. *Witnesses:* H. TUDER, WILLIAM BUN, ISAAC RICKS. *Clerk of the Court:* JOHN WYNNS.

MANER, JOHN.   Bertie County.

February 21, 1728–1729. May Court, 1729. *Sons:* WILLIAM, HENRY, JACOB. *Friend:* SOLOMON ALSTON. *Executor:* HENRY MANER (son). *Witnesses:* ELIZABETH SMITH, MARY ALSTON, JOHN ALSTON. *Clerk of the Court:* ROBT. FORSTER.

MANEY, JAMES.   Northampton County.

November 30, 1751. August Court, 1752. *Son and Executor:* JAMES. *Daughters:* JANE MAGETT (plantation bought of WM. TURNER), SUSANE SKINER (plantations bought of JOHN HOBBS, JOHN ROBENS and NATHAN BARNES, and a new survey on river). *Executors:* NICLAS MAGETT and CHARLES SKINER. *Witnesses:* JOHN MINSEY, DAVID JARNAGAND, THOS. JARNAGAND. *Clerk of the Court:* I. EDWARDS.

MARCKHAM, ANTHONY.   Albemarle County.

September 24, 1710. *Sons:* LEVY, JOSHUA, CHARLES, ANTHONY (to each is given a plantation). *Daughters:* MARY and TAMAR. *Wife:* JOY. *Executor:* LEVY MARCKHAM (son). *Witnesses:* FRANCIS DeLaMARE, EDWARD CHAPMAN. No probate.

MARKHAM, JOSHUA.   Pasquotank County.

August 6, 1746. April Court, 1747. *Devisees and legatees:* TIMER EVINS, BARTHOLOMEW EVINS, JOSHUA EVINS, ANTONY MARKHAM, JOSUA, CHARLES, ELIZABETH and MARY MARKHAM (to these are given negroes). *Executor:* ANTHONY MARKHAM. *Witnesses:* SAMUEL SCOLLAY, THOS. HAMLIN. *Clerk of the Court:* THOS. TAYLOR.

MARKHAM, LEVI.   Pasquotank County.

April 1, 1743. April Court, 1744. *Legatees:* WILLIAM MARKHAM CRANK, MARY, ANN and ELIZABETH CRANK. *Executrix:* ELIZABETH CRANK. *Executors:* ANTHO. MARKHAM and WILLIAM WALLIS. *Witnesses:* TERENCE SWEENY, WILLIAM JAMES, ANNE BOYD. *Clerk of the Court:* THOS. TAYLOR.

MARR, JOSEPH.   Craven County.

March, 1745. *Wife and Executrix:* ALIF. Three children mentioned, but not named. Dates and names of witnesses illegible.

MARSDEN, ALICE.   New Hanover County.

March 24, 1755. March 1, 1759. Wilmington. *Daughters:* ALICE and
PEGGY MARSDEN. *Granddaughter:* ALICE MOBSON. *Executor:* ARTHUR
MOBSON (son-in-law). *Witnesses:* ISAAC FARIES, JOHN DAVIS, JUNR.,
ANTHONY WARD. Proven before ARTHUR DOBBS.

MARSDEN, THOMAS.   New Hanover County.

September 23, 1739. *Father:* RICHARD MARSDEN. *Mother:* ELIZABETH
MARSDEN, "of Halifax, in ye County of York in England. *Brother:*
WILLIAM MARSDEN. *Executors:* JOHN SWANN and THOMAS JONES. *Wit-
nesses:* WILLIAM DUTTEN, WILL CARR, JNO. MARSHALL. No probate.
Coat of arms on seal.

MARSHALL, JOHN.   Edgecombe County.

October 24, 1757. February Court, 1758. *Sons:* JOHN ("plantation I
now live on"), HUMPHREY (plantation over Tar River at the head of
Middle Creek), ABSOLEM. *Daughters:* ELIZABETH MARSHALL, PRISCILLA
MARSHALL, GOODWIN TUCKER (to these are given negroes). *Wife and
Executrix:* AMY. *Executor:* JOHN MARSHALL (son). *Witnesses:* BENJA.
HAILE, BENJ'N NEVILLE, THOS. MARSHALL. *Clerk of the Court:* JOS.
MONTFORT.

MARSHALL, WILLIAM.   Bertie County.

September 4, 1738. May Court, 1739. *Wife:* MARGARET. *Other lega-
tees:* MARGARET ROBERTS, JOHN ROBERTS, SARAH PUKE, JAMES PARROT
PUKE, MARY KEEFE, WM. PEEKE, JOHN KEEP. *Executrix:* MARGARET
MARSHALL (wife). *Witnesses:* JOHN WYNNS, WILLIAM LEE, WILLIAM
LINN. *Clerk of the Court:* JNO. WYNNS.

MARSTON, ELIZABETH.   Bath County.

January 2, 1732. September 11, 1733. *Daughters:* MARY, ANN and
MOURNING MARSTON. *Executors:* ANN and MOURNING MARSTON. *Wit-
nesses:* JNO. COLLISON, JAMES ADAMS, ROGER JONES. *Clerk of the Court:*
JNO. COLLISON. *Justices of Beaufort and Hyde Precincts:* ROBERT TURNER,
BENJ. PEYTON, HENERY CROPTON.

MARTIN, ELIZABETH.   Craven County.

March 30, 1767. South River. *Daughters:* SARAH LOFTIN, ELIZABETH
MILL. *Grandsons:* ROBERT and ADAM WALLIS, SLOCUMB FERGUSON,
THOMAS PITTMAN. *Granddaughters:* SARAH MAHAINS, ANN STEVENS,
COMFT. ROLLINS, ELIZABETH HAMBLETON, PRUDENCE FULFORD, JEAN
WALLIS. *Brother:* JOHN CUMINGS. *Executor:* JAMES JONES. *Witnesses:*
THOMAS MCLIN, SAM'LL MASTERS, ROBERT OLIVER. No probate.

MARTIN, GEORGE.

October 6, 1734. March 8, 1734. *Wife and Executrix:* mentioned, but not named. *Witnesses:* W. SMITH, NATH. RICE, JOHN MONTGOMERY. A codicil to the will devises to EPHRAIM VERNON, brother-in-law of the testator, all lands taken up by patent. Date of codicil same as will, and same witnesses. Proven before GABRIEL JOHNSTON.

MARTIN, JOEL.   Bath County.

October 24, 1715. July 3, 1716. *Sons:* JOHN (land on Matchapungo Creek), WILLIAM (land in Newport Sound). *Daughters:* ANN MARTIN (320 acres of land), ELIZABETH PENNY, MARY WOODARD, FRANCES JARVIS. *Son-in-law:* JOHN PENNY. *Executors:* ELIZABETH PENNY, JOHN PORTER. *Witnesses:* JOHN DEON, HENRY SMITH, JNO. DRINKWATER. *Clerk of the Court:* JNO. DRINKWATER.

MARTIN, JOHN.   Pasquotank County.

December 25, 1741. January Court, 1741–1742. *Sons:* NATHANIEL, JOSEPH, JOHN, JOSHUA. *Daughters:* ELENER BRYANT, MARYANN JESSOP, ANN MARTIN, ELIZABETH MARTIN, JANE MORGIN. *Executors:* JOHN MORGIN (son-in-law), THOMAS JESSOP. *Witnesses:* WILLIAM DAVIS, JOSEPH PRITCHARD, BENJA. PRITCHARD. *Clerk of the Court:* THO. TAYLOR.

MARTIN, NATHANIEL.   Pasquotank County.

November 28, 1743. January Court, 1743. *Son and Executor:* JOSHUA (my land and plantation). *Daughter:* MIRIAM MARTIN. *Wife:* SARAH MARTIN. *Witnesses:* WILLIAM DAVIS, GEORGE DAWSON, WILLIAM BELLMAN. *Clerk of the Court:* THOS. TAYLOR.

MARTIN, THOMAS.   Craven County.

January 15, 1758. March 23, 1758. South River. *Wife and Executrix:* ELIZABETH. *Nephew:* ROBERT MARTIN, son of brother RICHARD MARTIN. *Other legatees:* SARAH LOFTIN, wife of LEONARD LOFTIN of Handcocks Creek; JOAN MARTIN FERGUSON, daughter of MARK FERGUSON. *Executor:* JOHN THOMLINSON, of Clubfoots Creek. *Witnesses:* JOHN CUMMINGS, ELISHA BELKNAP, STEPHEN WALLIS. Proven before ARTHUR DOBBS at Newbern.

MARTIN, WILLIAM.   Bertie County.

April 8, 1735. August Court, 1736. *Sons:* RICHARD ("plantation whereon I now live"), THOMAS, MOSES, JOHN. *Daughters:* MARY and ELSE MARTEN. *Wife and Executrix:* ELSE MARTIN. *Witnesses:* ALEXR. COTTEN, JOHN CARELL. *Clerk of the Court:* JNO. WYNNS.

MARTIN, WILLIAM.   Hyde County.

November 12, 1744. December 4, 1744. *Daughter:* ELIZABETH MAR-
TIN. *Wife and Executrix:* MARY. *Executors:* DANIEL BLIN (merchant
in Bath) and ALEXANDER FOREMAN. *Other legatees:* EDNE and RICHARD
MARTIN. *Witnesses:* JOS. TART, JOS. HOLLOWELL, THOMAS PARTREE.
Clerk of the Court: THOS. LOACK.

MARTIN, WILLIAM.   Beaufort County.

August 23, 1745. February 18, 1745. St. Thomas Parish. *Sons:* JOHN
(land on the Beaver Dams), JOEL, WILLIAM, JOSEPH (to each of the sons
is given a plantation). *Daughters:* ANN, ELIZABETH MARTIN. *Cousin:*
JOHN MARTIN. *Executors:* MARY MARTIN (wife), HENRY SNEAD, JOHN,
JOEL and WILLIAM MARTIN. *Witnesses:* JOHN ALDERSON, MARY ALDER-
SON, HENRY WOODARD. Proven before GAB. JOHNSTON at Eden House.

MARTIN, WILLIAM.   Beaufort County.

December 21, 1769. *Sons:* WILLIAM, THOMAS, JAMES, HENRY. *Daughters:* LURANE, MARY, ANNES, ANNE. These are named as "MARTIN,
alias SCOTT." *Executors:* MOSES HARE, HENRY BONNER, THOMAS JONES.
Witnesses: ALEX. GASTON, JOHN SMAW, JAMES LANE. No probate.

MASHBORNE, JETHRO.   Onslow County.

December 17, 1752. January Court, 1753. *Son:* EDWARD ("my plantation" and two negroes). *Daughters:* MARY and SARAH MASHBORNE.
Wife and Executrix: SUSANNA. *Executors:* CHARLES COX and DANIEL
MASHBORNE. *Witnesses:* JOHN JARMAN, WM. WHALEY, ELISABETH
PARKER. *Clerk of the Court:* WM. CRAY. Coat of arms on seal. Court
held for Onslow County at the house of JONATHAN MELTON on the Northeast.

MASKIL, WILLIAM.   Craven County.

February 21, 1753. November Court, 1753. *Brother:* DANIEL. *Wife
and Executrix:* DOROTHY. *Witnesses:* JAMES WHITING, CHARLES HOWARD.
ELIZABETH WHITING. *Clerk of the Court:* SOL. REW.

MASON, JOHN.   Currituck Precinct.

August 15, 1720. January 10, 1721. *Sons-in-law:* JAMES and MATTHIAS
TOLER. *Friend:* JOHN EVANS. *Wife and Executrix:* ANN. *Witnesses:*
RICHARD WILLIAMSON, DENNIS CALLIHERN, JOHN MARTYN. *Clerk of the
Court:* JO. WICKER.

MASON, JOHN.   Hyde Precinct.

February 15, 1737–1738. September Court, 1741. "In New Currituck." *Sons:* ROGER, THOMAS ("my dwelling plantation"). *Daugh-*

ters: MARY and MARGRET MASON. *Grandsons:* MASON TISON, JOHN MASON. *Other legatees:* THOMAS TISON and CHARLES HARRINGTON. *Wife and Executrix:* MARY. *Witnesses:* SAMUEL JASPER, JOHN TULE, THOM. SRETON CROMWELL. *Clerk of the Court:* H. BARROW.

MASON, JOHN.   Craven County.

February 27, 1747. September Court, 1748. *Sons:* THOMAS, JOHN, JOSEPH (to each is given about 100 acres of land). *Wife and Executrix:* ELIZEBETH. *Executor:* JEREMIAH PARSONS. *Witnesses:* SOUTHY REW, BENJAMIN MASON, JAMES BUSH. *Deputy Clerk:* PHIL. SMITH.

MASON, JNO., SR.   Hyde County.

January 9, 1751–1752. March 1, 1752. *Sons:* MOSES ("my dwelling plantation"), JOSHUA ("land on Roes Bay"), JOHN, JR. (land at Swanquarter Bay). *Daughters:* CHARITY, ANN and AGNES MASON. *Father:* ROGER MASON. *Brother:* ROGER MASON, JR. *Wife and Executrix:* CATHARINA. *Executors:* ROGER MASON, JR., and THOMAS MASON, JR. *Clerk of the Court:* FRAN. EGLETON.

MASON, MARY.   New Hanover County.

November 20, 1771. February 19, 1772. Wilmington. *Devisees and legatees:* ANN ROBESON (dwelling house on south side of Dock Street and west side of Second Street), JOHN ROBESON, RICHARD LOWRY (house at corner of Front and Princess Streets occupied by JOHN FORSTER), ROBERT BAIRD (tenements on Front Street "at present occupied by the reverend JAMES TATE and NEIL SCHAW"). *Executors:* JOHN ROBESON, ROBERT BAIRD and CORNELIUS HARNETT. *Witnesses:* A. MACLAINE, JA. MORAN, JOHN NUTT. Proven before JO. MARTIN.

MASON, ROGER.   Hyde County.

April 14, 1752. September Court, 1752. *Son:* ROGER (100 acres of land and one-half estate). *Daughter:* DORCAS. *Wife and Executrix:* SARAH (200 acres of land on Contentney). *Executors:* BENJAMIN and THOMAS MASON. *Witnesses:* THOMAS EASTER, HANNAH LEATH, SOLOMON CARTER. *Clerk of the Court:* FRANCIS EGLETON. Coat of arms on seal.

MASON, ROGER.   Hyde County.

December 23, 1754. June Court, 1756. *Sons:* BENJAMIN ("Gailars Hammocks and the upper old field"), THOMAS ("land up Roes down to the Great Bridges"), JOHN and ROGER MASON. *Grandsons:* CHRISTOPHER MASON, ROGER MASON, JR., DAVID MASON (land called the paupoy ridge), MOSES MASON. *Granddaughter:* SUSANNAH MASON. *Wife:* MARY. *Executors:* BENJAMIN and THOMAS MASON (sons). *Witnesses:* JOHN TULE, JEAN TULE, JACOB TULE. *Clerk of the Court:* STEPHEN DENNING.

16

MASSEY, HEZEKIAH.   Bertie Precinct.

April 15, 1727. August Court, 1727. *Sons:* HEZEKIAH, RICHARD and WILLIAM (100 acres of land to each), JOHN. *Daughters:* SARAH and LUCEY MASSEY. *Friend:* MATHEW SHEERING. *Wife and Executrix:* ELIZABETH. *Executor:* JOHN MASSEY (son). *Witnesses:* ABRAHAM BURTON, JOHN GREEN, SENIOR, THOMAS HICKS. *Clerk of the Court:* RT. FORSTER.

MASTERS, JOHN.   Craven County.

March 22, 1773. July 27, 1773. *Brothers and Executors:* THOMAS and JOSEPH MASTERS. *Wife:* JULYANN. *Witnesses:* THOS. COOKE, BENJ'N CUMMINGS, SARAH WHITEARD. Proven before Jo. MARTIN.

MASTERS, JOSEPH.   Craven County.

November 22, 1759. May 3, 1760. *Sons:* JOHN (plantation on the west side of Little Creek), THOMAS (land on Adams Creek), JOSEPH ("plantation whereon I now live"). *Wife and Executrix:* ARCALA. *Executors:* SAMUEL MASTERS (brother), THOMAS COOK. *Witnesses:* THOS. COOK, ELIZA WEST, WILLIAM NORTHAN, SOLOMON NORTHAN. Proven before ARTHUR DOBBS.

MASTERS, THOMAS.   Craven County.

October 27, 1746. *Sons:* JOSEPH, SAMUEL. *Wife and Executrix:* SARAH. *Witnesses:* THOS. COOK, PETER DUKE, DAVID RAMSEY. No probate. Testator mentions Indian slave.

MATHAM, RALPH.   Currituck County.

January 2, 1749. April 26, 1750. *Devisees:* BENJAMIN SIKES, NICH-OLAS LUNR (*Executor*). *Witnesses:* ROBERT STILL, WILLIAM STEVENSON, WILLIAM NORTON. Proven before GAB. JOHNSTON.

MATHERS, EDWARD.   Craven County.

July 17, 1753. *Daughters:* ANN GRAY, MARY MATHERS, ELEZEBETH WINFIELD, SARAH MATHERS, PRISCELLA MATHERS, MATHERS LURENIA MATHERS (*Executrix*). *Executor:* LAWRENCE HYLAND. *Grandson:* WILLIAM NEVILE. *Witnesses:* MARTEN HAGIN, THOS. MATCHETT, ELIZBETH RIGBE. No probate.

MATHEWS, CHARITY (wife of JAMES MATHEWS).

Tyrrell County.

January 20, 1771. May 16, 1772. *Daughters:* PENELOPE SPEIR (plantation on Conetoe), ELIZABETH HARDY, MARY ANDREWS, SUSSANAH SHER-RARD. *Other legatees:* JAMES CONNER WILLIAMS, son of JOSEPH JOHN WILLIAMS, WILLIAM WILLIAMS, THOMAS CARNAL, ELIZABETH BLANCHET. *Executors:* JAMES SHERRARD, JOHN EVERET, PENELOPY SPEIR. Proven before JO. MARTIN.

MATHEWS, THOMAS.   Chowan County.

October 6, 1732. October Court, 1732. *Legatees:* THOMAS WATERS, RICHARD HARECK. *Son-in-law:* SAMUEL BYFIELD. *Wife and Executrix:* PRECILLA. *Witnesses:* SARAH HARECK, WILLIAM HARE, JNO. MCWILLIAMS. *Clerk of the Court:* RT. FORSTER.

MATTHIAS, JOHN.   Perquimans County.

March 3, 1746–1747. April Court, 1748. *Son and Executor:* WILLIAM ("my plantation"). *Wife and Executrix:* ELIZABETH. *Witnesses:* DAVID and MARY BUTLER. *Clerk of the Court:* EDMUND HATCH.

MATTOCKE, JOHN.   Bath County.

October 12, 1732. September 4, 1733. *Daughters:* ANN and ELIZABETH MATTOCKE. *Wife:* MARY. No executor named. *Witnesses:* BEN WHEATLEY, WM. OWEN. *Clerk of the Court:* JNO. COLLISÓN.

MAUDLIN, EZEKIEL.   Perquimans Precinct.

March 25, 1732. April 17, 1732. *Sons:* JEREMIAH, JOSHUA and JAMES. *Wife and Executrix:* HANNAH. *Executor:* THOMAS WEEKES. *Witnesses:* ZEB. CLAYTON, JOHN STEVENS, TULLE WILLIAMS. *Clerk of the Court:* CHARLES DENMAN. Coat of arms on seal. Will recites that testator had sent to Boston for a negro and some goods.

MAUDLIN, THOMAS.   Perquimans County.

September 16, 1758. January Court, 1759. *Son:* JEREMIAH. *Wife:* SARAH. *Brother:* EDMUND CHANCEY. *Executors:* JOHN CLAYTON (father-in-law), RICHARD CLAYTON (brother-in-law) and WILLIAM TRUMBULL. *Witnesses:* WILLIAM TENNETT, EDMUND CHANCEY, JOSEPH BARCLIFT. *Clerk of the Court:* MILES HARVEY.

MAULE, JOHN.   Beaufort County.

December 11, 1773. February 16, 1774. *Son:* MOSES ("my manor plantation"; six negroes and mill on Blounts Creek with land adjoining). *Daughters:* ELIZABETH MAULE ("my Quarter Plantation" and six negroes), ANNE (400 acres of land and five negroes), PENELOPE (900 acres of land and five negroes), JEMIMA (land on Blounts and Nevils Creeks and in Pitt County and six negroes). *Wife:* ELIZABETH (seven negroes). *Executors:* MOSES HARE (brother-in-law), JOHN PATTEN, READING BLOUNT, JOSEPH BLOUNT. *Witnesses:* WILLIAM GERRARD, FORBIS GERRARD, JOHN NEVIL. Proven before JO. MARTIN.

MAULE, PATRICK.   Bath County.

April 19, 1736. Beaufort Precinct. *Wife:* ELIZABETH (five negroes "to be delivered after the tar kilns are off and the crop finished"; also plantation at Rumney Marsh with a dwelling house to be built "twenty foot long and sixteen foot wide"). *Son:* JOHN (five negroes, lands at Smiths Point and Blunts Creek and lot in Bath town). *Daughters:* SARAH (five negroes and land at Tranters Creek), BARBARA (four negroes and the land on Matchapungo Swamp), MARY (four negroes and lands on north dividing and Jacks Creeks). *Guardians for children:* JOHN and WILLIAM GRAY. *Executors:* JOHN and WILLIAM GRAY, JOHN CALDOM and ROBERT BOYD. *Witnesses:* BART. FLEMING, ELIZABETH MONTGOMERY, NEHEMIAH MONK. *Clerk of the Court:* JNO. COLLISON. Letters issued June, 1736. Probate not dated.

MAULE, WILLIAM.   Bertie Precinct.

February 25, 1726. March 30, 1726. *Wife:* PENELOPE (plantations called Scotts Hall and Mount Galland). *Daughter:* PENELOPE MAULE ("all the rest and residue of my Estate"). *Brother and Executor:* PATRICK MAULE. *Witnesses:* ROBERT FORSTER, JOHN NAIRN, JAMS EAGLES (?). Impression of head and Latin inscription on seal. Proven before RICHARD EVERARD.

MAULTSBY, JOHN.   Bladen County.

October 5, 1749. July 29, 1757. *Sons:* JOHN and WILLIAM. *Daughters:* HANNAH ROOTS, MARY and SARAH. *Wife and Executrix:* MARY. *Witnesses:* ROBT. FORSHA, JOHN JONES, WILLIAM HARRISON. *Clerk of the Court:* THOS. ROBESON. *Justices of the Peace:* CALEB HOWEL, E. CARTLIDGE. Coat of arms on seal.

MAULTSBY, JOHN.   New Hanover County.

May 17, 1757. November 6, 1757. Wilmington. *Mother:* MARY MAULTSBY. *Sisters:* HANNAH ROOTS and MARY MAULTSBY, SARAH SHEPHERD. *Nephews:* WILLIAM and JOHN MAULTSBY, ROGER ROOTS. *Executors:* THOMAS JONES and DANIEL DUNBIBIN. *Witnesses:* BENJ'N MORISON, JAMES ARLORD, FRAN. BETEITHELLY (or BATHELLY). *Clerk of the Court:* JA. MORAN.

MAYFIELD, PETER.   Albemarle County.

June 13, 1687. October 6, 1687. *Goddaughter:* ANN LOVE. *Wife and Executrix:* ANN. *Witnesses:* JOHN LARANCE, ROBERT WALLIS, THO. ROLFE. Proven before SETH SOTHELL.

MAYO, EDWARD.   Pasquotank County.

October 12, 1724. October 20, 1724. *Sons:* EDWARD ("my plantation"), JOSEPH. *Daughters:* MARY, ANN, ELIZABETH and SARAH MAYO. *Wife and Executrix:* MARY. *Executor:* THOMAS JESSOP (brother). *Witnesses:* CALEB SAWYER, WILLIAM JENNINGS, STEPHEN DELEMARE. *Clerk of the Court:* W. NORRIS.

MAYO, EDWARD.   Pasquotank County.

January 27, 1734–1735. February 14, 1734. *Wife and Executrix:*
MARY. *Daughter:* MARY. *Executor:* JOSEPH JESSOP (wife's father). *Wit-*
nesses: JOHN SCOTT, JEAN BUNDAY, JNO. PALIN. Proven before GAB.
JOHNSTON.

MEADS, TIMOTHY.   Albemarle County.

March 2, 1685. July 15, 1686. *Son:* JOHN. *Brother:* THOMAS MEADES,
of Littleworth, in Warwickshire, England. *Wife:* ANN. *Executors:* MR.
DANELL AKEHURST, ARNALL WHITE and HARDY WHITE. *Witnesses:* JOHN
HUNTT, WILLIAM BENTLEY, WILLIAM HOGBEN. Proven before SETH
SOTHELL.

MEAVIS (or MEVOIS), MARK.   Craven County.

January 11, 1762. February 4, 1762. *Sons:* JOHN ("my plantation"),
NATHAN (land on Trent River), BENJAMIN (land on Indian Grave Branch).
Daughters: LEAH and PIGO. *Executors:* EDMUND HATCH, JAMES FRAZIER
and EMANUELL SIMMONS. *Witnesses:* JAMES MCDONALD, JACOB BALL,
EMMANUEL SIMMONS. Proven before ARTHUR DOBBS.

MEDFORD, HENRY.   Halifax County.

December 19, 1773. February 17, 1774. *Sons:* JOHN, JAMES, HENRY
and DANIEL (to each is given a plantation). *Daughters:* MARY, FERREBEE
and ELIZABETH. *Wife:* ELIZABETH. *Executors:* JONATHAN CAIN and
JOHN MEDFORD. *Witnesses:* DANIEL HULL, THOMAS WEATHERSBEE.
Proven before JO. MARTIN.

MEEDS, SUSANNAH.   Pasquotank County.

March 26, 1755. June Court, 1755. *Sons:* TIMOTHY MEEDS, WILLIAM
DAVIS. *Daughters:* WINNIFRED DAVIS, ELIZABETH HIGHE, SARAH BAR-
CLIFT. *Executors:* TIMOTHY MEEDS, ROBERT HOSEA. *Witnesses:* ABRA-
HAM HOSEA, JOHN HOSEA, MARY CROCKER. *Clerk of the Court:* THOS.
TAYLOR.

MEEDS, THOMAS.   Pasquotank County.

March 8, 1750–1751. April Court, 1751. *Son and Executor:* TIMOTHY
("my plantation"). *Daughters:* ANN NIGHTS (two negroes), ELIZABETH
MEEDS (two negroes). *Wife and Executrix:* SUSSANAH. *Executor:* ISAAC
SWENY. *Witnesses:* JOSEPH SCOTT, JOHN BROTHERS, JOB WINSLOW.
Clerk of the Court: (signature missing).

MEED, TIMOTHY.   Pasquotank County.

July 6, 1751. January Court, 1751. *Sons:* JOHN and THOMAS ("my
land"). *Daughter:* MILLOSON MEED. *Wife and Executrix:* MARY. *Execu-*
tor: JOSEPH PENDLETON. *Witnesses:* THOS. MCKEELL, MARY ANN SMITH.
Clerk of the Court: THO. TAYLOR.

Meglohon, James.　　　　　　　　Bertie County.

July 4, 1750. September 4, 1750. *Son and Executor:* James ("my plantation"). *Wife:* Margerit. *Sons-in-law:* Christopher Hollyman, William Roads, Samuel Hollyman. *Daughter:* Alce Meglohon. *Witnesses:* Wm. Williford, Wm. Rasbuery, J. Parly. Proven before Gab. Johnston at Eden house.

Melton, Robert.　　　　　　　　Orange County.

April 24, 1759. November Court, 1759. *Sons:* James, Nathaniel, Nathan, Isesum, Ancel. *Executor:* Nathan Melton (son). *Witnesses:* James Sellars, Mary Stratton. *Clerk of the Court:* James Watson.

Merriday, Thomas.　　　　　　　Pasquotank County.

March 1, 1740. *Daughters:* Elizabeth ("my plantation in Pasquotank known as Lawsons"), Sarah and Mary ("the plantation whereon I now live"). *Wife and Executrix:* Elizabeth. *Witnesses:* Julius Caesar Clarke, John Jones. *Clerk of the Court:* Thos. Taylor. Coat of arms on seal.

Merritt, Charles.　　　　　　　Chowan County.

April 6, 1718. October 21, 1718. *Sons:* Charles, Nathaniel, William, John. *Daughters:* Ann, Sarah, Hardy. *Wife and Executrix:* mentioned, but not named. *Witnesses:* James Bryant, Peter Evans. *Clerk of the Court:* R. Hicks.

Merritt, John.　　　　　　　　Edgecombe County.

January 13, 1757. *Sons:* Thomas, John. *Daughter:* Pegee (wife of John Stone), Amee (wife of William Hanby), and Betty Merritt. *Wife and Executrix:* Mary. *Witnesses:* Jno. Haywood, Thos. Merritt. No probate.

Merrit, Nathaniel.　　　　　　　Edgecombe County.

April 10, 1735. February Court, 1735. *Wife and Executrix:* Mary. *Sons:* Nathaniel, Efrum, Benjamin. *Daughters:* Sarah and Mary Merrit. *Witnesses:* Frances Weldon, Henry Jones. *Deputy Clerk of the Court:* Thos. Kearny.

Mesler, Cearsmear.　　　　　　　Albemarle County.

May 2, 1696. October Court, 1696. *Son-in-law:* Richard Lowie. *Executrix:* Phillis Mesler. *Witnesses:* Thomas Luten, John Fener, Ruth Raner. *Clerk of the Court:* Nath. Chevin.

MESSEX, JOSEPH.   Onslow County.

February 27, 1754. July Court, 1754. Sons: LEVEN, JOSHUA, ARON and JOSEPH. Daughters: DOROTHY, SARAH, GRACE, ESTER. Wife and Executrix: GRACE. Witnesses: CHARLES WILLIAMSON, RICHARD WILLIAMSON, LEWIS JENKINS. Clerk of the Court: WILL. CRAY.

METCALF, CALEB.   Craven County.

December 31, 1736. This is a nuncupative will made in the presence of JOSHUA PLATT, WILLIAM HERRITAGE, ADAM MOORE and AARON WOOD, and bequeathes all estate to daughter, expressing desire that wife have no part of estate. WILLIAM HERRITAGE appointed Executor. Proven before GAB. JOHNSTON at Newton, March 15, 1736.

METS, GEORGE.   Bath County, Craven Precinct.

September 15, 1727. September 19, 1727. Son: GEORGE. Daughter: ANNE CURTISSE METS. Wife: SUSANNAH. Executors: ADAM MOORE and MATHIAS RISSONOVER. Witnesses: JOSHUA PLATT, PETER BALLARD. Clerk of the Court: C. METCALFE.

MEWBOORN, THOMAS.   Bertie County.

February 3, 1749. November Court, 1749. Sons: THOMAS, JOSHUA, NICHOLAS (a plantation to each), MOSES, GEORGE, JOHN, NICHOLESS. Daughter: MARY. Wife and Executrix: ELEANNAR. Witnesses: EDWARD RICE, THOMAS MEWBOORN. Clerk of the Court: JOHN LOVICK.

MIDDLETON, HENRY.   Tyrrell County.

March 6, 1738–1739. June Court, 1739. Sons: JAMES ("my manner plantation"), JOHN and HENRY. Daughter: MARY. Wife and Executrix: MARTHA. Executors: DANIEL GARRET and SAM'LL DURRANCE. Witnesses: THOS. LEE, BENJ. WALKER, ABIGAL WALKER. Clerk of the Court: JAMES CRAVEN.

MIDDLETON, JOHN.

June 26, 1718. July 8, 1718. Wife and Executrix: ELIZABETH. Daughter: MARY MIDDLETON. Witnesses: CHARLES DENMAN, WILL and ANN HALL. Clerk of the Court: RICH'D LEARY.

MIDDLETON, JOHN.   Onslow County.

December 25, 1741. April Court, 1744. Sons: JOHN and JAMES (plantation to be divided between them), SAMUEL, ISAAC. Daughters: ANN, SARAH, SABRA, SUSSANNA. Wife: SARAH. Executor: JOHN STARKEY. Witnesses: ABRAHAM MITCHELL, ALEXR. MITCHELL, SARAH MITCHELL. Clerk of the Court: ANDR. MURRAY.

MIDDLETON, JOHN.   Edgecombe County.

July 20, 1750. November Court, 1750. *Sons:* JAMES and EDWARD.
Daughters: ELIZABETH PERREY, JANE, SARAH and MILDRED MIDDLETON.
Wife and Executrix: MARY. *Witnesses:* AMBROSE JOSHUA SMITH, JUDITH
SMITH. *Clerk of the Court:* BENJ'N WYNNS.

MIDYETT, MATTHEW.   Currituck County.

December 21, 1734. July Court, 1735. Body Island. *Sons:* SAMUEL
(land on Albemarle Sound), JOHN ("one great periauger and sails"),
JOSEPH, MATTHEW and THOMAS. *Daughters:* ANN, CATERAN, DINA.
Executors: JOHN and JOSEPH MIDYETT. *Witnesses:* TULLE WILLIAMS,
JOSEPH OLOVER, MARY HUNTER. *Clerk of the Court:* JAMES CRAVEN.

MILLARD, CHARLES.

November 7, 1735. Cape Fear. *Legatees:* CORNELIUS HARNETT and
HUGH CAMPBELL (*Executor*). *Witnesses:* SOLOMON DAVIS, JOHN DAVEN-
PORT, MAGDALEN CAMPBELL. No probate.

MILLER, THOMAS.

February 20, 1693–1694. July 16, 1694. *Sons:* WILLIAM, RICHARD,
NATHANIEL and THOMAS. *Executor:* EDWARD MAYO. *Witnesses:* JOHN
HAWKINS, WILLIAM TEMPLE, JOHN CABEGE. *Clerk of the Court:* EDWARD
MAYO.

MILLER, THOMAS.   Pasquotank County.

March 30, 1722. July 27, 1722. *Executor and sole legatee:* WM. WILL-
SON. *Witnesses:* SAMUEL COCK, ANTHONY COCK, JOHN SCARBOROUGH.
Proven before RICH'D EVERARD.

MILLER, WILLIAM.   New Hanover County.

September 9, 1777. October 27, 1777. Wilmington. *Brothers:* DANIEL
and JAMES MILLER (of Luss in Dumbartonshire, North Brittain). *Father:*
JOHN MILLER, *sister:* ELEANOR MILLER, *brother:* JOHN MILLER (to these
three is given testator's interest in a brigantine, which he recites was
"built at this place"). *Brother-in-law:* JOHN COWAN ("an Island on the
Sound known by the name of Bermuda, and also a piece of land on
Smith's Creek"). *Wife and Executrix:* ANNA. *Executor:* ALEXR. HOSTLER.
Witnesses: JAMES GEEKIE, THOMAS BROWN, DAVID ROSS. Proven before
RICHARD CASWELL. *Justice of the Peace:* JONAS DUNBIBIN.

MILNER, JAMES.

September 18, 1771. January 13, 1773. Halifax Town. *Brother:*
ARTHUR MILNER ("my land estate in North Britain"). *Other legatees:*
MARGARET CATHCART, DOLLY HALL, JACOBINA WYNE, MARY and ELIZA-

BETH MONTFORT, JOSEPH MONTFORT, ANDREW MILLER, WILLIAM CATH-
CART, REV. WILLIAM WILLIE ("all my Hebrew and Greek books"), HENRY
SKIPWITH. *Executors:* JOSEPH MONTFORT, ANDREW MILLER, ABNER NASH,
HENRY SKIPWITH, DOUGLAS HAMILTON. *Witnesses:* MONTFORT EELBECH,
REBECA BAGLEY. Proven before JO. MARTIN. Codicil provides for sale
of negro servant, and devises lands purchased from one JACOB ODANIEL.
Coat of arms with motto: "Societas Scientia Virtus."

MILTON, JONATHAN.   Onslow County.
January 18, 1758. April Court, 1758. *Son:* JONATHAN. *Daughter:*
ANN. *Wife and Executrix:* PURIFY. *Witnesses:* THOMAS HILL, JOSEPH
THOMAS, FRANCES COOPER. *Clerk of the Court:* WILL CRAY. *Item:*
"all my *woods*, horses and mares be sold, etc."

MING, JOSEPH.   Chowan County.
December 1, 1750. April Court, 1751. *Sons:* THOMAS (2 plantations),
JOSEPH. *Daughters:* SARAH WILKINS, ANNARITO COLLINS, MARY MING.
Grandsons: JOSEPH WILKINS and JOSEPH COLLINS. *Wife and Executrix:*
RACHEL. *Executors:* THOMAS WARD, JOSEPH MING (son). *Witnesses:*
RACHEL CAMBEL, THOMAS WARD, THO. CALLAWAY. No probate officer.
Provision is made for three years' schooling to be given to son THOMAS,
"in addition to the one he now has."

MITCHELL, ABRAHAM.   Carteret County.
December 30, 1746. March Court, 1746. *Brothers:* ANTHONY, JOHN
and GEORGE. *Sister:* REBECKAH. *Wife:* not named. *Executors:* JOHN
MITCHELL and ESEKEL HUNTER. *Witnesses:* WILLIAM COOK, WILLIAM
WALLIS, PETER ARNOLD. *Clerk of the Court:* GEORGE READ.

MITCHELL, ABRAM.   Onslow County.
December 8, 1747. January Court, 1747. *Sons:* GEORGE (1 planta-
tion), ANTONY (land on Queens Creek). *Wife:* ANN. *Daughter:* RE-
BECCA. *Executor:* JOHN STARKEY. *Witnesses:* SARAH MIDDLETON, ED-
WARD BURKE, EDMOND THORLA. *Clerk of the Court:* THOS. BLACK

MITCHELL, JAMES.   Edenton, Chowan County.
April 22, 1745. July Court, 1745. *Son:* JAMES. *Wife and Executrix:*
CATHRINE. *Executors:* PETER PAYNE and SAMUEL STILLWELL. *Witnesses:* JAMES WALLACE, ANDRE RICHARD, ELIZ'TH WALLACE. *Clerk of
the Court:* EDMUND HATCH.

MITCHELL, RANDALL.   Edgecombe County.
September 24, 1756. June Court, 1758. *Brother:* WILLIAM MITCHELL.
Daughter-in-law: ELIZABETH LEAVET. *Wife and Executrix:* MARY. *Exec-
utor:* AQUILA SUGG. *Witnesses:* BAURLEAY BELCHER, JOSEPH HOWELLS,
BENJAMIN MITCHELL. *Clerk of the Court:* JOS. MONTFORT.

MOBLEY, JOHN.   Edgecombe County.

August 5, 1752.   May Court, 1753.   *Sons:* JOHN, MORDECA and EDWARD (one negro each).   *Brother:* EDWARD MOBLEY.   *Nephew:* SAMUEL MOBLEY (one negro).   *Wife and Executrix:* RACHELL (two negroes).   *Executor:* EDWARD MOBLEY (son).   *Witnesses:* JOHN WILLIAMS, JOHN WARD, LEWIS, ATKINS.   *Clerk of the Court:* BENJ'N WYNNS.

MOHOON, JOSIAH.   Halifax County.

January 1, 1772.   February 2, 1774.   *Sons:* JOSIAH and JAMES (one plantation to each), JOHN, JESSE.   *Daughters:* ANN and EDEE MOHOON. Testator bequeaths "remainder part of my estate * * * to give all my children an equal learning * * *."   *Executors:* NEEDAM BRYANT, ELIAS BRYANT, THOMAS HYMAN.   *Witnesses:* JOHN BRYAN, JAMES BURNET, WILLIAM BLAND.   Proven before JO. MARTIN.

MONEREIF, JOHN.   Currituck County.

June 22, 1712.   April Court, 1713.   *Sons:* THOMAS (160 acres of land), WILLIAM (160 acres adjoining THOMAS), JOHN (160 adjoining WILLIAM), GEORGE (gun and sword).   A great number of spoons, "poringers," pewter dishes and plates, etc., bequeathed to wife and children.   *Daughter:* MARY MONEREIF.   *Wife and Executrix:* MARY.   *Witnesses:* ADAM PEARRY, THOMAS DAVIS, DANIEL GLASCOE.   *Clerk of the Court:* JOS. WICKER.

MONS, THOMAS.   County not given.

January 5, 1693.   *Wife and Executrix:* ANN.   *Witnesses:* MATHEW SAYES, WILLIAM WATERS, THOMAS GILBERT.   *Clerk of the Court:* HENDERSON WALKER.

MONTGOMERY, ANN.   Chowan County.

August 28, 1741.   October 29, 1744.   *Legatees:* THOMAS JONS, REBECCA JONS, JANE SWAN, daughter of SAMUEL SWAN, at Cape Fear (one small diamond ring and "my staned taffety gound"); MARY TURNBULL, MARY BUCHAR, ANN ALLIN, SAMUEL SWAN ("the rest of the law books and a mourning ring"), JAMES TURNBULL.   *Executors:* JAMES TURNBULL and SAMUEL SWAN.   *Mother:* SARAH LASTER in England.   *Witnesses:* CULLEN POLLOCK, FRANCES POLLOCK, E. BELL.   Proven before E. MOSELEY, C. J. On seal is impression of a dog or lion and the word "canis."

MONTGOMERY, GEORGE.   Bath County.

January 19, 1722–1723.   July 2, 1723.   *Daughter:* ELIZABETH.   *Other legatees:* JAMES, JOSIAS and GEORGE MONTGOMERY.   *Executor:* ROBT. TURNER.   *Witnesses:* JOSEPH ENGLISH, EDWD. DODD, JNO. BROOK.   *Clerk of the Court:* JNO. BAPTISTE ASHE.

MONTGOMERY, JOHN.   Chowan County.

August 3, 1741. May 22, 1744. Testator devises all his estate to his
wife, ANNE, who is also appointed *Executrix*. *Witnesses:* JOS. ANDERSON,
JAMES CRAVEN, THE. GOOLD. Proven before GAB. JOHNSTON.

MONTICUE, THOMAS.   Perquimans County.

June 5, 1750. *Wife:* ELIZABETH. *Other legatees:* FRANCIS NIXON, ZACH-
ARIAH NIXON, HENRY PHELPS, SAMUEL NEWBY, JOHN NIXON, JOSEPH
RATLIFF. *Executor:* ZACHARIAH NIXON. *Witnesses:* JOSIAH BUNDY,
ABARAHAM HENDRIXON, JOSEPH RATLIFF. Provision is made in will for
bricking up the grave of the testator.

MOORE, DAVID.

March 25, 1670. All estate is bequeathed to one DAVID——— (name
illegible). *Witnesses:* JAMES BLOUNT, ROBERT BONEO. *Clerk of the Court:*
THOMAS HARRIS.

MOORE, EPAPHRODITUS.   Bertie County.

June 11, 1757. October Court, 1757. *Son:* JOHN (all the lands of tes-
tator). *Grandsons:* ELISHA WILSON, THOMAS MOORE (one plantation each,
both plantations lying on Fort Branch). *Daughters:* JUDATH HURST,
REBECKAH CAIN, CHARITY WALSTON, RACHEL WALSTON, MARY MOORE,
ANN MOORE, RACHEL STANDLY, GRACE MOORE, PENELOPE HARE, CHRIS-
TIAN MOORE. *Son-in-law:* JAMES HOWARD. *Wife:* not named. *Execu-
tors:* MARY and ANN MOORE. *Witnesses:* CHARLES HORN, DEMCY HOL-
LAND, LEWIS PERRY. *Clerk of the Court:* BENJAMIN WYNNS.

MOORE, JAMES.   Bertie Precinct.

November 28, 1735. December 11, 1735. *Wife:* SUSANAH (one negro).
Son: MORICE ("my plantation and also a plantation on Fishing Creek").
Daughter: SARAH. *Executor:* JOHN DAWSON. *Witnesses:* JAMES BARNS,
ROBERT TENELL, JOHN BROWN. Codicil dated November 30, 1735,
bequeaths live stock to wife. *Witnesses to codicil:* ROBT. RUFFIN, JAMES
TART, SAM'LL COTTEN. Proven before GAB. JOHNSTON.

MOORE, JOHN.   Perquimans County.

March 19, 1746. May 18, 1746. *Son:* CHARLES ("my plantation").
Daughter: MARY. *Wife:* RACHEL. *Executors:* JOHN HARVEY, CHRISTO-
PHER DENMAN, JOSHUA SKINNER. *Witnesses:* JONATHAN SKINNER, PETER
JONES, JOHN BEMBRIDGE. Proven before GAB. JOHNSTON.

MOOR, JOHN.   Perquimans County.

March 11, 1750. October 21, 1755. *Sons:* CORNELIUS, JOSEPH ("plantation lying in baley hack"), GIDEON ("the maner plantation"), JOSEPH.

Daughters: MIRIAM, SARAH and BETEY MOORE. *Wife and Executrix:* MARY. *Executor:* JOSEPH RATLIFF (brother-in-law). *Witnesses:* ZACH. NIXON, WILLIAM MORE, SAMUELL MORE. Proven before JNO. CLAYTON and JOSEPH SUTTON, *Justices.*

MOORE, JOHN.   Northampton County.

September 1, 1753. November Court, 1753. *Sons:* MARK, JOHN, IS-HAM, WILLIAM, NATHANIEL, RICHARD. *Daughter:* SARAH MOORE. *Wife and Executrix:* TABITHA MOORE. *Executors:* RICHARD MOORE and THOMAS PACE. *Witnesses:* GEORGE HARPER, JOHN MACDESLEY. *Clerk of the Court:* I. EDWARDS.

MOORE, JOHN.   Bertie County.

February 19, 1754. May Court, 1754. *Son:* BENJAMIN. *Daughter:* ANN. *Executors:* ELIZABETH MOORE (wife) and JOHN MOORE (uncle). *Witnesses:* JOHN PEETERICK, ANNE GAINS, HEZEKIAH HERRENDEN. *Clerk of the Court:* SAM'L ORMES.

MOOR, JOHN.   Bertie County.

March 11, 1754. May Court, 1754. *Sons:* SAMUELL and JOHN MOORE ("my lands"). *Daughter:* MARY BELL. *Wife and Executrix:* ANN. *Executor:* EPHRAIM WESTON. *Witnesses:* STEPHEN EVANS, ANN EVANS, JOS. HARDY. *Clerk of the Court:* SAM'L ORMES.

MOORE, JOSEPH.   Edgecombe County.

February 15, 1753. February Court, 1757. *Sons:* JOSEPH (plantation in Edgecombe County on Little Swamp and plantation in Bertie County on Rockquies Swamp), JAMES (land on Conehoe pocoson), HODGES (land on Conehoe), JESSEE and EZIEKEL ("my water mill"). *Daughters:* ANN MCGEE, MARTHA HINTON, CELIA MOORE (one negro girl each), MELIA MOORE. *Executors:* ANN MOORE (wife) and four sons. *Witnesses:* ELIZA-BETH WILLIAMS, MARY WHITMILL, WM. WILLIAMS. *Clerk of the Court:* JOS. MONTFORT.

MOORE, JOSHUA.   Perquimans County.

February 12, 1734–1735. February 24, 1734. *Brothers:* SAMUEL, JOHN, TRUEMAN. *Nephew:* CORNELIUS (son of JOHN). *Niece:* ELIZABETH NIXON. *Wife and Executrix:* ELIZABETH. *Witnesses:* ZACHARIAH NIXON, THOMAS WINSLOW, ZACHARIAH NIXON, JR. Proven before GAB. JOHNSTON.

MOORE, MARY.   Perquimans County.

March 24, 1753. April Court, 1756. *Sons:* THOMAS and NATHAN NEWBY (*Executors*). *Daughter:* MARY ROBINSON. *Other legatees:* JEM-

MIME, MARY, SARAH and JOHN ROBINSON, ELIZABETH NEWBY, ELIZABETH
HILL, ELIZABETH ELIOT. *Witnesses:* FRANCES JONES, RALPH FLETCHER,
ELIZABETH HILL. *Clerk of the Court:* MILES HARVEY.

MOORE, RICHARD.   Bertie County.

November 1, 1748. February Court, 1748. *Son and Executor:* JOHN
("all my lands"). *Brother and Executor:* JOHN MOORE. *Witnesses:* WIL-
LIAM RICE, THOMAS DAVIS, LUCREACY LEE. *Clerk of the Court:* JOHN
LOVICK.

MOORE, ROBERT.   Perquimans County.

February 22, 1749. January Court, 1750. *Sons:* SAMUELL ("my plan-
tation"), JOHN. *Daughters:* SARAH and RACHEL MOORE. *Grandchildren:*
MARY MOORE, MARTHA and MIRIAM MOORE, ELIAZOR CREESSIE. *Execu-
tors:* SAMUELL MOORE, RICHARD SKINNER, ABRAHAM SANDERS and JOSEPH
WHITE. *Witnesses:* JOSHUA JONES, JONATHAN PHELPS, ELIZABETH ELLIS.
Clerk of the Court: EDMUND HATCH.

MOORE, ROGER.   New Hanover County.

March 7, 1747–1748. May Court, 1758. Parish of St. Philips. *Sons:*
GEORGE, WILLIAM. *Daughters:* SARAH SMITH, MARY and ANNE MOORE.
Wife: MARY. The following lands are devised: Plantation called Kendall;
land on "Mr. Allens Creek"; lands between Therofaire and Black River
in the Neck known by the name of Maultsby's Point and lands on the Island opposite; land in fork of River known by name of Mount Misery; 500
acres on So. West River; land between JOB HOWE and MR. DALLISON; 3,025
acres near Saxpahaw Old Fields, bought of JOHN PORTER; lot in Brunswick
where "Mr. Ross at present dwells"; plantation called Orton where "I now
dwell"; 640 acres at Rocky Point; land on Smith Creek; 5,000 acres at Eno
Old Fields. To *daughters,* ANN and MARY MOORE, is bequeathed 3,600
pounds, 1,800 to each. To *son-in-law,* THOMAS SMITH, is devised lot in
Brunswick "where WILLIAM LORD at present dwells." *Grandmother of
daughters:* MRS. SARAH TROTT. *Aunt of daughters:* MRS. SARAH ALLEN.
About 250 negroes bequeathed. Will mentions mill at Brices Creek.
Executors: GEORGE and WILLIAM MOORE (sons). *Witnesses:* WM. FORBES,
RICH'D QUINCE, GEO. LOGAN, WM. ROSS, REBECCA COKE. *Clerk of the
Court:* ISAAC FARIES. Coat of arms on seal.

MOORE, SAMUEL.   Albemarle County.

January 9, 1693–1694. August 20, 1694. *Son:* SAMUEL. *Wife and
Executrix:* ABIGAIL. *Witnesses:* JNO. HAWKINS, JOHN CABBIDGE, SARAH
HAWKINS. *Clerk of the Court:* EDWARD MAYO.

MOORE, SAMUEL.   Onslow County.

October 11, 1750. April 2, 1751. *Sons:* SAMUEL (plantation on a branch of Stones Creek), THOMAS (250 acres of land). *Daughters:* SARAH, MARY and ALLETHEA. *Executors:* OBADIAH MOORE (brother) and THEOPHILUS WILLIAMS. *Witnesses:* HORATIUS WOODHOUSE, ROBERT NIXON, JOSHUA PAULL. *Clerk of the Court:* THOS. BLACK.

MOORE, SAMUELL.   Perquimans County.

October 25, 1751. January Court, 1752. *Wife and Executrix:* MARY. *Nieces:* MARY, HANNA and MARTHA MOORE (daughters of brother, JOHN MOORE). *Other legatees:* ELIZABETH ELLIOT, FRANCIS and NATHAN NEWBY, JOHN PERISHE, EDWARD DEWISE. *Friends:* RICH'D SKINNER, JOSEPH WHITE and ZACHARIAH NIXON. *Executor:* FRANCIS NEWBY. *Witnesses:* ZACH. NIXON, DANIEL SAINT. *Clerk of the Court:* EDMUND HATCH.

MOORE, SAMUEL.   Perquimans County.

May 26, 1754. January Court, 1756. *Sons:* JOSHUA, AARON, JONATHAN, JOHN (to each is given a plantation). *Daughters:* MARY and SARAH MOORE. *Wife and Executrix:* SARAH. *Witnesses:* JOHN ROBINSON, CORNELIUS MOORE, JOSEPH WHITE, JUNR. *Clerk of the Court:* MILES HARVEY.

MOOR, THOMAS.   New Hanover County.

February 3, 1755. February 4, 1755. "Late of New York now in Wilmington." This will appoints COSMAS FARQUHARSON, *Executor,* and he is directed to transmit all estate to New York "to be disposed of as my former Will in the Hands of MR. ALSOP and CARROLL Directs." *Witnesses:* CALEB MASON, SIMON PAYNE, RD. HARTLEY. *Clerk of the Court:* ISAAC FARIES.

MOORE, TITUS.   Bertie County.

April 26, 1753. January Court, 1757. *Son and Executor:* JAMES. *Wife and Executrix:* ELIZABETH. *Daughter:* MARY ODOM. *Witnesses:* NEEDHAM BRYAN, WILLIAM TURNER, PATIENCE TURNER. *Clerk of the Court:* BENJN. WYNNS.

MOORE, TRUEMAN.   Perquimans County.

December 12, 1752. April Court, 1753. *Sons:* WILLIAM, SAMUEL, THOMAS (to each is given a plantation), JESSE (land in Ballyhack). *Daughters:* JANE and MARY MOORE. *Friends:* JOHN WILSON, WILLIAM WHITE, JOHN MOORE and DANIEL SAINT. *Wife and Executrix:* LEAH. *Executors:* THOS. NICHOLSON and SAMUEL MOORE. *Witnesses:* WILLIAM WHITE, DANIEL SAINT, JOSEPH WINSLOW. *Clerk of the Court:* EDMUND HATCH.

MOORE, WILLIAM.   Perquimans County.

February 6, 1726–1727. October 31, 1732. *Sons:* WILLIAM, JOHN, JOSHUA, SAMUELL, TRUMAN (to each of the above is given a plantation). *Daughters:* ELIZABETH and JANE. *Cousin:* ROBERT BOGUE. *Wife and Executrix:* ELIZABETH. *Executors:* JOHN and JOSHUA MOORE. *Witnesses:* JOSEPH WINSLOW, JACOB HILL, J. JESSOP. Proven before GEO. BURRINGTON.

MORE, WILLIAM.   Perquimans County.

June 4, 1749. April Court, 1752. *Devisees:* TRUMAN MOORE and WILLIAM WILSON (land obtained from EDW. MOSLEY). *Wife and Executrix:* MARTHA. *Witnesses:* ROBT. NEWBY, JOSHUA HASKET, MARY SAVIG. *Clerk of the Court:* EDMUND HATCH.

MOORHEAD. JAMES.   Bladen County.

April 4, 1759. July Court, 1759. *Sons:* WILLIAM and JAMES. *Daughters:* JANE and SARAH. *Wife and Executrix:* SARAH. *Executor:* ALEXANDER MCCONKEY. *Witnesses:* PETER CATES, LAWRENCE BYRNE, MARY ARINTON. *Clerk of the Court:* J. BURGWIN.

MORGAN, JAMES (Son of WILLIAM MORGAN).
                                    Perquimans County.

January 26, 1740–1741. October Court, 1741. *Sons:* JACOB and CHARLES (land on Morgan's Swamp). *Daughters:* ELIZABETH and REBECKAH MORGAN. *Wife and Executrix:* HANNAH. *Executor:* THOMAS OVERMAN (brother-in-law). *Witnesses:* ZACHARIAH NIXON, CHARLES OVERMAN, JOS. ROBINSON. *Clerk of the Court:* EDMUND HATCH.

MORGAN, JANE.   Perquimans County.

February 4, 1742. March 22, 1742. *Sons:* JOHN ANDERSON, JAMES MORGAN. *Daughter:* SARAH PARSONS. *Daughter-in-law:* ANN MORGAN. *Granddaughters:* MARY and MIRIAM MORGAN, ELIZABETH COSAN, JANE ANDERSON. *Executors:* JOHN ANDERSON and JAMES MORGAN. *Witnesses:* ABRAHAM ELLIOTT, MARY ELLIOTT, JOSEPH RATLIFF. Proven before GAB. JOHNSTON.

MORGAN, JOHN.   Pasquotank County.

October 20, 1754. January Court, 1755. *Sons:* JOHN and JOSEPH (1 shilling). *Daughters:* RACHEL OVERMAN, ELIZABETH ELLIOT, MARY ELLIOT, HANNAH BOSWELL ("my manner plantation"). *Grandson:* JOSEPH BOSWELL. *Executors:* HANNAH and JOSEPH BOSWELL. *Witnesses:* GEORGE LOW, EDWARD WARDSWORTH. *Clerk of the Court:* THO. TAYLOR.

MORGAN, NATHAN.   Onslow County.

February 16, 1749. October 2, 1750. *Sons:* WILLIAM ("mannor house and one-half of mannor plantation"), GOER ("the other half of the land I now live on"). *Daughter:* SUKEE MORGAN. *Brothers:* WILLIAM MORGAN (*Executor*) and JOSEPH MORGAN. *Witnesses:* WILLIAM AMBROSE, FRANCIS SUMNER, JOSEPH STURGES. No probate.

MORGAN, ROBERT.   Pasquotank Precinct.

October 22, 1727. November 26, 1730. *Sons:* BENNET, JOSEPH, ROBERT and MOSES (a plantation to each), AARON. *Daughters:* ALLIS, ELIZABETH, ANN and JUDA. *Wife:* ELIZABETH. *Executors:* BENNET and JOSEPH MORGAN (sons). *Witnesses:* ABEL ROSS, TAMAR ROSS, JERUAS JONES, JAMES ADAMS. Proven before RICHARD EVERARD.

MORRELL, HUMPHREY.

March 10, 1732. *Grandsons:* JOSEPH and JOHN PEARS. *Daughter and Executrix:* ELIZABETH WATS. *Mother:* ELIZABETH MORREL. *Witnesses:* WILLIAM SIMES, ANN BURK, HENRY TUDOR. No probate.

MORIS, JOHN.   Craven County.

August 23, 1742. September 24, 1742. *Wife and Executrix:* MATHEW MORRIS. *Son:* JOHN. *Daughter:* MARY MORRIS. *Executors:* ABRAHAM BUSETT, JOHN HUDLER. *Witnesses:* WM. WICKLIFFE, THOMAS MORE, RICHARD MORGAN. *Clerk of the Court:* N. ROUTLEDGE.

MORRIS, JOHN.   Pasquotank County.

November 18, 1739. January Court, 1739. *Sons:* JOSEPH and JOHN ("my manner plantation"), ZACHARIAH, ISAC, AARON, JOSEPH. *Daughters:* HANNAH and SARAH MORRIS. *Wife and Executrix:* MARY. *Witnesses:* JOHN BELMAN, MARY ALBERTSON, JOSEPH ROBINSON. *Clerk of the Court:* JAMES CRAVEN.

MORRISS, JOHN.   Bertie County.

May 21, 1759. July Court, 1759. *Sons:* JOHN and WILLIAM ("plantation whereon I now live," lying on the main road to Bertie Courthouse), BENJAMIN, NATHAN, JACOB, JAMES EARLY, RICHARD. *Daughters:* MARY STALLINGS, ANN HOLMS, SARAH FARMER, ELIZABETH and JANE MORRIS. *Wife and Executrix:* REBEKAH. *Executors:* JOHN and WILLIAM MORRIS. *Witnesses:* WILLIAM WILLEFORD, JACOB STALLINGS, J. EARLY. *Clerk of the Court:* BENJ'N WYNNS.

MORRIS, THOMAS.   New Hanover County.

August 2, 1744. January 9, 1744. *Sons:* THOMAS, WILLIAM, SOLOMON, JAMES (land on Holly Shelter Creek). *Grandsons:* THOMAS and CHARLES

MORRIS. *Brother:* WILLIAM MORRIS. *Executors:* WILLIAM, SOLOMON and JAMES MORRIS (sons). *Witnesses:* CHAS. HARRISON, THOMAS STEERS, SUSANAH NICHOLS. *Deputy Clerk of the Court:* JAMES SMALLWOOD.

MORRISON, BENJAMIN.   New Hanover County.

April 14, 1760.   June 10, 1760.   Wilmington.   *Executor:* ALEXANDER DUNCAN. *Witnesses:* THOMAS TURNBULL, JAMES RUTHERFURD, HENRY TOOMER. Proven before ARTHUR DOBBS at Brunswick. No legatee named in will.

MORTIMER, JOHN.   New Hanover County.

June 14, 1765.   September 26, 1766.   Wilmington.   *Daughter:* HANNAH MORTIMER (lot in Wilmington on north side of Market Street). *Nephew:* JOHN CONAWAY. *Sister:* MARY MORTIMER. *Wife and Executrix:* REBECCA. *Executors:* DOCTR. SAMUELL GREEN and CORNELIUS HARNETT. *Witnesses:* MOSES JOHN DEROSSETT, WM. PURVIANCE, W. GREGORY. Proven before WM. TRYON. *Executors* qualified before MOSES JNO. DEROSSETT.

MOSELEY, EDWARD.   New Hanover County.

March 20, 1745.   August Court, 1749.   *Sons:* JOHN (plantation at Rockey Point, on the west side of the northeast branch of Cape Fear River, about 3,500 acres; lot and houses in Brunswick "where my Habitation usually is at Present"; plantation below Brunswick commonly called Macknights), EDWARD (plantation in Chowan County containing 2,000 acres in fee tail; lot and house in Wilmington; 600 acres of land opposite Cabbage Inlet; 500 acres in Tyrrell called Coopers; 450 acres in Tyrrell called Whitemarsh), SAMPSON (land on the east side of the northeast branch of Cape Fear River, lying between Holly Shelter Creek and the bald white sandhills, containing 3,500 acres), JAMES (lands on the east side of the northeast branch of Cape Fear River opposite Rocky Point plantation, containing 1,650 acres), THOMAS (1,880 acres of land on northwest branch of Cape Fear River). To SAMPSON, JAMES and THOMAS is devised "all my lands on the East side of Cape Fear River, on part whereof MR. BUGNION dwelleth." To five sons is devised "my large tract of Land in Edgecomb County called Clur, containing 10,000 acres," and fifty-six slaves. *Wife:* ANN (plantation on the Sound "whereon is a large Vineyard planted"; also 3,200 acres of land in Edgecomb called Alden of the Hill, lying on a branch of Fishing Creek, by "some called Irwins, by Other Butterwood"; also 1,650 acres on the west side of Neuse River, about twenty-four miles above Newbern; also twenty-one slaves, new chaise harness and pair of bay horses, ten cows and calves, ten steers and twenty sheep. *Daughter:* ANER (eleven slaves). *Friends:* SAMUEL SWANN, JOHN SWANN, JEREMIAH VAIL, ALEXANDER LILLINGTON, JAMES HASELL. *Mother-in-law:* MRS. SUSANNAH HASELL. *Brother-in-*

law: JAMES HASELL, JR. *Sisters-in-law:* MRS. MARY VAIL, MRS. JOHN PORTER and ELIZABETH, late wife of COL. MAURICE MOORE. *Executors:* JOHN and EDWARD MOSELEY (sons) and ANN MOSELEY (wife). *Witnesses:* ELEAZR ALLEN, ROGR. MOORE, WM. FORBES, MATT. ROWAN. Some interesting provisions in will: "I Recommend it to my Dear and loving wife that one of my sons as shall be thought best qualified for it be bred to the law, it being highly necessary in so large a family, and to him I give all my law books, being upwards of 200 volumes, which are now or shall be in my closet," etc. "*Item:* I give to my dear wife Blome's History of the Bible in folio, 3 volumes in folio of Arch Bishop Tillotson's Works, four volumes in Octavo of Dr. Stanhope's, on the Epistles & Gospels, and all the Books of Physick. *Item:* I give to my daughter, ANN HUMPHRIES, 3 Volumes in folio on the Old & New Testament, and I will that my executors buy for her the work of the Auther of the whole Duty of Man. I give to the oldest of my sons that shall not Study the Law, Chambers Dictionary, 2 Volms in folio, and LeBlond of Gardening in Quarto; and the rest of my books, about 150 Volumes, to be divided among my other three Sons. *Item:* I give and bequeath unto my Eldest Son, JOHN, my large Silver Tea Kettle, Lamp & Server for it to stand on, weighing in all about 170 ounces; To my Son EDWARD, my large silver Coffee Pot Pott; to my son SAMPSON, my large Silver Tea Pot; to my Son JAMES, my Large Silver Tankard, & To my Son THOMAS, a pair of Large Square Silver Servers, my cases of Knifes, Forks, Spoons, Salts, Casters & Other my plate to be divided between my Wife & Daughter * * *." "*Item:* it is my will that the profits arising from the labour of my Two Sons' Slaves & their part of the profits arising by the stocks be laid out in purchasing Young Female slaves * * *." "*Item:* When it shall be necessary to give all or any of my sons Other Education that is to be had from the Common Masters in this Province, for I would have my children well educated, it is then my will that such expence be defrayed out of the profits of such Child's estate, etc."

Codicil to will dated June 9, 1748, gives to son WILLIAM, "born since my said last Will was made," the tract of land in Edgecomb called Alden of the Hill and 300 acres contiguous thereto, and also emancipates three slaves, with the provision, however, that "if it shall not be allowed them, then it is my will that my executrix shall place them jointly or severally, as they shall choose, on any of my lands, to make what they shall judge most for their advantage, rendering one-tenth part of the profits to my executrix." *Witnesses to codicil:* JOHN COCHRAN, JOHN HANCOCK, JOHN COOKE. *Clerk of the Court:* ISAAC FARIES. Coat of arms on seal is illegible, and coat of arms on seal to codicil is said by testator to be "MR. SAMPSON's (my Wife's Father), mine being lately lost:" All land devised to sons is devised in fee tail, showing that entails existed at the time of the will.

MOSLER, CEARSMER. Chowan Precinct.

May 2, 1696. *Wife and Executrix:* PHILIS. *Witnesses:* THOMAS LATEN, JOHN JONES, RICHARD RANER. No probate. Will almost illegible.

MOSS, GRACE. Craven County.

June 7, 1771. August 6, 1771. *Daughter:* ANN CONWAY. *Niece:* SIDNEY PITMAN. *Son:* JOSEPH MOSS. *Executors:* THOMAS and JOHN NELSON. *Witnesses:* JAMES SEAVERN, JR., DENEL MOZOR, ELEANOR CLASH. Proven before JAS. HASELL. Provision is made for education of son.

MOUND, NOAH. Edgecombe County.

February 1, 1752. February Court, 1752. This is a nuncupative will proven before SAM'LL WILLIAMS by ELIZA WEBB and JOSEPH ISEN-MANGER, in which all estate of testator is left to AQUILA SUGG, who is also appointed *Executor. Clerk of the Court:* BENJ'N WYNNS.

MOUNTEAGUE, ELIZABETH. Perquimans County.

September 20, 1756. July Court, 1757. *Legatees:* JOSIAH RAPER, MIRIAM OVERMAN, NAOMY NEWBY, HANNAH NEWBY, JOSEPH ROBINSON, SAMUEL NEWBY, THOMAS NICHOLSON, WILLIAM HASKIT, CHRISTOPHER and JOSEPH NICHOLSON. *Witnesses:* THOMAS, CHRISTOPHER and JOSEPH NICHOLSON. *Witnesses:* JOHN OVERMAN, SARAH BARROW, JOHN TAYLOR. *Clerk of the Court:* MILES HARVEY.

MOUNTICUE, THOMAS. Perquimans County.

June 5, 1750. October Court, 1750. *Devisees and legatees:* FRANCIS NIXON (all lands and houses), ZACHARIAH NIXON, HENRY PHELPS (one negro man), SAMUEL NEWBY and JOHN NIXON (ten pounds in good "mer-chantable barrel pork"), JOSEPH RATLIFF, ZACHARIAH NIXON, JR., and MEHETABLE NIXON. *Wife and Executrix:* ELIZABETH. *Executor:* ZACHA-RIAH NIXON. *Witnesses:* JOSAH BUNDY, ABRAHAM HENDRIXON, JOSEPH RATLIFF. *Clerk of the Court:* EDMUND HATCH.

MOY, JOHN. Currituck County.

January 3, 1735. July 1, 1735. *Son:* JOHN ("my maner plantation"). *Daughter:* JANE MOY. *Wife and Executrix:* ANNIE. *Witnesses:* JOHN WAR-DEN, RICHARD BRADLEY. *Clerk of the Court:* JAMES CRAVEN.

MOYE, THOMAS. Bertie Precinct.

March 26, 1721–1722. May Court, 1723. *Wife and Executrix:* ELIZA-BETH. *Wife's sons:* THOMAS and JOHN PHILLIPS. *Witnesses:* JNO. SIMP-SON, THOMAS BOYKIN, ISABELL JOYNER. *Clerk of the Court:* RT. FORSTER.

MULKEY, PHILIP.   Edgecombe Precinct.

December 17, 1736. May Court, 1737. *Sons:* DAVID (land on Beaver Ponds), PHILIP ("my plantation"). *Daughters:* JANE, EVE, SCARBROUGH, JUDITH. *Son-in-law:* GEORGE LAWS. *Friends:* BACKLEY KIMBROUGH and JOHN HARDY (land at plumtree). *Wife and Executrix:* SARAH. *Executor:* JAMES SMITH. *Witnesses:* RICHARD HERRING, JOHN CALIHAN, JONATHAN MULKEY. *Clerk of the Court:* THOS. KEARNY.

MULLEN, ISAAC.   Perquimans County.

August 24, 1743. October Court, 1743. *Son:* JOSEPH ("my plantation"). *Wife and Executrix:* ELIZABETH. *Daughter:* REBECCA. *Executors:* ABRAHAM and JACOB MULLEN (brothers). *Witnesses:* SAMUEL BARCLIFT, JOSEPH PERSHER, JOHN ANDERSON. *Clerk of the Court:* EDMUND HATCH.

MULLEN, JACOB.   Perquimans County.

November 5, 1757. January Court, 1758. *Sons:* ISAAC and ABRAHAM ("my plantation containing 229 acres"), JACOB (76 acres of land), THOMAS (land on Suttons Creek). *Daughter:* HANNAH MULLEN. *Executors:* WILLIAM TOMBLIN and WILLIAM HASKET. *Witnesses:* JAMES GIBSON, JAMES PEIRCE, FRANCIS LAYDEN. *Clerk of the Court:* MILES HARVEY.

MUMFORD, JOSEPH.   Onslow County.

October 3, 1732. *Sons:* JOSEPH ("all my lands"), EDWARD. *Daughter:* ELIZABETH MUMFORD. *Executors:* EDWARD HOWARD, THOMAS FULLARD. *Witnesses:* JAMES MURRAY, EDWARD HOWARD, ELIZABETH MURRAY. *Clerk of the Court:* WM. CRANFORD.

MUNDAY, WILLIAM.   Albemarle County.

December 3, 1688. January 28, 1688. *Son:* WILLIAM. *Daughter:* ELIZABETH MUNDAY. *Wife and Executrix:* EMMAY. *Executor:* JOHN STOCKUM. *Witnesses:* JOHN JONES, WILLIAM HANCOCK, ELIZA STOCKUM, JOHN WINGATE. Proven before SETH SOTHELL.

MUNS, THOMAS.   Albemarle County.

January 5, 1693. *Wife:* ANNE MUNS, sole heir and Executrix. *Witnesses:* MATHEW SAYES, WM. WALTERS, THOS. GILBERT. Proved at Chowan. *Clerk of Court:* HENDERSON WALKER.

MURDEN, JEREMIAH.   Pasquotank County.

August 3, 1745. November 20, 1750. *Son and Executor:* ROBERT ("the manner plantation"). *Daughter:* MARY. *Granddaughter:* MARY SPENCE. *Witnesses:* JOHN JONES, ISAAC JONES, JOHN CAMMILL. Proven before GAB. JOHNSTON.

MURPHY, EDMOND.   Craven County.

March 4, 1745. *Sons:* BENJAMIN and JOSUA ("all my lands"), EDMUND. *Wife and Executrix:* ELIZABETH. *Witnesses:* JAMES TUCKER, WM. FLOOD, · PAUL PHILLIPS. No probate.

MURPHY, JEREMIAH.   Craven County.

November 26, 1750. May Court, 1752. *Son:* THOMAS. *Executors:* GEORGE LANE, THOMAS MURPHY and JOHN LANE. *Witnesses:* JOHN·MURPHY, JANE CARRUTHERS, JNO. CARRUTHERS, JR. *Clerk of the Court:* PHIL. SMITH.

MURPHY, THOMAS.   Craven County.

October 7, 1746. February 27, 1746. *Sons:* THOMAS (plantation on Trent River), JEREMIAH, JOHN. *Daughter:* BRIDGETT MURPHY. *Wife and Executrix:* SARAH. *Witnesses:* JOHN JOHNS, JOHN ABBOTT, JOHN PETER REMM. Proven before GABRIEL JOHNSTON.

MURPHEY, WILLIAM.   Edgecombe County.

January 23, 1736. May Court, 1737. *Daughters:* MARY and MARTHA MURPHEY (one plantation each), ESTHER MURPHY (negroes). *Other legatees:* WILLIAM HURST, JOSEPH BRADSHAW. *Wife and Executrix:* ANN. *Executors:* JOHN EDWARDS and ISAAC RICKS. *Witnesses:* JOHN POPE, WM. GOODWIN, JOHN STRICKLAND. *Deputy Clerk of the Court:* THOS. HARVEY.

MURRAY, ANDREW.   Onslow County.

February 9, 1745–1746. April 2, 1746. *Devisee:* JAMES HURLEY. *Executor:* STEPHEN LEE. *Witnesses:* FOYE DEXTER, E. CHADWICK, DANIEL SHESLOW, JAMES HOYLE, ELIZABETH HOYLE. *Clerk of the Court:* GEO. CLOPTON.

NAYLER, WILLIAM.   Albemarle County.

April 13, 1696. September 30, 1696. Little River. *Daughters:* MARGARET and MARY "living in Virginia." *Executor:* JOHN KING. *Witness:* MARTHA PLATER. *Clerk of the Court:* W. GLOVER.

NEALE, ABNER.   Craven County.

January 5, 1770. October 14, 1772. *Sons:* ABNER (land on Adams Creek), RICHARD (land bought of WILLIAM CARRUTHERS and MATHEW GODFREY), CHRISTOPHER and PHILIP (to each is given land bounded and described in will), MATHEW (lands on Browns Creek), BARRE (land on Goose Creek). *Daughters:* WINIFRED THOMAS, MARY PITTMAN, wife of JOSEPH PITTMAN, HANNAH NEALE, ELIZABETH NEALE, PATIENCE NEALE. *Grandchildren:* JOHN, ABNER, SARAH and WINIFRED THOMAS. Eight negroes bequeathed. *Wife:* ELIZABETH. *Friends:* JAMES JONES, JOHN

BRYAN, THOMAS COOK, SAMUEL MASTERS, PARMENAS HORTON and JOHN
THOMLINSON. *Executors:* CHRISTOPHER and RICHARD NEALE (sons) and
ROGER JONES. *Witnesses:* ELIJAH JARMAN, ROBERT TURNER, BENJAMIN
CUMMINGS. Proven before Jo. MARTIN.

NEALE, CHARLES.   Albemarle County.

January 7, 1698–1699. *Daughters:* DORCAS, MARY. *Guardian to daughter:* JOHN MACKEELL. *Son:* CHARLES (negroes). *Wife and Executrix:*
MARY. *Witnesses:* JOHN MACKEELL, FRANCIS DELAMARE, JOHN WOODHOUSE, THOMAS BOYD, JOY MARKHAM. *Clerk of the Court:* N. CHEVIN.

NEALE, HENRY.

July 13, 1734. April 30, 1735. *Wife's son:* JOHN SIMPSON. *Sons:*
SAMUEL and HENRY ("my negroes"), THOMAS. *Daughters:* JANE and
ELIZABETH NEALE (one negro each). *Wife:* SUSANAH. *Executors:* JANE
HUSBANDS (sister), SAMUEL HAZELL (cousin), JOSEPH CLARK. *Witnesses:*
THOS. HALL, HANNAH HALL, ELIZ. BRIAN. Proven before GAB. JOHNSTON,
at Cape Fear.

NEEDHAM, THOMAS.   Pasquotank County.

October 6, 1740. July Court, 1743. *Sons:* JOHN, GEDEON, THOMAS (a
plantation to each), CHRISTOFER (one shilling). *Daughter:* ANN. *Executor:* JOHN NEEDHAM (son). *Witnesses:* DENNIS SAWYER, ROBERT TORKSEY. *Clerk of the Court:* THOS. TAYLOR.

NESSFEILD, JOHN.   Bladen County.

March 27, 1764. April 20, 1764. *Wife and Executrix:* ANN. *Other
legatees:* THOMAS WHITE and wife, ANN. *Executor:* JOHN ROBESON of Wilmington. *Witnesses:* HU. WADDELL, JAMES BAILEY, EDW. BRYAN. Proven
before ARTHUR DOBBS. Testator provides for sale of all his estate; proceeds to be invested in young female slaves for use of wife and children.
Impression of dove with olive branch on seal.

NEVIL, BENJAMIN.   Halifax County.

November 15, 1758. September Court, 1759. *Sons:* BENJAMIN ("plantation whereon I now live"), JESSE (plantations in Edgecombe and Granville Counties). *Daughter:* ELIZABETH NEVIL (one negro). *Wife and
Executrix:* ELIZABETH. *Witnesses:* JOHN MARSHALL, AMY MARSHALL,
ROBART SANDERS. *Clerk of the Court:* JOS. MONTFORT.

NEVILL, FRANCIS.

April 16, 1735. April 20, 1735. Little River. *Legatees:* JAMES COLLINS
and wife, LUCE; JOHN ARMOR ("my bote"), "Old Madum Britt my ring

the pose in thy brest my heart dothe rest." *Executor:* JAMES COLLINGS. *Witnesses:* THOMAS BEDFORD, WILLIAM ALLIN. *Clerk of the Court:* JOHN PARKER. *Justice of the Peace:* JNO. PALIN.

NEWBY, BENJAMIN.   Pasquotank County.

November 13, 1739. January Court, 1739. *Sons:* JOSEPH (tract of land), BENJAMIN ("the manner plantation"). *Daughter:* SARAH NEWBY. *Wife and Executrix:* SUSANAH. *Executor:* JOHN OVERMAN. *Witnesses:* JAMES NEWBY, JOHN ROBINSON, JOHN LOW. *Clerk of the Court:* JAMES CRAVEN.

NEWBY, EDWARD.

August 6, 1717. *Brother:* WILLIAM. *Father and Executor:* GABRIEL NEWBY. *Witnesses:* BENJAMIN SANDERS, NATHAN and WILLIAM NEWBY. Original missing. Recorded in Book 1712–1722, page 270.

NEWBY, FRANCIS.   Perquimans County.

March 18, 1743–1744. April Court, 1744. *Sons:* ROBERT and JESSE ("my plantation"), MARK and FRANCIS. *Daughters:* MARGARET and SARAH (one negro each). *Executors:* ROBERT, MARK, FRANCIS and JESSEE NEWBY. *Witnesses:* SUSANNAH WOOD, MARY WILSON, RT. WILSON. *Clerk of the Court:* EDMUND HATCH.

NEWBY, FRANCIS.   Perquimans County.

January 8, 1752. July Court, 1752. *Brothers:* THOMAS NEWBY, NATHAN NEWBY (all "my lands and houses"), JOHN ROBINSON. *Mother and Executrix:* MARY MOOR. *Witnesses:* ZACH. NIXON, RALPH FLETCHER, ELESABETH NIXON. *Clerk of the Court:* EDMUND HATCH.

NEWBY, GABRIEL.

March 26, 1733. March 1, 1735. *Sons:* JOSEPH (plantation of 300 acres), JESSE (300 acres of land), SAMUEL ("my maner plantation" and also two negroes), FRANCIS. *Grandson:* WILLIAM NEWBY (300 acres of land). *Other legatees:* RICHARD and MARY MOORE. *Wife and Executrix:* MARY. *Witnesses:* WILLIAM HILL, THOMAS MUSE, THOMAS NICHOLSON. Proven before W. SMITH, C. J.

NEWBY, JAMES.   Pasquotank County.

November 24, 1739. January Court, 1743. *Son:* JACOB. *Son-in-law:* EDWARD WARD. *Daughters:* SARAH, MAGDALENE and MARY NEWBY. *Wife and Executrix:* HANAH. *Witnesses:* HENRY RAPER, THOMAS OVERMAN, JOSEPH ROBINSON. *Clerk of the Court:* THO. TAYLOR.

NEWBY, JOSEPH.   Perquimans County.

January 22, 1726. April 21, 1735. *Wife and Executrix:* MARY. No other legatee mentioned. *Witnesses:* NATHAN NEWBY, PETER PEARSON, J. JESSOP. *Clerk of the Court:* JAMES CRAVEN. Coat of arms on seal.

NEWBY, JOSEPH.   Perquimans County.

May 2, 1752. July Court, 1752. *Wife:* ELISABETH. *Daughter:* MARY. *Executors:* SAMUEL NEWBY and JOSEPH WHITE (uncles). *Witnesses:* SAMUEL MOÒRE, SARAH MOORE, ZACHARIAH MORRIS. *Clerk of the Court:* EDMUND HATCH. Coat of arms on seal.

NEWBY, MARY.   Perquimans County.

October 13, 1739. January Court, 1739. *Son:* JOSEPH MAYO. *Daughter:* ELIZABETH WILLSON. *Grandchildren:* JOHN WILLSON, EDWARD, JEMIMA and ISABELL NEWBY. *Niece:* ELIZABETH WINSLOW. *Executors:* JOHN WILLSON and SAMUEL NEWBY (sons-in-law). *Witnesses:* WILLIAM SITGREAVES, SARAH ELLIT, MIRIAM BOGUE. *Clerk of the Court:* JAMES CRAVEN.

NEWBY, NATHAN.   Perquimans County.

April 1, 1735. October Court, 1735. *Sons:* THOMAS (plantation on Cypress Swamp), FRANCIS ("land whereon I now live"), NATHAN (230 acres of land). *Daughter:* MARY NEWBY. *Wife and Executrix:* MARY. *Executor:* THOMAS NEWBY (brother) and ZACHARIAH NIXON. *Witnesses:* ZACHARIAH NIXON, SENR., FRANCIS TOMES, MARY GIBENS. *Clerk of the Court:* JAMES CRAVEN.

NEWBY, SAMUEL.   Perquimans County.

December 9, 1737. January Court, 1737. *Friends:* JOHN NIXON and ZACHARIAH NIXON. *Cousins and Executors:* THOMAS OVERMAN and JEMES NEWBY. *Witnesses:* ZACHARIAH NIXON, JOSEPH ROBINSON, MARY NIXON. *Clerk of the Court:* JAMES CRAVEN.

NEWBY, WILLIAM.

January 11, 1718–1719. *Wife and Executrix:* ANN. *Witnesses:* SARAH LATON, SARAH PEIRCE, GABRIEL NEWBY. Original missing. Recorded in Book 1712–1722, page 279.

NEWNAM, THOMAS.

September 21, 1723. November 22, 1723. "Now residing at Edenton in North Carolina as Missionary from the Honble the Society for propagating the Gospel in Foreign Parts." *Wife, Exeeutrix and sole legatee:* FRANCES. *Witnesses:* C. GALE, SARAH LLOYD and JOHN FRYARS. Proven before CHRISTOPHER GALE, *Chief Justice.* Coat of arms on seal representing a winged lion.

NEWSUM, JOEL.   Northampton County.

January 10, 1751. February Court, 1752. *Sons:* HOSEA and JOHN ("my plantation to be divided between them"), DAVID, JOEL, WILLIAM and ISAAC (the rest of estate to be divided among them). *Daughter:* MARY NEWSUM. *Executors:* WILLIAM HILYARD (brother), JOHN DUKE. *Witnesses:* ROBT. PEELLE (Quaker), JOHN DICKINSON, ALEXANDER O'QUIN. *Clerk of the Court:* I. EDWARDS.

NEWTON, CHRISTOPHER.   Perquimans County.

May 11, 1759. July Court, 1759. *Wife and Executrix:* SARAH. *Daughter:* CONSTANT. *Witnesses:* THOMAS GILBERT, WALTER NEWTON. *Clerk of the Court:* MILES HARVEY.

NEWTON, THOMAS.   Bladen County.

September 7, 1765. *Son:* JOHN ("my saw mill"). *Daughter:* JANE NEWTON. *Wife and Executrix:* MARY ("my negroes"). *Executor:* CORNELIUS HARNETT. *Witnesses:* WILL'M BARTRAM, JACOB MEZIES. No probate.

NICE, WILLIAM.

April 24, 1757. May Court, 1758. "On Board the Brigantine Hawke of War, THOMAS WRIGHT, Commander." *Sisters:* JANE and KATHERINE NICE in the shire of Murray in Great Britain. *Mother:* JENNET NICE. *Executor:* THOMAS CUNINGHAM. *Witnesses:* JOHN BLYTH, BENJAMIN STONE. *Clerk of the Court:* JA. MORAN.

NICHOLAS, NATHANIEL.   Bertie County.

September 17, 1755. October Court, 1755. This is a nuncupative will proven by THOMAS HUDSON, GEORGE HANDLY and WILLIAM WILLEFORD, and gives to *sons,* JOSAH and WILLIAM NICHOLAS, one plantation each. *Daughter:* ELIZABETH. *Justice:* JOHN BROWN. *Clerk of the Court:* BENJN. WYNNS.

NICHOLSON, JOSEPH.   Albemarle County.

August 6, 1679. January Court, 1697–1698. Plantation on Perquimans River to *brother,* JOHN NICHOLSON. *Brothers:* BENJAMIN, SAMUEL, JOHN, NATHANIEL, CHRISTOPHER. *Executors:* SAML. and JOHN NICHOLSON. *Witnesses:* GABRIEL NUBY, MARY NUBY, THOS. OVERMAN. *Clerk of the Court:* JOHN STEPNEY.

NICHOLSON, NATHANIEL.   Perquimans County.

March 12, 1731–1732. July Court, 1737. *Son:* JONATHAN ("my plantation"). *Daughters:* SARAH and ELIZABETH NICHOLSON. *Wife and Executrix:* SARAH. *Executor:* ZACHARIAH NIXON. *Witnesses:* ALIXANDER STUARD, PETER ALBARDSON. *Clerk of the Court:* JAMES CRAVEN.

NICHOLSON, SAMUEL.

March 22, 1727–1728. No date of probate. *Daughters:* SARAH and ELIZABETH NICHOLSON. *Friend:* SARAH GLOSTER. *Wife and Executrix:* ELIZABETH. *Executor:* JOHN ANDERSON (son-in-law). *Witnesses:* ZACHARIAH NIXON, JOHN KEATON, ELISABETH MONTECUE. *Clerk of the Court:* CHARLES DENMAN.

NICHOLSON, WILLIAM. Currituck County.

1721. October Court, 1723. *Sons:* JOSIAH ("my manner plantation"). ANTHONY and THEOFILUS NICHOLSON. *Daughters:* SOPHIA, NAOMY and ——— NICHOLSON. *Executor:* JOSIAH NICHOLSON (son). *Witnesses:* DOYLEY LATTER, ANDREW HUDDEY, JOHN CRABB. *Clerk of the Court:* JO. WICKER.

NICKOLLS, JAMES. Currituck County.

July 13, 1742. October Court, 1743. *Sons:* JAMES ("ye manard plantation"), CALEB (plantation), WILLIS (plantation over the River called Dunkins). *Daughters:* SARAH and FRANKEY NICKOLLS. *Executor:* JOHN ETHERIDGE. *Witnesses:* JAMES BUTT, DARCKES THOMAS, WILLIAM ETHERIDGE. *Clerk of the Court:* JOHN LURRY.

NICKOLSON, CHRISTOFER. Perquimans County.

May 17, 1723. July 23, 1723. *Son:* THOMAS ("my plantation"). *Daughters:* MARIAM, DABORA, MARY and ANN NICKOLSON. *Wife and Executrix:* MARY. *Executor:* SAMUEL NICKOLSON (brother). *Witnesses:* JEAMES NEWBY, SOLOMON POOL, RICHARD POOL. *Clerk of the Court:* RICHARD LEARY.

NICKOLSON, JOSIAH. Currituck County.

January 22, 1749–1750. April County Court, 1750. *Sons:* JOHN and JOSIAS ("my land to be divided between them"). To JOHN is also given one negro, and to *son* WILLIAM is given one negro. *Daughter:* CLARE. *Wife and Executrix:* HANNAH. *Witnesses:* BENJAMIN CRABB, PACHANCE EVRAGE, ALEXANDER TRAQUAIR. *Clerk of the Court:* RICH'D McCLURE.

NICKSON, THOMAS. Northampton County.

December 1, 1752. February Court, 1753. *Brothers:* JOSEPH and HENRY NICKSON. *Sister:* SARAH JINER. *Executors:* ABRAHAM STEVENSON, JUNR., and WILLIAM ANDREWS. *Witnesses:* WILLIAM TURNER, MARTHA MORE. *Clerk of the Court:* I. EDWARDS.

NICOLS, JOHN.

April 26, 1710. August 12, 1712. *Son:* SAMUEL (land on Sutens Creek). *Daughters:* MARY and HANNAH NICOLS. *Wife and Executrix:* PRESSILLA. *Executor:* SAMUEL NICOLS (father). *Witnesses:* FRANCIS FISHER, ANN DARMAN, HANNAH MODLING. No probate officer.

NIXON, ELIZABETH.   Perquimans County.

March 19, 1747–1748. January Court, 1748. *Son-in-law:* JOHN ANDERSON. *Daughters:* ELIZABETH ANDERSON, SARAH JONES. *Grandsons:* SAMUEL, JOHN and JOSEPH ANDERSON. *Granddaughter:* SARAH ANDERSON. *Friend:* ELIZABETH ALBERTSON, daughter of JOSHUA ALBERTSON. *Executors:* JOHN ANDERSON and JOSEPH ANDERSON. *Witnesses:* THOMAS OVERMAN, JOSHUA ALBERTSON, THOMAS NICHOLSON. *Clerk of the Court:* EDMUND HATCH.

NIXON, JOHN.   Pasquotank Precinct.

February 4, 1687–1688. August 8, 1692. *Wife and Executrix:* EM. *Daughter:* ANN NIXON. *Witnesses:* HENDERSON WALKER, RICHARD PLATER, FRANCIS TOMES, EDWARD MAYO. *Clerk of the Court:* FRANCIS TOMES.

NIXON, RICHARD.   Craven County.

March 5, 1745–1746. June Court, 1746. *Son:* RICHARD (land on Topsail Sound). *Daughters:* GARTRY NIXON (land on southwest), MARY NIXON (land on New Topsail Creek). *Wife and Executrix:* MARY (three negroes). *Executors:* THOMAS GRAVES (brother-in-law), JOHN FONVIELLE. *Witnesses:* JOHN OLIVER, WHEELWRT. PEARSON. *Clerk of the Court:* JNO. RICE. Will provides for investment of proceeds of sale of part of estate in young negroes.

NIXON, ZACHARIAH.   Perquimans County.

September 28, 1739. October Court, 1739. *Sons:* JOHN, PHINEAS, ZACHARIAH, BARNABY (to each is given a plantation, and to all four is given a sawmill and gristmill). *Friend:* MICHAEL MURPHY (land known by the name of Oak Ridge). *Daughter:* REBEKAH TOMS (one negro). To wife is given one-half of negroes. *Executors:* JOHN, PHINEAS and ZACHARIAH NIXON (sons). *Grandchildren:* JOSHUA and MARY MOORE. *Witnesses:* THOMAS OVERMAN, JOHN CHARLES, JOSEPH ROBINSON. OVERMAN and ROBINSON were Quakers. *Clerk of the Court:* JAMES CRAVEN.

NIXON, ZACHARIAH.   Perquimans County.

July 9, 1752. July Court, 1752. *Sons:* FRANCIS, ZACHARIAH (to each is given lands and a lot in Nixon town). *Daughter:* MEHETIBLE NIXON. *Wife and Executrix:* ELIZABETH. *Executor:* JOSEPH WHITE. *Witnesses:* JOHN NIXON, PHINEUS NIXON, MARK NEWBY. *Clerk of the Court:* EDMUND HATCH.

NOBLE, SAMUEL.   Carteret County.

December 26, 1776. January 14, 1776. "As it is customary to bequeath Both The Mortle and Immortal Parts I leave one to the Discression of my Executor and the other to the Marcies of God through my Lord & Savour

Jesus Christ." *Sons:* MARK (land between Miery Branch and White Oak River), WILLIAM (100 acres of land), SAMUEL ("plantation whereon I now live lying between the Black Swamp & Mire branch"). *Daughters:* MARY MAGDILIN BARRY, BETTIE, RACHEL and NANCY NOBLE. *Nephew:* JAMES HOUSTON. *Executors:* MARK, WILLIAM and SAMUEL NOBLE. *Witnesses:* JOHN MUNDINE, BRICE WILLIAMS, LEVI WEST. Proven before RICHARD CASWELL.

NOBLE, WILLIAM.   Bath County.

October 22, 1723. June Court, 1724. *Sons:* SAMUEL and WILLIAM (land to be divided between them), JOSEPH (land on White Oak River), JAMES. *Daughter:* HANAH NOBLE. *Wife and Executrix:* ELISABETH. *Witnesses:* ROBERT SMITH, JOHN STARKEY, THOMAS HOLSTON. *Clerk of the Court:* JOHN BAPTISTE ASHE.

NOBLELAND, JOHN.   Edgecombe County.

August 12, 1755. November Court, 1755. *Daughters:* MATHEW and REBECCA NOBLELAND, MARY COTTON. *Wife and Executrix:* MARY. *Witnesses:* WM. OGILVIE, NATHANIEL MERRITT, WILLIAM RAINWATER. *Clerk of the Court:* JOS. MONTFORT.

NORCOM, JOHN.   Chowan Precinct.

July 26, 1728. September 30, 1728. *Sons:* THOMAS ("plantation I now live on"), STEPNEY, WILLIAM, JOHN, CORNELUS, JEAMES. *Daughters:* SARAH, MARY, ELISABETH. *Wife:* JEAN. *Executor:* THOMAS NORCOM. *Friends:* WILLIAM EGERTON, JOHN CHASTEN, JOHN SIMONS, ABRAHAM WARREN. Proven before RICHARD EVERARD.

NORCOM, JOHN.   Chowan County.

February 4, 1745. April Court, 1746. *Daughters:* SARAH and ANN. *Wife and Executrix:* ANN. *Executor:* JOHN HALSEY. *Witnesses:* JOHN PEIRCE, LEVY HAUGHTON, MARY SHELDIN. *Clerk of the Court:* JAMES CRAVEN.

NORCOM, MARY.   Chowan County.

May 19, 1718. November 1, 1721. *Sons:* JOHN NORCOM (*Executor*), THOMAS NORCOM. *Daughters:* SARAH, wife of JAMES SMITH; MARY, wife of THOMAS BLICHENDEN. *Granddaughter:* MARY HOPTON. *Grandson:* ABRAHAM WARRIN. *Witnesses:* THOMAS WHITTIS, CORNELIUS LEARY, RICH'D LEARY. *Clerk of the Court:* R. HICKS.

NORCOM, THOMAS.   Perquimans Precinct.

May 13, 1707. October 29, 1707. *Sons:* THOMAS and WILLIAM ("my plantation"), JOHN. *Daughters:* ELIZABETH, MARY and SARAH NORCOM.

Grandson: THOMAS NORCOM. *Wife and Executrix:* mentioned, but not named. *Witnesses:* JAMES MING, WALTER TANER. *Clerk of the Court:* J. KNIGHT.

NORCOM, THOMAS.   Perquimans County.

April 23, 1741. April Court, 1744. *Son:* THOMAS ("plantation I now live on left me by the will of my father THOMAS NORCOM"). *Grandson:* RICHARD WHIDBEE (plantation on Sound side joining Lacinse's Creek; also three negroes). *Nephew:* JOHN NORCOM, son of brother, JOHN NORCOM. *Wife and Executrix:* SUSANNA. *Witnesses:* SAMUEL STANDING and JOSEPH ARNOLD. *Clerk of the Court:* EDMUND HATCH.

NORCOM, THOMAS.   Perquimans County.

May 12, 1748. October Court, 1748. *Wife:* MARTHA. *Son:* FREDERICK. *Executor:* JOHN HALSEY. *Witnesses:* GEORGE CHARLTON, MARY HALSEY. *Clerk of the Court:* EDMUND HATCH.

NORFLEET, JAMES.   Perquimans Precinct.

November 28, 1732. January 15, 1732–1733. *Sons:* JOHN ("my plantation, orchards and houses", still, worm and cap, one large silver tankard weighing 33 oz. 16 pwt.; three negroes); THOMAS (three negroes and silver cup, spoon and tobacco box). Cattle divided between sons. *Daughters:* MARY, SARAH, MARGARET and FELISHA NORFLEET. *Wife:* MARY. *Executors:* THOMAS NORFLEET (brother) and WILLIAM HINTON. *Witnesses:* JOHN GORDON, SENR., JOHN GORDON, JUNR., GEORGE GORDON, MARMADUKE NORFLEET. *Clerk of the Court:* CHARLES DENMAN.

NORFLEET, JOHN.   Chowan County.

September 10, 1753. April Court, 1754. *Sons:* ABRAHAM (plantation on Rockahock Creek), JACOB (plantation and houses), JOHN and JAMES *Daughter:* PATIENCE. *Wife and Executrix:* ELISABETH. Gristmill and still ordered to be sold and proceeds divided among children; also island containing 316 acres to be so divided. *Executors:* JOHN and JAMES NORFLEET (sons). All negroes bequeathed to wife. *Witnesses:* DAVID JONES, WILLIAM GWINN, LUKE SUMNER. *Clerk of the Court:* WILL HALSEY.

NORFLEET, MARMADUKE.   Halifax County.

June 29, 1762. November 6, 1762. *Brother:* LEMUEL HOGAN. *Sister:* ELIZABETH NORFLEET (three negroes and silver punch bowl and tankard). *Other legatees:* children of JOHN YOUNG and JOSHUA BEEL. *Executor:* JAMES HOGAN (father-in-law). *Witnesses:* JOHN MORRIS, ELISABETH NORFLEET, THOS. JOYNER, THOMAS KITCHING. Proven before ARTHUR DOBBS, at Newbern.

NORFLEET, MARY.   Perquimans County.

October 12, 1742. January Court, 1742. *Daughters:* MARGARET and
FELISHA NORFLEET. *Executor:* JAMES SUMNER. *Witnesses:* JOSEPH RID-
DICK, JOHN GORDON, JOSEPH GORDON. *Clerk of the Court:* EDMUND HATCH.
Impression of ship on seal.

NORFLEET, THOMAS.   Edgecombe County.

January 23, 1745. August Court, 1746. *Sons:* THOMAS and MARMA-
DUKE (all land of testator to be divided between them; to each is given
three negroes and to MARMADUKE is given one silver tankard and one still
"and worms"). *Daughters:* SARAH, FARBEY, SUSANAH, MARY, ELISBETH.
Wife and Executrix: RUTH. *Executor:* MARMADUKE NORFLEET (brother).
Witnesses: ROBERT HILLIARD, JOHN BLUNT. *Clerk of the Court:* RT. FOR-
STER.

NORMAN, JOHN.   Onslow County.

March 6, 1753. October 2, 1753. *Sons:* JOHN and WILLIS (to each is
given land), PETER (land on Ashes banks). *Daughter:* SARAH NORMAN.
Wife and Executrix: MARY. *Witnesses:* ELIZABETH CARY, JOB HUNTER,
JNO. HUNT. *Clerk of the Court:* JOHN MILTON. Coat of arms on seal.

NORRIS, WILLIAM.   Pasquotank County.

March 24, 1724. *Wife, Executrix and sole legatee:* SUSANAH. *Witnesses:*
DAN'LL GUTHRIE, ZACHARIAH FEILD. *Clerk of the Court:* JOHN PARKER.

NORTHEM, JOHN.   Currituck Precinct.

1712. July 14, 1714. *Wife and Executrix:* ELIZABETH. *Sons:* JOHN
and PHILIP ("plantation whereon I now live known by the name of Powels
Point"). Two negroes bequeathed to each of sons. *Witnesses:* DANIEL
MCFARLAND, JOHN WHEDBEE, JOHN BASSFORD. *Clerk of the Court:* JO.
WICKER.

NORTON, JOHN.   Currituck County.

September 30, 1744. July 2, 1745. *Sons:* WILLIAM, JOHN, JONATHAN,
ASAC. *Daughters:* ABGILL, METABLE, HANAH. *Executors:* WM. and JOHN
NORTON (sons). *Witnesses:* JONA. TAGNESS, MARGARET RUSSELL, MARY
NORTON. *Clerk of the Court:* RICH'D MCCLURE.

NORTON, WILLIAM.   Bladen County.

December 1, 1746. September Court, 1751. *Sons:* WILLIAM, DANIEL,
JACOB, THOMAS. *Daughter:* ELIZBETH. *Executors:* JACOB and THOMAS
NORTON. *Witnesses:* WM. LEWIS, JOHN MITCHELL, JOSIAH LEWIS. *Clerk
of the Court:* THOS. ROBESON.

NORWOOD, GEORGE.   Northampton County.

April 21, 1749.   August Court, 1749.   *Sons:* SAMUEL (300 acres of land on the River; "one-third part of my still, one-half of my Quince orchard, one-third part of the fruit of my apple orchard, one of the three Pare trees that which stands nearest the river called Norwood's Pare and four of the Catteron Pare trees"), WILLIAM (cattle at Nutbush and one negro). *Grandsons:* GEORGE NORWOOD, son of NATHANIEL (240 acres of land, one horse and one negro girl), NATHANIEL NORWOOD, son of NATHANIEL (310 acres of land at the mouth of Green's Creek, and one negro), JOHN NORWOOD, son of WILLIAM (160 acres of land on Green's Creek, and one negro girl). *Granddaughters:* ELIZABETH, MARY and SARAH, daughters of NATHANIEL NORWOOD. "I give Ten Pounds, Twelve shilling and Six pence Virginia Money to be made in rings with the first letters of my name engraven on them for each grand child I have." *Executors:* WILLIAM, NATHANIEL and SAMUEL NORWOOD (sons). *Witnesses:* JOHN JUSTIS, WILLIAM WOOTEN. *Clerk of the Court:* I. EDWARDS.

NORWOOD, THOMAS.   Craven County.

December 26, 1757.   March 24, 1758.   *Son:* WILLIAM (one shilling). *Wife, Executrix and sole legatee:* FRANCES. *Witnesses:* HENRY INCE, SISSELY NORWOOD.   Proven before ARTHUR DOBBS.

NORWOOD, WILLIAM.   Craven County.

December 30, 1747.   November 14, 1748.   *Sister:* MARY LANE. *Niece:* MARY NEVIN. *Brother:* THOMAS NORWOOD. *Nephew:* JOHN NORWOOD. *Executors:* WALTER LANE and BARNABAS RUSSELL. *Witnesses:* THOS. PEARSON, JOSEPH BALCH, W. BETTS, THOMAS PEARSON, JUNR.   Proven before E. HALL, *Chief Justice.*

NUSUM, RICHARD.   Bertie County.

February 11, 1753.   August Court, 1753.   *Wife:* ELIZABETH. *Daughter:* MARY SKINNER. *Grandchildren:* MARY ANDREWS, MARTHA SKINNER. REBECCA, SARAH, LYDIA and ELBE SKINNER (all children of MARY). *"Grandson-in-law" and Executor:* WILLIAM ANDREWS. *Witnesses:* ABRAHAM HARRELL, JOHN HARRELL, FRANCIS HARRELL. *Clerk of the Court:* SAM'L ORMES.

OATES, JAMES.   Albemarle Precinct.

July 24, 1703.   January Court, 1703–1704.   *Son:* JOSEPH OATES.   *Wife:* ELIZABETH OATES.   JONATHAN EVINS.   *Executrix:* ELIZABETH OATES. *Witnesses:* JOSEPH SMITH, JAMES COLES.   *Clerk of the Court:* THO. SNODEN.

O'BRIAN, DARBE.   Perquimans Precinct.

February 18, 1723–1724. July 6, 1725. *Legatees:* JOSEPH POTTLE,
JOASHAY WILLEBEE, WILLIAM EVANS (*Executor*). *Witnesses:* ANTHO.
HATCH, JOSEPH GODFREY, TEMPERANCE PENRICE. Proven before GEO.
BURRINGTON.

O'DANIEL, OWEN.   Bertie Precinct.

March 12, 1735–1736. May Court, 1736. *Wife and Executrix:* ELIZA-
BETH. *Executors:* JAMS ROBERTS, LEWIS FRYER and MICHL. RUSSEE.
Witnesses: WILLIAM KENNADAY, FRA. HOBSON, ROBT. ANDERSON. *Clerk
of the Court:* JNO. WYNNS.

ODEON, CHARLES.   Beaufort County.

March 11, 1733. June Court, 1736. *Son:* RICHARD (lands on Town
Creek, "at the mouth of the Creek I now live on," and "plantation I now
live on"). *Wife and Executrix:* ELISABETH. *Witnesses:* WM. THORNE,
WILLIAM CRAWLEY, JNO. WOODARD. *Clerk of the Court:* JOHN COLLISON.

ODOM, JACOB.   Bertie Precinct.

February 16, 1735–1736. November Court, 1736. *Sons:* RICHARD,
THOMAS, ABRAHAM (to each is given land). *Daughter:* SARAH ODOM. *Wife
and Executrix:* SUSAN. *Witnesses:* JOHN THOMAS and JOHN JENKINS.
Clerk of the Court: JNO. WYNNS.

ODOM (spelled also ODEOM), JOHN.   Beaufort County.

October, 1740. March Court, 1741. *Son:* JOHN ("my plantation and
three negroes"). *Daughters:* MARTHA, ANN, LIDEA and EDY ODOM. *Executors:* JOHN ODOM (son) and LEVI ALDERSON. *Witnesses:* SIMON ALDER-
SON, CHARLES WHITEHURST, JOHN ALDERSON. *Clerk of the Court:* JNO.
FORBES.

ODOM, RICHARD.   Chowan County.

August 12, 1727. January 24, 1728. *Sons:* RICHARD and JOHN, ABRA-
HAM, JACOB and ARON (to each is given a plantation). *Daughters:* ANN,
SARAH, ELIZABETH and JANE ODUM. *Wife:* ANNE. *Executors:* RICHARD
and ABRAHAM ODUM (sons). *Witnesses:* EDWARD WARREN, EDWARD
VANN, JAMES BRADY and RICHARD TAYLOR. Proven before C. GALE, C. J.

ODYER, DENNIS.   Johnston County.

February 16, 1746. June Court, 1746. *Daughter:* MARY ODYER. *Wife:*
ANN. *Executors:* AMBROSS ARIS and JOHN CLARK. *Clerk of the Court:*
WILL HODGES; court held at the house of FRANCIS ARINGER on Nuce River.

O'FEYE, DANIELL.   Pasquotank Precinct.

January 18, 1708. *Executor and sole legatee:* JOHN KEMBELL. *Witnesses:* JOHN DANE, JOHN SPARNOR, JOHN ISKET. *Clerk of the Court:* JOHN BISHOP.

OLDFIELD, RICHARD.   Onslow County.

April 19, 1773. September 9, 1773. *Sons:* PITTS ("my house and plantation"), RICHARD, REUBEN, PETER. *Daughters:* NANCE, SARAH and EXSPERANCE OLDFIELD. *Wife:* MARY. *Executors:* PETER STARKEY, EDWARD MORLY. *Witnesses:* WILLIAM CONNAWAY, MARY PITTS, GAIN PITTS. Proven before JO. MARTIN.

OLIVER, FRANCES.   Chowan County.

February 27, 1754. October Court, 1756. *Son-in-law:* JOHN DAVISON of Edenton. *Executor:* JOHN DAVISON. *Other legatees:* Brothers and sister in Virginia, not named. Negroes emancipated. *Witnesses:* ANTHONY CARTEEL, ELIZABETH FLOOD, LEONARD COTTON. *Clerk of the Court:* THOMAS JONES. *Executor* qualified before PETER HENLEY.

OLIVER, JOSEPH.

March 29, 1734. June 11, 1737. *Sons:* THOMAS and JOHN (*Executors*). *Daughter:* SIDNEY OLIVER. *Witnesses:* JOHN MACKEEL, THOMAS MACKEEL and MARTHA MASON. Proven before W. SMITH, C. J.

OLIVER, MOSES.   Chowan Precinct.

January 1, 1728–1729. January 9, 1728. *Executor:* CHARLES RICKETTS. *Legatees:* Children of CHARLES RICKETTS, not named. *Witnesses:* ROBERT JEFFREYS, JOHN GLOVER. Proven before RICHARD EVERARD.

OLIVER, THOMAS.   Hatteras, in Currituck County.

February 4, 1743–1744. April Court, 1745. *Sons:* JOSEPH (plantation called Oyster shell banks), THOMAS (plantation called Peachtree Ridge). *Daughter:* SARAH OLIVER. *Wife and Executrix:* PHEBE. *Executor:* JOB CARR (father-in-law). *Witnesses:* GEORGE HOWARD, ELIZABETH JACKSON, GEORGE SCARBOROUGH. *Clerk of the Court:* RICHD. MCCLURE.

O'NEAL, MICHAEL.   Currituck County.

September 15, 1721. January 10, 1721–1722. *Sons:* CHARLES ("my dwelling plantation"), MICHAEL. *Wife and Executrix:* DEBORAH. *Daughters:* MARY and ELIZABETH O'NEAL and SARAH WALKER. *Friend:* HUMPHREY VINCE. *Witnesses:* ANDREW PEACOCK, WILLIAM BELL, JOHN CRABB. *Clerk of the Court:* JO. WICKER.

18

O'NEAL, MICHAEL.   Currituck Precinct.

March 3, 1722–1723.   April 9, 1723.   *Sons:* MICHAEL (plantation at Coinjock), THOMAS.   *Daughter:* SARAH O'NEAL.   *Wife and Executrix:* THOMAZIN.   *Witnesses:* THOMAS PARKER, ELIZABETH HANER, RICHD. CHURCH.   *Clerk of the Court:* JO. WICKER.

O'QUIN, PATRICK.   Northampton County.

November 23, 1751.   February Court, 1752.   *Sister:* CHARITY GLASSON. *Executor:* THOMAS DEENS.   *Witnesses:* JOHN BROWN, THOMAS COOK, JOHN KNIGHT.   *Clerk of the Court:* I. EDWARDS.

ORINDELL, EDWARD.   Chowan County.

November 11, 1732.   January 8, 1732.   *Sons:* EDWARD ("my plantation"), THOMAS ("land on the Great Swamp").   *Daughters:* RACHEL, MARY and REBECKAH ARENDELL.   *Wife and Executrix:* ISEBELL.   *Executor:* THOMAS PEIRCE.   *Witnesses:* HESHTAN NOE, JOHN BENNET, FRANCIS PETTET.   Proven before GEO. BURRINGTON.

ORMOND, WYRIOTT.   Beaufort County.

March 9, 1773.   December 1, 1773.   *Wife:* ELIZABETH PENELOPE ORMOND (six negroes, one English bay horse and £500 in money).   *Daughters:* NANCY and SARAH ORMOND.   All profits of estate to be invested in young negroes for benefit of daughters.   "My principal desire is that of the education of my daughters * * * and that no expence be thought too great provided etc."   *Executors:* ROGER ORMOND (brother) and GEORGE BARROW.   Will proven by RICHARD CASWELL, THOMAS RESPESS and THOMAS RESPESS, JR., before JO. MARTIN.

OSBORNE, OBEDIAH.   Onslow County.

August 8, 1758.   October Court, 1758.   *Wife and Executrix:* ELISEBETH (six negroes and all other estate).   *Witnesses:* EDWARD WARD, ENOCH WARD.   *Clerk of the Court:* WILL CRAY.

OTTWELL, ISAAC.   Bath County.

October 28, 1732.   Town Creek.   *Daughters:* ELIZABETH and MARY OTTWELL.   *Friends:* EDWARD SALTER and JOHN ODEON.   *Witnesses:* PATRICK MAULE, ABRAHAM ADAMS, ROGER JONES, ANN WARREN.   *Clerk of the Court:* JNO. COLLISON.

OVERMAN, CHARLES.   Pasquotank County.

August 8, 1755.   *Sons:* SAMUEL (plantation), THOMAS, BENJAMIN, ENOCH (two negroes).   *Daughters:* ANN MORGAN, MARY ARMOUR, ELIZABETH ARMOUR, HANNAH DESON.   *Wife:* ANN.   *Executors:* THOMAS NICHOLSON and JOSEPH ROBINSON.   *Witnesses:* JOSEPH MORRIS, DAVID JACKSON, MARY TART.   *Clerk of the Court:* THOS. TAYLOR.

OVERMAN, JACOB.

September 12, 1715. *Son:* EPHRAIM. *Daughter:* MARGARET MACKY. *Wife:* DOROTHY. *Executors:* WILLIAM HAIG and THOS. MACKY. *Witnesses:* JAMES BELL, ROBERT WHEATLEY, THOMAS WOODLEY. No probate.

OVERMAN, JAMES. Pasquotank County.

March 20, 1745–1746. July Court, 1746. *Son:* THOMAS. *Daughter:* HANNAH. *Wife and Executrix:* SUSANNAH. *Witnesses:* THOS. OVERMAN, SAMUEL NEWBY, CHARLES OVERMAN. *Clerk of the Court:* THOS. TAYLOR.

OVERMAN, JOHN. Pasquotank County.

January 29, 1744–1745. April Court, 1745. *Sons:* JOHN ("my mannor plantation"), WILLIAM. *Daughters:* ELIZABETH and SARAH OVERMAN. *Wife and Executrix:* MARY. *Executor:* THOMAS OVERMAN (brother). *Witnesses:* CHARLES OVERMAN, JAMES OVERMAN, JOHN WHITE. *Clerk of the Court:* THOS. TAYLOR.

OVERMAN, JOSEPH. Pasquotank County.

September 22, 1739. October Court, 1739. *Brothers:* EPHRAIM, NATHAN and ISAAC OVERMAN. *Friend and Executor:* NATHANIEL MARTIN. *Witnesses:* JOHN NORRIS, THOMAS PALEN and JOHN MARTIN. *Clerk of the Court:* JAMES CRAVEN.

OVERTON, JOHN. Onslow County.

March 20, 1737–1738. July 4, 1739. *Sons:* JOHN, JAMES, AARON. MOSES, DAVID, JESSE. *Daughters:* SARAH, MARY, NAOMY, ELIZABETH SUSANNAH and ANGEL OVERTON. *Wife and Executrix:* ELIZABETH. *Witnesses:* WM. CRANFORD, JOHN HANSLY. *Clerk of the Court:* WM. CRANFORD. Coat of arms on seal.

OVERTON, ROBERT. Currituck County.

November 12, 1750. April Court, 1753. *Wife, Executrix and sole legatee:* ALES. *Witnesses:* JAMES BURNHAM, CALEB SIKES, EPHRAIM BRIGHT. *Clerk of the Court:* WILLIAM SHERGOLD.

OWENS, JOHN. Tyrrell County.

September 16, 1748. March Court, 1750. *Sons:* ZACHARIAH, THOMAS, JOHN (to each is devised a plantation). *Daughter:* SARAH OWENS. Stock mark of daughter: "crop in ye right ear and over keel in ye left." Stock mark of son JOHN: "a slit in the right ear and a crop in the left"; of son THOMAS: "a crop and over keel on right ear"; of son ZACHARIAH: "a crop and underkeel the left ear." *Wife:* ANN. *Executors:* WIFE and son ZACHARIAH. *Witnesses:* NATHANEL SPEENCE WESTE, THOMAS and JAMES FOX. *Clerk of the Court:* EVAN JONES. Coat of arms on seal.

OXENWALL, PETER.   Craven Precinct.

September 9, 1730. September Court, 1730. *Wife, Executrix and sole legatee:* ELIZABETH. *Witnesses:* WILLIAM CARRAWAY, JOHN CARRAWAY, JOHN WARD. *Deputy Clerk of the Court:* CALEB METCALF.

PACE, JOHN, SENIOR.   Bertie Precinct.

March 25, 1726–1727. August Court, 1727. *Sons:* JOHN and WILLIAM (*Executors*), GEORGE. *Daughters:* FRANCIS, ANN, ELIZABETH, MARY MELTON. *Wife:* not named. *Witnesses:* ABRAHAM BURTON, JOHN BOBITT, FRANCIS GARNET. *Clerk of the Court:* RT. FORSTER.

PACE, RICHARD.   Bertie Precinct.

March 13, 1736. February Court, 1738. *Sons:* WILLIAM and THOMAS (plantation to each), RICHARD. *Daughters:* ANN STEWARD, REBECKA BRADFORD, AMY GREEN, FRANCIS GREEN, TABITHA MOORE, MARY JOHNSON, SARAH HOUSE. *Wife:* REBECCA. *Executors:* WILLIAM and THOMAS PACE (sons). *Witnesses:* J. EDWARDS, WILL'M BOONE, BENJAMIN DUKES. *Clerk of the Court:* JOHN WYNNS. Impression of lion rampant on seal.

PACQUINET, MICHAEL.   Beaufort County.

March Court, 1747. Will illegible.

PAGETT, EDWARD.   Chowan Precinct.

February 28, 1727–1728. April 18, 1728. *Brother:* SAMUEL. *Wife and Executrix:* not named. Lands on Bear Creek and "manner plantation" devised to wife. *Witnesses:* WILLIAM ASHLEY, JOHN ROBINSON. Proven before RICHARD EVERARD. Original missing. Recorded in Book 1722–1735, page 138.

PAINE, JOHN.   Craven County.

December 29, 1753. March 2, 1754. *Son and Executor:* THOMAS. *Wife:* ANN. *Witnesses:* CASON SCOTT, ANN SNOW, JOHN SPEIGHT. *Clerk of the Court:* JOHN SNEAD.

PAINE, JOHN.   New Hanover County.

January 9, 1767. March 14, 1767. Wilmington. All estate is devised and bequeathed to *wife,* CATHERINE, and *daughter,* CATHERINE MUSGROVE PAINE. Thirteen pounds proclamation money is ordered paid into the hands of "the church wardens of every County in this province, to be by them distributed among the poor inhabitants of the said several Counties." *Mother:* MARY BREWTON. *Sister:* ELIZABETH, wife of FRANCIS ARTHUR in Georgia. *Executors:* MAURICE MOORE and WILLIAM HILL. *Witnesses:* MARY SNOW, ANN MOUAT, WILLIAM MOUAT. Proven before WM. TRYON.

PAINE, SAMUEL.   Currituck County.
January 17, 1715. February 17, 1715. *Legatees:* JOHN MCKENNY,
RACHEL MCKENNY (daughter of JOHN), JAMES, JOHN and GEORGE CAROON.
Executors: JAMES and JOHN CAROON. *Witnesses:* THOMAS CROCKER,
KATHERINE JONES, JAMES TOMOOTH. *Deputy Clerk of the Court:* THOS.
BUTT. *Clerk:* JO. WICKER.

PALIN, HENRY, JR.   Pasquotank Precinct.
January 30, 1700. April 16, 1700. *Sons:* JOHN and THOMAS. *Wife
and Executrix:* ANNE. *Friends:* RICHARD and ELIZABETH HEAT (lands
on Flatty Creek). *Witnesses:* JOHN ROBISON, HUGH CAMPBELL, RICHARD
HEATT. *Clerk of the Court:* THOMAS ABINGTON.

PALIN, JOHN.   Pasquotank County.
August 16, 1737. October Court, 1737. *Son:* JOHN ("my manner
plantation"). *Nephews:* THOMAS and HENRY PALIN. *Daughter:* MARY
CLEARK ("plantation and land at little flatty creek"). *Other legatees:*
GRISELL BULL (2 negroes), MILLICENT BULL (one negro), SARAH and
CHARLETTA BULL (one negro), ANN GEORGE, JOHN PALIN (1 negro).
To son and daughter is bequeathed ten negroes. *Wife and Executrix:*
SARAH. *Witnesses:* DAVID GEORGE, W. REED, MARY GLAISTER. *Clerk
of the Court:* JAMES CRAVEN. Coat of arms on seal.

PALIN, JOHN.   Pasquotank County.
February 15, 1755. December Court, 1755. *Legatees:* SARAH PALMER,
daughter of BENJAMIN PALMER; SAMUEL SWANN, son of WILLIAM SWANN;
ANN WINSLOW. *Executors:* CLARK PEOPLES and JOSEPH SCOTT. *Witnesses:* WILLIAM and THOMAS HOSKINS. *Clerk of the Court:* THOS. TAYLOR.

PALIN, THOMAS.   Pasquotank County.
August 1, 1733. July Court, 1734. *Sons:* HENRY and THOMAS (lands
on Little Flatty Creek). *Daughters:* ANN PALIN, MARY, wife of JOHN
ROSS. *Wife and Executrix:* SUSANNA. *Witnesses:* THOMAS COOK, THOMAS
DAVIS and JOHN PALIN. *Clerk of the Court:* JAMES CRAVEN.

PALIN, THOMAS.   Pasquotank County.
October 22, 1750. *Sons:* THOMAS and HENRY (land and slaves).
Daughter: ANNE. *Wife:* ELIZABETH. No executor named. *Witnesses:*
JOHN HOPKINS, ANNE HOPKINS, THOS. GRAINGER. No probate.

PALMER, JOSEPH.   Pasquotank County.
October 4, 1744. October Court, 1744. *Brothers:* ROBERT PALMER,
BENJAMIN PALMER. *Nephew:* MALICHI PALMER. *Cousin:* THOMAS
PALMER. *Sister:* SARAH PINDLETON. *Witnesses:* JNO. MCKEEL, EMANUEL
KNIGHT, THOMAS PALMER. *Executors:* ROBERT and BENJAMIN PALMER.
Clerk of the Court: THO. TAYLOR.

PALMER, ROBERT.   Pasquotank County.

October 5, 1740. October Court, 1740. *Sons:* ROBERT, BENJAMIN,
JOSEPH (negroes and land given to each of sons). *Grandsons:* ROBERT
and THOMAS PENDLETON, EVAN JONES. *Daughter:* SARAH PENDLETON.
Granddaughter: NANSE PENDLETON. *Wife and Executrix:* MARY ANN.
Witnesses: JOHN HASELL, WILLIAM RYALL, JAMES GEORGE. *Clerk of the
Court:* JAMES CRAVEN.

PALMER, THOMAS.

January 31, 1720–1721. April Court, 1721. *Son:* THOMAS. *Daughter:* MARY PALMER. *Executor:* ROBERT PALMER (brother). *Witnesses:*
ANN IMSON, MARY ———, MATTHEW PRITCHARD. *Clerk of the Court pro
tem.:* JNO. PALIN.

PAQUINET, MICHAEL.   Carteret County.

February 20, 1772. March 6, 1772. *Sons:* JAMES ("plantation whereon
I now live"), JOHN ("100 acres of land on Cane Creek"), ISAIAH (200
acres of land on Broad Creek). *Daughters:* CHARITY, MARY, MARGARET
and REBECKAH PAQUINET. *Wife and Executrix:* MARY. *Witnesses:* JOHN
RUSBULL, SEVERN SCOTT, WM. ROBERTSON. Proven before JO. MARTIN.

PARKER, AZRICAM.   Currituck Precinct.

February 18, 1738. *Sons:* JAMES and THOMAS. *Daughter:* SARAH
PARKER. *Wife and Executrix:* THOMEZON. *Witnesses:* JOSIAS LITTLE,
TIMMOTHY JONES, MICHAEL O'NEAL. *Clerk of the Court:* WILLIAM SHER-
GOLD.

PARKER, FRANCIS.   Edgecombe County.

April 26, 1746. August Court, 1757. *Sons:* FRANCIS, JOSEPH, SIMON
(plantation). *Daughters:* ELIZABETH FOREMAN, CHARITY BRETT, CATH-
ERINE HODGES. *Wife and Executrix:* ELIZABETH. *Witnesses:* GERRARD
WALL, JOHN KNIGHT, WALTER MCFARLAN. *Clerk of the Court:* JOS.
MONTFORT.

PARKER, JOSEPH.   Chowan County.

November 15, 1749. January Court, 1749. *Daughters:* MARY CANNON,
RUTH PARKER, LENINA PARKER. *Sons:* JACOB, TOBE, NATHAN, JOSEPH.
Witnesses: JEREMIAH CANNON, MARY CANNON. *Clerk of the Court:* WILL
MEARNS.

PARKER, MARY.   Edgecombe County.

August 11, 1753. August Court, 1754. *Grandson and sole legatee:*
EDMOND GODWIN. No executor named. *Witnesses:* BENJAMIN BRAND,
MOSES COLEMAN, CORNELIUS JORDAN. *Clerk of the Court:* BENJAMIN
WYNNS.

PARKER, PETER.   Currituck Precinct.

May 2, 1722. July Court, 1722. *Sons:* WILLIAM, WICKER. *Daughters:* SARAH GRIGORY, MARY PARKER, JANE PARKER (land called Beach Ridge), JOANAH PARKER. *Wife and Executrix:* HANAH. *Witnesses:* RICHD. DAUGE, JANE DAUGE, ANN BELL. *Clerk of the Court:* JO. WICKER.

PARKER, PETER.   Currituck County.

April 23, 1750. This is a nuncupative will, proven before STEPHEN WILLIAMS by EDWARD and ELIJAH COX, JOANAH and MIRIAM FEREBEE, and bequeaths all estate to his small children, not named. *Clerk of the Court:* RICHARD MCCLURE.

PARKER, RICHARD.   Chowan County.

September 22, 1749. April Court, 1752. *Sons:* RICHARD, DANIEL, FRANCIS, STEPHEN (about 2,000 acres of land to be divided between the foregoing sons), JONATHAN, JONAS, JACOB, PETER. *Daughters:* ELIZABETH HUNTER, ANN SPRAY, ALICE DAUGHTRY, PATIENCE PARKER. *Grandsons:* RICHARD and WILLIAM PARKER. *Wife and Executrix:* not named. *Witnesses:* JOHN WILLIAMSON, WILLIAM DOUGHTIE, JOHN MOORE. *Clerk of the Court:* JAS. CRAVEN.

PARKER, SIMON.   Edgecombe County.

December 31, 1758. March Court, 1759. *Sons:* FRANCIS, SIMON, WILLIAM, ROBERT (to each is devised a plantation), JAMES. *Daughters:* JUDAH, SARAH, WINNE, CHARITIE and RUTH PARKER. *Wife:* JUDITH. *Executors:* FRANCIS PARKER (brother) and JAMES KNIGHT (brother-in-law). *Witnesses:* CHARLES DANIELL, GIRRARD WALL, MARY CULLENDER. *Clerk of the Court:* JOS. MONTFORT.

PARKER, THOMAS.   Chowan County.

January 23, 1717. October Court, 1717. *Sons:* THOMAS, JOSEPH, JOHN and WILLIAM. *Daughters:* SARAH and FRANCES. *Wife and Executrix:* JEANE. *Witnesses:* JOHN PARKER, HENRY LAM, BENJAMIN EVANS. *Clerk of the Court:* R. HICKS.

PARKER, THOMAS.   Currituck County.

March 16, 1753. March Court, 1755. *Wife:* REBECKAH. *Executors:* EZRICAM PARKER and MICHAEL O'NEIL. *Witnesses:* THOS. TAYLOR, WILLIAM BRABELL, JOHN LURRY. *Clerk of the Court:* WILLIAM SHERGOLD.

PARKER, WILLIAM.   Chowan County.

December 27, 1750. July Court, 1751. *Sons:* JAMES, WILLIAM, THOMAS, BENJAMIN, JOHN. *Daughters:* MARY FRYER and JUDITH DUKE.

Wife and Executrix: ANN.   *Witnesses:* WILLIAM WATERS, HENRY GRIFFEN, DEMSEY SUMNER.   *Clerk of the Court:* JAMES CRAVEN.   Impression of head of Roman soldier on seal.

PARKES, HENRY.   Craven County.

February 27, 1733–1734.   September 17, 1734.   *Godson:* HENRY GRUM. *Wife:* CATHERINE.   No executor.   *Witnesses:* JNO. BRYAN, BENJAMIN GRIFEN.   *Clerk of the Court:* CALEB METCALFE.

PARLEPOUGH, HENRY.   Craven County.

January 27, 1735–1736.   March 17, 1735–1736.   *Executor and sole legatee:* JOHN VENDRICK.   *Witnesses:* JOHN BRYAN, JOHN JACOB HOAVER, SARAH THOMAS.   Proven before RICHARD EVERARD.

PARRISH, JOHN.   Perquimans Precinct.

October 14, 1738.   March 24, 1738.   *Son:* JOHN (plantation and orchard).   *Daughter:* ANNE BARCLIFT (wife of JOHN).   *Grandson:* JOHN BARCLIFT.   *Wife:* MARGERY.   *Executor:* JOHN BARCLIFT, SR.   *Witnesses:* JAMES GIBSON, SAMUEL WRIGHT.   Proven before W. SMITH, C. J.

PARRISHE, WILLIAM.   Edgecombe Precinct.

January 20, 1735–1736.   August Court, 1736.   *Daughter:* SARAH PARRISH.   *Wife and Executrix:* MARY.   *Witnesses:* BUCKLEY KIMBROUGH and ISAAC WINSTON.   *Clerk of the Court:* THOS. KEARNEY.

PARROT, JACOB.   Bertie Precinct.

November 3, 1738.   November 18, 1738.   *Son:* JOHN.   *Daughter:* MARY PARROT.   *Wife:* MARTHA.   *Executors:* WILLIAM FELLTWOOD, EDWARD RASOR.   *Witnesses:* LAMB HARDY, LOVICK YOUNG, SARAH MORPHEW. Proven before W. SMITH, C. J.

PARSONS, SAMUEL.   Perquimans County.

May 12, 1745.   July Court, 1745.   *Sons:* SAMUEL (land on Beaver Cove), BARNABY, JOHN.   *Daughters:* SARAH ARNELL, MARY PARSONS.   *Wife and Executrix:* SARAH.   *Witnesses:* JOHN ANDERSON, LAURENCE ARNEL and JOHN BOYLE.   *Clerk of the Court:* EDMUND HATCH.

PARSONS, THOMAS.   Craven County.

February 13, 1747–1748.   December Court, 1749.   *Sons:* JOHN (one plantation), JEREMIAH, THOMAS (one plantation to each).   *Daughters:* SARAH and MARY PARSONS, ELIZABETH MAISON.   *Executor:* JOHN MAISON. *Witnesses:* THOS. MASTERS, THOS. COOKE, THOS. WARREN LEE.   *Clerk of the Court:* PHIL. SMITH.

PARYER, JOHN. Craven County.

May 1, 1737. June 20, 1738. *Legatees:* WALPOLIA GILLETH, wife of JOHN GILLETH; JOHN WAXDALE. *Executors:* JOHN SIMON, JOHN WAXDALE, WALPOLIA GILLETH. *Witnesses:* PENELLOPE PARROTT, WILLIAM COOPPER, NATHL. PARROTT. *Clerk of the Court:* JAMES COOR.

PASMORE, JOHN. Edgecombe County.

May 19, 1754. November Court, 1754. *Sons:* GEORGE, JOHN, ROBERT, JOSEPH. *Daughters:* ELIZABETH SAMMON, SARAH PASMORE. *Wife:* SARAH. *Executors:* GEORGE and JOHN PASMORE (sons). *Witnesses:* JOHN JACKSON, MOSES PENDRY, JAMES SAMON. *Clerk of the Court:* BENJAMIN WYNNS.

PATCHITT, JOHN. Chowan Precinct.

March 14, 1710–1711. *Wife:* ELIZABETH. *Son:* JOHN ("my planta-tion"). *Executor:* not named. *Witnesses:* DAVID JONES and WILLIAM TANNER. Original missing. Recorded in Book 1712–1722, page 36.

PATTENSON, HENRY. New Hanover County.

July 7, 1751. *Wife:* ANNE. *Witnesses:* THOS. NEWTON, JOHN WALKER. *Clerk of the Court:* ISAAC FARIES.

PATTERSON, GEORGE. Bertie County.

November 19, 1749. December 30, 1749. *Wife and Executrix:* MARY. *Other legatees:* JOHN BURNS, ANN THOMSON, GRISELL BURNS, ANDREW BURNS. *Executors:* JOHN and ANDREW BURNS. *Witnesses:* THOMAS RYAN, ANDREW THOMSON, JAMES FLOOD and DAVID THOMSON. Proven before GAB. JOHNSTON.

PATTERSON, ROBERT.

June 4, 1717. February 15, 1721. *Son:* JOHN. *Daughters:* ELIZABETH and JANET PATTERSON. *Wife and Executrix:* JANET. *Other legatees:* SIMON SIMONS, JOHN PARKE, ANDREW ROSS, ANDREW ROSS, JR., of Nanse-mond County, Va. *Witnesses:* JAMES LONG, JOSIAH BRIDGERS, WILLM. HAWETT, WILLIAM MOORE, JAMES ALLENN, J. FEHENDEN. Proven before CHAS. EDEN.

PAUL, WILLIAM. Northampton County.

May 9, 1744. *Wife, Executrix and sole legatee:* MARY. *Witnesses:* R. WILLIAMS, WM. RUSHING, JOHN PAULL. No probate.

PAYNE, PETER. Chowan County.

March 18, 1754. April Court, 1755. Edenton. *Sons:* WILLIAM (houses and lots in Edenton, silver hilted sword and two negroes), MICHAEL (one negro). *Daughters:* MARY CAROLINA and SARAH EMELIA PAYNE. *Executors:*

JOHN RIEUSSET, JOHN CAMPBELL, THOMAS BARKER. *Witnesses:* JAMES
TROTTER, JOHN MCKILDO, MARY MESIGOOD. *Clerk of the Court:* WILL
HALSEY. Testator pays his respects to JAMES CAMPBELL of Edenton, in the
following language: "she (wife of testator) shall not keep or hold any cor-
respondence with JAMES CAMPBELL of Edenton whom I know to be a man
of infamous character, etc."

PEARCE, ROBERT.   Edenton.

July 11, 1729. Of the city of Exeter, but now of Edenton. This is a
nuncupative will made before C. GALE, G. ALLEYN and ANNE JENOURE and
appoints JOHN LOVICK *Executor* and desires that all remainder of estate
after payment of debts be forwarded to wife at the house of one JOHN HAR-
RIS in Exon, in Devon County, England.

PEARCY, LAZARUS.   Craven County.

April 11, 1760. *Sons:* JOHN, JAMES, EDMON, EPHREM. *Wife and Executrix:* not named. *Witnesses:* EDMUND PEARCE, THOMAS PEARCY, HEZE-
KIAH PEARCE. No probate.

PEARSON, JOHN.   Pasquotank County.

October 8, 1753. June Court, 1755. *Wife and Executrix:* PHEBE. *Witnesses:* MARY JUSTIS, JAMES JUSTIS, JOHN SNOW. *Clerk of the Court:* THOS.
TAYLOR.

PEARSON, RACHEL.   Perquimans County.

June 25, 1750. January Court, 1750. *Sons:* PETER, JOHN and JONA-
THAN PEARSON. *Daughters:* RACHEL BOGUE, MARY WINSLOW, BETTY
BAGLEY. *Executors:* JOHN WINSLOW and ROBERT BOGUE (sons-in-law).
Witnesses: JOSHUA HOBART, ARTHUR CROXEN, JOHN MOORE. *Clerk of the
Court:* EDMUND HATCH.

PEARSON, THOMAS.   Craven County.

December 7, 1748. December Court, 1748. *Sons:* WHEELWRIGHT
(land on "News" River), THOMAS (silver watch), HAMMOND. *Daughters:*
MARY, ELIZABETH, ANNA and EASTER PEARSON. *Parents:* THOMAS and
ELIZABETH PEARSON of Boston. *Executors:* WHEELWRIGHT, THOMAS and
MARY PEARSON (children). *Witnesses:* FRS. STRINGER, JOHN SHINE,
LEM'LL HARVEY. *Clerk of the Court:* PHIL. SMITH.

PEEKE, JAMES.   Bertie County.

November 23, 1728. February Court, 1728. *Son:* WILLIAM. *Execu-
tors:* GEORGE WYNN, THOMAS BANKS and RICHARD OLDNER. *Witnesses:*
ELIZABETH DAVIS, MARTHA LEE, TRIDDLE KEEFE. *Clerk of the Court:* RT.
FORSTER.

PEELLE, JUDITH.   Northampton County.

June 22, 1756. August Court, 1756. *Sons:* JOHN, ROBERT, JOSEPH, JOSIAH, JOSHUA. *Daughters:* SARAH DUKE, MARY GRANBERRY. *Executor:* WILLIAM GRANBERY (son-in-law). *Witnesses:* WILLIAM RUTLAND, ABRAM BRUCE. *Clerk of the Court:* I. EDWARDS.

PEET, WILLIAM.

February 8, 1722–1723. March 12, 1722. "Late of Long Islan in the province of New York." *Sole legatee:* JAMES BULLIN of Chester, in "Penselvany." *Executor:* JAMES NEWBI. *Witnesses:* VALENTINE WALLIS, ANN WALLIS. Proven before WM. REED.

PEGGS, JOHN.   Pasquotank County.

March 20, 1755. June Court, 1755. *Sons:* JOSEPH and JOHN PEGGS (one plantation to each, together with a negro). *Daughters:* MARY and ANN PEGGS. *Executors:* WILLIAM DAVIS, JOHN SMITHIN. *Witnesses:* THOS. HAMLIN, ROBART HOSEA, JONATHAN HOWELL. *Clerk of the Court:* THOS. TAYLOR.

PEGGS, MARGARET.   Pasquotank Precinct.

February 27, 1729. March 14, 1729. *Daughters:* MARY GREGORY, JANE BARECOCK, MIRIAM GREGORY. *Sons:* JOHN PEGGS and PETER BROWN. *Grandsons:* JOHN BROWN, THOMAS BARECOCK. *Granddaughter:* MARY SMITHSON. *Executor:* JOHN PEGGS (son). *Witnesses:* W. MINSON, THOMAS WOODLEY, DANIEL RECKXAKER. Proven before RICHARD EVERARD.

PEIRCE, JOSEPH.   Perquimans County.

1736. October 8, 1736. *Son:* THOMAS ("my plantation whereon I now live"). *Daughters:* MIRIAM (land known as Morises), REBECKAH ("my still"). *Wife and Executrix:* ALIS. *Executor:* THOMAS PEIRCE (brother). *Witnesses:* JOSIAH GILBERT, HANNAH GILBERT, JOSEPH CREECY. Proven before GAB. JOHNSTON.

PENDER, PAUL.   Bertie County.

April 18, 1748. August Court, 1748. *Sons:* JOHN, JOSEPH, SOLOMON, PAUL. *Daughters:* MARY LAURENCE, ELIZABETH LEE, RACHEL ELLIS, CHRISTIAN DAVIS. *Wife:* ELIZABETH. *Executor:* PAUL PENDER (son). *Witnesses:* ALEX. COTTEN, JACOB LASHER. *Clerk of the Court:* JOHN LOVICK.

PENDLETON, HENRY.   Pasquotank County.

March 18, 1727–1728. April 18, 1748. *Daughters:* ELIZABETH WOODLEY, wife of THOMAS; MARY, wife of JOHN BROTHERS; SARAH, wife of JOSEPH REDING; ANNE, wife of THOMAS DAVIS. *Sons:* THOMAS, JOHN.

Grandson: HENRY PENDLETON. *Executor:* THOMAS PENDLETON (son).
Witnesses: SARAH BULL, MARTHA KELLY, JNO. PALIN. Proven before
GAB. JOHNSTON.

PENDLETON, THOMAS.   Pasquotank County.

February 21, 1732. April Court, 1732. *Sons:* THOMAS and JOSEPH
("the manner plantation"), GEORGE, TIMOTHY (plantation called Masons
Neck). *Daughters:* ELIZABETH (plantation called Robinsons), ANNE
KNIGHT. *Wife:* SARAH. *Executors:* THOMAS and JOSEPH PENDLETON
(sons). *Witnesses:* DANIEL ROCKSAKER, WILLIAM DAVIS, J. SWEENY.
Clerk of the Court: W. MINSON.

PENDLETON, THOMAS.   Pasquotank County.

May 10, 1749. April 18, 1750. *Daughters:* PENELOPE JORDAN, MARY,
ELIZABETH. To daughters are given plantations at New Begon Creek, and
also an Island in Currituck Sound called Collinton, and also a number of
negro slaves. *Wife:* not named. *Executor:* JOSEPH JORDAN. *Witnesses:*
DEMSEY CONNER, ROBERT JORDAN, TIMOTHY PENDLETON. Proven before
GAB. JOHNSTON.

PENDLETON, THOMAS.   Pasquotank County.

February 21, 1750–1751. July Court, 1751. *Daughters:* MARY, ELIZA-
BETH, TEMINA PENDLETON. *Son:* ROBERT PENDLETON. *Wife and Exec-
utrix:* SARAH. *Executor:* BENJAMIN PALMER. *Witnesses:* WILL. GREGORY,
JOHN HOSEA, DEMSEY CONNER. *Clerk of the Court:* THOMAS TAYLOR.
Coat of arms on seal.

PENRICE, FRANCIS.   Perquimans County.

May 13, 1756. April Court, 1758. *Sons:* FRANCIS, SAMUEL, EDWARD.
Daughters: MARY LONG, ELIZABETH LONG, ANN SUTTON, HANNAH PEN-
RICE. *Executors:* HANNAH and EDWARD PENRICE (son and daughter).
Witnesses: JOSHUA SKINNER, WM. AINTON. *Clerk of the Court:* MILES
HARVEY.

PENRICE, THOMAS.   Chowan County.

September 5, 1739. October Court, 1739. *Brother, Executor and sole
legatee:* FRANCIS PENRICE. *Witnesses:* JOSHA HOBART, LUKE GREGORY,
MARY PENRICE. *Clerk of the Court:* JAMES CRAVEN.

PERISH, JOHN.   Perquimans County.

February 12, 1755. April Court, 1759. *Sons:* JOHN, JAMES, JOSEPH,
SAMUEL (to each is given land), JOSIAH. *Daughters:* ELINDER, BETTIE and
MARY PERISH, JEAN BUNDY. *Executors:* JOHN and JOSIAH PERISH (sons).
Witnesses: THOMAS HOLLOWELL, PETER PEARSON, CORNELIUS MOORE.
Clerk of the Court: MILES HARVEY.

PERISHE, SARAH. Perquimans County.

May 29, 1754. April Court, 1760. *Sons:* SIMON, JAMES. *Daughters:* SARAH, JANE and MORNEN. *Executors:* JAMES PERISHE (son), JOSEPH PERISHE (brother). *Witnesses:* JAS. PIERCE, THOMAS STANTON. *Clerk of the Court:* MILES HARVEY.

PERKINS, HENRY. Currituck County.

July 2, 1715. July 12, 1715. *Wife and Executrix:* ELIZABETH. *Witnesses:* PETER POYNER and JOSEPH POYNER. *Clerk of the Court:* JO. WICKER.

PERRY, JEREMIAH. Chowan Precinct.

October 18, 1694. October Court, 1694. *Wife and Executrix:* JANE PERRY. *Other legatees:* CHRISTIAN and THOS. BLOUNT. *Witnesses:* THO. POLLOCK, ALEX. MCFARLAND, NEAL MCMING, JOHN BUNTIN. *Clerk of the Court:* NATHL. CHEVIN. *Clerk in Secretary's office:* W. GLOVER.

PERRY, PHILIP. Perquimans County.

July 5, 1751. October Court, 1751. *Sons:* JESSE (lands on Little River known by the name of Sandy Hook), PHILIP ("plantation whereon I now live"). *Daughters:* SARAH, MARY, RACHEL, JUDE, ELIZABETH and MIRIAM. *Executor:* JACOB PERRY, son of JACOB PERRY. *Witnesses:* MOSES FEILD, BENJAMIN PERRY, ELIZABETH PERRY. *Clerk of the Court:* EDMUND HATCH.

PERSONS, JOHN. Perquimans County.

December 29, 1753. April Court, 1754. *Daughter:* MIRIAM PERSONS. *Wife and Executrix:* MARY. *Executor:* SAMUEL PERSONS (brother). *Witnesses:* JOHN WHEDBEE, GABRIEL COSAN, JOSEPH PERSHOE. *Clerk of the Court:* WILLIAM SKINNER.

PERSON, PETER. Perquimans Precinct.

March 1, 1751. April Court, 1755. *Sons:* JONATHAN, NATHAN, PETER, JOHN. *Daughters:* RACHEL, MARY and BETTY PERSONS. *Brother:* NATHAN NEWBY. *Wife and Executrix:* not named. *Witnesses:* JESSE NEWBY, WILLIAM BOGUE, WILLIAM HASKIT. *Clerk of the Court:* JAMES CRAVEN.

PETERSON, JACOB. Albemarle County.

January 13, 1697. July Court, 1698. One shilling in silver to REBONAH BOORD, *daughter-in-law;* one shilling each to *daughters* ELIZABETH, CONSTANT. *Daughter:* ANN PETERSON, plantation bought from JNO. DURANT. *Executrix:* MARY PETERSON. *Witnesses:* MARTHA FAGEETT, JAMES FAGEETT, STEPHEN MAINWARING. *Clerk of the Court:* JOHN STEPNEY.

PETERSON, JACOB.   Albemarle County.

1697. This is a nuncupative will leaving everything to *wife*, REBEC-
KAH. Proven before JOHN WHEDBE by EDWARD and MARY GELFF.

PETIT, FRANCIS.   Chowan Precinct.

October 29, 1710. August 12, 1712. *Son:* FRANCIS. *Cousin:* JOHN
CHESTNE. *Daughter:* SARAH. *Wife and Executrix:* MARY. *Executor:*
THOMAS PEIRCE (brother of wife). *Friend:* JOHN BARROW. *Witnesses:*
JONATHAN WILLIAMS, SARAH BARROW, FRANCIS SMITH. No probate
officer.

PEYTON, ROBERT.   Bath County.

January 8, 1733. September 10, 1754. *Sons:* THOMAS, ROBERT, WIL-
LIAM (lands up Derhams Creek), AMBROSE. To each of sons is given a
plantation. *Daughters:* SARAH PEYTON, DOROTHY PORTER. *Wife and
Executrix:* MARY. *Witnesses:* THOMAS GAINS, ELIZABETH BELL, BRYANT
KELLY, SOLOMON ROBSON. *Clerk of the Court:* JOHN SNEAD.

PFIFER, JOHN.   Mecklenburg County.

August 14, 1775. January 22, 1777. *Son:* PAUL PFIFER. *Daughters:*
MARGARET, ANN ELIZABETH PFIFER. *Wife:* CATHERINE. *Executors:*
MARTIN PFIFER (father) and PAUL BARRINGER (father-in-law). *Witnesses:* BENJAMIN PATTON, WILLIAM WALLACE, SAMUEL PATTON. *Clerk
of the Court:* SAML. MARTIN. Provision is made for sending son to college
and educating daughters.

PHELPS, GODFREY.   Tyrrell County.

February 7, 1750. September Court, 1751. *Sons:* CUDBERD, GODFREY,
JOHN (to each is given a plantation; to JOHN "the manner plantation").
Daughters: SARAH and ELIZABETH PHELPS. *Wife and Executrix:* ELIZA-
BETH. *Executor:* JOSHUA PHELPS. *Witnesses:* JOHN PAGETT, JOSHUAY
PHELPS, JOSEPH SPRUILL. *Clerk of the Court:* EVAN JONES.

PHELPS, HENRY.   Perquimans County.

May 19, 1752. July Court, 1752. *Son:* JONATHAN ("all my lands and
plantations * * * the fourth part of my negroes * * * Foxes Journals
first and second part &c." *Wife and Executrix:* MARGARET. *Daughter:*
ELIZABETH PHELPS. *Executors:* JONATHAN PHELPS (brother) and ZACHA-
RIAH NIXON (father-in-law). *Witnesses:* FRANCIS TOMES, FRANCIS NIXON
and SARAH NEWBY. *Clerk of the Court:* EDMUND HATCH.

PHELPS, JONATHAN.   Perquimans Precinct.

March 11, 1688. April 4, 1689. *Son:* JONATHAN. *Wife:* HANNAH.
Proven before RICHARD STANRICK, THO. IMPERS, DAVID SHERNOLD. This
will is very badly mutilated and so faded as to be illegible.

PHELPS, JONATHAN.   Perquimans County.

December 4, 1732. January Court, 1732. *Sons:* HENRY ("manner plantation"), JONATHAN (300 acres land on Perquimans River). *Daughter:* ELIZABETH PHELPS. Eight negroes and four horses bequeathed to wife and children. *Wife and Executrix:* ELIZABETH. *Executor:* CHARLES DENMAN. *Witnesses:* R. CHEASTEN, ELLEXANDER HOWARD, JAMES ANDERSON. *Clerk of the Court:* CHARLES DENMAN.

PHELPS, SAMUEL.   Perquimans Precinct.

April 21, 1728. July Court, 1728. *Sons:* JONATHAN, JOHN (land in "balehack"), WILLIAM, JAMES. *Wife:* not named. *Executors:* JONATHAN PHELPS (brother), JONATHAN PHELPS (son), ABRAHAM SANDERS and ROBERT WILLSON. *Witnesses:* ABRAHAM SANDERS, RALPH BOSEMAN, CHARLES DENMAN. *Clerk of the Court:* R. EVERARD.

PHELPS, WILLIAM.   Perquimans County.

April 15, 1752. April Court, 1752. *Legatees:* JOHN HARVEY and JAMES LITTESON (cousins), WILLIAM BARKER, SARAH ELIOT, SAMUEL LITTESON. *Executors:* JOHN HARVEY and JAMES LITTESON. *Witnesses:* JOSHUA HOBART, MARGERY MOORE, DERBE MOORE, PENNINAH CHANCEY. *Clerk of the Court:* EDMUND HATCH.

PHENNEY, GEORGE.

June 3, 1736. June 23, 1737. Surveyor Generall of His Majesties Customs Southern District on the Continent of America." *Legatees:* RALPH NODEN, of London; ELIZABETH KIRK, of London. *Nephew:* JOSEPH HARRISON. *Wife and Executrix:* PENELOPE. *Witnesses:* SAMUEL SCOTT, THOMAS ASHLEY, T. BUTLER. Proven before W. SMITH.

PHILLIPS, DANIEL.   Currituck County.

July Court, 1726. *Sons:* JAMES, DANIEL, SAMUEL, BENJAMIN. *Daughters:* MARY DUK, MARGRITT PHILLIPS. *Wife and Executrix:* ABIGALL. *Witnesses:* JOHN MASHELL, WILLIAM SCOTT, ANDR. DUKE. *Clerk of the Court:* J. MARTYN.

PHILLIPS, PAUL.   Craven County.

June 5, 1746. June Court, 1751. *Son:* PAUL. *Grandsons:* PAUL PHILLIPS and PAUL FLOOD. *Daughters:* RACHEL YENSHAW, RUTH SANDERS. *Son-in-law:* WILLIAM FLOOD. *Wife and Executrix:* REBECCA. *Witnesses:* LUKE GRACE, LEONARD LOFTIN, PETER HENDRICKSON. *Clerk of the Court:* CHAS. YOUNG.

PHILLIPS, THOMAS.   Craven County.

June 22, 1743. December 23, 1743. *Wife and Executrix:* ISABELL.
Sons: JOHN, MASON, THOMAS, JAMES, MARK, WILLIAM. *Daughter:* MARY.
Witnesses: ROBERT PATERSON, HENRY SUMERLIN. *Clerk of the Court:* N.
ROUTLEDGE.

PHILLIPS, THOMAS.   Northampton County.

April 4, 1751. May Court, 1751. *Sons:* THOMAS and MARK (one plantation to each), WILLIAM. *Daughters:* PATTY SIMPSON, MARY PHILLIPS.
Wife and Executrix: PATTY. *Executor:* WILLIAM PHILLIPS (son). *Witnesses:* SIMON SIMPSON, BEN. EDWARDS, CHRISTOPHER EDWARDS. *Clerk of
the Court:* I. EDWARDS.

PHILLIPS, WILLIAM.   Beaufort County.

October 6, 1740. December Court, 1751. *Son:* SAMUEL (land at Swan
Point). *Sister:* ANN WILLIAMS. *Wife and Executrix:* ELIZABETH. *Wit-
nesses:* THOMAS MOORE, RICHARD ALLEGOOD, JOHN MCKEEL. *Clerk of the
Court:* WILLIAM ORMOND.

PHILPOTT, JOHN.   Albemarle County.

November 19, 1694. JOHN LAWSON, son of NATHL. LAWSON (plantation
now living on, ten cows and 6,000 pounds pork to buy a negro), JOHN
LAWSON. *Wife:* MARY PHILPOTT. Plantation adjoining home lands to
son-in-law, WM. WOOLLARD. *Executors:* DANIEL AKEHURST and JOHN
LAWSON. *Witnesses:* THO. ROLFE, DANIEL HAWKINS, JOHN CABEGE.
(No probate.)

PICKENS, ANDREW.

November 4, 1756. *Sons:* JOHN and ANDREW ("my plantation").
Daughter: JEAN PICKENS (saddle horse). *Wife and Executrix:* NANCY.
Witnesses: ROBERT MCCLENACHAN, JOHN PICKENS. No probate.

PICKERIN, RICHARD.   Bertie County.

January 25, 1739. February Court, 1739. *Legatees:* MARY, JAMES and
ROGER SNELL. *Executor:* ROGER SNELL. *Witnesses:* J. HILL. *Clerk of
the Court:* RT. FORSTER.

PIERCE, JOHN.   Perquimans County.

September 13, 1682. *Sons:* THOMAS, JOHN and JOSEPH. *Daughter:*
REBECKAH. *Other legatees:* THOMAS DAW, WM. BUNDY. *Wife:* not
named. *Executors:* WILLIAM BUNDY and JONATHAN PHELPS. *Witnesses:*
ROBERT WILSON, FRANCIS TOME and JOHN STANLEY. No probate.

PIERCE, JOHN.   Perquimans County.

October 9, 1726. January 10, 1726. *Sons:* COPELAND, THOMAS. *Daughters:* MARY, ELIZABETH and HANNAH. *Wife and Executrix:* SARAH. *Brothers-in-law:* PETER JONES, JOHN WILLIAMS. *Witnesses:* REBECKAH LONG, RACHEL WEIGHT, THOMAS PIERCE. *Clerk of the Court:* RICHARD LEARY.

PIERCE, JOSEPH.   Perquimans Precinct.

June 6, 1700. *Brother:* THOMAS PIERCE. *Wife and Executrix:* DAMARIS. *Witnesses:* TIMOTHY CLEARE, WM. and THOS. WINSLOW. *Clerk of the Court:* THOS. SNODEN.

PIERCE, THOMAS.   Perquimans Precinct.

February 12, 1731–1732. March 30, 1732. *Sons:* THOMAS, JOSEPH, JOHN. *Daughter:* MARY JONES (1 negro). *Grandchildren:* THOMAS PIERCE, MARY PIERCE. *Wife and Executrix:* MARY. *Executor:* PETER JONES (son-in-law). *Witnesses:* MILES GALE, RICHARD SKINNER, ABRAHAM SANDERS. Proven before GEORGE BURRINGTON.

PIERCE, THOMAS.   Chowan County.

April 6, 1755. October Court, 1756. *Daughters:* MARY NIXON, SARAH MORRIS, JAMIMA NEWBY, KESIAH NEWBY, KERRENHAPPUCH PIERCE. *Grandson:* PIERCE NIXON. *Brother-in-law:* PETER JONES. *Executors:* PHENIASS NIXON, JOHN MORRISS, ROBERT NEWBY, NATHAN NEWBY (sons-in-law), and JOSEPH WHITE. *Witnesses:* JOHN SIMONS, CORNELUS LEARY, MARY CREECY. *Clerk of the Court:* THOMAS JONES.

PIKE, SAMUEL.   Pasquotank Precinct.

December 11, 1716. *Sons:* SAMUEL and BENJAMIN, JOHN. *Daughters:* SUSANNAH PIKE and ANN PIKE. *Wife and Executrix:* JANE PIKE. *Witnesses:* JOHN MARTIN, JOHN MOOR. No probate.

PILKINGTON, SETH.   Beaufort County.

October 7, 1751. March Court, 1754. *Daughters:* SARAH CAUTANCHE (seven negroes), WINIFRED PILKINGTON (ten negroes and "plantation whereon I now live, situated on Lemuel Cherry herring runn"). *Wife's daughter:* ANN LILLINGTON. *Wife's granddaughters:* CATHERINE LOCKHART and MARY EVANS. *Executors:* MICHAEL CAUTANCHE (son-in-law), WINIFRED PILKINGTON (daughter). *Witnesses:* JOHN FRY, WM. STUBBS, MICHAEL CAUTANCHE, JR. *Clerk of the Court:* WALLEY CHAUNCEY.

19

PILSON, GRACE.   Craven County.

September 17, 1743.   December 23, 1743.   *Sister:* MARY FOX, of Perth
Amboy, near New York (7 negroes, 3 large looking-glasses).   *Kinswomen:*
GRACE FOX (4 negroes, 1 silver tankard, 1 looking-glass, 1 gold chain and
two gold rings), ELLINOR FOX (2 gold rings, 1 pr. gold earrings).   *Brother:*
THOMAS FOX (silver watch).   *Friend:* RICHARD SCOTT (1 negro man).
Executors: RICHARD BIDDER and THOMAS PEARSON.   *Witnesses:* JAMES
COOR, JOSHUA ACKIS, WILLIAM WEBB, JAMES WHITING.   Proven before
GAB. JOHNSTON.   Impression of watchdog on seal.

PILSON, THOMAS.   Craven County.

February 17, 1742–1743.   September 9, 1743.   *Brother:* CHARLES PIL-
SON.   *Sister:* ELIZABETH WHEELER.   *Wife and Executrix:* GRACE (plantation and 10 negroes).   *Witnesses:* JOHN WEST, CHRISTOPHER DAWSON,
NICHOLAS PUREFOY.   *Clerk of the Court:* N. ROUTLEDGE.   *Executor* qualified before J. MONTGOMERY, C. J.

PIMBROUGH, DANIEL.

April 22, 1688.   August 2, 1688.   *Legatees:* ELIZABETH LILLINGTON,
WILLIAM CALLOWAY, son of CALEB CALLOWAY, WILLIAM and ELIZABETH
FETTERTON, children of WILLIAM FETTERTON.   *Executor:* CALEB CALLO-
WAY.   *Witnesses:* ALEXR. LILLINGTON, JOHN DURANT, ROBERT HERMAN.
Proven before DANIEL AKEHURST and EDWARD MAYO.

PINKETT, ELINOR.   Beaufort County.

May 17, 1757.   March Court, 1758.   *Sons:* WILLIAM DANIEL PINKETT,
THOMAS and ZACHARIAH PINKETT (one negro to each).   *Son-in-law:*
WILLIAM MOORE.   *Daughter:* HANNAH PINKETT.   *Granddaughter:* RACHEL
CASON.   *Executors:* WILLIAM DANIEL PINKETT and THOMAS PINKETT.
Witnesses: GEORGE MOYE, JR., WILLIAM PROCTER, MARGARET SMITH.
Clerk of the Court: WALLEY CHAUNCEY.

PIPKIN, JOHN.   Chowan County.

May 21, 1745.   July 18, 1745.   *Sons:* PHILIP, LEWIS and ISAAC, JOHN
and DANIEL (to each is devised a tract of land), JOSEPH (1 negro), JESSE
(1 negro).   *Wife and Executrix:* MARTHA (1 negro).   *Witnesses:* HENRY
GOODMAN, JR., TIMOTHY GOODMAN, HENRY GOODMAN, SR.   *Clerk of the
Court:* EDMUND HATCH.

PIRENT, JAMES.   Edgecombe County.

March 7, 1757.   May Court, 1757.   *Son:* JAMES ("plantation whereon
I now live").   *Daughters:* TATION, MARY and SARAH.   *Executors:* ARTHUR
and JOSHUA BELL.   *Witnesses:* JAMES HOGAN, JOSHUA BELL, WILLIAM
HOLLOWAY.   *Clerk of the Court:* JOS. MONTFORT.

PITMAN, BENJAMIN.   Edgecombe County.

August 3, 1755. May Court, 1756. *Sons:* MOSES, MICAH, SAMSON, JACOB. *Daughters:* PATIENCE FAULK, MARY BOTTOM, ABIGAL PITMAN, LUCY PITMAN, CELA PITMAN, JEMIMA PITMAN. *Wife and Executrix:* ANN. *Witnesses:* JOHN STREATER, JOHN JAMESON, JOHN MURPHREE. *Clerk of the Court:* JOS. MONTFORT.

PITMAN, THOMAS.   Edgecombe County.

April 4, 1754, February Court, 1755. *Sons:* LOT, THOMAS and seven others mentioned, but not named. *Daughters:* two mentioned, but not named. *Brothers:* ROBERT and AMBROSE PITMAN (*Executors*). *Wife:* ANNE. *Witnesses:* JNO. HOPKINS, AMBROSE PITTMAN, JOHN FORT. *Clerk of the Court:* BENJAMIN WYNNS.

PLATER, RICHARD.   Pasquotank Precinct.

September 8, 1705. January Court, 1705. *Legatees:* JOHN HUNT, JOHN MCKEEL, HUGH CAMPBELL, ANTHONY HATCH. Estate in the Kingdom of England devised to mother, DOROTHY PLATER, of Linn, in the County of Norfolk, and MRS. SARAH BEATHER. *Executor:* HUGH CAMPBELL. *Witnesses:* JOSEPH MING, ANTHONY MARCKHAM, JR., JOHN FOURRE. *Clerk of the Court:* J. KNIGHT.

PLATO, THOMAS.   Pasquotank Precinct.

March 12, 1735–1736. *Daughters:* MARTHA, SUSANNAH and MARY PLATO. *Executors:* ANTONY MARCKHAM and JOHN BOYD. *Witnesses:* THOS. WARD, ANTHONY MARCKHAM, JNO. MCKEEL. No probate.

PLOMER, SAMUEL SABANE.

April 12, 1755. May 2, 1755. Surgeon. *Legatees:* PENELOPE and CHARLOTTE BLACKHALL, daughters of DR. ABRAHAM BLACKHALL; SARAH ROWDEN, daughter of SARAH BLACKHALL; CAPT. JOSEPH HERON, SARAH SHARP, ELIZABETH PLOMER SHARP. *Executors:* JOHN CAMPBELL and CHARLES ELLIOT. *Witnesses:* BEN WHEATLEY, JOHN HARVEY, RO. LENOX. Proven before ARTHUR DOBBS. Impression of man's head on seal.

PLOWMAN, JOHN.   Chowan County.

July 1, 1721. August 4, 1721. *Legatees:* JOHN PLOWMAN WHITE (plantation and seven slaves), THOMAS LOVICK, MARY WHITE, JOHN PLOWMAN ASHLEY, GOVERNOR EDEN, JOHN LOVICK, NICHOLAS CRISP, ISAAC HILL (last-named three persons appointed Executors). *Witnesses:* JAMES CASTELLAW, JAS. WINRIGHT, J. CABB. Proven before CHARLES EDEN.

POLLOCK, ESTHER.   Chowan County.

May 30, 1712. March Court, 1723. *Executors:* THOMAS LUTEN and
THOMAS LUTEN, JR. *Other legatees:* GOVERNOR EDWARD HYDE, MRS.
ANN STEWART, HENDERSON LUTEN. Lands on Sasefrick River in Snell
County, Maryland, and lands in "this province given me by my late hus-
band, WILLM. WILKISON; lands at Sandy Point." *Witnesses:* ROBERT
HICKS, JAMES BEASLEY, JNO. PORTER, JUNR., CONRAD EICHHORN. *Clerk
of the Court:* W. BADHAM.

POLLOCK, GEORGE.

October 18, 1736. July 29, 1738. *Brother:* CULLEN POLLOCK (land
on Salmon Creek, Chowan River, on the "South Shore," on Moratock
River and Canaho Creek; 4,700 acres on north side of Moratock; 710
acres of land on Trent River). *Nephews:* CULLEN and THOMAS POLLOCK
(5,000 acres of land at the Haw Fields; 3,300 acres on Tarr River; 2,200
acres on Coor Creek; 220 acres on Coor Creek; 150 acres at Bennys Creek;
500 acres on Wecone Creek; 640 acres on Moratock). *Brother-in-law and
Executor:* COL. ROBERT WEST (lands on Trenters and Horn Creeks; island
called "the Crow" in Currituck County; sum of money to purchase
patents for lands). *Witnesses:* THOMAS ASHLEY, WILLIAM FRYLEY, NE-
HEMIAH WARRING. Proven before W. SMITH, C. J. The original of this
will is missing. Abstract made from recorded copy No. 82 in Book 4,
Land Grant Records.

POLLOCK, JAMES.   Chowan Precinct.

February 23, 1700. *Legatees:* BULLAH BLOUNT (houses and lands),
WILLIAM WARD, THOMAS POLLOCK, EDMOND PEARSE, JOHN WACKER.
Witnesses: THOMAS BLOUNT, SAM'LL SWANN, THOMAS COOPPER. *Clerk of
the Court:* N. CHEVIN.

POLLOCK, THOMAS.   Chowan County.

August 8, 1721. August Court, 1753. *Sons:* THOMAS, CULLEN and
GEORGE. *Daughter:* MARY, wife of THOMAS BRAY. The following lands
are devised: 1,550 acres on Chowan River between MR. KING and THO.
DANIEL; lands purchased of THOS. DANIEL, JOHN RASBERRY, JAMES WILKE-
SON, MARTIN FREDERICK RASOR; five tracts of lightwood land on Samon
Creek; "land where FIREBENT built ye mill"; 10,000 acres on Mill Creek;
2,560 acres in fork of Raquis called Springfield; 2,500 acres on Moratock
River called Canecarora (Coueconora); 640 acres on Bridges Creek at Week-
acanaan; 2,800 acres on Cassayah called Rosefield; land on Moratock
adjoining BOWMAN; land purchased of RICH'D ROSE; land on Moratock
Bay; 900 acres of land on Nuce River fork called New Bern; land bought of
MAJOR ROBERT WEST; lands adjoining "land where I now live"; lands adjoining that bought of CARY GOBBEE; land adjoining PARROTS; land where

SAM'LL EDMUNDS lives; land where JOHN GRIFFIN lives near Bavie Swamp; where WILSON lived at Weekacoon Creek; where JOHN MAINARD lived at Pettishore; 2,400 acres of land called Crany Island; 2,200 acres on the south side of Neuse River and west side of Core Creek; 710 acres on Trent River called "ye halfe-way House"; 220 acres on the east side of Core Creek; on the south shore where LEONARD LOFTEN lives; 360 acres on Boag Sound; 215 acres in the fork of Chesters Creek on White Oak River; 150 acres on Neuse River at the head of Bennys Creek; 5,000 acres to the south of Neuse River; 640 acres on Neuse River called Wilkeson's Point; 8,900 acres on the east branch of Salmon Creek; lands lying on South Lancaster. About seventy-five negroes are bequeathed to three sons. The following items may be of interest: "I give * * * one hundred pound to be paid in Boston and 5,000 feet of plank which I have sent for from Boston." "I give * * * lands, mortgages * * * whether in America or Scotland." "* * * what pitch and tarr ye hands in ye woods makes until ye first of aprill next." "* * * I have expended and laid out for a house at Black Rock * * * ten pound more for New England plank." "And whereas also I have been out and expended upon a House for my son CULLEN on the south shore when Mr. WEST the Carpentare is paid for what worke he hath done thereto (to-wit) the covering the house, doeing the Dormant Windoes and making up the Gavell end of the said house and when CULLEN hath what Glass is in the house." "Mr. COKE * * * is to have all the lands that are necessary for him for burning the bricks or what other worke he hath occasion for * * *." *Executors:* THOMAS, CULLEN and GEORGE (sons). *Witnesses:* JOHN BURNNELL, DAVID HENDERSON, WILLIAM HARDY, LAWRENCE SARSOR, JAMES CASTELAW, JAMES CASTELAW, ROBERT WICKS, THOMAS NEWMAN (or NEWNAM), WILLIAM LITTLE, JOSEPH SKITTLETHORP. *Clerk of the Court:* FR. FOSTER. Also SAMUEL ORMES.

POLLOCK, THOMAS.   Bertie County.

April 16, 1732. January 20, 1732. *Sons:* CULLEN, THOMAS, GEORGE. *Wife:* not named. The following lands are devised: plantation called Black Rock; plantation called Great Quarter; plantation called Manuels or Crickits; land on Salmon Creek and Chowan River; 8,900 acres adjoining the aforesaid land; land on Trent River containing 10,000 acres; 2,560 acres in fork of Raquis called Springfield; land at Unaroye Meadows; two tracts nigh Tuskarora Indian Town; 300 acres on Moratuck River; 235 acres on Moratuck River; four tracts on Fishing Creek; land on Briery Branch. *Other legatees:* JACOB PARAT and JOHN HAILES, MRS. ELIZ. DICKSON. About 50 negroes are bequeathed. The following item may be of interest: "I will & order and give by this will to all such persons who are setled on my lands at Trenton Condition of a Certain Writing I give to JACOB MILLER that those already settled thare have leases on ye same terms I promised them." *Witnesses:* GEORGE POLLOCK, FRANCIS RASOR,

JACOB PARAT, ROBERT MINOR, ELIZABETH DICKSON. *Executors:* GEORGE and CULLEN POLLOCK (brothers), ROBERT WEST. Will proven before W. LITTLE, C. J.

POOL, SOLOMON.   Pasquotank County.

July 30, 1739. *Sons:* JOSEPH, SOLOMON, JACOB ("my manner plantation"). *Daughter:* SARAH POOL. To each of children is bequeathed one negro. *Wife and Executrix:* GRACE. *Witnesses:* CHARLES TAYLOR, SOLOMON POOL, JOSEPH ROBINSON. Probate illegible.

POPE, EDWARD.   Pasquotank County.

January 26, 1721–1722. April Court, 1722. *Wife, Executrix and sole legatee:* SARAH. *Witnesses:* W. NORRIS, LUCY JACKSON, EDWARD MAYO. *Clerk of the Court:* EDMD. GALE.

POPE, RICHARD.   Pasquotank Precinct.

June 23, 1701. July 15, 1701. *Son:* EDWARD. *Daughter:* MARY POPE. *Wife and Executrix:* ANN. *Witnesses:* EDWARD MAYO, MATTHEW PRITCHARD, SAMUEL PIKE, GEO. ELLIS, THO. ABINGTON. *Clerk of the Court:* THOS. ABINGTON.

POPE, SAMUEL.   Craven County.

January 5, 1758. February 4, 1758. *Sons:* SAMUEL (land on Core Creek), JOHN and WILLIAM. *Daughters:* ELIZABETH and MARY POPE. *Wife:* SARAH. *Executors:* GEORGE POPE and JOHN TURNER. *Witnesses:* ROBERT TAYLOR, GEORGE POPE, BETTY LANE. *Deputy Clerk of the Court:* PETER CORNEGY.

POPE, WILLIAM.   Edgecombe County.

January 15, 1749. February Court, 1749. *Sons:* JACOB (three negroes), WEST and STEPHEN (one negro each). *Daughters:* REBECCA POPE and JULIAN NEWSOM. *Grandsons:* WILLIAM TAYLOR (two negroes), WILLIAM POPE ("my plantation"). *Executors:* JACOB POPE (son) and JOSEPH NEWSOM (son-in-law). *Witnesses:* HENRY WEST, JOSEPH PEARCE, ARTHUR WALL, JOHN JORDAN. *Clerk of the Court:* BENJAMIN WYNNS. Testator came to this state from Isle of Wight County, in Virginia, and devised to son STEPHEN plantation in said County.

PORSELL, GARRIT.   Albemarle County.

January 31, 1724–1725. August 2, 1725. *Sons:* EDMAN and GARRITT. *Daughters:* MARY, CATHEN, ELIZABETH. *Wife and Executrix:* ELIZABETH. *Witnesses:* WILLIAM WILSON, JOHN SCARBROUGH, WILLIAM WAITE. Proven before RICHARD EVERARD.

PORTER, JOHN, Merchant.   Albemarle County.

January 8, 1712.   August 7, 1712.   *Wife:* MARY, lands in Chowan Precinct.   *Son:* EDMUND, lands in Chowan after death of wife.   *Son:* JOHN PORTER, tract of land in Bath County called "Chocowinateh."   *Son:* JOSHUA, land called "Quarry's."   *Son:* MATTHEW PORTER, 2,000 acres in Bath County, "on other side of river," bought of RICHARD SMITH.   *Son-in-law:* JNO. LILLINGTON and *wife* SARAH, mentioned.   *Daughter:* ELIZA, three negroes.   *Executrix:* MARY PORTER.   *Witnesses:* JNO. ALLEN, M. D., JOHN WEBBER.   *Notary Public:* JOANE MILLS (WCH.).   Original missing. Recorded in Book of Wills No. 2, page 5.   This will is proven before JONA THOMAS, Mayor, of Bridgewater, in Sommersett County, England, on the ———— day of February, 1712.

PORTER, JOHN.   "Cape Fair."

October 11, 1727.   January 6, 1728.   *Son:* JOHN.   *Daughter:* SARAH PORTER.   *Wife and Executrix:* SARAH PORTER.   *Witnesses:* SETH PILKINGTON, JOHN WORTH, J. KNIGHT.   Proven before RICHARD EVERARD. Device on seal.

PORTER, JOHN PEYTON.   Beaufort County.

April 29, 1750.   March Court, 1755.   *Wife:* ELIZABETH (plantation on east side of Durham's Creek called the Garrison containing 644 acres). *Daughters:* MARY PORTER, SARAH PORTER (plantation on east side of Durhams Creek commonly called Hardings, adjoining the plantation called the Garrison).   Another tract beginning at SNEADS line "from thence to the Savanna, from thence to the Horsepen Swamp, from thence to the Dismall."   Negroes are to be kept on the above described tract "to make Tar, Turpentine in order to raise money, etc."   Negroes, cattle and other personal property divided between wife and children.   *Executors:* MICHAEL COTANCHE and NATHAN RICHARDSON.   *Witnesses:* THOMAS LOUGH, WILLIAM TRIPP, CHARLES LAWTHER.   *Clerk of the Court:* WALLEY CHAUNCEY.

PORTER, JOHN.   Hyde County.

November 20, 1750.   December Court, 1751.   *Sons:* WILLIAM and JOHN ("land whereon I now live including the Houses and plantation").   *Daughter:* PATIENCE PORTER.   *Wife:* ELISABETH.   *Executors:* THOMAS and JOHN SMITH.   *Witnesses:* THOMAS and MARY SMITH, MARY RHODES.   *Clerk of the Court:* THOMAS LOVICK.

PORTER, JOHN SWANN.   New Hanover County.

No dates.   Rocky Point.   House, land, watercourses, etc., devised to JOHN BAPTISTE ASHE, son of SAMUEL ASHE, with remainder to JOHN MOORE, SAM'L SWANN, JR., SAMUEL ASHE (youngest son of SAMUEL) and CINCINNATUS ASHE (son of SAMUEL).   Seven slaves are bequeathed to executors for education of two mulatto boys, emancipated by deeds

executed in 1773, which boys were formerly the property of ANN MOSE-
LEY ("now wife of HUGH MUNROE"). To these mulatto boys are be-
queathed slaves. *Executors:* SAMUEL SWANN, JR., and JOHN BAPTISTE
ASHE. No signature, date, witnesses or probate.

PORTER, JOSHUA.   Bath County.
    January 17, 1733. September 14, 1734. *Son:* JOHN PEYTON PORTER
(land "whereon I now live on Derhams Creek"). *Daughter:* ELIZABETH
(1,000 acres of land on Derhams Creek, together with negro slaves).
Cousin: JOHN FRY. *Other legatees:* ANN LILLINGTON and ELIZABETH FRY
(cousins of testator), WILLIAM TRIPPE, PHILIP CREMER. *Wife:* DOROTHY.
Executors: EDMUND PORTER (brother), PATRICK MAULE and SETH PILK-
INGTON (brothers-in-law), EDWARD MOSELEY and JOHN TRIPPE. *Witnesses:* CHURCHILL READING, JOHN CALDOM, WILLIAM WHITFORD. Proven
before GEORGE BURRINGTON. Original missing. Recorded in Book 1722–
1735, page 329.

PORTER, MARY.   Chowan Precinct.
    November 12, 1717. January 21, 1717. *Sons:* JOHN (one negro; one-
half dozen Russia leather chairs); EDMUND (one negro; one-half dozen silver spoons, etc.); JOSUA (land at Yawpim adjoining "MR. CLAYTON and
MR. CLARK"; the following personal property: "My negroe woman known
by the name of Edy one Ticken feather bed & bolster and two pillows one
feather bed covered with Canvas and bolster and one Pillowe three pillow
cases Suitable two pair fine sheets, two pair coarse sheets one set of red
watered Curtains and Wallons one Spotted Worsted Rug, Red Rug, Two
pair good blankets 1 flowered Bed coverlid Bedstead that stood in the Hall
Chamber Six Rusia leather chairs one of the large lookeing glasses and my
largest and one midling iron pott the large andirons a large double brass
Skillet and Trevit one brass Candlestick one pair brass Scales and weights,
one pair of Stilliards two Diaper towels a pewter mustard pott the Coarsest
of brass ridles my Dantzick locke Chests a lime sifter a Case of Knives and
forks a Cross cut Sawe a writeing Desk four Pewter Porringers one earthen
Porringer ten Pewter Plates iron pestle Ash Table 1 large Soup Pewter dish
one large small Dito one midle sized Dito 1 large and 1 small Pewter bason
2 earthen bason and 2 pewter Do one set of wedges and six wooden chairs
2 joint stooles to wooden turned chairs 2 Iron tramels 1 brass butter ladle
1 small brass Ketle, 1 pewter chamber pott Milland Salt, 1 Iron chafing
dish the half of my crop now in the ground and one pottle pewter pott and
a pint Pewter pott one Glass Gallon Bottle and one broad Axe"). *Daughters:* ELIZABETH PORTER ("six silver spoons each weighing ten shillings
sterling and one iron pott and pott hooks and twelve soup plates"). SARAH
LILINGTON ("my negro woman called Maria 1 chest of drawers, six painted
Chairs now in her possession one pair of iron fire doggs one small Cedar
table 1 pair of fine sheets two pair Coarse Sheets and two pillow cases Two

Diaper towells my largest quilt one Lignum Vitae Spice Mortar one large Soup Dish one midle sized pewter dish 1 small pewter bason 1 brass Skimer 1 small Iron Kettle the least of my painted trunks two Earthen Bason and Plates 1 English Flasket 1 large glass bottle 1 stone jugg 1 pewter Chamber pott 1 bed pann three of my other which she likes best and the full third part of the Cotten and Wooll that shall belong to me at my decease"). To *daughter* ELIZABETH in addition to above-named legacies is bequeathed the following personal property: "my Indian woman called Judith and her daughter named Sukey 1 chest of drawers one oval table my best Sett of red Curtains and Valent belonging to my lodging rooms three pair fine sheets two pair Coarse Sheets four pillow cases My Green Rugg made of worsted 1 pair of the best rose blankets the least of my quilts my Callico counterpane and Jester Cloath my Bible my Spice box 1 warmeing pann 1 pair Chamber doggs with brass 1 Black trunk and one painted trunk a large brass Keetle and Two Skimers a Brass Shield and Two Iron potts one linked Tramel a brass Flam one Copper Chocolate pott 1 white rugg 1 Grid-iron four matted chairs my Silver Salt Marked I p M and Silver peper box with the Same marke one large pewter Soup dish 1 shallow Do two midling pewter dishes 1 large and one Small pewter basons 10 pewter plates Six painted chairs five pewter porringers 1 pr brass candlesticks, Snuffers and snuff dish my Smoothing iron heaters and Frame 1 gallon Stone Jugg 1 Glass Cruit two glass cups one mustard pott two pewter Chamber potts three earthen Bason 1 large Dish Do & Two plates 1 Tin pudding pann 1 Spitt 1 leaden pann and 2 painted brushes a brass Shovel and Tongs a large looking Glass the best of the Bew panns 1 pewter Salt 1 glass decanter 2 tin dish covers 1 brass Ridle a large turned Elbow chair 1 Drippen Pan 1 case of bottles one-half of my Sheep and Cattle one silver tankard." *Grand-daughters:* SARAH PORTER, MARY and SARAH LILLINGTON. *Other legatee:* ROBT. HERRICK. *Executors:* JOHN and JOSHUA PORTER (sons). *Witnesses:* J. LOVICK, MARY HARVEY. *Clerk of the Court:* R. HICKS.

PORTER, NICOLESS.   Johnston County.

August 24, 1749. September Court, 1749. *Daughters:* JEANE PORTER ("mannor plantation"), ELIZABETH PORTER and ANN PORTER (143 acres of land to each), AGNES PORTER (143 acres of land). *Son:* SAMUELL ("my pole cat land"). *Wife and Executrix:* ELIZABETH. *Executor:* JAMES FAR-MER. *Witnesses:* NEEDHAM BRYAN, MARY DEES. *Clerk of the Court:* RICHARD CASWELL.

PORTER, SAMUEL.   Bladen County.

September 30, 1757. October Court, 1757. *Sons:* JAMES, JOHN, HUGH and SAMUEL. *Executors:* PETER LOARD and WILLIAM MCREE. *Witnesses:* MATTHEW BYRNE, NATHL. PLATT, JOHN LOCK. *Clerk of the Court:* J. BUR-GWYN.

PORTORWIN, PETER.

August 23, 1729.   June 10, 1730.   *Sons:* JOSEPH and SAMUEL.   *Sons-in-law:* JOHN SNOW, FRANCIS DESHUNG.   *Witnesses:* JOHN ARTER, THOMAS HUTCHINGS, ANTHONY MARCK.   Proven before RICHARD EVERARD.

POTTEL, JOSEPH.   Perquimans County.

February 1, 1747–1748.   August 4, 1749.   *Daughter and sole legatee:* ELISABETH POTTEL (Bible, gold ring and riding horse, saddle and bridle). *Executor:* PATRICK POOL.   *Witnesses:* JOSEPH NEWBY, RALPH FLETCHER, SAMUEL MOORE.   Proven before GAB. JOHNSTON.

POWELL, GEORGE.   Bertie Precinct.

March 24, 1735–1736.   May Court, 1736.   *Sons:* CADE, LEWIS, GEORGE, MOSES (to each is bequeathed a negro).   *Executor:* CADER POWELL (son). *Witnesses:* WM. MOOR, CHARLES HORNE, EDMON DOD.   *Clerk of the Court:* JNO. WYNNS.

POWELL, JOHN.   Albemarle County.

February 20, 1723–1724.   *Wife:* ANN.   *Sons:* JOHN and BROOKS POWELL (wife and sons in England and are appointed Executors).   *Friends:* WILLIAM DOWNING and JOSHUA TURNER.   *Witnesses:* MARY DOWNING, JOHN FREEMAN, JOS. FREEMAN.   No probate.

POWELL, THOMAS.   Northampton County.

July 20, 1752.   February Court, 1754.   *Daughters:* KEZIAH and ANN POWELL.   *Wife and Executrix:* ELIZABETH.   *Son:* MATTHEW.   *Witnesses:* JOHN DEW, HENARY HORTON, BARNEBE JOHNSON.   *Clerk of the Court:* I. EDWARDS.

POWELL, WILLIAM.

December, 1748.   Will illegible.

POWERS, GEORGE.   Currituck County.

March 27, 1754.   June Court, 1755.   *Sons:* WILLIAM, GEORGE (plantation between JOSEPH SANDERSON and JOHN WOODHOUSE), CALEB (plantation known as Dicks Field).   *Daughters:* LYDDA ETHERIDGE, JEAN ETHERIDGE, ABIGAL POWERS.   *Wife and Executrix:* ISABEL.   *Witnesses:* JAMES BURNHAM, WILLIAM MARSHAL, RICHARD ETHERIDGE.   *Clerk of the Court:* WILLIAM SHERGOLD.

POWERS, ISBELL.   Currituck County.

November 23, 1757.   December Court, 1757.   *Sons:* WILLIAM, GEORGE and CALEB.   *Daughters:* ISBELL, MARY ETHERIDGE, JEANE ETHERIDGE,

ABBEGALL PINER. *Grandson:* JAMES ETHERIDGE. *Witnesses:* WILLIS ETHERIDGE, ELIZABETH MARSHALL, THOS. RICHARDS. *Clerk of the Court:* WM. MEARNS.

POWERS, WILLIAM.   Chowan Precinct.

November 26, 1747. April 14, 1748. *Sister:* AUSTICE (of Cork in Ireland). *Friend and Executor:* BENJAMIN HILL. *Witnesses:* ABRA. BLACKALL, JOSEPH HARRON, ALEXR. MCCULLOCH. Proven before E. HALL, C. J. Testator bequeathes to sister, leases on the following lands in Ireland: Oaten fields, Leckineene Monetane Shanahane, Knockanearkamas, The Bullock Fields, Fort Fields, Currobrodah.

POYNER, JAMES.   Currituck County.

May 7, 1744. March Court, 1755. *Sons:* HUMPHREY and ROBERT. *Wife and Executrix:* SARAH. *Witnesses:* EDWARD COXE, RICHARD ROGERS, SAML. SIMMONS. *Clerk of the Court:* WILLIAM SHERGOLD.

POYNER, JOS.   Currituck County.

August 19, 1712. *Sons:* WILLIAM and JOSEPH. *Wife:* ELIZABETH. *Executors:* HUMPHREY VINCE and *father*, who is not named. *Witnesses:* JOS. WICKER, RUTH WICKER, HENRY SWANN. No probate.

POYNER, PETER.   Currituck County.

July 6, 1710. April 12, 1715. *Sons:* PETER, JOSEPH, ROBERT and WILLIAM (to each is devised land), THOMAS and JAMES. *Daughter:* ELIZABETH. *Granddaughter:* MARY POYNER. *Friend:* SAMUEL BARBER. *Wife and Executrix:* ELIZABETH. *Witnesses:* HUMPHREY VINES (or VINCE), ELIZABETH DAVIS, JOS. WICKER. *Clerk of the Court:* JO. WICKER.

POYNER (or POINER), WILLIAM.   Currituck County.

April 27, 1753. March Court, 1755. *Son:* NATHANIEL ("plantation whereon I now live and plantation in Moyocke"). *Daughter:* ELIZABETH POYNER (plantation on the Beaver Dam). *Executors:* WILLIAM SHERGOLD and CALEB WILLSON. *Witnesses:* SAML. SIMMONS, JONATHAN POYNER, JOHN CHITTOM. *Clerk of the Court:* WILLIAM SHERGOLD.

POYNER, PETER.   Currituck County.

June 22, 1758. December Court, 1758. *Sons:* PETER, JOEL, BENJAMIN (plantation known by the name of Beach Ridge), NATHAN. *Daughters:* SOPHIA BARCO, MARY MERCER, ESTER SALYER, ABIA PINER, KIZIAH POYNER (or PINER), GEMIMA PARKER. *Wife:* SOPHIA. *Executor:* NATHAN (son). *Witnesses:* WILLIAM BRAY, JOSHUA BALL, REUBEN BALL. *Clerk of the Court:* WM. MEARNS.

POYNER, WILLIAM.   Currituck Precinct.

March 14, 1722. July 9, 1723. *Sons:* WILLIAM and SAMUELL (lands on Currotuck Bay). *Daughter:* MARYANN POYNER. *Wife and Executrix:* LIDEE. *Witnesses:* HANNER MEEGS, THOS. SWANN, WM. LUFMAN. *Clerk of the Court:* JO. WICKER.

PRATT, JOB.   Perquimans County.

December 7, 1736. January Court, 1736. *Son:* JOHN. *Wife:* not named. *Executors:* JOSHUA PRATT (brother), JOHN WILKINS. *Friend:* LUKE GREGORY. *Witnesses:* DAN'L HALL, JOSEPH and JEREMIAH PRATT. *Clerk of the Court:* JAMES CRAVEN.

PRATT, JOHN.   Bertie County.

November 4, 1740. August 2, 1742. *Wife, Executrix and sole legatee:* CHRISTIAN (formerly CHRISTIAN CHAMARD). *Witnesses:* HANH. GALE, SARAH CLAYTON, GEORGE PARRIS. Proven before J. MONTGOMERY, C. J.

PRATT, JOHN.   Chowan County.

August 30, 1743. January Court, 1743. *Brother and Executor:* JOSHUA. *Witnesses:* DAVID BUTLER, JOSEPH MING. *Clerk of the Court:* RICHARD McCLURE.

PRATT, JOSEPH.   Perquimans County.

August 29, 1737. October Court, 1737. *Brothers:* JEREMIAH ("my half of the mill and dwelling house"), JOSHUA. *Executors:* NATHANIEL CARRUTHERS and JOSHUA PRATT (brother). *Witnesses:* NATH'L CARRUTHERS, JOSHUA PRATT and JEREMIAH PRATT. *Clerk of the Court:* JAMES CRAVEN.

PRESCOTT (or PRESCOATE), JOHN.   Beaufort County.

September 21, 1772. March 9, 1773. *Sons:* JOHN, AARON, WILLIAM, BENJAMIN, SIMON. *Daughters:* ANNE McKINGBUSH, ESBELL WILLIAMS, HANNAH PRESCOTT. No executor named. *Witnesses:* MOSES POOLE, JOHN BREFFILL. Proven before Jo. MARTIN.

PRESCOTT, MOSES.   Carteret County.

February 11, 1751. December Court, 1751. *Sons:* WILLIS ("plantation whereon I now live on Bouge Sound"), WILLIAM, MOSES, THOMAS and RUSSELL. *Daughters:* MARY PRESCOTT and SARAH PURDUE. *Wife:* MARY. *Executor:* WILLIAM PRESCOTT (son). *Witnesses:* THO. AUSTIN, MARTHA PRESCOTT, GEORGE McKEAN. *Clerk of the Court:* GEORGE READ.

PRESCOTT (spelled also PRESTCOAT and PRESCOOT),
                    WILLIAM.   Craven County.

March 17, 1744–1745. September Court, 1745. *Sons:* MOSES, WILLIAM, RICHARD, JOB (land between Troters Creek and Panters Creek).
Daughter: MARY PRESCOAT. *Granddaughter:* ELIZABETH PRESCOTT. *Wife and Executrix:* MARY. *Witnesses:* JOHN CARROLL, DANIEL CONERLY, AARON WOOD. *Clerk of the Court:* JNO. RICE.

PRESCOTT, WILLIAM.   Beaufort County.

October 13, 1755. September Court, 1756. *Son:* THOMAS (two plantations on west side of Durrams Creek). *Wife:* AMEY. *Executors:* JAMES BRINSON and JOHN ROE. *Witnesses:* JOHN ADAMS, ANN ADAMS. *Clerk of the Court:* WALLEY CHAUNCEY.

PRICE, PETER.   Beaufort County.

February 3, 1734–1735. March 11, 1734. *Legatees:* MARTHA DICKISON, ELIZABETH, ALIN, JOHN, SARAH, MARTHA, MARY and EZEKIEL DICKISON, JAMES MCKEEL, FRANCIS KNIGHT (*Executrix*). *Witnesses:* BAR. FLEMING, THOS. LEWIS, SARAH LEWIS. *Clerk of the Court:* JOHN COLLISON.

PRICE, RICE.   New Hanover County.

September 27, 1756. *Sons:* RICHARD, JAMES, EDMOND (to each is bequeathed negroes). *Wife and Executrix:* TOMZIN. *Executor:* RICHARD PRICE. *Witnesses:* JOHN ROGERS, HENRY HARKER, WM. PEARSE. *Clerk of the Court:* JA. MORAN.

PRICE, THOMAS.   Albemarle County.

September 18, 1689. February Court, 1696. *Godson:* ARCHIBALD MCDANIEL. MARY HUMFREYS, JOAN MCDANIEL, JOHN SAWYER. *Witnesses:* MICHAEL CONNER, JOHN SAWYER, GARRETT KEEN. *Clerk of the Court:* WM. GLOVER. (*Executor:* DANIEL PHILLIPS. Appointed by Court.)

PRICE, THOMAS.   Edgecombe County.

August 24, 1750. May Court, 1751. *Sons:* WILLIAM, THOMAS and JOHN. *Daughters:* ELIZABETH and RACHEL. *Wife:* not named. *Witnesses:* JOHN HOOKS, WILLIAM RADDAM and JOHN HOOKS, JR. *Clerk of the Court:* BENJAMIN WYNNS.

PRICE, WILLIAM.   Perquimans County.

September 21, 1756. January Court, 1757. *Daughters:* RACHEL and ELIZABETH PRICE, MARY and CHRISTIAN PRICE. *Wife and Executrix:* SARAH. *Witnesses:* ISAAC LILLEY, ABRAHAM RIDDICK, ELIZABETH STALLING. *Clerk of the Court:* MILES HARVEY.

PRICKLOVE, ELIZABETH.   Perquimans Precinct.

July 23, 1728. *Daughters:* LEAH SMITH, RACHEL WILLSON, PRISCILA SANDERS, REBECCA CHANCEY, JUDITH. *Grandchildren:* JOHN SMITH, SELVANUS WILLSON, JUDETH and PRESCILLA SANDERS. *Executor:* DANIEL CHANCY. Proven before RICH'D EVERARD by ELIZABETH ELIOT.

PRICKLOWE, SAMUEL.

January 20, 1702–1703. *Sons:* SAMUEL and FRANCIS. *Wife and Executrix:* PENINAH. *Witnesses:* FRANCIS PINVIC, SIMOND TRUMBULL, JOHN ANDERSON. No probate.

PRINGLE, ALEXANDER.   Craven Precinct.

January 29, 1738–1739. March 1, 1739–1740. *Wife, Executrix and sole legatee:* JANE. *Witnesses:* NICHOLAS FOX, ABRAHAM JESSOP, MARGARET WADE. Proven before GAB. JOHNSTON.

PRITCHARD, BENJAMIN.   Pasquotank County.

February 15, 1740. January Court, 1752. *Brother:* JOSEPH PRITCHARD. *Sister:* SARAH PRITCHARD. *Executors:* brother and sister abovementioned. *Witnesses:* WILLIAM DAVIS, JONATHAN REDDING and JOHN BROOKS. *Clerk of the Court:* THOS. TAYLOR.

PRITCHARD, DAVID.

October 2, 1697. January Court, 1697. *Sons:* THOMAS, HENRY, JAMES, SAMUEL, DAVID. *Executors:* GEORGE HARRIS and RICHARD MADREN. *Witnesses:* RICHARD MADREN, GEORGE HARRIS, PHILIP EVANS. *Clerk of the Court:* EDWARD MAYO.

PRITCHARD, DAVID.   Pasquotank Precinct.

October 20, 1707. January 2, 1707. *Devisees:* JAMES, HUGH and SARAH PRITCHARD (land on Nabs Creek). SAMUEL and RICHARD PRITCHARD (the relationship of testator to these parties is not set out). *Wife and Executrix:* mentioned, but not named. *Witnesses:* PAT GORMACKE, RICHARD MADREN, ANNA MADREN. *Clerk of the Court:* JNO. PALEN (or PALIN).

PRITCHARD, HARBERT.   Bertie Precinct.

September 23, 1738. February Court, 1738. *Sons:* JOHN, WILLIAM and JAMES. *Executor:* JONATHAN STANDLEY, JR. *Witness:* ANN WILLIAMS. *Clerk of the Court:* JNO. WYNNS.

PRITCHARD, JAMES.   Pasquotank County.

June 5, 1754. December Court, 1755. *Wife, Executrix and sole legatee:* SUSANAH. *Witnesses:* WM. COALE, THOS. TAYLOR, ELIZABETH TAYLOR. *Clerk of the Court:* THOS. TAYLOR.

PRITCHARD, JEAN.   Pasquotank Precinct.

October 25, 1707. January 20, 1707. *Executors:* SAMUEL and JAMES
PRITCHARD, PATRICK GORMACKE. No legatees mentioned. *Witnesses:*
GEORGE HARRIS, GEORGE HARRIS, JR., ——— WINBERNE, RICHARD
GRAY. *Clerk of the Court:* JNO. PALIN.

PRITCHETT, ABRAHAM.   Beaufort County.

January 9, 1749. June Court, 1750. *Sons:* PHILIP, JOSHUA, PETER,
ABRAHAM, JAMES (to each is given land and slaves). *Daughters:* SARAH
and ELIZABETH. *Wife:* MARGETT. *Executors:* PHILIP and JOSHUA PRIT-
CHETT (sons). *Witnesses:* JOHN WALLIS, WILLIAM BELL, JAMES FLANNA-
KIN. *Clerk of the Court:* LEVI ALDORSON.

PRITCHETT, JACOB.   Beaufort County.

May 4, 1756. September Court, 1756. "On the South Devidings
Creek and on the South side of Pamplico River." *Sons:* SIMON and
STEPHEN PRITCHETT. *Daughter:* ANNE PRITCHETT. *Other legatees:* JAMES
HERINTON (land called Prisces Neck), JOHN HERINTON. *Wife:* REBECKER.
Executors: NICHOLAS DAW and JOHN WALLIS. *Witnesses:* MARY TIN-
DESLY, ABIGAL DAW, JEANE COLLEBAR. *Clerk of the Court:* WALLEY
CHAUNCEY.

PRITCHETT, MARGARET.   Beaufort County.

January 12, 1756. March Court, 1756. *Sons:* PETER, JAMES, ABRA-
HAM, PHILIP, JOSHUAY. *Daughter:* SARAH BOND. *Granddaughters:* ELISA-
BETH, SARAH and MARGET PRITCHETT. *Executor:* PETER PRITCHETT
(son). *Witnesses:* THOMAS CAMPAN, MARY TILDESBY. *Clerk of the Court:*
WALLEY CHAUNCEY.

PRITLOWE, JOHN.   Perquimans Precinct.

September 8, 1720. May 1, 1728. *Daughters:* RACHEL WILLSON,
JUDITH SANDERS, ELIZABETH ELIOT. *Grandson:* JOHN SMITH. *Wife and
Executrix:* ELIZABETH. *Witnesses:* JOSEPH JESSOP and ROBERT MOORE.
Proven before RICHARD EVERARD.

PROUSE, ANNE.

December 14, 1682. *Brother:* CHARLES PROUSE. *Friend:* ELIZABETH
WILLIAMS. *Witnesses:* ARNOULD WHITE, WILLIAM MABERY. No probate.

PUGH, FRANCIS.   Bertie Precinct.

July 5, 1733. October 4, 1736. *Sons:* JOHN ("plantation whereon I
now live"), THOMAS (land "at the Emperors Fields which I bought of
CHRISTIAN HITTEBURGH"). Lands at Grindale Creek and lands in Bertie
and Edgecombe Precincts divided between two sons; lands in Virginia

ordered to be sold.   Negroes divided between wife and children.   "It is my will that my wife have the management of the ferry where HENRY HORNE lives * * *."   Provision for overplus after payment of debts to be laid out in young negroes.   *Wife and Executrix:* PHEREBE.   *Executors:* COL. ROBERT WEST and CULLEN POLLOCK.   *Witnesses:* NEEDHAM BRYAN, HENRY HORNE and WILL'M JONES.   *Clerk of the Court:* JOHN WYNNS.   Codicil provides for completion of brigantine, and lading and sending same to Great Britain—cargo, tobacco and black walnut.   "It is my will & desire that after my sloop Carolina return from New England * * * that my executors purchase a cargo and send the said sloop to the West Indies."   *Witnesses:* JOHN CHANCEL, SAM'L SABAN PLOMER, PETER BRITTON.   Codicil proven before GAB. JOHNSTON.

PUGH, JOHN.

April 14, 1740.   August 5, 1740.   *Wife:* HANNAH.   *Son:* JOHN. *Brothers and Executors:* THEOPHILUS and DANIEL PUGH (all estate of testator, both in Virginia and North Carolina, bequeathed to these two brothers in trust for son JOHN).   *Witnesses:* ABRAHAM BLACKALL, MILES GALE, JAMES CRAVEN.   Proven before W. SMITH, C. J.

PURCELL, NEILL.   Craven County.

March 5, 1752.   February Court, 1753.   *Wife, Executrix and sole legatee:* SARAH.   *Witnesses:* FAREBE WILLIAMS, R. MOORE, JNO. SNEAD. *Clerk of the Court:* SOL. REW.

PURDY, GEORGE.

July 10, 1733.   August 2, 1733.   All estate is left to *wife*, who is not named.   *Executors:* RICHARD SANDERSON, EDWARD SALTER.   *Witnesses:* GEORGE BURRINGTON, J. POWELL, THOMAS SHERWIN.   Proven before WILLIAM LITTLE.

PURKENS, DAVID.   Bath County.

April 26, 1733.   March 15, 1734.   *Sons:* JAMES, JONATHAN.   *Daughters:* ELISABETH WORLEY, MARY PUTTNELL, AFFERECA HARVEY, ANN JONES, REBECKAH and SARAH PURKENS.   *Wife and Executrix:* MARY. *Witnesses:* SIMON ALDERSON, JOEL MARTIN, JAMES PIRKINS.   *Clerk of the Court:* JNO. COLLISON.

PURSER, ROBERT.   Bath County.

May 10, 1733.   September 11, 1733.   *Sons:* RICHARD ("plantation I now live on called Ecrepint," on South Dividing Creek), JAMES and BENJAMIN.   *Daughter:* MARY PURSER.   *Executors:* WILLIAM DAW and JACOB PRITCHETT.   *Witnesses:* JOHN LEE, JACOB PRITCHETT, HUMPHRY HAWKINS.   *Clerk of the Court:* JNO. COLLISON.

PURYER, ROBERT.   Edgecombe County.

December 25, 1758. June Court, 1759. *Sons:* ROBERT ("my planta-
tion"), WILLIAM. *Daughters:* MARY, MARGARET, ELIZABETH and ANN.
Wife and Executrix: FRANCES. *Executor:* MOSES HORNE. *Witnesses:*
WILLIAM HOBGOOD, RACHEL TANER. *Clerk of the Court:* JOS. MONTFORT.

PUTNELL, WILLIAM.

November 7, 1733. December Court, 1734. Duck Creek. *Sons:*
AARON, JOHN. *Wife and Executrix:* MARY. *Brothers:* THOMAS and JOHN
WORSELY. *Witnesses:* ROBT. GREAVY, EDD. DOE, JNO. CLIFFORD and
ROGER JONES. *Clerk of the Court:* JNO. COLLISON.

QUINN, LOFTIN.   Carteret County.

February 17, 1766. *Sons:* WILLIAM and THOMAS. *Daughter:* MAR-
GRETT QUINN. *Wife and Executrix:* MARY QUINN, formerly MARY CANADY.
Executor: JAMES FREZER. *Witnesses:* WILLIAM and SARAH COALE, ABI-
GAIL COALE. Proven before JO. MARTIN.

RAGLAND, FREDERICK.   Northampton County.

August 2, 1757. February Court, 1758. *Brothers and Executors:*
GEORGE and WILLIAM. *Witnesses:* JAMES PARHAM, ROGER TAYLOR,
EPHRAIM MACGUFFIE. *Clerk of the Court:* I. EDWARDS.

RAGLAND, STEPHEN.   Northampton County.

March 1, 1746. February Court, 1747. *Sons:* STEPHEN, GEORGE,
WILLIAM and FREDERICK (plantation to each), EVEN. *Daughter:* AGNESS
(one Indian slave). *Wife:* MARY. *Executors:* EVEN and GEORGE RAG-
LAND (sons). *Witnesses:* ROBERT HICKS, JOHN HAMILTON, JOHN WEBB.
Clerk of the Court: I. EDWARDS.

RAMAN, WILLIAM.   Albemarle County.

October 12, 1713. *Sons:* THOMAS and EDWARD (plantation to each).
Daughters: ELIZABETH SCARBOROUGH, SARAH and MARY RAMAN. *Wife
and Executrix:* SARAH. *Witnesses:* JNO. HAWKINS, THOMAS PASSINGHAM.
No probate.

RAPHELD, WILLIAM.

January 20, 1757. March Court, 1757. *Sons:* BENJAMIN, WILLIAM,
THOMAS, ISAAC. *Wife and Executrix:* ANN. *Witnesses:* JOHN ROUTEN,
WILLIAM RAPHELD. *Clerk of the Court:* FR. WARD.

RASOR, FRANCES.   Bertie County.

April 20, 1747. December 18, 1748. *Son:* EDWARD RASOR. *Daughters:* ELIZABETH HARDY, CHRISTINA BELL. *Daughter-in-law:* ELIZABETH RASOR. *Granddaughter:* FRANCES HARDY. *Executor:* LAMB HARDY (son-in-law). *Witnesses:* WILLIAM HARDY, THOMAS and CHARITY TODD. Proven before E. HALL, C. J.

RASBUARY, JOHN.   Bertie County.

September 11, 1749. February Court, 1749. *Sons:* WILLIAM RASBUARY, THOMAS YAITS, ARTHUR PINNER. *Grandson:* JOHN RASBUARY. *Daughters:* REBECKAH PINNER, BRIDGET YAITS, ELIZABETH WILLIAMS, ANN BEVERLER, MARY UNKERS, CHRISTIAN LOID. *Executors:* BRIDGET RASBUARY (wife), WILLIAM and HOSEA RASBUARY. *Witnesses:* ISAAC HILL, EDWARD WILLIAMS. *Clerk of the Court:* JOHN LOVICK.

RATLIF, DAMARIS.

February 12, 1734. February 24, 1734. *Son:* JOSEPH. *Daughters:* MARY MORE, SARAH WINSLOW. *Sons-in-law:* JOHN MORE, THOMAS WINSLOW. *Granddaughter:* BETTY MORE. *Executors:* ZACHARIAH NIXON (brother), JOHN MORE and THOMAS WINSLOW. *Witnesses:* RICHARD DAVIS, MARY GILBART. Proven before GAB. JOHNSTON.

RATLIFF, RICHARD.   Perquimans Precinct.

June 17, 1724. July 14, 1724. *Sons:* THOMAS and JOSEPH (lands in Virginia and North Carolina). *Daughters:* ELIZABETH, MARY, SARAH, HULDAH. *Wife and Executrix:* DAMARIS. *Executor:* CORNELIUS RATLIFF (brother). *Witnesses:* ZACHARIAH NIXON, FRANCIS CROXTON, MARY NICHOLSON. *Clerk of the Court:* RICHD. LEARY.

RATTLIF, SAMUEL.

February 31, 1733. July 11, 1733. *Son:* ISAAC (plantation on Saman Creek). *Daughters:* ELISABETH and ISBELL. *Other legatees:* PARTHANEY and WILLIAM BALL. *Executors:* NATHANEL HILL and THOMAS ASHLEY. *Witnesses:* WILLIAM BYRD and ANN BALL and WILLIAM ASHLEY. Proven before GEORGE BURRINGTON.

RAWLINGS, BENJAMIN.   Edgecombe Precinct.

December 10, 1738. February Court, 1738. *Legatees:* ROBERT LOCKALEAR, DAVID COLTRAINE, EDMOND KEARNY (son of THOS. and SARAH), JAMES FLOOD, BENJAMIN HILL, JR. (son of BENJAMIN and SARAH), HENRY HILL, SARAH KEARNY, ELIZABETH ALSTON (wife of JOSEPH JOHN), WILLIAM ALSTON, ELIZABETH WILLIAMS (wife of SAMUEL). *Executors:* THOS. KEARNY and DAVID COLTRAINE. *Witnesses:* SAM'L WILLIAMS, R WHITTINGTON, WILLIAM LEE. *Clerk of the Court:* RT. FORSTER.

RAWLINGS, JOHN.   Northampton County.

March 26, 1747. November Court, 1747. *Daughters:* LUCY and
SUSANNAH RAWLINGS. *Wife and Executrix:* HANNAH RAWLINGS. *Witnesses:* ART. HARRIS, GEORGE JORDAN, WM. RAWLINGS and GEORGE
JORDAN, SENR. *Clerk of the Court:* RT. FORSTER.

RAYFIELD, WILLIAM.   Pasquotank Precinct.

August 4, 1722. March 23, 1731. Of Allegator in the Precinct of
Pasquotank. *Sons:* WILLIAM, JAMES (land called the Wild Cat Neck),
JOHN. *Wife and Executrix:* ANN. *Executor:* EDWARD LININGTON. *Witnesses:* EDWD. LININGTON, JOHN COMES, SETH PHELPS, RICHARD PUFFENGHALL. Proven before GEORGE BURRINGTON.

RAYFORD, MATTHEW.   Bladen County.

July 21, 1752. April Court, 1758. *Sons:* MATTHEW, ROBERT, WILLIAM and PHILIP. *Daughters:* MARY, ANNE, MOURNING, REBECKAH,
GRACE and DRUSILLA. *Wife and Executrix:* MOURNING. *Executor:* ISAAC
BUSH. *Witnesses:* MARGARET ARMSTRONG, FRANK ARMSTRONG and
THOMAS JONES. *Clerk of the Court of Cumberland County:* JAMES SIMPSON.

RAYMOND, THOMAS.

June 26, 1730. July 31, 1730. "Dover in ye County of Kent, Kingdom of Great Brittain." *Daughter:* ELIZABETH RAYMOND. *Other legatees:* JOB BROOK, ELIZABETH (daughter of Jos. BELL), JAMES WAINWRIGHT (book called Lexicon Technicon), JOHN STARKEY, PETER STARKEY.
Executors: JOHN STARKEY and THOMAS NELSON. *Witnesses:* RICHD.
RUSTULL, PETER STARKEY, JOHN STARKEY. Proven before RICHARD
EVERARD.

READ, GEORGE.   Carteret County.

May 26, 1753. September Court, 1753. *Son:* ROBERT (land in Carteret and in Barbadoes). *Daughters:* SARAH and FRANCES READ, MARTHA
(wife of ISRAEL CHRISTIAN). *Wife and Executrix:* ANN. *Friends:*
THOMAS LOVICK and DAVID SHEPARD. *Witnesses:* GEORGE COGDELL,
GRIGG YARBOROUGH, JACOB SHEPARD. Signature of probate officer
missing.

READING, CHURCHILL.   Bath County.

September 19, 1734. February 14, 1734. *Nephews:* CHURCHILL CALDOM, JOHN and JACOB BLOUNT. *Brother-in-law:* JOHN CALDOM. *Wife
and Executrix:* MARTHA (four negroes). *Executors:* ROBERT WEST,
THOMAS WORSLEY and JOHN CALDOM. *Witnesses:* EDW. TRAVIS, HARMAN
HILL and EDWARD SALTER. Proven before GAB. JOHNSTON.

READING, JOSEPH.   Pasquotank County.
June 29, 1731. August 3, 1731. *Sons:* SAMUEL, THOMAS, JOHN,
JONATHAN and JOSEPH. *Daughters:* MARY, MIRIAM and SARAH READING,
ANN PENDLETON. *Wife and Executrix:* SARAH. *Witnesses:* DAVID BOLES,
DANIEL RHODES and BENJA. PRITCHARD. Proven before GEO. BURRING-
TON.

READING, LIONEL.   Bath County.
July 12, 1708. February 18, 1725. *Sons:* NATHANIEL, CHURCHILL.
Daughters: SARAH DUPUIS and MARY READING, ANN READING. Negroes
bequeathed to sons and daughters. *Wife:* not named. *Executors:* DAVIS
DUPUIS and HUMPHREY LEGG. *Witnesses:* JAMES LEIGH, HENRY BROOK,
JOHN LAWSON. Proven before RICHD. EVERARD.

READING, THOMAS.   Beaufort County.
January 24, 1749. March Court, 1748–1749. *Niece:* MARGARET CAL-
DOM. *Nephew:* CHURCHILL CALDOM (husband of MARGARET and son of
sister, ANN CALDOM). *Executors:* ABRAHAM DUNCAN and RICHARD
EVANS. *Witnesses:* MARY DUNCAN, MARY POWERS, JOHN McKENNY.
Clerk of the Court: JOHN FORBES. *Executor* qualified before GAB. JOHNS-
TON.

REAVIS, EDWARD.   Northampton County.
February 21, 1750. February Court, 1752. *Son:* JESSE. *Daughters:*
JUDE and MARY REAVIS. *Wife and Executrix:* SARAH. *Executor:* CAPT.
JOHN PERSON of Virginia. *Witnesses:* ARTHR. HARRIS, JOHN GILLIAM,
ARTHUR JORDAN. *Clerk of the Court:* I. EDWARDS.

RECKSAKER, DANIEL.   Pasquotank Precinct.
February 27, 1732–1733. May 16, 1733. *Legatees:* MARY ANN MITCH-
ELL (daughter), SARAH PINDLETON (Executrix). *Witnesses:* WILLIAM
DAVIS, WILLM. AMBLER. Proven before WM. LITTLE, *Chief Justice.*

REDDITT, WILLIAM.   Bertie County.
August 24, 1739. October 29, 1739. *Sons:* JOHN (plantation on the
south side of Buckelsberry Swamp), WILLIAM, JOSEPH, JOEL, ISAAC (to
each is devised a plantation). *Daughters:* MARGARET, ANN, MARTHA and
MARY REDDITT. *Other legatee:* THOMAS YEATES. *Wife and Executrix:*
SUSSANNAH. *Executors:* JOHN REDDITT (son) and JOHN OXLEY. *Wit-
nesses:* GEORGE, ROBERT and MARY LAWRENCE. Proven before W.
SMITH, C. J.

REDDING, JOHN.   Perquimans County.
January 28, 1754. April Court, 1754. "I give and bequeath to
ELIZABETH FULLENTON, my dearly beloved and intended wife, my plan-

tation next to JESSE EASON'S." *Cousin:* JOHN ELLIS. *Executors:* JOHN DAVIS and JOSHUA SMALL (brothers-in-law). *Witnesses:* JESSE EASON, JOSEPH SKETO and JOHN HARRIS. *Clerk of the Court:* WILL. SKINNER.

REDING, JOSEPH.   Perquimans County.

October 26, 1751. January Court, 1753. *Sons:* JAMES and JOHN (lands at Ballahack). *Daughters:* MARY, RACHEL and CHARITY. *Executors:* JAMES and JOHN (sons). *Witnesses:* STURGISS EDERINGAME, ABRAHAM BALLARD, JESSE EASON. *Clerk of the Court:* EDMUND HATCH.

REDDING, WILLIAM.   Halifax County.

October 26, 1773. February 3, 1774. *Son:* JOSEPH. *Daughters:* PATTY BROWN, MARY, ANN and AMEY REDDING. *Wife and Executrix:* ANN. *Executors:* JAMES BROWN (son-in-law) and WILLIAM WILLIAMS. *Witnesses:* JAMES DAVIS, MARTHA HOOKS. Proven before Jo. MARTIN.

REED, ANDREW.   Perquimans Precinct.

February 29, 1723. July Court, 1728. *Grandsons:* WILLIAM and ANDREW WOODLEY, JONATHAN KEETON (to WILLIAM is bequeathed an Indian slave). *Daughter:* ELIZABETH KEETON (Executrix). *Granddaughter:* MARY WOODLEY. *Witnesses:* RICHD. SKINER, RICHD. RATLIF. *Clerk of the Court:* R. EVERARD.

REED, JOSEPH.   Anson County.

1750. July Court, 1751. *Son:* WILLIAM. *Wife and other children,* not named. Plantation near the Catawba River. *Executors:* JOHN BRANDON and JOHN NESBET. *Witnesses:* JOSEPH CATE, JOHN RAILY, JOHN ARTLEDGE. *Clerk of the Court:* M. BROWN.

REELL, PETER.   Craven County.

November 19, 1739. November 24, 1739. *Sons:* PETER, JOSHUA, JAMES. *Daughters:* ELIZABETH and MARY. *Wife and Executrix:* MARY. *Executors:* SIMON BRIGHT and RICHARD EVANS. *Witnesses:* JOHN BERRY, JOHN JAMES, JOHN HILL. Proven before W. SMITH, C. J.

REESE, OWEN.   Pasquotank County.

April 7, 1745. July Court, 1745. *Sons:* JOHN and OWIN. *Daughters:* BETTY, SARAH, MARY and ANN REESE. *Wife and Executrix:* MARY. *Executor:* DANIELL WILLIAMS. *Witnesses:* JOHN BURNHAM, DAVID and WILLIAM CARTRIGHT. *Clerk of the Court:* THOS. TAYLOR.

REGAN, DANIEL.

November 27, 1727. *Son:* DANIEL. *Brother:* THOMAS. *Daughters:* ANN, SARAH, MARY and PRISCILLA REGAN. *Other legatee:* THOMAS GOODSON. *Wife and Executrix:* SARAH. *Witnesses:* WM. BALDWIN, THOMAS REGAN. No probate.

REGGONS, JOSEPH.   Bertie County.

April 2, 1727. August Court, 1727. *Son:* JOSEPH. *Daughters:* MARTHA, MARY, HANNAH, OLIVE REGGONS. *Son-in-law:* JOHN WEEB. *Wife and Executrix:* ELIZABETH. *Witnesses:* WM. BOLDIN, DANIELL REGGONS, THOMAS REGGONS. *Clerk of the Court:* RT. FORSTER.

RELF, JOHN.   Pasquotank County.

September 22, 1742. January Court, 1742. *Sons and Executors:* CORNELIUS and JOHN. *Witnesses:* JOHN and MARY BELL, CORNELIUS JONES. *Clerk of the Court:* THO. TAYLOR.

RELF, MARY.   Pasquotank Precinct.

January 13, 1724–1725. April Court, 1725. *Brother:* WILLIAM RELF. *Brother's grandchildren:* THOMAS and MARY RELF. *Daughters:* SARAH CHANCE, SUSANAH CHANCE. *Son-in-law:* THOMAS PALIN. *Granddaughters:* MARY and ANN PALIN. *Son and Executor:* ROBERT KEEL. *Witnesses:* JAMES SPENCE, ALEXANDER SPENCE, DOROTHY ADAMS. *Clerk of the Court:* JOHN PARK.

RELFE, THOMAS.

April 10, 1704. No probate. *Wife and Executrix:* MARY. *Son:* THOMAS. *Daughter:* DOROTHY RELFE. *Other legatee:* WILLIAM ROADS. *Witnesses:* JOHN BISHOP, ROBERT KEEL, MARY BISHOP.

RENFROW, JOHN.   Edgecombe County.

May 30, 1748. August Court, 1748. *Sons:* ENUCH, JACOB, GEORGE, WILLIAM and JAMES. *Wife:* TOMESON. *Executor:* MATTHEW McKINNEY. *Witnesses:* JOHN HAYWOOD, NATHANIEL HOLLY, JOHN EVANS. *Clerk of the Court:* BENJN. WYNNS.

RESTON, THOMAS.   New Providence.

March 31, 1723. December 17, 1724. *Wife and Executrix:* ANN. *Witnesses:* WILLIAM JONES, WILLIAM WILLIAMS, WILLIAM WALTERS, JOHN FRENCH. Proven before E. MOSELEY.

REW, SOUTHY.   Craven County.

January, 1754. February Court, 1754. *Sons:* SOLOMON ("plantation whereon I now live on the East side of Owens Creek"), THOMAS (land on Owens' Creek), BEVERLY (land on South River known as Butchers), SOUTHY (two lots in Newbern), SOLOMON. *Daughters:* MARY and EUPHAMA. *Wife:* MARY. Negroes to be divided between wife and children. *Executors:* JOHN STARKEY and SOLOMON REW. *Witnesses:* JOHN SNEAD and CHARLES COGDELL. *Clerk of the Court:* SOL. REW.

REYNAUD, BENJAMIN. Currituck Precinct.

April 8, 1712. *Son and Executor:* MOSES. *Witnesses:* JOSEPH WALTER, ROSMUS HERSLEFF, DANIEL RICE. Original missing. Recorded in Book 1712–1722, page 24.

RHODES, HENRY. Onslow County.

September 14, 1751. October Court, 1751. *Sons:* HENRY ("my mannor plantation"), THOMAS. *Son-in-law:* DANIEL MASBONE. *Granddaughter:* ELIZABETH MASHBONE. *Wife and Executrix:* MARY. *Witnesses:* THOMAS RHODES, PATIENCE JOHNSON, JOSHUA PAULL. *Clerk of the Court:* THOS. BLACK.

RHODES, HENRY. Dobbs County.

December 21, 1773. January 25, 1774. *Sons:* JACOB, HENRY, WILLIAM, JAMES. *Daughters:* MARY RINCEY, BABREY RHODES, RACHEL and SARAH RHODES. *Wife:* ELIZABETH. *Executors:* BEEAMAN RHODES, WILLIAM JONES and JOSEPH FEW. *Witnesses:* JOHN FILLYAW, MOSES COX, ROBERT WINSETT. Proven before JO. MARTIN.

RHODES, RICHARD. Pasquotank Precinct.

March 2, 1693–1694. *Wife and Executrix:* ELISABETH. *Witnesses:* RICHARD MADREN, SARA DAVIS, JOHN SKIPAR. *Clerk of the Court:* EDWARD MAYO.

RHODES, WILLIAM. Pasquotank County.

January Court, 1734. *Sons:* THOMAS and WILLIAM. *Daughters:* SARAH, DOROTHY, ELIZABETH and MARY RHODES. *Wife and Executrix:* ELIZABETH. *Executor:* WILLIAM RELFE. *Witnesses:* FRANCIS MARTIN, COMFORT CAMMILL, JAMES BIGGERS. *Clerk of the Court:* JOS. SMITH.

RHOADS, WILLIAM. Tyrrell County.

August 29, 1753. September Court, 1753. *Sons:* WILLIAM ("my manner plantation"), JOHN. *Daughter:* MARGARET COLLINGS. *Wife:* ELIZABETH. *Executors:* WILLIAM and JOHN RHOADS (sons). *Witnesses:* THOMAS BEDFORD, JOHN BROWNING, CHRISTOPHER BUTTERY. *Clerk of the Court:* EVAN JONES.

RICE, BENJAMIN. Beaufort County.

September 12, 1745. June Court, 1746. *Sons:* ZEBULON, BANJAMIN, JAMES, EVEN, CLANERLY, EPHRIM, HEZEKIAH, GIDEON. *Wife and Executrix:* MARY. *Witnesses:* JAMES HUMES, NATHANIEL DRAPER, THOMAS WILLIA. *Clerk of the Court:* JOHN FORBES.

RICE, EDWARD.   Bertie County.

December 8, 1752. May Court, 1753. *Son:* JOHN. *Daughters:* MARY
and BETTY RICE. *Wife and Executrix:* ANN. *Executor:* THOMAS SLATTOR.
Witnesses: JOHN COKE, SR., JAMES HAIR, WALTER and ELIZABETH JOANES.
Clerk of the Court: BENJAMIN WYNNS.

RICE, JOHN.   Chowan County.

May 20, 1745. January Court, 1753. *Wife:* SARAH. *Brother and Executor:* EDWARD RICE. *Witnesses:* HARDY HURDELL, BENJAMIN BERREMAN,
THOMAS ROWNTREE. *Clerk of the Court:* JAMES CRAVEN.

RICE, LUCY.

February 15, 1720–1721. This is a nuncupative will proven by ROBERT
PALMER and THOMAS PALIN before JNO. PALIN and names *daughters,* MARY
and CELY.

RICE, MARY.   New Hanover County.

July 9, 1753. February 21, 1754. *Executors:* THOMAS CAMBER and
PENNY BUSSY (sister). Proven before MATT. ROWAN. Coat of arms on
seal. This will is so torn as to render all other names illegible.

RICE, MORGIN.

October 26, 1684. No date of probate. *Legatee:* SARAH BURNBY,
daughter of JOHN BURNBY, who is appointed Executor. *Witnesses:* WIL-
LIAM BURNBY, ANTHONY HATCH. Coat of arms on seal.

RICE, NATHANIEL.   New Hanover County.

December 6, 1752. February 27, 1753. *Son:* JOHN. *Sisters-in-law:*
HANNAH and PENNY BURSEY. *Wife's niece:* ELIZABETH DALE. *Wife and
Executrix:* MARY. *Niece:* ELIZABETH TWINER of Rumsey, in Hampshire.
Executors: JAS. HASELL, SAM'L and JOHN SWANN. *Witnesses:* JAMES POR-
TERFIELD, DAVID LINDSAY, ARC. MACLAINE. *Clerk of the Court:* ISAAC
FARIES.

RICHARDS, JOHN.   Pasquotank County.

July 11, 1741. July 14, 1741. *Son-in-law:* LAW. PRIDEES. *Wife and
Executrix:* MARY. *Witnesses:* THO. WEEKES, JOHN NELSON, JR., THEOPH-
ILUS MANN. *Clerk of the Court:* THOS. TAYLOR.

RICHARDS, MARY.   Pasquotank County.

October 31, 1743. November 19, 1743. *Daughter:* FRANCES PREDY.
Son-in-law and Executor: LAWS PREDY. *Witnesses:* J. HULL, ANDREW
MOORE, J. HARDY. Proven before J. MONTGOMERY. *Justice of the Peace:*
JAS. CRAVEN. Coat of arms on seal.

RICHARDS, RICHARD.   Edgecombe County.
October 23, 1758. December Court, 1758. *Sons:* JOHN, JESSE and
RICHARD. *Wife and Executrix:* REBECCA. *Executor:* DAVID CRAWLEY.
Witnesses: WM. KINCHEN, WM. HAYES, JOHN GREEN. *Clerk of the Court:*
JOS. MONTFORT.

RICHARDSON, DANIEL.   Pasquotank Precinct.
February 28, 1723. March 5, 1723. *Legatees:* GEORGE BURRINGTON
(one negro), JOHN LOVICK (one negro), —— GOFF, MARGARET BERNS-
BEE, MRS. ANN KNIGHT, wife of LEWIS MCALIXANDER KNIGHT. *Execu-
tors:* GEORGE BURRINGTON, JOHN LOVICK and —— GOFF. *Witnesses:*
PATRICK OGLESBEE, WILLIAM JEFFREYS, BARTHOLOMEW SCOTT, THOMAS
RAYMOND. Proven before GEORGE BURRINGTON.

RICHARDSON, GEORGE.   New Hanover County.
November 15, 1750. *Executor and sole legatee:* JEHU DAVIS, SENR.
Witnesses: SAML. and THOS. NEALE, ANTHY. WARD. *Clerk of the Court:*
JA. MORAN.

RICHARDSON, JOHN.   Perquimans County.
November 28, 1743. January Court, 1743. *Son:* JAMES. *Daughter:*
ANNE RICHARDSON. *Wife and Executrix:* MARY. *Witnesses:* JAMES GIB-
SON, JOHN PARRISH. *Clerk of the Court:* EDMUND HATCH.

RICHARDSON, JOHN.   Craven County.
September 11, 1773. September 16, 1773. (Newbern.) *Legatees:* WIL-
LIAM EVEN (one negro "now in possession of WILLIAM BROOK SIMPSON
Attorney in Newport Rhode Island and one negro man on board my sloop
called the Betsey"), PETER GORDON (son of PATRICK GORDON, of New-
bern). *Executors:* JOSEPH CRISPIN and RIGDON BRICE. *Witnesses:* JAMES
GREEN, JAMES PARRATT, BENJN. GREENAWAY. Proven before JO. MARTIN.

RICHARDSON, STEPHEN.   Pasquotank County.
February 7, 1722. July 16, 1723. *Sons:* JOHN ("plantation whereon I
live called the Poplars Havin"), STEPHEN (land called the White Oak
Neck), RICHARD (land called Blewbootens Neck, the said RICHARD to allow
THOMAS BETTYS to live on said land if he, the said BETTYS shall build a
house "twenty five foot long and fifteen foot wide and plant ought a or-
chard of apells trees thirty foot Destent for the Great Stones Sort and
Twenty five foot aney other Sort &c."), LEBBEOS and JOSEPH. *Daughter:*
ELIZABETH. *Wife and Executrix:* MARY. *Trustees:* JOHN and JAMES
TREWBLOOD. *Witnesses:* JAMES GREVES, KATHERINE GREVES and HAN-
NAH EVERTON. *Clerk of the Court:* W. NORRIS.

RICHMOND, HENRY.

September 15, 1714. December 4, 1714. *Wife:* not named. *Cousin and Executor:* CALEB BUNDY. *Witnesses:* CHARLES BULL and MARY STANTON. No probate.

RICKITSON, GORDIUS.   Craven County.

September 25, 1773. March 19, 1774. New Bern. *Sons:* JESSE, BENJAMIN, GORDIUS. *Daughter:* BATHSHABA. *Wife and Executrix:* ABIGAIL. *Witnesses:* JOHN GRANADE, JOHN MERKER, EDW. WHITTY. Proven before JO. MARTIN.

RICKS, BENJAMIN.   Chowan County.

March 31, 1719. November 30, 1721. *Brothers:* JAMES, ROBERT, ABRAHAM and ISAAC RICKS. *Nephew:* ROBERT RICKS, JR. (land on Notaway River). *Sister:* JANE RICKS. *Other legatees:* PATIENCE RICKS (niece) and WILLIAM BROWN, son of BEALE BROWN. *Wife and Executrix:* SARAH. *Witnesses:* BRIDGET ROGERS, MARY ROGERS, JOHN PHIPPS. Proven before C. EDEN, *Governor.*

RICKS, ISAAC.   Edgecombe County.

March 11, 1748. October 28, 1748. *Sons:* ABRAHAM and ROBERT and JOHN (two negroes to each). *Daughters:* MARY POP and MARTHA RICKS. *Wife and Executrix:* SARAH. *Witnesses:* JOHN CROWELL, RICHARD RICHARDS. Proven before E. HALL, *Chief Justice.*

RIDDICK, JOSEPH.   Perquimans County.

September 20, 1759. October Court, 1759. *Sons:* JOSEPH (plantation bought of THOMAS WARD), KADAK (plantation bought of WILLIAM ROUNTREE, MOSES FIELDS and JAMES PRICE; also plantation bought of WILLIAM MOORE and WILLIAM WILLSON lying in Ballahack), ISAAC (lands bought of JOHN BARCLIF and GEORGE SHELL "that lyes over Little River upon deep Creek"). *Daughter:* MARY RIDDICK. *Wife and Executrix:* HANNAH. *Executor:* ROBERT RIDDICK (brother). *Witnesses:* JOSEPH PERRY, BENJAMIN PERRY, JOB RIDDICK. *Clerk of the Court:* MILES HARVEY.

RIDGE, THOMAS.

February 17, 1747–1748. *Sons:* GODFREY and WILLIAM. *Daughters:* ANNE and MARY RIDGE. *Wife and Executrix:* ELIZABETH. *Witnesses:* BENJAMIN BURGESS, ELIZABETH McGEE, DANIEL McPETERS. *Clerk of the Court:* JOHN DUNN.

RIGBY, WILLIAM.   New Hanover County.

December 18, 1743. June Court, 1744. Wilmington. Lands on Long Creek, Lockwood's Folly, Black River and lot in Wilmington to be divided between MARGERY RIGBY (mother), JOHN RIGBY (brother) and ALICE MARSDEN. Brigantine "on her return from the West Indies" to be sold and proceeds applied to payment of debts. *Executor:* RUFUS MARSDEN (brother-in-law). *Witnesses:* JAMES SMALLWOOD, THOMAS FINNEY, JOSEPH GARY. *Clerk of the Court:* JAMES SMALLWOOD.

RIGNEY, BENJAMIN.   Beaufort County.

December 3, 1750. March 12, 1750. *Daughter:* MARY RIGNEY. *Brother:* JAMES RIGNEY. *Niece:* HANNAH RIGNEY. *Wife and Executrix:* FEBE. *Executors:* WILLIAM WAGGENER and READING BLOUNT. *Clerk of the Court:* WILL. ORMOND.

RIGNEY, JOHN.   Beaufort Precinct.

June 14, 1725. April Court, 1726. *Daughter:* ELISABETH. *Executor:* BENJAMIN SLADE (land called the Fork on condition that he "cause my daughter to be teached to read the Bible distinctly and putt her in school"). *Other legatee:* HENRY TRIP. *Witnesses:* JOHN SLADE, WILLIAM SATTERTHWAITE, GI. HOLLIDAY. *Clerk of the Court:* THOMAS JONES. Original missing. Recorded in Book 1722–1735, page 33.

RIORDAME, DENIS.   Currituck County.

January 18, 1723–1724. July 14, 1724. *Wife and Executrix:* SARAH. *Daughter:* ANGELICA. *Other legatees:* THOMAS and WM. VINCE. *Witnesses:* JO. WICKER, SAMUEL SIMMONS, ANN IRELAND, DAVID LEGGETT. *Clerk of the Court:* HENRY SWANN.

RISENOUER, MATTHEW.   Craven County.

November 18, 1747. September Court, 1747. *Sons:* JOHN and JACOB (Executors). *Daughter:* CATREN SMITH. *Wife:* ELISABETH. *Witnesses:* JACOB TAYLER, GASPER GRANADE, PAUL IVES. *Clerk of the Court:* WILL. HEDGES.

RITEGA, JACOB.   Pasquotank Precinct.

March 25, 1735. April Court, 1739. *Daughters:* MARGARET and MIRIAM RITEGA. *Son-in-law:* WILLIAM POWERS. *Wife and Executrix:* PHILLIS. *Witnesses:* WILLIAM LEWIS, THOMAS GASKILLS. *Clerk of the Court:* JOS. SMITH.

RIUSSETT, JOHN.

October 11, 1737. January 17, 1737. Bath Town. "Late of the city of London." *Sons:* JOHN and DAVID RIUSSETT. *Executors:* JOHN MONTGOMERY, THOMAS JONES and PETER RANDON. *Witnesses:* JOHN GARZIA, PETER RANDON. Proven before W. SMITH, C. J.

RIUSSETT, PETER.   Bath County.

January 14, 1734. February 21, 1734. *Nieces:* ANN GALABER, JANE
CAILA, MARY COVEE. *Nephew:* PETTER RANDOWN. *Son:* JOHN BELL.
Brother: JOHN RIUSSETT. *Executors:* EDWARD SALTER and OLIVER BLACK-
BURN. *Other legatee:* CHURCH OF BATH. *Witnesses:* OLIVER BLACKBURN,
PETER RANDON, MATHIAS COLLIER. Proven before GAB. JOHNSTON.

ROBERTS, ANDREW.   Craven Precinct.

January 22, 1722. June Court, 1723. *Sons:* JOHN and ANDREW.
Daughters: ANN and ELIZABETH. *Executor:* ADAM MORE. *Witnesses:*
WM. WILLSON, NATHANIEL BARAN. *Clerk of the Court:* CALEB METCALFE.

ROBERTS, JAMES.   Craven County.

July 24, 1745. This is a nuncupative will proven before DANL. SHINE by
JAMES CONAWAY, and names *Sons:* SAMUEL and JAMES. *Daughter:* MAR-
GRET ROBERTS. *Wife:* ISABLE.

ROBERTS, JAMES.   Craven County.

April 4, 1774. New Bern. *Sons:* RICHARD, JAMES and WILLIAM. *Wife
and Executrix:* ELIZABETH. *Witnesses:* ALEX. GARTEN, JOHN MACKAY,
JAMES COOR. Proven before JO. MARTIN.

ROBERTS, JOSEPH.   Craven County.

January 15, 1774. This is a nuncupative will proven by JAMES FRAZER
and CYNTHIA ROBERTS before JO. MARTIN and names *wife*, ELIZABETH.
Daughters: SALLY and SABONAH. *Father-in-law:* MICAJAH FRAZIER.

ROBERTSON, HENRY.   Edgecombe County.

June 23, 1749. February Court, 1752. *Sons:* HIGDON, HENRY, PETER,
LEWIS (Executor). *Daughter:* DEBORAH ROBERTSON. *Witnesses:* A. J.
SMITH, WILLIAM OGILVIE, CHRISTOPHER OGILVIE. *Clerk of the Court:*
BENJN. WYNNS.

RORERTSON, JAMES.   Pasquotank County.

January 17, 1753. October Court, 1754. *Sons:* MORDECAI ("my man-
ner plantation"), MALACHI ("my Road plantation"). *Daughter:* SALLEY.
Wife and Executrix: SARAH. *Executor:* THOMAS TAYLOR. *Witnesses:*
SAMUEL OKELY, WILLIAM WOODLY, MARY TAYLOR. *Clerk of the Court:*
THOMAS TAYLOR.

ROBINS, JAMES.

November 27, 1725. January 11, 1725. Bath Town. *Brother:* FRANCES
ROBINS (one saddle horse). *Wife and Executrix:* MARGARET. *Executor:*
THOMAS BOYD. *Witnesses:* CHARLES HOLYDAY, RICHARD FRENCH, WM.
SPARRY. Proven before RICHARD EVERARD.

ROBINS, JOSEPH.   Rowan County.

November 18, 1754. *Sons:* JOSEPH, WILLIAM and JOHN. *Daughter:*
ELENOR. *Wife and Executrix:* ELENOR. *Executor:* JOHN NATION (brother-
in-law). *Witnesses:* A. J. SMITH, CH. NATION, RICHARD ROBINS. No
probate.

ROBINSON, CHARLES.   Anson County.

December 29, 1754. *Sons:* CORNELIUS, TOWNSEND and CHARLES.
Daughters: SARAH and ELIZABETH. *Wife and Executrix:* SARAH. *Witnesses:* WILLIAM DOWNS, JOHN STON, JAMES DENSON. No probate.

ROBINSON, HUMPHREY.   Chowan County.

July 15, 1752. July Court, 1752. *Legatees:* ELIZABETH and SUSANNAH
CLELAND (lands in Chowan, houses and lots in Edenton and negroes), JOHN
CLELAND, JOHN COOPER. *Executors:* JOHN CLELAND, JOHN WILKINS. No
witnesses and no probate.

ROBINSON, JAMES.   Albemarle County.

March 12, 1699–1700. All lands and other property to CORNELIUS
JONES, Executor. *Witnesses:* THOMAS MILLER, WILLIAM WOOLARD, JOHN
POWELL. No probate.

ROBINSON, JOHN.   Perquimans County.

October 1, 1757. January Court, 1758. *Sons:* THOMAS and ROWLAND.
Daughter: SARAH ROBINSON. *Wife:* MARY. *Executor:* JOSEPH ROBINSON
(brother) and THOMAS ROBINSON (son). *Witnesses:* JOHN NIXON, JOSHUA
MORRIS, SARAH ROBINSON. *Clerk of the Court:* MILES HARVEY.

ROBINSON, JOSEPH.   Perquimans County.

June 8, 1717. July 9, 1717. *Son:* JOHN. *Daughter:* SARAH ROBIN-
SON. *Wife and Executrix:* JANE. *Witnesses:* NICHOLAS GUYOR, TIMOTHY
CLARE and ELIZABETH WINSLOW. *Clerk of the Court:* RICHARD LEARY.

ROBINSON, THOMAS.   Albemarle County.

March 4, 1718–1719. April 2, 1719. Little River in the County of
Albemarle. *Sons:* JOSEPH and JOHN (land and negroes). *Daughter:*
ANNE ROBINSON. *Executors:* ZACHARIAH NIXON, FRANCIS TOMES and
JOHN SYMONS. *Witnesses:* JOSEPH MING, JOSIAH BINGHAM, SAMUEL
SHERER. Proven before FRANCIS FOSTER. Also before CHARLES EDEN.

ROBINSON, THOMAS.   Chowan County.

April Court, 1755. *Son:* WILLIAM. *Wife and other children:* mentioned, but not named. *Executors:* JOHN HALSEY and JOHN VAIL. *Witnesses:* SAMUEL BENBURY, HANNAH CLAY, SARAH ARINGTON. *Clerk of
the Court:* WILL. HALSEY.

RODGERS, JOSEPH.   Bath County.

January 2, 1704–1705. *Granddaughters:* ELIZABETH DEARAM, LYDIA
COCKERUM. *Grandsons:* JOSEPH COCKERUM and CHARLES HOPTON.
Indian slave freed. *Wife and Executrix:* MARY. *Witnesses:* HENERY
LOCKEY, JOHN PROCTER. *Clerk of the Court:* LEVI TRUEWHITT.

ROE, EDWARD.

May 3, 1696. July 19, 1696. *Sons:* EDMOND, EBENEZER, VALLENTINE.
Daughter: DEBORAH. *Wife and Executrix:* SARAH. *Witnesses:* DANIEL
FEE, GEORGE ELLES, ELEBETH FEE. *Clerk of the Court:* EDWARD MAYO.
Coat of arms on seal.

ROE, JAMES.   Craven County.

July 13, 1737. March Court, 1737–1738. *Executor:* FRANCIS STRINGER.
Witnesses: DAN'LL SHINE, JAMES MORE. *Clerk of the Court:* JAMES COOR.

ROE, LUKE.   Craven County.

December 30, 1774. January 12, 1775. *Brother:* THOMAS ROE.
Nephew: BENJAMIN (son of THOMAS ROE). *Brother-in-law:* JOSHUA
TAYLOR (riding horse and saddle). *Other legatees:* JACOB and other chil-
dren of JOSHUA TAYLOR. *Executor:* PETER PHYSIOC. *Witnesses:* MAT-
THEW STEPHENS, NANCE STEPHENS, PETER PHYSIOC. Proven before
JAMES HASELL.

ROE, ROBERT.   Beaufort County.

December Court, 1756. Formerly of Princess Anne County, now of
Beaufort. *Son:* KITLEY. *Daughters:* BETTY and DOLLY. *Wife and
Executrix:* DOROTHY. *Witnesses:* JAMES DEGGE, JOHN CHAPMAN and
HENRY TRIPPE. *Clerk of the Court:* WALLEY CHAUNCEY.

ROGERS, EMANUEL.   Bertie Precinct.

November 21, 1727. May Court, 1729. *Wife:* DEBORAH. *Daughters:*
ELIZABETH and MARY. *Executor:* JOHN GRAY. *Witnesses:* RICHD.
HAYNSWORTH, DANIEL CRAWLEY. *Clerk of the Court:* RT. FORSTER.

ROGERS, JOHN.   Bertie Precinct.

March 4, 1724. July 7, 1726. *Son and Executor:* JOHN. *Witnesses:*
MARY and JOHN RODGERS. Proven before RICHARD EVERARD.

ROGERS, JOSEPH.   Northampton County.

February 18, 1752. February Court, 1752. *Sons:* JOSEPH, AARON,
ISOM, REUBEN, JOHN, DRURY, MICHAEL. *Daughters:* FAITH ROGERS,
SARAH TARVER, MARY LOWREY. *Executors:* JOHN and JOSEPH ROGERS
(sons). *Witnesses:* NATHN. WILLIAMS, ELY WILLIAMS, NATHAN WIL-
LIAMS. *Clerk of the Court:* I. EDWARDS.

ROGERS, RICHARD.   Onslow County.

July 4, 1749. October Court, 1749. *Wife and Executrix:* SARAH.
Witnesses: JOHN DUDLEY, EZEKIEL HUNTER, JOS. STURGES. *Clerk of the
Court:* THOMAS BLACK.

ROGERS, ROBERT.   Chowan Precinct.

December 13, 1736. June 11, 1739. *Grandsons:* ROBERT DANIELL
and WILLIAM ROGERS. *Son and Executor:* ROBERT. *Daughter:* ELIZA-
BETH (wife of SIMON DANIEL). *Other legatees:* THOMAS and MARY GAL-
LOWAY. *Witnesses:* JOHN WILLIAMS, JANE WILLIAMS, RICHARD TAYLOR.
Proven before W. SMITH, C. J.

ROGERS, THOMAS.   Bertie County.

August Court, 1749. *Sons:* THOMAS and ROBERT. *Daughter:* MARY.
No executor. *Witnesses:* WILLIAM LATTIMORE, JOHN LITLE (or LILLE).
No probate officer.

ROGERS, THOMAS.   Bertie County.

February 14, 1754. May Court, 1754. *Son:* THOMAS. *Daughters:*
MARY and FRANCES ROGERS. *Wife and Executrix:* MARY. *Witnesses:*
RICHARD TOMLINSON, RICHARD BRADLEY, ROBERT ROGERS. *Clerk of the
Court:* SAML. ORMES.

ROGERS, WILLIAM.   Albemarle County.

April 25, 1690. *Legatee:* JONATHAN BATEMAN. No executor. *Witnesses:* JOHN HOLLFAND, JOHN TWIGGER, HANAH EDY. No probate.

ROLFE, THOMAS.

October 15, 1688. February 2, 1690–1691. "Of Yawpim." *Cousin:*
JOHN LOVETT. *Wife and Executrix:* ELIZABETH. *Witnesses:* REBECCA
WYATE, LAWRENCE CRUISE, HENDERSON WALKER, THOMAS LONGE.
Clerk of the Court: RICHARD PLATER.

ROOSE, WILLIAM (of Boston, Mariner).

September 26, 1722. This is a nuncupative will proven by RICHARD
FARRELL, JANE SPARROW and SAMUEL BERNARD before JOHN SOLLEY, and
is so torn that the names of the legatees cannot be ascertained.

ROPER, WILLIAM.   Chowan Precinct.

August 18, 1729. February 7, 1729–1730. *Executor and sole legatee:*
JACOB BUTLER. *Witnesses:* CORNELIUS LEARY and WILLIAM STACY.
Proven before RICHARD EVERARD.

ROSIER, NATHL.   Albemarle County.

July 1, 1703. April 5, 1704. *Legatees:* WILLIAM JONES (*Executor*)
and HENRY LYSLES. *Witnesses:* HENRY LYSLES, JOHN LEWERTON,
ROBERT ONEALE. *Clerk of the Court:* N. CHEVIN.

ROURK, EDMOND.   Bladen County.

May 15, 1769. December 16, 1769. "Parish of St. Martins in the
County of Bladen." *Son and Executor:* SAMUEL. *Daughter:* MARY ADDI-
SON. *Other legatee:* HENRY McCoY. *Wife:* DOROTHY. *Witnesses:* MARY
ADDISON, DAVID MORLEY. Proven before WILLIAM TRYON.

ROWAN, MATTHEW.   New Hanover County.

April 18, 1760. July 15, 1760. *Niece:* ROSE ROWAN (daughter of
brother ANDREW ROWAN). *Nephew:* MATHEW ROWAN (son of brother
ATCHEYSON). *Niece:* ANN ROWAN (daughter of brother WILLIAM).
Other legatees: RICHARD LYON of Spring Hill in Bladen County, MAR-
GARET ROWAN (niece), MILDRED LYON, daughter of JOHN (ten negroes),
MARY LYON (daughter of RICHARD LYON), FREDERICK GREGG of Wil-
mington (land on the northeast side of Northeast River, opposite to
Stag Park in New Hanover County; one gold watch). Eleven negroes
and land on White Marsh, in Bladen County, bequeathed to FREDERICK
GREGG and RICHARD LYON, in trust for ESTHER ROWAN (wife of ROBERT).
ELIZABETH, wife of ARCHIBALD MacLAINE (daughter-in-law). Lands on
Northwest River adjoining HENRY SIMMONDS; land on said river adjoin-
ing JUDGE LENARD and Nelltown in Bladen County, and land in Craven
County opposite Newbern, lying on Trent River, in all about 1,800
acres, devised to Executors to be sold. All remainder of estate is devised
and bequeathed to JOHN, the son of JANE STUBBS of Bath, "commonly
called and known by the name of JOHN ROWAN." *Executors:* JOHN
ROWAN, FREDERICK GREGG, RICHARD LYON. *Witnesses:* SAML. WATTERS,
GEO. GIBBS, THOS. CLARK. Proven before ARTHUR DOBBS. *Executors*
qualified before CORNELIUS HARNETT, J. P. Coat of arms on seal.

ROW, VALENTINE.   Pasquotank County.

March 8, 1739. October Court, 1740. *Sons:* GEORGE and VALENTINE
("my plantation"). *Daughters:* DEBORAH, MARY and SARAH ROW. *Executor:* GEORGE ROW (son). *Witnesses:* RICHARD and THOMAS PRICHARD,
JOHN HARRIS. *Clerk of the Court:* JAMES CRAVEN.

ROWELL, ELIZABETH.   Northampton County.

January 20, 1745–1746. May Court, 1746. *Son and Executor:* SAMUEL.
Daughter: MARY ROWELL. *Witnesses:* THOMAS HOLT, JOHN GILL, SAMUEL
TARVER. *Clerk of the Court:* RT. FORSTER.

ROWNTREE, FRANCIS.

September 30, 1730. *Wife and Executrix:* not named. *Sons:* FRANCIS, WILLIAM, JESSE, MOSES and JOHN (lands lying in North Carolina and in Nansemond County, Virginia, where testator formerly lived). *Daughters:* REBECCA, SUSANNA, ELIZABETH and CHRISTIAN. *Witnesses:* THOMAS TASLER, THOMAS HOBBS, ISAAC PICKINSON. No probate.

ROUNTREE, FRANCIS.   Johnston County.

July 13, 1748. September Court, 1748. *Sons:* KADOR, FRANCIS, WILLIAM, MOSES. *Wife and Executrix:* MARY. *Executor:* MOSES COLEMAN. *Witnesses:* THEOPHILUS COLEMAN, JOHN BAREFOOT, TARLOW OQUIN. *Deputy Clerk of the Court:* RICHARD CASWELL.

ROUNTREE, HANNAH.   Perquimans County.

September 12, 1758. January Court, 1759. *Sisters:* SARAH HOLLOWELL, LIDY and ANN ROUNTREE. *Brother:* MOSES ROUNTREE. *Mother:* SARAH LELLY. *Brother-in-law:* ELISHA LELLY. *Executor:* NICHOLAS STALLINGS. *Witnesses:* JOE HOLLOWELL, ELIAS STALLINGS, ABNER HOLLOWELL. *Clerk of the Court:* MILES HARVEY.

ROUNTREE, JESSE.   Craven County.

October 17, 1777. November 21, 1777. *Sons:* JESSE, JOHN ("plantation called the Oald Meating House"), WILLIAM. *Daughters:* MARY and ELIZABETH. *Wife:* not named. *Executors:* JOHN ROUNTREE and JAMES FRIZLE. *Witnesses:* THOMAS COLEMAN, MOAB ROUNTREE, EDWD. FITZPATRICK. Proven before RICHARD CASWELL.

ROUNTREE, MOSES.   Perquimans County.

July 21, 1755. October Court, 1755. *Son:* MOSES (plantation and two negroes). *Daughters:* SARAH HOL————, HANAH, LEDY and ANN ROUNTREE. *Wife and Executrix:* SARY. *Executor:* NICHOLAS STALLINGS. *Witnesses:* JOSHUA WHITE, JOHN WHITE, ABRAM HILL. *Clerk of the Court:* MILES HARVEY.

ROUNTREE, THOMAS.   Chowan County.

December 1, 1746. July Court, 1748. *Sons:* CHARLES and THOMAS (to each is devised several tracts of land in Chowan County). *Grandsons:* WILLIAM WALLACE, THOMAS ROUNTREE. *Son-in-law:* ELIAS STALLINGS. *Wife:* ELIZABETH. *Executors:* CHARLES and THOMAS ROUNTREE (sons). *Witnesses:* THOS. WALTON, JOHN FREEMAN. *Clerk of the Court:* WILL. MEARNS.

21

ROWNTREE, THOMAS.   Chowan County.

August 6, 1773. January 15, 1774. *Daughters:* ELIZABETH SMALL, SARAH STALLINGS, MARY, RUTH, RACHEL, JUDITH and CHRISTIAN ROWNTREE. *Granddaughter:* SARAH SMALL. *Executor:* AARON HILL. Testator devises lands on Catrin Creek. *Witnesses:* HENRY WALTON, THOMAS SPIVEY. Proven before JO. MARTIN.

RUCKES, THOMAS.   Chowan County.

November 9, 1747. April Court, 1748. *Daughters:* MARY, TAMEY and SARAH. *Sons:* DEMSEY, JACOB, JESSE, JOSEPH and THOMAS (the two latter are appointed Executors). *Witnesses:* JACOB ODOM, JAMES BRADY, JACOB RODGERS.

RUSSELL, HABAKKUK.   Carteret County.

March 9, 1754. June Court, 1754. *Sons:* DAVID and ABRAHAM. *Daughters:* REBECKAH, SARAH, ABIGAIL and ANN SOPHIA RUSSELL. *Wife:* ANN. *Executors:* GEORGE READ and GEORGE MCKANE. *Witnesses:* LAKKESTER LOVET, HENRY HARTSELL, SAMUEL JORDAN. *Clerk of the Court:* GEORGE READ.

RUSSELL, JOHN.   Onslow County.

November 4, 1751. July 3, 1753. *Sons:* JAMES, PETER and MICHAEL. *Daughters:* MARY and ELIZABETH. *Wife:* ELIZABETH. *Executors:* JOHN and PETER STARKEY. *Witnesses:* WILLIAM BARBER, AARON BARBER, WM. FIELDEN. *Clerk of the Court:* WILL CRAY.

RUSSELL, THOMAS.   Craven County.

January 4, 1744. March Court, 1744–1745. *Son:* JOHN. *Daughters:* MARY SMITH and JEMIMA CULLING. *Other legatee:* JOHN SMITH, son of WINFREE SMITH. *Wife and Executrix:* ELIZABETH. *Witnesses:* PETER DUKE, JOHN WILLIAMS, WILLIAM MELLAR. *Deputy Clerk of the Court:* N. ROUTLEDGE.

RUSTULL (RUSSELL), RICHARD.   Carteret County.

March 15, 1739. June Court, 1747. Core Sound. *Son:* JOHN (land on East side of Newport River). *Daughter:* MARY RUSTULL. *Executors:* RICHARD RUSTULL (father) and HENERY STANTON. *Witnesses:* MARY STANTON, HENRY STANTON, JUNR., ALICE STANTON. *Clerk of the Court:* GEORGE READ.

RYALL, CHARLES.   Onslow County.

November 28, 1754. *Sons:* SAMUEL and THOMAS. *Grandson:* CHARLES AUGUSTUS NICKSON. *Executor:* SAMUEL RYALL (son). *Witnesses:* JAMES DENSON, ROBERT NIXON, JOB BROOKES. *Clerk of the Court:* WILL. CRAY.

RYAN, DAVID.   Bertie County.

January 9, 1762. November 13, 1762. *Brothers:* JAMES and GEORGE. *Sisters:* ELIZABETH CAMPBELL and MARY LACKEY. *Executors:* JAMES RYAN, CORNELIUS CAMPBELL, RICHARD LACKEY and JOHN HILL. *Witnesses:* J. PEARSON, JOS. FRITH, WILLIAM SHAW. Proven before ARTHUR DOBBS.

RYAN, THOMAS.   Bertie County.

January 29, 1753. March Court, 1753. *Sons:* DAVID (land "lying in the bottom of Cashy Neck on the thourough-fare commonly known by the name of The Old House"; 1,500 acres of land on Cypress Swamp and four negroes), JAMES (350 acres of land), JAMES (1,120 acres of land and three negroes), GEORGE (plantation in Rocquis formerly known as JAMES CASTELLO'S Islands; plantation at head of Salmon Creek and water mill; two plantations in Chowan and 150 acres of land on Cashy River; three negroes), THOMAS ("The Manor house & Plantation" and also 500 acres of land). *Daughter:* MARY RYAN (two plantations on Chowan River; two plantations on Black Walnut Swamp and two negroes), ELIZABETH CAMPBELL. *Son-in-law:* CORNELIUS CAMPBELL (plantation in Tyrrell County lying on Albemarle Sound and two plantations in Bertie County together with two negroes). *Wife and Executrix:* MARTHA (three negroes). *Executors:* CAPT. JOHN CAMPBELL, CORNELIUS CAMPBELL and THOMAS TURNER. Provision is made for education of children and sale of brig to pay debts. *Witnesses:* EDWD. UNDERHILL, DAVID ALLEN, HUMPHRY NICHOLS. *Witnesses to codicil:* DAVID ALLEN, ELIZABETH ASHBURN, MARY CAPHART. *Clerk of the General Court:* JNO. SNEAD.

RYDING, JONATHAN.   Bertie County.

May Court, 1754. *Son:* JOSEPH ("my mannor plantation"). *Daughters:* MARTHA, ELIZABETH and DOROTHY RIDING. No executor. *Witnesses:* MARK GIBBINS, ELISAH WHITFIELD, EDWARD COLLINS. *Clerk of the Court:* SAMUEL ORMES.

SADLER, RICHARD.   Chowan County.

November 30, 1753. July Court, 1754. *Wife and Executrix:* MARGARET. *Witnesses:* HENRY BONNER, JAMES and DEBORAH THOMPSON. *Clerk of the Court:* WILL. HALSEY.

SADLER, WILLIAM.   Chowan Precinct.

April 13, 1727. April Court, 1727. *Sons:* WILLIAM and RICHARD (plantation divided between them). *Wife and Executrix:* ELIZABETH. *Executor:* MAJR. HENRY BONNER. *Witnesses:* ROBERT JEFFREYS, EDWD. HOWCOTT, WILLIAM THOMPSON. *Clerk of the Court:* RT. FORSTER.

SALISBERY, JAMES.   Pasquotank County.

August 16, 1758.   September Court, 1758.   *Sons:* JAMES, JOHN, JOSEPH, WILLIAM.   *Daughters:* ELIZABETH and FRANCES SALISBERY.   *Executors:* JAMES SALISBERY (son) and JOSEPH REED.   *Witnesses:* THOMAS ARMOUR, JOSEPH COMMANDER, DAVID SINCLAIR.   *Clerk of the Court:* THOS. TAYLOR.

SALTER, EDWARD.   Bath County.

January 6, 1734.   February 5, 1734.   *Son:* EDWARD.   *Daughters:* SARAH, MARY and SUSANNAH.   *Sons-in-law:* MILES HARVEY and JOHN HARVEY.   *Wife:* ELIZABETH.   Following lands devised: 306 acres on south side of Pamlico River called Mount Colvert; land purchased of JOHN SWANN; lands on Bear Creek, Pamlico River and the Beaver Dam of Grays Creek, "whereon JOHN ARRINGTON now dwells." About 25 negroes, one periauger, one brigantine named The Happy Luke, one pair silver spurs, Richard Bloom's History of the Bible and other books "of Divinity, Law and History," large China Punch bowl bequeathed.   Brigantine ordered laden with tar and sent to Boston, there to be sold and proceeds invested in young negroes; provision is made for insurance of said vessel with Jacob Windall & Co., in the sum of 1,200 pounds.   *Daughter*, SARAH, is left in care of MRS. SARAH PORTER of Cape Fear.   Provision is made for education of son "to make him a compleat merchant."   *Executors:* EDWARD MOSELEY, JOHN ODEON, JOHN CALDAM, THOMAS BONNER, WILLIAM WILLIS, WILLIAM ADAMS.   Proven before GAB. JOHNSTON.   Coat of arms on seal.   *Witnesses:* WALLEY CHAUNCEY, BENJAMIN RIGNEY, WALTER DIXSON, ROGER JONES.

SANDERS, ABRAHAM.   Perquimans County.

April 6, 1750.   October Court, 1751.   *Sons:* JOHN (plantation whereon RICHARD WATERS lives), BENJAMIN ("plantation whereon I now live"), ABRAHAM (5s).   *Daughters:* JUDE BOIS, ELIZABETH SANDERS.   *Wife:* JUDE.   *Executors:* RICHARD SANDERS and JOSEPH WHITE.   *Witnesses:* JOHN MURDAUGH, JOHN and ELIZABETH WHITE.   *Friends:* RICHARD SKINNER and JOHN HARVEY.   *Clerk of the Court:* EDMUND HATCH.

SANDERS, ANN.   Perquimans County.

May 12, 1752.   July Court, 1752.   *Sons:* JOSEPH, BANJAMIN and JOHN SANDERS.   *Daughters:* ELIZABETH NEWBY and LYDIA SANDERS.   *Granddaughter:* ANN NEWBY.   *Executors:* JOHN and JOSEPH SANDERS (sons).   *Witnesses:* THOS. NEWBY, JOSHUA ELLIOT, THOMAS ELLIOT.   *Clerk of the Court:* EDMUND HATCH.

SANDERS, BENJAMIN.   Perquimans County.

September 30, 1744.   October Court, 1744.   *Sons:* BENJAMIN ("dwelling plantation"), JOSEPH and JOHN.   *Daughters:* BETTY and LIDA.   *Wife*

and Executrix: ANN.   *Executor:* SAMUEL NUBE (son-in-law).   *Witnesses:*
JOSHUA ELIOT, ANN ELLIOT.   *Clerk of the Court:* EDMUND HATCH.

SANDERS, JOHN.   Onslow County.

January 6, 1732–1733. April 3, 1733. New River. *Brother:* ROB-
ERT SANDERS. *Other legatees:* STEPHEN, RICHARD and EASTER WIL-
LIAMS (children of JOHN WILLIAMS), EDWARD and STEPHEN HOWARD
(sons of STEPHEN HOWARD), THOMAS FARNELL. *Sister:* ANN WILLIAMS.
Executor: ROBERT SANDERS (brother). *Witnesses:* JOB BROOKES, STEPHEN
HOWARD, JAMES FOYLE. *Clerk of the Court:* WILLIAM CRANFORD.

SANDERS, JOHN.   Chowan County.

August 18, 1751. October Court, 1751. *Sons:* FRANCIS ("plantation
I now live on"), JOHN (plantation on Cypress Swamp where THOMAS
RUTTER lives), ROBERT, JESSE, THOMAS. To each of above-named sons
is bequeathed negroes. *Daughters:* MILLE, FERIBE and ELIZABETH SAN-
DERS. *Wife and Executrix:* MARY. *Witnesses:* JOHN LOE (or LOCE), JR.,
JOHN LOE (or LOCE), SR., JACOB RUTH. *Clerk of the Court:* JAMES CRAVEN.

SANDERS, MARY.   Bertie County.

June 1, 1734. August Court, 1734. *Son:* ISAAC. *Daughters:* MARY
and CHRISTINA ELIZABETH SANDERS. *Grandson:* ISAAC SNODEN. *Godson:* JOHN WILLSON. *Executors:* GEORGE WYNNS and ROBERT EVANS.
Witnesses: JOSEPH THOMPSON and BENJN. WYNNS. *Clerk of the Court:*
BENJAMIN WYNNS.

SANDERS, WILLIAM.   Edgecombe County.

June 5, 1756. February Court, 1757. *Sons:* HENRY (land on Panther
Branch), WILLIAM ("the Mannor plantation"). Land called Simmonses
Neck to be sold. *Wife and daughters:* not named. *Executors:* JOSEPH
SHAW, JR., JOHN BRADFORD, TRISTRIM LOWTHER and SOLOMON WIL-
LIAMS. *Witnesses:* WM. IRBY, JOHN GRICE, WM. HORNSBY. *Clerk of
the Court:* JOSEPH MONTFORT.

SANDERSON, BAZIL.

January 22, 1721–1722. April 2, 1722. "Island of Antegua." *Lega-
tees:* WILLIAM HILL, of Antegua, ELIZABETH SANDERSON (wife of BAR-
THOLEMY SANDERSON), JOHN LOVICK (saddle and bridle and gold studs),
HENRY CLAYTON, WILLIAM LITTLE, WILLIAM BADHAM, MARY BADHAM
(wife of WILLIAM), SARAH HAZARD (wife of ROBERT). *Sisters:* KATHE-
RINE DYE and FRANCES PEATE (both of London). *Executors:* BART.
SANDERSON, KATHERINE DYE, JOHN LOVICK and HENRY CLAYTON.
Proven before Court at Edenton by WILLIAM LITTLE. *Clerk of the Court:*
W. BADHAM.

SANDERSON, BENJAMIN.   Craven County.

October 1, 1757. January 3, 1758. *Sons:* JOSEPH, BENJAMIN (*Executor*). *Daughter:* DINA FOSCUE, HANNAH BARBER. *Granddaughter:* SARAH FOSCUE (one negro). *Executor:* BENJAMIN BROCKETT. *Witnesses:* WILLIAM GARDNER, SIMON FOSCUE, JOHN GRANADE. Proven before ARTHUR DOBBS.

SANDERSON, JOSEPH.   Currituck County.

January 13, 1743. October Court, 1746. *Wife:* JULIA. *Sons:* RICHARD ("the manner plantation," also the plantation on Sandy Banks known as Pawmers, and other tracts of land, location not given), SAMUEL and JOSHUA (plantation and land to each), THOMAS and WILLIAM (plantation to each), BENJAMIN (1 negro and land on North River), JOSEPH (land on Sandy Banks). *Executor:* JOHN LURRY. *Witnesses:* JOHN WOODHOUSE, WILLIAM BAGLY, SAMUEL JARVES. *Clerk of the Court:* RICHARD McCLURE.

SANDERSON, JOSEPH.   Currituck County.

April 26, 1758. December Court, 1758. *Sons:* JOSEPH ("plantation whereon I now live"), RICHARD (plantation known as the Deep Branch), CALEB (70 acres land). *Daughters:* JULIAN, ANN, LIDA and SUSANNAH SANDERSON. *Wife:* CESIAH. *Executor:* JOSEPH SANDERSON (son). *Witnesses:* JOHN WOODHOUSE, GEORGE POWERS, SAMUELL SALLYER. *Clerk of the Court:* WM. MEARNS.

SANDERSON, JOSEPH.   Craven County.

February 12, 1774. March 19, 1774. *Sons:* JESSE, THOMAS, JOSEPH, BENJAMIN, SHADRACH, JOHN, JAMES, ISAAC (land at Miskeeto Point). Negroes bequeathed to each of sons. *Daughters:* PRUDENCE FOSTER, LIDDY LEE. *Executors:* JESSE SANDERSON (son), THOS. LEE (son-in-law), EDWARD WHITLEY. *Witnesses:* THOS. FOY, JOHN MEEKET, WILLIAM GRIFFITH. Proven before JO. MARTIN.

SANDERSON, JULIAN.   Currituck County.

July 31, 1749. April 17, 1752. *Granddaughters:* ELIZABETH CHURCH and ANN WHITE. *Executor:* HENRY WHITE (son-in-law). *Witnesses:* SAMUEL JONES, MARGITT BARRIT, EASTHER WHITE. *Clerk of the Court:* WILLIAM SHERGOLD.

SANDERSON, RICHARD.   Perquimans County.

August 17, 1733. October 15, 1733. *Son:* RICHARD ("ye Island of Ocreecock," three negroes and one Indian slave; "the mannor plantation"; "all my lots in Ronoak Town"; "two thirds of ye Sea Flower Brigantine"; one-half of sloop Swallow). *Son-in-law:* TULLY WILLIAMS (five negro slaves; 140 acres of land in Perquimans bordering on son RICHARD and JOHN WILLOUGHBY; one-third of Sea Flower Brigantine and one-half of sloop Swallow). *Nephews:* JOSEPH and RICHARD SANDERSON. *Brother-in-law:* HENRY WOODHOUSE (one Mustee fellow). *Sister:* SUSANNA ERWIN. *Daughter:* ELIZABETH POLLOCK. *Cousin:* ELIZABETH DICKSON. *Nephew:* HEZEKIAH WOODHOUSE (land "on ye Sandy Bank by the name of Point Lookout"). *Daughter:* GRACE (wife of TULLY WILLIAMS). *Executors:* RICHARD SANDERSON (son) and TULLY WILLIAMS (son-in-law). *Witnesses:* CLEMT. HALL, THOMAS SNOWDEN, THOMAS TRUMBAL. *Clerk of the Court:* CHARLES DENMAN.

SANDERSON, RUTH.

(Wife of COL. RICHARD SANDERSON of Little River). September 4, 1727. January 29, 1727. *Relatives:* THOS. HARVEY, MILES GALE of Boston (two negroes each), PENELEAP LETTELL, wife of WILLIAM LITTLE (one negro), ELIZABETH CLAYTEN (one negro). *Executors:* THOS. HARVEY and MILES GALE. *Witnesses:* JOSHUA WHEREY, ELIZABETH HARVEY. Proven before RICHARD EVERARD.

SARSON, LAURENCE.   Bertie Precinct.

May 6, 1726. "Formerly of the County of Suffolk in Great Brittain but now of Bertie precinct," etc. *Devisees and legatees:* WILLIAM WATERS (land on Salmon Creek), JAMES WATERS, brother of WILLIAM (land on the "east end of the Great Pocoson"), KATHERINE ARNOLD, SARAH WATERS. *Executor:* THOMAS LOVICK. *Witnesses:* JAMES CASTLETON, HERCULES COYTE. Coat of arms on seal. Attached to this will is a lease from testator to one HUGH HYMAN, dated January 24, 1723, of a plantation called Bucklesbury on the condition that the said HYMAN "clear on the plantation six thousand corn hills att five foot distant * * * and to raise and plant out at twelve foot distance three hundred peach trees." Lease witnessed by JOHN DUKINGFIELD, JOHN SHORT. No probate to will. Coat of arms on seal.

SAWYER, CHARLES.   Pasquotank County.

October 21, 1750. January Court, 1750. *Sons:* JOHN (plantation on North River), JESSE (land on North River), CHARLES ("land I now live on," riding horse and cattle); WILLIS (land adjoining Butterworth, JOHN SAWYER, etc.). *Daughters:* DOROTHY and MIRIAM. To each of above-named children is bequeathed a negro. *Wife:* not named. *Executor:* WILLIS SAWYER. *Witnesses:* BENNETT MORGAN, LODWICK WILLIAMS, S. S. PLOMER. *Clerk of the Court:* THOS. TAYLOR.

SAWYER, DANIEL.   Pasquotank County.

May 15, 1749. April Court, 1752. *Sons:* CORNELIUS, ISAAC and EZEKIEL (land divided among them). *Daughters:* TAYMER, BETTY and SARAH

SAWYER. *Wife:* MARY. *Executors:* CORNELIUS and ISAAC (sons). *Witnesses:* GRIFFITH GRAY, JOHN SAWYER, JOAB DAUGE. *Clerk of the Court:* THO. TAYLOR.

SAWYER, HENRY.   Pasquotank County.

June 24, 1728. August 3, 1729. *Sons:* CHARLES, BENJAMIN, DANIEL. *Daughters:* TAMER, CAEN and ELIZABETH WILLIAMS, CHARITY GRAY and SUSANNER WILLIAMS. *Executors:* DANIELL and BENJAMIN SAWYER (sons). *Witnesses:* CORNELIUS ROSE, JOHN KELLY, WILLIAM ———— . Proven before RICHARD EVERARD.

SAWYER, JEREMIAH.   Pasquotank County.

October 10, 1755. June Court, 1756. *Sons:* ROBERT and CHARLES (land divided between them). *Son-in-law:* THOS. HAYSTENS. *Daughter:* BRIDGET JOLLEY. *Grandson:* WILLIS HAYSTENS. *Executor:* CHARLES SAWYER (son) *Witnesses:* JOS. JONES, WILLIAM HIXSON. *Clerk of the Court:* THO. TAYLOR.

SAWYER, JOHN.   Albemarle County.

December 22, 1713. *Sons:* JOHN, THOMAS, ROBERT, SOLOMON (a plantation to each). *Grandson:* CHARLES GRANDY. *Wife and Executrix:* JEAN. *Witnesses:* THOMAS and ROBERT SAWYER, TIMOTHY READING. No probate.

SAWYER, JOHN.   Pasquotank County.

June 2, 1743. January Court, 1743. *Sons:* JOHN, TULLE (plantation called Gumberry), STEPHEN, WILLIAM (land in Currituck known as Peters Ridge). To each son is given negroes and a horse. *Daughters:* GRACE and SARAH. *Wife and Executrix:* ABIGAL. *Witnesses:* WILLES SAWYER, SARAH SAWYER. *Clerk of the Court:* THOS. TAYLOR.

SAWYER, JOSHUA.   Pasquotank County.

May 19, 1753. July Court, 1753. *Sons:* JOSHUA and DAVID (plantation divided between them), WILLIAM, NATHAN, JESSE. *Daughters:* MARY and SARAH SAWYER. *Executor:* JOSHUA SAWYER (son). *Witnesses:* ROBERT MURDEN, JOSHUA JENNINGS, JACOB MITCHELL. *Clerk of the Court:* THOS. TAYLOR.

SAWYER, ROBART.   Pasquotank County.

April Court, 1735. *Sons:* JEREMIAH (land adjoining JOHN SPENCE), JOSEPH and ZACHARIAH ("plantation whereon I now live"), DENIS (land on Sawyers Creek), JOHN SCARBOROUGH (land called the light place). *Daughter:* ESTER SAWYER (land between DENIS SAWYER and the light place). *Granddaughter:* SUSANNAH SAWYER (land called the Great Island). *Wife and Executrix:* FRANCES. *Witnesses:* CHARLES and DANIEL SAWYER, SAMUELL SIMMONS. *Clerk of the Court:* JOSU SMITH.

SAWYER, SOLOMON.   Pasquotank County.

August 15, 1742. October Court, 1742. *Sons:* JOHN ("my manner plantation"), SOLOMON (plantation known by the name of Dogwood Ridge). *Daughters:* CHARITY, ELISABETH, MARY, PETTYATH and CHRISTIAN SAWYER. *Witnesses:* BARTLETT MORGAN, THOMAS HASTINS. *Clerk of the Court:* THOS. TAYLOR.

SAWYER, THOMAS.

October 22, 1750. January Court, 1750. *Daughters:* DOLLY SMITHSON, JEMIMA, MARY and MIRIAM SAWYER. *Son-in-law and Executor:* JOHN SMITHSON. *Wife and Executrix:* ELISABETH. *Witnesses:* HENRY NICKELES, WILLIAM HARRIS, HEZ. CARTWRIGHT. *Clerk of the Court:* THOS. TAYLOR.

SAWYER, THOMAS.   Pasquotank County.

May 19, 1756. June Court, 1756. *Sons:* ALEXANDER, JOSEPH, THOMAS, SAMUEL ("my plantation"). *Daughters:* JANE HUMPHRIES, TAMER WILLIAMS, CATTREN and REBECKAH SAWYER. *Grandsons:* SAMUEL HASTINGS, MAIKD MORGAN. *Granddaughter:* ANNE SAWYER. *Daughter-in-law:* SARAH SAWYER. *Executors:* SAMUEL and REBECKAH SAWYER (son and daughter). *Witnesses:* BENJAMIN SAWYER, GRIFFITH GRAY, BENTT. MORGAN. *Clerk of the Court:* THOS. TAYLOR.

SAWYER, WILLIS.   Pasquotank County.

April 3, 1753. April Court, 1753. *Wife and Executrix:* HANOR (plantation on Pasquotank River). *Daughter:* BETTY SAWYER. *Brother:* CHARLES SAWYER. *Father:* CHARLES SAWYER. *Witnesses:* WILLIAM SYMONS, BETY SYMONS, ANN SAWYER. *Clerk of the Court:* THOS. TAYLOR. Executrix qualified before JARVIS JONES.

SCANER, ISAAC.   Albemarle County.

August 6, 1693. October 2, 1693. *Friends:* WILLIAM JACKSON and ELIZABETH NIXON. *Neighbors:* WILLIAM SIMSON, ROBERT LEWIS, JOHN GODFREY, ANN BOYSE. No executor appointed. *Witnesses:* WILLIAM TANNER, WILLIAM JACKSON, THOMAS SYMONS. *Clerk of the Court:* EDWARD MAYO.

SCARFE, JOHN.   Pasquotank County.

February 15, 1751. April Court, 1751. *Sons:* JAMES, JOHN, EDWARD, JONATHAN, ISRAEL. *Daughters:* ANNE RICHARDSON, MARY JONES. *Wife:* MARY. *Witnesses:* WILLIAM ABERCROMBIE, JAMES GREVES, WILLIAM RODES. Codicil to this will of even date and witnessed by same parties appoints *wife* and *son* JAMES as Executors, and makes bequests to *grandson,* JOHN SCARFE. *Clerk of the Court:* THOS. TAYLOR.

SCARBROUGH, CHARLES.   Pasquotank County.

January 20, 1750–1751.   *Son:* BENJAMIN (land on Poplar Swamp).
Daughter: LYDA SCARBROUGH.   *Wife and Executrix:* JOICE.   *Witnesses:*
JAMES FORBES, JOHN SCARBROUGH, ELIZABETH TORKSEY.   No probate.

SCARBROUGH, JOHN.   Pasquotank County.

December 27, 1754.   June Court, 1756.   *Daughters:* SARAH BURGES
(three negroes), TAMAR SCARBROUGH ("my plantation").   *Executor:* WIL-
LIAM BURGES.   *Witnesses:* PAUL SHARP, BENJAMIN WILLSON, THOMAS
CLUF and BENJAMIN TORKSEY.   *Clerk of the Court:* THOMAS TAYLOR.

SCARBROUGH, MACRORA.   Perquimans County.

January 31, 1752.   February 18, 1752.   *Sons:* BENJAMIN, MACRORA and
WILLIAM.   To BENJAMIN is given plantation "whereon I now dwell called
Springfield," with four negroes, six silver spoons, silver-headed cane, silver
shoe buckles, knee buckles, 14 silver vest buttons, black walnut desk and
also half of land at Yawpim, called Point Pleasant.   To MACRORA is devised land at Oak Ridge and four negroes, a silver can, silver watch and
black walnut desk.   To WILLIAM is given land bought of MR. HARVEY and
ROBERT WILSON.   *Daughter:* ELIZABETH SCARBROUGH.   *Wife and Executrix:* ELIZABETH.   *Trustees:* JOHN SCARBROUGH (brother), EDMUND HATCH
(brother-in-law) and WILLIAM BURGIS.   *Witnesses:* WALTER KIPPIN,
JOSHUA HOBART, CORNELIUS MULLIN, ROBERT AVERY, MARTHAANN KIP-
PIN.   Proven before GAB. JOHNSTON.   Coat of arms on seal.

SCHWANNER, MATHIAS TOBIAS.   Tyrrell County.

September 21, 1743.   March Court, 1744.   *Sons:* JOHN, SAMUEL, WIL-
LIAM and MATHIAS (land on the "Right hand of the road as thou goest up-
ward the said County on the westward side of Tuk Creek, and four negro
slaves").   *Grandson:* WILLIAM BRYAN (son of DARBY BRYAN).   *Daughters:* SARAH BRYAN, MARY SCHWANNER.   *Wife and Executrix:* JANE.   *Witnesses:* WILLIAM BARRETT, ROBERT LANIER, ROBERT LANIER DANIEL.
Clerk of the Court: THOMAS LEE.

SCOLLAY, ELIZABETH.   Bertie County.

December 1, 1766.   January 12, 1767.   *Sons:* THOMAS POLLOCK (three
negroes and one teapot, milk pot, tankard, two salts, three table, one soup
and all teaspoons).   CULLEN POLLOCK ("all my books and a mourning
ring").   *Other legatees:* children of TULLY WILLIAMS, children of RICHARD
SAUNDERSON; DR. ROBERT LENNOX and *wife,* FANNY; JOHN SCOLLAY, of
Boston (one negro man); PEGGY CATHCART, daughter of DOCTOR WILLIAM
CATHCART (negro girl); SARAH BLOUNT, daughter of JOSEPH (one negro
girl); SOPHIA RASOR, daughter of EDWARD RASOR (one negro girl); FANNAY
CATHCART, daughter of WILLIAM (one negro girl); THOMAS BLOUNT, son of

JOSEPH BLOUNT. *Former husband:* THOMAS POLLOCK. *Executors:* THOMAS POLLOCK, ROBERT LENOX, RICHARD SAUNDERSON and JOSEPH BLOUNT. *Witnesses:* HARDY HARDISON, FREDERICK HARDISON. Proven before WILLIAM TRYON.

SCOLLAY, SAMUEL.

February 18, 1752. *Friends:* THOMAS GILFORD, of Busty in Zetland; MAGNIS HENDERSON, of Guards in Zetland; GEORGE TRIEL, of Broh in Orkney, in the Island of Sandy (fifty pounds to each), "MRS. MARGARET STEWART, alias TRIEL, late Lady of Eleoness in Orkney, in the Island of Sandy" (twenty pounds); MRS. MARY TULINTON, alias DAVIS, relict of ROBERT DAVIS, shipbuilder in Leath, Scotland; HUGH BLACKBURN, of Norfolk; DR. WILLIAM CATHCART, ROBERT TODD, of Norfolk. *Brother:* JERMAN ROBERT SCOLLAY, of Lerwick in Zetland. *Sons-in-law:* THOMAS and CULLEN POLLOCK (land on "the Plank Bridge" in Pasquotank County). To TULLY WILLIAMS is bequeathed his father's sword and cattle at Kettyhauk. *Wife and Executrix:* not named. *Executors:* THOMAS and CULLEN POLLOCK. *Witnesses:* ANN ANDERSON, ED. RASOR, JOHN NICHOLLS. Proven before GAB. JOHNSTON.

SCOTT, JOHN.   Pasquotank County.

September 13, 1738. January 8, 1738. *Daughters:* ELIPHEL and HANNAH SCOTT. *Wife and Executrix:* SARAH. *Witnesses:* DAVID GEORGE, JOSEPH JORDAN. *Clerk of the Court:* JOS. SMITH.

SCOTT, JOHN.   Craven County.

October 4, 1764. September 27, 1773. Newbern. *Wife and Executrix:* MARTHA. *Executor:* JAMES REED. *Witnesses:* HANNAH LANGSONE, FRANK ROMBOUGH, JAMES DAVIS. *President of the Island of Antigua:* THOS. JARVIS. Will proven before JO. MARTIN and also before THOS. JARVIS.

SCOTT, JOSEPH.

October 26, 1685. *Son and Executor:* JOSHUA. *Clerk of the Court:* EDWARD MAYO. Remainder of will illegible.

SCOTT, JOSHUA.   Albemarle County.

January 8, 1685–1686. *Daughters:* GRACE and SARAH SCOTT (lands, orchards, etc.). *Wife and Executrix:* MARY. *Witnesses:* JOHN KINSAY, RICHARD EVENS, JOHN WOLFENDEN. No probate.

SCOTT, MARY.   Perquimans County.

March 17, 1691–1692. October 3, 1692. *Daughters:* HEPTHENIA WALKING, JULYANAH TAYLOR. *Granddaughter:* JOHENAH TAYLOR. No executor. *Witnesses:* ANTHONY DAWSON ——— BUTLER. *Clerk of the Court:* JOHN STEPNEY.

SCOTT, MATTHEW.   Pitt County.

August 26, 1771. December 6, 1771. *Brothers:* WILLIAM and JAMES
SCOTT, fullers and clothiers in Pennsylvania. *Father:* JOHN SCOTT (plantation and storehouse in Woodstock). Testator desires all bonds, notes, lot
and houses near one CLARK'S, lot and house in Woodstock town, Bay Boat,
periauger and seine to be delivered to one SAMUEL PURVIANCE, in Baltimore, in payment of account due him, said PURVIANCE, by testator and
CALHON trading as partners. *Executors:* JAMES SCOTT (brother) and MRS.
ELIZABETH SPEIR. *Witnesses:* SUSANNA EVANS, RICHD. EVANS. Proven
before Jo. MARTIN.

SCOTT, RICHARD.   New Hanover County.

March 6, 1756. April 16, 1762. *Wife and Executrix:* MARY (stock
marked and branded as set out in will and also dwelling plantation). *Son-
in-law:* OSWELL SILL. *Other legatees:* WILLIAM, son of RICHARD EARLE;
ELIZABETH, daughter of JOHN SIMPSON. *Witnesses:* ELIZABETH MORRIS,
ALICE HUDSON, JOHN EARLE. Proven before ARTHUR DOBBS.

SCOTT, STEPHEN.

March 12, 1711. September 11, 1716. *Sons:* EDWARD ("plantation I
now live on on Newbegun Creek"), STEPHEN and HENRY (plantation to
each), JOHN and JOSHUA. *Daughters:* SARAH and ELIZABETH SCOTT.
Wife and Executrix: ELIZABETH. *Witnesses:* MATTHEW PRITCHARD, JOHN
SHEARLY, BENJAMIN PRITCHARD. Proven before CHARLES EDEN.

SCOTT, STEPHEN, SR.   Pasquotank County.

November 21, 1752. January Court, 1753. *Sons:* JOSEPH (land on
Beaver Dam Swamp, one-half of "plantation whereon I now live, together with one negro man"), SAMUEL (half of the "plantation whereon I
now live," land known by the name of the Rigg, land known as New-
begun Creek meeting-house land, seven negroes and one "New England
mare & colt" and one silver watch). *Daughter:* MARY CONNER, wife of
JOHN CONNER (three negroes and one riding horse). *Grandchildren:*
JOSEPH and MARY SCOTT (6 negroes), MARY, JOHN and CADO CONNER
(5 negroes), STEPHEN and WILLIAM SCOTT (2 negroes). *Executors:*
JOSEPH and SAMUEL SCOTT (sons). *Witnesses:* ROBERT JORDAN, KATH-
ARNA WHITE, THOMAS NICHOLSON. *Clerk of the Court:* THOMAS TAYLOR.
Device on seal.

SEAGRAVE, ADAM.   Currituck Precinct.

October 7, 1723. January 14, 1723–1724. *Legatees:* JOHN SMITH
(Executor), SAMSON WOODHOUSE. *Witnesses:* HENRY WOODHOUSE,
THOMAS LARRY, JOHN STONE. *Clerk of the Court:* JOS. WICKER.

SEARS, WILLIAM.   Albemarle County.

August 29, 1679. *Wife and Executrix:* ANN. *Brother:* THOMAS SEARS ("now in Bermudas"). *Friend:* RICHARD ROADES. *Witnesses:* RALPH COATES, DANIEL FRISSELL. No probate. Impression of ship on seal.

SEAY, JAMES.   Bertie County.

May 18, 1772. January 6, 1774. *Sons:* ISAAC, JOHN, JAMES (plantation to each). *Daughters:* ONEY SEAY, MARY BROWN. *Executors:* ISAAC SEAY, ARTHUR BROWN, JOEL BROWN (son-in-law). *Witnesses:* EZEKIEL TOMLINSON, JOSEPH HORNE, ANN WILLIAMS. Proven before Jo. MARTIN.

SETTON, NATHANIEL.   Perquimans Precinct.

February 23, 1724–1725. March 30, 1725. *Legatees:* JOHN WARD, RUTH GLOSTER, JOSEPH SETTON, ELISABETH WHEDBEE, PATHANNA SETTON, JAMES ANDERSON, THOMAS SETTON, GEORGE SETTON and RICHARD WHEDBEE. *Executors:* RICHARD WHEDBEE and THOMAS SETTON. *Witnesses:* RICHARD DAVES, RICHARD SKINNER, REBECKA SETTON. *Clerk General Court:* SAMUEL SWANN.

SHACKLEFORD, JAMES.   Carteret County.

July 10, 1759. September Court, 1759. *Sons:* JAMES (600 acres "of my Quarter of the Banks"), JOSEPH (plantation formerly belonging to Jo. WICKER), PELEG. Negroes divided among children. *Wife and Executrix:* KEZIAH. *Witnesses:* ANANIAS CAVENAGH, THOMAS ADDISON, ANDREW HENDERSON, ROBERT FINNEY. *Clerk of the Court:* WM. ROBERTSON.

SHACKELFORD, JOHN.   Carteret County.

March 25, 1734. September Court, 1734. *Son:* JAMES ("land on Bancks lying to the Eastward of Old Topsail Inlet, called by the name of Shackelfords Banks"; island named Carrot Island and one negro). *Daughters:* MARY, ELIZABETH and ANN SHACKELFORD (one gold ring to each), SARAH MOSS (wife of JOSEPH). *Grandsons:* JOHN and WILLIAM ROBERTS. *Wife and Executrix:* ANN. *Executor:* JOHN SHACKELFORD (son, to whom is devised all remainder of estate after legacies mentioned). *Witnesses:* SAMUEL CHADWICK, EPHRAIM CHADWICK. *Clerk of the Court:* JAS. WINRIGHT.

SHARP, JACOB.   Bertie County.

October 30, 1748. January 27, 1748. *Son:* STARKEY ("all my lands and Manner plantation"). *Wife and Executrix:* ELISABETH. *Nephew:* SAMUEL TANNER. *Friends:* WILLIAM HOOKER, WM. WITHERIN, JOHN BAKER, of Littletown, PETER EVANS (*Executor*). *Witnesses:* WILLIAM WILLINGTON, ISAAC LASSITER, MARY LASSITER. Proven before GAB. JOHNSTON.

SHARWOOD, DAVID.   Perquimans Precinct.

November 16, 1722. April 9, 1723. *Sons:* JONATHAN and DAVID (a plantation to each). *Wife and Executrix:* JANE. *Executor:* SAMUELL PHELPS. *Witnesses:* GABRIELL NEWBY, SAMUEL PHELPS, JAMES CITESON (or CYTISON). *Clerk of the Court:* RICHD. LEARY.

SHAVER, JOHN.   Bath County.

October 25, 1730. December Court, 1730. *Friends and Executors:* JOHN THOMAS, THOMAS BLAKE, THOMAS FLIBUS and NICHOLAS ROUTLEDGE. *Witnesses:* JACOB HOOVER, R. ATKINS. *Clerk of the Court:* C. METCALFE.

SHEARD, DAVID.   Perquimans County.

August 10, 1740. December 3, 1740. *Son:* THOMAS ("my plantasion and all my lands"). *Daughters:* ELIZABETH and MARY SHEARD. *Executors:* WILLIAM and JOHN JONES. *Witnesses:* JOHN ANDERSON, JEREMIAH BARNES, ROBERT HALL. Proven before W. SMITH, C. J.

SHEARER, ROBERT.   Bertie Precinct.

October 7, 1727. *Sons:* ROBERT and ARTHUR (land on Little Swamp), JOHN (land called the "Poynt Land"), WILLIAM. *Daughters:* PRUDENCE and SUSANNAH. *Wife and Executrix:* ELIZABETH. *Overseers:* JOHN DEW and ARTHUR WILLIAMS. *Witnesses:* HENRY GAY, JOSEPH BOON. No probate.

SHELLEY, JOHN PHILIP.   Edgecombe County.

June 28, 1749. August Court, 1749. *Sons:* PHILIP (land on Swift Creek and four negroes), DANIEL (land on Swift Creek at the mouth of Tumbling Run, and two negroes). *Daughter:* JUDETH SHELLEY (two negroes). *Executor:* THOMAS MANN. *Witnesses:* WILLIAM SMITHES, JEREMIAH MALPASS, MARGARET TERRY. *Clerk of the Court:* BENJAMIN WYNNS. Impression of head on seal.

SHEPARD, DAVID.   Carteret County.

May 30, 1774. January 13, 1775. *Sons:* SOLOMON (land on west side of Black Creek bought of LANKISTHUR LOVETT, land on Boague Sound known as Smith's Hammock, land on the head of Broad Creek and three negro men), ELIJAH ("plantation whereon I now live," land on south side of Newport River called Snow Neck, land on Boague Sound known as Bartrom's Point, and four negroes). To two above-named sons is devised land on south side of Newport River known as Read's Neck. To heirs of son JACOB is devised land on Boague Sound called Whitehall, land on Newport River known as Mount Pleasant, and another tract on north side of Newport River, together with one negro man. *Grandsons:*

DAVID (son of SOLOMON SHEPARD, plantation on Boague Sound at the mouth of Goose Creek, known as Townley's Point, and one negro), JOHN (son of JACOB SHEPARD), SOLOMON and ABSOLOM SHEPARD (to SOLOMON is given a plantation on Boague Sound and three negroes), DAVID WARD, DAVID SANDERS (one negro), DAVID TAYLOR. *Daughters:* SARAH WALLIS (five negroes), REBECKAH SANDERS (one negro), ABIGAIL WARD (six negroes), ELISABETH TAYLOR (negroes). *Wife:* not named. *Executors:* SOLOMON and ELIJAH SHEPARD (sons), COL. WILLIAM THOMSON. *Witnesses:* CORNELIUS CANADY, ELISABETH CANADY, GIDEON CANADAY. Proven before JAS. HASELL.

SHEPARD, THOMAS.   Currituck County.

March 20, 1721–1722. July 10, 1722. *Daughters:* ELIZABETH and GWINEFOLD SHEPARD. *Son:* SAMSON ("my plantation"). *Wife and Executrix:* RUTH. *Witnesses:* JO. WICKER, HUMPH. VINCE. *Clerk of the Court:* JO. WICKER.

SHERARD, JOHN.   Northampton County.

October 21, 1751. August Court, 1753. *Sons:* JOSEPH, WILLIAM, ROBERT (plantation devised to each), THOMAS. *Daughter:* CHARITY SHERARD. *Wife:* not named. Two negroes bequeathed. *Witnesses:* JOHN DAWSON, WILLIAM BRIDGERS, AGNES LASSITER, JOHN BRIDGERS. *Clerk of the Court:* I. EDWARDS.

SHERWOOD, THOMAS.   Albemarle County.

December 22, 1693. April 17, 1694. *Wife and Executrix:* ELIZABETH ("one-half the plantation I now live on, including the mantion house"). *Daughter:* SARAH. *Executor:* GEORGE MUSCHAMP. *Witnesses:* WILLIAM RAWLINSON, ELIZABETH RAWLINSON, BARBARA MIDLETON. *Clerk of the Court:* EDWARD MAYO.

SHETTS, JACOB.   Craven County.

September 25, 1751. *Daughters:* ZILLPMAN JOHN, CEVEL SHETTS, CATRRON FELD. *Wife:* CEVEL. *Executors:* LEWIS BRYAN and JOHN CORNOT. *Witnesses:* HARDY BUSH, SAML. FEILD, CATHRINE BUSH. No probate.

SHINE, DANIEL.   Craven County.

May 5, 1757. August Court, 1757. *Sons:* JOHN (1 shilling), THOMAS (1 negro), WILLIAM (2 negroes), JAMES ("all the rest of my estate, negroes, lands, horses, cattle, hogs, etc."). *Daughter:* ELIZABETH VAUGHAN. *Executors:* JAMES SHINE and JOHN OLIVER. *Witnesses:* FARLD GREEN, JOHN WILLIAMSON, CHARLES SHENEWOLF. *Deputy Clerk of the Court:* PETER CONWAY. Impression of stag on seal.

SHIRLEY, JAMES.

December 9, 1737. February 18, 1737. Cape Fear. *Son:* DESMINIERE. *Daughters:* SUSANNAH and ANN SHIRLEY. *Wife and Executrix:* ANN. *Witnesses:* DUN. CAMPBELL, ARMAND DeROSSETT, M. D., DR. ROGER ROLFE. Proven before GAB. JOHNSTON at Newton.

SHIRORD, ALEXANDER.   Bertie Precinct.

July 10, 1731. *Sons:* ALEXANDER ("my plantation in Virginia"), AARON, JOHN ("plantation where I now live"). *Daughters:* MARTHA, CATREN and ELIZABETH. *Wife and Executrix:* MARY. *Witnesses:* ALXR. DOWNING, WILLIAM HOMES, WILLIAM WORRELL. No probate.

SHORTER, WILLIAM.   Northampton County.

December 7, 1752. May Court, 1753. *Son:* BENJAMIN ("my planta-tion"). *Other legatee:* DORCAS HUGGINS. *Wife and Executrix:* ELIZA-BETH. *Witnesses:* THOS. PACE, JOHN MOORE. *Clerk of the Court:* I. EDWARDS.

SHROCK, PETER.   Bertie County.

July 11, 1750. July 10, 1751. *Brothers:* MYCHEL, GEORGE and JOHN CAPHEART. *Father and Executor:* GEORGE CAPHEART. *Witnesses:* EDY CETER, JNO. CRICKET, JR. Proven before GAB. JOHNSTON, at Eden House.

SHUBRIDGE, WILLIAM.   Onslow County.

January 30, 1744–1745. April Court, 1746. *Grandchildren:* WILLIAM and ELISABETH AHAIR, SHUBRIDGE and WILLIAM RAMSEY. *Executors:* JOHN AHAIR and SAMUELL RAMSEY (sons-in-law), JOHN STARKEY. *Wit-nesses:* JOHN GILLETT, WILLIAM RAMSEY, DENIS OMAR. *Clerk of the Court:* GEO. CLOPTON.

SHUTE, GYLES.   Bath County.

February 11, 1729–1730. June Court, 1730. *Sons:* PHILIP, SAMUEL ("plantation I now live on lying on the Mouth of Towne Creek"), JOSEPH. *Daughter:* PENELOPE SHUTE (gold ring). *Wife and Executrix:* CHARITY. *Witnesses:* ISAAC OTTIWELL, JOHN MATTOCKE, JOHN LAWSON. *Clerk of the Court:* JNO. MATTOCKE. Device of some description on seal.

SHUTE, REBECCA.

May 28, 1732. August 12, 1732. Port Royall, in the Island of Jamaica. *Daughter :* REBECCA SHUTE (plantation in Cape Fear with negroes, etc.). *Mother:* MARY EARLE. *Friend:* JNO. EARLE. *Executors:* MARY and JOHN EARLE. *Witnesses:* GEORGE CAVANISS, JOHN PHIPPS, JACOB PHIPPS, JOSIAH EASON. *Clerk of the Court at Port Royall:* LOUIS GALDY. *Justice of the Peace, North Carolina:* W. BADHAM. Coat of arms on seal.

SIGLEY, JOHN.   Beaufort County.

May 10, 1750. December Court, 1754. *Son:* AARON. *Daughters:* ANN
and JEAN SIGLEY. *Wife and Executrix:* MARGRET SIGLEY. *Witnesses:*
COLEMAN ROE, HENRY LOCKEY. *Clerk of the Court:* WALLEY CHAUNCEY.

SILVERTHORN, GILFORD.   Hyde Precinct.

April 5, 1737–1738. March 7, 1737. *Sons:* JOHN, SABASTIN (*Executor*).
Daughter: MARY. *Wife and Executrix:* MARY. *Witnesses:* ROGER MASON,
NICKLES BOOTY, JOHN MASON. *Clerk of the Court:* J. MARDNER.

SILVERTHORN, SABASTIN.   Hyde County.

December 22, 1751. March Court, 1752. *Son:* JOHN ("my manner
plantation"). *Daughters:* LYDIA, MARY, AGNES and SARY SILVERTHORN.
Wife and Executrix: MARY. *Executor:* BENJAMIN MASON. *Witnesses:*
ROGER MASON, JR., JONATHAN BELL and MARK REW. *Clerk of the Court:*
FRANCIS EGLETON.

SILVESTER, RICHARD.   Beaufort County.

January 11, 1728. June 10, 1729. *Son:* RICHARD WILLIAM SILVESTER
(land at Bridge Town in Norfolk County, Virginia; also two tracts of land
on Machapungo River). *Other legatee:* WILLIAM WORMINTUN ("two bitts
of Ground in Virga att ye Bridge Town"). *Wife:* not named. *Grandsons:*
EBENEZER and HENRY SLADE. *Witnesses:* JOHN SMITH, JILES WILLIAMS,
JAMES ARTREE. No executor named. *Clerk of the Court:* JNO. MATTOCKE.

SIMMONS, BULLOCK.   Currituck County.

April 14, 1746. October Court, 1746. *Sons:* SOLOMON and WILLIS.
Daughter: MARY SIMMONS. *Wife and Executrix:* ELISABETH. *Witnesses:*
THOMAS LEGITT, WILLIS SIMMONS, ROBERT SIMMONS. *Clerk of the Court:*
RICHARD MCCLURE.

SIMMONS, EDWARD.   Edgecombe Precinct.

October 5, 1735. November Court, 1735. *Daughters:* ELIZABETH and
JANE HOLLEY, TOMAZIN, HANNAH. *Grandchildren:* JOHN and MARY JACK-
SON. *Wife and Executrix:* MARY. *Witnesses:* ANDREW JOHNSON, FRANCIS
JOHNSON, BEN. RAWLINS. *Clerk of the Court:* RT. FORSTER.

SIMMONS, FRANCIS.   Currituck County.

October 25, 1757. December 20, 1757. *Son:* SAMUEL. *Brother and
Executor:* JOHN SIMMONS. *Witnesses:* SAMUEL HOLSTEAD, JOHN BRABBELL,
WILLIAM CHITTUM. *Clerk of the Court:* WM. MEARNS.

22

SIMMONS, HENRY.   Currituck County.
   March 4, 1753. March Court, 1755. *Sons:* HILARY, SOLOMON, ASA,
THOMAS. *Daughters:* RHODA and ABIAH. *Wife and Executrix:* DEBORAH.
Witnesses: JAMES PHILLIPS, JOHN SIMMONS, SOLOMON SIMMONS. *Clerk of
the Court:* WILLIAM SHERGOLD.

SIMMONDS, HENRY.   Bladen County.
   January 9, 1758. January Court, 1758. *Brothers:* WILLIAM SIMMONDS,
BENINJR MOORE. *Sisters:* ANN MOORE, JUDITH DAVIS. *Other legatee:*
EDMUND FOGARTY. *Executors:* BENINJR MOORE, WILLIAM SIMMONDS,
THOS. HALL. *Witnesses:* MARY SMITH, JOHN GRANGE, SAM'L WATTERS.
Clerk of the Court: J. BURGWIN. Impression on seal of two fighting cocks
under a crown.

SIMMONS, HENRY.   Onslow County.
   August 7, 1770. April 18, 1774. *Sons:* EDWARD, JAMES, HENRY, JO-
SEPH, ELIJAH, SAMUEL and BENJAMIN (to these sons is devised lands on
Holstons Creek, Browns Harrows, etc.). *Wife and Executrix:* MARTHA.
Witnesses: THOS. DULANEY, MARY WARD, THOS. DULANEY. Proven before
JO. MARTIN.

SIMMONS, JACOB.   New Hanover Precinct.
   February 24, 1735–1736. June 16, 1736. Shallotte. *Sons:* JOHN (land
on Little River and the Sound), JACOB (250 acres of land in the fork of
Shallotte). *Daughter:* MARY SIMMONS. *Wife and Executrix:* MARY. *Trustee for minor son:* JONATHAN SWAIN, of Lockwoods Folly. *Witnesses:*
PHEEBE MILLER, THOMAS HOPCRAFT, JEHOSHAPHAT HALLANDS. Proven
before GAB. JOHNSTON.

SIMMONS, JAMES.   Currituck County.
   August 15, 1753. March Court, 1755. *Son:* ISLES. *Brother:* SAMUEL
SIMMONS. *Executor:* WILLIAM FERREBEE. *Witnesses:* SAMUEL SIMMONS,
PETER SPRALLIN, GEORGE FISHER. *Clerk of the Court:* WM. SHERGOLD.

SIMMONS, MARY.   Perquimans County.
   September 19, 1722. July 14, 1724. *Son:* THOMAS PEIRCE. *Daughter:*
REBECKAH TOMES. *Grandchildren:* SARAH, JOSEPH, THOMAS, JOSEPH
PEIRCE, MARY JONES, SARAH PETTELL, MARY and ISAIAH SMITH. *Execu-
tor:* THOMAS PEIRCE (land on Sound side). *Witnesses:* BENJAMIN SANDERS,
CHARLES DENMAN. *Clerk of the Court:* RICHD. LEARY. *Executor* qualified
before C. GALE, C. J.

SIMMONS, MATTHEW.   Albemarle County.
   February 16, 1691–1692. *Daughters:* ANN and MARGARET SIMMONS.
Remainder of will illegible.

SIMMONS, NICHOLAS.

Will illegible.

SIMMONS, THOMAS.   Currituck County.

February 22, 1755. September Court, 1755. *Sons:* THOMAS, SAMUEL and SAMPSON ("my plantation to be divided between them"), EDOM, CALEB and ASALEL. *Daughters:* MARY SIMMONS and ELIZABETH MUNCREEF and SARAH MERCER. *Wife and Executrix:* SARAH. *Witnesses:* BENJAMIN PRESCOOT, BENJAMIN COWEL, ELISABETH COWEL. *Clerk of the Court:* WILLIAM SHERGOLD.

SIMONS, ANDREW.   Beaufort County.

January 6, 1746–1747. April 7, 1752. *Sons:* WILLIAM, THOMAS, JOHN JOSHUA ("This Beaverdam plantation whereon I now live"), GEORGE and LEVI (100 acres of "Beaverdam land" to each). *Wife and Executrix:* MARY. *Executor:* JOHN ODEON. *Witnesses:* ROBT. CUTLER, JOHN CARROL, EDWARD POYNER. Proven before GAB. JOHNSTON, at Bath Town. Impression of winged dragon on seal.

SIMONS, ARGILL.   Chowan Precinct.

April 13, 1714. December 17, 1714. *Son:* JOHN. *Daughter:* MARGREAT. *Cousin and Executor:* FRANCES FOSTER. *Witnesses:* THOMAS HORTON, SARAH GRAY, P. SMITH. Proven before CHARLES EDEN. Device on seal.

SIMONS, JOHN.   Chowan Precinct.

June 2, 1731. June 25, 1732. *Sons:* JOHN, ARGILL. *Executors:* FRANCIS BEASLEY, EDWARD STANDING. *Witnesses:* JAMES BEASLEY, FRANCIS HARRISON. Proven before GEO. BURRINGTON.

SIMONS, JOHN.   Craven County.

July 14, 1741. September 24, 1742. *Sons:* JOHN, DANIEL, MANUELL, BENJAMIN, BUSETT (to each is devised a plantation). *Daughters:* KATHERINE BANTER, MARY and ELIZABETH SIMONS. *Brother:* ABRAHAM BUSETT. *Wife:* MARGERETT (two negroes). No executor named. *Witnesses:* MARTIN FRANCK, JOHN GOURLAY, CIVILL FRANCK. *Clerk of the Court:* N. ROUTLEDGE.

SIMONS, JOHN.   Craven County.

December 22, 1760. *Son:* WILLIAM. *Wife and Executrix:* MARY. *Executor:* THOMAS SIMONS (brother). Land on Bay River and Trent sold for debts. *Witnesses:* WILLIAM FULSHER, ANTHONY MOORE, ROBERT BURNEY. No probate.

SIMPSON, ALEXANDER.

November 29, 1737. June 9, 1738. "Late of the Parish of Kennoway in the shire of Fife in that part of Great Britain called Scotland." *Executor and sole legatee:* JOHN CALDOM. *Witnesses:* R. EVERARD, HARMAN HILL, THOMAS HARVEY, WALLEY CHAUNCEY. Proven before GAB. JOHNSTON. Coat of arms on seal.

SIMPSON, WALTER.   New Hanover County.

November 9, 1758. February Court, 1759. *Executor and sole legatee:* JOHN GARNES. *Witnesses:* BENJN. MORISON, ALEXANDER ADAMSON and ROBERT MCNAIR. *Clerk of the Court:* JA. MORAN.

SIMS, ROBERT.   Bertie Precinct.

February Court, 1729. *Sons:* ROBERT ("my dwelling plantation"), THOMAS (land lying upon Oachoneche Neck), JAMES (land on Conaconara Swamp). *Brother and Executor:* JOHN SIMS. *Other devisee:* JOHN FYBASH. *Witnesses:* WILLIAM BOON, ELIAS FORD, NATHANIEL COOPER. *Deputy Clerk of the Court:* THOS. CREW.

SIMSON, JOHN.   Knott's Island, in Currituck County.

March 19, 1744–1745. March Court, 1754. *Sons:* JAMES ("plantation I live on"), SOLOMON ("plantation THOMAS EVANS now lives on"), JOSHUA. *Wife:* SARAH. *Daughter:* MARY EVANS. *Executor:* THOMAS EVANS (son-in-law). *Witnesses:* HENRY WHITE, HILRA WHITE. *Clerk of the Court:* JOHN SNOAD.

SIMSON, WILLIAM.   Albemarle County.

January 15, 1693–1694. April 17, 1694. *Sons:* WILLIAM and JOHN (negro to each). *Wife:* DORITY. *Executors:* JOHN THOMLIN and JOHN RAPER. *Witnesses:* ROBERT LOWRY and CHARLES TAYLOR. *Clerk of the Court:* EDWARD MAYO.

SINCLAIR, SAMUEL.   Hyde County.

January 3, 1755. January 7, 1755. *Daughters:* ANN, CATHERINE, FRANCES and LUCIE. *Grandchildren:* WILLIAM and ANN THOMAS. *Wife and Executrix:* ELISABETH. *Executors:* JOHN STARKIE and STEPHEN LEE. Sawmill and land to be sold for debts. *Witnesses:* SAMUEL SWANN, THOMAS LOVICK, WILL MONAT. Proven before ARTHUR DOBBS.

SINGLETON, JOHN.   Northampton County.

October 29, 1754. May Court, 1755. *Wife and Executrix:* MARTHA. *Other legatee:* ANNE MORRIS, daughter of wife (500 acres of land and one negro). *Executor:* GEORGE ROBERTSON. *Witnesses:* ARTHUR DICKESON, MATT HUBBARD, ARTHUR DICKESON, JR. *Clerk of the Court:* I. EDWARDS.

SINGLETON, SAMUEL.   Dobbs County.

December 4, 1762. *Son:* SPYERS ("my plantation"). *Daughter:* MAR-
THA CASWELL. *Executors:* HANNAH (wife), RICHARD CASWELL, BENJA-
MIN CASWELL (son-in-law). *Witnesses:* ARTHUR YOUNG, FRANCIS WIL-
LIAMS. Proven before ARTHUR DOBBS.

SITGREAVES, WILLIAM.   Carteret County.

July 26, 1744. March Court, 1747. Port Beaufort. *Sons:* WILLIAM
and THOMAS. *Executors:* STEPHEN FORD, MARY LINGARD (aunt, residing in Philadelphia). *Witnesses :* MICHEL PAQUINET, MARY PAQUINET,
MICHEL PAQUINET. *Clerk of the Court:* GEORGE READ.

SITTERSON, JAMES.   Perquimans County.

January 13, 1748. January Court, 1750. *Wife:* HANNAH SITTERSON.
Sons: JAMES and SAMUEL. *Daughter:* MARY BARKER. *Executors:* Wife,
HANNAH, and *son*, JAMES. *Witnesses:* JOHN HARVEY, JOHN NICKOLS,
THOMAS NICKOLS. *Clerk of Court:* EDMUND HATCH.

SKINNER, JOHN.   Perquimans County.

July 26, 1769. December 12, 1771. *Wife and Executrix:* SARAH.
Son: STEVEN (silver shoe buckles, knee buckles and stock buckle, and
all remainder of estate real and personal. Provision is made for his
schooling in Carolina and other parts). *Executors:* EVAN, JOSHUA and
WILLIAM SKINNER (brothers). *Witnesses:* DUKE BOGUE, WILLIAM JACK-
SON, JOSHUA SKINNER, JR. Proven before Jo. MARTIN.

SKINNER, RICHARD, JR.   Perquimans County.

January 10, 1746. January Court, 1746. *Wife and Executrix:* SARAH.
Executor: JOHN HARVEY. *Witnesses:* SAMUEL STANDIN, ABRAM SANDERS,
JOSHUA SKINNER. *Clerk of the Court:* EDMUND HATCH.

SKINNER, RICHARD.   Perquimans County.

May 18, 1752. July Court, 1752. *Sons:* SAMUEL ("my plantation"),
EAVENS ("plantation where JOHN SIMPSON now lives in Chowan"),
JOSHUA (plantation on the Sound Side "formerly called Fendall's," being
land purchased of CHRISTIAN REED), WILLIAM ("my backe plantation"),
JOHN (plantation lying on the Sound side called "Petifers," being land
purchased of CHRISTIAN REED). *Wife:* SARAH ("land where THOMAS
MUNDS now lives in Chowan County"). Negroes divided among sons.
Friends: JOSEPH WHITE, JOHN and BENJAMIN HARVEY. *Executrix:*
SARAH SKINNER (wife). *Witnesses:* JOS. WHITE, PETER JONES and JOHN
HARVEY. *Clerk of the Court:* EDMUND HATCH.

SLADE, GEORGE.   Chowan Precinct.

June 3, 1710. *Wife and Executrix:* MARY. *Other legatee:* JAMES
PATCHETT. *Witnesses:* DANIEL LEIGH, RICHARD LAWRENCE, WILL NEW-
LAND. Original missing. Recorded in Book 1712–1722, page 32.

SLADE, HEZEKIAH.   Hyde County.

January 10, 1752. March Court, 1752. *Son:* JEREMIAH. *Daughters:*
DINAH and REBECCA. *Wife and Executrix:* SARAH. *Executor:* BEN-
JAMIN JEWEL. *Witnesses:* THOS. SMITH, BENJAMIN SLADE, JAMES HAM-
ILTON. *Clerk of the Court:* FRANCIS EGLETON.

SLADE, JOHN.   Hyde County.

September 6, 1743. December Court, 1743. *Sons:* JOHN ("the plan-
tation whereon I now live"), BENJAMIN (land bought of JOHN SMITH
COOPER), HEZEKIAH and WILLIAM HODGES SLADE (land bought of FRAN-
CIS BANKS). *Daughters:* MARY (wife of BENJAMIN JEWEL), SARAH and
KEZIA SLADE. Stock marks of children are as follows: WM., "under
square ye left ear"; BENJN., "crop & an under bit and one slit in the
Right ear"; SARAH, "under square the right ear". *Wife and Executrix:*
ABIGAIL. *Witnesses:* RICHARD LEATH, WILLIAM WILKINSON, URIAH
COLLINS. *Clerk of the Court:* WILLIAM BARROW.

SLADE, SAMUEL.   Beaufort County.

March 17, 1746. December Court, 1746. *Daughters:* ELIZABETH
(wife of WILLIAM DUNBARR), HANNAH (wife of WILLIAM FOSQUE), JANE
(wife of JAMES BLOUNT), SUSANNAH ("my manner plantation"). *Grandchildren:* SAMUEL BLOUNT, MARY BLOUNT (1 slave to each), MARY DUN-
BARR (1 negro), SAMUELL DUNBARR (plantation on south side of Pamtico
River "att the head of Blount's Creek and on a Branch known by the
name of good neighborhood branch"). *Executors:* BENJAMIN RIGNEY
and JACOB NEVELL. *Witnesses:* THOS. JAMES, PHILIP SHUTE, MARY
DUNBAR. *Clerk of the Court:* JOHN FORBES.

SLAUGHTER, MICHAEL.   Chowan County.

February 2, 1741. February 6, 1741. Edenton. *Daughters:* ANAH,
ABIGAIL, ELIZABETH, NANCY, REBECKAH and DEBORAH SLAUGHTER.
Wife and Executrix: ELIZABETH. *Witnesses:* JOHN PARK, ROBERT and
ABIGAL FRENCH. Proven before GAB. JOHNSTON.

SLOBOCK, JACOB.   Carteret County.

October 13, 1755. March Court, 1756. *Son:* NATHAN. *Executor and
brother-in-law:* JAMES SMITH. *Witnesses:* PHILEMON HUNTT, AMOS SMALL,
SARAH SMALL. *Clerk of the Court:* JOHN SMITH.

SLOCKUM, ANTHONY.   Albemarle County.

November 26, 1688. *Son:* JOHN ("plantation I now live upon"). *Grandsons:* JOHN SLOCKUM, SAMUEL SLOCKUM (200 acres of land), JOSEPH (200 acres of land), THOMAS and JOSEPH GILBERT. *Granddaughter:* SARAH GILBERT. *Executor:* JOHN SLOCKUM (son). *Witnesses:* JOHN WIMPELE, WILLIAM DOBSON, NICHOLAS CRISP. No probate.

SLOCOMB, JOHN.   Craven Precinct.

March 28, 1722. September 19, 1722. *Sons:* JOHN ("my dwelling plantation"), JOSEPH (land known as JOSIAS SLOCUM's), JESEWAY and JOSIAS (land on Mill Branch and one Mustee boy). *Daughter:* ELISABETH SLOCOM (land on Mill Branch and one mustee boy). Proven before RICHARD GRAVES by CAPT. WILLIAM HANDCOCK. *Clerk of the Court:* C. METCALFE. No signature of testator or witnesses.

SLOCUMB, JOHN.   Craven County.

December 17, 1759. *Cousins:* JOSEPH and JOHN CHARLES SLOCUMB. *Mother:* MARY SLOCUMB. *Wife:* MARY. *Executors:* JOHN DONELSON, JACOB TAYLOR. *Witnesses:* GRIGG YARBOROUGH, HUGH HOWY. No probate.

SLOCOM, SAMUEL.   Bath County.

May 8, 1712. April 25, 1713. *Brothers:* WILLIAM and SOLOMON SMITH, and JOHN SLOCOM. *Sister:* ISEBLE SMITH. *Other legatee:* MARGET DAVIS. *Witnesses:* WM. BRICE, LOUIS THOMAS, ANN BRICE. Proven before WM. BRICE. *Clerk of the Court:* J. PALIN.

SMALL, BENJAMIN.   Carteret County.

January 11, 1751. March Court, 1752. *Sons:* BENJAMIN (plantation bought of DAVID BALY), JONAS (land adjoining BENJAMIN), AMOS (100 acres of land adjoining THOMAS JESSOP), JOHN KNITE SMALL ("my manna plantation"). *Daughter:* SARAH JESSOP. *Wife and Executrix:* MIRIAM. *Witnesses:* HENRY STANTON, PATIENCE BULL. *Clerk of the Court:* GEORGE READ.

SMALL, BENJAMIN.   Carteret County.

June Court, 1756. *Sons:* BENJAMIN and JONAS SMALL. *Wife:* not named. *Executor:* JOHN LOVET (father-in-law). *Witnesses:* LEWIS WELCH, JOHN KNIGHTS SMALL. *Clerk of the Court:* JNO. SMITH.

SMELAGE, EDWARD.   Onslow County.

December 9, 1744. New River. *Daughter:* SARAH SMELAGE. *Wife and Executrix:* ANNE. *Witnesses:* WILLIAM MARCHMENT, DAVID BUMPUS, THOMAS BUMPUS. No probate.

SMEWIN, HENMAN.   Albemarle County.

July 17, 1673.   November 3, 1673.   *Friend and Executor:* THOMAS EAST-CHURCH, who is appointed guardian for JOHN, MARGARET and ELIZABETH WHITE, children of HENRY WHITE, dec'd.   *Witnesses:* GEORGE WALKER, THO. HASSOLD.   *Clerk of the Court:* THOMAS HARRIS.

SMITH, ANDREW.

March 22, 1756.   April 14, 1760.   Cape Fear.   *Wife and Executrix:* ANN. *Witnesses:* ISAAC WALDRON, JACOB WALDRON, RACHEL WALDRON.   Proven before ARTHUR DOBBS.

SMITH, EDWARD.   Pasquotank Precinct.

July 10, 1690.   July Court, 1690.   *Witnesses:* THO. DAVIS, DAVID PRICHARD, ANN BARTLETT.   *Clerk of the Court:* PAUL LATHUM.   Will illegible.

SMITH, EDWARD.

August 20, 1727.   June 10, 1735.   *Executor and sole legatee:* ROGER MOORE.   *Witnesses:* JNO. MOORE, JUSTINA MOORE, RICHARD JAMES PARKER.   *Clerk of the Court:* HUGH CAMPBELL.

SMITH, GEORGE.   Bertie County.

March 1, 1735.   April 16, 1736.   *Sons:* RICHARD and GEORGE ("the manner plantation"), JOHN and LEWIS (land at Cottanoe).   *Daughter:* MARY (plantation in Tyrrell).   *Wife and Executrix:* ELIZABETH (two negroes).   *Witnesses:* EDWARD COLLINS, THOMAS GAINS, CHARLES ARRINGTON.   Proven before W. SMITH, C. J.

SMITH, GEORGE.   Northampton County.

January 21, 1745–1746.   February Court, 1746.   *Sons:* WILLIAM, JEREMIAH ("my plantation").   *Daughters:* MARTHA JONES, ELIZABETH BALDWIN, MARY BARRETT, SUSANNAH, SARAH, RACHEL and CAROLINE PENELLOPE SMITH, ELIZABETH SMITH.   *Executors:* JEREMIAH SMITH and THOMAS BARRETT.   *Witnesses:* JAMES SMITH, JAMES JONES.   *Clerk of the Court:* RT. FORSTER.

SMITH, HENRY.   Craven County.

August 4, 1748.   November 2, 1748.   *Sons:* DAVID ("plantation I now live on" and all cattle in his mark "which is a crop in the right ear and slit in ye left Ear"), HENRY (land on Nuse River), JOHN (one negro boy "and one gray mare that has been much bit with wolves"), SAMUEL (one negro). *Daughters:* SARAH (cattle), NANNEY (one negro boy), ELIZABETH (one mustee boy), OLIF (one negro) and REBECKAH SMITH (one negro). *Executor:* DAVID SMITH (son). *Witnesses:* HENRY GARRALD, CHARLES SMITH, JOHN HARDEE. Proven before E. HALL, C. J.

SMITH, JAMES. Perquimans County.

December 8, 1735. April Court, 1736. *Sons:* JAMES ("plantation I now live on"), SOLOMON (land called Forte Point), JOHN (land called Beaver Dam Neck). *Daughters:* ELIZABETH SMITH ("1 mulatter boy"), MARY SMITH. *Wife and Executrix:* ANN. *Executor:* MACKRORA SCARBOROUGH. *Witnesses:* FRANCIS PENRICE, SAMUELL BOUNDS, JOHN HARMAN. *Clerk of the Court:* JAMES CRAVEN.

SMITH, JAMES. Craven County.

March 27, 1745. April 8, 1745. *Son and Executor:* JAMES. *Daughters:* MARY and MARTHA SMITH. *Wife and Executrix:* MARTHA. *Executor:* WILLIAM BRICE. *Witnesses:* THOMAS SMITH, BENJAMIN SANDERSON, JNO. SNOAD. Proven before GAB. JOHNSTON.

SMITH, JAMES. Beaufort County.

September 3, 1744. March Court, 1749. *Wife and Executrix:* ANN ("my manner plantation"). *Executor:* JAMES DODLEY. *Witnesses:* JAMES SINGLETON, MARY DUDLEY, JOHN SMITH. *Clerk of the Court:* JOHN ALDORSON.

SMITH, JEREMIAH.

June 10, 1720. July 12, 1720. *Wife:* MARGARET. *Executor:* THOMAS SIMMONS. *Witnesses:* THO. TAYLOR, ESTER TAYLOR, THO. TAYLOR, JR. *Clerk of the Court:* JO. WICKER.

SMITH, JOHN. Bertie Precinct.

December 12, 1728. August Court, 1729. *Son:* JOHN ("my manour plantation"). *Daughters:* MARY and JANE SMITH. *Wife and Executrix:* JUDITH. *Executors:* JAMES BOONE and THOMAS MACKELENDING. *Witnesses:* GEORGE WHITE, WILLIAM JONES and CHARITY WHITE. No probate.

SMITH, JOHN. Chowan Precinct.

January 30, 1731–1732. *Wife and Executrix:* ELIZABETH. *Witnesses:* JOHN CHAMPEN, HUMPHREY WEBB, RICHARD BOND. No probate.

SMITH, JOHN. Hyde County.

December 17, 1748. March 7, 1748. *Sons:* WILLIAM (lands on Matchapungo River and Slades Creek), THOMAS, JAMES, BENJAMIN, JOHN (plantation to each), SAMUEL (lands known as Mouse harbor). *Daughters:* MAR-

THA and ELIZABETH. *Wife and Executrix:* MARY. *Witnesses:* JONATHAN JASPER, CATHERINE JASPER, URIAH COLLINS. *Clerk of the Court:* THOS. LOACK.

SMITH, JOHN. Craven County.

August 15, 1768. October 9, 1770. Newbern. *Son:* JOHN TRINK SMITH ("all my estate"). *Mother:* MARTHA SMITH. *Mother-in-law:* HANNAH FRINK and her daughter HANNAH FRINK (twenty pounds to each). *Wife:* DEBORAH. *Daughter-in-law:* SARAH OUTERBRIDGE (two negroes). *Son-in-law:* RAMSEY WHITE OUTERBRIDGE (two negroes). *Sister:* HANNAH FRINK. *Uncle and Aunt:* JOHN and PRUDENCE HARDY, in Blossom Street, Norton Falgate, London. *Other legatee:* RICHARD SALTER, of Newgate in London. *Executors:* JAMES REED, RICHARD BLACKLEDGE, JACOB SHEPPARD and JAMES COOR. *Witnesses:* JOSEPH CRISPIN, MARY HAWK, FRANCIS CHILD. Proven before WM. TRYON.

SMITH, JOHN. Hyde County.

March 20, 1772. *Sons:* JOSHUA, THOMAS and STEPHEN SMITH (land and negroes), JOHN (one negro). *Grandson:* JOHN SMITH. *Executors:* STEPHEN, JOSHUA and THOMAS SMITH (sons). *Witnesses:* SAMUEL DAVIS, THOMAS MACKWILLAMS, ABIGAL SLAID. No probate.

SMITH, JOSEPH. Perquimans County.

October 2, 1724. July 17, 1732. *Sons:* JOHN, JOSEPH (land in Ballyhack). *Daughter:* ELISABETH SMITH. *Wife and Executrix:* LEAH. *Executor:* SAMUEL PHELPS. *Witnesses:* ROBERT WILSON, LUKE NOBLIN, THOMAS ELLIOT. *Clerk of the Court:* CHARLES DENMAN.

SMITH, LEVI. Currituck Precinct.

August 29, 1709. January 10, 1715–1716. *Son:* JEREMIAH. *Wife and Executrix:* SARAH ("all my estate"). *Witnesses:* THO. TAYLOR, EDWD. TAYLOR, JOS. WICKER. *Clerk of the Court:* JOS. WICKER.

SMITH, NICHOLAS. Beaufort County.

April 14, 1751. June Court, 1751. *Son and Executor:* SIMON. *Wife and Executrix:* MARY. *Witnesses:* ANDREW and RICHARD BROWN, THOMAS WILLIAMS. *Clerk of the Court:* WILLIAM ORMOND.

SMITH, RICHARD. Pasquotank County.

January 10, 1750–1751. April Court, 1751. *Wife and Executrix:* MARY ANN SMITH. *Executor:* HENRY PENDLETON. *Witnesses:* HENRY PENDLETON, GEORGE PENDLETON, ANN MEADS. *Clerk of the Court:* THO. TAYLOR.

SMITH, RICHARD.   Northampton County.

July 26, 1751. February Court, 1756. *Legatees:* DRURY and MARY ALDRIDG and RICHARD SMITH (grandson). *Executors:* HENRY ARTHUR SMITH (son), ROBERT STURT. *Witnesses:* JOHN PETERSON, ROBERT STUART, WM. COCKE. *Clerk of the Court:* I. EDWARDS.

SMITH, RICHARD.   Edgecombe County.

December 17, 1756. May Court, 1757. *Sons:* RICHARD, STEPHEN, WILLIAM (to each is devised 73 acres of land), BENJAMIN ("my plantation"). *Wife and Executrix:* SARAH. *Witnesses:* JOHN DOYLE, CHARLES DODSON. *Clerk of the Court:* JOS. MONTFORT.

SMITH, ROBERT.   Perquimans Precinct.

February 13, 1692–1693. May 1, 1693. *Son:* JOSEPH. *Daughter:* ELIZABETH. *Son-in-law:* SAMUEL WOOD. *Executors:* WILLIAM and JOHN GODFREY. *Witnesses:* THOMAS STEELE, ELIZABETH GODFREY, SAMUEL WOOD. *Clerk of the Court:* EDWARD MAYO.

SMITH, ROBERT.   Bertie County.

January 26, 1726. May Court, 1726. *Son:* ROBERT (one plantation). *Daughters:* ELIZABETH and MARY SMITH. *Wife and Executrix:* MARY. *Executor:* BARRABY MELTON. *Witnesses:* WILLIAM LOW, JOHN LOW, JOHN WERHAM. *Clerk of the Court:* RT. FORSTER.

SMITH, SARAH.   Currituck Precinct.

February 22, 1721–1722. *Son and Executor:* THOMAS TAYLOR. *Witnesses:* CORNELIUS JONES, ANN PEACOCK, AND. PEACOCK. *Clerk of the Court:* JOHN MARTYN.

SMITH, THOMAS.   Albemarle County.

November 4, 1706. *Legatees:* MARGRITT CUTTLER and JAMES WARD (*Executor*). *Witnesses:* JNO. ALLCOCK, STEPHEN SWAINE, PATRICKE CAVYELTON. No probate.

SMITH, THOMAS.   Beaufort County.

December 12, 1752. March Court, 1753. *Son:* JAMES. *Daughter:* MARY SMITH. *Wife and Executrix:* MARY. *Witnesses:* GEORGE GERRARD, THOMAS HENLY, SAMLL. TAYLOR. *Clerk of the Court:* WILLIAM ORMOND.

SMITH, THOMAS.   Edgecombe County.

March 10, 1757. May Court, 1757. *Wife and Executrix:* not named. *Executor:* BENJAMIN HAILE. *Witnesses:* JOHN and SUSANA JONES. *Clerk of the Court:* JOSEPH MONTFORT.

SMITH, WILLIAM.

December 28, 1716. October 24, 1724. Little River. *Wife and Executrix:* ELISABETH. *Witnesses:* RO. BUCKNER, JOHN FOURRE. *Clerk of the Court:* JOHN CORNICK. Will proven before GEORGE BURRINGTON.

SMITH, WILLIAM.   Pasquotank Precinct.

March 14, 1719–1720. May 11, 1734. *Son:* JOHN ("my land and plantation"). *Daughter:* LYDIA SMITH. *Wife and Executrix:* ELIZABETH SMITH. *Executors:* JOHN SMITH (brother), WM. RELFE. *Witnesses:* W. NORRIS, WM. RELFE, RICHARD RELFE. Proven before NATH. RICE.

SMITH, WILLIAM.   Tyrrell County.

February 12, 1741–1742. March 16, 1742. *Sons:* THOMAS, SAMUEL and JOHN (1 shilling to each). *Wife and Executrix:* ELIZABETH. *Witnesses:* WINEFORD COMBS, MARY MACKEY, ANN MACKE. Proven before W. SMITH, C. J. *Clerk of the Court:* W. DOWNING.

SMITH, WILLIAM.   Chowan County.

March 30, 1743. July Court, 1743. *Legatees:* ROBERT HALTON (box of china at ABRAHAM BLACKALL'S), BENJAMIN HILL, DAVID COLETRANE, JAMES CRAVEN, JOSEPH ANDERSON, JOSEPH HARREN, DR. WILLIAM CATHCART and DR. ABRAHAM BLACKALL, THOMAS JONES, GABRIEL JOHNSTON, JAMES TROTTER. *Executors:* GABRIEL JOHNSTON and ROBERT HALTON. *Witnesses:* T. BARKER, WILLIAM HERRITAGE, ALEXR. MC-CULLOCH. *Clerk of the Court:* RICHD. McCLURE.

SMITH, WILLIAM.   Craven County.

September 4, 1749. March 20, 1749. *Sons:* JAMES ("my plantation"), RICHARD. *Daughters:* MARY and ELIZABETH (one mulatto slave to each), SARY ANN SMITH. *Wife and Executrix:* SARAH. *Witnesses:* LEVI TREWHITT, ANDREW BASS, ISABELLA KEITH. *Clerk of the Court:* PHIL. SMITH.

SMITH, WILLIAM.   Chowan County.

April 26, 1755. July Court, 1755. "Late of the Shire of Perth in North Britain, but now of Chowan Precinct in Carolina." *Brothers:* JOHN and JAMES SMITH. *Sister:* ISABEL SMITH, relict of THOMAS EMERS. *Executor:* WILLIAM MEARNS. *Witnesses:* THOMAS BARKER, ROBERT LENOX. *Clerk of the Court:* THOMAS JONES.

SMITHSON, THOMAS.   Pasquotank County.

November 2, 1743. January Court, 1743. *Sons:* JOSHUA ("plantation whereon I now live to him and his ears, and so from eair to eair so long as there is a SMITHSON to be found"), JOSEPH and JOHN (land to each). *Daughters:* MERIAM and DORKIS SMITHSON (1 negro to each), MARY MURDEN, TAMER NORRIS. *Wife and Executrix:* ANN. *Witnesses:* EDMOND JACKSON, RICHARD PRICHARD. *Clerk of the Court:* THO. TAYLOR.

SMITHWICK, ANN.   Bath Precinct.

November 5, 1711. *Executors and legatees:* Brothers and sisters, not named. *Witnesses:* CHARLES HOPTON, ——— GATLING. No probate.

SMITHWICK, EDWARD.   Chowan County.

January 21, 1715. October 16, 1716. *Sons:* EDWARD, SAMUEL and JOHN. *Daughter:* SARAH (land on Morattock River). *Executors:* WILLIAM CHARLTON and LUKE MIZELL. *Witnesses:* ROBERT ANDERSON, STEPHEN ALDERSS. *Clerk of the Court:* R. HICKS.

SMITHWICK, JOHN.

August 28, 1696. January Court, 1696. Archdaill. *Wife and Executrix:* HANNA. *Daughter:* SARY SMITHWICK. *Witnesses:* THOMAS HARLOE, CHARLES SMITH. *Clerk of the Court:* CHARLES DENMAN.

SNEDEKER, GARRET.   New Hanover County.

July 7, 1770. August 24, 1770. *Wife:* MARGARET. *Brothers:* TUNIS and THEODORANS SNEDEKER. *Nephew:* THEODORANS WARING, son of JAMES WARING (land on the Widow Moore's Creek). No executor appointed. *Witnesses:* DANIEL AUSTIN, ANNE AUSTIN, FRANCIS TOMLINSON. Proven before WM. TRYON.

SNELL, ROGER.

June, 1708. November 26, 1708. *Son:* ROGER. *Wife and Executrix:* ELIZABETH. *Daughter:* KATHERINE. *Witnesses:* WILL FRILIE, WILLIAM BOULER, NICHOLAS TYLOR. Proven before STEPHEN CARY, *Governor.*

SNELL, ROGER.   Duplin County.

October 27, 1758. April 11, 1759. *Sons:* JAMES (land and two negroes), ROGER ("my plantation and three negroes"). *Daughters:* PURTHANY SNELL, MARY KING, REBECCA HERRING (negroes to each). *Sons-in-law:* ABRAHAM HERRING and MICHAEL KING. *Wife:* ANN. *Executors:* MICHAEL KING and GEORGE BELL. *Witnesses:* JOHN KING, JOHN CANADY, JESSE BELL. *Clerk of the Court:* JOHN DICKSON.

SNELLIN, ISRAEL.   Albemarle County.

August 31, 1700. September 6, 1700. *Daughter:* RACHELL SNELLIN (plantation after decease of *wife,* HANNAH SNELLIN). *Daughter:* ESTER

SNELLIN. *Executors:* HANNAH SNELLIN, ISAAC WILLSON. *Witnesses:* SAMUEL NICHOLSON, JOSEPH PEINE, FRANCIS TOMES, JR. *Secretary of State:* SAML. SWANN.

SNOAD, HENRY.   Beaufort County.

May 20, 1752. December 12, 1752. *Sons:* JOHN PEYTON SNOAD ("plantation whereon I now live, plantation I bought of JOHN LANE, my silver watch, silver-hilted sword, silver shoe and knee buckles, six silver spoons, silver can, gold sleeve buttons, mahogany desk, gilt framed looking-glass and large china bowl"), BENJAMIN SNOAD (plantation in the Cow-pen Neck, plantation at the mouth of White Oak River on Queens Creek, "my silver-hilted sword that was my father's, six large silver spoons, black walnut looking-glass and all my china"). *Daughter:* ANN SNOAD (plantation at the mouth of Blount's Creek, six silver spoons, silver tea tongs and silver pepper box). *Sister:* MARY LANE (money "to purchase head stones for her son, JOHN SNOAD LANE, who lies buried in my orchard"). *Friends and Executors:* WALLEY CHAUNCEY (1 horse, bridle and saddle and one case pistols and gun. To wife of WALLEY, AUNT CHAUNCEY, is bequeathed 40s for ring), JAMES BONNER (gun and sword), JOHN HARDEE. *Apprentice:* WILLIAM OGLESBY. *Witnesses:* SAMUEL BOUTWELL, ANNE WILLOUGHBY, GRIFFITH HOWELL. *Clerk of the Court:* WILL. ORMOND.

SNOAD, JOHN.   Beaufort County.

June 21, 1743. September 1, 1743. *Sons:* HENRY ("my plantation," land on Little Beaver Dam, Maule's Neck; land on Herring Run, the north side of Pamlico River; land on Grindell Creek), WILLIAM (lands on Pamlico River and in the fork of May's Beaver Dam), JOHN (land on Grindell Creek). To each of sons is bequeathed negroes. *Daughters:* MARY, ANNE and ELIZABETH SNOAD (negroes to each). To sons HENRY and WILLIAM is bequeathed two periaugers. *Son-in-law:* JOHN FRY. *Wife:* ELIZABETH (6 negroes). *Executors:* WILLIAM MARTIN and WALLEY CHAUNCEY (brothers-in-law), HENRY SNOAD (son). *Witnesses:* HENRY, ELIZABETH and ZACHR. LUCAS. Proven before J. MONTGOMERY.

SNOAD, WILLIAM.   Beaufort County.

March 15, 1746. April 8, 1747. *Wife:* PATIENCE (lands on White Oak and Queens Creeks). *Other legatees:* MARY LANE, ANNE BONNER, ELIZABETH SNOAD (sisters). *Executors:* THOMAS BONNER, SIMON JONES, EDWARD SALTER and JAMES BONNER. *Witnesses:* JOEL MARTIN, ANN MARTIN, SARAH MARTIN, ANN SALTER, MARY BRICKLE. Proven before E. HALL, C. J.

SNODEN, SAMUEL.   Pasquotank County.

December 5, 1750. July Court, 1753. *Wife and Executrix:* SARAH. *Other legatee:* GRACE, daughter of GEORGE SNODEN. *Executor:* ROBERT BAILEY. *Witnesses:* JAMES GREGORIE, ROBERT BAILEY, DEBORAH SUTTON. *Clerk of the Court:* THO. TAYLOR.

SNODEN, THOMAS.   Perquimans County.

February 24, 1727–1728. October Court, 1736. *Sons:* JOHN (land in Bertie and stock in his mark, "the said mark being upon Record"), JOSEPH (land in Bertie), WILLIAM, GEORGE and SAMUEL (land in Perquimans divided among them), SOLOMON and LAMUELL. *Executors:* SAMUEL SWANN and JNO. SNODEN. *Witnesses:* RICHARD ROBINS, ABRAHAM JENETT, THOS. TRUMBLE. *Clerk of the Court:* JAMES CRAVEN.

SNOUCK, DANIEL.   Perquimans Precinct.

June 1, 1712. *Friends:* THOMAS LILY, JOHN, SARAH, MARGARET and ELIZABETH LILY (children of THOMAS). *Wife and Executrix:* MARGRETT. *Executor:* WILLIAM KITSHING. *Witnesses:* WILLIAM CARMAN, TIMOTHY TAYLOR, FRANCIS JOHNES. *Clerk of the Court:* RICHARD LEARY.

SNOWDEN, JOSEPH.   Perquimans County.

November 20, 1740. January Court, 1740. *Brothers:* JOHN, GEORGE and WILLIAM SNOWDEN. *Niece:* THOMSON SNOWDEN. *Executors:* JOHN and WILLIAM SNOWDEN (brothers). *Witnesses:* BENJAMIN BAPTISS, AARON MOSES, WILLIAM LAYDEN. *Clerk of the Court:* EDMUND HATCH.

SNOWDON, ELIZABETH.   Perquimans County.

May 31, 1744. January Court, 1744. *Sons:* WILLIAM, FRANCIS, GEORGE and ISACK LAYDEN. *Granddaughter:* ELIZABETH LAYDEN. *Grandsons:* ROBERT and JOSEPH WARREN. *Executors:* GEORGE and FRANCIS LAYDEN (sons). *Witnesses:* SAMLL. SWANN, SARAH SWANN, MARY SWANN. *Clerk of the Court:* EDMUND HATCH.

SOANE, JOHN.   Bertie County.

March 16, 1732–1733. August Court, 1733. *Sons:* HALLEDAY and WILLIAM. *Daughters:* ELIZABETH and ANNA. *Wife and Executrix:* HANNAH. *Witnesses:* LEWIS BRYAN, ELIZABETH DUNCAN. *Clerk of the Court:* RT. FORSTER.

SOLLEY, JOHN.   Pasquotank County.

June, 1751. April Court, 1752. *Sons:* THOMAS (land on Neuse River bounding on Beards Creek), JOSEPH ("my plantation whereon I now live").

To each son is given two negroes. *Daughters:* MARY CLEVES, ANN WIAT. *Executor:* JOSEPH (son). *Witnesses:* TABITHA EMERSON, THOMAS EMERSON, JOHN GRAY. *Clerk of the Court:* THO. TAYLOR.

SOMERSET, SEYMORE.   Northampton County.

December 20, 1751. February Court, 1752. *Sons:* JOHN ("my plantation"), SEYMORE. *Daughters:* EASTER SOMERSETT, ELIZABETH EARP (*Executrix*). *Witnesses:* EDWARD EARP, MANUAL EARP, WM. WINBORNE. *Clerk of the Court:* I. EDWARDS.

SOTHELL, SETH.   Albemarle County.

January 20, 1689–1690. February Court, 1693–1694. *Executrix:* ANNA SOTHELL. THOMAS HARTLEY (plantation for five years, Signory on Flatty Creek and Pasquotank River until death). *Father-in-law:* EDWARD FOSTER (plantation at Cuscopincum and 30 head of cattle). WILLIAM DUNKINFIELD, WILLIAM WILKESON and HENDERSON WALKER (five pounds each for gold ring), EDWARD WADE (plantation on Little River until death). ANNA BLUNT, *wife* (all estate and personal property not otherwise willed). *Witnesses:* WM. WILKESON, HENDERSON WALKER, JOHN LOWES, WILL. WOLLARD, SARAH WOLLARD. *Clerk of the Court:* EDWARD MAYO.

SOUTHERLAND, JOHN.   Donwoody County, Virginia.

March 27, 1771. April 5, 1771. *Son:* FENDALL. *Daughters:* ELIZABETH, SARAH and MARY ANN. *Wife:* ANN (lot in Peters Burg). *Executor:* FENDALL SOUTHERLAND (brother). *Witnesses:* WILLIAM ROBERTSON, JOSEPH BELL, WM. ROBERTS. Proven before WILLIAM TRYON.

SOWELL, CHARLES.   Bertie Precinct.

November 25, 1738. February Court, 1738. *Sons:* RICHARD (land on Bear Swamp), THOMAS (plantation "where ADAM HARRELL now dwells"), LEWIS (land on horse swamp), CHARLES ("my manner plantation"). *Daughters:* ELIZABETH, HANNAH, MARY and SARAH SOWELL. *Wife and Executrix:* MARTHA. *Executor:* BENJAMIN WYNNS. *Witnesses:* EBANAZAR SLASON, THOMAS SOWELL, RICHARD HOLMES, ELIZA HARRELL, JNO. WYNNS. *Clerk of the Court:* JNO. WYNNS.

SOWELL, JOHN.   Bertie County.

March 28, 1750. February Court, 1755. *Sons:* JOHN (land), JAMES (one negro), FRANCIS. *Daughters:* MARY, ELIZABETH, FERIBY, ANN. *Wife and Executrix:* ANN. *Executor:* JAMES JONES. *Witnesses:* ADHAM HARRILL, JOHN FREEMAN, PAUL BUNCH. *Clerk of the Court:* SAML. ORMES.

SOWELL, RICHARD.   Bertie County.

July 5, 1751.   August Court, 1751.   *Sons:* RICHARD, AARON ("my maner plantation").   *Wife:* MARTHA.   *Executors:* JOHN and OBEDIAH SOWELL. *Witnesses:* ELEAZR. QUINBY (?), AARON OLIVER, WILLIAM BENNET.   *Clerk of the Court:* SAML. ORMES.

SOWERBY, HENRY.   Northampton County.

June 22, 1747.   August Court, 1747.   *Son:* JOHN ("my plantation" and one negro).   *Wife and Executrix:* SARAH.   *Witnesses:* CHAS. STEVENS, BENJAMIN DeBERRY, ELIZA STEVENS.   *Clerk of the Court:* RT. FORSTER.

SPARKMAN, JOHN.   Chowan County.

April 19, 1728.   October Court, 1728.   *Grandsons:* JOHN and STEPHEN SPARKMAN (land on the "Liking Root Branch").   *Sons:* JOHN, RICHARD, THOMAS, WILLIAM.   *Daughters:* SARAH and MARY SPARKMAN.   *Executor:* JOHN GREEN.   *Witnesses:* JOHN WIGGINS, JOHN HORNE, JOHN GREEN. *Clerk of the Court:* RT. FORSTER.

SPARKMAN, JOHN.   Chowan County.

April 25, 1738.   July 14, 1739.   *Sons:* THOMAS, JOHN.   *Wife:* SARAH. *Executors:* ROBERT and WILLIAM REDDICK.   *Witnesses:* THOMAS PILAND, THOMAS HARRELL, THOMAS HARRELL.   Proven before W. SMITH.

SPARNON, JOSEPH.   Pasquotank County.

May 15, 1718.   *Legatees:* WILLIAM BRETTNO, WILLIAM and ANN BRETTNO (children of WILLIAM), JOHN BLISH, ABRAHAM THOMAS.   *Executor:* not named.   *Witnesses:* JOSEPH COOPER, THOMAS SHEPARD, ELIZABETH COOPER, JOHN BELL.   No probate.

SPARROW, THOMAS.

May 20, 1717.   May 27, 1717.   *Sons:* SOLOMON ("my maner plantation"), JOHN and KINSEY (plantations above the "maner" plantation), SOLOMON (cattle).   *Wife:* not named.   *Brother and Executor:* THOMAS HARDING.   *Witnesses:* JAMES LEIGH, ELIEZER LILLINGTON, JOHN LILLINGTON.   Proven before CHAS. EDEN.

SPEIGHT, FRANCIS.   Chowan County.

October 16, 1749.   January Court, 1749.   *Sons:* MOSES (plantation at Contenteny and four negroes), JOHN and JOSEPH (land on wolfpit valley). *Brother:* WILLIAM SPEIGHT.   *Wife and Executrix:* KATHERN.   *Witnesses:* JOHN SANDERS, FRANCIS SANDERS, DANIEL CARCH.   *Clerk of the Court:* WILL. MEARNS.

SPEIR, ELIZABETH.   Pitt County.

October 9, 1773. March 23, 1774. *Nephews:* JOSEPH WARREN (two negroes), WILLIAM SMYDICK, MARKE MESELL (three negroes). *Other legatees:* MARY SMYDICK, JOHN SMYDICK, EDMOND SMYDICK, FAMALER SMYDICK, MARY MEESEL, ELIZABETH WARREN, JOSEPH WARREN, JAMES and MATHEW SCOTT, WILLIAM MEESEL. *Executors:* MARK MEESEL and JOSEPH WARREN, JR. *Witnesses:* GEO. EVANS, JOHN HARDEE, MAJOR HARRIS. Proven before JO. MARTIN.

SPEIR, JAMES.   Bertie County.

December 12, 1731. February Court, 1731. *Son:* JAMES (plantation on Ahoskie). *Wife and Executrix:* ANN ("my manner plantation" and two negroes). *Daughters:* MORNING SPEIR, SARAH EVERITT. *Daughters-in-law:* SARAH and PATIENCE STALLINGS. *Witnesses:* ROBERT GREAVES, CULMER SESSOMS, JNO. SUTTON. *Clerk of the Court:* RT. FORSTER.

SPEIR, JOHN.

January 8, 1761. June Court, 1767. *Wife:* ELIZABETH (negro boy and other chattels). *Daughters:* CLEARE HARDEE ("all my lands in North Carolina"), PATIENCE JEFFREYS, APSELE HOLLAND. *Executors:* JOHN and WILLIAM SPEIR (brothers) and ALEXANDER STEWART. *Witnesses:* WM. SPEIR, ALEXR. STEWART, JOHN SPEIR, JUNR. *Clerk of the Court:* AMB COX BAYLEY.

SPELLER, HENRY.   Bertie Precinct.

April 5, 1727. *Son:* THOMAS ("plantation I now dwell on lying on the North side of Moratock River"). *Daughter:* ANN SPELLER (land on Smithwick Creek below Scewocca). *Wife:* PATIENCE. *Executor:* THOMAS PARRIS, of Edenton (brother). *Witnesses:* WILLIAM LITTLE, THO. BETTERLEY, W. BADHAM, ANN ISMAY. No probate. Impression of lion rampant on seal.

SPELLER, PATIENCE.   Bertie Precinct.

February 3, 1738–1739. February Court, 1738. *Sons:* JAMES SWAIN and THOMAS SPELLER (one mulatto boy to each), RICHARD SWAIN. *Daughters:* PATIENCE RAY, ANNE WARD (negroes to each). *Grandchildren:* SARAH, JOHN and ELIZABETH SMITHWICK, WILLIAM SWAIN. *Executors:* JAMES SWAIN and THOMAS SPELLER (sons). *Witnesses:* CHARLTON MIZELL, PHILIP WARD. *Clerk of the Court:* JOHN WYNNS.

SPENCE, ALEXANDER.   Pasquotank Precinct.

August 2, 1734. April Court, 1735. *Sons:* JAMES (240 acres of land on the Eastern Shore in Maryland), ALEXANDER, JOSEPH (land on Pasquotank River), ROBERT (land adjoining RICHARD FERRIL, ABEL ROSS, JOHN TRUE-

BLOOD), TRUMAN (appointed *Executor*).   *Daughters:* JANE and CATHERINE SAWYER.   *Witnesses:* JEREMIAH MURDEN, THOMAS SAWYER, EVIN LURRY. *Clerk of the Court:* JOS. SMITH.

SPENCE, JAMES.   Pasquotank Precinct.

March 20, 1739–1740.   October Court, 1740.   *Sons:* ALEXANDER, DAVID, JAMES.   *Daughters:* BRIDGET SPENCE and BETTY MARDRUM.   *Wife and Executrix:* SARAH.   *Witnesses:* JOHN JONES, BERD BANGER, ELIZABETH PERISHE.   *Clerk of the Court:* JAMES CRAVEN.

SPENCE, JAMES.   Pasquotank County.

November 19, 1753.   April Court, 1755.   *Sons:* ALEXANDER, JOHN and JAMES.   *Daughters:* SARAH COOK, LETTESHA, AREY and DOROTHY SPENCE. *Wife and Executrix:* ELIZABETH SPENCE.   *Witnesses:* SAMUEL SMITH, SAML. EDNYE, DAVID DAVIS.   *Clerk of the Court:* THOS. TAYLOR.

SPENCE, JOHN.   Pasquotank County.

March 14, 1735–1736.   April 13, 1736.   *Sons:* DAVID and ALEXANDER (lands divided between them).   *Daughters:* DOROTHY DAVIS, ELIZABETH SPENCE.   *Granddaughter:* REACHELL SAWYER.   *Executors:* CHARLES SAW- YER and JOHN DAVIS.   *Witnesses:* GEO. ROWE, ALEXANDER LEFLEAR, ELIZABETH LEFLEARE.   *Clerk of the Court:* JOS. SMITH.   Device on seal: Letters S. S., three circles and square.

SPIGHT, MARY.   Bertie County.

February 25, 1740–1741.   May 7, 1743.   *Sons:* MOSES, ISAAC (*Executor*). *Daughter:* RACHEL and RUTH JORDAN, ZILPAH BLANCHARD.   *Granddaugh- ters:* MARY and ELIZABETH SPIGHT.   *Cousins:* JACOB HINTON, RUBEN HINTON, WILLIAM, BETTIE and MARY HINTON, JOSEPH PEREY (*Executor*). *Witnesses:* GUY HILL, MOSS ROWNTREE, THOMAS ROWNTREE.   Proven before GAB. JOHNSTON, at Edenton.

SPIGHT, THOMAS.   Perquimans Precinct.

April 9, 1737.   April 27, 1737.   *Sons:* ISAAC ("plantation whereon I now dwell"), MOSES.   *Daughters:* RACHEL and RUTH JORDEN and ZILPAH BLANCHARD.   *Wife and Executrix:* MARY.   *Witnesses:* RICHARD PEARCE, GEFERY HUBBARD, THOS. ROWNTREE.   Proven before W. SMITH, C. J.

SPIGHT, THOMAS.   Craven County.

October 3, 1756.   November Court, 1756.   This is a nuncupative will proven before JOHN CLITHERALL by JOHN SPEIGHT, PHRUSAN SPEIGHT and ANN PAYN.   *Wife:* ELIZABETH (one negro).   *Sister:* PRUSANE SPIGHT. *Other legatees:* JOHN and SIMON SPIGHT.   *Clerk of the Court:* WM. POWELL.

SPIVEY, THOMAS.   Chowan Precinct.

December 23, 1729. February 5, 1729–1730. *Sons:* JACOB (plantation) and BENJAMIN, WILLIAM and THOMAS (12 pence and a Bible). *Son-in-law:* WILLIAM HILL (90 acres land). *Daughter:* MARY HILL. *Grandchildren:* JACOB SPIVEY, SARAH, MARY and SUSANAH HILL. *Other legatee:* MARKE CHAPEL. *Executor:* JACOB SPIVEY (son). *Witnesses:* WILLIAM WESTTON, ROBART BLANCHARD, THOMAS MANSFIELD. Proven before RICHARD EVERARD.

SPRATTEN, HENRY.   Currituck County.

January 10, 1750. April Court, 1751. *Wife and Executrix:* MARY. *Daughter:* ESTHER SPRATTON. *Brother:* PETER SPRATTON. *Brother-in-law:* THOMAS TATUM. *Witnesses:* ROBERT FLETCHER, WILLIAM WHITE. *Clerk of the Court:* RICHD. MCCLURE.

SPRING, ARON.   Beaufort County.

April 18, 1755. June Court, 1756. *Sons:* ROBERT ("my plantation"), JAMES and ABRAHAM (440 acres of land divided between them). *Daughters:* DINAH (wife of WILLIAM JESSOP), ELIZABETH SPRING. *Wife:* MARTHA. Negroes bequeathed to children. *Executor:* JOHN BARROW (brother-in-law). *Witnesses:* THOMAS BARROW, LITTLETON EBORN, JUN. *Clerk of the Court:* WALLEY CHAUNCY.

SPROT, THOMAS.   Anson County.

January 15, 1757. *Daughters:* MARY and ANN BARNET, JEAN NEEL, SUSANNAH POLK, MARTHA SPROT (land on Sugar Creek). *Sons:* THOMAS (land on Twelve Mill (Mile) Creek), JOHN CLARK. *Executors:* ANDREW SPROT and THOMAS POLK. *Witnesses:* WILLIAM BARNET, JAMES SPROT, JAS. CAMPBELL. No probate.

STACEY, CHARLES.   Chowan Precinct.

January 2, 1724–1725. July 19, 1725. *Wife and Executrix:* MARY. *Witnesses:* DAVID BUTLER, JAMES WARD, GEORGE DEAR. Proven before C. GALE, C. J.

STAFFORD, JOHN.   Bath County.

May 15, 1733. March Court, 1735. *Sons:* WILLIAM (plantation on South side of Broad Creek), JOHN ("my plantation I now dwell on"), JOSHUA (180 acres land), EDWARD (land on Creek Swamp), THOMAS (land on Broad Creek). *Daughter:* DINAH STAFFORD. *Executor:* JOHN STAFFORD (son). *Witnesses:* MARY, DARKIS and THOMAS BATTERS. *Clerk of the Court:* JOHN COLLISON.

STAFFORD, WILLIAM.   Currituck Precinct.

    February 17, 1727–1728. April 9, 1728. *Sons:* JOHN and EDWARD (1 shilling to each), WILLIAM ("my plantation"), SAMUEL (300 acres of land). *Daughters:* ANN, FRANCES and MARY STAFFORD. *Wife and Executrix:* JEAN. *Executor:* PHILIP NORTHAN. *Witnesses:* MARY JOHNS, GEORGE POWERS. *Clerk of the Court:* J. MARTYN.

STAFFORD, WILLIAM.   Currituck County.

    August 28, 1742. October Court, 1742. *Sons:* JAMES ("plantation whereon I now live"), WILLIAM. *Wife and Executrix:* FRANCES. *Executor:* RICHARD HODGES. *Witnesses:* SOLOMON BRIGHT, WILLIAM BOWIN. *Clerk of the Court:* JOHN LURRY.

STAFFORD, WILLIAM.   Pasquotank County.

    November 12, 1750. *Sons:* JOHN and STEPHEN (land to each). *Daughters:* SUSANNAH and MARY. *Wife and Executrix:* ELENDER. *Other legatee:* RACHEL REW. *Executor:* WILLIAM WAYMAN. *Witnesses:* JAMES DUFFY, JOB NICKOLES, HEZ. CARTWRIGHT. No probate.

STAFFORD, WILLIAM.   New Hanover County.

    August 31, 1765. October Court, 1765. *Sons:* RICHARD, WILLIAM and JOHN (plantation divided between them and one negro each), SAMUEL (plantation in Pitt County lying on SAML. TISON'S branch, and one negro), SETH (plantation). *Daughters:* MARY MAY, ANN FORBES, PRUDENCE STONE and ELIZABETH STAFFORD. *Wife:* ELIZABETH. *Executors:* WILLIAM and JOHN STAFFORD (sons). *Witnesses:* JOHN ALEXR. WILLEY, CHAS. HOLLINGSWORTH. *Clerk of the Court:* JNO. BURGWIN.

STALLINGS, LOTT.   Chowan County.

    November 5, 1749. January 31, 1749. *Son:* SAMUEL (land in Belleyhack known by the name of Elbo). *Son-in-law:* ISAAC HILL (land adjoining THOS. NEWBY). *Daughter:* ANN STALLINGS. *Granddaughter:* SARAH HILL. *Executor:* SAMUEL STALLINGS (son). *Witnesses:* JAMES COPELAND, BENJ. BERRYMAN, GILBERT SCOTT. Proven before GAB. JOHNSTON at Eden House.

STAMP, RICHARD.   Pasquotank Precinct.

    October 20, 1721. April 17, 1722. *Sons:* THOMAS ("my plantation"), RICHARD (225 acres of land). *Daughters:* MARY, ANN, ELIZABETH and TAMER. To each of above-named children is bequeathed one negro. *Wife and Executrix:* MARY ANN. *Witnesses:* DANIEL RICHARDSON, JOSEPH OLIVER, MARGARETT BOURNSBY, MARY CALLIHAN. *Clerk of the Court:* EDMUND GALE. Impression of church spire on seal.

STAMP, THOMAS.   Pasquotank Precinct.

October 9, 1729. *Brothers:* BENJAMIN PALMER and RICHARD STAMP
(*Executor*). *Mother:* MARY ANN PALMER. *Witnesses:* JOHN MCKEELL,
JOHN CLARKE, WILLIAM ASKINES. *Clerk of the Court:* WM. MINSON.

STANDING, EDWARD.   Chowan Precinct.

July 9, 1718. January 17, 1721. *Sons:* WILLIAM (land on Cossia),
SAMUEL, EDWARD. *Daughter:* SARAH STANDING. *Wife and Executrix:*
SARAH ("my manner plantation"). *Witnesses:* JNO. HARLOE, ROBERT
STASEY, THOMAS HEARTH (or HEATH). *Clerk of the Court:* W. BADHAM.

STANDIN, SAMUEL.   Perquimans County.

March 28, 1752. April Court, 1752. *Sons:* SAMUEL and WILLIAM
(plantation to each), EDWARD (250 acres of land and one negro man).
Daughters: MARY and PENELOPE STANDIN. *Wife:* not named. *Execu-
tors:* JOHN HARVEY, WILLIAM WYATT and JOSHUA SKINNER. *Witnesses:*
JOHN NICKOLS, THOS. NICKOLS, ELISABETH SUTTON. *Clerk of the Court:*
EDMUND HATCH. Device on seal: man mounted on lion.

STANDIN, WILLIAM.   Perquimans County.

November 4, 1759. April Court, 1760. *Son:* JOHN (plantation and
two negroes). *Daughter:* SARAH (two negroes). *Wife and Executrix:*
MARY. *Executor:* WILLIAM WYATT. *Witnesses:* JOHN CREECY, THOMAS
STRATTON, ABRAHAM JENNETT. *Clerk of the Court:* MILES HARVEY.
Provision is made for schooling of son JOHN, "to read, rite and cifer as
far as the rule of three."

STANDLEY, JONATHAN.   Bertie County.

March 5, 1773. April 3, 1773. *Sons:* DAVID (plantation on Rocquis
and one negro), EDMOND (Pine woods land and one negro). *Daughters:*
ELISABETH ROADES, JEMIMA KITTRELL, ESTHER SPIVEY, SUSANNAH
BAKER, MARY STALLINS, MARTHA STANDLEY. *Wife:* ANN (land at Lum-
ber Bridge, three negroes, one "smoaking chair," etc.). *Executors:*
DAVID STANDLEY (son) and THOMAS ROADES (son-in-law). *Witnesses:*
CADER CHERRY, SOLLOMON CHERRY, MARTHA CHERRY. Proven before
JO. MARTIN.

STANFIELD, JOHN.   Orange County.

August 4, 1755. September Court, 1755. *Sons:* JOHN (land on Haw
River), THOMAS (land known as the Meeting-house tract), SAMUEL ("plantation whereon I now live"). To THOMAS and SAMUEL is also devised
land near the Rich Hills. *Wife:* HANNAH. *Executors:* JOHN JONES and

JOSEPH MADDOX. Codicil provides for education of three sons. *Witnesses:* THOMAS LINDLEY, HUGH LAUGHLIN, THOMAS LOWE. *Clerk of the Court:* JAS. WATSON.

STANFORD, LEVIN.   Beaufort County.

December 16, 1772. May 15, 1773. *Daughter:* SARAH SHUFORD. *Executor:* JAMES BRINSON. *Witnesses:* MOSES POOLE, JOHN and NANCY COVINGTON. Proven before JO. MARTIN.

STANSELL, JOHN.   Tyrrell County.

August 22, 1750. March Court, 1750. *Sons:* JOHN and GODFREY. *Daughters:* ELIZABETH BARBRE, REBECKAH STANSELL, MARY BENTELY. *Wife and Executrix:* SARAH. *Witnesses:* EDMUND SMITHWICK, REBECKAH STANSELL, SAMUEL SMITHWICK. *Clerk of the Court:* EVAN JONES.

STANTON, HENRY.   Carteret County.

May 1, 1751. September Court, 1751. *Sons:* HENRY (land called the Swimming Point), JOSEPH (land on Queens Creek), BENJAMIN, JOHN (land called Bare Banks). *Wife and Executrix:* LIDDY. *Daughters:* HANNAH SPOONER, MARY ALBURTSON, SARAH STANTON. *Witnesses:* ELIAS ALLERTSON, THOMAS WHITE, ISAAC WHITE. *Clerk of the Court:* GEORGE READ.

STANTON, MARY.

February 2, 1720-1721. April Court, 1721. *Sons:* JOHN and ROBERT ARMOUR, ELIJA STANTON. *Daughters:* MARY BROTHERS, ANN KELLY. *Other legatees:* MARY STANTON and REBECCA BROTHERS. *Executor:* ELIJA STANTON (son). *Witnesses:* SAMUEL GUTHRIE, TERRENCE SWEENY, MARY ARMOUR. *Clerk pro tem.:* JNO. PALIN. Fleur-de-lis on seal.

STANTON, THOMAS.   Pasquotank Precinct.

August 25, 1720. October 18, 1720. *Wife and Executrix:* MARY. *Witnesses:* JOHN BUNDY, RICHD. SAMS, ANN MEIDS. *Clerk of the Court:* W. NORRIS.

STASEY, THOMAS.   Chowan Precinct.

April 19, 1697. July 5, 1697. *Sons:* JOHN, THOMAS and CHARLES. *Wife and Executrix:* REBECKAH. *Witnesses:* KATHERINE WATTS, FRANC SEGRAVE, LUSEAH SEGRAVE. *Clerk of the Court:* N. CHEVIN.

STEELL, ALEXANDER.   Onslow County.

September 18, 1751. January Court, 1751. *Sons:* PETER and JAMES (plantation on Trent River). *Daughters:* ELIZABETH, SARAH, MARGARET,

ANN and RACHELL. *Wife and Executrix:* MARY. *Executors:* PETER STEELL (son) and JOHN STARKEY. *Witnesses:* SUSANNA BARBARA, MITCHELL BARBARA, RICHARD BARBER. *Clerk of the Court:* THO. BLACK.

STEELE, AMBROSE.   Beaufort County.

December 25, 1724. April Court, 1725. *Son:* AMBROSE (land in town of Freehold, in the County of Monmouth, in East Jersey). *Wife:* REBECKAH. Land at Neuse leased of CULLEN POLLOCK ordered sold. *Executors:* WILLIAM LITTLE, CORNELIUS FOWLER and EDWARD SALTER. *Witnesses:* WILLIAM LITTLE, DEBORAH PILSON, J. STONOR and THO. UNDAY. Codicil witnessed by J. STONOR, DEBORAH PILSON and WILLIAM BEVAN. *Clerk of the Court:* JNO. SWANN. *Justice:* THOS. BOYD.

STEELY, THOMAS.   Chowan County.

May 28, 1719. June 4, 1719. *Brother:* THOMAS HAWKINS. *Sister:* JANE ADDERLY. *Witnesses:* JAMES SMITH, JAMES and ELIZABETH HAWKINS. No probate.

STEPHENS, EDWARD.   Johnston County.

October 19, 1751. December Court, 1751. *Sons:* EPHRAIM, EDMUND, JACOB (plantation to each). *Daughters:* SARAH, PATIENCE, MORNIN. *Executors:* WILLIAM STEPHENS (brother) and EPHRAIM STEPHENS (son). *Witnesses:* ARTHUR FORT, BENNET BLACKMAN, RACHEL STEPHENS. *Clerk of the Court:* CHAS. YOUNG.

STEPHENSON, GEORGE.   Edgecombe County.

June 25, 1753. August Court, 1754. *Nephews:* JOSEPH STEPHENSON (son of brother, WILLIAM), JESSE and WILLIAM STEPHENSON (sons of brother, CHARLES). *Executor:* WILLIAM STEPHENSON. *Witnesses:* HENRY HORN, ELIZABETH HORN, SION HORNE. *Clerk of the Court:* BENJAMIN WYNNS.

STEPNEY, JOHN.   Perquimans County.

November 11, 1750. January Court, 1750. *Sons:* JOHN (three plantations, one lying on Indian Creek, and one negro), SAMUEL ("plantation whereon I now live" and plantation on Indian Creek, together with one negro). *Daughters:* SARAH, MARY, MARCEY, ELIZABETH and RACHEL. *Wife and Executrix:* SARAH. *Executors:* JOHN STEPNEY (son) and ZACHARIAH NIXON. *Witnesses:* THOMAS CALLAWAY, WILLIAM WYATT, LEVY HAUGHTON. *Clerk of the Court:* EDMUND HATCH.

STEPNEY, JOHN.   Perquimans County.

February 2, 1754. April Court, 1754. *Sons:* WILLIAM, JOHN. *Daughter:* MARY STEPNEY. *Wife and Executrix:* ELIZABETH. *Executor:* WILLIAM WYATT. *Witnesses:* JOSHUA HARMAN, BREATHARD TRUELOVE. *Clerk of the Court:* WILLIAM SKINNER.

STEVENS, JAMES. Bath County.

September 5, 1739. November 15, 1739. *Wife and Executrix:* JENET. *Witnesses:* RICHARD CHEEK, JOHN QUIN, JAMES CHEEK. Proven before GAB. JOHNSTON.

STEVENS, JEREMIAH. Currituck County.

August 24, 1757. September Court, 1757. *Daughters:* EASTER and ELIZABETH STEVENS. *Executor:* SAMUEL JARVIS. *Witnesses:* JOHN LURRY, WILLIAM FEREBE, JOHN BARNES. *Clerk of the Court:* WM. MEARNS.

STEVENS, THOMAS. Craven County.

June 11, 1751. June Court, 1751. *Sons:* JOHN ("my plantation"), THOMAS. *Daughters:* SARAH, MARY and FRANCES STEVENS. *Wife:* MARY. *Executors:* THOMAS STEVENS (sons), BENJAMIN BROCKIT. *Witnesses:* JOHN GRANADE, JOHN KINSEY, SARAH BROCKETT. *Clerk of the Court:* CHAS. YOUNG.

STEVENS, THOMASEN. Currituck County.

April 20, 1748. October 5, 1748. *Sons:* MICHAEL ONEAL, JOHN STEVENS. *Daughter:* MARY STEVENS. *Executors:* THOMAS PARKER and JOHN STEVENS. *Witnesses:* THO. TAYLOR, GILBIRD PORTWOOD, JAMES MERCER. *Clerk of the Court:* RICHD. MCCLURE.

STEVENS, WILLIAM. Chowan Precinct.

October 24, 1697. January Court, 1697. *Legatees:* ROBERT WEST, THOMAS GILLAM (*Executor*). *Witnesses:* HENDERSON WALKER, JOHN HOULDBROOK, ANN WALKER. *Clerk of the Court:* N. CHEVIN.

STEVENS, WILLIAM. Beaufort County.

February 22, 1750. March 13, 1750. *Son:* JAMES ("my plantation"). *Wife and Executrix:* PENNELOPE. *Witnesses:* RICHARD NEWMAN, EZEKIEL DICKINSON, SALATHIEL MIXON. *Clerk of the Court:* WILLIAM ORMOND. Will almost illegible.

STEVENSON, CHARLES. Northampton County.

July 4, 1748. November Court, 1751. *Sons:* BENJAMIN, GEORGE, WILLIAM and JESSE (land divided among them). *Daughters:* MARTHA, SUSANNA and OLIVE. *Wife:* ELIZABETH. *Executor:* WILLIAM STEVENSON (son). *Witnesses:* JOHN DAWSON, ABRM. HOOD, EDWARD STREATER. *Clerk of the Court:* I. EDWARDS.

STEVENSON, WILLIAM. Perquimans County.

July 18, 1738. July Court, 1739. *Grandsons:* WILLIAM ("1 Church Bybel and silverware marked W. S."), JOHN, JOSEPH and THOMAS STEVEN-

SON ("all the residue of my estate"). *Son and Executor:* JOHN. *Witnesses:* WILLIAM AMBLER, JOSEPH BUNCOMBE, JAMES TURNBULL. *Clerk of the Court:* JAMES CRAVEN.

STEWARD, WILLIAM. Perquimans Precinct.

August 11, 1709. *Wife and Executrix:* ELIZABETH. *Sons:* WILLIAM and JOSEPH. *Daughters:* MARY and PATIENCE. *Witnesses:* ——— FRENCH and ELIZ. FRENCH. No probate. The signature of JOHN LAWSON appears on the back of this will.

STEWARD, WILLIAM. Perquimans Precinct.

April 11, 1711. *Sons:* WILLIAM and JOSEPH. *Daughters:* PATIENCE, ELIZABETH and MARY. *Wife and Executrix:* ELIZABETH. *Witnesses:*——— FRENCH and ——— FRENCH. *Clerk of the Court:* EDWD. BENWICKE.

STEWART, JOHN. Craven County.

October 13, 1741. June 22, 1742. *Legatees:* JACOB TOMSON, JOHN, son of RICHARD BYRD; ELIZABETH, daughter of SAMUEL PRESENT. *Executors:* DENIS ODYER (father-in-law), RICHARD BYRD. *Witnesses:* JNO. HERRING, RICHARD BYRD. *Registrar:* EDWARD GRIFFITH.

STEWART, JOHN. Bertie County.

August 5, 1773. December 13, 1774. *Wife and Executrix:* JENNET. *Executors:* ANDREW BUNN and GEORGE LOCKHART. *Witnesses:* GEORGE MATTHEWS, THOMAS CLARKSON, MATTHEW CRAWFORD. Proven before JO. MARTIN.

STEWART, LEVI. Currituck County.

July 15, 1752. January Court, 1753. *Sons:* JOHN ("plantation I now live on"), LEVI (one negro). *Wife and Executrix:* ANN (one negro). *Witnesses:* JOSEPH STEWART, JOHN BENNET, WILLIS MILLER. *Clerk of the Court:* WILLIAM SHERGOLD. Impression of head on seal.

STIBALL, RICHARD. Chowan County.

September 18, 1695. April Court, 1695. *Daughters:* MARY, PASHENCE. *Executors:* WILLIAM PREVES, WILLIAM CHALTON. *Witnesses:* WILLIAM PREVES, WILLIAM CHALTEN, ARTHUR CARLETON. *Clerk of the Court:* N. CHEVIN.

STIRING, GEORGE. Carteret County.

March 29, 1745. June Court, 1745. *Sons:* GEORGE, JOHN and HENRY. *Wife and Executrix:* MARY. *Daughters:* ELIZABETH and JOYCE STIRING. *Witnesses:* WILLIAM SALTER, HENRY SMITH. *Clerk of the Court:* GEORGE READ.

STOAKLEY, JOSEPH.   Pasquotank County.

December 12, 1729. January 3, 1729–1730. *Sons:* ISAAC, JOSEPH. *Daughter:* MARY STOAKLEY. *Other legatees:* ISACK DELLEMAR, WILLIAM CARTRIGHT. *Wife and Executrix:* ANN. *Witnesses:* THOMAS MERREDAY, JOHN RICKS, WM. MINSON. Proven before RICHARD EVERARD. To children is bequeathed six negroes and one gold ring each.

STOCKLEY, THOMAS.   New Hanover County.

September 5, 1757. February Court, 1758. *Brothers:* CAPEWELL STOCKLEY (*Executor*), PETER STOCKLEY. *Sister:* ANN STOCKLEY. *Sons:* JOHN and THOMAS. *Witnesses:* JOHN WILKINSON, JONATHAN STURGES, JACOB STOCKLEY. *Clerk of the Court:* JA. MORAN.

STONE, JOHN.   Perquimans County.

October 14, 1744. January Court, 1744. *Sons:* JOHN, WILLIAM and MOSES. *Wife and Executrix:* MARY (land on Veases Creek). *Executor:* RALPH FLETCHER. *Witnesses:* JOHN PERRY, JOHN MUNDLEN, ROGER KENYON. *Clerk of the Court:* EDMUND HATCH.

STONE, RICHARD.   Currituck County.

August 19, 1749. October Court, 1749. *Daughters:* ALES and AMAY STONE, MARY PARKER. *Son-in-law:* JOHN PARKER. *Wife and Executrix:* SINNA. *Executor:* PETER DAUGE. *Witnesses:* JOHN WHITEHURST, PETER DAUGE. *Clerk of the Court:* RICHARD McCLURE.

STRICKLAND, JOSEPH.   Northampton County.

September 25, 1755. November Court, 1755. *Son:* AXEM ("my plantation"). *Daughters:* RACHEL STRICKLAND (land on Great Branch), ABEGILL STRICKLAND, OLLIEF STRICKLAND. *Wife and Executrix:* ELISABETH. *Executor:* JOSEPH SIKES. *Witnesses:* WILLIAM MOORE, JOHN POWELL. *Clerk of the Court:* I. EDWARDS.

STRICKLAND, WILLIAM.   Bertie County.

May Court, 1728. *Sons:* WILLIAM, JOHN (100 acres of land at Roanoak), JOSEPH (100 acres of land at Roanoak), MATTHEW, SAMUEL ("my dwelling plantation"). No wife or executor named. *Witnesses:* NATHANIEL COOPER and ELIAS FORD. *Clerk of the Court:* RT. FORSTER.

STRINGER, FRANCIS.   Craven County.

January 8, 1749. March 30, 1753. *Mother:* MARY STRINGER (plantation on Contentne bought of HENRY SUMMERLIN and two negroes). *Brothers-in-law:* JOHN SHINE (land on Stoney Town Creek, in Chowan County bought of DERHAM HANDCOCK), DANIEL SHINE (land on Falling Creek).

Brother: WILLIAM STRINGER (lots in Newbern). *Daughter:* ELIZABETH STRINGER (eight slaves). *Other legatees:* ANNE GOFFEE, JOHN STRINGER, son of GEORGE STRINGER of Core Creek; WILLIAM BOND, GEORGE STRINGER, son of brother RALPH; and THOMAS STRINGER (land commonly called Dover). Provision is made for fund for poor of parish. *Wife:* HANNAH (eight negroes). *Executors:* DANL. SHINE, JAMES GREEN and THOMAS GRAVES. *Witnesses:* ABNER NEALE, JNO. KANNADY, JOHN JONES, JOS ATHERLY. Codicil witnessed by JNO. OLIVE and JNO. CANNADY bequeaths slaves to wife. Proven before MATT. ROWAN.

STRINGER, MARY.   Chowan County.

April 27, 1744. May 10, 1748. *Sons:* JOHN and FRANCIS SANDERS (*Executors*). *Daughters:* MARY DAWSON, MARTHA SUMNER. *Grand-daughters:* FRUSAN MORRIS, ELIZABETH COTTING and MARY GARDNER. *Witnesses:* EDWARD HARE, HENRY CLAYTON, EDWARD HARE, JR. Proven before GAB. JOHNSTON.

STRINGFIELD, RICHARD.   Northampton County.

July 19, 1747. November Court, 1747. *Sons:* JAMES, RICHARD, JOSEPH (*Executor*). *Witnesses:* THOMAS SHORN, SAMUEL WARREN. *Clerk of the Court:* RT. FORSTER.

STROWDE, JOHN.   Currituck County.

January 28, 1693. January 25, 1703–1704. *Daughters:* MARY and ELIZABETH ("all my estate"). *Executor:* JOHN BENNETT. *Witnesses:* WILLIAM STAFFORD, MARY BENNETT, RICHARD EVERINGTON. *Clerk of the Court:* EDWD. TAYLER.

STUART, JOHN.   Chowan Precinct.

January 5, 1702–1703. January Court, 1706–1707. *Wife and Executrix:* not named. *Daughter:* MARY. *Witnesses:* WM. WILKINS, ALEXR. GILLAGIN. *Clerk of the Court:* N. CHEVIN.

STUART, JOHN.   New Hanover Precinct.

June 27, 1736. July 9, 1736. *Legatees:* SARAH SMITH, HENRIETTA STUART (sister, of Inverness in North Britain). *Executors:* THOMAS WARDROPER (Surveyor General of the Province) and JAMES MURRAY, of Brunswick. *Witnesses:* JAMES FERGUS, WM. ELLISON. Proven before W. SMITH, C. J.

STUBBS, RICHARD.   Tyrrell County.

February 25, 1754, March Court, 1754. *Brothers:* EVERITT ("my manner plantation"), WILLIAM, THOMAS, JOHN. *Sister:* MARY. *Other legatee:* ANN JONES.   *Executors:* THOMAS and EVERETT STUBBS.   *Witnesses:* DAVID AIRS, ESTHER WALKER, MARY STUBBS.   *Clerk of the Court:* EVAN JONES.

STUBBS, THOMAS.   Beaufort County.

January 17, 1738.   August 7, 1737.   (Letters issued May 23, 1739.) *Sons:* WILLIAM ("my maner plantation lying near Moratock Bridge"), THOMAS (plantation on Flat Swamp "on Pantico Road"), EVERET ("land on Pantico Road"), JOHN (land on Coneke Creek called Briles Neck), RICHARD (land called Saverges).   *Daughters:* HANAH and MARY.   *Wife and Executrix:* MARY.   *Witnesses:* JAMES DWIGHT, NATHANIEL EVERET. *Clerk of the Court:* ANDERSON SAGG.

STUBBS, WILLIAM.

December 8, 1756.   June Court, 1757.   Bath Town.   *Son:* WILLIAM. *Daughter:* MARGARET.   *Wife and Executrix:* JANE.   *Witnesses:* JOHN ALDORSON, SAMUEL THOMSON, PETER CAILA.   *Clerk of the Court:* WALLEY CHAUNCEY.

SUGG, GEORGE.   Beaufort County.

October 29, 1758.   November Court, 1758.   *Sons:* NIMROD (land on Tison Creek), JOEL, GEORGE and ALLEN SUGG.   *Daughters:* LUCEY TISON, FANNY and SARAH SUGG.   *Executors:* AQUILA SUGG, ABRAHAM TISON, JOEL and ALLEN SUGG.   *Witnesses:* THOS. TILDESLEY, FRIEDRICH SERGNT, JOHN ANDERS.   Proven at Enfield Court.   I. EDWARDS, *Clerk of the Court.*

SUMNER, JAMES.   Perquimans County.

March 26, 1750.   May 14, 1750.   *Sons:* LUKE (two plantations), JAMES (three plantations), SETH (land on Sutton's Creek), DAVID (plantation "where DAVID KELLEY now lives"), ROBERT, WILLIAM and JOSIAH (200 pounds current money of Virginia to each).   To each of sons is bequeathed negro slaves, and to JOSIAH is devised houses and lots in Suffolk, Virginia.   *Daughters:* MARY and PENELOPE (200 pounds in money and two negroes to each).   *Wife and Executrix:* MARY.   *Witnesses:* THOMAS HURDLE, DEMSEY SUMNER.   Good impression of castle on seal.

SUMNER, JOHN.   Chowan County.

April 18, 1754.   January Court, 1755.   *Sons:* SAMUEL ("plantation whereon I now live"), WILLIAM (land bought of JOSEPH and GRIGORY STALLINGS and JOHN KNIGHT, and three negroes), JACOB (land on west side of Orapeak Swamp known as Kilmaney, six negroes), JOSEPH (land at Tar River bought of ABRAHAM ODUM, and five negroes), MOSES (land bought of WILLIAM WEBB in Bertie County, and four negroes).   *Daugh-*

ter: ELISABETH BATTLE (four negroes). *Wife and Executrix:* ELISABETH (nine negroes). *Witnesses:* JOSEPH JONES, JOHN BENTON, SR., JASEN CAMPBELL, ROSANNA RIDDICK, JETHRO BENTON. *Clerk of the Court:* WILL HALSEY. Impression of coronet on seal.

SUMNER, RICHARD.   Bertie County.

April 12, 1729. May Court, 1729. *Son and Executor:* JAMES ("my manner plantation"). *Wife:* MARY. *Daughter:* CHARITY SUMNER. *Executor:* JAMES BRYANT (father-in-law). *Witnesses:* JAMES WOOD, EDWARD GREEN, JOHN SUTTON. *Clerk of the Court:* RT. FORSTER.

SUTTON, GEORGE.

March 11, 1699. No probate. *Son:* RICHARD. *Daughters:* ELIZABETH (plantation at the Richland), DEBORAH (plantation at the hickory land). *Wife:* not named, and no executrix appointed.

SUTTON, JOSEPH.   Perquimans County.

January 20, 1694–1695. April Court, 1696. *Sons:* JOSEPH, CHRISTOPHER, GEORGE and NATHANIEL. *Wife and Executrix:* DELIVERANCE. *Witnesses:* JENKIN WILLIAMS, FRANCIS FOSTER, WILLIAM BARROW. *Clerk of the Court:* W. GLOVER.

SUTTON, JOSEPH.   Perquimans County.

January 11, 1723–1724. March 10, 1723. *Sons:* GEORGE and JOSEPH ("plantation I now live on"). To JOSEPH is also given two negroes, and to GEORGE two negroes. *Daughters:* PASHENCE and ELIZABETH (six silver spoons, one silver cup and silver tankard). *Grandson:* THOMAS SUTTON. *Executors:* RICHARD WHIDBEE (brother) and GEORGE SUTTON (son). *Witnesses:* RICHARD RATLIFF, WILLIAM WOOD, WILLIAM BARBER. Proven before GEO. BURRINGTON.

SUTTON, JOSEPH.   Perquimans County.

January 15, 1723–1724. March 26, 1724. *Son:* CHRISTOPHER (land and negroes). *Daughters:* SARAH and ELIZABETH (land called Edghill Leavels), MARY (land on Sutton's Creek), HANNAH (land on Sipros (Cypress) Swamp). *Brothers:* GEORGE and NATHANIEL SUTTON. *Wife and Executrix:* REBECKAH. *Executors:* PETER JONES and RICHARD WHIDBY. *Witnesses:* FRANCIS CRAXTON, RICHARD RATTLIFF, WILLIAM JONES. Proven before GAB. JOHNSTON.

SUTTON, MARY.   Perquimans County.

November 14, 1738. January Court, 1738. *Mother:* REBECKA DENMAN. *Sisters:* SARAH THOMAS and ELIZABETH MOULIN. *Brother and*

Executor: CHRISTOPHER SUTTON (plantation on Sutton's Creek). *Cousin and Executor:* JOSEPH SUTTON. *Witnesses:* BENJAMIN BAPTIST, ANN BARBER. *Clerk of the Court:* JAMES CRAVEN.

SUTTON, NATHANIEL.

December 20, 1682. March 12, 1682. *Sons:* GEORGE ("plantation whereon I now live"), JOSEPH (plantation where EDWARD POULTER lives), NATHANIEL (150 acres of land). *Daughter:* REBECKAH. *Cousin:* JOHN GODBY. *Wife:* not named. *Witnesses:* EDWARD POULTER, JOHN KINSE. *Clerk of the Court:* THOS. SNODEN.

SUTTON, THOMAS.   Bertie County.

February 3, 1750–1751. March 2, 1750. *Sons:* THOMAS, WILLIAM, GEORGE, JOSHUA, JASPER (land divided among these sons). *Daughters:* PARTHENIA, MARY, ELIZABETH, JUDITH. *Wife:* ELIZABETH. *Executors:* JOHN HARDISON and EDWARD RASOR. *Witnesses:* PETER WINANTS, ARTHUR WILLIAMS, ELIZABETH RASOR. Proven before GAB. JOHNSTON at Eden House. Eight negroes are divided among children.

SWAIN, JEREMIAH.   Tyrrell County.

June 28, 1746. September Court, 1746. Scuppernong. *Wife and Executrix:* MARY. *Son:* JOHN ("my plantation"). *Brother:* JAMES SWAIN (100 acres of land). *Witnesses:* JOHN SWAIN, WILLIAM TARKINGTON, MARY WEST. *Clerk of the Court* in 1746: JAMES CONNOR; in 1747: JOSIAH HART.

SWAIN, JOHN.   Tyrrell County.

April 6, 1749. December Court, 1749. *Sons:* JAMES: (land on Riders Creek), JOHN (plantation on the Sound Side), WILLIAM and STEPHEN ("the manor plantation"). *Daughters:* ELIZABETH MARY HOOKER, ROSANNA and MARTHA SWAIN. *Grandson:* JOHN SWAIN (son of JEREMIAH). *Wife and Executrix:* MARY. *Witnesses:* JOSEPH SPRUILL, JOANNE CHESTON, MARGARET GENKKENS. *Clerk of the Court:* EVAN JONES.

SWAIN, WILLIAM.   Tyrrell County.

December 15, 1752. March Court, 1753. *Brothers:* JOHN and JAMES SWAIN. *Wife and Executrix:* MAREY. *Witnesses:* JOSEPH SPRUILL, WILLIAM RHOADS, MARTHA SWAIN. *Clerk of the Court:* EVAN JONES.

SWAINE, STEPHEN.   Chowan County.

January 24, 1712–1713. *Sons:* JOHN, JAMES, RICHARD (plantation devised to each). *Daughters:* ELIZABETH SPRUILL, MARY and PATIENCE SWAINE. *Wife and Executrix:* PATIENCE. Proven before J. PALIN, *Clerk of the Court*, by the deposition of THOS. SNODEN.

SWANN, SAMUEL.   Perquimans County.

January 8, 1753.   April Court, 1753.   *Daughters:* MARY, wife of RICH-ARD CLATEN (lands on sound side, and lands lying to westward of afore-said), SARAH, ANN, ELIZABETH, MARTHA, JANE and MARGARET.   *Other legatees:* JESSE HENDLEY ("one-half my Allegator land"), JOHN VAIL (brother).   *Executors:* JOHN and JEREMIAH VAIL (brothers).   *Witnesses:* JOHN SMITH, SUSANNAH VAIL (?), WILLIAM WOLLARDS.   *Clerk of the Court:* EDMUND HATCH.   SWANN seal used.

SWANN, SAMUEL.   Perquimans Precinct.

September 12, 1707.   April 20, 1708.   *Sons:* WILLIAM (bible and seal ring), SAMPSON, HENRY and THOMAS (land between Muddy Creek and Marshy Gutt; lightwood on Grassy Point land, one pitch kettle "to Boyle Tarr"; "all the goods I have sent for from London—shagathee, shalloon and silk to make them a suit"); SAMUEL and JOHN.   *Daughters:* ELIZABETH and SARAH SWANN.   *Brother:* RICHARD BLAND, of Virginia.   *Wife and Executrix:* ELIZABETH ("my plantation whereon I now live during her life and then to son, SAMUEL").   *Witnesses:* ELIZABETH THICKPEN, ANN MOSELEY, JOHN LILLINGTON, FRANCIS FOSTER, EDWD. MOSELEY.   *Clerk of the Court:* J. KNIGHT.   Impression of what seems to be a coronet on seal. Letters testamentary with a copy of will is annexed to this will, signed by W. GLOVER and sealed with the seal of the proprietors—A cross surrounded by coat of arms of the eight lords proprietors.

SWANN, THOMAS.   Pasquotank County.

May 7, 1733.   August 9, 1733.   *Sons:* SAMUEL (one plantation), WIL-LIAM (plantation bought of ROBERT WALLIS).   "But in case either of my said sons shall sell, alien, mortgage or any other way convey either of ye sd plantations hereby given out of ye name of SWANN then it shall and may be lawful for ye other of my sd sons to reenter and take possession of the same."   *Daughters:* REBECCA and ELIZABETH SWANN (land at Moyock, in Currituck).   To each of sons is bequeathed a horse, bridle and saddle.   All estate, consisting of negroes, lands, cattle, etc., is given to wife for educa-tion of children.   *Wife and Executrix:* ELIZABETH.   *Executor:* EDWARD MOSELEY.   *Witnesses:* BANJA. PRITCHARD, MARY EDWARDS, SAML. WISE. Proven before GEORGE BURRINGTON.   Coat of arms on seal illegible.

SWIFT, EPHERAM.   White Oak, in Onslow County.

November 4, 1744.   *Sons:* EPHERAM, EBENEZER.   *Wife:* PHEBY.   *Exec-utor:* JOHN STARKEY.   *Witnesses:* THOS. CUMMINS, EMEL JONES, FRANCIS REAVIS.   No probate.   Portion of this will is missing.

SWINSON, RICHARD.   Chowan County.

April 24, 1716.   July Court, 1716.   *Sons:* RICHARD ("my plantation"), JOHN (200 acres of land), WILLIAM (land on Creek).   *Son-in-law:* RICHARD

KANADY (land "from pecoson to the Little Bridges"). *Wife and Executrix:* ELIZABETH. *Witnesses:* MARY SWINSON, GI. HALLIDAY. *Clerk of the Court:* R. HICKS.

SYERS, GERRARD.

March 29, 1755. "Late of Perth Amboy but now of Cape Fear." *Wife and Executrix:* JANE. *Other legatees:* PHILIP KEARNY, of Perth Amboy; ANDREW GOUTEY (sea books and instruments). *Executors:* CORNELIUS HARNETT and DANIEL DUNBIBIN. *Witnesses:* SAML. DUNBIBIN, JOHN EDE, JNO. LYELL. Proven before ARTHUR DOBBS. Impression of anchor and ropes on seal.

SYMONS, BENJAMIN.   Pasquotank County.

October 24, 1748. *Son:* ABRAHAM (plantation and one negro). *Daughters:* ANN, MARY and HANNAH SYMONS. *Wife and Executrix:* ELIZABETH. *Executor:* WILLIAM SYMONS (uncle). *Witnesses:* JOSEPH BAILEY, JOHN DAVIS, HANNAH SYMONS. No probate.

SYMONS, JEREMIAH.   Pasquotank County.

March 30, 1713. December 12, 1713. *Sons:* JEREMIAH, WILLIAM and SAMUELL (plantation divided between them). *Daughters:* TAMER, wife of SAMUEL RUNDEY; DEBORAH, wife of WM. CHANCEY; SARAH, wife of THOS. ROBINSON; MARY SYMONS (to these are bequeathed negroes), ANN OVERMAN and ELIZABETH SYMONS. *Executors:* JEREMIAH SYMONS, SAMUELL BUNDEY and CHARLES OVERMAN. *Witnesses:* W. NORRIS, JOHN SYMONS, HENRY WHITE. No probate.

SYMONS, JEREMIAH.   Pasquotank County.

November 1, 1740. January Court, 1740. Little River in the County of Pasquotank. *Sons:* BENJAMIN, JEREMIAH ("my manor plantation"). *Daughters:* SARAH READING, ANN SPENCE, HANNAH SYMONS. *Wife and Executrix:* RACHEL. *Witnesses:* WILLIAM SYMONS, JEHOSAPHAT SYMONS, JAMES OVERMAN. •*Clerk of the Court:* THO. TAYLOR.

SYMONS, JOHN.   Pasquotank County.

November 13, 1741. January Court, 1741. *Sons:* THOMAS and PETER (plantation divided between them). All estate is bequeathed to aforementioned sons. No executor or other legatees named. *Witnesses:* WILLIAM SYMONS, AARON MORRIS, JONATHAN WHITE. *Clerk of the Court:* THOS. TAYLOR.

24

SYMONS, JOHN.   Pasquotank Precinct.

September 11, 1748. January 19, 1748. *Wife and Executrix:* ELIZA-
BETH (two negroes). *Executor:* JOSEPH ROBERTSON. *Witnesses:* MARY
SYMONS, JOSEPH SYMONS, JONATHAN LANGWITHTHA. Proven before GAB.
JOHNSTON.

SYMONS, RACHEL (relict of JEREMIAH).   Pasquotank Co.

October 12, 1748. April 11, 1749. *Daughters:* SARAH READING, ANN
SPENCE and HANNAH SYMONS. *Son:* BENJAMIN. *Grandson:* ABRAHAM
SYMONS. *Granddaughter:* ANN REDDING. *Executor:* BENJAMIN SYMONS
(son). *Witnesses:* TERENCE SWEENY, ROBERT LOWRY, JEHOSHAPHAT
SYMONS, RACHEL SYMONS. Proven before E. HALL, C. J.

SYMONS, THOMAS.   Pasquotank Precinct.

January 20, 1702–1703. February 16, 1706. *Sons:* JOHN and PETER
(plantation to each). *Wife and Executrix:* REBECCA. *Witnesses:* JEAMS
WHITE, JOHN MOVIS, JOHN WHITE, ZACHARIAH NIXON. *Clerk of the Court:*
THO. ABINGTON.

SYMONS, THOMAS.   Pasquotank County.

February 30, 1757. March Court, 1758. *Sons:* JOHN, ABRAHAM,
THOMAS (to each is devised land). *Daughters:* MIRIAM and ANN. *Wife
and Executrix:* ANN. *Witnesses:* JEHOSHAPHAT SYMONS, NATHAN OVER-
MAN, JOHN SANDERS. *Clerk of the Court:* THO. TAYLOR. Coat of arms on
seal.

SYMS, WILLIAM.   Edgecombe County.

October 24, 1755. *Daughter:* SARAH WHOOPER (plantation lying on
Kehukey). *Son:* WILLIAM. *Executor:* JOHN WHITAKER. *Witnesses:*
THOS. TAYLOR, MARY TREE, XTR. HAYNES. No probate.

TARKINGTON, JOHN.

November 14, 1715. August 2, 1716. "Scoppernun." *Son:* WILLIAM
(lands). *Daughters:* MARY and REBECCA TARKINGTON. *Wife and Executrix:* MARTHA. *Executor:* EDWARD PHELPS "of Scoppernun" (Scuppernong). *Witnesses:* JOHN WINGET, MARY LASON, J. WATKINS. *Clerk of
the Court:* R. HICKS.

TARKINGTON, WILLIAM.   Tyrrell County.

February 21, 1747. September Court, 1748. *Sons:* JOHN (land on
Sheep Neck Branch), JOSHUA, BENJAMIN and JOSEPH, WILLIAM and ZEBU-
LON (to each is given land). *Daughters:* ANN, SARAH and JOANNA. *Wife
and Executrix:* mentioned, but not named. *Witnesses:* MATTHEW CAS-
WELL, EDWARD PHELPS, ELIZABETH CASWELL. *Clerk of the Court:* EVAN
JONES.

TART, JOSEPH. Hyde County.

June 19, 1748. September 6, 1748. *Sons:* NATHAN and JOSEPH. *Daughters:* MARY MCCEALE and TABITHA TART. *Wife and Executrix:* SARAH (plantations in Hyde and Beaufort). *Executors:* RICHARD NEWMAN and RICHARD LEIRMONT. *Witnesses:* WILLIAM MORE, JACOB CONER, RD. LEIRMONT. *Clerk of the Court:* THOMAS LOACK.

TATUM, NATHANIEL. Edgecombe County.

November 9, 1750. February Court, 1750. *Sons:* EDWARD, NATHANIEL, PETER and JOSE. *Daughter:* REBECKER TATUM. All lands divided among children. One negro bequeathed to children. *Wife and Executrix:* ELIZABETH. *Witnesses:* JAMES CANE, ELLENER WEVER, REBECCA CANE. *Clerk of the Court:* BENJN. WYNNS.

TAYLOR, ABRAHAM. Johnston County.

April 2, 1751. December Court, 1751. *Sons:* ROBERT, JACOB, JOSEPH and ABRAHAM. *Daughters:* PRUDENCE TAYLOR, ANNE CALTON, RACHEL BEEZLEY. *Grandchildren:* DINAH and ABRAHAM TAYLOR. *Wife:* EDE. *Executor:* JOSEPH TAYLOR (son). *Witnesses:* HENRY ROBERTS, SARAH PRIVAT, J. ATKINSON. *Clerk of the Court:* CHAS. YOUNG.

TAYLOR, ANDREW. Northampton County.

March 1, 1759. April Court, 1759. *Sons:* CALEB (plantation and two negroes), DEMSY (one negro). *Daughters:* GRACE and JUDITH. *Wife and Executrix:* ANNE. *Witnesses:* I. EDWARDS, JOHN HAYES, SAMUEL HAYES. *Clerk of the Court:* I. EDWARDS.

TAYLOR, ANN.

February 4, 1764. March 16, 1764. This is a nuncupative will proven by SAMUEL SWANN before ARTHUR DOBBS, and bequeaths negroes to grandchildren of SAML. SWANN, and an annuity to one MRS. SAUNDERS.

TAYLOR, EBENEZER.

April 21, 1711. *Cousins:* SAMUEL and ELINOR CROSS. *Wife:* AGNES (house and plantation). *Brothers:* SAMUEL TAYLOR, BENJAMIN TAYLOR. Library bequeathed to son of BENJAMIN who entered the ministry. Land on Forsters Creek ordered sold. *Son-in-law:* GOWEN LONDON. *Brother:* EDWARD WALKER (*Executor*). *Executor:* SAMUEL CROSS. *Witnesses:* EBENEZER TAYLOR, GIDEON JOHNSON, SAMUEL and JOSEPH WRAGG. No probate. Original missing. Recorded in Book 1712–1722, page 273.

TAYLOR, EDWARD.

December 3, 1710. *Daughters:* SARAH, DORCAS, ANNE. *Wife:* SARAH. *Executrix:* SARAH TAYLOR. *Witnesses:* TIMOTHY EIVES, RACHEL EIVES, AZRIKAM PARKER, JR. *Clerk of the Court:* ROBT. BUCKNER.

TAYLOR, JANE (widow of NATHANIEL).   Carteret Precinct.

April 17, 1754.   This is a nuncupative will, proven before ENOCH WARD by FRANCIS DAVIS.   All estate of testatrix is bequeathed to one ISHMAEL TAYLOR, who was formerly a slave of her husband.   Deposition approved by NATHANIEL RICE.

TAYLOR, JOHN.   Chowan County.

March 19, 1715–1716.   September Court, 1716.   *Son:* JOHN.   *Wife and Executrix:* MARTHA.   *Executors:* HENRY and WILLIAM CONER.   *Witnesses:* JERE. VAIL, ROBERD STECEY.   *Clerk of the Court:* R. HICKS.

TAYLOR, JOHN.   Craven County.

March 24, 1772.   March 28, 1772.   *Sons:* ABSOLAM, JOHN.   *Grandson:* JOHN TAYLOR.   *Daughters:* VIOLATER GARDE, TAMER TAYLOR, COURTNEY TAYLOR.   *Granddaughter:* ALSE GARDE.   *Executor:* BAZELL SMITH.   *Witnesses:* JACOB SIKES, ANN SIKES, ELIZABETH THOMPSON.   Proven before JO. MARTIN.

TAYLOR, LEMUELL.   Perquimans Precinct.

November 3, 1719.   July Court, 1720.   *Son:* LEMUELL (plantation and one negro).   *Wife and Executrix:* JEAN.   *Witnesses:* DANELL HALL, JAMES CHESON, JO. OATES.   *Clerk of the Court:* WM. HABEL.

TAYLOR, LUKE.   Chowan County.

December 18, 1773.   February 8, 1774.   *Sons:* JOHN and THOMAS (plantation divided between them).   *Wife:* DEBORAH.   *Executors:* JOSEPH CREECY, JOHN WILKINS and JOHN TAYLOR.   Proven before JO. MARTIN.

TAYLOR, NATHANIEL.

April 3, 1734.   May 13, 1734.   *Wife and Executrix:* JANE (silver plate and remainder of estate).   *Witnesses:* JAMES BELL, FRANCIS DAVIS, HENRY BLURTON.   Proven before NATHL. RICE.

TAYLOR, RALPH.   New Hanover County.

November 18,·1757.   February Court, 1758.   Wilmington.   *Wife and Executrix:* MARY.   *Executors:* BENJAMIN MORRISON and WILLIAM LORD.   *Witnesses:* ARMAND DEROSSET, DANIEL DUNBIBIN and ARTHUR MABSON.   *Clerk of the Court:* JA. MORAN.   Provision made for payment of debts due merchants in Liverpool.

TAYLOR, ROBERT.   Albemarle Precinct.

September 7, 1700.   *Wife:* ANN TAYLOR (all real and personal estate).   *Executrix:* ANN TAYLOR.   *Witnesses:* THO. ROLFE, THO. LEWISS, ROBT. LOVE.   No probate.

TAYLOR, ROBERT.   Edgecombe County.

September Court, 1758. *Sons:* ROBERT and EDWARD (1 shilling to each), JOSEPH, WILLIAM, HENRY, RICHARD, THOMAS, BILLINGTON, NIM-. ROD and HUDSON. *Daughters:* JUDITH and RACHEL TAYLOR, ANN HUSE. *Wife and Executrix:* ANN. *Witnesses:* WILLIAM HUDSON, JAMES VAULX, WM. HUDSON, JR. *Clerk of the Court:* JOS. MONTFORT.

TAYLOR, SAMUEL.   Northampton County.

1746. *Sons:* ROBERT ("my plantation" and two negroes), ETHD. (land and two negroes), HARRY (lands). *Daughters:* ELIZABETH and MARTHA TAYLOR (negro and increase). *Wife:* CELA. *Executor:* ETHD. TAYLOR (son). Bequests made to *son,* SAMUEL TAYLOR, "in case he returns to Meherrin to enjoy same." No signature, witnesses or probate.

TAYLOR, THOMAS, SR.   Currituck Precinct.

August 20, 1734. July Court, 1736. *Sons:* EDWARD (negroes) and THOMAS. *Daughters:* SARAH (wife of JEREMIAH STEPHENS), BRIDGET (wife of SAMUEL JARVES), BETHIA TAYLOR. *Grandsons:* BENJAMIN TAYLOR and EZEKIEL PHILLIPS. *Wife and Executrix:* EASTHER. *Witnesses:* STEPHEN WILLIAMS, SOLO. JARVES, J. MARTYN. *Clerk of the Court:* JOS. SMITH.

TAYLOR, WILLIAM.   Pasquotank County.

December 30, 1772. January 23, 1773. *Brother:* JAMES TAYLOR. *Wife and Executrix:* MARY (four negroes). *Executors:* JOHN RICHARDSON (brother-in-law) and CALEB NASH. *Witnesses:* W. NORRIS, JOHN CRAWFORD, JER. SEDLEY. Proven before Jo. MARTIN.

TERNELL, JACOB.

December 18, 1711. July 1, 1713. Little River. *Cousins:* ANN HILL, ROUGER HILL ("my land in Kakcomak"). *Executor:* RICHARD HILL (brother). *Witnesses:* JOHN MACKIE, JOHN SMITH, EDWD. ———. Proven before JOHN NELSON.

TERRILL, WILLIAM.   Albemarle County.

June 3, 1682. Little River. *Sons:* WILLIAM, "in Weymouth, New England" (plantation on Little River, commonly called the Quarter), GIDEON, "of Weymouth afsd" (land on Little River and Deep Creek). *Daughter:* MARY (wife of WILLIAM MANSON). *Other legatees:* MARY, daughter of NATHANIEL BAXTER; JOHN, son of RICHARD TULE. *Executors:* GEORGE DURRANT of "Bertey Point," JOHN HUNT of Little River. *Witnesses:* SAM WOODROW, WILLIAM HUGHES, NATHANIEL BAXTER. No probate. Impression of swan on seal.

TESTER, ROBERT.

January 8, 1695. January 13, 1696. This is a nuncupative will, proven before JOHN STEPNEY by THOMAS and KATHERINE CLARK, and names *legatees:* JOHN HOPKINS and ROBERT TESTER.

THOMAS, BARNABEE.

October 5, 1735. December 11, 1735. *Son:* ELISHA (plantation and two negroes). *Wife:* SARAH ("ye use of all my negroes, she using them as a Christen ought to do"). *Brother and Executor:* PHILIP. *Witnesses:* WILLIAM THOMAS, JNO. DAWSON, JACOB CARR. Proven before GAB. JOHNSTON.

THOMAS, FRANCIS.   Chowan County.

September 16, 1738. January 15, 1739. *Sons:* STEPHEN, JOHN and WILLIAM, FRANCIS ("plantation I live on, called the forck of the Duckinstool"). *Daughter:* ELIZABETH THOMAS. *Wife and Executrix:* MARY. *Witnesses:* JOHN JORDAN, EDMOND CONELL, JAMES WILLIAMS. Proven before W. SMITH, C. J.

THOMAS, FRANCIS.   Bladen County.

June 8, 1756. October Court, 1756. *Son:* GEORGE. *Wife and Executrix:* JOAN. *Witnesses:* THOS. HALL, LUCY HALL, THOMAS SMITH. *Clerk of the Court:* J. BURGWIN.

THOMAS, JOHN.   Northampton County.

March 18, 1745. May Court, 1746. *Son:* JOSEPH (plantation and negro). *Wife and Executrix:* ANN. *Witnesses:* I. EDWARDS, JOHN GOODALL, MATTHEW LOWRY. *Clerk of the Court:* RT. FORSTER.

THOMAS, JOSEPH.   Bertie Precinct.

December 10, 1735. February Court, 1735. *Sons:* JOSEPH, MIKEL, LUKE and JAMES (lands divided among them). *Daughter:* CHARITY THOMAS. To sons is also given negroes. *Wife:* ELISABETH. *Executor:* JOHN SPIVEY. *Witnesses:* FRANS. HOBSON, WM. SIMONS. *Clerk of the Court:* JNO. WYNNS.

THOMAS, JOSEPH.   Bertie County.

April 26, 1752. April Court, 1758. *Sons:* MICHAEL (640 acres of land "now in the possession of GRIFFIN SUMMERELL," together with stock of cattle and hogs and two negroes), JOSIAH (land "on which NATHANIEL KEEL lives," together with cattle, etc., and one negro boy), JOSEPH ("my plantation," stock and one negro). *Daughters:* MARY (land adjoining JOHN SPIVEY, and one negro), ELISABETH THOMAS (land "Whereon

JUDITH THOMAS now lives"). *Wife and Executrix:* ANN. *Executors:* THOMAS WHITMILL and ARTHUR WILLIAMS. *Witnesses:* JOSIAH COLLINS, NATHANIEL KEEL, JOSEPH KEEL, RICHARD SPARKMAN. *Clerk of the Court:* BENJAMIN WYNNS.

THOMAS, JOSEPH.   Edgecombe County.

October 24, 1757. June Court, 1758. *Daughters:* MARY, PRISCILLA and CHARITY THOMAS (to each is devised lands on Pigg Basket Creek, and one negro), MORNING ("my plantation"). *Wife and Executrix:* MOURNING (or MORNING). *Executor:* JOHN THOMAS (brother). *Witnesses:* MICAJAH THOMAS, WILLIAM DEFNALL, MOURNING THOMAS. *Clerk of the Court:* JOS. MONTFORT.

THOMAS, JOSIAH.   New Hanover County.

January 30, 1751. May Court, 1752. *Brothers:* HANNANIAH and AZRIAH THOMAS. *Cousin:* JAMES WILLIAMS (lot "on the Town Sandhills"). *Daughter:* ANN THOMAS (lot in Wilmington, ten acres "of ye aforesaid Sand Hills, and plantation whereon I now live"). *Wife and Executrix:* HANNAH (land on Long Creek). *Witnesses:* MARY ANN DUBOSE, ELIZABETH CARTER. *Clerk of the Court:* ISAAC FARIES.

THOMAS, LOUIS.   Craven County.

October 30, 1730. March 16, 1730–1731. *Wife and Executrix:* ANN MARTHA. *Daughter:* ELIZABETH THOMAS. *Son-in-law:* JOHN MICHEL SHILFER. *Witnesses:* JOSHUA PLATT, JOHN PAGE. *Clerk of the Court:* C. METCALFE.

THOMAS, LUKE.   Edgecombe County.

June 20, 1751. August Court, 1751. *Brother and Executor:* JACOB THOMAS ("my plantation," together with one negro). *Sister:* MARY THOMAS (one negro). *Other legatee:* EZEKIAH KEEL. *Witnesses:* EDWD. BROWN, JOHN TANNER, ELIZABETH KEEL. *Clerk of the Court:* BENJAMIN WYNNS.

THOMAS, MORGAN.

1709. *Legatees:* JAMES MARTIN and JOHN ANDERSON. *Witnesses:* JAMES LUTON, EDWARD HARPER. No executor or probate.

THOMAS, THOMAS.   Bladen County.

March 6, 1758. April Court, 1758. *Sons:* SAMUEL, JOSEPH, CORNELIUS, THOMAS (land in Craven on Flat Swamp), JOHN and AMOS (land on Dunn's Creek). *Daughters:* PHEBE, MARTHA and ELIZABETH THOMAS, PRISCILLA DUNN. *Wife and Executrix:* PRUDENCE. *Witnesses:* JOSIAH EVANS, JONATHAN EVANS. *Clerk of the Court:* J. BURGWIN.

THOMSON, DAVID.   Duplin County.

March 6, 1773. October 26, 1773. *Sons:* WILLIAM (two negroes, and land lying between Buck Hall and the spring branch), DAVID (two negroes, and land on Cow Marsh), JAMES (two negroes, and land on Buck Hall), STEPHEN ("my plantation," three negroes, and "my large Book called Burket on the New Testament"). *Daughters:* AMELIA and MARTHA THOMSON (three negroes to each). *Sons-in-law:* ROGER SNELL and JESSE DARDEN (one negro to each). *Executors:* ANDREDO THOMSON (brother) and ROGER SNELL. *Witnesses:* HENRY HOLLINGSWORTH, JOHN THOMSON and THOMAS THOMSON. Proven before JO. MARTIN.

THOMPSON, JOHN.   Craven County.

1738. September 27, 1738. *Son:* WILLIAM (half of all estate). *Brother:* ALEXANDER THOMPSON. *Wife:* AGNES. *Executors:* WILLIAM THOMPSON (brother) and FRANCIS STRINGER (surgeon). *Witnesses:* JOSEPH SLOCUMB, JOHN THOMPSON, JR., WILLIAM BOND. *Clerk of the Court:* JAMES COOR. Crest on seal.

THOMPSON, JOHN.   Chowan County.

August 8, 1755. *Son:* ROBERT. *Wife:* MARY (three negroes and plantation). *Other legatees:* WILLIAM THOMPSON (son of JAMES THOMPSON) and MARY TULLINGTON (daughter of MATTHIAS TULLINGTON). *Executors:* MATTHIAS TULLINGTON, JOHN LEWIS and HENRY BONNER. *Witnesses:* MICAJAH BUNCH, THOMAS LUTEN, WILLIAM JONES. No probate. Impression of head on seal.

THOMS, JOSEPH.   Perquimans Precinct.

February 9, 1728. March Court, 1727–1728. *Brothers:* JAMES and JOHN. *Other legatees:* JOSEPH, MARY, SARAH and DAMMERES RATLEFF. *Executor:* RICHARD DAVIS. *Witnesses:* THOMAS RATLIFF, HANNAH NICKLESON. Proven before RICHARD EVERARD.

THORAGOOD, FRANCIS.   Bath County.

June, 1714. April Court, 1716. *Sons:* FRANCIS, ADAM and EARLEY. *Daughters:* SARAH and ANN THORAGOOD. *Wife and Executrix:* ANN. *Witnesses:* JOSEPH FULFORD and ROBERT TURNER. *Clerk of the Court:* JNO. DRINKWATER.

THORNTON, JOHN.   Granville County.

November 10, 1754. September 2, 1755. *Wife and Executrix:* SARAH (three negroes). *Son:* FRANCIS (lands in Granville). *Daughter:* MARY THORNTON (lands in Virginia and Northampton County). *Executor:* ROBERT JONES, JR. *Witnesses:* WILLIAM PERSON, MARY JORDAN, WILLIAM LANKFORD. *Clerk of the Court:* DANIEL WELDON.

THURSTON, JOHN.   Albemarle County.

April 10, 1692. *Son and Executor:* JOHN. *Witnesses:* FRANCIS TOMES, THOMAS HOLMSON (?), SAMUEL NICKELLSON. No probate.

TIBBIT, JOHN.   Carteret County.

April 9, 1755. June Court, 1755. This is a nuncupative will proven by EPHRAIM BULL and names: *Wife and Executrix:* SARAH (land and negro). *Son:* GEORGE TIBBIT and *daughters,* MARY HOPKINS, AVES SOLE, ANNE BALA and ALSEY HILL.

TIGNER, JAMES.   Craven County.

November 25, 1749. March 20, 1749. *Sons:* THOMAS, WILLIAM and TOULSON (lands divided among them). *Daughter:* MARY ANN TIGNER. *Wife and Executrix:* SUSANNAH. *Witnesses:* ABNER NEALE, EDMUN CULLEN, DANIEL SMITH. *Clerk of the Court:* PHIL. SMITH.

TIMMERMAN, JOHN GASPER.   Craven Precinct.

May 21, 1722. September Court, 1722. *Legatees:* SEVILLA TIMMERMAN (wife) and MARY MAGDALEN TIMMERMAN (daughter). *Witnesses:* JACOB MILLER, JOHN LEILKER MILLER, JACOB SHEETS. *Clerk of the Court:* CALEB METCALFE.

TISON, SAMUEL.   Bath County.

May 1, 1736. September 16, 1736. Buford Parish. *Son:* MAGER. *Daughter:* SARAH TISON ("all cattle marked with smooth crop on ye right ear and half flower deluse on ye under side of ye left ear"). *Wife and Executrix:* MARGERA. *Executors:* CORNELIUS and THOMAS TISON. *Witnesses:* JNO. HARDEE, EDMD. TISON, JNO. KING. Provision is made for land on Horn Creek or Little Contentnea to be patented for son MAGER, and to daughter SARAH is devised land on Swift Creek. *Clerk of the Court:* JNO. COLLISON.

TISSON, MATHIAS.   Bath County.

April 5, 1710. *Sons:* JOHN, EDWARD, EDMOND, THOMAS, SAMUEL (land on Slaids Creek), MATHYAS. *Daughter:* SUSANNA. *Wife and Executrix:* MARY. *Witnesses:* BENJAMIN SANDERSON, BENJAMIN SLADE, CHARLES SMITH. No probate.

TOMES, FRANCIS.   Perquimans County.

September 5, 1729. No probate. *Daughters:* MARY NEWBY (plantation bought of JAMES THICKPEN, also a tract of land on Usess Creek bought of WILLIAM MORE), ELIZABETH PHELPS ("land I had in exchange from STEPHEN GIBBONS for my land called ye Image," also plantation adjoining RACHELL BARROW called Clagisters), PRISCILLA JONES, MARGARET TOMES (land on Bull Branch), PLEASANT WINSLOW (land on Usess Creek). *Son:* FRANCIS (land "whereon I now live"). Negroes bequeathed to children. *Wife and Executrix:* REBECKAH. *Friends:* JOSEPH and THOMAS JESSOP and WILLIAM MORE and THOMAS WINSLOW. *Executor:* NATHAN NEWBY (son-in-law). *Witnesses:* J. JESSOP, RICHARD CHESTEN, RALPH FLETCHER, R. EVERARD. Letters granted October 6, 1729.

TOMES, JOSHUA.   Perquimans Precinct.

March 4, 1731–1732. April Court, 1732. *Son:* FOSTER (land and negroes). *Daughters:* SARAH TOMES (one negro), HANNAH MAUDLIN and MERIAM SUTTON. *Son-in-law:* CHRISTOPHER SUTTON. *Grandsons:* JOSHUA and WILLIAM SHERRO. *Wife and Executrix:* REBECKAH (plantation and three negroes). *Executors:* FOSTER TOMES (son), JOSEPH SUTTON and CHARLES DENMAN. *Witnesses:* CHARLES DENMAN, MARGARET and JOHN CHARLES. *Clerk of the Court:* CHARLES DENMAN.

TOMLIN, JOHN.   Perquimans Precinct.

July 7, 1715. *Son:* WILLIAM (plantation, live stock, etc.). *Brother and Executor:* WILLIAM TOMLIN. *Witnesses:* ALBERT ALBERTSON, SR., ALBERT ALBERTSON, JR., and THOMAS STAFFORD. No probate.

TOMLINSON, JOHN.   Albemarle County.

October 14, 1697. March Court, 1697–1698. *Children:* WILLIAM and MARY, JOHN and ELIZABETH. Land called "Cabin Neck" to be divided between *sons*, WILLIAM and JOHN. *Executrix:* ELIZABETH TOMLINSON. *Witnesses:* JACOB OVERMAN, DOROTHY OVERMAN. *Clerk of the Court:* WM. GLOVER.

TOMS, MARY.   Perquimans Precinct.

March 30, 1713. January Court, 1717–1718. *Legatees:* WILLIAM PLATER, VESTY LEWIS, ELISABETH PRITLOW, RACHELL LORENCE, ELIZABETH, daughter of *brother*, WILLIAM NICKOLLSON. *Executors:* JOSEPH and MARY GLOSTER. *Witnesses:* RALPH FLETCHER, JEAN FLETCHER, EDWARD THOMAS, JAMES BALES, ELIZABETH IEEDLETT (?), JAMES THECKPU. *Clerk of the Court:* RICHARD LEARY.

TOMSON, JACOB.   Johnston County.

May 25, 1750. June Court, 1750. *Sons:* THOMAS and JACOB THOMSON. *Executors:* THOMAS LUES and RICHARD BYRD. *Wife:* MARY. *Witnesses:* MIKEL RASHER, ROBERT BYRD. *Clerk of the Court:* RICHARD CASWELL. Courthouse on Walnut Creek.

TOMSON, WILLIAM (son of JOHN TOMSON).

June 11, 1736. July 27, 1736. "County of Medlesex, London March." *Legatees:* JOHN TOMSON ("fine house and two acres of land called ye

Charey Gardens in Barken being eight miles from London"). *Wife and Executrix:* SUSANNAH. *Witnesses:* JOSEPH THORNE, JOHN STINSON, ANTHONY WHITE, JUDATH STRATCH (?).   Proven before GABRIEL JOHNSTON. Impression of head on seal.

TOOKE, JAMES.   Pasquotank Precinct.

February 6, 1719–1720.   April Court, 1720.   *Legatees:* JOHANNAH SCOTT (sister), JAMES TOOKE SCOTT (plantations known as Proctors and Floyds), THOMAS SCOTT, MARY SCOTT, ELIZABETH and SARAH SCOTT, MARY RICKS, JOHN SYMONS, JOHN TAWNYHILL, JOHN SCOTT, JOHN, SARAH and WILLIAM EVERIGIN, THOMAS and JOSEPH COMMANDER, JAMES COMMANDER. *Executors:* THOMAS COMMANDER and WILLIAM EVERIGIN. *Witnesses:* EVAN JONES, DAVID PRINCE, ANNE PALMER, DANIEL MACKEEL. *Clerk of the Court:* W. NORRIS.

TOOPS, JOSEPH.

July 26, 1755.   *Brother:* JOHN TOOPS ("in Jermaney"). *Executors:* GEORGE SMITH and CHARLES HUNTER. *Witnesses:* JONATHAN HUNT, JAMES MACAY, ZEBULON STOUT.   No probate.

TORKSEY, ELIZABETH.   Pasquotank County.

January 25, 1758.   March Court, 1758.   *Son:* JOHN TORKSEY. *Executor:* ABEL GALLUP. *Witnesses:* JUDITH WHITE and FRANCES BROCKSAT. *Clerk of the Court:* THOMAS TAYLOR.

TORKSEY, JOHN.   Pasquotank County.

November 10, 1745.   April Court, 1747.   *Sons:* THOMAS (one negro), BENJAMIN ("my plantation"). *Daughters:* ELIZABETH and SUSANA (four negroes). *Executors:* THOMAS and BENJAMIN (sons). *Witnesses:* WM. BURGES, JOHN RIGHT (WRIGHT) and ABASANA PERKINS. *Clerk of the Court:* THOS. TAYLOR.

TORKSEY, PHILLIP.   Albemarle County, Pasquotank
                                                      Precinct.

January 16, 1720–1721.   July 20, 1727.   *Sons:* PHILLUP and JOHN TORKSEY, ROBERT MORGIN and HENRY HAMAN. *Executors:* ROBERT MORGAN and *wife,* not named. *Witnesses:* ROBERT and SARAH HARRISON, MARY GILBART, WILLIAM GRIFFIN. *Clerk of the Court:* THO. WEEKES. Executors qualified before WM. WILLSON.

TORKSEY, PHILIP.   Pasquotank County.

February 25, 1755.   June Court, 1755.   *Brothers:* EZEKIEL and JOHN TORKSEY. *Cousin:* MARGARET NEEDHAM (one negro). *Wife and Executrix:* ELISABETH. *Witnesses:* WM. BURGES, ABEL GALLEP, BENJAMIN TORKSEY. *Clerk of the Court:* THOS. TAYLOR.

TORVERSON, JAMES.   Albemarle County.

August 5, 1675. *Executor and sole legatee:* THOMAS JARVIS. *Witnesses:*
PAUL LATHUM, THOMAS DEWBERY. Proven before SETH SOTHELL.

TOTEWINE, WILLIAM.   Craven County.

April 5, 1776. February 7, 1777. *Sons:* WILLIAM (plantation on Flat
Swamp), SIMON (silver shoe buckles and "Rifeld Gun"), WINDER (horse,
saddle and bridle), COLBORN. *Executor:* WILLIAM TOTEWINE (son). *Witnesses:* JOSIAH HOLT, RACHEL BANKS. Proven before RICHARD CASWELL.

TOWNSEN, JOHN.   Perquimans County.

August 10, 1737. October Court, 1739. *Brother and Executor:* WIL-
LIAM TOWNSEN. *Daughter of brother:* ANN TOWNSEN. *Witnesses:* ZACH.
CHANCEY, PRISCILLA SANDERS, REBECCA CHANCEY. *Clerk of the Court:*
JAMES CRAVEN.

TRANTER, JOHN.   Bath County.

December 15, 1723. *Wife and Executrix:* ANNE. *Other legatees:* HENRY
and ROBERT WHITHURST, SAMUEL, WILLIAM and ELINOR WHITHURST.
Witnesses: THOMAS MOUNT, J. BAPTA. ASHE. No probate.

TRAVIS, EDWARD.   Beaufort County.

December 30, 1739. December Court, 1740. Parish of St. Thomas.
Sons: JOHN, WILLIAM, THOMAS (land "where I now dwell in the fork of
Goose Creek"). *Daughter:* MARY TRAVIS. To *son*, THOMAS is bequeathed
negroes. *Executors:* SIMON ALDERSON and JOHN BOYDE. *Witnesses:*
JNO. BOYDE, BENJAMIN HAWKINS, ROBERT CURTIS. *Clerk of the Court:*
ROG. JONES.

TREMAIN, JONATHAN.   Onslow County.

July 3, 1739. January 4, 1742. *Friends:* ROGER MOORE and WILLIAM
DRY. *Executors:* JOHN and PETER STARKEY. *Witnesses:* JANTT. NOBLE,
CHAR. HAY and JOSEPH NOBLE. *Clerk of the Court:* WM. CRANFORD.

TROTTER, WILLIAM.   Perquimans Precinct.

March 28, 1729. December 16, 1729. *Daughter:* DOROTHY TROTTER
("my plantation"). *Wife and Executrix:* MARY. *Sisters:* ELISABETH
NEWBY and ELISABETH TROTTER. *Witnesses:* FRANCIS NEWBY, MOSES
and MARGARET ELLIOT. Proven before RICHD. EVERARD. Nuncupative
codicil dated December 10, 1729, and proven before EZEKIEL MAUDLIN by
WILLIAM GREEN, JESSE NEWBY and WILLIAM MORRIS, devises lands in
York County, Virginia, to daughter.

TROWELL, JOSEPH.   Perquimans County.

January 29, 1735. April Court, 1736. *Wife and Executrix:* TABITHA.
Son: JOSEPH. *Witnesses:* SAM. TAYLOR, JAMES BEASLY. *Clerk of the
Court:* JAMES CRAVEN.

TRUEBLOOD, AGNES.   Pasquotank Precinct.

September 15, 1692.   October 3, 1692.   *Sons:* JOHN and AMOS.   *Daughters:* MARY and ELIZABETH TRUBLOOD.   Negroes bequeathed to above-named.   No witnesses.   No executor.   *Clerk of the Court:* PAUL LATHUM.

TRUEBLOOD, JOHN.   Pasquotank County.

October 28, 1734.   January 14, 1734.   *Sons:* JOHN ("my manner plantation," also plantation on Arrannuse Creek known by the name of Cretches Old Field, and one negro), FISKER (land known by the name of Ieve Neck), DANIEL (one negro).   *Daughters:* MIRIAM and ELIZABETH TRUBLOOD (negroes given to each).   *Wife and Executrix:* SARAH (negroes).   *Executors:* ABEL ROSS (brother) and JARVIS JONES.   *Witnesses:* JOHN SAULS, WILLOUGHBY RICE and DUGLESS ROOD.   *Clerk of the Court:* JAMES SMITH.

TRUITT, JOSEPH.   Craven County.

March 29, 1755.   August Court, 1756.   *Sons:* LEVI ("my plantation and riding horse"), JOHN.   *Wife and Executrix:* PERSILLAR.   *Witnesses:* LUKE RUSSELL, JEMINEA RUSSELL, JAMES SMITH.   *Clerk of the Court:* WM. POWELL.

TRUMBULL, THOMAS.

October 22, 1733.   November 8, 1733.   *Son:* WILLIAM (plantation and one negro).   *Daughter:* SARAH TRUMBULL.   Two other children mentioned, but not named, to each of whom is bequeathed a negro.   "My desire is that each one of my children shall have a maire branded by my executors and their brand recorded."   *Wife and Executrix:* ELIZABETH.   *Executors:* SAMUEL BARTLETT and JEAMES TURNULL.   *Witnesses:* RICHARD SANDERSON, THOMAS CLARK, JOHN SNODEN.   Proven before GEO. BURRINGTON.

TUCKER, NATHANIEL.   Onslow County.

January 7, 1750.   April 2, 1751.   *Brother:* HENRY TUCKER.   *Executor:* JOHN STARKEY.   *Witnesses:* J. ROBERTS, JNO. HOLMES, ANN FRAZER.   *Clerk of the Court:* THOS. BLACK.

TULLEY, JANE.   Pasquotank Precinct.

August 1, 1729.   October 11, 1732.   *Grandson and Executor:* DAVID BOLES.   *Other legatees:* MARY and DANIEL RODES, JR.   *Witnesses:* JONATHAN HIBBS, WILLM. LEE and DANIEL RODS.   *Clerk of the Court:* W. MINSON (or H. MINSON).

TULY (or TULLE), THOMAS.   Hyde County.

December 3, 1740.   June Court, 1741.   *Sons:* THOMAS, JOHN, NATHANIEL and ANTHONY TULY.   *Daughters:* MARY LEITH, SARY TULY, ELIZA-

BETH EASTER, RACHEL JUEL. *Wife and Executrix:* not named. *Witnesses:* EDW. HADLEY, FOSTER JONES (or JAMES), EZEKIEL RICHARDS. *Clerk of the Court:* W. BARROW.

TURBAVELL, RICHARD.   Bertie Precinct.

December 4, 1725. May Court, 1726. *Sons:* JOHN (land on "ye reedy run"), FRANCIS (land on Moratock River), WILLIAM ("plantation where he lives"), WALTER ("plantation where I now live"). *Daughter:* ELIZABETH TURBAVELL. *Grandchildren:* DANIEL and MARY COLSON. *Executor:* WILLIAM TURBAVELL (son). *Witnesses:* JOHN HOG, RICHARD CAERTON (?), JOHN HATCHER. *Clerk of the Court:* RT. FORSTER.

TURNBULL, JAMES.   Tyrrell County.

September 26, 1753. June Court, 1754. *Legatees:* YREOT ORMOND, THOMAS BARKER, MARY PANTRY (niece), ROBERT and JAMES PANTRY (land at Scuppernong called the Brak Oake, and the Rich Levills), MARY TURNBULL BUTCHER, BELL BUTCHER (lands called Bell's gift, Gards Island and land in Edenton), HENRY JORDAN, ELIZABETH HANMORE, DANIEL HANMORE. Periauger and canoes ordered sold for debts. *Executors:* MARY BUTCHER and WILLIAM GARDNER. *Witnesses:* ANN DENEM, JOHN MATHEWS, CHARLES DENEM, JAMES TATTERTON. *Clerk of the Court:* EVAN JONES.

TURNER, HENRY.   Henrico County, Va.

January 17, 1712–1713. *Son:* ABELL (plantation on Falling Creek in Henrico County). *Daughters:* JOAN, ELIZABETH, ANN, HANNAH, JANE, MARY. *Wife and Executrix:* PATIENCE. *Witnesses:* JAMES FLEMMING, ARTHUR DOUGALL, WILLIAM FISHER. *Clerk of the Court:* EDWD. BONWICKE (or RENWICKE).

TURNER, HENRY.   Edgecombe County.

January 20, 1748–1749. February Court, 1748. *Sons:* JOSEPH and THOMAS TURNER (land on the "Cattale Marsh"), SOLOMON (land on Deep Creek). *Daughters:* SARAH, MARY and OLLIF (negro to each). *Wife and Executrix:* MARY (three negroes). To sons is also bequeathed negroes. *Executor:* MATTHEW JOYNER. *Witnesses:* MATTHEW JOYNER, JAMES HARRIS, MARMADUKE NORFLEET. *Clerk of the Court:* BENJN. WYNNS.

TURNER, JOHN.

October 30, 1715. *Cousins:* EDWARD and WILLIAM TURNER. *Brother:* WILLIAM TURNER. *Executor:* JOHN SYMONS. *Witnesses:* HENRY ARNOLD and MARY WHITE. No probate.

TURNER, JOHN. Perquimans Precinct.

March 3, 1717–1718. April 8, 1718. *Brother:* WILLIAM BASTABELL. *Other legatees:* THOMAS PEIRCE (*Executor*) and MARY PIERCE. *Witnesses:* WM. WOOD, CATTRON DAVIS, THOMAS PEIRCE. *Clerk of the Court:* RICHARD LEARY. Impression of head on seal with letters "o a v."

TURNER, RICHARD. Perquimans Precinct.

April 14, 1719. *Daughters:* ELIZABETH NEWBY and HANNAH BASTABLE. *Son-in-law:* WILLIAM BASTABLE. *Grandson:* SAMUEL NEWBY. *Wife and Executrix:* BRIDGET. *Witnesses:* ROBERT WILSON, SAMUEL PHELPS, JAMES LITTLESON. *Clerk of the Court:* RICHD. LEARY.

TURNER, ROBART. Perquimans County.

April 15, 1742. July Court, 1743. *Son:* JOSEPH. *Daughter:* MARY TURNER. *Wife and Executrix:* ANN. *Witnesses:* PETER ALBORDSON, THOMAS JESSOP. *Clerk of the Court:* EDMUND HATCH.

TURNER, ROBERT. Beaufort County.

March 6, 1745. March Court, 1745. *Sons:* ROBERT (in England), JOHN (land on South Dividing Creek, lot No. 27 in Bath Town, large Bible, sermon books, law books, silver watch, mourning ring). *Daughters:* ANN WILLIAMS, SARAH GRAVES (land on Nevil's Creek), MARY BENSON (land on Nevil's Creek). *Sons-in-law:* JOHN BENSON (lot No. 38 in Bath Town), THOMAS WILLIAMS (lot No. 39 in Bath Town), THOMAS GRAVES. *Grandson:* ROBERT WILLIAMS ("my plantation"). *Executors:* JOHN TURNER, THOMAS WILLIAMS, THOMAS GRAVES, JOHN BENSON. *Witnesses:* HENRY WEST, JACOB NEVILL, SAMLL. TAYLOR, WILLM. LANE. *Clerk of the Court:* JOHN FORBES.

TURNER, WILLIAM. Albemarle County.

April 28, 1696. July 27, 1698. Little River. *Sons:* WILLIAM and JOSHUA (plantation to each). *Daughter:* SARAH TURNER. *Wife and Executrix:* KATHERINE. *Witnesses:* RICHARD PLATER, HUGH CAMPBELL, HENRY PALIN, THOMAS SIMMONS. *Clerk to Council:* W. GLOVER.

TURNER, WILLIAM. Albemarle County.

October 28, 1696. Little River. *Sons:* WILLIAM (orchard on Little Creek), JOHN (plantation bought of PATRICK BALEY). *Daughter:* SARAH TURNER. *Executors:* MATTHEW KELLY and JAMES DAVIS. *Witnesses:* RICHARD PLATOR, HUGH CAMBELL, HENRY PALIN, THOMAS SIMONS. This is a copy made by J. KNIGHT. No probate.

TURNER, WILLIAM.

May 23, 1709. October 17, 1709. *Sons:* WILLIAM and EDWARD. *Brother:* JOHN. *Wife and Executrix:* not named. *Witnesses:* THOS. TWEDIE, ZACHARIAS NIXON, ELIZABETH NIXON. *Clerk of the Court:* THOS. ABINGTON.

TURNER, WILLIAM.   Pasquotank County.

December 23, 1749. April Court, 1750. *Son:* JAMES. *Wife and Executrix:* ELIZABETH (estate divided between son and wife). *Executor:* EZEKIEL TURNER (brother). *Witnesses:* JOSEPH MORRIS, WILLIAM TURNER, PATRICK POOL. *Clerk of the Court:* THOS. TAYLOR.

TURNER, WILLIAM.   Pasquotank County.

April 6, 1753. July Court, 1753. *Sons:* EZEKIEL (land on Gumbridge Branch, on CHARLES OVERMAN'S line), JOSEPH (land on Gumbridge Branch), WILLIAM ("two lotts lying next to Nixonton), JOHN ("my plantation"). *Grandson:* JAMES TURNER (two lots next to son WILLIAM'S). *Wife and Executrix:* KESIAH. *Witnesses:* ISAAC PARKER, SAML. OVERMAN and RT. WILSON. Codicil dated April 13, 1753, and witnessed by RT. WILSON, ISAAC SWEENIE and JAMES GREGORIE, gives negro man to son WILLIAM. *Clerk of the Court:* THOMAS TAYLOR.

TWEOX, JAMES.

May 5, 1711. *Son:* ROBERT ("all cattle in his possession," "land he now lives on, running from ye south side of his new dwelling house to a place called Selpshis (?) Swamp"). JOHN LAWSON (one horse, and land beginning at Mahomets Swamp running to WM. HARDY'S line), MARY LAWSON, JUNR., SAML. HARDY (son of WM. HARDY). *Wife:* ANN TWEOX. "Plantation I now live on" to MARY LAWSON (widow of NATHL. LAWSON). ROBERT TWEOX, JOHN LAWSON and MARY LAWSON to have privilege of grinding at mill, and daughter of MARY LAWSON, provided she marry and "seat in this Neck." *Witnesses:* GEORGE GLADSTENIES, JOSEPH CANINGS, JOHN SNELL (?). *Clerk of the Court:* ROBERT BUCKNER.

TWIDDY, THOMAS.   Pasquotank Precinct.

April 12, 1705. August 19, 1706. *Wife, Executrix and sole legatee:* ELENER. *Witnesses:* THOMAS STAFFORD, RICHARD POOL, JOHN RAPER. *Clerk of the Court:* THO. ABINGTON.

TWIGG, WILLIAM.   Chowan County.

June 20, 1741. July Court, 1741. *Legatees:* ELIZABETH HALE (30 pounds "bill money of this province"), MARY MARSH ("that came in with me into North Carolina," one silver tankard, two silver salts, one silver punch ladle, two silver spoons). *Daughter:* MARY ANN TWIGG, of

London.   *Executor:* MILES GALE.   *Witnesses:* BENJAMIN TALBOT, KATH-
ERINE DELOGG and PRISTER PERRY.   *Clerk of the Court:* JAMES CRAVEN.
Coat of arms on seal.

TYLER, MOSES.   Bladen County.

June 25, 1762.   August 9, 1762.   *Sons:* NEEDHAM ("my plantation"),
OWEN ("my cattle"), MOSES (one negro).   *Daughters:* PENELEBY, ELISA-
BETH, CHRISTIAN and LUCRETIA TYLER.   *Wife and Executrix:* SARAH.
Executor: JOS. HOWARD.   *Witnesses:* ROBERT STEWART, ITHAMAR SIN-
GLETARY, JOHN FLOYD.   Proven before ARTHUR DOBBS.

TYLER, THOMAS.   Bath County.

June 5, 1722.   July Court, 1722.   *Executor and sole legatee:* JOHN
JORDAN.   *Witnesses:* THOMAS MCKENNY and DAVID BLAIR.   *Clerk of the
Court:* RT. FORSTER.

TYNER, NICHOLAS.   Northampton County.

December 12, 1752.   November Court, 1753.   *Grandson:* JAMES TYNER
(lands on Gaulberry).   *Other children:* NICHOLAS and JOHN TYNER (the
children of JAMES TYNER, decd.), WILLIAM TYNER, SARAH WOODARD,
ELIZABETH JOHNSON and ANN CORBETT.   *Executor:* WILLIAM TYNER
(son).   *Wife:* ELIZABETH.   All estate divided among children above-
named.   *Witnesses:* J. DEW, WILLIAM CORBETT.   *Clerk of the Court:*
I. EDWARDS.

UNDAY, THOMAS.   Bath County.

October 13, 1722.   July Court, 1725.   *Wife and Executrix:* MARTHA
(houses and lot in Bath town).   *Witnesses:* ROBERT FORRESTER, JAMES
ROBINS, RALPH SEYMOUR.   *Clerk of the Court:* JOHN SWANN.

UPTON, EDWARD.   Pasquotank County.

July 7, 1753.   January Court, 1755.   *Sons:* EDWARD and JOSHUA (lands
adjoining MATTHEW WINN).   *Daughters:* SARAH FIRBISH, SABELLA, ELIZA-
BETH, SUSANNA and ANN UPTON.   *Wife and Executrix:* ELIZABETH.   *Witnesses:* EDWARD and MARY SCOTT, ABRAHAM MILLER.   *Clerk of the Court:*
THOS. TAYLOR.

UPTON, JOHN.   Pasquotank Precinct.

June 30, 1715.   *Sons:* JOHN (plantation known as Buckingham), WIL-
LIAM, JOSEPH and THOMAS (plantation on Pasquotank River), EDWARD
(plantation known as Abington).   *Daughters:* MARY and RUTH.   *Wife and
Executrix:* not named.   *Witnesses:* GRIFFITH GRAY, METHUSALEM VAUGHAN.
Clerk of the Court: W. NORRIS.

UPTON, THOMAS.   Pasquotank County.

May 19, 1750.   July Court, 1750.   *Sons:* WILLIS ("my maner plantation"), THOMAS and WILLIAM (land known as Johnskintown).   *Daughters:* ELIZABETH, MERAM and CHARETON UPTON.   *Wife and Executrix:* CHRISTIAN.   *Witnesses:* JOHN UPTON, ISAAC SAWYER, JOSEPH TEMPLE.   *Clerk of the Court:* THO. TAYLOR.

URQUHART, WILLIAM.   Chowan County.

September 5, 1738.   September 26, 1738.   (Edenton).   *Legatees:* JAMES MITCHELL of Edenton, ROBERT ANDERSON of New York (*Executor*). *Witnesses:* ROBERT INNES, JAMES WALLACE, JA. BALLENTINE.   Proven before W. SMITH, C. J.

VALLENTINE, RICHARD.

June 4, 1731.   December 7, 1731.   Northwest branch of Cape Fear River.   *Devisees:* JOHN BENNITT, of Pennsylvania (estate on Cape Fear River), JAMES BENNITT, son of JOHN (one-half of estate in Pennsylvania), RUTH BENNITT, daughter of JAMES (one-half of estate in Pennsylvania), ANN BENNITT (wife of JAMES).   *Executors:* JOHN CLAYTON, of Cape Faire River, THOMAS LINDLEY, of Philadelphia.   *Witnesses:* EDWD. WINGATE, JEFF. POLLARD.   Proven before R. MOORE, DA. EVANS and JNO. CLAYTON, *Justices.*

VANLUVEN, CHRISTOPHER.   Bertie County.

September 23, 1732.   November 1, 1732.   *Sons:* JOHN and HENRY. *Wife and Executrix:* ELISABETH.   *Witnesses:* MARTIN FREDERICK RASOR, THOMAS ASHBURN.   Proven before GEORGE BURRINGTON.

VAN PELT, JOHN.

November 22, 1734.   June 17, 1748.   City of New York, Mariner. *Sons:* JOHN (land in Bertie known as JOHN SWANN's plantation), DANIEL, (land in Bertie known as Chinckapin Neck and JOHN WILSON's plantation). *Daughters:* MARY and ELSLIE (five lots in Bath Town).   *Wife:* MARY. *Executor:* JOHN VAN PELT (son).   *Witnesses:* ANDREW MOOR, JOHN PRATT, HENRY DEMEYER.   Proven before GAB. JOHNSTON.

VANN, EDWARD.   Chowan County.

February 14, 1738.   June 4, 1752.   *Son:* EDWARD (land on Swamp). *Daughters:* ANN VANN, SARAH, ELIZABETH.   *Executor:* EDWARD VANN (son).   *Wife:* not named.   *Witnesses:* JOHN VANN, WILLIAM VANN, JOHN LEWIS.   Proven before GAB. JOHNSTON.

VANN, JOSEPH.   Chowan County.

April 27, 1752.   April Court, 1753.   *Sons:* GEORGE, JACOB ("my manner plantation").   *Daughters:* ANN LANGSTON, DARKES, MARY, ELIZABETH and

JUDEY.   *Executors:* GEORGE and ELIZABETH VANN (children).   *Witnesses:* JACOB ODOM, THOMAS LANGSTONE, SARY LANGSTONE.   *Clerk of the Court:* JAMES CRAVEN.

VANN, WILLIAM.   Chowan Precinct.

April 16, 1735.   August 11, 1740.   *Son:* EDWARD (lands between THOMAS NORICE and STEPHEN SHEPARD; land on the Lands Ridge between JOSEPH BRADDY and JAMES BRADDY).   *Daughters:* SARRAH HOGH, ANN VANN. *Grandson:* WILLIAM VANN, son of EDWARD.   *Wife and Executrix:* SARRAH. *Witnesses:* JAMES and JOHN BRADY, HENRY GOODMAN.   Proven before W. SMITH, C. J.

VARNUM, JACOB.   Chowan County.

September 25, 1715.   March 29, 1716.   Boston in New England. Chowan in North Carolina.   "Mariner."   *Wife:* not named.   *Other legatee:* WILLIAM GARDINER ("one sad coloured Broad Cloth Coat and breeches and Vest, ye Vest and breeches being in Boston").   *Executor:* ANTHONY ALEXANDER.   *Witnesses:* JOHN BLISH, JOHN MIXON, JOHN NEWMAN, GRIFF JONES.   *Clerk of the Court:* R. HICKS.   Impression of head on seal.

VAUGHAN, JOHN.   Northampton County.

August Court, 1750.   *Sons:* WILLIAM and JOHN.   *Daughters:* LUCEY, MOLLIE and FANNY.   *Wife and Executrix:* CASSIAH.   *Witnesses:* SAMUEL TARVER (*Executor*), WILLIAM BAKER, JOHN MANDER.   *Clerk of the Court:* I. EDWARDS.

VAUGHAN, VINSON.   Northampton County.

June 29, 1749.   August Court, 1749.   *Sons:* VINSON (350 acres of land and three negroes), JOSHUA (one negro), NOEL HUTCHENS (one negro). *Daughters:* MARGARET BREATHAN, SARAH VAUGHAN, NAOMY VAUGHAN (one negro to each).   *Executors:* JOHN BRETHEN and FRANSES VAUGHAN.   *Witnesses:* RICHARD BROWN, JOHN BREEDING, JOHN BROWN.   *Clerk of the Court:* I. EDWARDS.

VEALE, WILLIAM.   New Hanover County.

June 11, 1760.   November 22, 1760.   Wilmington.   *Son:* WILLIAM.   *Wife and Executrix:* ABIGAIL.   *Executor:* DANIEL DUNBIBIN.   *Witnesses:* JOHN CAMPBELL, THOMAS MUTTED (?), JOHN FORSTER.   Proven before ARTHUR DOBBS.

VINCE, HUMPHREY.   Currituck County.

April 4, 1738.   January Court, 1739.   *Cousins:* JAMES and SARAH POYNER, PETER, son of JAMES (plantation and negroes), WILLIAM and VINCE WHITE.   *Other legatees:* JOSIAS NICKOLS, SARAH SIMMONS, THOMAS MEGGS,

LAZARUS and JOHN FLOWER, ANDREW PEACOCK, LUKE WHITE (cousin). *Executor:* JAMES POYNER. *Witnesses:* THOS. TAYLOR, JOSHUA DEEL, MARY TAYLOR. *Clerk of the Court:* WM. SHERGOLD.

VINCE, THOMAS. Currituck County.

August 31, 1721. October 10, 1721. *Sons:* THOMAS and WILLIAM. *Daughters:* HANNAH VINCE, MARGRETT WHITE, SARAH POYNER. *Grandchildren:* MARGRETT WHITE, WILLIS POYNER. *Executor:* HUMPHREY VINCE (brother). *Witnesses:* JO. WICKER, WILLIAM PARKER. *Clerk of the Court:* JO. WICKER.

VINES, SAMUEL. Beaufort County.

March 15, 1740. *Sons:* JOHN (plantation on Goose Creek), SAMUEL and WILLIAM (plantation "wherein I now dwell" called the Point). *Daughters:* FRANSES, ELIZABETH, MARY, REBECCA and ESTER. *Wife and Executrix:* MARY. *Witnesses:* JOHN LAWSON, MARTHA ELLIOTT, ROGER JONES. *Clerk of the Court:* ROGER JONES.

VINSENT, STEPHEN.

September 26, 1696. April 13, 1698. *Wife and Executrix:* MARY. *Witnesses:* JOHN BILLETT, ALSE BILLETT, ———? *Clerk of the Court:* EDWARD MAYO.

WADE, JOHN. Pasquotank County.

Will not dated. October Court, 1750. *Daughters:* MARY and MAGDALENE WADE. *Executors:* ROBERT LOWRY, WILLIAM DAVIS and JOHN SKINNER. *Witnesses:* JOSIAH CARTRIGHT, ROBERT PALMER, THOMAS WILCOCKS. *Clerk of the Court:* THOMAS TAYLOR.

WADE, JOSEPH. Orange County.

January 3, 1757. March Court, 1757. *Sons:* JOHN (one dollar), JAMES (three negroes, land on Eno River). *Daughters:* MARY STRAWTHER, SUSANNAH HART, ELIZABETH TALLY, LUCY POWELL (two negroes), SARAH FOUNTIN (one negro). *Wife:* SARAH. *Grandson:* JOSEPH STRAWTHER. *Executors:* JAMES WADE (son) and JOSEPH POWELL (son-in-law). *Witnesses:* WILLIAM BURFORD, SAMUEL BURTON. *Clerk of the Court:* JOSEPH WATSON.

WADE, MARY. Pasquotank County.

December, 1736. January Court, 1736. *Sister and Executrix:* MAGDALEN WADE. *Witnesses:* JOSHUA MARKHAM, SARAH LOWRY. *Clerk of the Court:* JAMES CRAVEN.

WAHAB, JAMES. Currituck County.

October 15, 1772. March 25, 1774. Hatteras Banks. *Daughters:* SARAH and BARBARA (negroes to each). *Sons:* JOBE (land at Armiskeat and at Wissockin Creek), JAMES, WILLIAM (land at Hatteras Banks). *Executors:* JAMES and JOB WAHAB (sons). *Witnesses:* JOSEPH WILLIAMS, GEORGE PRICE, ANDREW DONALDSON. Proven before JO. MARTIN.

WAIDE, ALICE. Chowan County.

April 25, 1700–1701. *Grandsons:* THOMAS and JOHN HAWKINS, THOMAS and JAMES LONG. *Granddaughters:* MARY and ELIZABETH LONG. *Daughter:* ELIZABETH LONG. *Executor:* JOHN HAWKINS. *Witnesses:* GEORGE SLAID, VINES CROPLEY, GEORGE SWAINE. *Clerk of the Court:* N. CHEVIN.

WAIN, THOMAS. Beaufort County.

November 16, 1747. *Son and Executor:* JOHN. *Daughter:* SARAH WHARTON. *Granddaughter:* MAHETABEL WHATNOUGH. *Witnesses:* JOHN FOURER. JOHN HARRISON, WILLIAM DOWS. No probate.

WAINS, THOMAS. Craven County.

Will illegible.

WALBUTTEN, ROBERT. Bertie Precinct.

March 25, 1733. July 31, 1733. *Wife and Executrix:* SARAH. *Sons:* JOHN and SMITHWICK (lands). *Daughter:* SARAH. *Witnesses:* ROBERT ROGERS, HUGH HIGHMAN, JOSEPH WIGHT. Proven before GEORGE BURRINGTON.

WALDRON, JACOB.

May 13, 1763. October Court, 1765. *Sons and Executors:* ISAAC and JACOB. *Brother:* CORNELIUS WALDRON. *Executor:* RICHARD QUINCE. *Witnesses:* RICHARD QUINCE, REVELL MUNROE, PARKER QUINCE. *Clerk of the Court for Wilmington District:* J. BURGWIN.

WALKER, HENDERSON.

October 27, 1701. July 4, 1704. *Wife and Executrix:* ANN. *Other legatees:* MAJ. SWANN ("my swoard"), JOHN, GEORGE and SARAH LILLINGTON, ELIZABETH WALKER. *Witnesses:* PR. GODFREY, ROBERT HARMAN, GEORGE CHAMBERY. *Clerk of the Court:* N. CHEVIN.

WALKER, JOHN. Albemarle County.

January 12, 1709. *Wife and Executrix:* ELISABETH. *Sons:* JAMES, THOMAS (land called Barsees Neck). *Daughter:* SARAH. *Executors:* THOMAS and ROBERT WEST. *Witnesses:* ELIZABETH POWELL, ZACHARIAH GARKIN, WILL MITCHELL. Original missing. Recorded in Book 1712–1722, page 37.

WALKER, THOMAS.   Craven County.

February 19, 1753. March 19, 1753. *Son:* JOHN. *Daughters:* SARAH and MARY. *Executors:* BENJAMIN CUMMINGS, THOMAS TIGNER. *Witnesses:* ABNER NEALE, CHRISR. NEALE, JOHN CUMMINGS. Proven before JAS. HASELL, C. J.

WALL, JOSEPH.   Beaufort County.

December 29, 1755. September Court, 1756. *Sons:* JAMES, JOSEPH and HOWEL ("lands on Bear Creek and ye horse pen"), ROBERT. *Daughters:* MARY BALLARD, ANN and ELIZABETH WALL. *Wife and Executrix:* DEBORAH. *Witnesses:* SAMUEL PHILLIPS, JAMES WALL, JOSEPH WALL. *Clerk of the Court:* WALLEY CHAUNCEY.

WALL, JOSHUA.   Currituck County.

November 10, 1744. April Court, 1745. *Sons:* JOSHUA, THOMAS and JOSEPH. No executor. *Witnesses:* THOMAS ROBB, MARY ROOUSALL (RUSSELL), PATTRICK GOODIN. *Clerk of the Court:* RICHARD McCLURE.

WALL, JOSHUA.   Currituck County.

January 16, 1749. April Court, 1752. Hatteras Banks. *Brother:* THOMAS. *Wife and Executrix:* MARY. *Witnesses:* JOSEPH WILLIAMS and JOSHUA CAMPBELL. *Clerk of the Court:* WILLIAM SHERGOLD.

WALL, RICHARD.   Northampton County.

February 29, 1752. August Court, 1755. *Sons:* SAMPSON (1 negro), RICHARD, ARTHUR, SAMUEL. *Daughters:* JUDITH DELOATCH, SARAH BOYKIN, PRECILA BENSON, JANE LEWIS. *Wife:* LUCY. *Witnesses:* CHAS. CAMPBELL, JAMES LEWIS. *Clerk of the Court:* I. EDWARDS.

WALL, SARAH.   Edgecombe County.

November 2, 1754. June Court, 1756. *Sons:* HENRY, ARTHUR and JOHN WALL. *Grandson:* WILLIAM FRENCH. *Daughter:* FAITH. *Executor:* JOHN WALL (son). *Witnesses:* HENRY, ELIZABETH and SIHON HORN. *Clerk of the Court:* JOS. MONTFORT.

WALLACE, THOMAS.   Currituck County.

January 26, 1746–1747. April 27, 1747. *Wife and Executrix:* SARAH ("my perriauger"). *Daughter:* BARBARA WALLACE. *Witnesses:* CHRIS. BUTLER, ELIZABETH MATTHEWS. Proven before GAB. JOHNSTON.

WALLACE, THOMAS.   Chowan County.

October 28, 1750. January Court, 1750. *Sons:* WILLIAM, JONATHAN, JOHN. *Daughters:* JUDITH and SUSANAH (lands in Bertie County), ELIZABETH WALLACE (land on "the old Soune Neck"), MARY WALLACE (land on the east side of the "old Toune Road to Warreck"). *Wife and Executrix:* ELISABETH. *Witnesses:* THOMAS and TIMOTHY WALTON. *Clerk of the Court:* WILL MEARNS.

WALLACE, WILLIAM.   Martin County.

September 19, 1774. February 13, 1775. *Son:* WILLIAM (plantation and six negroes). *Daughters:* KEZIAH, DINAH, QUOTINA, AGNESS, ALBA (one negro to each). *Wife and Executrix:* MARTHA. *Witnesses:* JAMES RAWLINS, WILLIAM LEWELLING, DAVID TAYLOR, WILLIAM BOWERS. Proven before JO. MARTIN.

WALLER, THOMAS.   Albemarle County.

June 30, 1687. July 10, 1687. *Son:* GEORGE. *Daughters:* ANNE and ELIZABETH. *Wife and Executrix:* not named. *Witnesses:* JOHN HALLAN, WILLIAM BILLINGS, JOHN HARRIS, JOHN DURANT. Proven before SETH SOTHELL.

WALLIS, ANDREW.   Craven County.

March 18, 1742–1743. *Sons:* JAMES, ANDREW. *Wife and Executrix:* MARY. *Witnesses:* WILLIAM WICKLIFFE, JOS. WILSON, ROBERT JARMAN. No probate.

WALLIS, JOHN.   Onslow County.

November 21, 1748. April Court, 1751. *Son and Executor:* RICHARD. *Wife:* ELIZABETH. *Witnesses:* ARTHUR ROYALL, JOHN ROYALL, JOB BROOKES. *Clerk of the Court:* THOMAS BLACK.

WALLIS, STEPHEN.   Craven County.

April 28, 1757. August Court, 1757. *Sons:* BENJAMIN (lands), ROBERT and STEPHEN (*Executors*). *Wife:* SUSANA. *Witnesses:* BERRY NELSON, SARAH NELSON, JOHN CUMMINGS. *Clerk of the Court:* PETER CONWAY.

WALLIS, WILLIAM.   Beaufort County.

December 29, 1748. March Court, 1749. *Sons:* WILLIAM and JOHN (land and negroes). *Daughters:* LIDIA BOND, ABIGAL DAW (negroes to each). *Wife and Executrix:* MARY WALLIS. *Executor:* NICHOLAS DAW. *Witnesses:* PHIL. PRITCHETT, JOHN BENSTED, JEAN BRANNOCK. *Clerk of the Court:* JOHN ALDORSON.

WALSTON, LONDON.   Bath County.

May 26, 1728. April Court, 1728. *Devisees:* THOMAS BATTERS (*Executor*), MARY BATTERS, daughter of THOMAS (land on "Papleco River" adjoining Blunts Town). *Witnesses:* JAMES BACKALDER, THOMAS RIGNE, MARY CORDING. *Clerk of the Court:* THOMAS JONES.

WALTERS, MARY.   New Hanover County.

April, 1756. May 25, 1756. *Brothers:* JOHN and JOSEPH WALTERS.
Sisters: ELIZABETH WALTERS and MARY GRAINGER. *Son:* WILLIAM
WALTERS. *Other legatees:* BARBARA MURRAY, ISABEL MACNEIL, KATHER-
INE MACLAINE (daughter of ARCHIBALD MACLAINE). *Executor:* JAMES
MURRAY (lands on Black River). *Witnesses:* B. MURRAY, ANN BRITTON,
WALTER ———. Codicil dated April 21, 1756, bequeaths estate to
sister, MARY GRAINGER, in event of death of son. *Witnesses to codicil:*
JOSEPH and ELIZABETH WALTERS. Proven before ARTHUR DOBBS.
Clerk of the Court: ISAAC FARIES.

WALTON, THOMAS.   Chowan County.

November 12, 1750. July 5, 1751. *Son and Executor:* WILLIAM.
Daughters: ELIZABETH TROTMAN, SUSANAH WALTON, JUDETH ROUNTREE,
ANN HUNTER, SARAH PERY (1 negro). *Grandson:* THOMAS WALTON
(plantation). *Witnesses:* WILLIAM WALTON, HARDY HUNTER, TIMOTHY
WALTON. Proven before GAB. JOHNSTON at Eden House.

WAMAN, WILLIAM.   ·Pasquotank County.

March 18, 1721. July 18, 1721. *Sons:* WILLIAM, ROBERT and JOHN.
The following lands are devised: land on Nobesbruke Creek, lands be-
tween DAVID PRICHARD and BENJAMIN LONEWELL, lands between the
mouth of Pasquotank River and Flatty Creek. *Daughter:* ELENDER
WAMAN. *Wife and Executrix:* HANNAH. *Witnesses:* JNO. MCKEELE,
JNO. FOURRE, THOMAS REES. *Clerk of the Court:* EDMUND GALE.

WAR, WILLIAM.   Northampton County.

December 16, 1754. May Court, 1756. *Sons:* HENRY, THOMAS (200
acres of land on the Horse Hole). *Daughter:* ANN WAR. *Wife:* ANN.
Executor: WILLIAM WINBORNE. *Witnesses:* THOMAS FLANNER, PHILIP
WINBORNE. *Clerk of the Court:* I. EDWARDS.

WARD, ENOCH.   Carteret County.

February 13, 1750. March Court, 1750. *Sons:* RICHARD and ENOCK.
Daughters: ANN, MARY, ELIZABETH, SARAH, ABIGALL and SUSANAH (lands
on Banks). *Son-in-law:* JOSEPH SUTTON (husband of daughter ANN).
Other devisee: JAMES SHACKELLFORD. *Wife:* MARY. *Executors:* RICHARD
WARD and EDWARD SIMPSON. *Witnesses:* ANANIAS CAVENAGH, JOSHUA
and JOHN SIMPSON. *Clerk of the Court:* GEO. READ. Five negroes
bequeathed.

WARD, JOHN.   Chowan County.

May 9, 1747. December 16, 1748. *Sons:* THOMAS, JAMES and JOSEPH
(land bought of GEORGE TURNIDGE), WILLIAM, JOBE, AMOS (plantation

known by the name of the Indian Creek), BENJAMIN. *Daughters:* ELIZABETH TOMSON, CATTERINE EVINS. *Wife and Executrix:* CATTERENE WARD. *Witnesses:* THOMAS ROWNTREE, CHARLES COPELAND, JOHN COPELAND. Proven before GAB. JOHNSTON.

WARD, JOHN.   Tyrrell County.

March 5, 1748–1749. September Court, 1750. *Sons:* MICHAEL, JOHN (1 negro and "all cattle running on Little Cantanknee"), DAVID. *Daughters:* ELIZABETH NOBLE (100 acres of land), DORCAS OVERSTREET (land lying on Little Cantanknee). *Executors:* MICHAEL and JOHN (sons). *Witnesses:* GRIFFITH HOWELL, JOHN BUTLER, ELIZABETH BUTLER. *Clerk of the Court:* EVAN JONES.

WARD, THOMAS.   Chowan County.

October 16, 1750. July Court, 1751. *Wife and Executrix:* CHRISTIAN. *Son:* MICHAEL ("the Shop Plantation"). *Witnesses:* WILLIAM WRIGHT, HARDY and JOSEPH HURDLE. *Clerk of the Court:* JAMES CRAVEN.

WARMING, ABRAHAM.   Albemarle County.

No date or probate. *Legatees:* JOHN WHEATLEY, WILLIAM WINSEY. *Witnesses:* JOHN LEWIS, ELINOR LUTON, THOMAS LUTEN, JOHN CHANDLER.

WARRIN, ABRAHAM.   Perquimans County.

October 26, 1739. July Court, 1740. *Son:* HENRY (plantation "I now live on"). *Other children:* mentioned, but not named. *Other legatees:* JOHN and JEAMES CHESSON, CHRISTOPHER DENMAN. *Creditors:* SARAH and SUSANNAH SUTTEN. *Wife and Executrix:* SARAH. *Executor:* RICHARD SKINNER. *Witnesses:* JOHN CREESE, MARY CREESE, JOHN STEPNEY. *Clerk of the Court:* JAMES CRAVEN.

WARREN, HENRY.   Matchepungo Creek, in Bath County.

February 15, 1716. April 2, 1717. *Son:* ABRAHAM (lands). *Daughters:* MARY, ELIZABETH and ANN (cattle to each). *Wife and Executrix:* ELIZABETH. *Executor:* JOHN PORTER, of Bath. *Witnesses:* JOHN MARTIN, WILLIAM HARRIS, GI. HALLIDAY. Codicil of even date and witnessed by same persons bequeaths negro to son, ABRAHAM. *Clerk of the Court:* JNO. DRINKWATER.

WARREN, ROBERT.   Edgecombe County.

Not dated. June Court, 1759. *Daughters:* MARY WARREN (one negro), SARAH, JANE and MILSSON WARREN. *Wife and Executrix:* MARGRET. *Executor:* GEORGE DAWKINS. *Witnesses:* BENJAMIN MERRYMAN, WILLIAM LANE. *Clerk of the Court:* JOSEPH MONTFORT.

WARREN, SARAH.   Perquimans Precinct.

October 1, 1730. *Sons-in-law:* ABRAHAM JONES, JOHN ARNOLD (*Executor*). *Other legatee:* ANN CRAWTHERS, daughter of NATHAN CRAWTHERS. *Witnesses:* JOHN FALCONER, ABRAHAM WARREN, SARAH WARREN. No probate.

WARREN, WILLIAM.

October 3, 1723. November 26, 1723. *Friend and Executor:* JOSEPH REDING. *Witnesses:* ALEXR. CRUIKSHANK, DUGLIS ROD. Proven before WILLIAM REED.

WATERS, WILLIAM.   Onslow Precinct.

January 18, 1751. July Court, 1754. *Son:* JOSIAS. *Daughter:* MARY. *Wife and Executrix:* MARTHA. *Witnesses:* LEWIS JENKINS, JOHN AVIRETT. *Clerk of the Court:* WM. RAY.

WATKINS, THOMAS.   Perquimans County.

January 3, 1754. January Court, 1754. *Legatees:* JOHN and RICHARD WHEDBEE, JOHN MORRIS and SAMUELL NEWBY. *Executor:* JOHN WHIDBEE. *Witnesses:* WILLIAM FOSTER, POTSEFULL PIERCE, MARY WHEDBEE. *Clerk of the Court:* EDMUND HATCH.

WATKINS, WILLIAM.   Pitt County.

November 9, 1771. October 14, 1773. *Sons:* JOHN and WILLIAM. *Sons-in-law:* FRANCIS BUCK, JAMES CASON, WILLIAM ORMOND, JAMES JONES. *Daughters:* SARAH BUCK, ELIZABETH, ANN and RACHEL. *Wife and Executrix:* CHRISTIAN. *Witnesses:* CATHERINE CROFTON, JOHN SALTER, RANDEL McDANIEL. Proven before Jo. MARTIN.

WATSON, JOHN.   New Hanover County.

January 3, 1743–1744. March Court, 1743. "Of ye Sound." *Sons:* JOHN, JOSEPH and JONATHAN. *Daughter:* SARAH. *Wife and Executrix:* SARAH. *Witnesses:* ARCHD. NICKELLS, JOSEPH JONES, FRANCIS BEALE. *Clerk of the Court:* JAMES SMALLWOOD.

WATSON, JOHN.   New Hanover County.

December 15, 1773. March 3, 1774. *Son:* JOHN. *Daughters:* ELIZABETH WATSON, MARY, wife of SAMUEL MARSHALL, SARAH, wife of NIXON CHESTER. *Wife and Executrix:* ANN. *Witnesses:* JNO. ROBESON, JOHN GAILLARD, WILLM. NICHOLS. Proven before Jo. MARTIN.

WAXDALE, JOHN.   Bath County.

November 12, 1733. December Court, 1734. Trent River. *Son:* JOHN. *Wife and Executrix:* WALPOLIA. *Witnesses:* DAVID DUPUIS, WILLIAM DUPUIS, JOHN SIMONS, JOHN PARKER, JAMES CLEMENT. *Clerk of the Court:* CALEB METCALFE.

WAXDALE, JOHN.   Craven County.

March 5, 1738–1739.   December 18, 1739.   *Daughters:* LOVICE, MARGA-
RET, KATHERINE, MARIAM, ANNACIVILLA.   *Executors:* ABRAHAM BUSSETT,
PHILIP MILLER.   *Witnesses:* HUGH STANALAND, NATHANIEL PARROTT.
Clerk of the Court: JAMES COOR.

WAYMAN, WILLIAM.   Pasquotank County.

March 9, 1737.   July Court, 1740.   *Legatees:* MARY, HANER, THAMER,
THOMAS and ROBERT LOWRY.   *Executor:* ROBERT LOWRY.   *Witnesses:*
ROBERT and MARY LOWRY.   *Clerk of the Court:* JAMES CRAVEN.

WEAVER, JOHN.   Chowan County.

September 18, 1750.   October Court, 1750.   *Legatees:* JOHN POLSON
(*Executor*) and CALEB POLSON, son of JOHN.   *Witnesses:* MARY STUART,
GEORGE POLSON, DEMSEY SUMNER.   *Clerk of the Court:* WILLIAM MEARNS.

WEAVER, WILLIAM.   Bertie Precinct.

February Court, 1735.   *Sons:* WILLIAM, JOHN (land at Pea Hill), HENRY
(land on Fountains Creek), EDWARD, THOMAS (one "Clankibone pot").
Brother: STEPHEN WEAVER.   *Wife and Executrix:* not named.   *Witnesses:*
JOHN COOK and JOHN ARNOL.   *Clerk of the Court:* JOHN WYNNS.

WEBB, ANTHONY.   Bertie County.

August 27, 1748.   November Court, 1750.   *Sons:* SAMUEL, WILLIAM
(plantation on Deep Creek "whereon I now live" and two negroes).   *Daughters:* PERSILLO, KEZIER, ANNE.   *Wife:* MARTHA.   *Executor:* WILLIAM.
Witnesses: WILLIAM and JOHN BARTON, ISAAC PIERCE.   *Clerk of the Court:*
SAMUEL ORMES.

WEBB, HENRY.   Orange County.

January 10, 1756.   March Court, 1759.   *Sons:* WENTWORTH and JOHN
(negro to each).   *Wife and Executrix:* ELIZABETH.   *Witnesses:* GEORGE
LAWS, ELIAS DOWNES.   *Clerk of the Court:* JAMES WATSON.

WEBB, JOHN.   Northampton County.

February 11, 1749.   February Court, 1749.   *Sons:* JOLLEY, JAMES and
JESSE.   *Daughter:* JUDITH WEBB (estate divided among children above
named).   *Wife and Executrix:* ELIZABETH.   *Witnesses:* ROBERT HICKS,
WILLIAM RAGLAND.   *Clerk of the Court:* I. EDWARDS.

WEBB, SAMUEL.   Bertie County.

May 24, 1754.   May Court, 1754.   *Sons:* BENJAMIN and SAMUEL (lands
on Horse Creek).   *Daughters:* PENELOPE, ANN and ELIZABETH WEBB

(negro to each). *Wife and Executrix:* MARGET. *Witnesses:* MOSES SUMNER, TAMER WILLIFORD, EASTER WILLEFORD. *Clerk of the Court:* SAMUEL ORMES.

WEBSTER, ELISABETH.   Carteret County.

March 4, 1754. June Court, 1754. *Sons:* JOHN WEBSTER, JOSEPH, JAMES and SAMUEL NOBLE, BENJAMIN WEBSTER. *Daughters:* HANNAH ROBERTS and RACHEL HOURTON. *Executor:* SAMUEL NOBLE (son). *Witnesses:* MOSES HOUSTON, RACHEL PEARSON, HANNAH SIMMONS. *Clerk of the Court:* GEO. READ.

WEBSTER, JOHN.   Carteret County.

July 8, 1745. February 27, 1746. *Sons:* JOHN, JOSEPH, BENJAMIN. *Daughters:* ELIZABETH and MARY. *Executors:* PETER PEERY and NICHOLAS HUNTER. *Witnesses:* MOSES HOUSTON, JAMES NOBLE, RICHARD WILLIAMSON. Proven before GAB. JOHNSTON.

WEBSTER, JOHN.   Hyde County.

December 25, 1773. April 6, 1774. *Sons:* RICHARD, SAMUEL, JAMES and HENRY. *Daughter:* MARY. *Wife and Executrix:* LYDIA. *Executors:* SAMUEL SMITH and WILLM. PORTER. *Witnesses:* JOHN MARKDORY (?), RICHARD CAPPS. Proven before Jo. MARTIN.

WEBSTER, WILLIAM.   Hyde County.

October 16, 1745. February 3, 1745. *Son:* WILLIAM (plantation and two negroes). *Wife and Executrix:* ANN. *Grandchildren:* JOHN THOROGOOD WEBSTER and ANN WEBSTER, children of JAMES WEBSTER, deceased (one negro girl to each). *Witnesses:* JOHN WEIGHT, LODWICK MARTIN, THOMAS LOACK. *Clerk of the Court:* THOMAS LOACK.

WEEKES, BENJAMIN.   Carteret County.

November 9, 1744. June Court, 1745. *Sons:* ISAAC, JARBUS, THEFFLUS, ARCHELAS, BENGUMEN. *Daughters:* LIDDA WITTON, MARY WILLIMS, CHRISTIAN WEAKS, THANKFULL HICKS, ELIZABETH WEEKS. *Wife and Executrix:* MARY. *Witnesses:* JEHOSHAPHAT HOLLANDS, FRANCIS BURNS, THOMAS PERSON. *Clerk of the Court:* GEORGE READ.

WELCH, JOHN.   Chowan County.

April 23, 1730. *Sons:* EDWARD and JOHN (plantation to each, JOHN'S lying on Cockfighting Branch), JAMES (land on Cockfighting Branch). *Daughter:* SARAH (150 acres of land). *Wife and Executrix:* ELIZABETH. *Witnesses:* JOHN and JAMES PARKER, BENJAMIN EVANS. No probate.

WELCH, NATHANIEL.   Pasquotank County.
February 13, 1734–1735. April Court, 1735. *Legatees:* TERENCE
SWEENY, THOMAS GASKILL, ELIZABETH GASKILL, JOSEPH PENDLETON,
DANIEL DUNN, JOHN CORP. *Executor:* TERENCE SWEENY. *Witnesses:*
JOHN SMEDLEY, THOMAS PENDLETON. *Clerk of the Court:* JOS. SMITH.

WELLS, WILLIAM.
January 31, 1742–1743. *Sons:* WILLIAM and NATHANIELL, JOHN and
JOSEPH (lands), HENRY. *Daughters:* SARAH EVANS, ELIZABETH ———.
Executor: JOHN STARKEY. *Witnesses:* JOHN DUDLEY, JOHN McGRAH, EPH.
SWIFT. No probate. County not given.

WENHAM, ROBERT.
May 16, 1735. August 9, 1735. *Sons:* ROBERT (*Executor*), WILLIAM.
Witnesses: FRANCIS BROWN, JOHN GREEN, JOHN GOURDON. Proven before
W. SMITH, C. J.

WEST, ARTHUR.   Bertie County.
April 12, 1727. May Court, 1730. *Devisees and legatees:* ROBERT, son
of HENRY WEST (land on Fishing Creek), NATHANIEL HICKMAN (land on
Fishing Creek). *Brother:* JOSEPH WEST. *Sister:* MARY WEST. *Wife and
Executrix:* MARY. *Witnesses:* ARTHUR WHITCHED, WILLIAM WEST, EDWARD
TOWERSON. *Clerk of the Court:* RT. FORSTER.

WEST, CHARLES.   Pasquotank County.
August 8, 1747. October Court, 1748. *Sons:* LEMUEL (four negroes),
JONATHAN (three negroes and cattle), HEZEKIAH (two negroes). *Daughters:*
WINEFRUIT WEST (two negroes), DINAH WEST. *Grandson:* BENJAMIN
WEST, son of CHARLES, dec'd (plantation known as Cowpen Neck and Rol-
linseas). *Wife and Executrix:* DINAH. *Executors:* LEMUEL WEST (son)
and THOMAS MACKEEL (son-in-law). *Witnesses:* JOHN GUTHRAY, ANN
DANIEL, JOHN McKEEL. *Clerk of the Court:* THOS. TAYLOR.

WEST, HENRY.   Beaufort County.
August 14, 1752. December Court, 1752. *Sisters:* MARY SOJORNER,
SARAH PEYTON, CEILA TYNES. *Nephew:* JOHN PEYTON. *Niece:* HOL-
LAND APPLEWHITE. *Executors:* JOHN GILES, MICHAEL COUTANCHE, WIL-
LIAM PEYTON and THOMAS PIERCE. *Witnesses:* THOMAS and JOHN
JASPER, JOHN PORTER. *Clerk of the Court:* WILL ORMOND. Original
missing. Abstract made from recorded copy.

WEST, JOHN.   Chowan Precinct.
July 16, 1713. *Wife and Executrix:* ELIZABETH. *Witnesses:* LAW-
RENCE SARSON, ELIZABETH ROSE. Original missing. Recorded in Book
1712–1722, page 27.

WEST, JONATHAN.   Pasquotank County.

August 28, 1751. July Court, 1751. *Legatees:* LAMUEL and HEZEKIAH
WEST, THOMAS MCKEEL, WILLIAM WOODLEY, DINAH and BENJAMIN
WEST. Negroes are divided among above-named. *Executors:* THOMAS
WOODLY and THOMAS MACKEEL. *Witnesses:* JONATHAN HOWELL, ISAAC
COX, ANTHONY WHITE. *Clerk of the Court:* THOMAS TAYLOR.

WEST, PETER.   Bertie County.

July 31, 1749. ʹMay Court, 1751. *Daughters:* SARAH WEST, ELIZA-
BETH COTTON (four negroes). *Son:* PETER (lands and negroes). *Grand-
son:* WILLIAM WEST. *Executor:* CHARLES HORNE. *Witnesses:* HENRY
WINBORNE, BRYAN HARE, WUSTRUM (?) ROGERS. *Clerk of the Court:*
SAMUEL ORMES.

WEST, ROBERT.   Chowan Precinct.

March 28, 1689. June 4, 1689. *Sons:* ROBERT, THOMAS, JOHN and
RICHARD (lands and negroes). *Wife and Executrix:* MARTHA. *Witnesses:* JAMES DAMERELL, JAMES HARLA. Proven before SETH SOTHELL.

WEST, THOMAS.   Bertie County.

November 6, 1756. April Court, 1757. *Wife and Executrix:* ELIZA-
BETH. *Daughter:* ELIZABETH WEST. *Son:* WILLIAM. (7 negroes divided
among foregoing). *Executor:* ROBERT WEST (brother). *Witnesses:* JOHN
CORBERT, WM. FLEETWOOD, JOSEPH WHITE. *Clerk of the Court:* BENJN.
WYNNS.

WEST, WILLIAM.   Bertie Precinct.

July 28, 1735. *Legatees and Executors:* ROBERT WEST, JR., and
THOMAS WEST, his brother (all estate devised and bequeathed to these
two). *Witnesses:* WILLIAM LATTIMER, ROBERT WEST. No probate
officer.

WEST, WILLIAM.   Beaufort County.

December 4, 1744. December 10, 1745. *Daughters:* SARAH PEYTON
(negro), CAHIA TYNES, MARY SOJOURNER. *Grandson:* JACOB SOJOURNER.
Wife and Executrix: SUSANNA. *Executor:* HENRY WEST (son). *Witnesses:* RICHRD. JONES, MARY SMITH, JEREMIAH SMITH. *Clerk of the
Court:* JOHN FORBES.

WEST, WILLIAM.   Edgecombe County.

November 26, 1749. February Court, 1749. *Son and Executor:* WIL-
LIAM (lands on Rocky Swamp, together with water mill). *Brother:*
HENRY WEST. *Nephew:* WILLIAM WEST (son of HENRY). *Daughter:*
MARY WILLIAMS. *Witnesses:* WALLIS JONES, JOHN LONG, JOEL JONES.
Clerk of the Court: BENJAMIN WYNNS.

WEST, WILLIAM.   Craven County.

February Court, 1750. *Sons:* JOHN, DANIEL, WILLIAM, SAMEWILL (SAMUEL). *Daughters:* MARY LANE, ELIZABETH and LYDIA WEST. *Wife and Executrix:* REBECKOR. *Executors:* JOHN LANE and DANIEL DAUGHITY. *Witnesses:* JONATHAN MCKFARSON, DANIEL DAUGHITY, ELIZABETH DAUGHITY. *Clerk of the Court:* PETER CONWAY.

WESTON, WILLIAM.   Bertie County.

November 12, 1747. February Court, 1748. *Sons:* EPHRAIM, JOHN and WILLIAM (lands "upon the Loosing Swamp" and other tracts described in will), MALICHI and THOMAS WESTON ("plantation whereon I live"). *Daughter:* RACHEL WESTON. *Wife:* CATHERINE. *Executors:* JOHN and WILLIAM (sons). *Witnesses:* JOSEPH WATFORD, MOSES GREEN. *Clerk of the Court:* JOHN WESTON.

WHALTONE, THOMAS.   Chowan County.

May 8, 1719. June 8, 1719. *Wife:* ANNE, of King and Queen County in Virginia. All estate is left to wife and seven children, not named. *Executor:* JOHN PLOWMAN. *Witnesses:* AB. COKBURNE, JOHN WHITE, MARY WHITE. Proven before Governor CHARLES EDEN. Impression of what appears to be cherub with wings on seal.

WHARREY, ANTHONY.   Perquimans Precinct.

September 17, 1716. July 8, 1718. *Son:* JOSHUA. *Wife and Executrix:* SARAH. *Executor:* THOMAS HARVEY. *Witnesses:* FRANCIS SMITH. SAMUELL WYATT, ANN RAY. *Clerk of the Court:* RICHARD LEARY.

WHARY, JOSHUA.   Perquimans Precinct.

January 28, 1729. August 18, 1730. *Brother:* ANTHONY WHARY. *Sisters:* ELIZABETH, RACHEL, SARAH and MARY WHARY. *Executor:* ROBERT BEVINES. *Witnesses:* JOHN ARNAL, ELIZABETH ARNAL, JOHN STEPNEY. Proven before GAB. JOHNSTON.

WHEATLEY, JOHN.   Chowan County.

December, 1706. January 1, 1706–1707. *Daughters:* ELIZABETH, ANN and MARTHA. *Wife and Executrix:* ANNE (land on Indian Towne Creek). *Executor:* SAMUEL PASCKEL. *Witnesses:* THOMAS LUTON, HENRY BONER, NATHL. CHEVIN. *Clerk of the Court:* NATHL. CHEVIN.

WHEATLEY, SAMUEL.   Tyrrell County.

January 21, 1739–1740. June Court, 1740. *Wife and children:* mentioned, but not named. *Executors:* SAMUEL WHEATLEY and WILLIAM KENNEDY. *Witnesses:* WM. KENNEDY, SARY PELL, MARY WENTHAM. *Clerk of the Court:* THOMAS LEARY.

WHEDBEE, RICHARD.   Perquimans County.

January, 1746. July Court, 1746. *Sons:* JOHN (plantation and one negro), RICHARD (land known as Broken Beeches and one negro), GEORGE (three negroes), BENJAMIN and JOSEPH (two negroes to each). *Daughters:* ELIZABETH PRATT, DEBORAH WILKENS, SARAH HASKENS (two negroes to each). *Wife and Executrix:* HANNAH (two negroes). *Executors:* CHRISTIAN and JOSEPH REED (brothers-in-law). *Witnesses:* SAMUEL SNOWDEN, ELIZABETH REED, CATHERINE DAVIS. *Clerk of the Court:* EDMUND HATCH.

WHEEDBEE, ANN.   Pasquotank County.

September 24, 1750. January Court, 1750. *Sons:* WILLIAM BOYD and THOMAS BOYD. *Other legatees:* ELIZABETH BAILEY, WINIFORT BOYD, ANN BAILEY. *Executors:* ANTHONY MARCKHAM and WILLIAM BOYD. *Witnesses:* JOHN WILKINS, JOSEPH COMMANDER. *Clerk of the Court:* THOS. TAYLOR.

WHELLER, HENRY.   Bertie Precinct.

June 24, 1726. November Court, 1727. *Sons:* EMPRER, HENRY, JOHN. *Daughter.* SARAH. *Wife and Executrix:* ANNE. *Witnesses:* ROBERT SIMES, ANDREW IRELAND. *Clerk of the Court:* ROBERT FORSTER.

WHIDBE, GEORGE.   Pasquotank Precinct.

March 22, 1718. July 29, 1718. *Sons:* RICHARD, GEORGE (land on Alegator River), JOHN. *Cousin:* RICHARD WHIDBE. *Daughter:* RUTH WHIDBE. *Executors:* GEORGE and RICHARD WHIDBE (sons). *Witnesses:* JOHN MIXON, AUTHO. ALLEXANDER, REBECKAH BALEY. *Clerk of the Court:* R. HICKS.

WHIDBE, GEORGE.   Albemarle County.

April 21, 1722. *Daughters:* ANN and ELIZABETH (land on Cow Ridge). *Brother:* RICHARD WHIDBEE. *Other legatees:* JOHN GARDENER (son of JANE GARDENER) and JOHN WHIDBEE (son of JOHN WHIDBEE). *Wife and Executrix:* WINEFORD. *Witnesses:* JOSEPH WINSHIP, WILLIAM HUDSON, WILLIAM WILLSON. Proven before WM. REED, *"Presidente of North Carolina."*

WHIDBEE, GEORGE.   Pasquotank County.

June 16, 1749. August 11, 1749. *Brothers:* JOHN and RICHARD WHIDBEE. *Nephews:* GEORGE (son of RICHARD), JOHN and THOMAS WHIDBEE (sons of JOHN). To above-named is bequeathed negroes. *Wife and Executrix:* ANN. *Witnesses:* ANTHONY MARKHAM, JNO. MCKEEL. Proven before GAB. JOHNSTON at Eden House. Coat of arms on seal.

WHIDBE, RICHARD.   Tyrrell County.
   March 29, 1736. June Court, 1740. *Cousin and Executor:* GEORGE
PHILPS. *Other legatee:* CUDBATH PHILPS. *Witnesses:* JOHN WOODLAND,
THOMAS and JANE BEST. *Clerk of the Court:* THOMAS LEARY.

WHITE, ABRAHAM.   Pasquotank County.
   January 7, 1746. January Court, 1746. *Brother:* JOHN WHITE.
Nephew: JAMES WHITE, son of JOHN (plantation). *Wife and Executrix:*
SARAH. *Executor:* JAMES WHITE (brother). *Witnesses:* AARON MORRIS,
THOMAS SYMONS, JOSEPH ROBINSON. *Clerk of the Court:* THOMAS TAY-
LOR. Device on seal.

WHITE, ARNOLD.
   March 22, 1690. *Daughter:* ELIZABETH. *Son and Executor:* ARNOLD.
Brother: HENRY WHITE. *Witnesses:* STEPHEN MUNDEN, WILLIAM MAN,
JEAMS DAVIS. *Clerk of the Court:* HENDERSON WALKER.

WHITE, ARNOLD.   Perquimans County.
   April 24, 1751. July Court, 1752. *Sons:* SAMUEL and ARNOLD (plantation divided between them). *Wife and Executrix:* ELIZABETH. *Witnesses:* PETER PARKER, JACOB OVERMAN, MARY PARKER. *Clerk of the
Court:* EDMUND HATCH.

WHITE, GEORGE.   Craven County.
   October 7, 1741. September 22, 1744. *Sons:* GEORGE and LUKE.
Daughters: SARAH and PERSILLA. *Wife:* FRANCESS. *Witnesses:* ROBERT
CLARK, JOHN WHITE, EDWD. VANN. Proven before GAB. JOHNSTON.

WHITE, GEORGE.   Chowan County.
   April, 1747. Will illegible.

WHITE, HENRY.
   November 14, 1669–1670. May 16, 1670. *Wife:* ELENER. *Son:* ARNULL.
No executor appointed. *Witnesses:* GEORGE RICHARDS, HENRY MAN-
NERLY. *Clerk of the Court:* THOS. HARRIS. *Justice:* PETER CARTERET.

WHITE, HENRY.   Albemarle County.
   September 19, 1706. *Sons:* HENRY, ARNOLD, ISACK, ROBERT and JOHN.
(Negroes and "maner" plantation devised and bequeathed to sons.) *Daugh-
ters:* CONTENT, MARY and NAOMY. *Wife and Executrix:* not named. *Wit-
nesses:* ZACHARIAH NIXON, JOHN SYMONS, JOHN MARTIN, JEREMYAH
SYMONS, JOHN RAPER. No probate.

WHITE, HENRY.   Pasquotank County.

March 25, 1739. April Court, 1739. *Sons:* THOMAS and ISAAC (all estate left to these two sons). *Executors:* HENRY STANTON and WILLIAM BURDEN (or BENDER). *Witnesses:* WILLIAM SYMONS, JOHANA WHITE, BENJAMIN NEWBY. *Clerk of the Court:* JOSEPH SMITH. *Clerk of Carteret County:* JOHN SIMPSON.

WHITE, HENRY.   Currituck County.

December 22, 1751. September 10, 1754. *Sons:* HILARY (two negroes), HENRY, JOSEPH (land at Navis Creek), CALEB (plantation called Dunkeleys), JOSHUA, CHURCH. To four sons is given land over Indian Creek, and also plantation at Black Water. *Daughter:* MARY. *Executors:* HILARY and HENRY WHITE (sons). *Witnesses:* JOS. CAMPBELL, CHARLES WILLIAMS, WILLIAM DUDING (?). *Clerk of the Court:* JOHN SNOAD.

WHITE, JOHN.   Albemarle County.

April 4, 1690–1691. *Legatees:* WILLIAM and ELIZABETH EDLETON, JAMES RIGG (*Executor*). *Wife and Executrix:* MARGRET. *Witnesses:* JOHN STEPNEY, STEPHEN HANREFFE (?), THOMAS LEFFER (?). Signature of probate officer illegible.

WHITE, JOHN.   Hyde County.

April 7, 1724. April Court, 1726. *Wife and Executrix:* SARAH. *Witnesses:* ROBERT PEYTON, PATRICK MAULE. *Clerk of the Court:* THOMAS JONES. *Executrix* qualified before SAMUEL SLADE. Coat of arms on seal.

WHITE, JOHN.   Perquimans Precinct.

February 16, 1730–1731. March 10, 1730. *Son:* JOHN. *Daughters:* RACHEL WHITE (land bought of FRANCIS NUBE (NEWBY), SARAH, ELIZABETH and HULDE. *Sister:* MARY. *Wife and Executrix:* SARAH. *Witnesses:* JOHN LILLE, JAMES ———, WILLIAM WHITE. Proven before GEORGE BURRINGTON.

WHITE, JOHN.   Carteret County.

April 11, 1744. February 26, 1745. *Brother:* ROBERT WHITE, of the County of Norfolk, in Great Britain. *Executors:* JOHN STARKEY and SAMUELL WILSON. *Witnesses:* RALPH CAVES, SARAH STARKEY, JACOB BIDDLE. Proven before GAB. JOHNSTON.

WHITE, JOHN.   Pasquotank County.

May 19, 1754. July Court, 1754. *Son:* SAMUEL. *Sister:* ELIZABETH WHITE. *Wife:* ANN. *Other legatee:* JOHN MAN. *Executor:* JAMES DAVIS. *Witnesses:* TIMOTHY MEEDS, JAMES DAVIS, WILLIAM BUNDY. *Clerk of the Court:* THOMAS TAYLOR.

WHITE, LUKE.   Currituck County.

June 8, 1757.   March Court, 1758.   *Sons:* VINSON (land called Absalom Poiner's), JOSHUA (plantation and one negro).   *Daughters:* CHRISTIAN WHITE, KEZIAH ELLES, wife of MICHAEL ELLES, MARY, wife of JOHN TOMSON.   *Wife and Executrix:* MARGARET.   *Witnesses:* WILLIAM BRAY, JOSEPH POYNER, JOHN WHEATLEY.   *Clerk of the Court:* WM. MEARNS.

WHITE, MEDIA.   Bertie County.

August 27, 1744.   January 17, 1749.   Chowan.   *Wife and Executrix:* ELIZABETH.   *Witnesses:* ABIGAIL WHITE, JOSEPH BUTTERTON, SARAH BUTTERTON.   Proven before GAB. JOHNSTON.   Impression of winged dragon on seal.

WHITE, NEHEMIAH.   Pasquotank County.

September 5, 1751.   July Court, 1751.   *Sons:* BENJAMIN and JOSHUA (land to each).   *Daughters:* SARAH, MARY and MARTHA WHITE.   *Wife and Executrix:* MARTHA.   *Executor:* JOSEPH PRITCHARD (brother-in-law).   *Witnesses:* JOSEPH COMMANDER, ROBERT WHITE, JOSEPH ROBINSON.   *Clerk of the Court:* THOMAS TAYLOR.

WHITE, ROBERT.   Albemarle County.

April 19, 1698.   Probate illegible.   *Sons:* VINCENT and ROBERT.   *Daughter:* MARY.   *Friend:* THOMAS JONES.   *Executor:* VINCENT WHITE (son).   *Witnesses:* EPHREAM COSTE, JOHN FOURRE, FRANCIS DeLAMARE.

WHITE, ROBERT.   Pasquotank Precinct.

January 1, 1732.   April 16, 1733.   *Sons:* JONATHAN and ZEFENIAH ("the manah plantation adjoining ROBERT LOWRY"), JOSEPH ("back land" and two negroes).   To each of sons is bequeathed negroes.   *Daughters:* ANN and ELIZABETH WHITE.   *Wife and Executrix:* REBECKAH.   *Witnesses:* AARON MORRIS, ROBART DAVIS, HENRY WHITE.   Proven before GEO. BURRINGTON.

WHITE, ROGER.   Albemarle County.

September 10, 1686.   *Wife and Executrix:* JOAN.   *Other legatees:* WILLIAM MORRISON, RICHARD WILLIAMSON and GEORGE LONODAY (?).   *Witnesses:* WM. CHAPMAN, GEORGE LONODAY (?), RICHARD WILLIAMSON, THOMAS WALLEN.   No probate.

WHITE, SARAH.   Hyde County.

January 6, 1726.   April Court, 1727.   *Legatees:* BENJAMIN MORDICKE (plantation on Machepungo River), ELIZABETH MONTGOMERY, JOHN SNOAD, JR., ARDLEY THOROWGOOD, SARAH BELL (*Executrix*).   *Witnesses:* GI. HALIDAY, WILLIAM WEBSTER.   *Clerk of the Court:* THOMAS JONES.

WHITE, THOMAS.   Albemarle County.

March 11, 1695.   No probate.   *Wife and Executrix:* DIANA.   *Other legatee:* WILLIAM COLLINS.   *Witnesses:* DEBORA WILLOBY, WILLIAM COLLINS, THOMAS HASSOLD.

WHITE, THOMAS.   .   Chowan County.

April 26, 1752.   January Court, 1754.   *Wife and Executrix:* SARAH. *Son:* not named.   *Children of wife:* JOB and JOHN CHARLTON, MARY CRECY, SUSANAH LEARY.   *Executors:* JOB and JOHN CHARLTON, LEVI CRECY.   *Witnesses:* J. BENBURY, M. POTTER, JOSH. PRATT.   *Clerk of the Court:* WILL HALSEY.   Impression on seal: man mounted on horse or lion.

WHITE, THOMAS.   Carteret County.

November 28, 1757.   December 8, 1757.   *Sons:* HENRY (plantation), THOMAS (one negro).   *Executors:* HENRY STANTON and ISAAC WHITE (brother).   *Witnesses:* EPHRAIM BULL, JAMES BROWN, KATHERINE WHITE. *Clerk of the Court:* WILLIAM ROBERTSON.

WHITE, WILLIAM.   Chowan County.

December 14, 1723.   April 14, 1724.   *Wife and Executrix:* MARY.   *Daughter:* MARY.   *Witnesses:* JEREMIAH PRATT, THOMAS MERCER.   Proven before C. GALE, C. J.

WHITE, WILLIAM.   Currituck County.

March 10, 1753.   March Court, 1755.   *Sons:* HENRY, WILLOUGHBY (lands to each), LUKE, JAMEY (negro to each).   *Daughters:* CORTNA, LOVE and MERIAM WHITE (negroes).   *Wife and Executrix:* MARGARET.   *Witnesses:* GEORGE POWERS, SAM. SIMMONS, THOMAS MILLER.   *Clerk of the Court:* WILLIAM SHERGOLD.

WHITE, WILLIAM.   Cumberland County.

May 5, 1774.   July 13, 1774.   *Granddaughter:* CATRINE KNOWLAN. *Nephews:* JAMES and GERALD WHITE.   *Brother:* JAMES WHITE.   *Executors:* WM. MCREE, JAMES WHITE, JOSEPH KEMP.   *Witnesses:* GRIFFITH JONES, MARY WHITE, MARY WHITE.   Proven before JO. MARTIN.

WHITEHEAD, ALICE.   Craven County.

March 12, 1741–1742.   June 21, 1743.   *Brother:* EDWARD WHITEHEAD of London.   *Nephews:* JAMES and ROBERT WHITEHEAD (sons of brother, EDWD.).   *Niece:* ELIZABETH WHITEHEAD (daughter of brother, EDWARD). *Other legatees:* TABITHA SMITH, MILDRED TRAVERS, THOMAS (son of JOHN FEARN), MARY (wife of JOHN FEARN), ANN BENDIS, SARAH BENDIS, MARY (wife of JAMES COOR, youngest daughter of THOMAS SMITH of New River), NICHOLAS ROUTLEDGE of New Bern, MADAM HANNIS (wife of JOSEPH HANnis), Susannah (wife of William Herritage), William Brice, Joseph Hannis, Jr. (*Executor*), Manuel and Peter ("two Portugee servants"). Codicil revokes legacy of two Portugese slaves and gives them their freedom. All legacies are in money or clothing. *Witnesses:* Thomas Hildersley Skerrett, Catherine Routledge, Henry Hertwell, Ralph Yeoman. Device on seal. *Clerk of the Court:* N. Routledge.

Whitehouse, Samuel.   Carteret County.

October 28, 1756. December Court, 1756. *Sons:* Robert (plantation at the Straights lying to the eastward of Old Topsail Inlet and one negro). *Son-in-law:* William Wilkins Taylor (plantation "on which I now live" on Bouge and Newport Sounds). *Daughters:* Esther and Anne Whitehouse. *Wife and Executrix:* Abigail. *Executor:* Valintine Wallis. *Witnesses:* Frances Shepard, John Ogelsbee, Geo. Mackane. *Clerk of the Court:* John Smith.

Whitehurst, Thomas.

"Lieutenant in the Royal Navy." March 22, 1765. June 23, 1766. Unto William Grenfell Lobb, youngest son of Jacob Lobb, commander of "His Majesty's sloop the Viper," is bequeathed money in hands of George Marsh of Savage Gardens, Tower Hill, London. Unto *sister*, Ann Whitehurst is devised lands known as Styles Copp within six miles of the town of Stafford, England; sister also named as *Executrix*. *Witnesses:* J. Eustace, Thomas Cobham, Thomas McGuire. Proven before Wm. Tryon. Impression of head on seal.

Whitley, Samuel.   Tyrrell County.

January 21, 1739–1740. March 4, 1739. Lands and property bequeathed to wife and children, who are not named. *Son-in-law:* William Archdecon. *Executors:* Samll. Whitley and William Kennedy. *Clerk of the Court:* Thomas Leary.

The original of this will missing. Abstract made from recorded copy No. 117, in Grant Book No. 4.

Whitley, William.   Northampton County.

August 15, 1751. April Court, 1759. *Sons:* Jacob, James, William, Arthur, Joseph. *Daughters:* Elizabeth, Julian and Susanna. *Wife and Executrix:* Julian. *Witnesses:* James Gay, Elisha Darden, Charles Barnes. *Clerk of the Court:* I. Edwards.

Whitmell, Thomas.   Bertie County.

November 23, 1735. December 13, 1735. *Sons:* Thomas, Lewis, William. *Daughters:* Sarah and Marth. Whitmell and Elizabeth Pollock. *Wife:* Elizabeth. The following lands devised: plantation (home) on Kesia River; land on Buck Swamp. Horses and other live stock, together with eight or ten negroes bequeathed to above-named. *Executors:* THOS. WHITMELL (son) and JOHN GRAY. *Witnesses:* SIMON GALE, GARRAD VAN UPSTALL, MARY CANNADY. Proven before GAB. JOHNSTON.

The original of this will missing. Abstract made from recorded copy No. 22, in Grant Book No. 4.

WHITNEY, JOSHUA.

December 26, 1735. January 21, 1735. *Sons:* DAVID, JEREMIAH, SAMUEL (one negro and one-fourth share of sloop Ketring to each), JOSEPH, FRANCIS. *Daughters:* KETRING (negro), RUTH. About 12 silver spoons and one silver tankard bequeathed to sons and daughters. *Wife:* MARTHA. *Executors:* DAVID and JEREMIAH WHITNEY (sons). *Witnesses:* JOHN and JEREMIAH BENTLEY, JAMES BLAIR. Proven before W. SMITH.

WIAT, JOHN.   Perquimans County.

April 9, 1738. June 15, 1739. *Son:* WILLIAM (lands and negroes). *Daughters:* SARAH STANDING (lands on Mings Creek and Bridge Creek), ELIZABETH OATES. *Brother:* JOSHEWAY LONG (land known as Normond's Folly). *Wife and Executrix:* RACHEL. *Executors:* WILLIAM WIAT and THOMAS PEIRCE. *Witnesses:* THOMAS CALLOWAY, WM. HOSKING, WILLIAM LONG. Proven before W. SMITH.

WIAT, THOMAS.   Perquimans Precinct.

April 28, 1735. July 23, 1735. *Brothers:* THOMAS LONG, SAMUELL WIAT, WILLIAM LONG, JOSHUA LONG (*Executor*). *Witnesses:* JOHN STEPNEY, WILLIAM HOSKINS (or HORKINS). No probate officer.

WICKER, RICHARD.   Currituck County.

January 30, 1699–1700. *Wife:* MARTHA. *Granddaughters:* ANNA and ELIZABETH (daughters of GEORGE BOOTH). *Other legatee:* ROBERT LINNEY. *Witnesses:* ANN THOMAS, PEETER PARKER, NATHANIEL TOMS. *Clerk of the Court:* WILL SWANN.

WICKLIFFE, WILLIAM.   Craven County.

September 30, 1753. December 15, 1754. *Son:* WILLIAM. *Daughters:* ELIZABETH, ALICE and KATHERINE WICKLIFFE. *Executors:* JOHN FRANKS (son-in-law), WILLIAM WICKLIFFE (son), JOHN STARKEY. *Witnesses:* JERE. VAIL, DANIEL DUPEE, SOUTHY REW. Proven before ARTHUR DOBBS.

WICKSTEAD, PALL.   New Hanover County.

August 4, 1738. August 12, 1738. This is a nuncupative will proven before MATT. ROWAN, J. P., by MARY BRYAN and FRANCIS BOYLAN, and bequeaths books to said ROWAN's children, and remainder of estate to said BOYLAN.

WILCOCKS, JOHN.   Craven County.

May 9, 1761. No probate. *Sons:* BENJAMIN (land bought of LEMUEL HATCH). THOMAS and STEPHEN. *Grandson:* JOHN WILCOCKS. Saw and grist mill mentioned. *Wife:* JANE. *Daughter:* ANN. *Executor:* LEMUEL HATCH. *Witnesses:* ELENER WILCOCKS, GERSHOM WOOD, EDMUND HATCH.

WILKINS, CHARLES.   Chowan Precinct.

January 23, 1733–1734. February 15, 1734. *Sons:* JOHN ("my plantation," bounded by Mattacomack Swamp and Queen Anne's Creek, and the road from Hoskins Bridge to Yawpim), WILLIAM (plantation called Britains and Fordyces, and also lands called the Wett Ground). *Daughters:* SARAH (wife of LUKE GREGORY), ANN, MARY and ELISABETH. *Brother-in-law:* NICHOLAS CRISP. *Wife:* not named. *Executors:* JOHN and WILLIAM (sons). *Witnesses:* SAMUEL and SARAH WARNER, EDWARD STANDIN. Proven before GAB. JOHNSTON.

WILKINS, JOHN.   Chowan County.

January 18, 1774. March 17, 1774. *Sons:* CHARLES ("thick neck" plantations in Perquimans and Chowan, together with three negroes), JOHN (plantation near Hoskins' Mill and plantation known as McClenny's, together with three negroes). *Daughters:* KATHERINE BAINS, DEBORAH TAYLOR, ELIZABETH WILKINS. *Wife and Executrix:* JUDITH (three negroes). *Executors:* ANDREW KNOX and THOMAS OLDHAM. *Witnesses:* CHARLES COPELAND, WILLIAM COPELAND, REBECCA BARBER. Proven before Jo. MARTIN.

WILKISON, PHILIP.   Bladen County.

February 24, 1757. July Court, 1758. *Sons:* THOMAS (land on Wilkeson's Creek), RICHARD, JOHN, WILLIAM. *Daughters:* ELIZABETH, MARY and MARGARET WILLIAMS. *Wife and Executrix:* MARTHA (negroes). *Witnesses:* BENJAMIN SLUYTER, THOMAS PLATT, ALEXANDER McCONKEY. *Clerk of the Court:* J. BURGWIN.

WILKISON, WILLIAM.

July 4, 1704. May 9, 1706. *Wife and Executrix:* ESTHER. *Other legatees:* WM. GLOVER, THOMAS LUTTEN, THOMAS BLUNT, JNO. BLUNT (1 ring to each). *Witnesses:* JAMES BENBERY, DANLL. LEIGH, SILAS SMITH, JAMES BEASLEY, JOHN SHAW, RACHELL BACKER. *Clerk of General Court:* J. KNIGHT.

WILLCOX, JEREMIAH.   Pasquotank County.

April 22, 1754. July Court, 1754. *Son:* STEPHEN (lands on sound side). *Daughters:* SARAH and RUTH. *Wife and Executrix:* ELIZABETH.

Other legatee: ELIZABETH WAKEFIELD. *Executor:* ZACHARIAH KEETON. *Witnesses:* NATHAN OVERMAN, JOB NICHOLS. *Clerk of the Court:* THO. TAYLOR.

WILLIAMS, ANTHONY.   Chowan County.

December 3, 1717. April Court, 1718. *Sons:* LEWIS, WILLIAM, JOHN, ANTHONY (land on Beach Swamp). *Daughters:* SARAH, MARY and ELLINORE WILLIAMS. *Wife and Executrix:* MARTHA (land at Catawatsky). *Other devisee:* JAMES CORLEE (land on Holly Swamp). *Father-inlaw:* JOHN EARLY. *Witnesses:* WILLIAM CRANFORD, PETER WEST, PRECILLA WEST. *Clerk of the Court:* R. HICKS.

WILLIAMS, ANTHONY.   Duplin County.

July 3, 1751. April Court, 1752. *Sons:* STEPHEN (plantation and negroes), BENJAMIN (land "I now live on called the Beaverdam Neck"). To son BENJAMIN is also given two negroes, and son STEPHEN is requested to build for him a "sufficient dwelling of ye Bigness of twenty and sixteen foot." *Daughters:* MARY (wife of MOSES POWELL), PENELLIPY WILLIAMS (one negro), PHERIBE WILLIAMS (one negro), EASTER WILLIAMS, SIVELITY WILLIAMS. *Cousin:* ANTHONY BEVELY. *Other devisee:* EDWARD CARTER. *Wife:* MARY. *Executors:* JOB BROOKES, WILLIAM HAIRS. *Witnesses:* SAMUELL JONES, GEORGE SMITH, JOHN WILLIAMS. *Clerk of the Court:* JOHN DICKSON.

WILLIAMS, ARTHUR.   Bertie County.

August 8, 1735. February Court, 1739. *Sons:* ARTHUR (water mill and lands on Creek), ROBERT (lands on Potecasi Creek above ye Wildcat Swamp, land on Mahering River at Walnut Field, lands called the Goose Pond), JOHN ("plantation I now live on" and land called the Reedy Branch), MOAB (lands on River and land on Pottecasi called the Roundabout). To JOHN and MOAB is bequeathed small water mill. All negroes divided among sons. *Executors:* ROBERT and WILLIAM (sons). *Witnesses:* ABRAHAM BURTON, NICHOLAS BOONE, NICHOLAS BOONE, JUNR. *Clerk of the Court:* JOHN WYNNS.

WILLIAMS, EDWARD.   Chowan County.

February 9, 1713–1714. July Court, 1714. *"Prodigall and disobedient"* son: JOHN. *Wife and Executrix:* MARY. *Witnesses:* JOHN BRYAN, LAWRENCE MAGUE. *Clerk of the Court:* EDWD. BENWICKE (or RENWICKE).

WILLIAMS, EDWARD.   Pasquotank County.

October Court, 1739. *Sons:* LEMAND, JOSIAH, LODWICK and JOSEPH (lands and negroes). *Daughter:* SARAH. *Wife and Executrix:* ELISEBETH. *Witnesses:* DANIEL SAWYER, B. MORGAN. *Clerk of the Court:* JAMES CRAVEN.

WILLIAMS, ELISHA.   Edgecombe County.

August 13, 1751. February Court, 1755. *Brothers:* SOLOMON WIL-
LIAMS, GEORGE WILLIAMS, DANIEL WILLIAMS, JOSHUA WILLIAMS, JOHN
WILLIAMS. *Nephew:* RICHARD WILLIAMS (son of JOHN). *Sisters:* MARY
CAR, ELIZABETH DAUGHTRY. *Executor:* JOSHUA WILLIAMS. *Witnesses:*
JAMES SMITH, DREW SMITH, GEORGE BELL. *Clerk of the Court:* BEN-
JAMIN WYNNS.

WILLIAMS, ELIZA.   Perquimans County.

November 8, 1745. December 3, 1745. *Sons:* JOHN and ANTHONY
HATCH. *Daughter:* PENELOPE WILLIAMS (1 negro). Ten silver spoons
bequeathed to son and daughter. *Other legatees:* BENJAMIN BAPTIST and
BRYAN FOSSETT. *Executors:* McRORA SCARBROUGH and EDMUND HATCH
(brother). *Witnesses:* SAMUEL SNOWDEN, SARAH SNOWDEN, FRANCIS
LAYDEN. Proven before E. HALL.

WILLIAMS, GEORGE.   Northampton County.

January 6, 1749–1750. May Court, 1750. *Sons:* ROBERT (one negro),
GEORGE (land bought of MATTHEW KINCHEN, and one negro), SAMUEL
(one negro), JACOB (one negro), WILLIAM (one negro). Lands lying on
Hopkins Howell's spring branch, and Kerby's Creek. *Daughters:* SARAH,
ANN and MELDRED. *Wife:* SARAH (seven negroes). *Other legatees:*
ETHEL TAYLOR and JAMES TURNER, JR. *Executors:* ROBERT WILLIAMS
(son). *Witnesses:* JNO. SIMPSON, ETHD. TAYLOR, NICHOLAS MONGER,
WILLIAM MONGER. *Clerk of the Court:* I. EDWARDS.

WILLIAMS, GEORGE.   Edgecombe County.

July 19, 1758. June Court, 1759. *Sons:* GEORGE ("my plantation"),
SAMUEL (land on Deer Creek bought of WILLIAM WHITEHEAD). *Daugh-
ter:* CLOE. *Deceased Sister:* LUCRETIA WILLIAMS. *Wife and Executrix:*
PRISCILLA. *Witnesses:* GEORGE CRUDUP, MOSES BAKER, JOHN NORWOOD.
Clerk of the Court: JOS. MONTFORT.

WILLIAMS, JAMES.   Bertie Precinct.

August 21, 1736. February Court, 1737. *Son:* EZEKIEL. *Daughters:*
FERIBE and JERUSHA WILLIAMS (two negroes). *Wife and Executrix:*
ELIZABETH. *Executor:* THEOPHILUS WILLIAMS (brother). *Witnesses:*
ROBERT HINES, WILLIAM STANDLEY, GEORGE PRICE. *Clerk of the Court:*
JNO. WYNNS.

WILLIAMS, JAMES.   Carteret County.

October 31, 1770. November 19, 1770. *Sons:* BRICE (land in Duplin
County on Stewart's Creek, and four negroes), BENJAMIN and JAMES
("plantation I now live on" divided between them, and five negroes

bequeathed to each). *Wife and Executrix:* SARAH ($\frac{1}{2}$ dozen cushion chairs, $\frac{1}{2}$ dozen chairs, silver spoons and other household furniture, together with three negroes). *Daughters:* CHRISTIAN NIXON, SARAH HATCH (negroes), CASSANDRA (three negroes), MARY (three negroes), CLARISSICA (three negroes). *Executor:* LEMUEL HATCH. *Witnesses:* STEPHEN BALL, STEPHEN YEATS, CHARLES MACKLAND. Proven before WM. TRYON.

WILLIAMS, JESSE.   Onslow County.

September 27, 1773. *Sons:* LOT (one negro and land on N. W. Branch of New River "above DR. CARRUTHERS' bridge at a place called Gerald's neck"), JESY (plantation and one negro), HILL (one negro and land on N. W. branch of New River adjoining MATTHEW GREGORY). *Daughters:* SARAH, ESTHER and HANNAH WILLIAMS (negro to each). *Wife:* ANNE (three negroes). *Executors:* OBED and UZ WILLIAMS (brothers). *Witnesses:* MOSES COX, MATTHEW GREGORY, BENJAMIN WILLIAMS. Proven before JO. MARTIN.

WILLIAMS, JOANNA.   Bertie County.

January 12, 1747–1748. July Court, 1756. *Sons and Executors:* RICHARD and THOMAS WILLIAMS. *Daughter:* ELIZA SMITH. *Grandchildren:* SIMON WILLIAMS, ARTHUR BROWN (negro boy to each), MARY SMITH, PENELOPE WILLIAMS, MARY HARRELL (negro to each). *Witnesses:* JOHN HARRELL, EASTHR CHITTAM. *Clerk of the Court:* BENJAMIN WYNNS.

WILLIAMS, JOHN.   Albemarle County.

January 29, 1727–1728. *Daughter:* MARY. *Brother:* NATHANIEL WILLIAMS (plantation). *Wife and Executrix:* SARAH. *Witnesses:* THOMAS and MARY PEIRCE, CHARLES CENMAN. *Clerk of the Court:* CHARLES DENMAN.

WILLIAMS, JOHN.

January 26, 1721. May 18, 1722. *Brothers:* THEOPHILUS, JAMES, ISAAC and ARTER WILLIAMS (lands at Runaroy). *Cousins:* JOHN WILLIAMS, ANTHONY HERRING. No executor named. *Witnesses:* JOHN and ANN WILLIAMS, MARY MONDS. Proven before THOS. POLLOCK, SENR.

WILLIAMS, JOHN.   Edgecombe County.

August Court, 1737. *Wife and Executrix:* ANN. *Sons:* JOHN and JOSHUA. *Daughter:* MARY. *Witnesses:* HENRY TANTON, THOMAS CARTA. *Clerk of the Court:* THOMAS KEARNY.

WILLIAMS, JOHN.   Bertie County.

March 13, 1745. January Court, 1758. *Sons:* ISAAC (one negro), ARTHUR ("my maner plantation"), THEOPHILUS (one negro). *Daughters:*

ANN HERRING, SARAH CASTELAW. *Grandson:* JOHN WILLIAMS. *Wife and Executrix:* ANN. *Witnesses:* WILLIAM BYRD, JOHN MOORE, THOMAS CASTELLAW. *Clerk of the Court:* BENJAMIN WYNNS.

WILLIAMS, JOSEPH.

1682. Will illegible.

WILLIAMS, JOSEPH.   Perquimans County.

June 28, 1772. *Sons:* JAMES and JOSEPH (plantation between Garrgut and the Mill Swamp "whereon I now live"), WILLIAM, NATHANIEL. *Daughters:* ELIZABETH, MARY and ANN WILLIAMS. *Wife and Executrix:* FRANCES. *Witnesses:* WILLIAM SKINNER, ROBERT HAINES, NICHOLAS BRAINER. *Clerk of the Court:* MILES HARVEY.

WILLIAMS, LEWIS.   Chowan County.

October 1, 1716. April 16, 1717. *Son:* ANTHONY. *Grandsons:* LEWIS WILLIAMS (land on Poplar Swamp), JOHN JONES, CHARLES SAWELL, JOSHUA PATCHETT. *Daughter:* PRISCILLA WEST (land on Katherine's Creek). *Wife and Executrix:* MARY (land at Catawatsky). *Witnesses:* WILLIAM CRANFORD, GRISSIE LITTLESON. *Clerk of the Court:* R. HICKS.

WILLIAMS, LODWICK.   Albemarle County.

November 7, 1684. December 1, 1684. *Son:* EDWARD. *Wife and Executrix:* HANNAH. *Witnesses:* THOMAS FRENCH, JOHN JONES. Proven before JOHN ARCHDALE.

WILLIAMS, LOTT.   Onslow County.

June 16, 1757. October Court, 1757. *Son:* BENJAMIN. *Daughter:* ANN. Negroes bequeathed to each. *Executors:* JESSE and OBED. WILLIAMS. *Witnesses:* BENJAMIN WILLIAMS, MOSES COX, JUNR., UZ WILLIAMS. *Clerk of the Court:* WILL CRAY.

WILLIAMS, MOAB.   Northampton County.

May 19, 1751. May Court, 1752. Lands on Potecasi Creek called the Roundabout, and also lands purchased of ROBERT EDWARDS. *Son:* DENTON (water mill and still). *Wife and Executrix:* SARAH WILLIAMS. *Father of wife:* JAMES DENTON (*Executor*). *Witnesses:* JOHN BROWN, ANNE WILLIAMS, JOHN THORN. *Clerk of the Court:* I. EDWARDS.

WILLIAMS, NATHAN.   Northampton County.

April 8, 1751. July Court, 1758. *Sons:* ELEY and NATHAN (lands on Plumtree and Cyprus Branch), THOMAS. *Daughters:* MARTHA WILLIAMS and four others, not named. *Wife and Executrix:* REBECCA (four negroes). *Witnesses:* CHAPLIN WILLIAMS, JOHN FORDHAM. *Clerk of the Court:* I. EDWARDS.

WILLIAMS, ROWLAND.   Northampton County.

March 8, 1754.   May Court, 1754.   *Son:* JOHN ("all my lands in North
Carolina").   *Daughters:* CASIAH BALL, MARTHA and LEWSY WILLIAMS.
Wife and Executrix: PHELIS.   *Witnesses:* WILLIAM ARMISTEAD, JAMES
WALLACE, FRA. JONES.   *Clerk of the Court:* I. EDWARDS.

WILLIAMS, SAMUEL.   Bertie Precinct.

April 16, 1736.   November Court, 1736.   *Legatees:* ELIZABETH and
SAMUEL WILLIAMS (children of GEORGE).   *Brother and Executor:* GEORGE.
Witnesses: JNO. SIMPSON, EDWARD HERRIN, WALTER PITTS.   *Clerk of the
Court:* JNO. WYNNS.

WILLIAMS, SAMUEL.   Edgecombe County.

November 18, 1748.   February Court, 1748.   *Sons:* SAMPSON and WIL-
LIAM (land "adjoining to the Taylor's in the Island as I leased of MRS.
JOHNSTON"), JACOB and GEORGE ("the manner plantation" and land on
Beaverdam Swamp), SAMUEL.   *Daughter:* CREESE WILLIAMS.   To sons
and daughter are bequeathed five negroes.   *Wife and Executrix:* JANE.
Witnesses: JOHN POPE, JOHN CRUDUP, MOURNING CRUDUP.   *Clerk of the
Court:* BENJAMIN WYNNS.

WILLIAMS, SAMUEL.   Edgecombe County.

October 21, 1753.   February Court, 1754.   *Sons:* WILLIAM, SOLOMON,
SAMUEL (land on Mush Island bought of ROBERT LANG), JOSEPH JOHN
WILLIAMS (about 800 acres of land bought of JOHN BURT and JOHN EGER-
TON, and adjoining YANCEY's line and the Reedy Branch).   To two last
named sons are devised 11 negroes.   *Grandson:* SAMUEL WILLIAMS.   *Wife:*
ELIZABETH.   *Executors:* PHILIP ALSTON and BENJAMIN WYNNS.   *Wit-
nesses:* THOMAS and EDMUND KEARNY, JAMES ALSTON.   *Clerk of the Court:*
BENJAMIN WYNNS.   Coat of arms on seal.

WILLIAMS, THOMAS.   Currituck County.

December 12, 1732.   Probate not dated.   *Sons:* SAMUEL (land called
the New Desire), JOSEPH (land on the Sand Banks).   *Wife:* MARY.   *Daughter:* MARY.   Negroes bequeathed to sons and daughter.   Wife appointed
Executrix.   *Witnesses:* MARGRET NORTON and CHARLY NORTON.   *Clerk of
the Court:* THOMAS LOWTHER.

WILLIAMS, THOMAS.   Beaufort County.

December 13, 1748.   December Court, 1753.   "Southwark Parish in the
County of Surry."   Will probated in Beaufort County, N. C.   *Wife and
Executrix:* ELIZABETH.   *Wife's children:* MARY WILLIAMS, WILLIAM FLAKE,
ARTHUR, ELIZABETH and ROBERT FLAKE.   *Witnesses:* CHAS. BINNS, WIL-
LIAM CLARK, JAMES CLARK, JOHN WILLIAMS, ROBERT FLAKE.   *Clerk of the
Court:* not given.

WILLIAMS, THOMAS. Beaufort County.

February 17, 1757. March Court, 1758. *Sons:* THOMAS (land on the East side of the mouth of Bath Town Creek, bought of WM. BAKER, and lot in Bath Town No. 39), CHARLES and JOHN (land in the fork of Cuckolds Creek), ROBERT. *Daughters:* TEMPERANCE, ANN, MARY, SARAH and HANAH WILLIAMS, ELIZABETH PRITCHARD. Land in the fork of Nevils Creek devised to *son,* CHARLES. Estate in England and Wales ordered divided among wife and children. *Wife and Executrix:* ANN. *Executors:* WYRIOTT ORMOND, JAMES ELLISON, COLEMAN ROE and THOMAS WILLIAMS. *Witnesses:* WILLIAM DOWD, JACOB NEVIL, JR., MOSES NEVIL. *Clerk of the Court:* WALLEY CHAUNCY.

WILLIAMS, WILLIAM. Currituck Precinct.

February 2, 1724–1725. No probate. *Sons:* THOMAS (plantation up Tulls Creek together with one negro), STEPHEN (land at the mouth of Tulls Creek), TULLE (land bought of WILLIAM SWANN together with one negro). To three sons is devised land up Tulls Creek called Long Leet. *Daughters:* JANE BRENT, ABIGAIL PHILLIPS (one negro to each). *Granddaughter:* MARY BRENT. *Grandson:* JONATHAN BRENT. To sons TULLE and STEPHEN is devised land called "Gibeses Island." *Wife and Executrix:* MARY. *Witnesses:* WILLIAM DAVIS, CHARLES BRENT, ROBERT ERVIN.

WILLIAMS, WILLIAM. Albemarle County.

December 9, 1711. April 15, 1712. *Wife and Executrix:* MARY. *Sons:* SAMUEL, JOHN (lands on Blak Water called Littel Town), STEVEN (lands). *Witnesses:* TREDELL KEEFE, LUIS WILLIAMS, ROBERT LANIER. *Clerk of the Court:* EDWARD BONWICKE.

WILLIAMS, WILLIAM. Edenton, Chowan County.

May 7, 1730. December 20, 1732. *Sons:* WILLIAM and THOMAS. *Daughters:* SARAH and ELIZABETH. *Wife and Executrix:* FRANCES. *Witnesses:* JAMES BREMEN, JOHN RICHARDS, JOHN MATTHEWS. Proven before GEO. BURRINGTON.

WILLIAMS, WILLIAM.

February 7, 1760. *Son:* JESSE. *Daughters:* ZELPHA and LUCY WILLIAMS. *Executor:* ISAAC BARRENTON. *Witnesses:* DAVID LEWIS, WILLIAM WEST, BENJAMIN WILLIAMS. No probate.

WILLIAMSON, CHARLES. Onslow County.

June 18, 1746. June 18, 1746. This is a nuncupative will proven before GABRIEL JOHNSTON by DANIEL RAYNER, JOHN SHEPHERD and SAMUEL RAYNER, and bequeaths all estate to *wife,* HANNAH.

WILLIAMSON, JOHN.   Onslow County.
  March 13, 1733–1734. October 2, 1734. New River. *Sons:* CHARLES
(land on southwest fork of New River), ZACHARY and JOHN (plantation on New River). *Daughter:* MARGARET. *Wife and Executrix:* ROSE.
Witnesses: ALLEXANDER FRAZER, PETER STARKEY, JOSEPH WATTS. *Clerk
of the Court:* WM. CRANFORD.

WILLIAMSON, RICHARD.   Carteret Precinct.
  January 15, 1723. *Sons:* WILLIAM, JOHN (land on White Oak River).
Daughters: MARY, JANE and ANNE WILLIAMSON. *Wife and Executrix:*
JANE. *Executors:* ENOCH WARD, JOHN STARKEY, JOHN ROBERTS, SARAH
and NATHANIEL PIGOTT. No probate.

WILLIS, WILLIAM.   Beaufort County.
  Will so torn as to be illegible.

WILLOUGHBY, THOMAS.   Pasquotank County.
  June 6, 1753. July Court, 1753. *Half-brother:* THOMAS EVINS. *Wife
and Executrix:* ANN. *Witnesses:* SOLOMON POOL, JOHN BAYLEY, PATRICK
POOL. *Clerk of the Court:* THOS. TAYLOR.

WILSON, CHARLES.
  County and all dates missing. *Witnesses:* COLEMAN ROE, EDETH ODEON.
Will illegible.

WILLSON, ELIZABETH.   Perquimans County.
  Only a portion of this will is found, and mentions *sons,* JAMES, ISAAC
and ROBERT. All dates missing.

WILLSON, ELIZABETH.
  December 18, 1753. Will so torn as to be illegible.

WILLSON, ISAAC.   Perquimans County.
  June 13, 1714. July 13, 1714. *Sons:* BENJAMIN, ROBERT and ISAAC.
Daughter: ANN. *Wife and Executrix:* ANN. *Witnesses:* JA. CAVANA,
THOMAS WILKISON. *Clerk of the Court:* HENRY CLAYTON.

WILLSON, MARGARET.
  April 14, 1706. *Daughters:* ELENOR and MARY. *Witnesses:* JOHN
DUNN, MATTHEW BRAYE, HANNAH WHITLOCK. Proven before PHIL.
TORKSEY.

WILLSON, ISAAC.   Perquimans Precinct.
  October 3, 1724. December 29, 1724. *Brothers:* ROBERT and BENJA-
MIN WILLSON. *Nephews:* JOSEPH WILLSON, ISAAC WILLSON (plantation

on Perquimans River "where CAPT. PETTIVER now lives"). *Niece:* RACHEL WILLSON. *Other legatees:* JOSEPH and THOMAS ELLIOTT. *Mother:* ANN PETTIVER. *Uncle and Executor:* RALPH BOZMAN. *Witnesses:* RUTH MINGE, ROBERT MORE, ELIZABETH FLOWER. Proven before EDWARD MOSELEY.

WILLSON, ROBERT. Perquimans Precinct.

April 28, 1693. January 11, 1696. *Grandchildren:* ROBERT and ANN WILLSON, SARAH and ESTER BELMAN. *Son:* ISAAC. *Daughter:* SARAH BELMAN. *Wife and Executrix:* ANN. Plantation devised to son, location of land not given. *Witnesses:* JOHN COPELAND, RICHD. RATCLYFE, ELIZABETH RATCLYFE. Proven before JOHN ARCHDALE, DANIEL AKEHURST, FRANCIS TOMES and SAMUEL SWANN, Justices of Court, sitting at house of SAMUEL SWANN.

WILLSON, SAMUEL. Onslow County.

October 13, 1758. April Court, 1759. *Wife and Executrix:* SARAH. *Nephew:* SAML. WILSON, son of brother ROBART, decd., "in Penselvany." *Witnesses:* EZEKIEL HUNTER, LEBBEUS HUNTER, REBKAH HUNTER. *Clerk of the Court:* WILLM. CRAY.

WILLSON, SARAH. Pasquotank County.

January 2, 1751–1752. April Court, 1754. *Sons:* WILLIAM, BENJAMIN (one negro), THOMAS (one negro). *Daughters:* REBECKAH FURBUSH, ELIZABETH BARTLET. *Executors:* BENJAMIN and THOMAS (sons). *Witnesses:* WILLIAM BARNARD, SAMUEL LOWMAN. *Clerk of the Court:* THOMAS TAYLOR.

WILLSON, WILLIAM. Tyrrell County.

June 19, 1740. June Court, 1741. *Sons:* PATTESON (land called Aoses), WILLIAM and THOMAS (land bought of CORNELIOUS FITCHPATRICK), BENJAMIN (land bought of BENJAMIN ALEXANDER). *Daughters:* REBECKA, SARAH and ROSAMAN (land called Pope land), MARY SCARBOROUGH, ELIZABETH BARCLIFTE. *Wife and Executrix:* SARAH (use of all negroes). *Witnesses:* BENJAMIN BIDGOOD, WILLIAM RAPYULD, BENJAMIN ALEXANDER. *Clerk of the Court:* W. DOWNING.

WILLSON, WILLIAM. Northampton County.

January 1, 1745. No probate. *Sons:* JOHN, ISAAC (land on south side of Tarr River), ELISHA MOORE WILSON. *Daughters:* CHARITY, ANNE, KATHERINE, ELINOR and MARY WILLSON. Negroes bequeathed to above-named. *Wife:* JUDITH. *Executor:* JOHN EDWARDS. *Witnesses:* ABRM. HOOD, JOHN GOODALL, MICHAEL TURNER.

WILSON, CALEB.   Currituck County.

1754. September Court, 1754. *Sons:* JAMES (land inherited from father, land bought of THOMAS BURGES, land bought of brother, JOSIAH WILSON, eight negroes and one silver tankard and gold ring), TATUM and WILLIAM (three negroes to each). *Nephew:* DANIEL SWEENEY. To son WILLIAM are bequeathed seven negroes and one gold ring. *Daughter:* LOVE WILSON (lands bought of THOMAS LOWTHER and "the Muncreefs," and five negroes). To TATUM is devised land bought of FRANCIS ETHERIDGE, BENJAMIN CROWELL, JOHN HUGHES and JOSEPH COOPER and seven negroes. Seven negroes over and above what had been already bequeathed are bequeathed to four children. *Wife and Executrix:* SARAH. *Executors:* JOSIAH WILSON (brother) and DANIEL SWEENEY. *Witnesses:* DREW HOLSTEAD, THOS. BURGES, MALACHI WILSON, JOS. NORBURY, WM. BLUNT. *Clerk of the Court:* JNO. SNOAD.

WILSON, ISAAC.   Perquimans County.

October 30, 1749. April Court, 1751. *Sons:* ROBERT, JAMES. *Daughters:* RACHEL and MIRIAM WILLSON. *Wife and Executrix:* ELIZABETH. *Witnesses:* JACOB PERRY, SENR., JACOB PERRY, ISRAEL PERRY. *Clerk of the Court:* EDMUND HATCH.

WILSON, JOSEPH.   Perquimans County.

April 24, 1752. July Court, 1752. *Daughters:* ELIZABETH (land on Wilson's Creek), MARY (land adjoining MATTHEW PRITCHARD). *Son:* REUBEN ("maner plantation"). *Wife and Executrix:* MARY. *Executor:* ROBERT NEWBY. *Witnesses:* JACOB WILSON, WILLIAM TOWNSEND, RACHEL WINSLOW. *Clerk of the Court:* EDMUND HATCH.

WILSON, PATTISON.   Pasquotank County.

March 15, 1746. July 12, 1746. *Son:* WILLIAM. *Daughter:* MARY. *Wife and Executrix:* ELIZABETH. *Executor:* WILLIAM WILSON (brother). *Witnesses:* JOHN SCARBROUGH, JOHN BELL, JOHN SQUIERS. *Clerk of the Court:* THOS. TAYLOR.

WILSON, ROBERT.   Albemarle County.

February 26, 1693. December Court, 1697. *Son:* ISAIAH WILSON. *Grandchildren:* ROBERT and ANN WILSON, SARAH and HESTER BOLMAN. *Son:* ISAACK WILSON. *Executrix:* ANN WILSON. *Witnesses:* JOHN COPELAND, RICHD. RATCLIFF, ELIZ. RATCLIFF. *Clerk of the Court:* W. GLOVER.

WILSON, ROBERT.   Pasquotank County.

April 22, 1757. June Court, 1758. Nixonton. *Grandsons:* RUBEN WILSON (lands between Reedy Branch and Ferry Causey), OBED. WINSLOW (land at Grassie Point), CALEB WINSLOW (land known by the name of the

Glade). *Sons:* ISAAC and SILVANUS. *Daughter:* RACHEL TOWNSEND. *Granddaughters:* ELISABETH and MARY WILSON (lands on Reedy Branch, etc.). Negroes bequeathed to granddaughters. *Executor:* BARNABY NIXON, JACOB WINSLOW. *Witnesses:* WILLIAM, GEORGE and ELISABETH WOOD. *Clerk of the Court:* THO. TAYLOR.

WILTON, WILLIAM.   Craven County.
    January 7, 1773. New Bern. *Wife:* JANE. *Executors:* TIMOTHY CLEAR, JOHN GREEN, WILLIAM RUMSEY. *Witnesses:* JOSEPH DOWSE, JOHN MACE, JAMES BIGGLESTON. Proven before Jo. MARTIN.

WIMBERLEY, JOHN.   Bertie County.
    September 2, 1742. November Court, 1749. *Sons:* EZEKIEL, BENJAMIN, JOHN, LEVY, MOSES (land and negroes bequeathed to sons). *Wife:* ELIZABETH. *Executors:* THOMAS WIMBERLEY (brother), JOHN SMITH (brother-in-law). *Clerk of the Court:* JOHN LOVICK.

WIMBERLY, THOMAS.   Bertie Precinct.
    October 22, 1731. February Court, 1732. *Sons:* GEORGE (land on Swift Creek and Tar River), JOSEPH (land between Tar River and Swift Creek). *Daughter:* SARAH WIMBERLEY. *Wife:* SUSANA. *Executors:* GEORGE and JOSEPH WIMBERLEY (sons). Negroes bequeathed to wife. *Witnesses:* JOHN DUFFIELD, SAMUEL WILLIAMS, ELINOR BRASWELL. *Clerk of the Court:* RT. FORSTER.

WIMBERLY, THOMAS.   Bertie County.
    January 27, 1751. February Court, 1752. *Sons:* ABRAHAM and six others mentioned, but not named. *Daughter:* JUDITH. *Wife and Executrix:* MARY. *Witnesses:* NEEDHAM BRYAN, WILLIAM LEVENER (?). *Clerk of the Court:* SAMUEL ORMES.

WINDLEY, ROBERT.   Albemarle County.
    July 31, 1688. Probate illegible. *Son and Executor:* WILLIAM. *Daughter:* LIDIA. *Other legatees:* JOHN PERRY, GEORGE PERRY, JOHN and ELIZABETH EATON. *Witnesses:* EDWARD and ELIZABETH SMITHWICK.

WINFELD, RICHARD.
    April 3, 1733. September 12, 1733. *Daughter:* ABIGALL, SUSANA, ELISABETH, MARY, ANNE, PRUDENCE. *Sons:* ROBERT and JOHN. *Wife and Executrix:* MARY. *Witnesses:* ROBERT SPRING, WILLIAM GRAY, JONAS WINFIELD. *Clerk of the Court:* JNO. COLLISON. *Justices of the Court at Bath Town:* ROBERT TURNER, BENJAMIN PEYTON, HENRY CROPTON.

27

WINGATE, SAMUEL.

January 9, 1770.   January 19, 1770.   "Formerly of Cape Fear but Now resident in the Island of Grenada."   *Wife and Executrix:* ALICE.   Schooner "Charming Peggy" ordered sent to CORNELIUS HARNET in Cape Feare to be sold for benefit of wife.   *Executor:* JOHN KNIGHT.   *Witnesses:* JOHN O'DONNELL, JOHN MACKEAND, ELIAS HOWELL.   Will proven before ULYSSES FITZMAURICE, "Lieutenant-Governor and Commander-in-Chief in and over the Southern Carribee Islands."   Proven in North Carolina before WILLIAM TRYON.   Executrix qualified before FREDERICK GREGG.   Impression of head on seal.

WINHAM, ROBERT.   Craven County.

January 19, 1754.   November Court, 1753.   *Wife and Executrix:* MARY (land on Broad Creek).   *Son:* WILLIAM.   *Executor:* JOHN LENFIELD.   *Witnesses:* ROBERT BIERNEY, WILLIAM WILLIAMS, KAZIA WILLIAMS.   *Clerk of the Court:* PETER CONWAY.

WINN, JOHN.   Pasquotank County.

December 18, 1739.   January Court, 1739.   *Son:* EZEKIAH.   *Daughter:* ELISABETH WINN.   *Nephew:* DANIEL TEMPLE.   *Sister:* BEETY WINN.   *Wife and Executrix:* DINAH.   *Executors:* ABEL ROSS and WILLOUGHBY PRICE.   *Witnesses:* WILL CRETCH, DANIEL TEMPLE, BETEY WINN.   *Clerk of the Court:* JAMES CRAVEN.

WINRIGHT, JAMES.   Carteret County.

August 13, 1744.   March Court, 1744.   Lands on Newport River between MR. LOVICK and DAVID SHEPARD ordered sold.   Land on Newport River called Newfoundland devised to wife, ANN, together with all negroes owned by testator.   Lots in Beaufort Town bought of JOHN PINDAR devised to wife.   *Sister:* ELIZABETH WHITE of Boston.   *Other legatees:* ELIZABETH and SUSANNAH MABSON, ANN (wife of JAMES BLOUNT), THOMAS FLYBUS.   Rents and profits of land and houses in Beaufort Town to be applied "for the encouragement of a sober Discreet Quallified Man to teach a School at Least Reading Writing Vulgar and Decimal Arithmetick in the aforesaid town of Beaufort, which said man shall be chosen and appointed by the Chairman of the Cartret County Court, etc."   *Other legatees:* THOMAS LOVICK, ROBERT READ, GEORGE READ, ARTHUR MABSON, WILLIAM WHITE (boat and sails), JAMES MALIN.   Lands on Suttons Creek ordered sold.   *Executors:* THOMAS LOVICK and GEORGE READ.   *Witnesses:* DAVID SHEPARD, DAVID SHEPARD "younger," WILLIAM DENNIS.   *Clerk of the Court:* GEORGE READ.

WINSHIP, JOSEPH.   Currituck County.

April 2, 1733. January Court, 1746. *Wife and Executrix:* APPELONE. *Witnesses:* JOHN COX, JOHN WILLIAMS, NICHOLAS LUND, SAM. WILLIAMS. *Clerk of the Court:* RICHD. MCCLURE.

WINSLOW, JOHN.   Perquimans County.

January 25, 1753. *Daughters:* ELIZABETH, HANNAH and EASTER. *Sons:* BENJAMIN and ISRAEL (lands divided between them), JOHN and JOSEPH. *Wife and Executrix:* EASTER. *Witnesses:* NICHOLAS STALLINGS, JOSHUA and THOMAS WHITE. *Clerk of the Court:* MILES HARVEY.

WINSLOW, JOHN.   Perquimans County.

April 17, 1754. July Court, 1754. *Sons:* JOSIAH (one negro), THOMAS and SAMUEL (lands divided between them). *Daughter:* MIRIAM. *Wife and Executrix:* MARY. *Witnesses:* WILLIAM WEEKES, THOMAS WEEKES, JR., BENJAMIN ROBERTS. *Clerk of the Court:* RICHARD CLAYTON.

WINSLOW, JOSEPH.   Perquimans County.

September 26, 1750. January Court, 1750. *Son:* JOSEPH (land on Core Neck). *Daughters:* LYDIA WINSLOW (lands near head of Little River), MARY WINSLOW, MIRIAM WINSLOW (land called Grassy Ridge). Negroes bequeathed to son. *Wife and Executrix:* PLEASANT. *Executors:* WILLIAM WHITE and FRANCIS TOMS. *Witnesses:* JOSHUA HOBART, TRUMAN MOORE, JOHN ROBERTSON. *Clerk of the Court:* EDMUND HATCH.

WINSLOW, THOMAS.   Perquimans County.

January 9, 1744. January Court, 1745. *Sons:* THOMAS and TIMOTHY (negro to each), JOHN (1 negro), JOB (plantation in Pasquotank County near Newbegun Creek). *Daughters:* ELIZABETH and MIRIAM (negroes to each). *Executors:* THOMAS and JOBE WINSLOW (sons). *Witnesses:* THOMAS HOLLOWELL, JOSIAH BOGUE, TRUMAN MOORE. *Clerk of the Court:* EDMUND HATCH.

WINSLOW, THOMAS.   Perquimans County.

January 21, 1746–1747. April Court, 1747. *Sons:* JESSE, THOMAS ("my manah plantation"). Negroes are bequeathed to above-named sons. *Daughter:* ELIZABETH WINSLOW. *Wife and Executrix:* SARAH. *Executors:* FRANCIS TOMES and ZACHARIAH NIXON. *Witnesses:* ABRAHAM ELLIOT and MARY WINSLOW. *Clerk of the Court:* EDMUND HATCH.

WINSLOW, TIMOTHY.   Perquimans County.

April 26, 1752. July Court, 1752. *Sons:* JACOB, TIMOTHY, OBED (land to each), CALEB (land on Little River). *Daughter:* MARY WINSLOW.

To sons and daughter are bequeathed negroes. *Wife and Executrix:* RACHEL. *Executor:* JOHN WINSLOW (brother). *Witnesses:* ESTHER WINSLOW, SARAH ELLIOT, THOMAS NEWBY. *Clerk of the Court:* EDMUND HATCH.

WINTER, JOSEPH.   Bath County.

December 1, 1735. December 12, 1735. *Executrix and sole legatee:* MARGRETT PENDERGEST. *Witnesses:* RICHD. RIGBY, ROBERT CONLAHANE, MARGRETT RIGBY. *Clerk of the Court:* JNO. COLLISON.

WINWRIGHT, ANN.   Carteret County.

March 7, 1751. June Court, 1751. Newport River. *Legatees:* SARAH and BETSEY (daughters of THOS. LOVICK), SARAH (wife of THOMAS LOVICK), PENELOPE LOVICK, SARAH BENNERS (mulatto boy), GEORGE PHENIS LOVICK, JOHN BENNERS. *Executors:* SARAH and PENELOPE LOVICK. *Witnesses:* JOHN BENNERS, DAVID EVANS. *Clerk of the Court:* GEORGE READ.

WOOD, EDWARD.   Chowan Precinct.

August 9, 1691. *Wife:* ALICE (land at Yaupim). *Executor:* FRANCIS HARDLEY. *Witnesses:* SAML. PRICKLOVE, JOHN SLOCOMB, ROBERT MELLYNE. No probate.

WOOD, EDWARD.   Onslow Precinct.

April 5, 1728. January 2, 1738. *Sons:* WILLIAM (lands on Harrys Creek), EDWARD (lands known as Broad Neck). To son WILLIAM is bequeathed cattle branded with his brand "as by record may appear." *Daughters:* SARAH and BETHIA. *Mother:* MARY. *Wife and Executrix:* ANN. *Other legatee:* DANLL. RAINER. *Witnesses:* JNO. MURFREY, JOHN MOORE, ELINOR MURFREY. *Clerk of the Court:* WILLIAM CRANFORD.

WOOD, JAMES, SR.   Northampton County.

June 25, 1751. March 18, 1752. Northwest Parish. *Sons:* JAMES (lands on Cuttowhisky Marsh and pasture lands on Cuttowhisky Swamp, together with five negro slaves), JOSEPH (land on Cuttowhisky, together with six negroes), JONAS ("plantation whereon I now live" on Cuttowhisky Marsh, together with six negroes and a still), MOSES (one shilling). Plantation at Coniritratt given to three sons. *Daughters:* ELIZABETH, SUSANNAH and MARY WOOD, MARY OUTLAW, SARAH DUFFIELD, ANN and CHARITY WOOD, ROSANNAH BOND, WINNY WOOD (negroes given to above-named daughters). *Sister:* SARAH KILLINGSWORTH. *Executors:* JOSEPH and JONAS WOOD (sons). *Witnesses:* BARNABA BAGGOTT, JOHN PARKER, WM. FRYER. Proven before GAB. JOHNSTON at Eden House.

WOOD, JOHN.   Johnston County.

August 4, 1748. June Court, 1750. *Daughters:* ALICE, MARY and ESTHER. *Son:* JOHN (land, cattle, etc.). *Wife:* JANE. *Executors:* JOHN WOOD (son) and JOHN SMITH. *Witnesses:* ROBERT and ANN BUTLER, WILLIAM BUTLER. *Clerk of the Court:* R. CASWELL. Courthouse on Walnut Creek.

WOOD, MOSES.   Bertie County.

March 8, 1757. April Court, 1757. *Brother:* JAMES WOOD, Executor. *Sister:* SARAH BAKER. *Witnesses:* THOMAS BAKER, JONATHAN WOOD, JOSEPH FARMER, THOS. CREW. *Clerk of the Court:* BENJAMIN WYNNS.

WOOD, THOMAS.   Hyde County.

July 19, 1740. December Court, 1740. *Sons:* SCARBROUGH (plantation), RICHARD, ABRAHAM and ISAAC. *Daughters:* RACHEL and SARAH WOOD. *Wife and Executrix:* NAOMI. *Witnesses:* URIAH COLLINS, LEMUEL WHYN, MARTHA WHYN. *Clerk of the Court:* W. BARROW.

WOOD, WILLIAM.   Pasquotank County.

November 4, 1732. April 15, 1733. *Friend and Executor:* ROBERT CARTRITT. *Witnesses:* ALEXANDER SPENCE, JER. SYMONS. Proven before GEO. BURRINGTON.

WOODHOUSE, HENRY.   Currituck County.

November 27, 1750. April Court, 1751. *Son:* HEZEKIAH (land and negroes). *Wife:* CESIAH (six negroes). *Daughter:* MARY WEST (three negroes). *Daughter-in-law:* MARY JARVES. *Friend:* ABRAHAM LEACH-FIELD. *Witnesses:* JOHN WOODHOUSE, THOMAS LURRY, PETER BAWM. *Clerk of the Court:* RICHARD MCCLURE.

WOODHOUSE, HORATIO.   Onslow County.

January 28, 1755. July Court, 1755. *Wife and Executrix:* CATHERINE. *Son:* JOHN (three negroes). *Daughter:* ALISS HAINES (wife of ERASMUS HAINES of Va.). *Executors:* HENRY RODES and WILLIAM CRAY. *Witnesses:* HENRY MOORE, CASSON MOORE, WM. WILLIAMS. *Clerk of the Court:* WILL CRAY.

WOODNOT, HENRY.   Chowan Precinct.

December 29, 1718. June 29, 1719. *Legatees:* ROBERT BELL (one negro), ISABELL FERGUSON (daughter of ANNE FERGUSON "and now the wife of ROBERT BELL"). Above-named legatees appointed Executors. *Witnesses:* ARTHUR DUGALL, THOMAS ROGERS, JAMES CASTELLAW. Proven before CHARLES EDEN.

WOODROW, ALEXANDER.

June 12, 1754. September 6, 1759. Wilmington. *Mother:* JEAN
WOODROW, of the City of Edenburgh. *Executor:* BENJAMIN MORRISON.
Witnesses: ALEX. MCALESTER, JOHN CAMPBELL, ALEXR. MCGILLIVRAY.
Clerk of the Court: A. MACLAINE.

WOODS, THOMAS.   Northampton County.

October 20, 1751. November Court, 1751. *Son:* JESSE. *Daughter:*
ANN WOODS. *Wife:* MARY. *Witnesses:* CHARLES COUNSELL, ANDREW
TAYLOR, MICHAEL COUNCILL. *Clerk of the Court:* I. EDWARDS.

WOOLARD, RICHARD.

January 22, 1706–1707. April 8, 1707. *Sons:* JOHN and RICHARD.
Daughters: HANNAH BOROS, ANN WOOLARD. *Wife and Executrix:* JANE.
Witnesses: JAMES WARD, WM. BREATHET, JNO. ALLCOCK. *Clerk of the
Court:* THOS. SNODEN.

WOLFENDEN, JOHN.   Perquimans County.

September 4, 1691. No probate. *Executor:* RICHARD EVANS. *Witnesses:* JOHN LILLY, STEPHEN MANWARING.

WOODARD, JOHN.   Bath County.

November 21, 1734. St. Thomas Parish. *Sons:* HENRY (land "adjoin-
ing the school house"), JOHN ("manner plantation"). *Daughter:* MARY
WOODARD (plantation on Pamplyco River). *Brother:* JOEL WOODARD.
Other legatee: ELIZABETH CORTNEY. *Executors:* WILLIAM MARTIN and
HENRY LUCAS. *Witnesses:* ROBERT SHEARD, HENRY ODOM, ELIZABETH
CORTNEY. *Overseers:* EDWARD SALTER and JOHN ODOM. No probate.

WOODLEY, THOMAS.   Pasquotank County.

March 20, 1752. January Court, 1753. *Grandchildren:* WILLIAM,
THOMAS, MARY, ELIZABETH and PEGGY TAYLOR. *Daughters:* MARY
SPEIGHT, ELIZABETH TAYLOR. *Son:* WILLIAM (lands and negroes).
Executors: THOMAS TAYLOR, WILLIAM GREGORY, WILLIAM WOODLEY
(son). *Witnesses:* JONATHAN REDING, JAMES PRICHARD, THOMAS TWEEDY.
Clerk of the Court: THOS. TAYLOR.

WOODWARD, SAMUELL.   Chowan County.

March 13, 1752. April Court, 1752. *Sons:* SAMUEL (250 acres of
land). EDWARD, RICHARD (negroes to each). *Daughter:* ELIZABETH
WHITE (negroes). *Wife:* SARAH. To sons is bequeathed tar—118 barrels. *Executors:* SAMUEL WOODWARD, LUKE WHITE. *Witnesses:* CHARLES
ROBERTS, RICHARD WOODWARD. *Clerk of the Court:* JAMES CRAVEN.

WOOLWARD, WILLIAM.   Albemarle County.
November 12, 1684. February 2, 1691–1692. *Wife:* SARAH. *Granddaughter:* MARGRETT HOLLBROCK. *Executor:* EDWARD WADE. *Witnesses:* GEORGE GUNNETTE, HENRY GOODMAN, HENRY BONNER, WILLIAM
CHARELTON, NICHOLAS DAW. *Clerk of the Court:* RICHARD PLATER.

WOMBWELL, BENJAMIN.   Beaufort County.
November 5, 1750. March Court, 1750. *Sons:* NATHAN, WILLIAM,
BENJAMIN and JORDAN (land on Tison's Creek). Land in "Miana Gov-
ernment in South Hampton" devised to Executors. *Wife and Executrix:*
ANNE. *Executor:* BENJAMIN BROWN. *Witnesses:* JOS. BARROW, JOHN
EVANS. *Clerk of the Court:* WILLIAM ORMOND.

WORDEN, JAMES.   Chowan County.
April 23, 1755. July Court, 1755. *Sons:* JOHN (saddle, clothes and
silver buckles), JAMES and WILLIAM ("such money as will buy him a
small Bible and pair of silver shoe buckles" to each). *Executor:* JOHN
HALSEY. *Witnesses:* STEPHEN and ELENER CREECH. *Clerk of the Court:*
THOMAS JONES. Coat of arms on seal.

WORKMAN, ARTHUR.
August 1, 1695. April 19, 1697. "Late of Jamaica but now of
Ronoch." *Legatees:* CAPT. JOHN HUNT (one silver tankard, value of
twelve pounds), MRS. ELIZABETH HUNT (gold mourning ring), ANTHONY
HATCH, son of MRS. ELIZABETH HUNT (plantation on Little River), JOHN
ROBINSON, CHARLES SADLER of Jamaica, THOMAS SHERWOOD of Jamaica,
MARY and MILLESAINT WORKMMAN (sisters, all estate in Kingdom of
Ireland), SARAH and HENRY FRANKLIN, MARY CLERKE (*Executrix*),
widow of JOHN CLERKE. *Witnesses:* JOHN HUNTT, JOHN ROBISON, RICH-
ARD PLATER, JOHN LEGG. *Clerk of the Court:* EDWARD MAYO.

WORLEY, JOHN.   Tyrrell County.
February 8, 1740–1741. March 3, 1740. *Son:* JOSHUA ("my maner
plantation"). *Daughters:* ELIZABETH LURRY (three negroes), PENELOPE
WEIGHT (cattle, "crop in ye right Eare and over Caele in left"). *Grand-
son:* JOHN NORCOMB (or NORKOM). *Executors:* JOSHUA WORLEY, THOMAS
LURREY and WILLIAM WEIGHT. *Witnesses:* EBENEZER SLAD, JOHN and
JANE ROGERS. Proven before W. SMITH, C. J.

WORLEY, LOVICK.   Tyrrell County.
January 24, 1754. March Court, 1754. *Daughter:* ANN GRAY WOR-
LEY. *Wife and Executrix:* ANN WORLEY. *Brother:* JOHN WORLEY.
Brother-in-law: WILLIAM GRAY. *Sisters-in-law:* LUCRETIA, AMELIA and

LOUISA GRAY. *Executors:* JAMES BLOUNT (uncle), THOMAS WHITMELL. *Witnesses:* DAVID JERNIGAN, THOMAS KINSY, DAVID CANADAY. *Clerk of the Court:* EVAN JONES.

WORSLEY, JOHN. Beaufort County.

1750. Probate not dated. *Sons:* ABRAHAM and STEPHEN. *Daughter:* DORCAS. *Wife and Executrix:* not named. *Witnesses:* JNO. BARROW, SAMUEL BARROW, LYDIA ODEON. *Clerk of the Court:* PHTT. PRITCHETT.

WORSLEY, JOHN.

October 17, 1760. *Half-brothers:* LEWIS BRYAN, ISAAC, THOMAS, WILLIAM, HARDY and NATHAN BRYAN. *Half-sister:* MARY BRYAN. *Mother:* SARAH BRYAN (Executrix). To above-named are bequeathed negroes, lands and horses. *Witnesses:* JOHN STEVENS, FREDERICK ISLER, FREDERICK BECTON. No probate.

WORSLEY, THOMAS. Bath County.

January 18, 1737. March Court, 1737. *Sons:* THOMAS (lands on Swift Creek), JOSEPH (lands on Swift Creek), JOHN (lands on Bear Creek). Negroes divided between sons. *Cousin:* RICHARD CLEMENS. *Wife:* SARAH. *Executors:* JOHN HODGSON, THOMAS and JOSEPH BLOUNT. *Witnesses:* R. EVERARD, PHILIP WILLIAMS, JOHN CALDOM. *Clerk of the Court:* ROGER JONES. Impression of lion rampant on seal.

WORTH, JOHN. Bladen County.

August 1, 1743. September Court, 1743. *Father:* JOHN WORTH, of New Jersey. *Sister:* ELIZABETH. *Cousin and Executor:* JOSEPH CLARK of New Hanover County. *Witnesses:* THOMAS WAMAN, E. VERNON, JOHN WILLIAMSON. *Clerk of the Court:* JOHN CLAYTON. Executor qualified before SAMUEL BAKER. Impression of dog on seal.

WOTSFORD, JOSEPH. Bertie County.

July 27, 1737. November Court, 1739. *Sons:* JOHN ("my mannor plantation"), JOSEPH. *Daughters:* MARY WOTSFORD, ELIZABETH VALLENTINE. *Other legatee:* MARTHA MAYNOR. *Wife and Executrix:* ELINOR. *Trustee:* WM. WESSON (brother). *Witnesses:* JNO. WYNNS, BENJAMIN HARGROVE, EDWARD TIDMON. *Clerk of the Court:* JOHN WYNNS.

WRIGHT, AUGUSTINE. Pasquotank County.

May 27, 1741–1742. April Court, 1742. *Brothers:* WILLIAM and CHARLES. *Mother and Executrix:* ELIZABETH. *Witnesses:* JOHN MARTIN, JOHN BROWN. *Clerk of the Court:* THOMAS TAYLOR.

WRIGHT, JOHN.   New Hanover County.

May 30, 1747. *Son:* SAMUEL. *Daughter:* SARAH WRIGHT. *Wife and Executrix:* ANN. *Witnesses:* JOHN LYON, WILLIAM VERNON, JOHN MERRICK. No probate.

WRIGHT, SAMUEL.   Perquimans Precinct.

September 9, 1717. July 29, 1718. *Sons:* THOMAS (land on Little River), SAMUEL. *Wife and Executrix:* not named. *Witnesses:* THOMAS STAFFORD, GEORGE GORDEN. *Clerk of the Court:* R. HICKS.

WRIGHT, SAMUEL.   Perquimans County.

March 6, 1754. April Court, 1754. *Sons:* THOMAS and SAMUEL. *Daughters:* MARY and HANNAH WRIGHT. *Wife and Executrix:* ELIZABETH. *Executor:* NATHANIEL WELCH. *Witnesses:* HANNER ELLET, JEMIME DOWDY, ISAAC SITTERSON. *Clerk of the Court:* RICHARD CLAYTON.

WYNNS, WILLIAM.   Bertie County.

December 3, 1757. April Court, 1758. *Wife and Executrix:* ELIZABETH. *Daughter:* PENELOPE. *Son:* "unnamed." *Executors:* BENJAMIN WYNNS (brother), JOHN HARRELL. *Witnesses:* THOMAS BONNIFANT, GEO. WYNNS, WILLIAM BARTON. *Clerk of the Court:* BENJAMIN WYNNS. Coat of arms on seal.

WYNNS, GEORGE.   Bertie County.

February 2, 1750–1751. May Court, 1751. *Sons:* JOHN (two negroes), JOSEPH (one negro), BENJAMIN (three negroes), WILLIAM (three negroes), GEORGE (lands and five negroes, copper brandy still). *Daughter:* MARY SESSUMS, wife of CULMEN SESSUMS (one negro); SARAH, wife of PETER EVANS (one negro). *Wife:* ROSE. *Executors:* BENJAMIN and WILLIAM (sons). *Witnesses:* JNO. BAKER, THOS. LEE, JNO. HARRELL, JAS. BOON. *Clerk of the Court:* SAMUEL ORMES.

WYNNS, JOHN.   Bertie County.

February 10, 1750. May Court, 1753. "Winnson." *Sons:* JAMES BOON ("the mannour plantation" and two negroes), WATKIN WILLIAM (Ferry plantation, and land called Blind Islands), JOHN AUGUSTUS (land called Bridge Neck, 400 acres of "lightwood land" and two negroes). *Daughters:* MARY ANNE (lands bought of PEEKE and HALLUM, and two negroes), SARAH AMELIA (plantation called Morrises and Cuba, and two negro slaves), WYNNEY CAROLINE (land called Sharpe's Neck, and two negroes). *Wife and Executrix:* SARAH. *Executors:* BENJAMIN and WILLIAM WYNNS (brothers), JAMES BOONE and WATKIN WILLIAM WYNNS (sons). *Witnesses:* JOS. WYNNS, STEPHN. HOOKER, WILLIAM HOOKER, JUNR., EPHRAIM HUNTER, BENJAMIN BASKER. *Clerk of the Court:* BENJAMIN WYNNS.

YEATS, JAMES.   Carteret County.

November 8, 1750. March Court, 1750. *Wife and Executrix:* MARY.
Executor: GEO. READ. *Witnesses:* MARY STEM, SAMUEL O'STEEN, GEO.
MCKEAN. *Clerk of the Court:* GEORGE READ.

YEATS, WILLIAM.   Bertie County.

December 3, 1751. May Court, 1752. *Daughters:* MARY YEATES,
SUSANNAH PIPKIN, MARTHA LANGSTON (one negro), JUDITH YEATES
(one negro), AMY YEATES (one negro). *Sons:* WILLIAM, ROBERT (land
n Bertie on Pottecasi Creek), RICHARD (land in Bertie on Blew Water
Branch and Raccoon Marsh adjoining BRYAN HARE; also one negro
man), CHARLES (land in Bertie on Cuttewhiski Swamp), DANIEL ("my
plantation"). *Wife and Executrix:* MARY. *Witnesses:* JNO. BRICKELL,
ISAAC CARTER, BRYAN HARE. *Clerk of the Court:* SAMUEL ORMES.

YOUNG, GEORGE.

March 12, 1696. 1698. *Son:* FOSTER. *Daughters:* ANN and MARY.
Friend: WM. LEDFORD. *Wife and Executrix:* PROTHESIA. *Witnesses:*
WILLIAM LEDFORD, SENIOR, WILLIAM LUDFORD, JUNIOR, HUMPHREY
LEGG. *Clerk of the Court:* N. CHEVIN.

SUPPLEMENT.

Records of the following wills were found after the foregoing pages had been printed:

ANSWELL (ANSELL or ANCELL), JAMES.   Currituck County.

September 12, 1738. April Court, 1740. *Son and Executor:* JOHN. *Daughter:* SARAH ROBERTS. *Grandson:* JAMES ROBERTS. "* * * My will and desire is that the negro wench called ESTOR which I gave to my son JOHN ANSELL by Deed be Sett att liberty During the term of sixty years and in case my Son JOHN should not allow her my Desire then all that I have given to him I give to my Daughter SARAH ROBERTS except five pounds * * *." *Witnesses:* HENRY WHITE, HILARY WHITE, LEADY WHITE. *Clerk of the Court:* WM. SHERGOLD. Original missing. Recorded in Book No. 4, Will No. 110, Record of Grants.

CHRISTIAN, CHRISTOPHER.   Montgomery County.

November 29, 1781. March Court, 1783. *Sons:* JOHN and JAMES. *Daughters:* PATTY and LUCY. *Friend:* PATTY COLLY. *Executors:* JOHN MACK, NICHOLAS CHRISTIAN and WILLIAM MACK. *Witnesses:* CHRISTO-PHER CHRISTIAN, DRURY COLLIER, THOMAS BULLOCK. *Clerk of the Court:* GEO. DAVIDSON.

JORDAN, JOSEPH.   Pasquotank County.

May 4, 1742. February Court, 1752. *Wife:* MARY. *Daughter:* MARY HENLEY. *Sons:* JOSEPH (" my Plantation whereon I now live, contain-ing Two hundred Acres of Land more or Less"); ROBERT (" Two Plan-tations on the River Side Called by the names of Overmans and Hacket, running as far as to the head of a Branch to the plantation called the Old plantation across from this Line where I live on by that line Called Lufmans line"), MICAJAH (" my Plantation called the Old Plantation withall the Woodland belonging to it Except that part I gave to my son Robert"). *Witnesses:* SAMUEL HUGHE, DEMPSEY CONNER, JOSEPH ROB-INSON. *Clerk of the Court:* THOMAS TAYLOR.

MARSH, EDWARD.   Guilford County.

May 18, 1778. September Court, 1779. *Son:* DARIUS MARSH (planta-tion whereon I now live). *Wife:* KATHERINE. *Other legatees:* KATHERINE and BRYANT (children). *Executors:* KATHERINE MARSH, ROBERT HAR-GROVE, JACOB SHEPPARD. *Witnesses:* ROBT. HARGROVE, AMORY SPINKS, JA. SHEPPARD. Will proven in Randolph County. *Clerk of the Court:* A. TATOM.

ROE, JOHN.   Richmond County.

November 15, 1780. March Court, 1783. *Sons:* EDWARD ROE (one shilling and no more), JOHN EDWARD ROE and SAMUEL ROE. *Daughters:* SARAH RICHARDSON PHILLIPS, JEAN ROE, RACHEL ROE. *Grandson:* SAMUEL SALSBURY CHEARS. *Other legatee:* MARTHA USSERY. *Wife:* SUSANNAH. *Executors:* SUSANNAH ROE and JOSEPH CHAPLAIN. *Witnesses:* JOSEPH HINES, JAMES DOWNING, WM. LEAGO. *Clerk of the Court:* WM. LOVE.

INDEX TO ABSTRACT OF WILLS.

[Names of testators are printed in capitals.]

28

34

37

39

APPENDIX.

INDEX TO WILLS.

BOOK 1 "A."

BOOK 1.

LIST OF WILLS IN GRANT BOOK No. 76.

Name.	Page.	Date.	Counties.
Allen, Andrew	278	1762	Dobbs and Craven.
Adair, James (deed of gift)	256	1759	Dobbs and Craven.
Adair, James (deed of gift)	259	1763	Dobbs and Craven.

LIST OF WILLS RECORDED IN GRANT BOOK 4.

Date, 1724–1743.

Name.	Number of Will.	County.
Alderson, Simon	131	Beaufort.
Andrews, Thomas	135	Bertie.
Abington, Joseph	10	Currituck.
Allin, John	35	
Answell, James	110	
Bond, Robert	71	Bath.
Brown, Richard	41	Bertie.
Brown, Walter	54	Bertie.
Boade, John	87	Bertie.
Battle, John	127	Bertie.
Ballard, John	59	Chowan.
Baker, Henry	81	Chowan.
Boyd, John	86	Chowan.
Badham, William	136	Chowan.
Bonner, Henry	162	Chowan.
Bright, Richard	111	Currituck.
Bryant, John	4	Edgecombe.
Burgess, Stephen	44	Pasquotank.
Bundy, Samuel	122	Pasquotank.
Boyd, John	168	Pasquotank.
Belman, John	133	Perquimans.
Boswell, George	156	Perquimans.
Blunt, Benjamin	114	Tyrrell.
Booth, George	2	
Beezley, Thomas	17	
Beasley, Samuel	27	
Bate, Henry Lawrence	113	
Branch, Francis	123	
Bright, Henry	134	
Baigeron, Judith	150	
Carter, Henry	33	Bath.
Crompton, Henry	56	Bertie.
Collins, John	138	Bertie.
Charlton, John	50	Chowan.
Crawford, W.	140	Chowan.
Craven, James	201	Chowan.
Cox, Thomas	143	Currituck.
Convey, Dennis	13	Pasquotank.

Name.	Number of Will.	County.
Cox, John	141	Onslow.
Chappel, Richard	11	
Chancey, W., Jr.	30	
Delamar, Francis	161	Bath.
Dias, Henry	76	Beaufort.
Dwight, Matthew	70	Chowan.
Davis, Isaac	146	Currituck.
Donohoe, Job	149	New Hanover.
Davis, Solomon	100	Pasquotank.
Davis, Richard	67	Perquimans.
Downing, William	92	
Etheridge, Henry	147	Currituck.
Everton, Jeremiah	164	Pasquotank.
Ferrel, Richard	124	Albemarle.
Forster, Robert	128	Bertie.
Green, Susannah	18	
Griffin, William	36	
Gale, Edmund	69	
Goffe, Arthur	74	
Gregory, Thomas	106	
Harrison, Vines	78	Albemarle.
Henderson, George	64	Bertie.
Hollbrook, John	126	Bertie.
Horth, Thomas	28	Chowan.
Houston, Thomas	14	Onslow.
Hall, Ann	163	Perquimans.
Haig, William	3	
Irving, Robert	65	Currituck.
Jessop, Joseph	46	Albemarle.
Jones, William	31	Bertie.
Jones, John	42	Bertie.
Jeffries, Eliza	151	Northampton.
Jeffries, Eliza	142	
Jones, Jonathan	108	Pasquotank.
Jackson, William	48	Perquimans.
Jewel, Thomas	57	
King, Michael	160	Bertie.
Ketchings, William	32	Perquimans.
Lovick, John	39	
Lilley, Thomas	52	
Leary, Richard	85	
Ludford, John	90	
Lillington, Elizabeth	154	
Man, Thomas	7	
Moys, John	9	
McKeels, Rebecca	15	

41

Name.	Number of Will.	County.
Moore, James	24	
Mauden, Thomas	45	
Martin, William	55	
Mackinne, Barnaby, Jr.	58	
Middleton, Henry	89	
Morris, John	103	
Macrary, Robert	115	
Mackgue, Lawrence	118	
Mason, John, Sr.	155	
Martin, John	157	
Mereday, Thomas	158	
Nicholson, Nathaniel	66	
Newby, Mary	99	
Newby, Benjamin	102	
Odeon, John	165	Beaufort.
Odeon, Charles	49	
Overman, Joseph	107	
Parish, John, Sr.	91	Albemarle.
Pugh, Francis	34	Bertie.
Purrei, Joseph	43	
Power, George	53	Bertie.
Prichards, Harbert	95	Bertie.
Pukerin, Richard	109	Bertie.
Peyton, Robart	121	Bertie.
Pratt, John	167	
Parke, Henry	21	Craven.
Parish, William	139	Edgecombe.
Plato, Thomas	26	Pasquotank.
Pools, Solomon	98	Pasquotank.
Pendleton, Henry	105	Pasquotank.
Palmer, Robert	125	Pasquotank.
Pratts, Job	62	Perquimans.
Pnenny, George	68	
Pollock, George	82	
Parrot, Jacob	84	
Pugh, John	112	
Redditt, William	116	Bertie.
Rogers, Robert	88	Chowan.
Roe, James	72	Craven.
Ritegas, Jacob	12	Pasquotank.
Spellers, Patience	79	Bertie.
Snoad, John	145	Beaufort.
Smith, George	63	Bertie.
Smith, James	51	Perquimans.
Sowell, Charles	80	Bertie.
Stafford, William	169	Currituck.
Simmons, Edward	16	Edgecombe.
Spence, Alexander	5	Pasquotank.
Spence, James	129	Pasquotank.
Spence, John	60	
Symons, Jeremiah	132	Pasquotank.

Name.	Number of Will.	County.
Snowden, Thomas	61	Perquimans.
Sharred, David	153	Perquimans.
Shackelford, John	19	
Shavers, John	20	
Stubs, Thomas	83	
Silberton, Gilford	77	
Simpson, Alexander	75	
Stevenson, William	93	
Scot, John	96	
Snowden, Joseph	132	
Symons, John	159	
Tayler, Thomas	47	
Thomas, Barnaba	23	
Townsens, John	101	Perquimans.
Trublood, John	6	Pasquotank.
Thomas, Joseph	37	
Vann, William	119	Chowan.
Williams, Thomas	22	Bertie.
Williams, John	94	
Williams, Edward	103	Pasquotank.
Wills, William	152	Onslow.
Winn, John	104	Pasquotank.
Wiat, John	97	Perquimans.
Weaver, William	38	Bertie.
Wade, Mary	137	Pasquotank.
Warrens, Abraham	120	Perquimans.
Whetley, Samuel	117	Tyrrell.
Whedbee, Richard	130	Tyrrell.
Whitmell, Thomas	22	Bertie.
Whitehead, Alice	144	Craven.
Whitney, Joshua	25	
Worth, John	148	Bladen.

INDEX TO WILL BOOK, No. 2, 1712-1722.

Name.	Will Book.	Page.
Avelin, Peter	1712–1722	2
Askue, John	1712–1722	31
Adams, James (inventory)	1712–1722	78
Alderson, Simon	1712–1722	80
Armor, William	1712–1722	276
Albertson, Mary	1712–1722	315
Bannfield, Walter	1712–1722	1
Borsene, John	1712–1722	3
Bodeet, Jacob	1712–1722	10
Brent, Thomas	1712–1722	25
Brett, William	1712–1722	34
Benbury, William	1712–1722	39
Bowrem, Edmund	1712–1722	42

Name.	Will Book.	Page.
Burnby, John	1712–1722	46
Bennet, John	1712–1722	49
Bell, George (jury before him)	1712–1722	58
Bell, John	1712–1722	316
Bonesly, John	1712–1722	61
Bounsell, Walter	1712–1722	62
Burke, Richard	1712–1722	73
Britt, William	1712–1722	73
Berry, Ed.	1712–1722	75
Berry, John	1712–1722	86
Berey, John (inventory)	1712–1722	184
Beard, James	1712–1722	76
Burchenhead, George (inventory)	1712–1722	76
Bray, William	1712–1722	81
Barrass, John	1712–1722	85
Browne, Daniele	1712–1722	86
Brown, William	1712–1722	152
Browne, James	1712–1722	284
Browne, John	1712–1722	300
Brown, Thomas	1712–1722	158
Baley, John	1712–1722	108
Blount, James	1712–1722	113
Blount, James (inventory)	1712–1722	255
Barrow, William	1712–1722	115
Barrow, John	1712–1722	146
Barrow, James	1712–1722	151
Barrow, James (inventory)	1712–1722	248
Barrow, John	1712–1722	174
Beasley, Francis	1712–1722	172
Beesly, Francis (inventory)	1712–1722	206
Beesly, Walter (inventory)	1712–1722	290
Beaseley, James	1712–1722	239
Beaseley, James (inventory)	1712–1722	278
Britnoe William (inventory)	1712–1722	184
Britnoe, William (inventory)	1712–1722	289
Barnes, Henry (inventory)	1712–1722	189
Blysh, John (inventory)	1712–1722	192
Busby, John (inventory)	1712–1722	207
Billet, John	1712–1722	223
Brice, William	1712–1722	227
Boyd, Winefred	1712–1722	242
Bonner, Katherine	1712–1722	252
Batchelor, Richd. (account)	1712–1722	256
Berkley, John, Eliz. Berkely and Sarah Catchmayd (letter).	1712–1722	281
Broem, William (inventory)	1712–1722	289
Branch, William	1712–1722	294
Bounds, Richard	1712–1722	298
Barcocks, Thomas	1712–1722	303
Boge, William	1712–1722	318
Barnsfield, Anne	1712–1722	319
Bundy, Caleb	1712–1722	328
Bundy, Caleb	1722–1722	322
Ball, Thomas	1712–1722	333
Beels, James	1712–1722	336
Barry, William	1712–1722	338

Name.	Will Book.	Page.
Gregory, Thomas (children's estate)	1712–1722	73
Gregory, Richard	1712–1722	235
Goodlett, Alexander	1712–1722	4
Goodlatt, Alexander (inventory)	1712–1722	60
Green, Farnifold	1712–1722	10
Green, Farnifold (order)	1712–1722	77
Giles, Mathias	1712–1722	14
George, Henry	1712–1722	34
Gladstains, George	1712–1722	44
Goodale, Gilbert	1712–1722	46
Graylin, Thomas (inventory)	1712–1722	58
Goodpatt, Thorough (inventory)	1712–1722	74
Goodgrave, Ann (order)	1712–1722	77
Gibson, Elinor	1712–1722	85
Gergamus, N.	1712–1722	90
Goreham, John	1712–1722	158
Griffen, Martin	1712–1722	165
Griffen, Martin (inventory)	1712–1722	186
Glover, Joseph (inventory)	1712–1722	199
Gardiner, James (inventory)	1712–1722	211 and 256
Grill, Richard	1712–1722	221
Grill, Richard (inventory)	1712–1722	250
Goble, Dederith	1712–1722	236
Godson, Benj. (inventory)	1712–1722	247
Gale, Christopher	1712–1722	291
Glanville, William	1712–1722	293
Garrett, Cowan	1712–1722	303
Glaister, Joseph	1712–1722	142
Grosvenor, William	1712–1722	322
Holebrough, Joseph	1712–1722	16
Harrington, Humphrey	1712–1722	19
Hodgson, John	1712–1722	24
Harrison, John	1712–1722	32
Hill, Isack	1712–1722	33
Harris, John	1712–1722	48
Hancock, John (inventory)	1712–1722	59
Hawkins, John	1712–1722	227
Hawkins, John	1712–1722	111
Hawkins, Sarah	1712–1722	340
Hooker, William	1712–1722	144
Houghton, George	1712–1722	171
Houghton, George (inventory)	1712–1722	249
Hudson, Edwd. (inventory)	1712–1722	185
Hall, Peter (inventory)	1712–1722	273
Haig, William (inventory)	1712–1722	200
Haig, Mary	1712–1722	169
Horner, Elinor	1712–1722	220
Horner, Elinor (inventory)	1712–1722	257
Halsey, Danll.	1712–1722	222
Hardy, John	1712–1722	233
Hewitt, Bartholomew	1712–1722	242
Hopkins, John	1712–1722	301
Heicklefeild, John	1712–1722	305
Haman, Thomas	1712–1722	320
Harvy, Dorothy	1712–1722	332

Name.	Will Book.	Page.
Hodges, James	1712–1722	343
Haig, William	1712–1722	167
Harman, Robert	1712–1722	269
Jones, Thomas (inventory)	1712–1722	74
Jones, Thomas (will)	1712–1722	29
Jones, Fran., admr. to Arthur Jones	1712–1722	9
Jones, Daniel	1712–1722	13
Jones, John	1712–1722	21
Jones, John (inventory)	1712–1722	187
Jones, Cornelius	1712–1722	93
Jones, Edwd.	1712–1722	245
Jones, Edwd. (inventory)	1712–1722	253
Jones, David (inventory)	1712–1722	255
Jones, Arthur (inventory)	1712–1722	278
James, Edward	1712–1722	321
Jordine, Solomon	1712–1722	296
Jennings, Ann (inventory)	1712–1722	251
Jennings, Ann (will)	1712–1722	224
Jennings, John (inventory)	1712–1722	253
Jennings, John (will)	1712–1722	223
Jordan, John	1712–1722	219
Johnson, Susannah	1712–1722	166
Johnson, Lewis	1712–1722	53
Jackson, Isaac	1712–1722	128
King, Henry	1712–1722	100
Knight, Simon (admr. to John Porter)	1712–1722	108
Knight, Tobias	1712–1722	147
Knight, Tobias (inventory)	1712–1722	263
Kerby, Thomas	1712–1722	173
Kent, John	1712–1722	219
Kent, John (inventory)	1712–1722	254
Kasewell, Fran.	1712–1722	41
Lewerton, Ephraim	1712–1722	30
Lewerton, John (inventory)	1712–1722	68
Lawson, John	1712–1722	39
Lawson, John	1712–1722	98
Long, James	1712–1722	51
Long, William	1712–1722	54
Long, Sarah	1712–1722	160
Long, Sarah (inventory)	1712–1722	194
Lee, Thomas	1712–1722	161
Lee, William (inventory)	1712–1722	191
Lepper, Thomas	1712–1722	163
Lepper, Thomas (inventory)	1712–1722	248
Lowden, John	1712–1722	171
Lowden. John (inventory)	1712–1722	185
Luis, Richard	1712–1722	176
Lewis, Thomas, Sen.	1712–1722	237
Lewis, Thomas (inventory)	1712–1722	260
Lockey, Henry (admstr.)	1712–1722	84
Ligo, John	1712–1722	117
Ligo, John (inventory)	1712–1722	118
Loftin, Leonard	1712–1722	317

Name.	Will Book.	Page.
Lowe, William	1712–1722	336
Lee, Thomas	1712–1722	343
Martin, Joel	1712–1722	131
Martin, James	1712–1722	244
Monereif, John	1712–1722	43
Mitchel, Archibald (inventory)	1712–1722	72
Mackarty, Timothy	1712–1722	157
Malbe, George	1712–1722	164
Moore, Richard (inventory)	1712–1722	189
Mathews, Edmund (inventory)	1712–1722	250
Meads, John (inventory)	1712–1722	255
Markham, Anthony (inventory)	1712–1722	265
Machley, Henry	1712–1722	323
Nicholson, Benjamin	1712–1722	15
Norcom, Mary	1712–1722	313
Newby, Edward	1712–1722	270
Newby, William	1712–1722	279
Nortly, David (James Nortly, admr.)	1712–1722	84
Oglebey, George (inventory)	1712–1722	254
Odeon, Elinor (inventory)	1712–1722	252
Porter, Mary	1712–1722	139
Porter, John	1712–1722	5
Porter, John	1712–1722	45
Patnel, John	1712–1722	24
Patchitt, John	1712–1722	36
Pettit, Mary	1712–1722	79
Parry, Adam (inventory)	1712–1722	204
Peirce, John (inventory)	1712–1722	204
Pearce, Joseph (inventory)	1712–1722	256
Prescot, Aron	1712–1722	279
Plowman, John	1712–1722	301
Palmer, Thomas	1712–1722	325
Pike, Samuel	1712–1722	150
Pruet, William (inventory)	1712–1722	189
Pope, Edward	1712–1722	337
Phelps, Edwd. (inventory)	1712–1722	196
Parker, Peter	1712–1722	229
Paterson, Robert	1712–1722	330
Robinson, Susanna	1712–1722	13
Robinson, John	1712–1722	238
Rountree, William (inventory)	1712–1722	247
Rice, Danll.	1712–1722	251
Relf, Thos.	1712–1722	270
Rice, Lucy	1712–1722	315
Reverly, John	1712–1722	41
Reynaud, Benjamin	1712–1722	24
Russel, Sarah (admrx. to Wm. Russel)	1712–1722	135
Robinson, Thomas	1712–1722	169
Robinson, Thomas (inventory)	1712–1722	208
Ross, William	1712–1722	342
Ricks, Benjamin	1712–1722	344

Name.	Will Book.	Page.
Scot, Stephen	1712–1722	106
Slade, Joseph (Ed. Traverse, admr.)	1712–1722	136
Slade, George	1712–1722	32
Sparrow, Thomas	1712–1722	120
Slocum, Saml.	1712–1722	8
Standing, Richd.	1712–1722	13
Standing, Edward	1712–1722	311
Sadler, William	1712–1722	35
Smith, Alexander	1712–1722	54
Smith, Mary	1712–1722	225
Smith, Mary (inventory)	1712–1722	249
Swain, Stephen	1712–1722	57
Swain, Stephen (inventory)	1712–1722	65
Stansel, John (inventory)	1712–1722	69
Sparnon, Joseph	1712–1722	155
Sparnon, Joseph (inventory)	1712–1722	202
Steely, Thomas	1712–1722	177
Steely, Thomas	1712–1722	199
Steely, Thomas (inventory)	1712–1722	272
Simon, Rebecca (inventory)	1712–1722	197
Simons, George	1712–1722	238
Snell, John (inventory)	1712–1722	211
Sayer, Thomas	1712–1722	233
Smithwick, Edwd. (inventory)	1712–1722	249
Sanderson, Richd. (inventory)	1712–1722	264
Sanderson, Basil	1712–1722	339
Spruill, Godfrey	1712–1722	271
Spruill, Godfrey (inventory)	1712–1722	280
Stone, Willm.	1712–1722	277
Stanton, Thos.	1712–1722	308
Stanton, Mary	1712–1722	309
Stanton, Thomas	1712–1722	324
Stamp, Richard	1712–1722	334
Toms, Francis (inventory)	1712–1722	78
Toms, Francis (will)	1712–1722	55
Toms, Mary	1712–1722	156
Tayler, John	1712–1722	98
Tayler, Lemuell (inventory)	1712–1722	260
Tayler, Ebenezer	1712–1722	273
Tayler, Peter	1712–1722	275
Tyler, Thomas	1712–1722	346
Thorowgood, Fran.	1712–1722	129
Thomas, Morgan	1712–1722	3
Tanner, Walter	1712–1722	18
Turner, Henry	1712–1722	26
Turner, Richard	1712–1722	175
Tomlins, John (inventory)	1712–1722	183
Tomlin, John (will)	1712–1722	212
Tooke, James	1712–1722	228
Thorp, Richd.	1712–1722	239
Tucker, Robert	1712–1722	243
Upton, John	1712–1722	241
Upton, John	1712–1722	326

INDEX TO WILL BOOK, No. 3, 1722-1735.

Name.	Will Book.	Page.
Bray, William, Senr.	1722–1735	130
Bromley, George	1722–1722	131
Bunch, Paul	1722–1722	138
Burket, John	1722–1735	172
Burket, John (inventory)	1722–1735	182
Ballard, Joseph, Senr.	1722–1735	198
Burgess, Stephen	1722–1735	200
Bailey, William (inventory)	1722–1735	228
Blanchard, John (inventory)	1722–1735	229
Barecock, William	1722–1735	237
Baros, Moses	1722–1735	269
Browning, John	1722–1735	280
Barclifts, William	1722–1735	285
Bryan, James	1722–1735	297
Bass, John	1722–1735	305
Church, Joseph	1722–1735	5
Clerk, George	1722–1735	8
Clerk, Thomas (inventory)	1722–1735	68
Clayton, Henry	1722–1735	40
Cambril, Alexander	1722–1735	50
Cape, John (inventory)	1722–1735	62
Clear, Timothy (inventory)	1722–1735	71
Clare, Hannah	1722–1735	118
Clare, Hannah (inventory)	1722–1735	177
Chesson, Ann	1722–1735	127
Chesson, Ann (inventory)	1722–1735	164
Chesson, James (inventory)	1722–1735	165
Cheston, James	1722–1735	105
Crisp, Nicholas	1722–1735	93
Cameril, Alexander and Ann (inventory)	1722–1735	108
Carman, William	1722–1735	137
Cotton, Jno.	1722–1735	141
Cockshell, Andrew (inventory)	1722–1735	158
Coward, William	1722–1735	166
Charles, Samuel (inventory)	1722–1735	167
Charles, Samuel (will)	1722–1735	186
Crossot, Joseph	1722–1735	191
Collens, James	1722–1735	192
Collens, Lucy	1722–1735	192
Cannings, Joseph	1722–1735	197
Copeland, William	1722–1735	14
Cartwright, Grace (inventory)	1722–1735	170
Chapman, Mary	1722–1735	207
Clapham, Joseph	1722–1735	315
Cartwright, William	1722–1735	260
Cartright, William, Senr.	1722–1735	354
Colson, Mary	1722–1735	298
Cane, William	1722–1735	302
Cromen, Martin	1722–1735	320
Chester, John	1722–1735	328
Creasy, Levi	1722–1735	330
Cook, Thomas	1722–1735	344
Deiptt, John	1722–1735	4
Davis, Hugh	1722–1735	36

Name.	Will Book.	Page.
Davis, Peter	1722–1735	104
Davis, William (inventory)	1722–1735	188
Davis, Jno. (inventory)	1722–1735	223
Discorah, Thomas	1722–1735	38
Discorah, Thomas (inventory)	1722–1735	188
Dauge, Richard (inventory)	1722–1735	82
Dunston, John	1722–1735	107
Dixon, Robert	1722–1735	125
Delamare, Stephen	1722–1735	254
Durant, Thomas	1722–1735	302
Darden, Joseph	1722–1735	326
Engel, Peter	1722–1735	22
Evans, Jeffry	1722–1735	60
Evans, Jonathan (inventory)	1722–1735	83
Evans, Hunt (inventory)	1722–1735	226
Evans, Thomas	1722–1735	258
Edy, John	1722–1735	107
Ellis, Francis (inventory)	1722–1735	166
Elleot, George	1722–1735	132
Elliott, Aaron (inventory)	1722–1735	169
Elliott, Thomas	1722–1735	203
Everendon, Thomas (inventory)	1722–1735	176
Eaton, James	1722–1735	209
Eubank, George	1722–1735	233
Easters, John	1722–1735	272
Early, Elenor	1722–1735	296
Eborn, Henry	1722–1735	310
Farrow, Francis	1722–1735	11
Felts, Humphrey	1722–1735	38
Flint, Richard (inventory)	1722–1735	87
Fry, Thomas (inventory)	1722–1735	92
Fry, Thomas (will)	1722–1723	101
Frost, William (inventory)	1722–1735	93
Farlee, James	1722–1735	97
Forster, James	1722–1735	107
Foster. Hannah	1722–1735	131
Foster, James (inventory)	1722–1735	169
Feltham, James	1722–1735	132
Fraser, David	1722–1735	228
Fourre, John	1722–1735	242
Freeman, John	1722–1735	243
Gunter, John	1722–1735	36
Guilbert, Francis	1722–1735	38
Guilbert, Francis (inventory)	1722–1735	85
Guilbert, Francis (inventory)	1722–1735	91
Guilbert, Joseph (inventory)	1722–1735	122
Gatlin, Edward	1722–1735	54
Gavins, Charles (inventory)	1722–1735	74
Garmack, James (inventory)	1722–1735	88
Griffith, John	1722–1735	135
Guthrie, Samuel (inventory)	1722–1735	169
Galley, John	1722–1735	203
Grey, Richard	1722–1735	209

Name.	Will Book.	Page.
Gray, Ann	1722–1735	239
Godley, John	1722–1735	255
Glesson, John	1722–1735	286
Hicks, Thomas	1722–1735	30
Hicks, Thomas (inventory)	1722–1735	77
Hicks, David	1722–1735	263
Hicks, Robert	1722–1735	297
Heclefield, John (inventory)	1722–1735	69
Hassell, Jane (inventory)	1722–1735	73
Hatch, Anthony	1722–1735	57
Hatch, Anthony (inventory)	1722–1735	189
Hill, George	1722–1735	26
Hill, Richard	1722–1735	181
Hill, John	1722–1735	238
Hardin, Thomas (inventory)	1722–1735	121
Hayman, Henry	1722–1735	122
Harrison, Daniel	1722–1735	143
Harrison, Danl. (inventory)	1722–1735	168
Henley, John	1722–1735	146
Hackley, Henry (inventory)	1722–1735	171
Henderson, Henman (inventory)	1722–1735	171
Hopton, Charles (inventory)	1722–1735	173
Hambleton, John	1722–1735	174
Handworker, Daniel	1722–1735	213
Harvey, Thomas	1722–1735	216
Harvey, Richard	1722–1735	278
Hollowell, Edmund	1722–1735	208
Hinton, John	1722–1735	240
Husbands, Richard	1722–1735	263
Hunter, William	1722–1735	265
Hawkins, Thomas	1722–1735	268
Hardison, Jasper	1722–1735	279
Howcott, John	1722–1735	283
Hall, Hezekiah	1722–1735	292
Hamilton, Jane	1722–1735	293
Hooks, John	1722–1735	296
House, Thomas	1722–1735	299
Hoskins, Thomas	1722–1735	304
Irby, Henry	1722–1735	290
Ismay, John	1722–1735	312
Jesper, Richard	1722–1735	28
Jasper, Richard, Senr. (inventory)	1722–1735	65
Jasper, Richard, Jun. (inventory)	1722–1735	93
Jones, Samuel	1722–1735	37
Jones, David (inventory)	1722–1735	66
Jones, John, Senr.	1722–1735	98
Jones, Frederick	1722–1735	115
Jones, John	1722–1735	193
Jones, Wm. Harding	1722–1735	251
Jones, William	1722–1735	306
Jones, William	1722–1735	308
Joy, William	1722–1735	39
Johnson, William	1722–1735	140

Name.	Will Book.	Page.
Nolam, James (inventory)	1722–1735	76
Navell, Francis (inventory)	1722–1735	88
Navell, Francis (will)	1722–1735	106
Nicholson, Samuel	1722–1735	119
Norcomb, Jno.	1722–1735	139
Norfleet, James	1722–1735	281
Obrian, Darby	1722–1735	31
Obrian, Darby (inventory)	1722–1735	89
O'Neal, Michael	1722–1735	52
Ogilby, Patrick	1722–1735	108
Ogleby, Patrick (inventory)	1722–1735	109
O'Neal, Michael (will)	1722–1735	153
Oliver, Moses	1722–1735	169
Oadam, Richard (inventory)	1722–1735	225
Orandle, Edward	1722–1735	271
Ottiwell, Isaac	1722–1735	285
Powell, John	1722–1735	23
Poyner, Joseph	1722–1735	46
Poyner, William (inventory)	1722–1735	223
Philips, Daniel	1722–1735	55
Phillips, Thomas (inventory)	1722–1735	227
Palmer, Thomas (inventory)	1722–1735	58
Palmer, Nathaniel (inventory)	1722–1735	159
Pavy, Weebly	1722–1735	87
Peirce, John	1722–1735	100
Pearse, Thomas	1722–1735	234
Pearce, Robert	1722–1735	212
Pace, John, Senr.	1722–1735	126
Pagett, Edward	1722–1735	137
Phelps, Samuel	1722–1735	145
Phelps, Humphrey (inventory)	1722–1735	175
Phelps, Jonathan	1722–1735	266
Pollock, Hester	1722–1735	152
Pollock, Thomas	1722–1735	309
Parris, Thomas	1722–1735	155
Parris, Thomas (inventory)	1722–1735	219
Pricklove, John and Elizabeth (inventory)	1722–1735	160
Pendleton, Thomas	1722–1735	245
Purdy, George	1722–1735	276
Purser, Robert	1722–1735	287
Putnell, William	1722–1735	291
Porter, Joshua	1722–1735	329
Pirkins, David	1722–1735	309
Richardson, Daniel	1722–1735	2
Rigney, John	1722–1735	32
Rigney, John (inventory)	1722–1735	86
Robins, James	1722–1735	33
Reading, Lionel	1722–1735	41
Reading, Lionel (inventory)	1722–1735	86
Rogers, John	1722–1735	52
Roggers, John (inventory)	1722–1735	228
Reston, Thomas	1722–1735	55
Rice, Lucy (inventory)	1722–1735	58
Ratliff, Samuel	1722–1735	318

Name.	Will Book.	Page.
Strickland, William	1722–1735	145
Stafford, William	1722–1735	148
Smithson, John (inventory)	1722–1735	166
Soan, John	1722–1735	325
Stephenson, Elizabeth	1722–1735	331
Taylor, Nathaniel	1722–1735	300
Taylor, Lemuel	1722–1735	29
Taylor, Jane	1722–1735	301
Turbervil, Richard	1722–1735	51
Thorowgood, Thomas (inventory)	1722–1735	68
Tannahill, John (inventory)	1722–1735	90
Torksey, Philip	1722–1735	106
Torksey, Philip (inventory)	1722–1735	168
Thomas, Joseph	1722–1735	121
Toms, Joseph (inventory)	1722–1735	166
Toms, Francis	1722–1735	201
Toms, Francis (inventory)	1722–1735	222
Toms, Joshua	1722–1735	247
Trotter, William	1722–1735	204
Tinnins, Mary	1722–1735	228
Tully, Jane	1722–1735	259
Unday, Thomas	1722–1735	47
Vanluven, Christopher	1722–1735	256
White, William	1722–1735	10
White, John	1722–1735	53
White, Sarah	1722–1735	99
White, Arnold (inventory)	1722–1735	225
White, Robert	1722–1735	324
White, Arnold, Senr.	1722–1735	205
Widbey, George	1722–1735	24
Wilson, Isaac	1722–1735	35
Wilson, Isaac (inventory)	1722–1735	224
Williams, William	1722–1735	48
Williams, Johanna (inventory)	1722–1735	90
Williams, John	1722–1735	119
Williams, William	1722–1735	264
Williams, Thomas	1722–1735	284
Warren, William	1722–1735	61
Wheeler, Henry	1722–1735	124
Walston, London	1722–1735	134
Wherry, Joshua	1722–1735	207
Wimberly, Thomas	1722–1735	244
Walburton, Robert	1722–1735	274
Wingfield, Richard	1722–1735	301
Wood, William	1722–1735	325
Young, Joseph	1722–1735	175
Zearge, Jacob	1722–1735	261

42

INDEX TO WILL BOOK, No. 4, 1738-1752.

Name.	Will Book.	Page.
Green, John	1738–1752	100
Gourley, John	1738–1752	101
Grange, John	1738–1752	131
Grant, Alexander	1738–1752	245
Griggs, Samuel	1738–1752	273
Gillitt, John	1738–1752	329
Hedges, Thomas	1738–1752	31
Higgins, Ann	1738–1752	41
Huggins, Edmond	1738–1752	181
Heneley, John	1738–1752	45
Hollis, James	1738–1752	114
Hutson, William	1738–1752	137
Hendrick, Francis	1738–1752	167
Hambleton, Joseph	1738–1752	183
Hodgson, John	1738–1752	186
Howcott, Edward	1738–1752	267
Harvis, John	1738–1752	322
Hunter, Nicholas	1738–1752	324
Hannis, Joseph	1738–1752	337
Hicks, John	1738–1752	292
Ingram, Abram	1738–1752	334
Keel, John	1738–1752	76
King, John	1738–1752	312
Lamberson, Henry	1738–1752	18
Laker, Juliana	1738–1752	82
Lord, William	1738–1752	85
Lawkins, John	1738–1752	212
Luton, Adam	1738–1752	248
Love, Daniel	1738–1752	92
Lockey, Joseph	1738–1752	361
Lyon James	1738–1752	367
Logan, Alexander	1738–1752	139
Lock, Thomas	1738–1752	122
Leath, Richard	1738–1752	296
Moseley, Edward	1738–1752	1
Mackferrell, John	1738–1752	17
Murphey, Edmond	1738–1752	34
Mitchel, Abram	1738–1752	53
Mason, John	1738–1752	57
Maskill, William	1738–1752	80
McDowell, John	1738–1752	200
Millard, Charles	1738–1752	218
Metcalfe, Caleb	1738–1752	219
Maule, Patrick	1738–1752	238
McCalpin, William	1738–1752	299
Murphy, Thomas	1738–1752	327
Marr, Joseph	1738–1752	336
Marsden, Thomas	1738–1752	226
Neal, Henry	1738–1752	196
Newby, Samuel	1738–1752	215
Norwood, William	1738–1752	51

Name.	Will Book.	Page.
Norman, John	1738–1752	87
Nixon, Zachariah	1738–1752	133
Nixson, Richard	1738–1752	357
Overton, John	1738–1752	77
Ohier, John	1738–1752	21
Owan, Daniel	1738–1752	23
Odyer, Dennis	1738–1752	252
Parker, Azricom	1738–1752	241
Purcell, Neal	1738–1752	14
Pollock, Thomas	1738–1752	66
Powell, William	1738–1752	59
Pringle, Alexander	1738–1752	170
Pearson, Thomas	1738–1752	277
Parsons, Thomas	1738–1752	304
Porter, Nicholas	1738–1752	314
Pritchett, Abraham	1738–1752	352
Paquinet, Michael	1738–1752	49
Russell, Thomas	1738–1752	19
Roberts, James	1738–1752	26
Risonover, Matthew	1738–1752	29
Rawlings, Banjamin	1738–1752	63
Rontree, Francis	1738–1752	116
Reading, Thomas	1738–1752	118
Rustull, Richard, Jr.	1738–1752	259
Rogers, Richard	1738–1752	263
Smith, James	1738–1752	24
Smith, John, Senr.	1738–1752	153
Smith, Edward	1738–1752	170
Smith, William	1738–1752	256
Smith, Henry	1538–1752	288
Smith, James	1738–1752	320
Sterring, George, Senr.	1738–1752	47
Sitgraves, William	1738–1752	55
Sanders, John	1738–1752	112
Stevens, James	1738–1752	128
Stafford, John	1738–1752	166
Sherley, James	1738–1752	172
Stuart, John	1738–1752	179
Sutton, Mary	1738–1752	221
Simmonds, Jacob	1738–1752	223
Swift, Ephraim	1738–1752	301
Stover, Jacob John	1738–1752	331
Tomson, William	1738–1752	188
Thompson, John	1738–1752	230
Tignar, James	1738–1752	286
Valentine, Richard	1738–1752	108
Vince, Humphrey	1738–1752	205
Waxdale, John	1738–1752	174
West, William	1738–1752	20
Wallis, Andrew	1738–1752	33

Name.	Will Book.	Page.
Wallis, William	1738–1752	264
Winn, Sam.	1738–1752	110
White, Henry	1738–1752	129
White, John	1738–1752	342
Wickstead, Pall	1738–1752	193
William, James	1738–1752	225
Wood, John	1738–1752	275
Walker, Thomas	1738–1752	284
Wain, Thomas	1738–1752	303
Wright, John	1738–1752	342

INDEX TO WILL BOOK, No. 5, 1749-1753.

Name.	Will Book.	Page.
Allen, Eleazar	1749–1753	11
Albertson, Joshua	1749–1753	229
Brown, Thomas	1749–1753	1
Benbow, Gershon	1749–1753	15
Bishop, George	1749–1753	24
Burnap, John	1749–1753	31
Bryan, Edward	1749–1753	36
Bryan, Simon	1749–1753	207
Brickell, James	1749–1753	61
Befret, Benjamin	1749–1753	79
Boulds, George	1749–1753	119
Bevin, Richard	1749–1753	125
Cranford, William	1749–1753	58
Cheek, Richard	1749–1753	144
Coker, Calep	1749–1753	205
Dexter, Hope	1749–1753	27
Dudley, Christopher	1749–1753	29
Davis, Thomas	1749–1753	166
Davis, Benja. and David Davis (power of attorney to John Sampson).	1749–1753	174
Dupee, Elias	1749–1753	190
Edmondson, Joseph	1749–1753	111
Fort, John	1749–1753	76
Frazier, John	1749–1753	133
Godfrey, Matthew	1749–1753	50
Giddins, Thomas	1749–1753	67
Grainger, Joshus	1749–1753	86
Godwin, William	1749–1753	199
Hall, Joseph	1749–1753	7
Huggins, John	1749–1753	98
Harket, George	1749–1753	103
Humes, James	1749–1753	129
Hunter, Robert	1749–1752	184
Hill, Banjamin	1749–1753	187
Hollowell, Rubin	1749–1753	223
Handcock, William	1749–1753	69

Name.	Will Book.	Page.
Holms, Ebenezer	1749–1753	138
Isler, Christian	1749–1753	148
Jennings, Thomas	1749–1753	92
John, Arthur	1749–1753	13
Jarrott, John	1749–1753	154
Jasper, Sam	1749–1753	163
Jackson, Thomas	1749–1753	217
Kingston, James	1749–1753	3
Kenyon, John	1749–1753	227
Lowell, Edmond	1749–1753	96
Lattemare, Elizabeth	1749–1753	204
Morris, Thomas	1749–1753	23
Mackay, William	1749–1753	25
Middleton, John	1749–1753	33
Mabson, Arthur	1749–1753	40
Murray, Andrew	1749–1753	74
McNary, Gilbert	1749–1753	81
Mason, Roger, Jr.	1749–1753	90
McClalland, Andrew	1749–1753	100
Martin, William	1749–1753	114
Mitchel, Abraham	1749–1753	141
Mewboorn, Thomas	1749–1753	196
Mobley, John	1749–1753	202
Mackinne, John	1749–1753	214
Norton, William	1749–1753	136
Nusum, Richard	1749–1753	182
Prescott, William	1749–1753	151
Pain, John	1749–1753	167
Rigby, William	1749–1753	21
Reel, Peter	1749–1753	47
Rice, Benjamin	1749–1753	52
Rice, Mary	1749–1753	192
Rice, Edward	1749–1753	212
Smelage, Edward	1749–1753	19
Slade, Samuel	1749–1753	45
Slade, John	1749–1753	55
Subridge, William	1749–1753	65
Simson, John	1749–1753	169
Tarkington, William	1749–1753	4
Tart, Joseph	1749–1753	8
Turner, Robert	1749–1753	105
Thomas, Josiah	1749–1753	127
White, George	1749–1753	20
White, Henry	1749–1753	171
Waine, Thomas	1749–1753	44
Watson, John		54
Weekes, Bingman	1749–1753	62

INDEX TO WILL BOOK, No. 6, 1750-1758.

Name.	Will Book.	Page.
Gainer, Samuel	1750–1758	81
Gomm, John	1750–1758	97
Giddings, William	1750–1758	269
Homes, Edward	1750–1758	9
Hall, John	1750–1758	46
Harbrett, Edward	1750–1758	78
Higgins, Michael	1750–1758	84
Holladay, William	1750–1758	124
Hassell, John	1750–1758	129
Harrington, Hezekiah	1750–1758	147
Harrell, Edward	1750–1758	170
Ives, Thomas	1750–1758	89
Jones, John	1750–1758	14
Jones, James	1750–1758	126
Jones, Thomas	1750–1758	173
Johnson, John	1750–1758	189
Johnston, Gabriel	1750–1758	153
King, Henry	1750–1758	17
Knight, William	1750–1758	40
Kemp, William	1750–1758	136
Lattimer, William	1750–1758	10
Lee, Thomas	1750–1758	39
Lockhart, James	1750–1758	149
McDowal, James	1750–1758	44
McRee, William	1750–1758	64
Moore, John	1750–1758	159
Moore, John	1750–1758	167
Moore, Thomas	1750–1758	179
Moore, John	1750–1758	192
Moore, Joseph	1750–1758	211
Mountague, Elizabeth	1750–1758	224
Meltons, Jonathan	1750–1758	264
Owense, John	1750–1758	5
Pollock, Cullen	1750–1758	23
Pilkington, Seth	1750–1758	103
Parker, Mary	1750–1758	122
Parker, Francis	1750–1758	196
Powel, Thomas	1750–1758	183
Pirent, James	1750–1758	201
Prescott, William	1750–1758	236
Russell, Habbakkuk	1750–1758	68
Redding, John	1750–1758	74
Rogers, Thomas, Senr.	1750–1758	169
Rogers, Thomas	1750–1758	141
Ryding, Jonathan	1750–1758	145
Roe, Robert	1750–1758	248
Stansell, John	1750–1758	11
Sutton, Thomas	1750–1758	12

INDEX TO WILL BOOK, No. 7, 1755-1758.

Name.	Will Book.	Page.
Daniel, John	1755–1758	41
Denson, James	1755–1758	55
Duckenfield, Nathaniel	1755–1758	144
Davis, William	1755–1758	186
Davison, John	1755–1758	261
Everett, John	1755–1758	86
Eliot, Moses	1755–1758	121
Eliot, Michael	1755–1758	194
Evans, Aberwall	1755–1758	204
Evans, Robert	1755–1758	213
Foraster, James	1755–1758	56
Falconer, Thomas	1755–1758	108
Fox, James	1755–1758	180
Gray, Allen	1755–1758	17
Gardner, John	1755–1758	48
Gardner, William	1755–1758	102
Gordon, Nathaniel	1755–1758	118
Gordon, John	1755–1758	227
Gillett, John	1755–1758	176
Griffen, Epenetus	1755–1758	178
Howard, Charles	1755–1758	33
Haughton, Charles	1755–1758	89
Hendrick, Jeremiah	1755–1758	123
Hunter, John	1755–1758	131
Harrell, John, Jr.	1755–1758	164
Hockings, John	1755–1758	173
Hooker, William	1755–1758	241
Hinton, Micajah	1755–1758	254
Hillard, William	1755–1758	52
Jordan, Arthur	1755–1758	51
Jones, Morris	1755–1758	82
Jones, John	1755–1758	112
Jones, David, Sr.	1755–1758	139
Johnson, John	1755–1758	141
Little, John	1755–1758	127
Lee, Richard	1755–1758	157
Laurence, George	1755–1758	160
Moore, Samuel	1755–1758	116
Moore, John	1755–1758	35
Moore, Titus	1755–1758	245
McCulloh, Henry	1755–1758	24
Mullen, Jacob	1755–1758	222
Mason, Roger	1755–1758	39
Nickson, Thomas	1755–1758	22
Nobland, John	1755–1758	155
Nicholas, Nathaniel	1755–1758	159
Norwood, Thomas	1755–1758	206
Oliver, Francis	1755–1758	71

Name.	Will Book.	Page.
Parker, Thomas	1755–1758	20
Pierce, Thomas	1755–1758	75
Payne, Peter	1755–1758	95
Plomer, Samuel S.	1755–1758	99
Peeble, Judith	1755–1758	120
Pitman, Benjamin	1755–1758	154
Price, William	1755–1758	188
Pritchett, Margaret	1755–1758	200
Powers, Isobell	1755–1758	233
Pope, Samuel	1755–1758	238
Ryall, Charles	1755–1758	8
Rountree, Moses	1755–1758	37
Read, George	1755–1758	57
Robinson, Charles	1755–1758	129
Robinson, Thomas	1755–1758	88
Robinson, John	1755–1758	217
Robins, Joseph	1755–1758	134
Syers, Gerard	1755–1758	1
Sumner, John	1755–1758	2
Stevenson, John	1755–1758	26
Seville, Stephen	1755–1758	32
Smith, Richard	1755–1758	43
Smith, William	1755–1758	92
Singleton, John	1755–1758	49
Speight, Thomas	1755–1758	126
Small, Benja.	1755–1758	184
Shine, Danll.	1755–1758	191
Spring, Aaron	1755–1758	202
Simmons, Francis	1755–1758	321
Syms, William	1755–1758	152
Trewett, Joseph	1755–1758	60
Thompson, John	1755–1758	100
Toops, Joseph	1755–1758	135
Woodhouse, Horatio	1755–1758	19
War, William	1755–1758	44
Wall, Richard	1755–1758	45
Worden, James	1755–1758	94
Whitehouse, Saml.	1755–1758	142
Williams, Joanah	1755–1758	163
Wallis, Stephen	1755–1758	190
Wade, Joseph	1755–1758	193
West, Thomas	1755–1758	256
Wood, Moses	1755–1758	258

INDEX TO WILL BOOK, No. 8, 1753-1768.

Name.	Will Book.	Page.
Arenton, Christopher	1753–1768	99
Anderson, George	1753–1768	155
Albertson, Isaac	1753–1768	179
Allen, Sarah	1753–1768	193
Alton, Andrew	1753–1768	270

Name.	Will Book.	Page.
Bradley, John	1753–1768	1
Barrow, Joseph	1753–1768	32
Barrow, William	1753–1768	221
Bell, William	1753–1768	107
Bond, Lewis	1753–1768	103
Bond, Vinyard	1753–1768	263
Ballard, Abraham	1753–1768	96
Blackall, Sarah	1753–1768	92
Brockett, Benja.	1753–1768	145
Bray, Henry	1753–1768	176
Brown, John	1753–1768	206
Barclift, John	1753–1768	242
Crocker, Peter	1753–1768	34
Clark, Robert	1753–1768	45
Chancey, Edmund	1753–1768	55
Carruthers, Robert	1753–1768	135
Connor, John	1753–1768	120
Connor, Demsey	1753–1768	83
Corps, John	1753–1768	81
Cooper, Joseph	1753–1768	82
Cloase, George	1753–1768	149
Campbell, James	1753–1768	186
Crutchfield, Edmund (depo.)	1753–1768	278
Davis, John	1753–1768	18
Davis, Thomas	1753–1768	161
Danbe, Daniel	1753–1768	40
Duggan, Thomas	1753–1768	110
Dalrymple, John	1753–1768	300
Dobbs, Arthur, Governor	1753–1768	290
Duncan, Alexander	1753–1768	302
Eaton, William	1753–1768	156
Eavans, Charles	1753–1768	225
Freshworter, John John	1753–1768	88
Grigory, Margaret	1753–1768	13
Grigory, William	1753–1768	20
Gregory, Richard	1753–1768	166
Griffin, Edward	1753–1768	113
Galluay, Thomas	1753–1768	94
Gardner, Martin	1753–1768	211
Galland, Mary	1753–1768	288
Hosea, Joseph	1753–1768	47
Hunter, Isaac	1753–1768	100
Hopkins, John	1753–1768	93
Hopkins, James	1753–1768	251
Hodges, James	1753–1768	179
Harrell, John	1753–1768	180
Houston, William	1753–1768	184
Horn, William	1753–1768	202
Hobby, Jacob	1753–1768	218
Haywood, John	1753–1768	223

Name.	Will Book.	Page.
Isham, James	1753–1768	24
Innes, James	1753–1768	191
Jordan, Joseph	1753–1768	26
Jones, Peter	1753–1768	42
Jones, Isham	1753–1768	50
Jones, William	1753–1768	208
Johnston, Saml.	1753–1768	133
Jasman, Thomas	1753–1768	148
Kelley, John	1753–1768	177
Kinchen, William, Jun.	1753–1768	197
Kince, Christian	1753–1768	215
Lelly, John	1753–1768	7
Long, Thomas	1753–1768	48
Long, Joshua	1753–1768	117
Long, William	1753–1768	233
Lawson, Saml.	1753–1768	137
Lashly, Patrick	1753–1768	154
Lynch, John, Sen.	1753–1768	162
Low, John	1753–1768	173
Moore, Trueman	1753–1768	37
Moore, Roger	1753–1768	62
MacKane, George	1753–1768	140
Messex, Joseph	1753–1768	140
Mckeel, Thomas, Senr.	1753–1768	78
Mackeel, Benjamin	1753–1768	80
Meed, Timothy	1753–1768	87
Morison, Benjamin	1753–1768	150
Morris, John	1753–1768	213
Meares, Mark	1753–1768	228
Maudlin, Thomas	1753–1768	230
Melton, Robert	1753–1768	254
Neville, Benjamin	1753–1768	189
Newton, Christopher	1753–1768	236
Norfleet, Marmaduke	1753–1768	267
Nessfield, John	1753–1768	280
Overton, Robert	1753–1768	86
Peyton, Robert	1753–1768	104
Poyner, Peter	1753–1768	168
Parker, Simon	1753–1768	200
Puryer, Robert	1753–1768	204
Perisho, John	1753–1768	261
Paine, John Captaine	1753–1768	298
Reding, Joseph	1753–1768	22
Ridge, Thomas	1753–1768	35
Rew, Southy	1753–1768	52
Robertson, James	1753–1768	121
Rhoads, William	1753–1768	75
Rowan, Matthew	1753–1768	151
Richards, Richard	1753–1768	219